BASIC ELECTRICAL ENGINEERING

M.E. (Electrical)
Formerly Lecturer in Department of Electronics Engg.
Vishwakarma Institute of Technology
Pune

Varsha U. Bakshi
B.E. (Electronics)
Assistant Director,
Noble Institute of Computer Training
Pune

TECHNICAL PUBLICATIONS
SINCE 1993
An Up-Thrust for Knowledge

BASIC ELECTRICAL ENGINEERING

First Edition : November 2020

Published by :

Amit Residency, Office No.1, 412, Shaniwar Peth, Pune - 411030, M.S. INDIA
Ph.: +91-020-24495496/97, Email : sales@technicalpublications.org
Website : www.technicalpublications.org

ISBN 978-93-332-2350-8

9 789333 223508

PREFACE

The importance of **Basic Electrical Engineering** is well known in various engineering fields. Overwhelming response to our books on various subjects inspired us to write this book. The book is structured to cover the key aspects of the subject **Basic Electrical Engineering**.

The book uses plain, lucid language to explain fundamentals of this subject. The book provides logical method of explaining various complicated concepts and stepwise methods to explain the important topics. Each chapter is well supported with necessary illustrations, practical examples and solved problems. All chapters in this book are arranged in a proper sequence that permits each topic to build upon earlier studies. All care has been taken to make students comfortable in understanding the basic concepts of this subject.

Representative questions have been added at the end of each section to help the students in picking important points from that section.

The book not only covers the entire scope of the subject but explains the philosophy of the subject. This makes the understanding of this subject more clear and makes it more interesting. The book will be very useful not only to the students but also to the subject teachers. The students have to omit nothing and possibly have to cover nothing more.

We wish to express our profound thanks to all those who helped in making this book a reality. Much needed moral support and encouragement is provided on numerous occasions by our whole family. We wish to thank the **Publisher** and the entire team of **Technical Publications** who have taken immense pain to get this book in time with quality printing.

Any suggestion for the improvement of the book will be acknowledged and well appreciated.

Authors
U. A. Bakshi
V. U. Bakshi

Dedicated to Gururaj, Apurva, Arjun and Pradnya

TABLE OF CONTENTS

Chapter - 2 Network Theorems	(2 - 1) to (2 - 56)

Chapter - 3   Steve State Analysis of Single Phase A.C. Circuits

Chapter - 6   Introduction to Earthing and Electrical Safety
(6 - 1) to (6 - 14)

Chapter - 7   Magnetic Circuits
(7 - 1) to (7 - 70)

Chapter - 8   Single Phase Transformer   (8 - 1) to (8 - 64)

Chapter - 10   Three Phase Induction Motor   (10 - 1) to (10 - 36)

Chapter - 11 Single Phase Induction Motors	(11 - 1) to (11 - 16)

Chapter - 12   Three Phase Synchronous Machines   (12 - 1) to (12 - 30)

Chapter - 13   Introduction to Power System   (13 - 1) to (13 - 12)

Chapter - 14   Additional Measuring Instruments   (14 - 1) to (14 - 16)

0

Basic Concept

Contents

0.1 Concept of Electric Charge

The matter on the earth which occupies the space may be solid, liquid or gaseous and is made up of many atoms which are of similar nature. According to modern electron theory, atom is composed of the three fundamental particles, which are invisible to bare eyes. These are the **neutron**, the **proton** and the **electron**. The proton is positively charged while the electron is negatively charged. The neutron is electrically neutral i.e. possessing no charge. Atom as a whole is electrically neutral as the number of protons is always equal to the number of electrons.

In all the atoms the electrons revolve around the nuclues in fixed orbits or shells. All the elctrons are under the force of attraction by the nucelus. The last shell is called valence shell and the electrons in this last shell are called valence electrons.

The valence electrons are very loosely bound to the nucleus and by absorbing external energy such electrons become free from the force of attraction of the nucleus. These electrons are called free electrons and are responsible for the conduction. When electrons are removed from an atom, it looses negative charge and becomes positively charged cation. While if an atom gains an excess electron it becomes negatively charged anion.

> This total deficiency or addition of excess electrons in an atom is called as its **charge** and the atom is said to be **charged**. The unit of charge is **coulomb.**

The charge on one electron is 1.602×10^{-19} C. Hence one coulomb of charge means the total charge possessed by $\dfrac{1}{1.602 \times 10^{-19}}$ electrons i.e. 6.24×10^{18} number of electrons.

> 1 coulomb = Charge on 6.24×10^{18} electrons

0.2 Electromotive Force and Current

A conductor is one which has abundant free electrons. The free electrons in such a conductor are always moving in random directions as shown in the Fig. 0.2.1. The small electrical effort, externally applied to such conductor makes all such free electrons to drift along the metal in a definite particular direction.

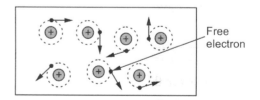

Fig. 0.2.1 Inside the piece of a conductor

This direction depends on how the external electrical effort is applied to the conductor. Such an electrical effort may be an electrical cell, connected across the two ends of a conductor. Such physical phenomenon is represented in the Fig. 0.2.2.

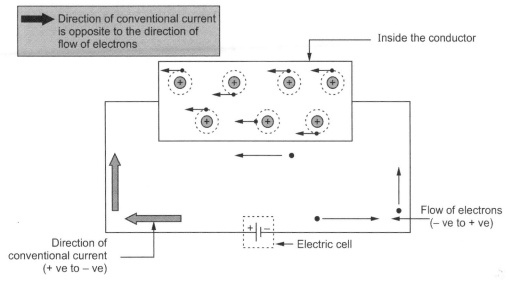

Fig. 0.2.2 The flow of current

An electrical effort required to drift the free electrons in one particular direction, in a conductor is called **Electromotive Force** (e.m.f.). **It is denoted as E and measured in volts.** Thus e.m.f. is an electromotive force which converts any other form of energy into an electrical energy.

When free electron gets dragged towards positive from an atom it becomes positively charged ion. Such positive ion drags a free electron from the next atom. This process repeats from atom to atom along the conductor. So there is flow of electrons from negative to positive of the cell, externally through the conductor across which the cell is connected. This movement of electrons is called an **Electric Current**. The movement of electrons is always from negative to positive while movement of current is always assumed as from positive to negative. This is called **direction of conventional current**.

0.3 Relation between Charge and Current

The current can be defined as **rate of flow of charge in an electric circuit** or in any medium in which charges are subjected to an external electric field.

The unit for the current is **Amperes** which is nothing but coulombs/sec.

Mathematically we can write the relation between the charge (Q) and the electric current (I) as,

$$I = \frac{Q}{t} \quad \text{Amperes}$$

where   I = Average current flowing   while   Q = Total charge transferred

             t = Time required for transfer of charge.

Definition of 1 ampere : *A current of 1 ampere is said to be flowing in the conductor when a charge of one coulomb is passing any given point on it in one second.*

0.4 Electric Potential and Potential Difference

When two similarly charged particles are brought near, they try to repel each other while dissimilar charges try to attract each other. This means, every charged particle has a tendency to do work.

This ability of a charged particle to do the work is called its **electric potential**. The unit of electric potential is **volt.**

The electric potential at a point due to a charge is one volt if one joule of work is done in bringing a unit positive charge i.e. positive charge of one coulomb from infinity to that point.

Mathematically it is expressed as,

$$\text{Electrical Potential} = \frac{\text{Work done}}{\text{Charge}} = \frac{W}{Q}$$

It is well known that, flow of water is always from higher level to lower level, flow of heat is always from a body at higher temperature to a body at lower temperature. Such a level difference which causes flow of water, heat and so on, also exists in electric circuits. In electric circuits, flow of current is always from higher electric potential to lower electric potential.

The difference between the electric potentials at any two given points in a circuit is known as **Potential Difference (p.d.)**. This is also called voltage between the two points and measured in **volts.** The symbol for voltage is V.

To maintain the flow of electrons i.e. flow of electric current, there must exist a potential difference between the two points.

No current can flow if the potential difference between the two points is zero.

Thus a voltage is potential difference which causes current to flow and converts electrical energy into some other form of energy such as heat. While electromotive force converts some other form of energy into electrical energy and maintains the flow of current. This is the difference between electromotive force and potential difference.

0.5 Resistance

The property of an electric circuit opposing the flow of current and at the same time causes electrical energy to be converted to heat is called resistance.

Higher the availability of the free electrons, lesser will be the opposition to the flow of current and lesser is the resistance. A conductor having high number of free electrons offer less resistance to the flow of current. The resistance is denoted by the symbol '**R**' and is measured in **Ohm** symbolically represented as Ω . We can define unit ohm as below :

Definition of 1 ohm : *The resistance of a circuit, in which a current of 1 ampere generates the heat at the rate of one joules per second is said to be 1 ohm.*

4.186 joules = 1 calorie	and	1 joule = 0.24 calorie

Thus unit 1 ohm can be defined as that resistance of the circuit if it develops 0.24 calories of heat, when one ampere current flows through the circuit for one second.

0.5.1 Factors Affecting the Resistance

1. Length of the material : The resistance of a material is directly proportional to the length. Length is denoted by '*l*'.

2. Cross-sectional area : The resistance of a material is inversely proportional to the cross-sectional area of the material. The cross sectional area is denoted by '*a*'.

3. The type and nature of the material : If the material is conductor, its resistance is less while if it is insulator, its resistance is very high.

4. Temperature : As temperature changes, the value of the resistance of the material changes.

So for a certain material at a certain constant temperature we can write a mathematical expression as,

$$R \propto \frac{l}{a}$$

The effect of nature of material is considered through the constant of proportionality denoted by ρ (rho) called **resistivity** or **specific resistance** of the material.

So finally,
$$R = \frac{\rho l}{a}$$

where l = Length in metres, a = Cross-sectional area in square metres

ρ = Resistivity in ohms-metres,   R = Resistance in ohms

The resistivity or specific resistance of a material depends on nature of material and denoted by ρ(rho). From the expression of resistance it can be expressed as,

$$\rho = \frac{Ra}{l} \quad \text{i.e.} \quad \frac{\Omega\text{-}m^2}{m} \quad \text{i.e.} \quad \Omega\text{-}m$$

It is measured in Ω - m.

Definition : *The resistance of a material having unit length and unit cross-sectional area is known as its specific resistance or resistivity.*

Key Point *A material with highest value of resistivity is the best insulator while with poorest value of resistivity is the best conductor.*

The examples of conductors are copper, gold, aluminium, bronze etc. while the examples of insulators are rubber, paper, wood, mica, glass etc.

0.5.2 Conductance

The reciprocal of a resistance R of any material is called conductance denoted as G. It is the indication of ease with which current can flow through the material. It is measured in **siemens** or **mhos**.

$$G = \frac{1}{R} = \frac{a}{\rho l} = \frac{1}{\rho}\left(\frac{a}{l}\right) = \sigma\left(\frac{a}{l}\right) \quad S$$

0.5.3 Conductivity

The quantity $(1/\rho)$ is called **conductivity**, denoted as σ (sigma). **Thus the conductivity is the reciprocal of resistivity. It is measured in siemens / m or mhos/m.**

Key Point *The material having highest value of conductivity is the best conductor while having poorest conductivity is the best insulator.*

1

D.C. Circuit Analysis

Syllabus

Circuit Concepts : Concepts of network, Active and passive elements, Voltage and current sources, Concept of linearity and linear network, Unilateral and bilateral elements, R, L and C as linear elements, Source transformation. Kirchhoff's laws; Loop and nodal methods of analysis; Star-delta transformation.

Contents

1.1 Introduction

In practice, the electrical circuit may consist of one or more sources of energy and number of electrical parameters, connected in different ways. The different electrical parameters or elements are resistors, capacitors and inductors.

The combination of such elements alongwith various sources of energy gives rise to complicated electrical circuits, generally referred as **networks**. The terms **circuit** and **network** are used synonymously in the electrical literature.

The d.c. circuits consist of only resistances and d.c. sources of energy. And the circuit analysis means to find a current through or voltage across any branch or element of the circuit.

1.2 Network Terminology

In this section, we shall define some of the basic terms which are commonly associated with a network.

1.2.1 Network

Any arrangement of the various electrical energy sources along with the different circuit elements is called an **electrical network**. Such a network is shown in the Fig. 1.2.1.

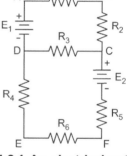

Fig. 1.2.1 An electrical network

1.2.2 Network Element

Any individual circuit element with two terminals which can be connected to other circuit element, is called a **network element**.

Network elements can be either active elements which supply power to the network or passive elements which store or dissipate energy.

1.2.3 Branch

A part of the network which connects the various points of the network with one another is called **a branch**. In the Fig. 1.2.1, AB, BC, CD, DA, DE, CF and EF are the various branches.

A branch may consist more than one element.

1.2.4 Junction Point

A point where three or more branches meet is called **a junction point**.

Point D and C are the junction points in the network shown in the Fig. 1.2.1.

1.2.5 Node

A point at which two or more elements are joined together is called **node**. The junction points are also the nodes of the network.

In the network shown in the Fig. 1.2.1, A, B, C, D, E and F are the nodes of the network.

1.2.6 Mesh (or Loop)

Mesh (or Loop) is a set of branches forming a closed path in a network in such a way that if one branch is removed then remaining branches do not form a closed path.

A loop also can be defined as a closed path which originates from a particular node, terminating at the same node, travelling through various other nodes, without travelling through any node twice.

In the Fig. 1.2.1 paths A-B-C-D-A, A-B-C-F-E-D-A, D-C-F-E-D etc. are the loops of the network.

However the exact difference between a mesh and a loop is that a mesh does not contain any other loop within it. Thus mesh is a smallest loop. A mesh is always a loop but a loop may or may not be a mesh. In the Fig. 1.2.1 paths A-B-C-D-A is a mesh while a path A-B-C-F-E-D-A is a loop.

Review Question

> 1. *Define branch, network element, node, junction point and a mesh related to an electrical network with the help of suitable example.*

1.3 Classification of Electrical Circuits   2008-09

The classification of electrical circuits is based on the behaviour and characteristics of various elements used in the network. The electrical circuits or networks are classified as,

1) Linear network : A network whose elements are always constant irrespective of changes in time, voltage, temperature etc. is called linear network. Ohm's law is applicable for such networks. Principle of superposition can be applied to such networks. The response of various elements is linear with respect to the input applied to them. Examples are networks using elements R, L and C.

2) Nonlinear network : A network whose parameters change their values with change in time, temperature, voltage etc. is called nonlinear network. Ohm's law is not applicable to such networks. Principle of superposition is not applicable to such networks. The response of the elements is not linear with respect to the excitation applied to them. Example is a network using diode as an element whose response is not linear.

3) Bilateral network : A circuit whose behaviour and characteristics is same irrespective of the direction of current through various elements is called bilateral network. Example is a network consisting R, L and C whose behaviour remains same though the direction of current through them changes.

4) Unilateral network : A circuit whose behaviour is dependent on the direction of current through various elements is called unilateral network. Example is a network consisting diode or transistors. The diode allows flow of current only in one direction.

5) Active network : A network consisting at least one source of energy is called an active network. Example is a network consisting at least one battery, voltage source, current source etc.

6) Passive network : A network which contains no energy source is called passive network. Example is a network consisting only elements such as R, L and C without any energy source.

7) Lumped network : A network in which all the network elements are physically separable from each other and shown to be concentrated at one place in a network is called lumped network. Example is a network consisting elements R, L and C.

8) Distributed network : A network in which the network elements are not physically separable but are distributed all along the length of the network is called distributed network. Example is a transmission line whose resistance is distributed all along its length and can not be shown concentrated at one place and hence not seperable.

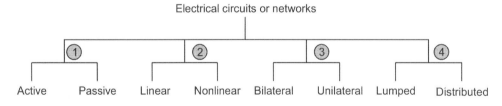

Fig. 1.3.1 Electrical circuits or networks

Review Questions

1. *How electrical circuits are classified ?*
2. *Explain linear and nonlinear networks.*
3. *Explain active and passive networks.*
4. *Explain unilateral and bilateral networks.*   **2008-09, Marks 4**
5. *Explain lumped and distributed networks.*

1.4 Energy Sources

2009-10

There are basically two types of energy sources ; voltage source and current source. These are classified as - i) Ideal source   and   ii) Practical source.

Let us see the difference between ideal and practical sources.

1.4.1 Voltage Source

Ideal voltage source : It is defined as the energy source which gives constant voltage across its terminals irrespective of the current drawn through its terminals. The symbol for ideal voltage source is shown in the Fig. 1.4.1 (a). This is connected to the load as shown in Fig. 1.4.1 (b). At any time the value of voltage at load terminals remains same. This is indicated by V- I characteristics shown in the Fig. 1.4.1 (c).

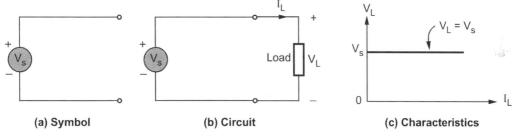

(a) Symbol   (b) Circuit   (c) Characteristics

Fig. 1.4.1 Ideal voltage source

Practical voltage source :   But practically, every voltage source has small internal resistance shown in series with voltage source and is represented by R_{se} as shown in the Fig. 1.4.2.

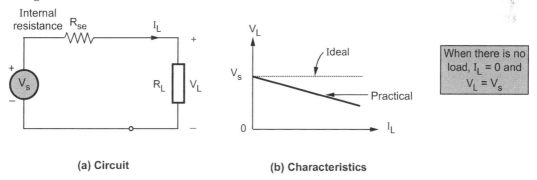

(a) Circuit   (b) Characteristics

Fig. 1.4.2 Practical voltage source

Because of the R_{se}, voltage across terminals decreases slightly with increase in current and it is given by expression,

$$V_L = V_s - I_L R_{se}$$

Key Point *For ideal voltage source,* $R_{se} = 0$.

1.4.2 Current Source

Ideal current source : It is the source which gives constant current at its terminals irrespective of the voltage appearing across its terminals. The symbol for ideal current source is shown in the Fig. 1.4.3 (a). This is connected to the load as shown in the Fig. 1.4.3 (b). At any time, the value of the current flowing through load I_L is same i.e. is irrespective of voltage appearing across its terminals. This is explained by V-I characteristics shown in the Fig. 1.4.3 (c).

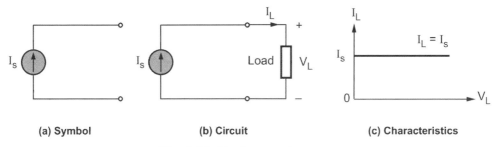

     (a) Symbol   **(b) Circuit**   **(c) Characteristics**

Fig. 1.4.3 Ideal current source

Practical current source : But practically, every current source has high internal resistance, shown in parallel with current source and it is represented by R_{sh}. This is shown in the Fig. 1.4.4.

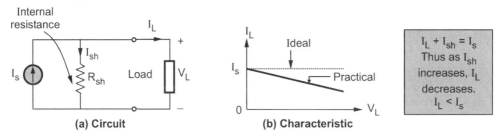

     (a) Circuit   **(b) Characteristic**

Fig. 1.4.4 Practical current source

Because of R_{sh}, current through its terminals decreases slightly with increase in voltage at its terminals.

Key Point *For ideal current source, $R_{sh} = \infty$.*

Both voltage sources and current sources are further classified as follows :

i) Time invariant sources : The sources in which voltage and current are not varying with time are known as **time invariant sources** or **D.C. sources**. These are denoted by capital letters.

ii) Time variant sources : The sources in which voltage and current are varying with time are known as **time variant or A.C. sources**. These are denoted by small letters.

These are shown in the Fig. 1.4.5 (a), (b), (c) and (d).

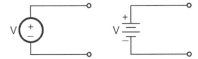

Fig. 1.4.5 (a) D. C. voltage source   **Fig. 1.4.5 (b) A. C. voltage source**

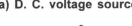

Fig. 1.4.5 (c) D. C. current source   **Fig. 1.4.5 (d) A. C. current source**

Independent sources : The sources which are discussed above are called independent sources because these sources does not depend on other voltages or currents in the network for their value. These are represented by a circle with a polarity of voltage or direction of current indicated inside.

1.4.3 Dependent Sources

Dependent sources are those whose value of source depends on voltage or current in the circuit. Such sources are indicated by diamond as shown in the Fig. 1.4.6 and further classified as,

i) Voltage dependent voltage source : It produces a voltage as a function of voltages elsewhere in the given circuit. This is called **VDVS.** It is shown in the Fig. 1.4.6 (a).

ii) Current dependent current source : It produces a current as a function of currents elsewhere in the given circuit. This is called **CDCS.** It is shown in the Fig. 1.4.6 (b).

iii) Current dependent voltage source : It produces a voltage as a function of current elsewhere in the given circuit. This is called **CDVS.** It is shown in the Fig. 1.4.6 (c).

iv) Voltage dependent current source : It produces a current as a function of voltage elsewhere in the given circuit. This is called **VDCS.** It is shown in the Fig. 1.4.6 (d).

Fig. 1.4.6 Types of dependent sources

K is constant and V_1 and I_1 are the voltage and current respectively, present elsewhere in the given circuit. The dependent sources are also known as **controlled sources**.

> 1. *Explain the difference between ideal and practical voltage source.*
> 2. *Explain the difference between ideal and practical current source.*
> 3. *Discuss the different types of voltage and current sources.*   **2009-10, Marks 5**

1.5 Ohm's Law

This law gives relationship between the potential difference (V), the current (I) and the resistance (R) of a d.c. circuit. **Dr. Ohm** in 1827 discovered a law called **Ohm's Law**. It states,

Ohm's Law : *The current flowing through the electric circuit is directly proportional to the potential difference across the circuit and inversely proportional to the resistance of the circuit, provided the temperature remains constant.*

Mathematically, $$I \propto \frac{V}{R}$$

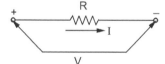

Where I is the current flowing in amperes, the V is the voltage applied and R is the resistance of the conductor, as shown in the Fig. 1.5.1.

Fig. 1.5.1 Ohm's law

Now $$I = \frac{V}{R}$$

The unit of potential difference is defined in such a way that the constant of proportionality is unity.

Ohm's Law : $I = \dfrac{V}{R}$ amperes or $V = I R$ volts or $\dfrac{V}{I} = $ Constant $= R$ ohms

The Ohm's law can be defined as,

The ratio of potential difference (V) between any two points of a conductor to the current (I) flowing between them is constant, provided that the temperature of the conductor remains constant.

Key Point *Ohm's Law can be applied either to the entire circuit or to the part of a circuit. If it is applied to entire circuit, the voltage across the entire circuit and resistance of the entire circuit should be taken into account. If the Ohm's Law is applied to the part of a circuit, then the resistance of that part and potential across that part should be used.*

1.5.1 Limitations of Ohm's Law

The limitations of the Ohm's law are,

1) It is not applicable to the nonlinear devices such as diodes, zener diodes, voltage regulators etc.

2) It does not hold good for non-metallic conductors such as silicon carbide. The law for such conductors is given by,

$$V = k\, I^m \quad \text{where k, m are constants.}$$

Review Question

> 1. *State Ohm's law and its limitations.*

1.6 Basic Circuit Parameters

The three basic circuit elements are resistor, inductor and a capacitor.

1.6.1 Resistance (R)

The property of a resistor made up of any material which opposes the flow of current through it is called resistance denoted as R. Its symbol is shown in the Fig. 1.6.1. The resistance is measured in ohms (Ω).

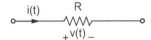

Fig. 1.6.1

The factors affecting the resistance R of a material are,

i) Length (l) ii) Area of cross-section (a) iii) Resistivity (ρ)

It is given by,
$$R = \frac{\rho l}{a} \ \Omega$$

The resistance also depends on the temperature. The voltage and current relationship is given by Ohm's law as,

$$i(t) = \frac{v(t)}{R} \qquad \text{and} \qquad v(t) = i(t)\, R$$

The power consumed is given by,

$$p(t) = v(t)\, i(t) = \frac{v^2(t)}{R} = i^2(t)R$$

If the voltage and current are d.c. i.e. constant given by V and I then,

$$I = \frac{V}{R}, \ V = IR, \ P = VI = \frac{V^2}{R} = I^2R$$

The power is measured in watts.

The energy consumed is given by,

$$W = \int_{-\infty}^{t} p(t)dt = \int_{-\infty}^{t} v(t)\, i(t)\, dt$$

The energy consumed is measured in joules (J).

For constant d.c. V and I, energy consumed in time 't' is,

$$W = VIt \ J$$

1.6.2 Inductance (L)

The coils having N number of turns made up various materials and having various sizes are called inductors.

The property of a coil which opposes any change in current passing through it is called an inductance denoted as L.

Inductance is treated as a circuit element which stores energy in the form of electromagnetic field. Its symbol is shown in the Fig. 1.6.2. The inductance property is measured in henries (H). In inductance, the voltage across it is proportional to the rate of change of current and constant of proportionality is an inductance L.

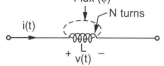

Fig. 1.6.2

$$\therefore \qquad v(t) = L\,\frac{d\,i(t)}{dt} \quad \text{and} \quad i(t) = \frac{1}{L}\int_{0}^{t} v(t)\,dt + i(0)$$

where i(0) = Initial current through an inductor

The current in inductance can not change instantly.

Mathematically inductance is the ratio of flux linkages (Nϕ) associated with it to the current (i) producing the flux.

$$L = \frac{N\phi}{i}$$

The power in the inductor is, $p(t) = v(t)\, i(t)$

The energy stored in an inductor is,

$$W = \int_{0}^{t} v(t)\, i(t)\, dt = \int_{0}^{t} L\,\frac{d\,i(t)}{dt}\, i(t)\, dt$$

$$\therefore \quad W = \int_0^t L\, i(t)\, d\, i(t) = \frac{L\, i^2(t)}{2} \quad \text{i.e.} \quad \boxed{W = \frac{1}{2} L\, i^2(t)\, J}$$

If the current flowing is constant I then $W = \frac{1}{2} LI^2 J$.

1.6.3 Capacitance (C)

Two conducting plates separated from each other by an insulating material is called a capacitor. The insulating material is called dielectric. The commonly used dielectrics are paper, air, mica etc.

The property of a capacitor to store an electrical energy in the form of electrostatic field, when a potential difference is applied across it is called capacitance denoted as C. Its symbol is shown in the Fig. 1.6.3. It is measured in farads (F).

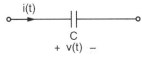

Fig. 1.6.3

The charge acquired by a capacitor is proportional to the voltage applied and a constant of proportionality is a capacitance C.

$$\therefore \quad \boxed{q = C\, v(t) \quad \text{or} \quad C = \frac{q}{v(t)}} \quad \ldots q = \text{Charge in coulombs}$$

Its current can be obtained by differentiating above equation,

$$\frac{dq}{dt} = C\frac{dv(t)}{dt} \quad \text{but} \quad \frac{dq}{dt} = \text{Current } i(t)$$

$$\therefore \quad \boxed{i(t) = C\frac{d\, v(t)}{dt} \quad \text{and} \quad v(t) = \frac{1}{C}\int_0^t i(t)\, dt + v(0)}$$

where $v(0) = $ Initial voltage across the capacitor

The voltage across capacitance C can not change instantly.

The power in the capacitor is, $\boxed{p(t) = v(t)\, i(t)}$ in watts.

The energy stored can be obtained as,

$$W = \int_0^t v(t)\, i(t)\, dt = \int_0^t v(t)\, C\frac{d\, v(t)}{dt}\, dt$$

$$\therefore \quad W = \int_{0}^{t} C \, v(t) \, d \, v(t) = \frac{C \, v^2(t)}{2} \quad \text{i.e.} \quad \boxed{W = \frac{1}{2} C \, v^2(t) \, J}$$

If the voltage across C is constant V then $W = \frac{1}{2} CV^2 J$.

1.6.4 Voltage-Current Relationships for Passive Elements

The three passive elements are resistance (R), inductance (L) and capacitance (C). The behaviour of these three elements alongwith the respective voltage-current relationship is given in the Table 1.6.1.

The behaviour of the three elements can be summarized as,

Element	Basic relation	Voltage across, if current known	Current through, if voltage known	Energy
R	$R = \dfrac{v}{i}$	$v_R(t) = R \, i_R(t)$	$i_R(t) = \dfrac{1}{R} \, v_R(t)$	$w = \displaystyle\int_{-\infty}^{t} i_R(t) \, v_R(t) \, dt$
L	$L = \dfrac{N\phi}{i}$	$v_L(t) = L \dfrac{di_L(t)}{dt}$	$i_L(t) = \dfrac{1}{L} \displaystyle\int_{-\infty}^{t} v_L(t) \, dt$	$w = \dfrac{1}{2} L \, i^2(t)$
C	$C = \dfrac{q}{v}$	$v_C(t) = \dfrac{1}{C} \displaystyle\int_{-\infty}^{t} i_C(t) \, dt$	$i_C(t) = C \dfrac{dv_C(t)}{dt}$	$w = \dfrac{1}{2} C \, v^2(t)$

Table 1.6.1 Behaviour of basic circuit elements

Note that in the Table 1.6.1, v_R, v_L and v_C are the voltages across R, L and C respectively while i_R, i_L and i_C are the currents through R, L and C respectively.

If voltage and current are d.c. then use V and I instead of v(t) and i(t).

Review Questions

1. *Which are the three basic elements ? Explain their behaviour in brief.*
2. *Explain the voltage-current relationship for basic circuit elements.*

1.7 Series and Parallel Combinations of Elements

Analysis of complicated electrical circuits can be simplified by using the equivalent of series and parallel combinations of various elements. The following tables give the method of finding the equivalent of 'n' elements connected in series and parallel.

The Table 1.7.1 gives the equivalent of 'n' basic elements in series,

Element	Equivalent
'n' Resistances in series	$R_{eq} = R_1 + R_2 + R_3 + ... + R_n$
'n' Inductors in series	$L_{eq} = L_1 + L_2 + L_3 + ... + L_n$
'n' Capacitors in series	$\dfrac{1}{C_{eq}} = \dfrac{1}{C_1} + \dfrac{1}{C_2} + ... + \dfrac{1}{C_n}$

Table 1.7.1 Series combinations of elements

The Table 1.7.2 gives the equivalent of 'n' basic elements in parallel,

Element	Equivalent
'n' Resistances in parallel	$\dfrac{1}{R_{eq}} = \dfrac{1}{R_1} + \dfrac{1}{R_2} + ... + \dfrac{1}{R_n}$
'n' Inductors in parallel	$\dfrac{1}{L_{eq}} = \dfrac{1}{L_1} + \dfrac{1}{L_2} + ... + \dfrac{1}{L_n}$
'n' Capacitors in parallel	$C_{eq} = C_1 + C_2 + ... + C_n$

Table 1.7.2 Parallel combinations of elements

Key Point *The current through series combination remains same and voltage gets divided while in parallel combination voltage across combination remains same and current gets divided.*

Examples for Understanding

Example 1.7.1 *Two capacitances C_1 and C_2 of values of 10 μF and 5 μF, respectively are connected in series. What is the equivalent capacitance of the combination ?*

Solution : $C_1 = 10 \ \mu F$ and $C_2 = 5 \ \mu F$

∴ $C_{eq} = \dfrac{C_1 C_2}{C_1 + C_2} = \dfrac{10 \times 10^{-6} \times 5 \times 10^{-6}}{10 \times 10^{-6} + 5 \times 10^{-6}} = 3.333 \times 10^{-6} = \mathbf{3.33 \ \mu F}$

Example 1.7.2 *Find the equivalent resistance between the two points A and B shown in the Fig. 1.7.1.*

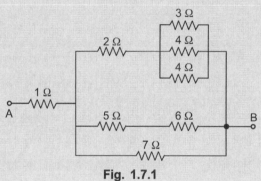

Fig. 1.7.1

Solution : Identify combinations of series and parallel resistances.

The resistances 5 Ω and 6 Ω are in series, as going to carry same current.

So equivalent resistance is 5 + 6 = 11 Ω

While the resistances 3 Ω , 4 Ω, and 4 Ω are in parallel, as voltage across them same but current divides.

∴ Equivalent resistance is, $\dfrac{1}{R} = \dfrac{1}{3} + \dfrac{1}{4} + \dfrac{1}{4} = \dfrac{10}{12}$ i.e. R = $\dfrac{12}{10} = 1.2 \ \Omega$

Replacing these combinations redraw the figure as shown in the Fig. 1.7.1 (a).

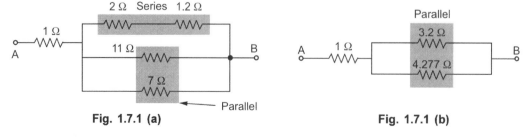

Fig. 1.7.1 (a)   **Fig. 1.7.1 (b)**

Now again 1.2 Ω and 2 Ω are in series so equivalent resistance is 2 + 1.2 = 3.2 Ω while 11 Ω and 7 Ω are in parallel.

Using formula $\dfrac{R_1 R_2}{R_1 + R_2}$ equivalent resistance is $\dfrac{11 \times 7}{11 + 7}$ = $\dfrac{77}{18}$ = 4.277 Ω .

Replacing the respective combinations redraw the circuit as shown in the Fig. 1.7.1 (b).

Now 3.2 and 4.277 are in parallel.

$\therefore$ Replacing them by $\dfrac{3.2 \times 4.277}{3.2 + 4.277}$ = 1.8304 Ω

$\therefore$ R_{AB} = 1+ 1.8304 = **2.8304** Ω

Review Question

1. *Find the equivalent resistance across the terminals PQ of the network shown in the Fig. 1.7.2.*

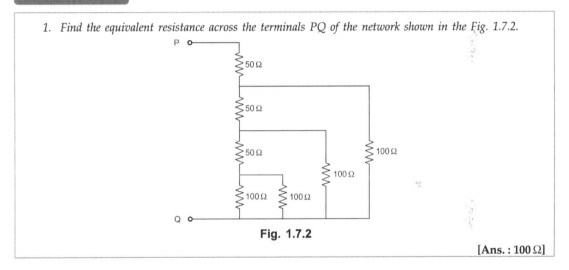

Fig. 1.7.2

[Ans. : 100 Ω]

1.8 Short and Open Circuits

In the network simplification, short circuit or open circuit existing in the network plays an important role.

1.8.1 Short Circuit

When any two points in a network are joined directly to each other with a thick metalic conducting wire, the two points are said to be short circuited. **The resistance of such short circuit is zero.**

The part of the network, which is short circuited is shown in the Fig. 1.8.1. The points A and B are short circuited. The resistance of the branch AB is $R_{sc} = 0 \ \Omega$.

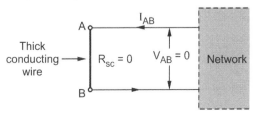

Fig. 1.8.1

The curent I_{AB} is flowing through the short circuited path.

According to Ohm's law,

$$V_{AB} = R_{sc} \times I_{AB} = 0 \times I_{AB} = 0 \text{ V}$$

Key Point *Thus, voltage across short circuit is always zero though current flows through the short circuited path.*

1.8.2 Open Circuit

When there is no connection between the two points of a network, having some voltage across the two points then the two points are said to be open circuited.

As there is no direct connection in an open circuit, **the resistance of the open circuit is ∞.**

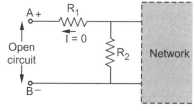

The part of the network which is open circuited is shown in the Fig. 1.8.2. The points A and B are said to be open circuited. The resistance of the branch AB is $R_{oc} = \infty \ \Omega$.

Fig. 1.8.2

There exists a voltage across the points AB called open circuit voltage, V_{AB} but $R_{oc} = \infty \ \Omega$.

According to Ohm's law,

$$I_{oc} = \frac{V_{AB}}{R_{oc}} = \frac{V_{AB}}{\infty} = 0 \text{ A}$$

Key Point *Thus, current through open circuit is always zero though there exists a voltage across open circuited terminals.*

1.8.3 Redundant Branches and Combinations

The redundant means excessive and unwanted.

Key Point *If in a circuit there are branches or combinations of elements which do not carry any current then such branches and combinations are called redundant from circuit point of view.*

The redundant branches and combinations can be removed and these branches do not affect the performance of the circuit.

The two important situations of **redundancy** which may exist in practical circuits are,

Situation 1 : Any branch or combination across which there exists a short circuit, becomes redundant as it does not carry any current.

If in a network, there exists a direct short circuit across a resistance or the combination of resistances then that resistance or the entire combination of resistances becomes **inactive** from the circuit point of view. Such a combination is redundant from circuit point of view.

To understand this, consider the combination of resistances and a short circuit as shown in the Fig. 1.8.3 (a) and (b).

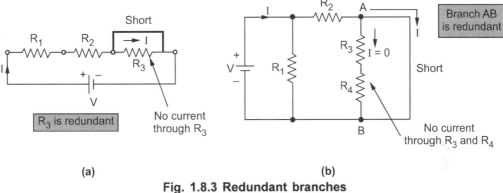

(a)   **(b)**

Fig. 1.8.3 Redundant branches

In Fig. 1.8.3 (a), there is short circuit across R_3. The current always prefers low resistance path hence entire current I passes through short circuit and hence resistance R_3 becomes redundant from the circuit point of view.

In Fig. 1.8.3 (b), there is short circuit across combination of R_3 and R_4. The entire current flows through short circuit across R_3 and R_4 and no current can flow through combination of R_3 and R_4. Thus that combination becomes meaningless from the circuit point of view. **Such combinations can be eliminated while analysing the circuit.**

Situation 2 : If there is open circuit in a branch or combination, it can not carry any current and becomes redundant.

In Fig. 1.8.4 as there exists open circuit in branch BC, the branch BC and CD can not carry any current and are become redundant from circuit point of view.

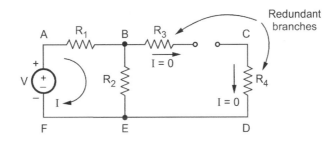

Fig. 1.8.4 Redundant branches due to open circuit

1.9 Voltage Division in Series Circuit of Resistors

Consider a series circuit of two resistors R_1 and R_2 connected to source of V volts.

As two resistors are connected in series, the current flowing through both the resistors is same, i.e. I. Then applying KVL, we get,

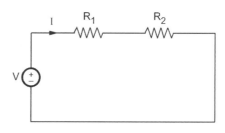

Fig. 1.9.1

$$V = I R_1 + I R_2$$

$$\therefore \quad I = \frac{V}{R_1 + R_2}$$

Total voltage applied is equal to the sum of voltage drops V_{R1} and V_{R2} across R_1 and R_2 respectively.

$$\therefore \quad V_{R1} = I \cdot R_1$$

$$\therefore \quad V_{R1} = \frac{V}{R_1 + R_2} \cdot R_1 = \left[\frac{R_1}{R_1 + R_2}\right] V$$

Similarly, $V_{R2} = I \cdot R_2$

$$\therefore \quad V_{R2} = \frac{V}{R_1 + R_2} \cdot R_2 = \left[\frac{R_2}{R_1 + R_2}\right] V$$

So this circuit is a **voltage divider circuit**.

Key Point *So in general, voltage drop across any resistor, or combination of resistors, in a series circuit is equal to the ratio of that resistance value to the total resistance, multiplied by the source voltage.*

Example 1.9.1 *Find the voltage across the three resistances shown in the Fig. 1.9.2.*

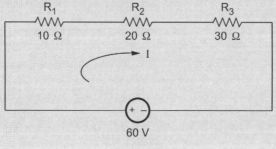

Fig. 1.9.2

Solution : $I = \dfrac{V}{R_1 + R_2 + R_3}$ ... series circuit

$$= \dfrac{60}{10 + 20 + 30} = 1 \text{ A}$$

$\therefore \qquad V_{R1} = I R_1 = \dfrac{V \times R_1}{R_1 + R_2 + R_3} = 1 \times 10 = \mathbf{10\ V}$

$\therefore \qquad V_{R2} = I R_2 = \dfrac{V \times R_2}{R_1 + R_2 + R_3} = 1 \times 20 = \mathbf{20\ V}$

and $\qquad V_{R3} = I R_3 = \dfrac{V \times R_3}{R_1 + R_2 + R_3} = 1 \times 30 = \mathbf{30\ V}$

Key Point *It can be seen that voltage across any resistance of series circuit is ratio of that resistance to the total resistance, multiplied by the source voltage.*

1.10 Current Division in Parallel Circuit of Resistors   2001-02

Consider a parallel circuit of two resistors R_1 and R_2 connected across a source of V volts.

Current through R_1 is I_1 and R_2 is I_2, while total current drawn from source is I_T.

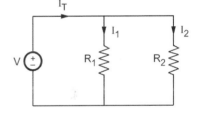

Fig. 1.10.1

$\therefore \qquad I_T = I_1 + I_2$

But $\quad I_1 = \dfrac{V}{R_1},\qquad I_2 = \dfrac{V}{R_2}$

i.e. $\quad V = I_1 R_1 = I_2 R_2$

$\therefore \qquad I_1 = I_2 \left(\dfrac{R_2}{R_1} \right)$

Substituting value of I_1 in I_T,

$\therefore \qquad I_T = I_2 \left(\dfrac{R_2}{R_1} \right) + I_2 \ = I_2 \left[\dfrac{R_2}{R_1} + 1 \right] \ = I_2 \left[\dfrac{R_1 + R_2}{R_1} \right]$

$\therefore \qquad$ 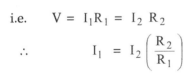 $\quad I_2 = \left[\dfrac{R_1}{R_1 + R_2} \right] I_T$

Now $\qquad I_1 = I_T - I_2 = I_T - \left[\dfrac{R_1}{R_1 + R_2} \right] I_T$

$\therefore \qquad I_1 = \left[\dfrac{R_1 + R_2 - R_1}{R_1 + R_2} \right] I_T$

$\therefore$

$$I_1 = \left[\frac{R_2}{R_1 + R_2} \right] I_T$$

Key Point *In general, the current in any branch is equal to the ratio of opposite branch resistance to the total resistance value, multiplied by the total current in the circuit.*

Example 1.10.1 *Find the magnitudes of total current, current through R_1 and R_2 if, $R_1 = 10\ \Omega$, $R_2 = 20\ \Omega$, and $V = 50\ V$.*

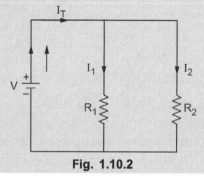

Fig. 1.10.2

Solution : The equivalent resistance of two is,

$$R_{eq} = \frac{R_1\,R_2}{R_1 + R_2} = \frac{10 \times 20}{10 + 20} = 6.67\ \Omega$$

$\therefore$

$$I_T = \frac{V}{R_{eq}} = \frac{50}{6.67} = \textbf{7.5 A}$$

As per the current distribution in parallel circuit,

$$I_1 = I_T \left(\frac{R_2}{R_1 + R_2} \right) = 7.5 \times \left(\frac{20}{10 + 20} \right) = \textbf{5 A}$$

and

$$I_2 = I_T \left(\frac{R_1}{R_1 + R_2} \right) = 7.5 \times \left(\frac{10}{10 + 20} \right) = \textbf{2.5 A}$$

It can be verified that $I_T = I_1 + I_2$.

The current distribution in parallel resistances is very frequently required in the network analysis and used as **current distribution rule** hereafter.

Example 1.10.2 *A d.c. circuit comprises 2 resistors; resistor A of value 25 Ω, and resistor B of unknown value, connected in parallel, together with a third resistor C of value 5 Ω connected in series with the parallel branch. Find the voltage to be applied across the whole circuit and the value of the resistor B, if the p.d. across C is 90 V and the total power consumed is 4320 W.*   **2001-02**

Solution :

$$V_C = I \times R_C$$

$$\therefore \quad 90 = I \times 5$$

$$\therefore \quad I = 18 \ A$$

$$R_{eq} = [R_A \parallel R_B] + R_C$$

$$\therefore \quad R_{eq} = \frac{25 \ R_B}{25 + R_B} + 5 = \frac{125 + 30 \ R_B}{25 + R_B}$$

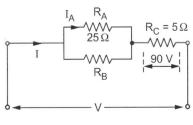

Fig. 1.10.3

Now $\quad P_T = I^2 \ R_{eq} \quad$ i.e. $\quad 4320 = 18^2 \times \left[\dfrac{125 + 30 \ R_B}{25 + R_B} \right]$

$$\therefore \quad 13.333 \ (25 + R_B) = 125 + 30 \ R_B$$

$$\therefore \qquad\qquad R_B = \frac{208.3333}{16.6667} = \mathbf{12.5 \ \Omega}$$

$$V = \text{Drop across } R_A \text{ or } R_B + 90 \qquad\qquad \dots R_A \text{ and } R_B \text{ in parallel}$$

$$= I_A \times 25 + 90 = \left[I \times \frac{R_B}{R_A + R_B} \right] \times 25 + 90 \quad \dots \text{ Using current division}$$

$$= \left[\frac{18 \times 12.5}{(25 + 12.5)} \right] \times 25 + 90 = \mathbf{240 \ V}$$

1.11 Source Transformation

Consider a practical voltage source shown in the Fig. 1.11.1 (a) having internal resistance R_{se}, connected to the load having resistance R_L.

Now we can replace voltage source by equivalent current source.

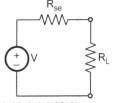

Fig. 1.11.1 (a) Voltage source

> **Key Point** *The two sources are said to be **equivalent**, if they supply equal load current to the load, with same load connected across its terminals*

The current delivered in above case by voltage source is,

$$I = \frac{V}{(R_{se} + R_L)}, \qquad R_{se} \text{ and } R_L \text{ in series} \qquad\qquad \dots(1.11.1)$$

If it is to be replaced by a current source then load current must be $\dfrac{V}{(R_{se} + R_L)}$

Consider an equivalent current source shown in the Fig. 1.11.1 (b).

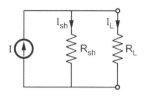

The total current is ' I '.

Both the resistances will take current proportional to their values.

Fig. 1.11.1 (b) Current source

From the current division in parallel circuit we can write,

$$I_L = I \times \frac{R_{sh}}{(R_{sh} + R_L)} \qquad ...(1.11.2)$$

Now this I_L and $\dfrac{V}{R_{se} + R_L}$ must be same, so equating (1.11.1) and (1.11.2),

$$\therefore \quad \frac{V}{R_{se} + R_L} = \frac{I \times R_{sh}}{R_{sh} + R_L}$$

Let internal resistance be, $R_{se} = R_{sh} = R$ say.

Then, $\quad V = I \times R_{sh} = I \times R \quad$ or $\quad I = \dfrac{V}{R_{sh}}$

$$\therefore \qquad \boxed{I = \frac{V}{R} = \frac{V}{R_{se}}}$$

Key Point *If voltage source is converted to current source, then current source $I = \dfrac{V}{R_{se}}$ with parallel internal resistance equal to R_{se}.*

Key Point *If current source is converted to voltage source, then voltage source $V = I R_{sh}$ with series internal resistance equal to R_{sh}.*

The direction of current of equivalent current source is always from **– ve to + ve, internal to the source.** While converting current source to voltage source, polarities of voltage is always as +ve terminal at top of arrow and –ve terminal at bottom of arrow, as direction of current is from –ve to +ve, internal to the source. **This ensures that current flows from positive to negative terminal in the external circuit.**

Note the directions of transformed sources, shown in the Fig. 1.11.2 (a), (b), (c) and (d).

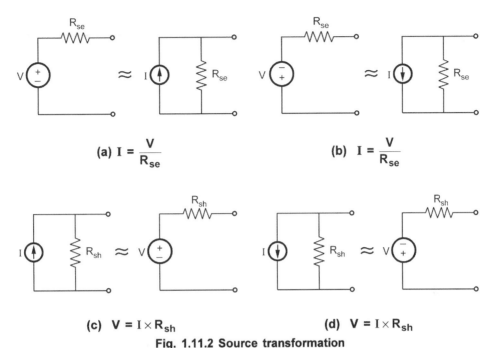

(a) $I = \dfrac{V}{R_{se}}$

(b) $I = \dfrac{V}{R_{se}}$

(c) $V = I \times R_{sh}$

(d) $V = I \times R_{sh}$

Fig. 1.11.2 Source transformation

Example 1.11.1 *Transform a voltage source of 20 volts with an internal resistance of 5 Ω to a current source.*

Solution : Refer to the Fig. 1.11.3 (a).

Then current of current source is,

$I = \dfrac{V}{R_{se}} = \dfrac{20}{5} = 4$ A with internal

parallel resistance same as R_{se}.

∴ Equivalent current source is as shown in the Fig. 1.11.3 (b).

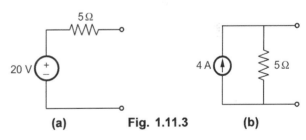

(a)   **Fig. 1.11.3**   (b)

Example 1.11.2 *Using source transformation find I.*

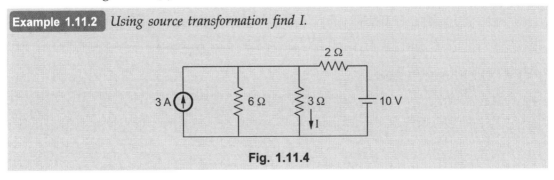

Fig. 1.11.4

Solution : Converting 10 V voltage source to current source,

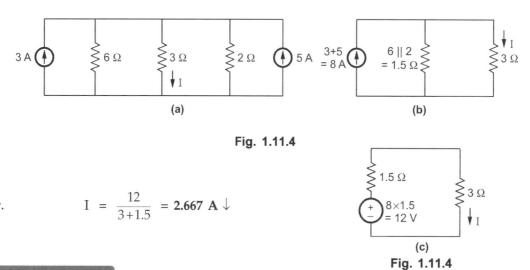

(a)   (b)

Fig. 1.11.4

∴ $I = \dfrac{12}{3+1.5} = \mathbf{2.667\ A} \downarrow$

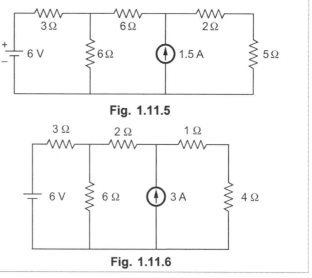

(c)

Fig. 1.11.4

1. *Explain how to convert voltage source into current source and vice-versa.*

2. *Using source transformations, determine the voltage across 5 ohm resistance for the circuit shown in Fig. 1.11.5.*

   [Ans. : 5.333 V]

Fig. 1.11.5

3. *For the circuit shown in Fig. 1.11.6, find the current in 4 Ω resistance by source transformation.*

   [Ans. : 1.778 A↓]

Fig. 1.11.6

1.12 Kirchhoff's Laws

In 1847, a German Physicist, **Kirchhoff,** formulated two fundamental laws of electricity. These laws are of tremendous importance from network simplification point of view.

1.12.1 Kirchhoff's Current Law (KCL)

Consider a junction point in a complex network as shown in the Fig. 1.12.1.

At this junction point if $I_1 = 2$ A, $I_2 = 4$ A and $I_3 = 1$ A then to determine I_4 we write, total current entering is $2 + 4 = 6$ A while total current leaving is $1 + I_4$ A

And hence, $I_4 = 5$ A.

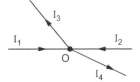

This analysis of currents entering and leaving is nothing but the application of Kirchhoff's Current Law. The law can be stated as,

Fig. 1.12.1 Junction point

> *The total current flowing towards a junction point is equal to the total current flowing away from that junction point.*

Another way to state the law is,

> *The algebraic sum of all the current meeting at a junction point is always zero.*

The word algebraic means considering the signs of various currents.

$$\sum I \text{ at junction point} = 0$$

> *Sign convention : Currents flowing towards a junction point are assumed to be positive while currents flowing away from a junction point assumed to be negative.*

E.g. Refer Fig. 1.12.1, currents I_1 and I_2 are positive while I_3 and I_4 are negative.

Applying KCL, $\qquad \sum I$ at junction O $= 0$

$$I_1 + I_2 - I_3 - I_4 = 0 \text{ i.e. } I_1 + I_2 = I_3 + I_4$$

The law is very helpful in network simplification.

1.12.2 Kirchhoff's Voltage Law (KVL)

> *"In any network, the algebraic sum of the voltage drops across the circuit elements of any closed path (or loop or mesh) is equal to the algebraic sum of the e.m.fs in the path".*

In other words, "the algebraic sum of all the branch voltages, around any closed path or closed loop is always zero."

$$\text{Around a closed path } \sum V = 0$$

The law states that if one starts at a certain point of a closed path and goes on tracing and noting all the potential changes (either drops or rises), in any one particular direction, till the starting point is reached again, he must be at the same potential with which he started tracing a closed path.

Sum of all the potential rises must be equal to sum of all the potential drops while tracing any closed path of the circuit. The total change in potential along a closed path is always zero.

This law is very useful in the loop analysis of the network.

1.12.3 Sign Conventions to be Followed while Applying KVL

When current flows through a resistance, the voltage drop occurs across the resistance. The polarity of this voltage drop always depends on direction of the current. The current always flows from higher potential to lower potential.

In the Fig. 1.12.2 (a), current I is flowing from right to left, hence point B is at higher potential than point A, as shown.

In the Fig. 1.12.2 (b), current I is flowing from left to right, hence point A is at higher potential than point B, as shown.

(a)   **(b)**

Fig. 1.12.2

Once all such polarities are marked in the given circuit, we can apply KVL to any closed path in the circuit.

Now while tracing a closed path, if we go from – ve marked terminal to + ve marked terminal, that voltage must be taken as positive. This is called **potential rise**.

For example, if the branch AB is traced from A to B then the drop across it must be considered as rise and must be taken as + IR while writing the equations.

While tracing a closed path, if we go from +ve marked terminal to – ve marked terminal, that voltage must be taken as negative. This is called **potential drop**.

For example, in the Fig. 1.12.2 (a) only, if the branch is traced from B to A then it should be taken as negative, as – IR while writing the equations.

Similarly in the Fig. 1.12.2 (b), if branch is traced from A to B then there is a voltage drop and term must be written negative as – IR while writing the equation. If the branch is traced from B to A, it becomes a rise in voltage and term must be written positive as   + IR while writing the equation.

Key Point

1) *Potential rise i.e. travelling from negative to positively marked terminal, must be considered as* ***Positive****.*

2) *Potential drop i.e. travelling from positive to negatively marked terminal, must be considered as* ***Negative****.*

3) *While tracing a closed path, select any one direction clockwise or anticlockwise. This selection is totally independent of the directions of currents and voltages of various branches of that closed path.*

1.12.4 Steps to Apply Kirchhoff's Laws to Get Network Equations

The steps are stated based on the branch current method.

Step 1 : Draw the circuit diagram from the given information and insert all the values of sources with appropriate polarities and all the resistances.

Step 2 : Mark all the branch currents with some assumed directions using KCL at various nodes and junction points. Kept the number of unknown currents minimum as far as possible to limit the mathematical calculations required to solve them later on.

Assumed directions may be wrong, in such case answer of such current will be mathematically negative which indicates the correct direction of the current. A particular current leaving a particular source has some magnitude, then same magnitude of current should enter that source after travelling through various branches of the network.

Step 3 : Mark all the polarities of voltage drops and rises as per directions of the assumed branch currents flowing through various branch resistances of the network. This is necessary for application of KVL to various closed loops.

Step 4 : Apply KVL to different closed paths in the network and obtain the corresponding equations. Each equation must contain some element which is not considered in any previous equation.

Key Point *KVL must be applied to sufficient number of loops such that each element of the network is included at least once in any of the equations.*

Step 5 : Solve the simultaneous equations for the unknown currents. From these currents unknown voltages and power consumption in different resistances can be calculated.

What to do if current source exists ?

Key Point *If there is current source in the network then complete the current distribution considering the current source. But while applying KVL, the loops should not be considered involving current source. The loop equations must be written to those loops which do not include any current source. This is because drop across current source is unknown.*

For example, consider the circuit shown in the Fig. 1.12.3. The current distribution is completed interms of current source value. Then KVL must be applied to the loop bcdeb, which does not include current source. **The loop abefa should not be used for KVL application**, as it includes current source. Its effect is already considered at the time of current distribution.

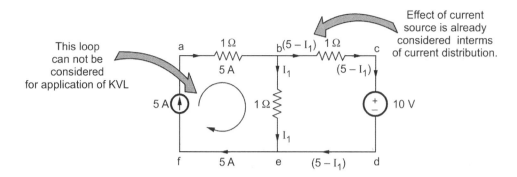

Fig. 1.12.3

1.12.5 Cramer's Rule

If the network is complex, the number of equations i.e. unknowns increases. In such case, the solution of simultaneous equations can be obtained by **Cramer's Rule** for determinants.

Let us assume that set of simultaneous equations obtained is, as follows :

$$a_{11}x_1 + a_{12}x_2 + \ldots\ldots + a_{1n}x_n = C_1$$

$$a_{21}x_1 + a_{22}x_2 + \ldots\ldots + a_{2n}x_n = C_2$$

$\therefore$
$$\vdots$$

$$a_{n1}x_1 + a_{n2}x_2 + \ldots\ldots + a_{nn}x_n = C_n$$

where $C_1, C_2, \ldots\ldots\ldots C_n$ are constants.

Then Cramer's rule says that form a system determinant Δ or D as,

$$\Delta = \begin{vmatrix} a_{11} & a_{12} & \cdots & a_{1n} \\ a_{21} & a_{22} & \cdots & a_{2n} \\ \vdots & & & \\ a_{n1} & a_{n2} & \cdots & a_{nn} \end{vmatrix} = D$$

Then obtain the subdeterminants D_j by replacing j^{th} column of Δ by the column of constants existing on right hand side of equations i.e. $C_1, C_2, \ldots C_n$;

$$D_1 = \begin{vmatrix} C_1 & a_{12} & \cdots & a_{1n} \\ C_2 & a_{22} & \cdots & a_{2n} \\ \vdots & & & \\ C_n & a_{n2} & \cdots & a_{nn} \end{vmatrix}, \quad D_2 = \begin{vmatrix} a_{11} & C_1 & \cdots & a_{1n} \\ a_{21} & C_2 & \cdots & a_{2n} \\ \vdots & & & \\ a_{n1} & C_n & \cdots & a_{nn} \end{vmatrix}$$

$$\text{and} \qquad D_n = \begin{vmatrix} a_{11} & a_{12} & \cdots & C_1 \\ a_{21} & a_{22} & \cdots & C_2 \\ \vdots & & \cdots & \vdots \\ a_{n1} & a_{n2} & \cdots & C_n \end{vmatrix}$$

The unknowns of the equations are given by Cramer's rule as,

$$X_1 = \frac{D_1}{D}, \ X_2 = \frac{D_2}{D}, \ \ldots\ldots\ldots, \ X_n = \frac{D_n}{D}$$

where $D_1, D_2, \ldots, D_n$ and D are values of the respective determinants.

Example 1.12.1 *In the circuit shown in the Fig. 1.12.4, find the current supplied by 7 V source.*

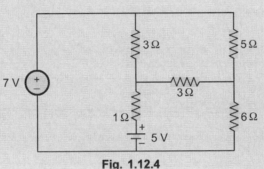

Fig. 1.12.4

Solution :

Step 1 : The circuit diagram is given.

Step 2 : Mark the various branch currents using KCL.

Step 3 : Mark the polarities for the drops due to branch currents as shown in the Fig. 1.12.4 (a).

Fig. 1.12.4 (a)

Apply KVL to the various loops,

Loop abcfha, $-3\,I_2 - (I_2 - I_3) - 5 + 7 = 0$

i.e. $\quad -4\,I_2 + I_3 = -2$ \hfill ...(1.12.1)

Loop cdefc, $-5\,(I_1 - I_2) + 3\,I_3 + 3\,I_2 = 0 \quad$ i.e. $\quad -5\,I_1 + 8\,I_2 + 3\,I_3 = 0 \quad$ ...(1.12.2)

Loop feghf, $-3I_3 - 6\,(I_1 - I_2 + I_3) + 5 + (I_2 - I_3) = 0$ i.e. $-6I_1 + 7I_2 - 10I_3 = -5$ ...(1.12.3)

$$\therefore \qquad D = \begin{vmatrix} 0 & -4 & 1 \\ -5 & 8 & 3 \\ -6 & 7 & -10 \end{vmatrix} = 285 \qquad \text{and} \quad D_1 = \begin{vmatrix} -2 & -4 & 1 \\ 0 & 8 & 3 \\ -5 & 7 & -10 \end{vmatrix} = 302$$

$$I_1 = \frac{D_1}{D} = \frac{302}{285} = \mathbf{1.0596 \ A} \uparrow$$

Example 1.12.2 *Apply Kirchhoff's laws to find potential difference between X and Y shown in the network.*

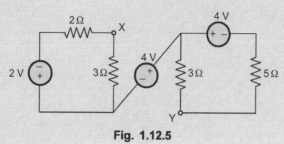

Fig. 1.12.5

Solution : Apply KVL to Loop A-X-B-C-A.

$$-2\,I_1 - 3\,I_1 - 2 = 0 \quad \text{i.e. ,}$$

$$-5\,I_1 = 2 \quad \text{i.e.} \quad I_1 = -0.4 \text{ A}$$

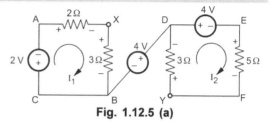

Fig. 1.12.5 (a)

Negative (–) sign indicates assumed direction is wrong.

Apply KVL to Loop D-E-F-Y-D

$$-4 - 5\,I_2 - 3\,I_2 = 0 \quad \text{i.e. } -8\,I_2 = 4$$

i.e. $I_2 = -0.5$ A

Negative (–) sign indicates assumed direction is wrong.

∴ With correct directions, the voltage drops across different resistances are as shown in the Fig. 1.12.5 (b).

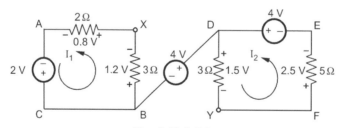

Fig. 1.12.5 (b)

To find V_{x-y}, consider path X-B-D-Y and write voltages, add them with same sign convention.

X o———ⱲⱲ———o B   (–+)   o D ———ⱲⱲ——— o Y

Fig. 1.12.5 (c)

i.e. $V_{x-y} = +1.2 + 4 - 1.5 = +3.7$ V

$V_{x-y} =$ **3.7 V with X negative w.r.t. Y**

Fig. 1.12.5 (d)

Review Questions

1. *State and explain Kirchhoff's laws.*

2. *Find the value of R and the current flowing through it in the network shown in the Fig. 1.12.6, when the current in the branch OA is zero.*

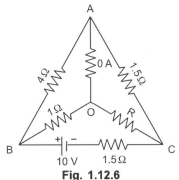

Fig. 1.12.6

[Ans. : 0.375 Ω, + 3.0769 A]

3. *The total power consumed by the network shown in Fig. 1.12.7 if 16 W. Find the value of R and the total current.*

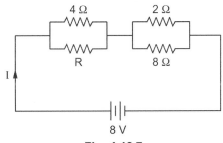

Fig. 1.12.7

[Ans. : 6 Ω, 2 A]

4. *A 8 ohm resistor is in series with a parallel combination of two resistors 12 ohm and 6 ohm. If the current in the 6 ohm resistor is 5 A, determine the total power dissipated in the circuit.*

[Ans. : 675 W]

5. *For Fig. 1.12.8 shows a d.c. two-source network; the branch currents I_1 and I_2 are as marked in it. Write, using Kirchhoff's laws, two independent simultaneous equations in I_1 and I_2. Solve these to find I_1.*

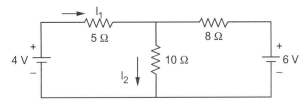

Fig. 1.12.8

[Ans. : 0.0705 A →]

6. Find the currents i_1, i_2, i_3 and powers delivered by the sources of the network in Fig. 1.12.9.

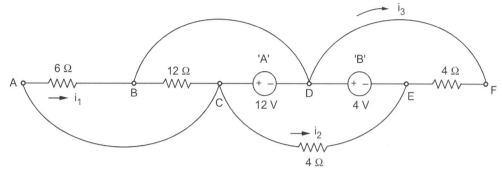

Fig. 1.12.9

[Ans. : 2 A, 4 A, 1 A, 84 W, 20 W]

7. A lamp rated 110 volt, 60 W is connected with another lamp rated 110 volt, 100 W across 220 volt mains. Calculate the resistance that should be joined in parallel with the first lamp so that both the lamps may take their rated power. [Ans. : 302.4256 Ω]

1.13 Star and Delta Connection of Resistances
2001-02, 2003-04, 2005-06, 2009-10, 2010-11, 2011-12

If the three resistances are connected in such a manner that one end of each is connected together to form a junction point called **Star point**, the resistances are said to be connected in **Star**.

The Fig. 1.13.1 (a) and (b) show star connected resistances. The star point is indicated as S. Both the connections Fig. 1.13.1 (a) and (b) are exactly identical. The Fig. 1.13.1 (b) can be redrawn as Fig. 1.13.1 (a) or vice-versa, in the circuit from simplification point of view.

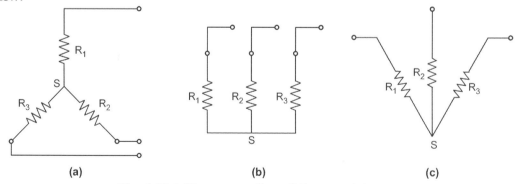

(a)   (b)   (c)

Fig. 1.13.1 Star connection of three resistances

Let us see what is delta connection ?

If the three resistances are connected in such a manner that one end of the first is connected to first end of second, the second end of second to first end of third and so on to complete a loop then the resistances are said to be connected in **Delta**.

Key Point *Delta connection always forms a loop, closed path.*

The Fig. 1.13.2 (a) and (b) show delta connection of three resistances. The Fig. 1.13.2 (a) and (b) are exactly identical.

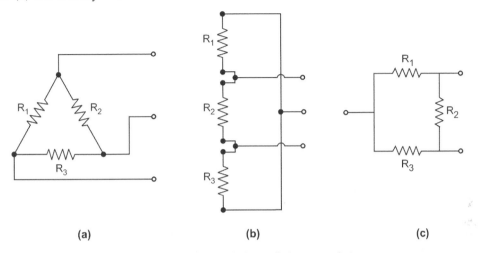

(a)   (b)   (c)

Fig. 1.13.2 Delta connection of three resistances

1.13.1 Delta-Star Transformation

Consider the three resistances R_{12}, R_{23}, R_{31} connected in Delta as shown in the Fig. 1.13.3. The terminals between which these are connected in Delta are named as 1, 2 and 3.

Now it is always possible to replace these Delta connected resistances by three equivalent Star connected resistances

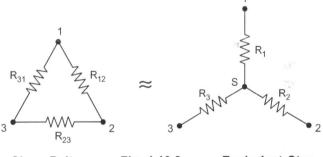

Given Delta   Fig. 1.13.3   Equivalent Star

R_1, R_2, R_3 between the same terminals 1, 2, and 3. Such a Star is shown inside the Delta in the Fig. 1.13.3 which is called **equivalent Star of Delta connected resistances**.

Key Point *To call these two arrangements as equivalent, the resistance between any two terminals must be same in both the types of connections.*

Let us analyse Delta connection first, shown in the Fig. 1.13.3 (a).

Now consider the terminals (1) and (2). Let us find equivalent resistance between (1) and (2). We can redraw the network as viewed from the terminals (1) and (2), without considering terminal (3). This is shown in the Fig. 1.13.3 (b).

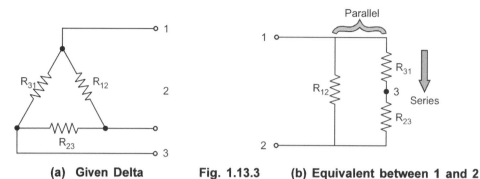

(a) Given Delta **Fig. 1.13.3** **(b) Equivalent between 1 and 2**

Now terminal '3' we are not considering, so between terminals (1) and (2) we get the combination as,

R_{12} parallel with $(R_{31} + R_{23})$ as R_{31} and R_{23} are in series.

∴ Between (1) and (2) the resistance is,

$$= \frac{R_{12}(R_{31} + R_{23})}{R_{12} + (R_{31} + R_{23})} \qquad \qquad \dots(a)$$

$$\left[\text{using } \frac{R_1 R_2}{R_1 + R_2} \text{ for parallel combination} \right]$$

Now consider the same two terminals of equivalent Star connection shown in the Fig. 1.13.4.

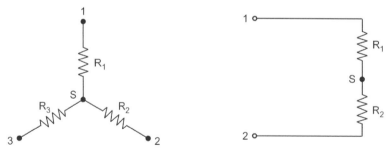

Fig. 1.13.4 Star connection **Fig. 1.13.5 Equivalent between 1 and 2**

Now as viewed from terminals (1) and (2) we can see that terminal (3) is not getting connected anywhere and hence is not playing any role in deciding the resistance as viewed from terminals (1) and (2).

And hence we can redraw the network as viewed through the terminals (1) and (2) as shown in the Fig. 1.13.5.

∴ Between (1) and (2) the resistance is = $R_1 + R_2$ ... (b)

This is because, two of them found to be in series across the terminals 1 and 2 while 3 found to be open.

Now to call this Star as equivalent of given Delta it is necessary that the resistances calculated between terminals (1) and (2) in both the cases should be equal and hence equating equations (a) and (b),

$$\frac{R_{12}\left(R_{31}+R_{23}\right)}{R_{12}+\left(R_{23}+R_{31}\right)} = R_1 + R_2 \qquad \qquad ...(c)$$

Similarly if we find the equivalent resistance as viewed through terminals (2) and (3) in both the cases and equating, we get,

$$\frac{R_{23}\left(R_{31}+R_{12}\right)}{R_{12}+\left(R_{23}+R_{31}\right)} = R_2 + R_3 \qquad \qquad ...(d)$$

Similarly if we find the equivalent resistance as viewed through terminals (3) and (1) in both the cases and equating, we get,

$$\frac{R_{31}\left(R_{12}+R_{23}\right)}{R_{12}+\left(R_{23}+R_{31}\right)} = R_3 + R_1 \qquad \qquad ...(e)$$

Now we are interested in calculating what are the values of R_1, R_2, R_3 interms of known values R_{12}, R_{23}, and R_{31}.

Subtracting (d) from (c),

$$\frac{R_{12}\left(R_{31}+R_{23}\right) - R_{23}\left(R_{31}+R_{12}\right)}{\left(R_{12}+R_{23}+R_{31}\right)} = R_1 + R_2 - R_2 - R_3$$

$$\therefore \qquad\qquad R_1 - R_3 = \frac{R_{12}\,R_{31} - R_{23}\,R_{31}}{R_{12}+R_{23}+R_{31}} \qquad \qquad ...(f)$$

Adding (f) and (e),

$$\frac{R_{12}\,R_{31} - R_{23}\,R_{31} + R_{31}\left(R_{12}+R_{23}\right)}{R_{12}+R_{23}+R_{31}} = R_1 + R_3 + R_1 - R_3$$

$$\therefore \qquad \frac{R_{12}\,R_{31} - R_{23}\,R_{31} + R_{31}\,R_{12} + R_{31}\,R_{23}}{R_{12}+R_{23}+R_{31}} = 2R_1$$

$$2R_1 = \frac{2\,R_{12}\,R_{31}}{R_{12}+R_{23}+R_{31}}$$

$$\boxed{R_1 = \frac{R_{12}\,R_{31}}{R_{12}+R_{23}+R_{31}}}$$

Similarly by using another combinations of subtraction and addition with equations (c), (d) and (e) we can get,

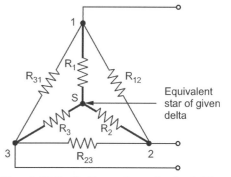

$$R_2 = \frac{R_{12} \, R_{23}}{R_{12} + R_{23} + R_{31}}$$

and

$$R_3 = \frac{R_{23} \, R_{31}}{R_{12} + R_{23} + R_{31}}$$

Fig. 1.13.6 Delta and equivalent Star

Easy way of remembering the result :

The equivalent star resistance between any terminal and star point is equal to the product of the two resistances in delta, which are connected to same terminal, divided by the sum of all three delta connected resistances.

1.13.2 Star-Delta Transformation

Consider the three resistances R_1, R_2 and R_3 connected in Star as shown in Fig. 1.13.7.

Now by Star-Delta conversion, it is always possible to replace these Star connected resistances by three equivalent Delta connected resistances R_{12}, R_{23} and R_{31}, between the same terminals. This is called **equivalent Delta of the given star**.

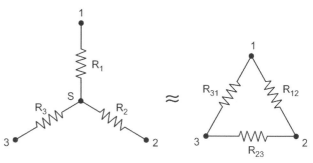

Given Star   Fig. 1.13.7   Equivalent Delta

Now we are interested in finding out values of R_{12}, R_{23} and R_{31} interms of R_1, R_2 and R_3.

For this we can use set of equations derived in previous article. From the result of Delta-Star transformation we know that,

$$R_1 = \frac{R_{12} \, R_{31}}{R_{12} + R_{23} + R_{31}} \qquad \qquad \dots(g)$$

$$R_2 = \frac{R_{12} \, R_{23}}{R_{12} + R_{23} + R_{31}} \qquad \qquad \dots(h)$$

$$R_3 = \frac{R_{23} \, R_{31}}{R_{12} + R_{23} + R_{31}} \qquad \qquad \dots(i)$$

Now multiply (g) and (h), (h) and (i), (i) and (g) to get following three equations.

$$R_1 R_2 = \frac{R_{12}^2 \, R_{31} \, R_{23}}{\left(R_{12} + R_{23} + R_{31}\right)^2} \qquad \ldots(j)$$

$$\therefore \qquad R_2 R_3 = \frac{R_{23}^2 \, R_{12} \, R_{31}}{\left(R_{12} + R_{23} + R_{31}\right)^2} \qquad \ldots(k)$$

$$R_3 R_1 = \frac{R_{31}^2 \, R_{12} \, R_{23}}{\left(R_{12} + R_{23} + R_{31}\right)^2} \qquad \ldots(l)$$

Now add (j) ,(k) and (*l*)

$$\therefore \qquad R_1 R_2 + R_2 R_3 + R_3 R_1 = \frac{R_{12}^2 R_{31} R_{23} + R_{23}^2 R_{12} R_{31} + R_{31}^2 R_{12} \, R_{23}}{\left(R_{12} + R_{23} + R_{31}\right)^2}$$

$$\therefore \qquad R_1 R_2 + R_2 R_3 + R_3 R_1 = \frac{R_{12} R_{31} R_{23} \left(R_{12} + R_{23} + R_{31}\right)}{\left(R_{12} + R_{23} + R_{31}\right)^2}$$

$$\therefore \qquad R_1 R_2 + R_2 R_3 + R_3 R_1 = \frac{R_{12} R_{31} R_{23}}{R_{12} + R_{23} + R_{31}}$$

But $\qquad\qquad \dfrac{R_{12} R_{31}}{R_{12} + R_{23} + R_{31}} = R_1 \qquad\qquad$ From equation (g)

$\therefore \qquad$ Substituting in above in R.H.S. we get,

$$\therefore \qquad R_1 R_2 + R_2 R_3 + R_3 R_1 = R_1 \, R_{23}$$

$$\therefore \qquad \boxed{R_{23} = R_2 + R_3 + \frac{R_2 \, R_3}{R_1}}$$

Similarly substituting in R.H.S., remaining values, we can write relations for remaining two resistances.

$$\boxed{R_{12} = R_1 + R_2 + \frac{R_1 \, R_2}{R_3}}$$

and $\qquad$ $$\boxed{R_{31} = R_3 + R_1 + \frac{R_1 \, R_3}{R_2}}$$

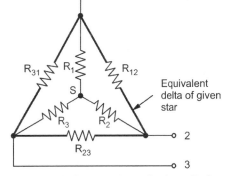

Fig. 1.13.8 Star and equivalent Delta

Easy way of remembering the result :

The equivalent delta connected resistance to be connected between any two terminals is sum of the two resistances connected between the same two terminals and star point respectively in star, plus the product of the same two star resistances divided by the third star resistance.

Result for equal resistances in star and delta :

If all resistances in a Delta connection have same magnitude say R, then its equivalent Star will contain,

$$R_1 = R_2 = R_3 = \frac{R \times R}{R + R + R} = \frac{R}{3}$$

i.e. **equivalent Star contains three equal resistances, each of magnitude one third the magnitude of the resistances connected in Delta.**

If all three resistances in a Star connection are of same magnitude say R, then its equivalent Delta contains all resistances of same magnitude of ,

$$R_{12} = R_{31} = R_{23} = R + R + \frac{R \times R}{R} = 3R$$

i.e. **equivalent delta contains three resistances each of magnitude thrice the magnitude of resistances connected in Star.**

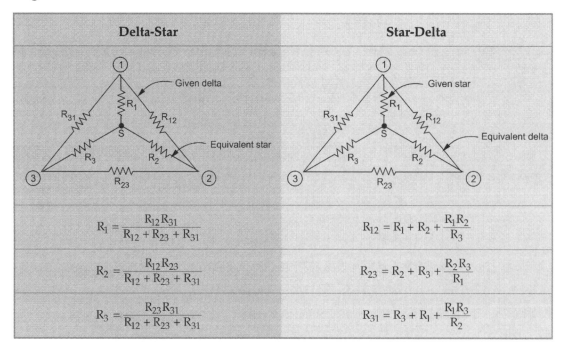

Delta-Star	Star-Delta
$R_1 = \dfrac{R_{12}R_{31}}{R_{12} + R_{23} + R_{31}}$	$R_{12} = R_1 + R_2 + \dfrac{R_1 R_2}{R_3}$
$R_2 = \dfrac{R_{12}R_{23}}{R_{12} + R_{23} + R_{31}}$	$R_{23} = R_2 + R_3 + \dfrac{R_2 R_3}{R_1}$
$R_3 = \dfrac{R_{23}R_{31}}{R_{12} + R_{23} + R_{31}}$	$R_{31} = R_3 + R_1 + \dfrac{R_1 R_3}{R_2}$

Table 1.13.1 Star-Delta and Delta-Star Transformations

Example 1.13.1 *Find equivalent resistance between points A-B.*

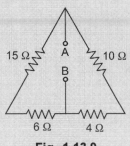

Fig. 1.13.9

Solution : Redrawing the circuit,

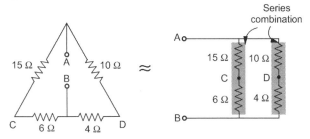

Fig. 1.13.9 (a)

$$R_{AB} = \frac{21 \times 14}{21 + 14} = 8.4 \ \Omega$$

Fig. 1.13.9 (b)

Example 1.13.2 *Find equivalent resistance between points A-B.*

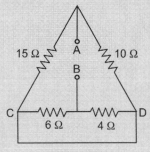

Fig. 1.13.10

Solution : Redraw the circuit,

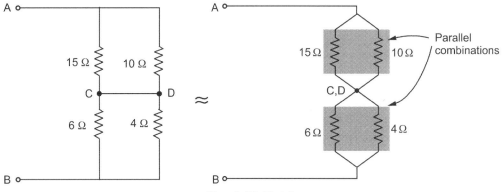

Fig. 1.13.10 (a)

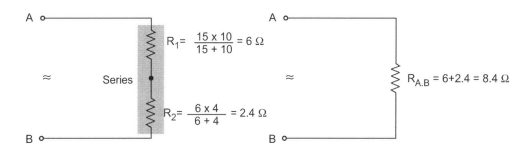

Fig. 1.13.10 (b)

$\therefore$ R_{AB} = **8.4** Ω

Example 1.13.3 *Calculate the effective resistance between points A and B in the given circuit in Fig. 1.13.11.*

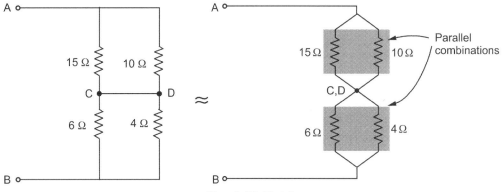

Fig. 1.13.11

Solution : The resistances 2, 2 and 3 are in series while the resistances 4, 2, and 5 are in series.

$\therefore$ $2 + 2 + 3 = 7\,\Omega$

and $4 + 2 + 5 = 11 \ \Omega$

The circuit becomes as shown in Fig. 1.13.11 (a).

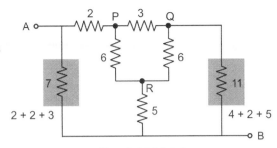

Fig. 1.13.11 (a)

Converting Δ PQR to equivalent star,

$$R_{PN} = \frac{6 \times 3}{6 + 3 + 6} = 1.2 \ \Omega$$

$$R_{PN} = \frac{6 \times 6}{6 + 3 + 6} = 2.4 \ \Omega$$

$$R_{QN} = \frac{6 \times 3}{6 + 3 + 6} = 1.2 \ \Omega$$

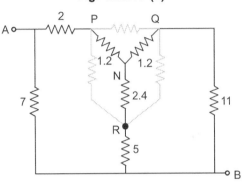

Hence the circuit becomes as shown in the Fig. 1.13.11 (b).

The resistances 2 and 1.2 are in series.

1.2 and 11 are in series.

5 and 2.4 are in series.

Fig. 1.13.11 (b)

$\therefore$ Circuit becomes after simplification as shown in the Fig. 1.13.11 (c).

The resistances 7.4 and 12.2 are in parallel.

$$\therefore \quad 7.4 \parallel 12.2 = \frac{7.4 \times 12.2}{7.4 + 12.2} = 4.6061 \ \Omega$$

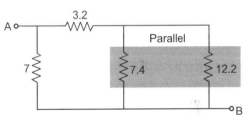

Fig. 1.13.11 (c)

So circuit becomes,

Now the two resistances are in parellel as shown in the Fig. 1.13.11(e).

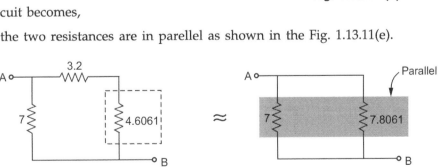

(d)   **(e)**

Fig. 1.13.11

$$\therefore \quad R_{AB} = \frac{7 \times 7.8061}{7 + 7.8061} = \textbf{3.69} \ \Omega$$

Example 1.13.4 *For the circuit given in Fig. 1.13.12, find current drawn from the source.*

2003-04, Marks 6

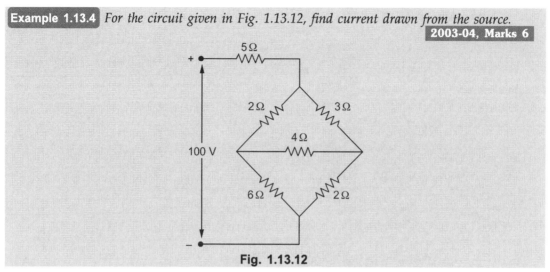

Fig. 1.13.12

Solution : Convert the delta of 2 Ω, 4 Ω and 3 Ω to star,

$$R_1 = \frac{2 \times 3}{2 + 4 + 3} = 0.667 \ \Omega$$

$$R_2 = \frac{2 \times 4}{2 + 4 + 3} = 0.888 \ \Omega$$

$$R_3 = \frac{4 \times 3}{2 + 4 + 3} = 1.333 \ \Omega$$

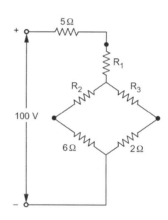

Fig. 1.13.12 (a)

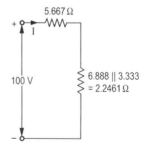

Fig. 1.13.12 (b)

Fig. 1.13.12 (c)

$$\therefore \qquad I = \frac{100}{5.667 + 2.2461} = \textbf{12.6372 A}$$

Example 1.13.5 *Find the resistance between A - B using star-delta transformation.*

2005-06, Marks 8

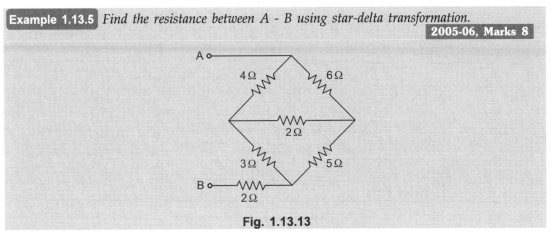

Fig. 1.13.13

Solution : Converting delta of 4 Ω, 6 Ω, 2 Ω to equivalent star,

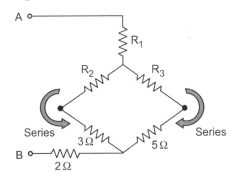

Fig. 1.13.13 (a)

$$R_1 = \frac{4 \times 6}{4 + 6 + 2} = 2 \ \Omega$$

$$R_2 = \frac{4 \times 2}{4 + 6 + 2} = 0.666 \ \Omega$$

$$R_3 = \frac{2 \times 6}{4 + 6 + 2} = 1 \ \Omega$$

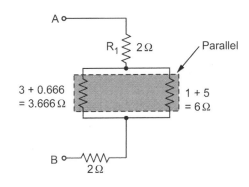

Fig. 1.13.13 (b)

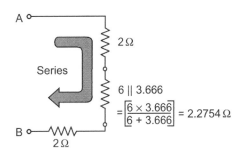

Fig. 1.13.13 (c)

$$\therefore \qquad R_{AB} = 2 + 2.2754 + 2 = \textbf{6.2754} \ \Omega$$

Example 1.13.6 *In the given circuit shown in Fig. 1.13.14, find the resistance between the point B and C.*

2009-10, Marks 5

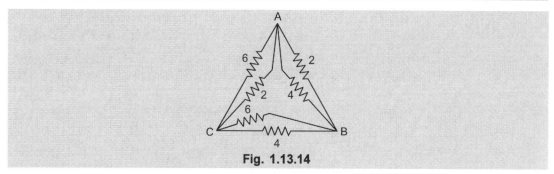

Fig. 1.13.14

Solution : Reducing the parallel combinations,

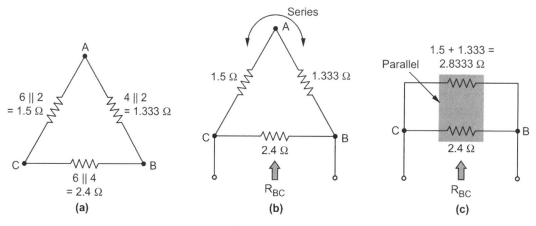

Fig. 1.13.14

$\therefore$ $\qquad$ R_{BC} = $(2.4 \| 2.8333)$ = **1.3 Ω**

Example 1.13.7 *Find the equivalent resistance for the following circuit and hence calculate the current supplied by the source.* **2010-11, Marks 10**

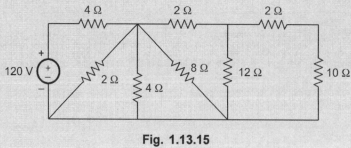

Fig. 1.13.15

Solution : The resistances 2 Ω, 4 Ω, 8 Ω are in parallel

$\therefore$ $\qquad$ $\dfrac{1}{R} = \dfrac{1}{2} + \dfrac{1}{4} + \dfrac{1}{8}$ $\qquad$ i.e. $\qquad$ $R' = 1.1428\ \Omega$

The circuit reduces as shown in the Fig. 1.13.15(a) .

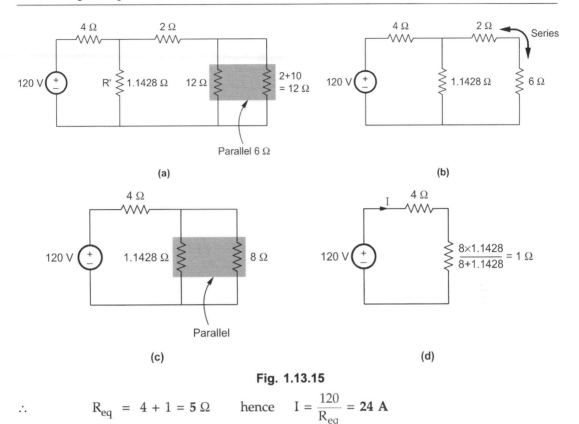

Fig. 1.13.15

$$\therefore \qquad R_{eq} = 4 + 1 = 5\ \Omega \qquad \text{hence} \qquad I = \frac{120}{R_{eq}} = 24\ A$$

Review Questions

1. *Explain star-delta transformation.*   **2009-10, Marks 5**

2. *Explain and derive the relations to convert delta connected resistances to equivalent star.*

3. *Find the resistance between the terminals XY of the bridge circuit shown in Fig. 1.13.16 by using delta-star transformation.*   **2001-02**

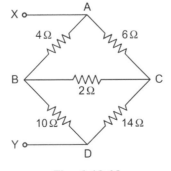

Fig. 1.13.16

[Ans. : 8.2337 Ω]

4. *For a given circuit shown in Fig. 1.13.17, find out the equivalent resistance between terminals X and Y.*

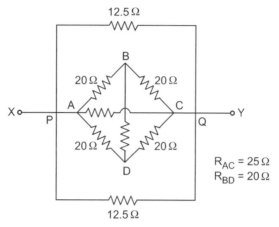

$R_{AC} = 25\,\Omega$
$R_{BD} = 20\,\Omega$

Fig. 1.13.17

[**Ans. : 4** Ω]

5. *Determine the resistance between the terminals X and Y for the circuit shown in Fig. 1.13.18.*

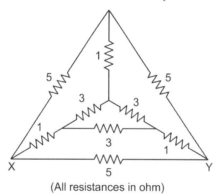

(All resistances in ohm)

Fig. 1.13.18

[**Ans. : 1.8181** Ω]

6. *Find the equivalent resistance across the terminals A and B shown in the Fig. 1.13.19.*

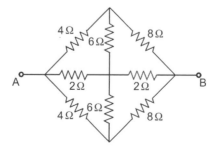

Fig. 1.13.19

All resistances are in ohms.   [**Ans. : 2.417** Ω]

7. Find the equivalent resistance across terminals X and Y.

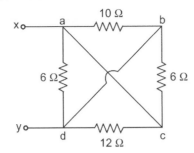

Fig. 1.13.20

[Ans. : 2.1053 Ω]

8. Calculate the resistance between terminals A-B.

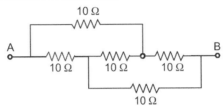

Fig. 1.13.21

[Ans. : 10 Ω]

9. Find the equivalent resistance between the terminals Y and Z.

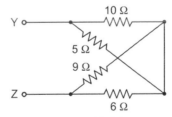

Fig. 1.13.22

[Ans. : 6.9333 Ω]

10. Find the equivalent resistance across AB for the circuit shown in below Fig. 1.13.23. Each resistance value is equal to 9 Ω.

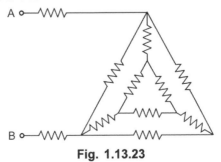

Fig. 1.13.23

[Ans. : 22.8 Ω]

11. *Find the equivalent resistance across AB, in the below circuit (shown in Fig. 1.13.24). All the resistances are equal and 5 Ω.*

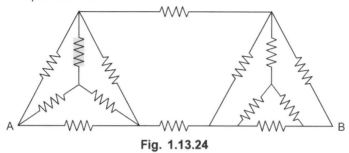

Fig. 1.13.24

[Ans. : 13.75 Ω]

1.14 Concept of Loop Current

A loop current is that current which simultaneously links with all the branches, defining a particular loop.

The Fig. 1.14.1 shows a network. In this circuit, I_1 is the loop current for the loop ABFEA and simultaneously links with the branches AB, BF, FE and EA.

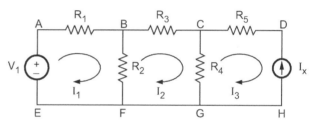

Fig. 1.14.1 Concept of loop current

Similarly I_2 is the second loop current for the loop BCGFB and I_3 is the third loop current for the loop CDFGC.

Observe :

1. For the common branches of the various loops, multiple loop currents get associated with them. For example to the branch BF, both I_1 and I_2 are associated.

2. The branch current is always unique hence a branch current can be expressed interms of associated loop currents.

> **The total branch current is the algebraic sum of all the loop currents associated with that branches.**

$$I_{BF} = I_1 - I_2 \text{ from B to F} \quad \text{and} \quad I_{CG} = I_2 - I_3 \text{ from C to G}$$

3. The branches consisting current sources, directly decide the values of the loop currents flowing through them.

The branch DH consists current source of I_x amperes and only the loop current I_3 is associated with the branch DH in opposite direction. Hence $I_3 = -I_x$.

4.   Assuming such loop currents and assigning the polarities for the drops across the various branches due to the assumed loop currents, the Kirchhoff's voltage law can be applied to the loops. Solving these equations, the various loop currents can be obtained.

     Once the loop currents are calculated, any branch current can be calculated.

Review Question

> 1. *Explain the difference between a branch current and a loop current.*

1.15 Loop Analysis or Mesh Analysis   2001-02, 2004-05, 2005-06, 2009-10, 2010-11, 2011-12

     This method of analysis is specially useful for the circuits that have many nodes and loops. The difference between application of Kirchhoff's laws and loop analysis is, in loop analysis instead of branch currents, the loop currents are considered for writing the equations. The another difference is, in this method, each branch of the network may carry more than one current. The total branch current must be decided by the algebraic sum of all currents through that branch. While in analysis using Kirchhoff's laws, each

branch carries only one current. The advantage of this method is that for complex networks the number of unknowns reduces which greatly simplifies calculation work.

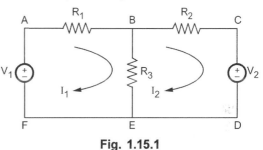

Fig. 1.15.1

     Consider following network shown in the Fig. 1.15.1. There are two loops. So assuming two loop currents as I_1 and I_2.

Key Point *While assume loop currents, consider the loops such that each element of the network will be included atleast once in any of the loops.*

     Now branch B-E carries two currents; I_1 from B to E and I_2 from E to B. So net current through branch B-E will $(I_1 - I_2)$ and corresponding drop across R_3 must be as shown below in the Fig. 1.15.2.

$$B \circ\!\!-\!\!\!\overset{R_3}{\wedge\!\!\wedge\!\!\wedge}\!\!-\!\!\circ E \qquad\qquad B \circ\!\!-\!\!\!\overset{R_3}{\wedge\!\!\wedge\!\!\wedge}\!\!-\!\!\circ E$$

$$\underset{+ \qquad -}{\xrightarrow{} (I_1 - I_2)} \qquad\qquad \underset{- \qquad +}{\xleftarrow{} (I_2 - I_1)}$$

Fig. 1.15.2

     Consider loop A - B - E - F - A,

     For branch B-E, polarities of voltage drops will be B +ve, E –ve for current I_1 while E +ve, B –ve for current I_2 flowing through R_3.

Now while writing loop equations assume main loop current as positive and remaining loop current must be treated as negative for common branches.

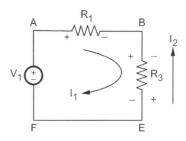

Writing loop equations for the network shown in the Fig. 1.15.3.

For loop A - B - E - F - A,

$$-I_1R_1 - I_1 R_3 + I_2R_3 + V_1 = 0$$

For loop B - C - D - E - B

$$-I_2R_2 - V_2 - I_2 R_3 + I_1R_3 = 0$$

Fig. 1.15.3

By solving above simultaneous equations any unknown branch current can be determined.

1.15.1 Points to Remember for Loop Analysis

1. While assuming loop currents make sure that atleast one loop current links with every element.

2. No two loops should be identical.

3. Choose minimum number of loop currents.

4. Convert current sources if present, into their equivalent voltage sources for loop analysis, whenever possible.

5. If current in a particular branch is required, then try to choose loop current in such a way that only one loop current links with that branch.

1.15.2 Supermesh

Key Point *If there exists a current source in any of the branches of the network then a loop **cannot** be defined through the current source as drop across the current source is unknown, from KVL point of view.*

For example, consider the network shown in the Fig. 1.15.4. In this circuit, branch B-E consists of a current source. So loop A-B-E-F-A cannot be defined as loop from KVL point of view, as drop across the current source is not known.

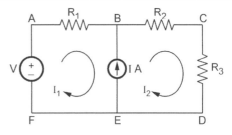

Fig. 1.15.4

In such case, **to get the required equation interms of loop currents, analyse the branch consisting of a current source independently.**

Express the current source interms of the assumed loop currents. For example, in the Fig. 1.15.4 analyse the branch BE. The current source is of IA in the direction of loop current I_2. So I_2 is more than I_1 and we can write an equation,

$$I = I_2 - I_1$$

So all such branches, consisting current sources must be analysed independently. Get the equations for current sources interms of loop currents. Then apply KVL to the remaining loops which are existing without involving the branches consisting of current sources. The loop existing, around a current source which is common to the two loops is called **supermesh**. In the Fig. 1.15.4, the loop A-B-C-D-E-F-A is supermesh.

1.15.3 Steps for the Loop Analysis

Step 1 : Choose the various loops.

Step 2 : Show the various loop currents and the polarities of associated voltage drops.

Step 3 : Before applying KVL, look for any current source. Analyse the branch consisting current source independently and express the current source value interms of assumed loop currents. Repeat this for all the current sources.

Step 4 : After the step 3, apply KVL to those **loops, which do not include any current source.** A loop cannot be defined through current source from KVL point of view. Follow the sign convention.

Step 5 : Solve the equations obtained in step 3 and step 4 simultaneously, to obtain required unknowns

Example 1.15.1 *Calculate current through 6 Ω resistance using loop analysis.*

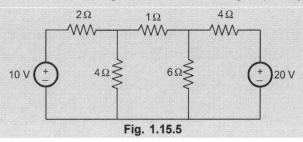

Fig. 1.15.5

Solution : Assume loop currents I_1, I_2 and I_3. Also show polarities of voltage drops for each loop, assuming corresponding loop current positive as shown in Fig. 1.15.5 (a).

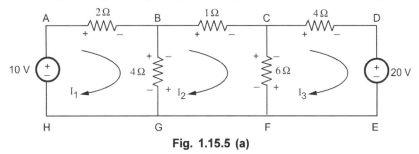

Fig. 1.15.5 (a)

Consider loop A - B - G - H - A, loop equation is,

$$-2I_1 - 4(I_1 - I_2) + 10 = 0 \qquad \text{i.e.} \qquad 6I_1 - 4I_2 = 10 \qquad \dots (1.15.1)$$

Consider loop B - C - F - G - B, loop equation is,

$$-1I_2 - 6(I_2 - I_3) - 4(I_2 - I_1) = 0 \qquad \text{i.e} \qquad 4I_1 - 11I_2 + 6I_3 = 0 \qquad \dots (1.15.2)$$

Consider loop C - D - E - F - C, loop equation is,

$$-4I_3 - 20 - 6(I_3 - I_2) = 0 \qquad \text{i.e.} \qquad 6I_2 - 10I_3 = 20 \qquad \dots (1.15.3)$$

Solving equations (1.15.1), (1.15.2) and (1.15.3) by Cramer's Rule,

$$I_2 = -1.1267 \text{ A} \qquad \text{and} \qquad I_3 = -2.676 \text{ A}$$

∴   Current through 6 Ω resistance $= I_2 - I_3 = -1.1267 - (-2.676)$

$$= \textbf{1.5493 A from C to F}$$

Example 1.15.2 *Find the current through branch a-b using mesh analysis.*

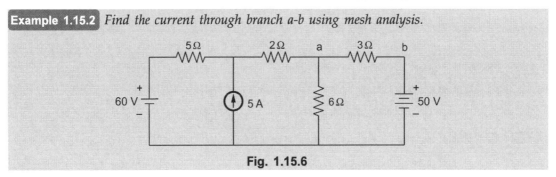

Fig. 1.15.6

Solution : The various loop currents can be assumed as shown in the Fig. 1.15.6 (a).

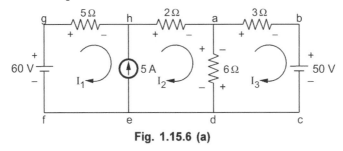

Fig. 1.15.6 (a)

As branch 'h-e' consists of a current source, before applying KVL, analyse the branch 'h-e' separately. From it we can express 5 A current source interms of the loop currents as,

$$I_2 - I_1 = 5 \qquad \dots (1.15.4)$$

Now apply KVL to other loops **without consisting the current source**.

Loop g-h-a-d-e-f-g, $-5I_1 - 2I_2 - 6I_2 + 6I_3 + 60 = 0$

∴ $- 5 I_1 - 8 I_2 + 6 I_3 = - 60$ ... (1.15.5)

Loop a-b-c-d-a, $- 3I_3 - 50 - 6 I_3 + 6 I_2 = 0$

∴ $6 I_2 - 9 I_3 = 50$ ... (1.15.6)

Solving equations (1.15.4), (1.15.5) and (1.15.6),

∴ $I_3 = - 1.7283 \text{ A}$

So current through branch ab is 1.7283 A flowing from b to a.

Example 1.15.3 *Using Mesh equation method, find the current in resistance R_1 of network given below.*   **2004-05, Marks 5**

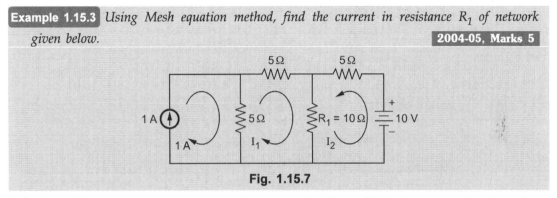

Fig. 1.15.7

Solution : The various polarities are shown in the Fig. 1.15.7 (a), as per the given loop currents.

Apply KVL to the loops I and II,

$- 5 I_1 - 10 I_1 - 10 I_2 - 5 I_1 + 5 \times 1 = 0$

∴ $+ 20 I_1 + 10 I_2 = 5$ ...(1.15.7)

$+ 5 I_2 - 10 + 10 I_2 + 10 I_1 = 0$

∴ $10 I_1 + 15 I_2 = 10$ ...(1.15.8)

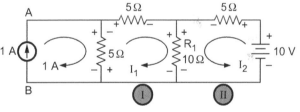

Fig. 1.15.7 (a)

Solving, $I_1 = - 0.125 \text{ A}, \quad I_2 = 0.75 \text{ A}$

∴ $I_{10 \,\Omega} = I_1 + I_2 = 0.75 - 0.125 = \textbf{0.625 A} \downarrow$

Example 1.15.4 *Using loop current method, find the current I_1 and I_2 in the following -*

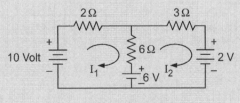

Fig. 1.15.8

2001-02, 2005-06

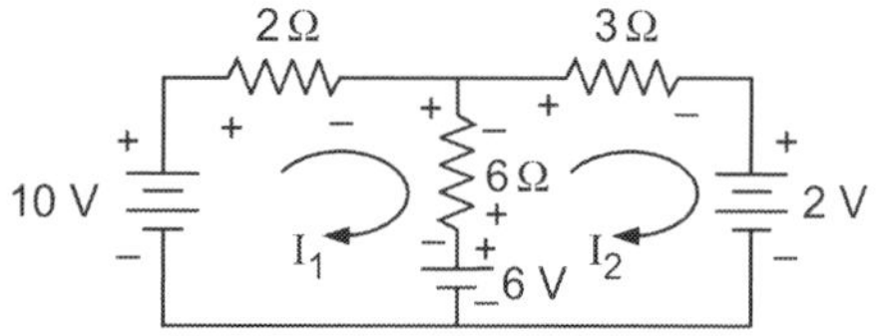

Fig. 1.15.8 (a)

Solution : Applying KVL to the two loops,

$$-2I_1 - 6I_1 + 6I_2 - 6 + 10 = 0$$

i.e. $$-8I_1 + 6I_2 = -4 \quad ...(1.15.9)$$

$$-3I_2 - 2 + 6 - 6I_2 + 6I_1 = 0$$

$\therefore$ $$6I_1 - 9I_2 = -4 \quad ...(1.15.10)$$

Solving the equations (1.15.9) and (1.15.10),

I_1 = **1.667 A**, I_2 = **1.555 A**

Example 1.15.5 *Calculate current through the galvanometer in the following bridge -*

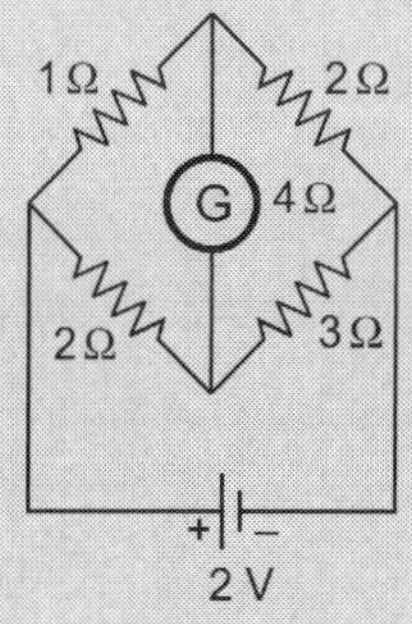

Fig. 1.15.9

2001-02, Marks 5

Solution : The various loop currents are as shown in the Fig. 1.15.9 (a).

Apply KVL to the three loops,

$$-4I_1 + 4I_2 - 2I_1 + 2I_3 - I_1 = 0$$

i.e. $$-7I_1 + 4I_2 + 2I_3 = 0 \quad ...(1.15.11)$$

$$-2I_2 - 3I_2 + 3I_3 - 4I_2 + 4I_1 = 0$$

i.e. $$4I_1 - 9I_2 + 3I_3 = 0 \quad ... (1.15.12)$$

$$-2I_3 + 2I_1 - 3I_3 + 3I_2 + 2 = 0$$

i.e. $$2I_1 + 3I_2 - 5I_3 = -2 \quad ...(1.15.13)$$

Solving (1.15.11), (1.15.12) and (1.15.13)

I_1 = 0.6818 A, I_2 = 0.659 A,

I_3 = 1.06818 A

$\therefore$ Current through galvanometer is,

I_G = $I_1 - I_2$ = 0.6818 − 0.659 = **0.0228 A** ↓

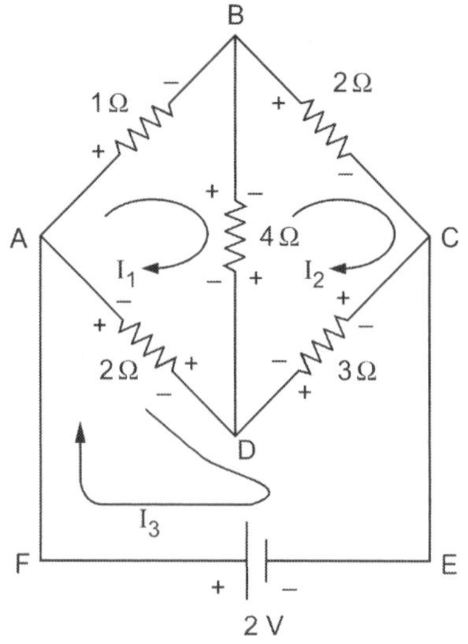

Fig. 1.15.9 (a)

Example 1.15.6 *Using mesh current method, determine current I_x in the following circuit :*

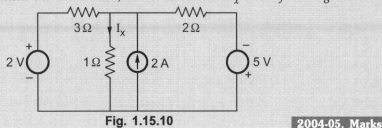

Fig. 1.15.10

2004-05, Marks 6

Solution : The various mesh currents are shown in the Fig. 1.15.10 (a).

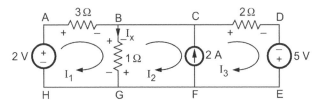

Fig. 1.15.10 (a)

From branch CF, $I_3 - I_2 = 2$ ...(1.15.14)

From branch BG, $I_1 - I_2 = I_x$ (Required)   ...(1.15.15)

Apply KVL to the loops without current source,

Loop A-B-G-H-A, $-3I_1 - I_1 + I_2 + 2 = 0$ i.e. $-4 I_1 + I_2 = -2$ ...(1.15.16)

Loop B-C-D-E-F-G-B, $-2I_3 + 5 - I_2 + I_1 = 0$ i.e. $I_1 - I_2 - 2 I_3 = -5$ ...(1.15.17)

Solving (1.15.14), (1.15.16) and (1.15.17) simultaneously,

$$I_1 = 0.6363 \text{ A}, \quad I_2 = 0.5454 \text{ A}, \quad I_3 = 2.5454 \text{ A}$$

∴ $I_x = I_1 - I_2 = \textbf{0.0909 A} \downarrow$

Example 1.15.7 *Find voltage V_1 across 6 ohm resistance in the following circuit using loop analysis method :*

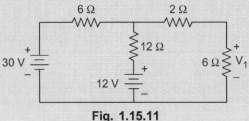

Fig. 1.15.11

2009-10, Marks 5

Solution : The loop currents are shown in the Fig. 1.15.11 (a).

Applying KVL to the two loops,

$$-6I_1 - 12I_1 + 12I_2 - 12 + 30 = 0$$

i.e. $18I_1 - 12I_2 = 18$ ...(1.15.18)

$-2I_2 - 6I_2 + 12 - 12I_2 + 12I_1 = 0$

i.e. $-12I_1 + 20I_2 = 12$ ...(1.15.19)

Solving, $I_1 = 2.333$ A, $I_2 = 2$ A

$\therefore$ $V_1 = I_2 \times 6 = 2 \times 6 = \textbf{12 V}$.

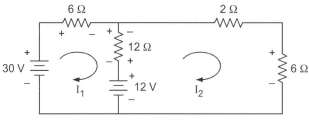

Fig. 1.15.11 (a)

Example 1.15.8 *Find the voltage drop across R_1 and R_2 (see Fig. 1.15.12). The resistance R_3 is not specified.*

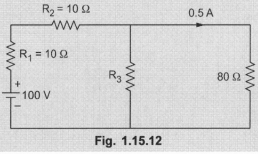

Fig. 1.15.12 **2010-11, Marks 5**

Solution : The current through 80 Ω is given to be 0.5 A

$\therefore$ Drop across 80 Ω = 80 $\times$ 0.5 = 40 V

The resistance R_3 is in parallel with 80 Ω hence drop across resistance R_3 is also 40 V as shown in the Fig. 1.15.12 (a).

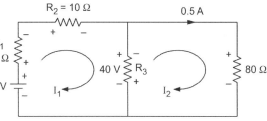

Fig. 1.15.12 (a)

Apply KVL to the loops,

$-I_1 \times 10 - 40 + 100 - 10 I_1 = 0$ i.e. $I_1 = 3$ A

$\therefore$ Drop across $R_1 = I_1 R_1 = 3 \times 10 = \textbf{30 V}$

$\therefore$ Drop across $R_2 = I_1 R_2 = 3 \times 10 = \textbf{30 V}$

Example 1.15.9 *Apply mesh analysis, obtain the current through 5 ohm resistance in the following circuit :*

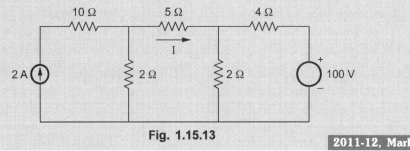

Fig. 1.15.13 **2011-12, Marks 10**

Solution : The mesh currents are shown in the Fig. 1.15.13 (a).

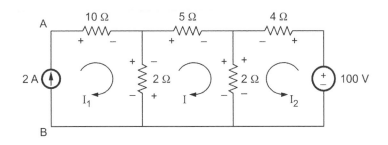

Fig. 1.15.13 (a)

Form the branch AB, $I_1 = 2$ A   ... (1.15.20)

Applying KVL to the remaining loops and using $I_1 = 2$ A,

$-5\,I-2\,I-2\,I_2-2\,I+2\,I_1 = 0$ i.e. $9\,I+2\,I_2 = 4$ ... (1.15.21)

$-4\,I_2-2\,I_2-2\,I+100 = 0$ i.e. $2\,I+6\,I_2 = 100$ ... (1.15.22)

Solving equations (1.15.21) and (1.15.22), $I = -3.52$ A

Thus, current through $5\,\Omega = I = -\mathbf{3.52\ A}$ i.e. $\mathbf{3.52\ A} \leftarrow$

Review Questions

1. *Explain the loop analysis method.*
2. *Calculate the current in the 50 ohms resistor in the network shown in the Fig. 1.15.14 using mesh analysis.*

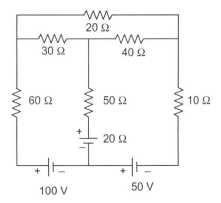

Fig. 1.15.14

[Ans. : – 0.4721 A i.e. 0.4721 A ↑]

3. Calculate the current in 20 ohm resistor in the circuit shown below.

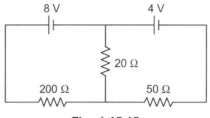

Fig. 1.15.15

[Ans. : 0.02667 A ↓]

4. Use mesh analysis to determine the three mesh currents in the circuits shown below.

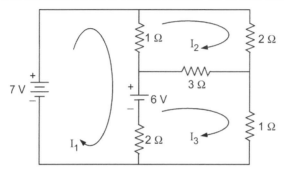

Fig. 1.15.16

[Ans. : $I_1 = 3$ A, $I_2 = 2$ A, $I_3 = 3$ A]

5. Using mesh analysis, calculate the current I_1 shown in the Fig. 1.15.17.

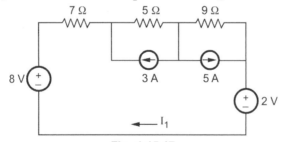

Fig. 1.15.17   [Ans. : 1.7142 A]

6. Calculate the voltage across branch AB in circuit shown, using loop analysis.

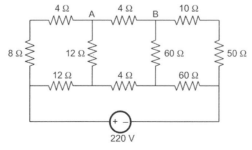

Fig. 1.15.18   [Ans. : 11.578 V]

7. *Calculate the current through 10 Ω resistance by loop analysis.*

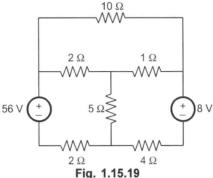

Fig. 1.15.19   [Ans. : 1.6082 A]

8. *In the circuit shown in the Fig. 1.15.20, use the loop analysis to find the power delivered to the 4 Ω resistor.*

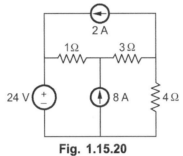

Fig. 1.15.20   [Ans. : 36 W]

1.16 Node Analysis

The node analysis method is based on the Kirchhoff's Current Law (KCL). In this method, one node is assumed as a **reference node** and its potential is assumed to be zero. This node is also called **zero potential node** or **base node** or **datum node.**

At the other nodes, the node voltage variables are assumed whose voltages are measured with respect to base node. These nodes are called **major nodes.**

The various branch currents are assumed and KCL equations are written at all the major nodes. The current variables are then expressed interms of assumed node voltage variables and branch resistances, by analysing each branch independently.

Using these expressions in the KCL equations, a set of simultaneous equations in terms of node voltage variables is obtained. Solving these equations, the required node voltages and hence any branch current of the network can be determined.

If there are N nodes including the reference node then we get (N – 1) number of equations in this method. Thus compared to loop analysis, we get one equation less in this method.

Explanation : Consider the network shown in the Fig. 1.16.1.

In this circuit, the common point of all the branches is considered as reference node as shown.

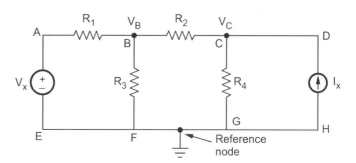

Fig. 1.16.1

The nodes B and C are the major nodes where node voltage variables are to be assumed.

Important : In node analysis, the branch B to E is considered as the entire branch for the analysis hence node A is not considered as the major node. Similarly branch C to H is considered as the entire independent branch hence node D is not considered as the major node. Generally the nodes where three or more branches meet are the major nodes where node voltage variables must be assumed.

Show the various branch currents preferably leaving the nodes. The direction of I_x is towards the node C and must be considered as it is.

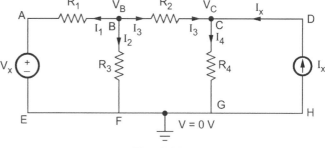

Fig. 1.16.2

Apply KCL at the nodes.

$- I_1 - I_2 - I_3 = 0$ ...at node B

$I_3 + I_x - I_4 = 0$ ...at node C

Express the current variables interms of node voltage variables by analysing each branch independently.

Important : For writing such equations use Ohm's law. The current through branch is potential difference across it divided by the resistance of the branch.

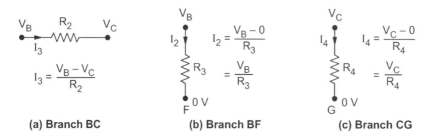

(a) Branch BC   (b) Branch BF   (c) Branch CG

Fig. 1.16.3

Important : The branches consisting independent voltage sources are important.

Consider branch BE shown in the Fig. 1.16.4 consisting source V_x.

If $V_x = 0$ V i.e. V_x is absent then our equation for I_1 would have been,

$$I_1 = \frac{V_B - 0}{R_1}$$

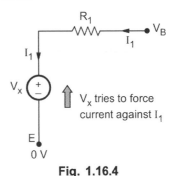

Fig. 1.16.4

But now V_x exists. So check that in which direction it tries to force current. Here V_x tries to force current from its positive terminal out which is opposite to assumed current I_1 hence V_x opposes V_B hence must be subtracted from V_B while writing equation for I_1.

$$I_1 = \frac{V_B - V_x - 0}{R_1} = \frac{V_B - V_x}{R_1}$$

Consider the various cases shown in the Fig. 1.16.5.

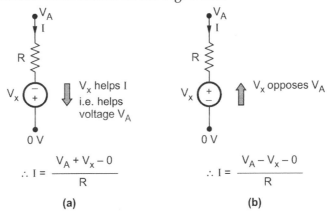

$$\therefore I = \frac{V_A + V_x - 0}{R} \qquad\qquad \therefore I = \frac{V_A - V_x - 0}{R}$$

(a)   (b)

Fig. 1.16.5

If the branch current is flowing towards the node from base node then base node is at higher potential hence equation becomes as shown in the Fig. 1.16.6.

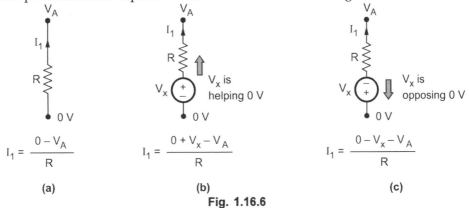

$$I_1 = \frac{0 - V_A}{R} \qquad\quad I_1 = \frac{0 + V_x - V_A}{R} \qquad\quad I_1 = \frac{0 - V_x - V_A}{R}$$

(a)   (b)   (c)

Fig. 1.16.6

Once the simultaneous equations are obtained then those can be solved to obtain required node voltages.

1.16.1 Points to Remember for Nodal Analysis

1. While assuming branch currents, make sure that each unknown branch current is considered at least once.

2. Convert the voltage source present into their equivalent current sources for node analysis, wherever possible.

3. Follow the same sign convention, currents entering at node are to be considered positive, while currents leaving the node are to be considered as negative.

4. As far as possible, select the directions of various branch currents leaving the respective nodes.

1.16.2 Supernode

Consider a circuit shown in the Fig. 1.16.7. In this circuit, the nodes labelled V_2 and V_3 are connected directly through a voltage source, without any circuit element. The region surrounding a voltage source which connects the two node directly is called **supernode**.

In such a case, the nodes in supernode region can be analysed seperately and the relation between such node voltages and a source voltage connecting them can be separately obtained. In the circuit shown in the Fig. 1.16.7 we can write,

$$V_2 = V_3 + V_x$$

In addition to this equation, apply KCL to all the nodes assuming different branch currents at the nodes. The current through voltage source, connecting supernodes must be expressed interms of node voltages, using these KCL equations. Then the resulting equations and supernode equation are to be solved simultaneously to obtain the required unknown.

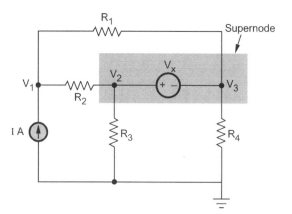

Fig. 1.16.7 Region of supernode

1.16.3 Steps for the Node Analysis

Step 1 : Choose the nodes and node voltages to be obtained.

Step 2 : Choose the currents preferably leaving the node at each branch connected to each node.

Step 3 : Apply KCL at each node with proper sign convention.

Step 4 : If there are supernodes, obtain the equations directly interms of node voltages which are directly connected through voltage source.

Step 5 : Obtain the equation for the each branch current interms of node voltages and substitute in the equations obtained in step 3.

Step 6 : Solve all the equations obtained in step 4 and step 5 simultaneously to obtain the required node voltages.

Key Point *If there are many number of branches in parallel in a network then node method is advantageous for the network analysis.*

Examples 1.16.1 *Using node voltage analysis, find the current I.*

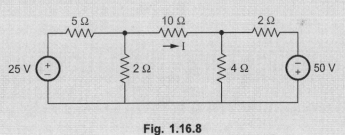

Fig. 1.16.8

Solution :

Step 1 : Show the node voltages.

Step 2 : Show the various branch currents.

Step 3 : Apply KCL at the two major nodes.

$$-I_1 - I_2 - I = 0$$

i.e. $I_1 + I_2 + I = 0$ ... (1.16.1)

$$I - I_3 - I_4 = 0$$ ... (1.16.2)

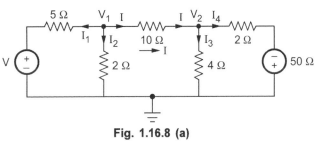

Fig. 1.16.8 (a)

Step 4 : Obtain the expressions for the branch currents.

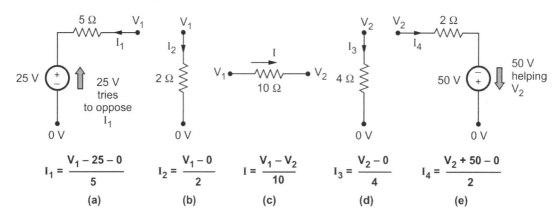

$$I_1 = \frac{V_1 - 25 - 0}{5}$$

(a)

$$I_2 = \frac{V_1 - 0}{2}$$

(b)

$$I = \frac{V_1 - V_2}{10}$$

(c)

$$I_3 = \frac{V_2 - 0}{4}$$

(d)

$$I_4 = \frac{V_2 + 50 - 0}{2}$$

(e)

Fig. 1.16.9

Step 5 : Using current expressions in the equations (1.16.1) and (1.16.2),

$$\frac{V_1 - 25}{5} + \frac{V_1}{2} + \frac{V_1 - V_2}{10} = 0 \quad \text{i.e.} \quad 0.8\,V_1 - 0.1\,V_2 = 5 \quad \text{... (1.16.3)}$$

$$\frac{V_1 - V_2}{10} - \frac{V_2}{4} - \frac{(V_2 + 50)}{2} = 0 \quad \text{i.e.} \quad 0.1\,V_1 - 0.85\,V_2 = 25 \text{ ... (1.16.4)}$$

Solving, $V_1 = 2.6119$ V, $V_2 = -29.1044$ V

∴ $I = \dfrac{V_1 - V_2}{10} = \dfrac{2.6119 - (-29.1044)}{10} = \textbf{3.1716 A} \rightarrow$

Examples 1.16.2 *Find the current in the 132 Ω resistance using node analysis.*

2001-02, Marks 5

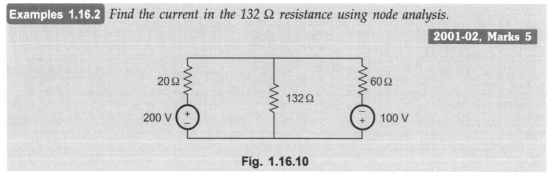

Fig. 1.16.10

Solution : Select the lowermost node as base node. There is only one node voltage present. The various branch currents are shown in the Fig. 1.16.10 (a).

KCL at the node is,

$$I_1 + I_2 + I_3 = 0 \quad\quad \text{...(1.16.5)}$$

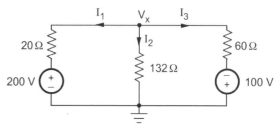

Fig. 1.16.10 (a)

Now analyse the branches,

$$I_2 = \frac{V_x - 0}{132} \qquad ...(1.16.6)$$

The node voltage V_x tries to force current downwards while polarities of 200 V source are such that it tries to force current upwards. So **200 V opposes V_x** hence net voltage deciding I_1 is $V_x - 200$.

$$\therefore \qquad I_1 = \frac{V_x - 200}{20} \qquad ...(1.16.7)$$

In 60 Ω branch, both V_x and 100 V tries to force current downwards hence both voltages help each other. Hence net voltage deciding I_3 is $100 + V_x$.

$$\therefore \qquad I_3 = \frac{V_x + 100}{60} \qquad\qquad\qquad\qquad ...(1.16.8)$$

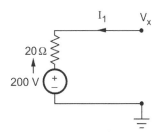

Fig. 1.16.10 (b)

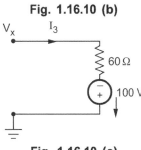

Fig. 1.16.10 (c)

Substituting (1.16.6), (1.16.7) and (1.16.8) in (1.16.5),

$$\frac{V_x}{132} + \frac{V_x - 200}{20} + \frac{V_x + 100}{60} = 0$$

$$\therefore \qquad\qquad\qquad V_x = \textbf{112.25 V}$$

$$\therefore \qquad\qquad I_{132\,\Omega} = I_2 = \frac{V_x}{132} = \textbf{0.8503 A} \qquad\qquad \textbf{...Ans.}$$

Examples 1.16.3 *Find the currents in the various resistors using nodal analysis.*

2005-06, Marks 10

Fig. 1.16.11

Solution : KCL at the three nodes,

$$10 - I_1 - I_2 - I_3 = 0, \qquad I_2 - I_5 - I_6 = 0, \qquad I_6 + I_1 - I_4 - 2 = 0$$

$$I_1 = \frac{V_A - V_C}{5} = 0.2V_A - 0.2V_C \qquad I_2 = \frac{V_A - V_B}{3} = 0.333\,V_A - 0.333\,V_B$$

$$I_3 = \frac{V_A - 0}{2} = 0.5\,V_A \qquad\qquad I_4 = \frac{V_C - 0}{4} = 0.25\,V_C$$

$$I_6 = \frac{V_B - V_C}{1} = V_B - V_C \qquad\qquad I_5 = \frac{V_B}{5} = 0.2\,V_B$$

Using in KCL equations,

$$10 - 0.2\,V_A + 0.2\,V_C - 0.333\,V_A + 0.333\,V_B - 0.5\,V_A = 0$$

i.e. $$\qquad 1.033\,V_A - 0.333\,V_B - 0.2\,V_C = 10 \qquad\qquad …(1.16.9)$$

$$0.333\,V_A - 0.333\,V_B - 0.2\,V_B - V_B + V_C = 0$$

i.e. $$\qquad 0.333\,V_A - 1.5333\,V_B + V_C = 0 \qquad\qquad …(1.16.10)$$

$$V_B - V_C + 0.2\,V_A - 0.2\,V_C - 0.25\,V_C - 2 = 0$$

$$\therefore \qquad 0.2\,V_A + V_B - 1.45\,V_C = 2 \qquad\qquad …(1.16.11)$$

Solving (1.16.9), (1.16.10) and (1.16.11),

$$V_A = 12.05\,V, \qquad V_B = 5.093\,V, \qquad V_C = 3.796\,V$$

$$\therefore \quad I_1 = \mathbf{1.6508\ A}, \qquad I_2 = \mathbf{2.3151\ A}, \qquad I_3 = \mathbf{6.025\ A}$$

$$I_4 = \mathbf{0.949\ A}, \qquad I_5 = \mathbf{1.0186\ A}, \qquad I_6 = \mathbf{1.297\ A}$$

Examples 1.16.4 *Using nodal analysis, find the current through 10 Ω resistor in Fig. 1.16.12.*

2003-04, Marks 5

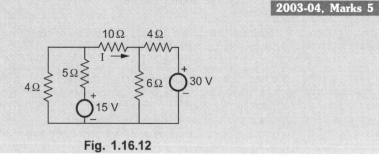

Fig. 1.16.12

Solution : The various node voltages and currents are shown in the Fig. 1.16.12 (a).

Apply KCL at two nodes,

$$+ I_1 + I_2 + I = 0 \qquad …(1.16.12)$$

$$I - I_3 - I_4 = 0 \qquad …(1.16.13)$$

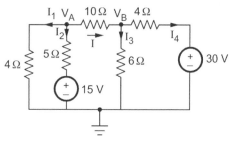

Fig. 1.16.12 (a)

From analysis of branches,

$$I_1 = \frac{V_A}{4} = 0.25 \ V_A,$$

$$I_2 = \frac{V_A - 0 - 15}{5} = 0.2 \ V_A - 3$$

$$I_3 = \frac{V_B}{6} = 0.166 \ V_B, \qquad I_4 = \frac{V_B - 0 - 30}{4} = 0.25 \ V_B - 7.5$$

$$I = \frac{V_A - V_B}{10} = 0.1 \ V_A - 0.1 \ V_B$$

Using in (1.16.12) and (1.16.13),

$0.25 \ V_A + 0.2 \ V_A - 3 + 0.1 \ V_A - 0.1 \ V_B = 0$ i.e. $0.55 \ V_A - 0.1 \ V_B = 3$

$0.1 \ V_A - 0.1 \ V_B - 0.166 \ V_B - (0.25 \ V_B - 7.5) = 0$ i.e. $0.1 \ V_A - 0.5166 \ V_B = -7.5$

Solving the two equations,

$$V_A = 8.389 \ V, \quad V_B = 16.14 \ V$$

$\therefore$ $I = \dfrac{V_A - V_B}{10} = -\ \textbf{0.7751 A} \ \ \text{i.e.} \ \ \textbf{0.7751 A} \leftarrow$

Examples 1.16.5 *For the circuit shown in Fig. 1.16.13, find voltages of nodes B and C and determine current in 8 Ω resistor.*   **2003-04, Marks 5**

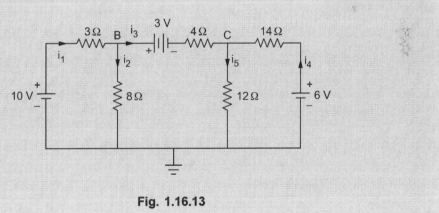

Fig. 1.16.13

Solution : Applying KCL at the nodes B and C for given currents,

$$i_1 - i_2 - i_3 = 0 \qquad \text{and} \quad i_3 + i_4 - i_5 = 0$$

From various branches,

$$I_2 = \frac{V_B - 0}{8}, \quad i_3 = \frac{V_B - V_C - 3}{4}, \quad i_5 = \frac{V_C}{12}$$

Now I_4 is the current arriving from base node to V_C hence base node is assumed more positive. While 6 V tries to force current in same direcon as I_4, helping the base node.

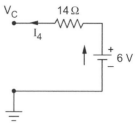

Fig. 1.16.13 (a)

Hence net voltage deciding I_4 is $(0 + 6 - V_C)$.

$$\therefore \quad I_4 = \frac{6 - V_C}{14}$$

Similarly, $I_1 = \dfrac{0 - V_B + 10}{3} = \dfrac{10 - V_B}{3}$

Substituting in KCL equations,

$$\frac{-V_B + 10}{3} - \frac{V_B}{8} - \left[\frac{V_B - V_C - 3}{4}\right] = 0 \quad \text{i.e.} -0.7083\, V_B + 0.25\, V_C = -4.0833$$

$$\frac{V_B - V_C - 3}{4} + \left[\frac{-V_C + 6}{14}\right] - \frac{V_C}{12} = 0 \quad \text{i.e.} \ 0.25\, V_B - 0.4047\, V_C = +0.32142$$

Solving the two equations,

$$V_B = \textbf{7.0138 V}, \quad V_C = \textbf{3.5385 V}$$

$$\therefore \quad I_{8\,\Omega} = i_2 = \frac{V_B}{8} = \frac{7.0138}{8} = \textbf{0.8767 A} \downarrow$$

Examples 1.16.6 *Find the current in the circuit given in Fig. 1.16.14.* **2006-07, Marks 5**

Fig. 1.16.14

Solution : Use the node analysis.

Applying KCL at the node,

$$-I_1 - I - 4 = 0$$

i.e. $\quad -I_1 - I = 4 \qquad \text{...(1.16.14)}$

Now $\quad I_1 = \dfrac{V_1 - 24}{6}$

$\quad I = \dfrac{V_1}{5}$

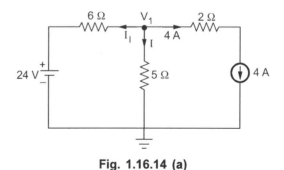

Fig. 1.16.14 (a)

$\therefore \qquad -\left[\dfrac{V_1-24}{6}\right] - \left[\dfrac{V_1}{5}\right] = 4$

$\therefore \qquad\qquad\qquad V_1 = 0\ V$

$\therefore \qquad\qquad\qquad I = \mathbf{0\ A}$

Examples 1.16.7 *Find current in 4 Ω resistor for a circuit shown in Fig. 1.16.15. Find the value of R.* **2006-07, Marks 10**

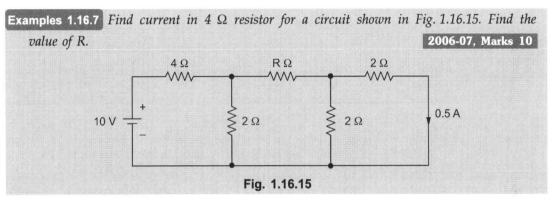

Fig. 1.16.15

Solution : Use node analysis

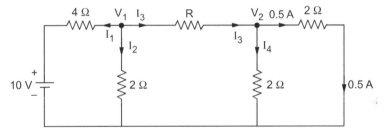

Fig. 1.16.15 (a)

Applying KCL at the two nodes,

$$-I_1 - I_2 - I_3 = 0 \quad \text{i.e.} \quad I_1 + I_2 + I_3 = 0 \qquad\qquad\qquad\qquad ...(1.16.15)$$

$$I_3 - I_4 - 0.5 = 0 \quad \text{i.e.} \quad I_3 - I_4 = 0.5 \qquad\qquad\qquad\qquad ...(1.16.16)$$

$$I_1 = \frac{V_1-10}{4}, \quad I_2 = \frac{V_1}{2}, \quad I_3 = \frac{V_1-V_2}{R}, \quad I_4 = \frac{V_2}{2}$$

From the branch of 2 Ω carrying 0.5 A, the voltage V_2 is obtained as,

$$V_2 = 0.5 \times 2 = 1\ V$$

From equation (1.16.15), $\quad \dfrac{V_1-10}{4} + \dfrac{V_1}{2} + \dfrac{V_1-1}{R} = 0 \quad$ i.e. $\left(0.75+\dfrac{1}{R}\right)V_1 - \dfrac{1}{R} = 2.5$

From equation (1.16.16), $\quad \dfrac{V_1-1}{R} - \dfrac{1}{2} = 0.5 \quad$ i.e. $\quad \dfrac{V_1-1}{R} = 1 \quad$ i.e. $V_1 = 1 + R$

$$\therefore \left(0.75 + \frac{1}{R} \right)(1 + R) - \frac{1}{R} = 2.5 \quad \text{i.e.} \quad (0.75\ R + 1)(1 + R) - 1 = 2.5\ R$$

$$\therefore \qquad\qquad 0.75\ R\ (R - 1) = 0 \quad \text{i.e.}\ R = 1\ \Omega$$

Thus current through $4\,\Omega$ is ,

$$I_1 = \frac{V_1 - 10}{4} = \frac{(1 + R) - 10}{4} = \frac{2 - 10}{4} = -\,2\ \text{A} \quad \text{i.e.} \quad \textbf{2 A} \rightarrow$$

Examples 1.16.8 *Find the currents in all the resistive branches of the circuit shown in Fig. 1.16.16 by i) KVL ii) KCL.*   **2007-08, Marks 5**

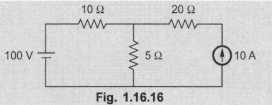

Fig. 1.16.16

Solution : i) By KVL means by loop analysis :

Key Point *As current source exists in a branch AB, it decides the corresponding loop current.*

$$\therefore \qquad I_2 = 10\ \text{A} \qquad ...\text{From AB}$$

Applying KVL to the first loop,

$$-\,10\ I_1 - 5\ I_1 - 5\ I_2 + 100 = 0 \quad \text{and} \quad I_2 = 10\ \text{A}$$

$$\therefore\ \ -\,15\ I_1 - 50 + 100 = 0$$

i.e. $$I_1 = \frac{-50}{-15} = 3.333\ \text{A}$$

ii) By KCL means by node analysis :

At the node,

$$-\,I_1 - I_2 + I_3 = 0 \qquad ...\text{KCL}$$

$$I_3 = 10\ \text{A}$$

$$I_1 = \frac{V - 100}{10}, \qquad I_2 = \frac{V - 0}{5}$$

$$\therefore\ \ -\left[\frac{V - 100}{10}\right] - \left[\frac{V}{5}\right] + 10 = 0$$

i.e. $$-\,0.3\ V = -\,20$$

$$\therefore \qquad V = 66.66\ \text{V}$$

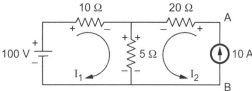

Fig. 1.16.16 (a)

Branch	Current
$10\ \Omega$	$I_1 = \textbf{3.333 A} \rightarrow$
$5\ \Omega$	$I_1 + I_2 = 10 + 3.333 = \textbf{13.333 A}$
$20\ \Omega$	$I_2 = \textbf{10 A}$

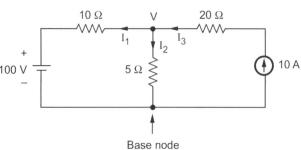

Base node

Fig. 1.16.16 (b)

Branch	Current
10 Ω	$I_1 = \dfrac{66.66 - 100}{10} = -\,\textbf{3.333 A i.e.} \rightarrow$
5 Ω	$I_2 = \dfrac{66.66}{5} = \textbf{13.333 A}$
20 Ω	$I_3 = \textbf{10 A}$

Examples 1.16.9 *Find the current in and voltage across the 2 Ω resistance in the following Fig. 1.16.17.*　　　　　　　　　　　　　　　　　　　　　　**2008-09, Marks 5**

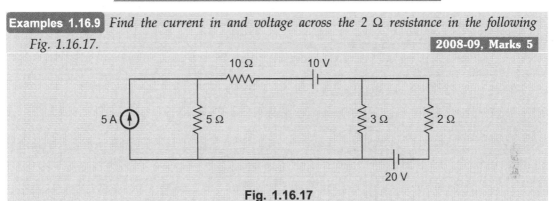

Fig. 1.16.17

Solution : Use Nodal analysis :

The node voltages and various currents are shown in the Fig. 1.16.17 (a).

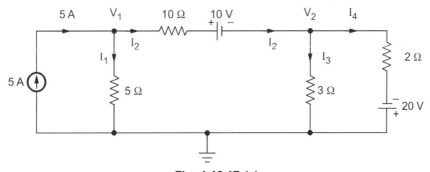

Fig. 1.16.17 (a)

At the two nodes,

$$5 - I_1 - I_2 = 0 \quad \text{... (1.16.17)} \quad \text{and} \quad I_2 - I_3 - I_4 = 0 \quad \text{... (1.16.18)}$$

$$I_1 = \frac{V_1 - 0}{5} = 0.2\, V_1, \qquad I_2 = \frac{V_1 - 10 - V_2}{10} = 0.1\, V_1 - 0.1\, V_2 - 1$$

$$I_3 = \frac{V_2 - 0}{3} = 0.3333\, V_2, \qquad I_4 = \frac{V_2 + 20}{2} = 0.5\, V_2 + 10$$

Using in equations (1.16.17) and (1.16.18),

$$5 - 0.2\, V_1 - [0.1\, V_1 - 0.1\, V_2 - 1] = 0 \quad \text{i.e.} \quad -0.3\, V_1 + 0.1\, V_2 = -6 \qquad \text{....(1.16.19)}$$

$$0.1\, V_1 - 0.1\, V_2 - 1 - 0.3333\, V_2 - (0.5\, V_2 + 10) = 0 \quad \text{i.e.} \quad 0.1\, V_1 - 0.9333\, V_2 = 11 \text{ ...(1.16.20)}$$

Solving $V_1 = 16.6667$ V, $V_2 = -10$ V

∴ $I_4 = 0.5 \times (-10) + 10 = 5$ A

∴ $I_{2\,\Omega} = \textbf{5 A}$ and $V_{2\,\Omega} = 2\,I_4 = \textbf{10 V}$

Review Questions

1. Explain the node analysis method.

2. Using nodal analysis, find current 'I' in the circuit shown in Fig. 1.16.18.

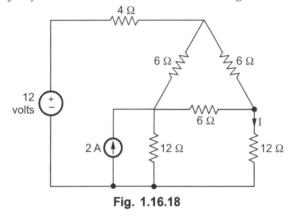

Fig. 1.16.18

[Ans. : 0.8583 A]

3. Using nodal method find current through 8 Ω resistor of Fig. 1.16.19.

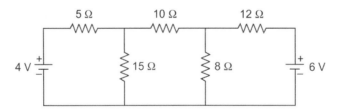

Fig. 1.16.19

[Ans. : 0.3193 A ↓]

4. Two batteries A and B are connected in parallel to a load of 10 ohm. Battery A has an emf of 12 V and an internal resistance of 2 ohm and battery B has an emf of 10 V and internal resistance of 1 ohm. Using nodal analysis, determine the currents supplied by each battery and load current.

2002-03

[Ans. : 1 A, 0 A, 1 A]

5. The Fig. 1.16.20 shows 2 batteries connected in parallel, each represented by an e.m.f. along with its internal resistance. A load resistance of 6 Ω is connected across the ends of the batteries. Calculate the current through each battery and the load.

2001-02

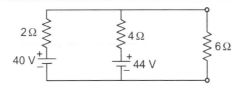

Fig. 1.16.20

[Ans. : 3.09 A, 2.55 A, 5.64 A]

6. *Using node analysis, determine current in each branch of the network shown in Fig. 1.16.21. Also find total power loss in the network.*   **2000-01**

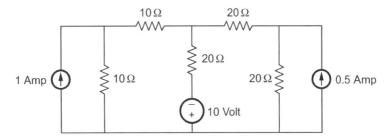

Fig. 1.16.21

[Ans. : $I_{10\,\Omega}$ = 0.6 A, 0.4 A, $I_{20\,\Omega}$ = 0.6 A, 0.2 A, 0.3 A, P_T = 15 W]

7. *Using nodal anlaysis, find V_x.*

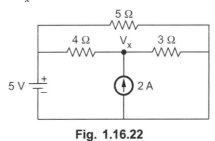

Fig. 1.16.22

[Ans. : 5.5714 V]

8. *Using node analysis find the current through 100 Ω resistor in the network shown.*

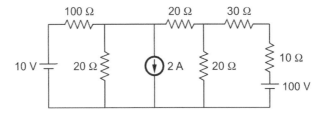

Fig. 1.16.23

[Ans. : 0.2 A]

9. By using Nodal analysis find V_1 and V_2.

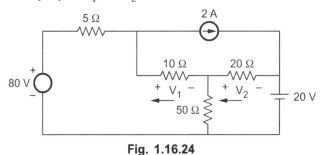

Fig. 1.16.24

[Ans. : 19.024 V, 21.463 V]

10. For the circuit below, using nodal analysis, find voltage at X.

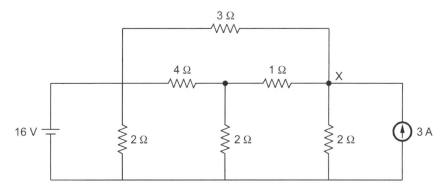

Fig. 1.16.25

[Ans. : 9.5878 V]

1.17 Short Answered and Objective Type Questions

Q.1   The mass of electron is _____kg.   `2009-10`

[Ans. : 9.107×10^{-31} kg]

Q.2   Is 'L' a linear element ? Explain the answer.   `2011-12`

Ans. : The voltage across 'L' is given by $L\dfrac{di}{dt}$ where 'i' is the current flowing through it. As long as L is constant and not dependent on circuit parameters, the relation is linear and hence 'L' is a linear element.

Q.3   If resistance of each branch is 3 ohms in a delta connected load, what would be the resistance of each branch in its star equivalent ?   `2011-12`

Ans. :   In delta, $R_{12} = R_{23} = R_{31} = R = 3 \ \Omega$

∴   Each R in star $= \dfrac{3 \times 3}{3+3+3} = \mathbf{1} \ \Omega$

Q.4   On what factors do the resistance of a conductor depends ?   `2012-13`

Ans. :   a) Length of the conductor.

b) Cross-sectional area of the conductor.

c) Specific resistance of the conductor.

d) Temperature.

Q.5   What is the difference between loop and mesh ?

Ans. :   The difference between a mesh and a loop is that a mesh does not contain any other loop within it. Thus a mesh is the smallest loop. A mesh is always a loop but a loop may or may not be a mesh.

Q.6   What is difference between ideal and practical voltage source ?

Ans. :   Ideal independent voltage source is defined as the energy source which gives constant voltage across its terminals irrespective of the current drawn through its terminals. Its internal resistance is zero.

Practically, every voltage source has small internal resistance shown in series with voltage source and is represented by R_{se}. Because of the R_{se}, there is voltage drop across R_{se} when current flows through the load and hence the voltage across terminals decreases with increase in current

Q.7   What is difference between ideal and practical current source ?

Ans. :   Ideal current source is the source which gives constant current at its terminals irrespective of the voltage appearing across its terminals. Its internal resistance is infinite.

Practically, every current source has high internal resistance and it is shown in parallel with the current source and represented by R_{sh}. Because of R_{sh}, current gets divided into two paths. Hence the current through its terminals towards the load decreases with increase in the voltage at its terminals.

Q.8   Draw the V-I characteristics of an ideal and practical voltage source.

Ans. :   Refer Fig. 1.4.1 (c) and Fig. 1.4.2 (b).

Q.9   Draw the V-I characteristics of an ideal and practical current source.

Ans. :   Refer Fig. 1.4.3 (c) and Fig. 1.4.4 (b).

Q.10   State Ohm's law.

Ans. :   The current flowing through the electric circuit is directly proportional to the potential difference across the circuit and inversely proportional to the resistance of the circuit, provided the temperature remains constant.

Mathematically it is stated as, $I = \dfrac{V}{R}$.

Q.11   A point where three or more branches meet is called ____.

a) node   b) junction point   c) datum   d) base   **[Ans. : b]**

Q.12 A circuit whose operation is dependent on the direction of current through elements is called ____.

    a) linear   b) bilateral   c) unilateral   d) lumped **[Ans. : c]**

Q.13 The law of Superposition cannot be applied to the ____ network.

    a) linear   b) bilateral   c) lumped   d) nonlinear

                                                   [Ans. : d]

Q.14 A circuit without any energy source is called ____.

    a) passive   b) active   c) linear   d) distributed

                                                   [Ans. : a]

Q.15 The transmission line is best example of ____ network.

    a) passive   b) nonlinear   c) distributed   d) lumped **[Ans. : c]**

Q.16 The load increases means load resistance ____.

    a) increases   b) decreases   c) remains constant   d) none of these

                                                   [Ans. : b]

Q.17 The electrical devices are connected in parallel because ____.
    a)   the circuit becomes simple.
    b)   the voltage remains constant hence operation of each becomes independent.
    c)   it consumes less power.
    d)   it requires less current.   **[Ans. : b]**

Q.18 For bettter performance of the source, the regulation must be ____.

    a) infinite   b) very high   c) constant   d) zero   **[Ans. : d]**

Q.19 For ideal voltage soruce, internal resistance is ____ ohms.

    a) infinite   b) zero   c) constant   d) none of these

                                                   [Ans. : b]

Q.20 For ideal current source, internal resistance is ____ ohms.

    a) infinite   b) zero   c) constant   d) none of these

                                                   [Ans. : a]

Q.21 For application of ohm's law, ____ of circuit must remain constant.

    a) voltage   b) current   c) resistance   d) inductance

                                                   [Ans. : c]

Q.22 The ohm's law cannot be applied to ____.

    a) resistance   b) inductance   c) capacitance   d) diode   **[Ans. : d]**

Q.23 The resistance is ____ proportional to length and ____ proportional to area of cross-section.

    a) directely, directly   b) directly, inversely
    c) inversely, directly   d) none of these   **[Ans. : b]**

Q.24 1 joule = ____ calories

     a) 0.21   b) 0.24   c) 0.28   d) 0.22   **[Ans. : b]**

Q.25 In a series circuit, ____ remains same.

     a) current   b) voltage   c) resistance   d) none of these
                                                                                  [Ans. : a]

Q.26 In a series circuit, the equivalent resistance is ____ of all the individual resistances.

     a) smallest   b) same as   c) largest   d) none of these
                                                                                         [Ans. : c]

Q.27 In a parallel circuit, ____ remains same.

     a) current   b) voltage   c) resistance   d) none of these
                                                                                         [Ans. : b]

Q.28 In a parallel circuit, the equivalent resistance is ____ of all the individual resistances.

     a) smallest   b) same as   c) largest   d) none of these
                                                                                         [Ans. : a]

Q.29 The voltage drop across 8 Ω resistance is ____ V.

     a) 100 V   b) 80 V   c) 220 V   d) 120 V   **[Ans. : d]**

Q.30 The voltage across the short circuit is ____.

     a) infinite   b) one   c) zero   d) none of these
                                                                                         [Ans. : c]

Q.31 In a circuit shown, the current through 5 Ω resistance is ____ A.

     a) 15 A   b) 20 A   c) 25 A   d) 4 A   **[Ans. : b]**

Q.32 If a voltage source of 50 V, 5 Ω is transformed to current source, the value of current source is ____ A.

     a) 10 A   b) 5 A   c) 50 A   d) 25 A   **[Ans. : a]**

Q.33 The algebraic sum of all the currents at a junction point is always zero is the statement of ____ law.

     a) KVL   b) Lenz's   c) Faraday's   d) KCL   **[Ans. : d]**

Q.34 The delta connection always forms a ____.

a) loop   b) open circuit   c) short circuit   d) none of these

[Ans. : a]

Q.35 If all the resistances in a delta are of 9 Ω then all the resistances in an equivalent star will be ____ Ω.

a) 27   b) 6   c) 18   d) 3   **[Ans. : d]**

Q.36 If all the resistances in a star are of 9 Ω then all the resistances in an equivalent delta will be ____ Ω.

a) 27   b) 6   c) 18   d) 3   **[Ans. : a]**

Q.37 In a given circuit, the total circuit resistance is ____ ohms.

a) 1000 Ω   b) 6.4 Ω   c) 1536 Ω   d) 1236 Ω   **[Ans. : c]**

Q.38 Refer to the Fig. 1.17.1, which of the following statement is true?

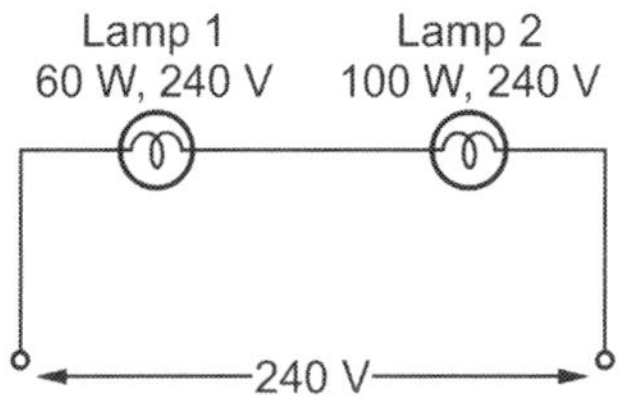

Fig. 1.17.1

a) Lamp 1 will be less brighter than Lamp 2.
b) Lamp 1 will be more brighter than Lamp 2.
c) Both the lamp will glow with equal brightness.
d) None of the above.   **[Ans. : b]**

Q.39 The practical voltage source has e.m.f. of E volts and internal resistance is r ohms. If it supplies a load current of I amperes, the terminal voltage is ____.

a) E   b) $\left(\dfrac{E}{r}\right)$ c) Ir   d) E - Ir

[Ans. : d]

Q.40 A practical voltage source of 100 V is connected across 10 Ω resistance and the terminal voltage across 10 Ω is found to be 80 V, then the internal resistance of the source is ____ Ω.

a) 2.5 Ω   b) 10 Ω   c) 5 Ω   d) 8 Ω   **[Ans. : a]**

Q.41 If 20 resistances, each of 1 Ω are connected in parallel then the equivalent resistance is ____ Ω

a) 0.01 Ω   b) 0.05 Ω   c) 20 Ω   d) 0.02 Ω   **[Ans. : b]**

Q.42 The current drawn by the resistance of 8 Ω in the circuit shown is ____ A.

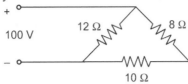

a) 1.555 A   b) 2.5555 A   c) 5.5555 A   d) 4.5555 A **[Ans. : c]**

Q.43 The total current drawn by the circuit shown from the supply is ____ A.

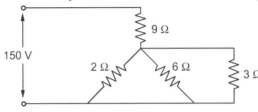

Fig. 1.17.2

a) 10 A   b) 5 A   c) 1 A   d) 15 A   **[Ans. : d]**

Q.44 If the 3 Ω resistance is removed from the circuit shown in the Fig. 1.17.2. The current drawn by the circuit is ____ A.

a) 14.285 A   b) 9.185 A   c) 2 A   d) 1.185 A **[Ans. : a]**

Q.45 The voltage across the parallel circuit shown in the Fig. 1.17.3 is ____ V.

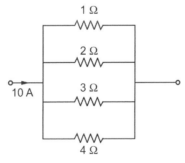

Fig. 1.17.3

a) 1.8 V   b) 4.8 V   c) 8.4 V   d) 2.8 V   **[Ans. : b]**

Q.46 In the circuit shown, there are ____ junction points.

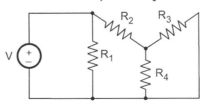

a) 2   b) 3   c) 4   d) 1   **[Ans. : c]**

Q.47 The current in 20 Ω resistance of the circuit shown in the Fig. 1.17.4. is _____ A.

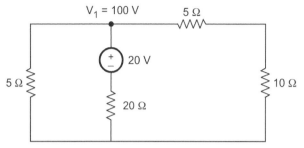

Fig. 1.17.4

a) 4 A   b) 5 A   c) 1 A   d) 10 A   [Ans. : a]

Q.48 _____ number of equations based on node basis are required to solve the circuit shown in the Fig. 1.17.5.

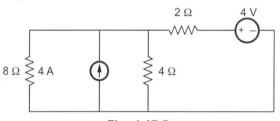

Fig. 1.17.5

a) 2   b) 3   c) 1   d) 4   [Ans. : c]

Q.49 _____ of the following is not bilateral.

a) Resistor   b) Inductor   c) Capacitor   d) Transistor
                                                                    [Ans. : d]

Q.50 Among following which conductor has highest conductivity ?   `2009-10`

a) Cu   b) Al   c) Ag   d) Mg   [Ans. : c]

Q.51 An ideal voltage source should have : _____ .   `2009-10`

a) large value of e.m.f.   b) small value of e.m.f.

c) zero source resistance   d) infinite source resistance   [Ans. : c]

Q.52 A 100 ohm resistor is needed in an electric circuit to carry a current of 0.3 A. Which resistor would you specify ?   `2010-11`

a) 100 ohm 5 W   b) 100 ohm 7.5 W   c) 100 ohm 10 W   d) None of these
                                                                    [Ans. : c]

Q.53 An inductor at $t = 0^+$ with zero initial condition act as : _____.   `2010-11`

a) Voltage source   b) Current source   c) Open circuit   d) None of these
                                                                    [Ans. : c]

Q.54 In star connection of resistance is R then in equivalent delta connection this value will be : _____.   `2010-11`

a) R/2   b) 3R/2   c) 3R   d) R/3   [Ans. : d]

❑❑❑

2 Network Theorems

Syllabus

Superposition theorem, Thevenin's theorem, Norton's theorem, Maximum power transfer theorem (Simple numerical problems).

Contents

2.1 Superposition Theorem   2002-03, 2004-05, 2006-07, 2007-08, 2008-09, 2009-10, 2010-11, 2011-12, 2012-13

This theorem is applicable for linear and bilateral networks. Let us see the statement of the theorem.

Statement : *In any multisource complex network consisting of linear bilateral elements, the voltage across or current through any given element of the network is equal to the algebraic sum of the individual voltages or currents, produced independently across or in that element by each source acting independently, when all the remaining sources are replaced by their respective internal resistances.*

Key Point *If the internal resistances of the sources are unknown then the **independent voltage sources** must be replaced by **short circuit** while the **independent current sources** must be replaced by an **open circuit**.*

The theorem is also known as Superposition principle. In other words, it can be stated as, the response in any element of linear, bilateral network containing more than one sources is the sum of the responses produced by the sources, each acting independently. The response means the voltage across the element or the current in the element. The superposition theorem does not apply to the power as power is proportional to square of the current, which is not a linear function.

2.1.1 Explanation of Superposition Theorem

Consider a network, shown in the Fig. 2.1.1, having two voltage sources V_1 and V_2.

Let us calculate, the current in branch A-B of the network, using superposition theorem.

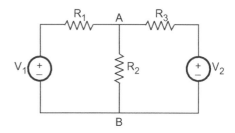

Fig. 2.1.1

Step 1) According to Superposition theorem, consider each source independently. Let source V_1 volts is acting independently. At this time, other sources must be replaced by internal impedances.

But as internal impedance of V_2 is not given, the source V_2 must be replaced by short circuit. Hence circuit becomes, as shown in the Fig. 2.1.1 (a).

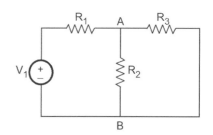

Fig. 2.1.1 (a)

Using any of the network reduction techniques discussed earlier, obtain the current through branch A-B i.e. I_{AB} due to source V_1 alone.

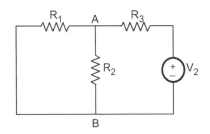

Fig. 2.1.1 (b)

Step 2) Now consider source V_2 volts alone, with V_1 replaced by a short circuit, to obtain the current through branch A-B. The corresponding circuit is shown in the Fig. 2.1.1 (b).

Obtain I_{AB} due to V_2 alone, by using any of the network reduction techniques discussed earlier.

Step 3) According to the Superposition theorem, the total current through branch A-B is the sum of the currents through branch A-B produced by each source acting independently.

$\therefore$ Total I_{AB} = I_{AB} due to V_1 + I_{AB} due to V_2

2.1.2 Steps to Apply Superposition Theorem

Step 1 : Select a single source acting alone. Short the other voltage sources and open the current sources, if internal resistances are not known. If known, replace them by their internal resistances.

Step 2 : Find the current through or the voltage across the required element, due to the source under consideration, using a suitable network simplification technique.

Step 3 : Repeat the above two steps for all the sources

Step 4 : Add the individual effects produced by individual sources, to obtain the total current in or voltage across the element.

Examples 2.1.1 *Using superposition theorem, determine currents in all resistances of the following network :*

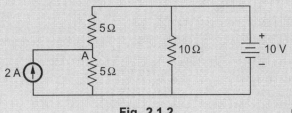

Fig. 2.1.2

2004-05, Marks 10

Solution : Step 1 : Consider 2 A source alone and short 10 V.

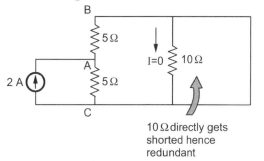

10 Ω directly gets
shorted hence
redundant

Fig. 2.1.2 (a)

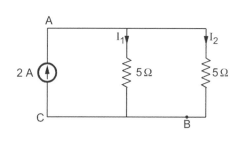

Fig. 2.1.2 (b)

By current distribution rule,

$$I_1 = I_2 = 2 \times \frac{5}{10} = 1 \text{ A}$$

∴ Current through upper   5 Ω = 1 A ↑

Current through lower   5 Ω = 1 A ↓

Current through 10 Ω = 0 A

Step 2 : Consider 10 V alone and open 2 A source

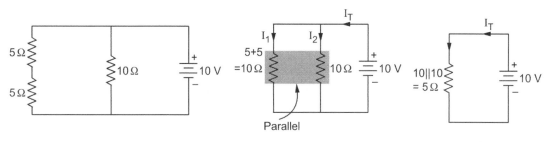

| Fig. 2.1.2 (c) | Fig. 2.1.2 (d) | Fig. 2.1.2 (e) |

∴ $$I_T = \frac{10}{5} = 2 \text{ A}$$

By current disribution rule, from the Fig. 2.1.2 (d),

$$I_1 = I_2 = I_T \times \frac{10}{10+10} = 1 \text{ A}$$

∴ Current through both 5 Ω = 1 A ↓

Current through   10 Ω = 1 A ↓

Step 3 : Thus the total currents are,

Through upper 5 Ω = 1 A ↑ + 1 A ↓ = **0 A**

Through lower 5 Ω = 1 A ↓ + 1 A ↓ = **2 A ↓**

   Through 10 Ω = 0 A + 1 A ↓ = **1 A ↓**

Examples 2.1.2 *Determine current through 8 Ω resistor in the following network using superposition theorem.*

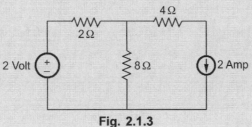

Fig. 2.1.3   2002-03, Marks 5

Solution : Step 1 : Consider 20 V alone, open 2 A source

$$I = \frac{20}{8+2} = 2\ A$$

∴ $I' = \textbf{2 A} ↓$

                  ...Due to 20 V alone

Step 2 : Consider 2 A alone and short 20 V source

Using current distribution rule,

$$I'' = I_T \times \frac{2}{2+8} = \frac{2\times2}{10}$$

$$= \textbf{0.4 A} ↑$$

                  ...Due to 2 A alone

∴ $I_{8\,\Omega} = 2A ↓ + 0.4\ A ↑ = \textbf{1.6 A} ↓$

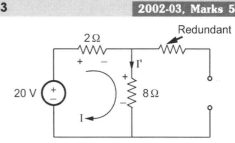

Fig. 2.1.3 (a)

Fig. 2.1.3 (b)

Examples 2.1.3 *In the circuit shown in Fig. 2.1.4 find the current through the 6 Ω register using Superposition theorem.*

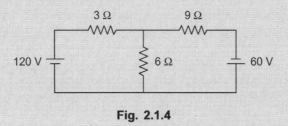

Fig. 2.1.4

2007-08, Marks 5

Solution : Refer example 2.1.4 and verify the answer as **9.091 A ↓**.

Examples 2.1.4 *Using superposition theorem, calculate the current in the AB branch in the circuit shown in below Fig. 2.1.5.*

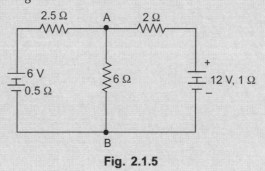

Fig. 2.1.5

2012-13, Marks 10

Solution : Step 1 : Consider 6 V source, replace 12 V by 1 Ω.

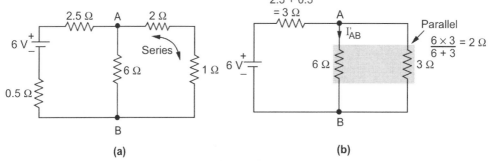

Fig. 2.1.5

From Fig. 2.1.5 (c),

$$I_T = \frac{6}{3+2} = 1.2 \text{ A}$$

Applying current division rule to Fig. 2.1.5 (b),

Fig. 2.1.5 (c)

$$I'_{AB} = I_T \times \frac{3}{3+6} = \frac{1.2 \times 3}{9} = 0.4 \text{ A} \downarrow$$ ... Due to 6 V source

Step 2 : Consider 12 V source, replace 6 V by 0.5 Ω.

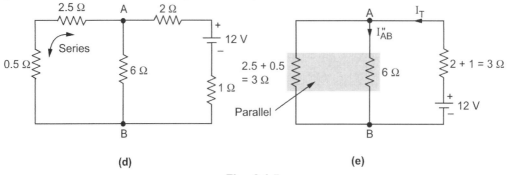

Fig. 2.1.5

From Fig. 2.1.5 (f),

$$I_T = \frac{12}{2+3} = 2.4 \text{ A}$$

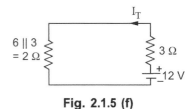

Fig. 2.1.5 (f)

Applying current division rule to Fig. 2.1.5 (e),

$$I''_{AB} = I_T \times \frac{3}{3+6} = \frac{2.4 \times 3}{9} = \textbf{0.8 A} \downarrow \qquad \text{... Due to 12 V source}$$

Step 3 : $I_{AB} = I'_{AB} + I''_{AB} = 0.4 \text{ A} \downarrow + 0.8 \text{ A} \downarrow = \textbf{1.2 A} \downarrow$

Examples 2.1.5 *For the circuit shown in the following figure, the value of R such that the same amount of power is supplied to the 10 Ω resistance by the current and by the voltage source will be _____ .*

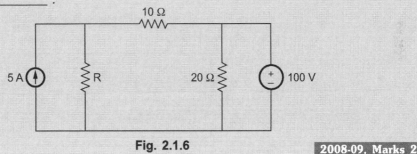

Fig. 2.1.6 2008-09, Marks 2

Solution : **i)** By Superposition, consider 5 A source alone, short 100 V.

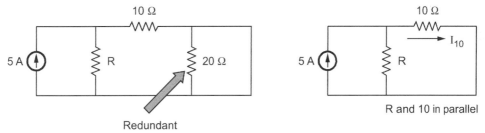

Fig. 2.1.7

$$\therefore \qquad I_{10} = \frac{5 \times R}{10 + R} \qquad\qquad\qquad \text{... (2.1.1)}$$

Consider 100 V alone, open the current source.

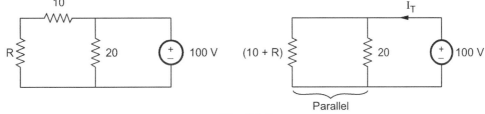

Fig. 2.1.8

$$\therefore \qquad I_T \;=\; \frac{100}{20||(10+R)} \;=\; \frac{100}{\dfrac{20\times(10+R)}{20+10+R}} \;=\; \frac{100(30+R)}{20\,(10+R)} \;=\; \frac{5(30+R)}{(10+R)}$$

$$\therefore \qquad I_{10} \;=\; \frac{I_T\times 20}{(20+10+R)} \;=\; \frac{5(30+R)}{(10+R)}\times\frac{20}{(30+R)} \;=\; \frac{100}{(10+R)} \qquad\qquad ...(2.1.2)$$

For same power, currents due to two sources must be same hence,

$$\frac{5R}{10+R} \;=\; \frac{100}{(10+R)} \qquad \text{i.e. } 5\,R = 100$$

$$\therefore \qquad R \;=\; \mathbf{20\ \Omega}$$

Examples 2.1.6 *Using Superposition theorem find the current in 20 Ω resistor of the circuit shown in Fig. 2.1.9.*

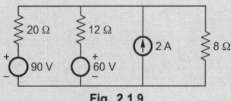

Fig. 2.1.9   2009-10, Marks 5

Solution : Step 1 : Consider 90 V source alone, short 60 V source and open 2 A source.

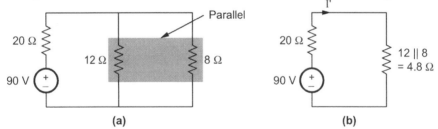

(a)   (b)

Fig. 2.1.9

$$I' \;=\; \frac{90}{20+4.8} \;=\; \mathbf{3.629A}\uparrow \qquad\qquad \text{... Due to 90 V alone}$$

Step 2 : Consider 60 V source alone, short 90 V source and open 2 A source.

The 20 Ω and 8 Ω are in parallel.

$$\therefore \qquad I_T \;=\; \frac{60}{12+(20||8)} \;=\; \frac{60}{12+5.7143} \;=\; 3.3871 \text{ A}$$

Fig. 2.1.9 (c)

Using current distribution rule,

$$I'' \;=\; I_T\times\frac{8}{8+20} \;=\; \mathbf{0.9677A}\downarrow \qquad\qquad \text{.. Due to 60 V alone}$$

Step 3 : Consider 2 A alone, short the two voltage sources.

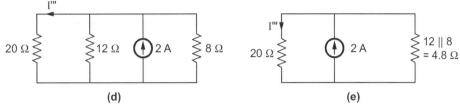

(d)   **(e)**

Fig. 2.1.9

Using current distribution rule,

$$I''' = 2 \times \frac{4.8}{20 + 4.8} = \textbf{0.3871A} \downarrow \qquad \text{... Due to 2 A alone}$$

$$\therefore \qquad I_{20\Omega} = I' + I'' + I''' = 3.629 \uparrow + 0.9677 \downarrow + 0.3871 \downarrow = \textbf{2.2742 A} \downarrow$$

Examples 2.1.7 *By means of superposition theorem find the current which flows through* R_2 *in the circuit of Fig. 2.1.10.*

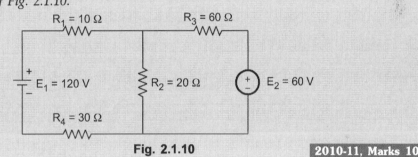

Fig. 2.1.10   **2010-11, Marks 10**

Solution : Step 1 : Consider $E_1 = 120$ **V, short** E_2

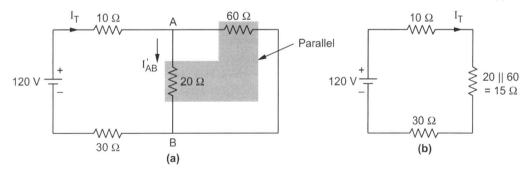

(a)   **(b)**

Fig. 2.1.10

$$\therefore \qquad I_T = \frac{120}{40 + 15} = 2.1818 \text{ A}$$

Using current division rule to the Fig. 2.1.10 (a).

$$\therefore \qquad I'_{AB} = \frac{I_T \times 60}{(20 + 60)} = \frac{2.1818 \times 60}{80} = \textbf{1.6363 A} \downarrow$$

Step 2 : Consider $E_2 = 60$ V only, short E_1

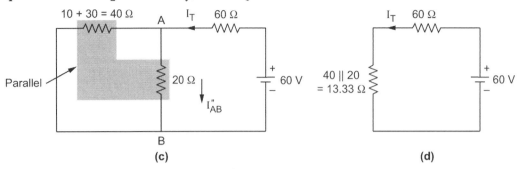

Fig. 2.1.10

$$\therefore \qquad I_T = \frac{60}{60+13.333} = 0.8181 \text{ A}$$

Using current division rule to the Fig. 2.1.10 (c).

$$\therefore \qquad I''_{AB} = I_T \times \frac{40}{40+20} = \frac{0.8181 \times 40}{60} = \mathbf{0.5454 \text{ A}} \downarrow$$

Step 3 : $I_{R2} = I'_{AB} + I''_{AB} = 1.6363 \text{ A} \downarrow + 0.5454 \text{ A} \downarrow = \mathbf{2.1817 \text{ A}} \downarrow$

Examples 2.1.8 *Find the current flowing through 10 Ω resistance in the following circuit. Use superposition theorem.*

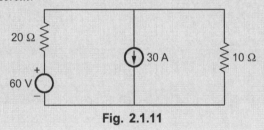

Fig. 2.1.11

2011-12, Marks 10

Solution : Case 1 : Consider 60 V alone, open 30 A source.

$$\therefore \qquad I'_{10} = \frac{60}{20+10} = 2 \text{ A} \downarrow$$

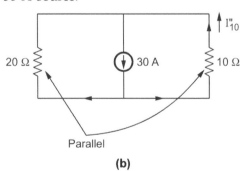

(a)   (b)

Fig. 2.1.11

Case 2 : Consider 30 A alone, short 60 V source. As 10 Ω and 20 Ω in parallel. using current division rule,

$$I''_{10} = 30 \times \frac{20}{20+10} = 20 \text{ A} \uparrow$$

$$\therefore \quad I_{10\Omega} = I'_{10} + I''_{10} = 2 \text{ A} \downarrow + 20 \text{ A} \uparrow = \mathbf{18 \text{ A}} \uparrow$$

Examples 2.1.9 *Determine the currents i_x and i_y in the following network. State theorem used.*

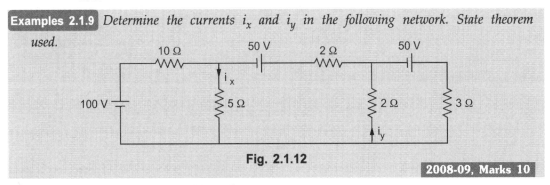

Fig. 2.1.12

2008-09, Marks 10

Solution : i) A) Use superposition theorem :

Case 1 : Consider 100 V, short 50 V sources.

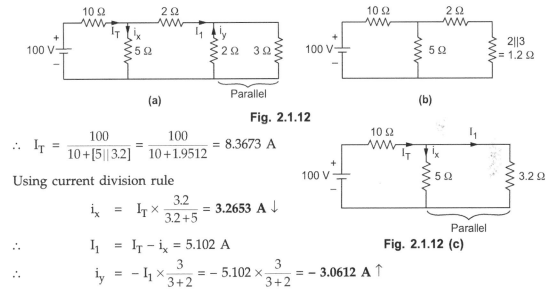

(a)   (b)

Fig. 2.1.12

$$\therefore \quad I_T = \frac{100}{10+[5||3.2]} = \frac{100}{10+1.9512} = 8.3673 \text{ A}$$

Using current division rule

$$i_x = I_T \times \frac{3.2}{3.2+5} = \mathbf{3.2653 \text{ A}} \downarrow$$

$$\therefore \quad I_1 = I_T - i_x = 5.102 \text{ A}$$

$$\therefore \quad i_y = -I_1 \times \frac{3}{3+2} = -5.102 \times \frac{3}{3+2} = \mathbf{-3.0612 \text{ A}} \uparrow$$

Fig. 2.1.12 (c)

i_y is negative as assumed upwards but actually flowing downwards.

Case 2 : Consider 50 V source.

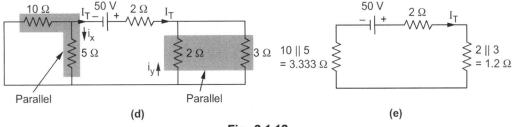

(d)   (e)

Fig. 2.1.12

$\therefore$ $I_T = \dfrac{50}{3.333 + 2 + 1.2} = 7.65306$ A

$\therefore$ $i_x = -I_T \times \dfrac{10}{10 + 5} = -5.102$ A $\downarrow$ ... (– ve as assumed downwards)

$\therefore$ $i_y = -I_T \times \dfrac{3}{2 + 3} = -4.5918$ A $\uparrow$ ... (– ve as assumed upwards)

Case 3 : Consider another 50 V source.

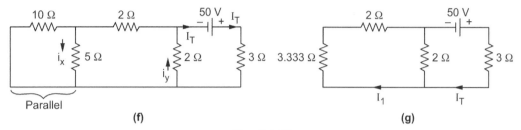

(f)   (g)

Fig. 2.1.12

$\therefore$ $I_T = \dfrac{50}{3 + [2 \| 5.333]}$

          $= \dfrac{50}{3 + 1.4545} = 11.2244$ A

$\therefore$ $i_y = I_T \times \dfrac{5.3333}{5.333 + 2} = 8.1632$ A $\uparrow$

$\therefore$ $I_1 = I_T - i_y = 3.06116$ A

$\therefore$ $i_x = -I_1 \times \dfrac{10}{10 + 5} = -2.0407$ A $\downarrow$ ... (– ve as assumed downwards)

Fig. 2.1.12 (h)

Hence algebraically adding all the results,

       $i_x = (3.2653$ A $\downarrow) + (-5.102$ A $\downarrow) + (-2.0407$ A $\downarrow)$

           $= -3.8774$ A $\downarrow$ i.e.   **3.8774 A** $\uparrow$

       $i_y = (-3.0612$ A $\uparrow) + (-4.5718$ A $\uparrow) + (8.1632$ A $\uparrow) = $ **0.5102 A** $\uparrow$

Examples 2.1.10 *Find current I in 8 Ω resistance using Superposition theorem as shown in Fig. 2.1.13.*

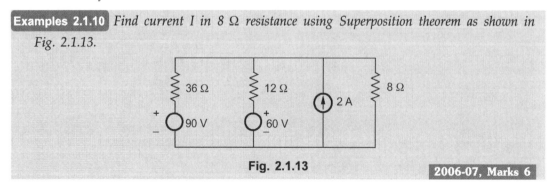

Fig. 2.1.13

2006-07, Marks 6

Solution : Refer example 2.1.6 for the procedure and verify the answer as **5.0293 A** $\downarrow$.

1. *State and explain superposition theorem.*   **2009-10, Marks 5**

2. *Find current flowing through* 3 Ω *resistance by Superposition theorem for the circuit shown in the Fig. 2.1.14.*

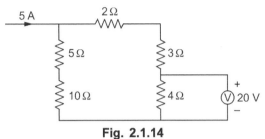

Fig. 2.1.14

[Ans. : 2.75 A ↓]

3. *Using Superposition theorem, calculate the current flowing in* 1 Ω *resistance for the network shown in Fig. 2.1.15.*

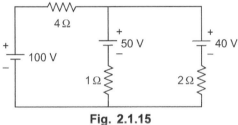

Fig. 2.1.15

[Ans. : 4.2826 A ↓]

4. *For the network shown in Fig. 2.1.16, find the current in the 2-ohm resistance by using superposition theorem.*

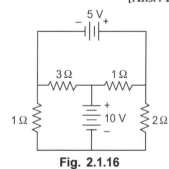

[Ans. : 3.5286 A ↓]

Fig. 2.1.16

5. *In the circuit shown, find current through branch AB by superposition theorem.*

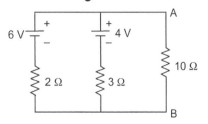

[Ans. : 0.4642 A ↓]

Fig. 2.1.17

6. Use superposition theorem to find the current through the 20 ohm resistance shown in the Fig. 2.1.18.

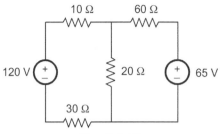

Fig. 2.1.18 [Ans. : 2.2272 A ↓]

7. Calculate current through the 15 Ω resistance using Kirchhoff's law and verify your answer using Superposition theorem as well. The circuit is shown in the Fig. 2.1.19.

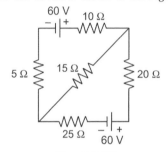

Fig. 2.1.19 [Ans. : 2.2857 A ↓]

8. Find the current through 4 Ω by superposition theorem.

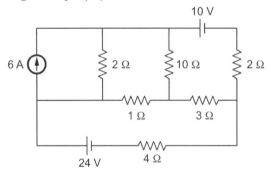

Fig. 2.1.20 [Ans. : 4.1021 A ←]

9. Using superposition principle find I.

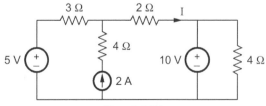

Fig. 2.1.21

[Ans. : 0.2 A →]

10. Find V_{ab} for the circuit below using superposition theorem.

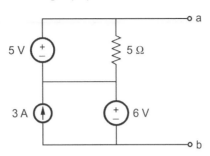

Fig. 2.1.22

[Ans. : 11 V with 'a' +ve]

11. Apply superposition theorem to find current i_3 in the circuit shown in the Fig. 2.1.23.

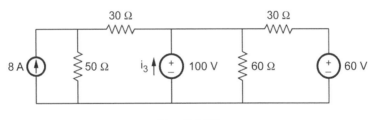

Fig. 2.1.23

[Ans. : 0.75 A ↓]

2.2 Thevenin's Theorem

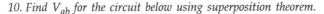

2001-02, 2002-03, 2004-05, 2005-06, 2006-07, 2008-09, 2009-10, 2010-11, 2012-13

Let us see the statement of the theorem.

Statement : *Any combination of linear bilateral circuit elements and active sources, regardless of the connection or complexity, connected to a given load R_L, may be replaced by a simple two terminal network consisting of a single voltage source of V_{TH} volts and a single resistance R_{eq} in series with the voltage source, across the two terminals of the load R_L. The voltage V_{TH} is the open circuit voltage measured at the two terminals of interest, with load resistance R_L removed. This voltage is also called **Thevenin's equivalent voltage**. The R_{eq} is the **equivalent resistance** of the given network as viewed through the terminals where R_L is connected, but with R_L removed and all the active sources are replaced by their internal resistances.*

Key Point *If the internal resistances are not known then **independent voltage sources** are to be replaced by the **short circuit** while the **independent current sources** must be replaced by the **open circuit**.*

2.2.1 Explanation of Thevenin's Theorem

The concept of Thevenin's equivalent across the terminals of interest can be explained by considering the circuit shown in the Fig. 2.2.1 (a). The terminals A-B are the terminals of interest across which R_L is connected. Then Thevenin's equivalent across the load terminals A-B can be obtained as shown in the Fig. 2.2.1. (b).

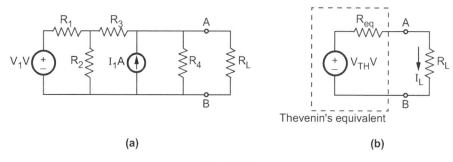

(a)   (b)

Fig. 2.2.1

The voltage V_{TH} is obtained across the terminals A-B with R_L removed. Hence V_{TH} is also called open circuit Thevenin's voltage. The circuit to be used to calculate V_{TH} is shown in the Fig. 2.2.2 (a), for the network considered above. While R_{eq} is the equivalent resistance obtained as viewed through the terminals A-B with R_L removed, voltage sources replaced by short circuit and current sources by open circuit. This is shown in the Fig. 2.2.2 (b).

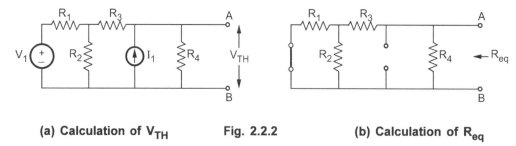

(a) Calculation of V_{TH}   **Fig. 2.2.2**   **(b) Calculation of R_{eq}**

While obtaining V_{TH}, any of the network simplification techniques can be used.

When the circuit is replaced by Thevenin's equivalent across the load resistance, then the load current can be obtained as,

$$I_L = \frac{V_{TH}}{R_L + R_{eq}}$$

By using this theorem, current through any branch of the circuit can be obtained, treating that branch resistance as the load resistance and obtaining Thevenin's equivalent across the two terminals of that branch.

2.2.2 Steps to Apply Thevenin's Theorem

Step 1 :   Remove the branch resistance through which current is to be calculated.

Step 2 :   Calculate the voltage across these open circuited terminals, by using any of the network simplification techniques. This is V_{TH}.

Step 3 :   Calculate R_{eq} as viewed through the two terminals of the branch from which current is to be calculated by removing that branch resistance and replacing all independent sources by their internal resistances. If the internal reistances are not known then replace independent voltage sources by short circuits and independent current sources by open circuits.

Step 4 :   Draw the Thevenin's equivalent showing source V_{TH}, with the resistance R_{eq} in series with it, across the terminals of branch of interest.

Step 5 :   Reconnect the branch resistance. Let it be R_L. The required current through the branch is given by,

$$I = \frac{V_{TH}}{R_{eq} + R_L}$$

2.2.3 Limitations of Thevenin's Theorem

The limitations of Thevenin's theorem are,

1. Not applicable to the circuits consisting of nonlinear elements.

2. Not applicable to unilateral networks.

3. There should not be magnetic coupling between the load and circuit to be replaced by Thevenin's theorem.

4. In the load side, there should not be controlled sources, controlled from some other part of the circuit.

Examples 2.2.1 *Replace the network of following figure to the left of terminals ab by its Thevenin equivalent circuit. Hence determine I.*

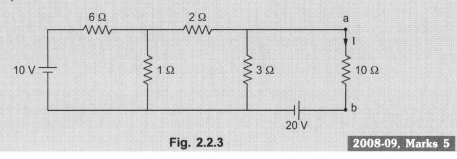

Fig. 2.2.3   2008-09, Marks 5

Solution :

Step 1 : Remove the 10 Ω branch.

$$R_L = 10 \, \Omega.$$

Step 2 : Calculate the open circuit voltage V_{TH}.

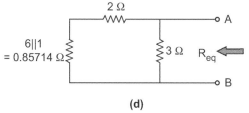

Fig. 2.2.3 (a)

Applying KVL to the two loops,

$$- 6I_1 - I_1 + I_2 + 10 = 0 \qquad \text{i.e.} \quad -7\,I_1 + I_2 = -10 \qquad ...(2.2.1)$$

$$- 2\,I_2 - 3\,I_2 - I_2 + I_1 = 0 \qquad \text{i.e.} \quad I_1 - 6\,I_2 = 0 \qquad ...(2.2.2)$$

Solving, $I_1 = 1.4634$ A, $\quad I_2 = 0.2439 \, \Omega$

Tracing the path ACDB as shown in the Fig. 2.2.3 (b),

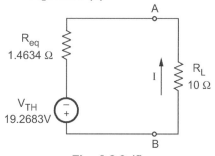

$$\therefore \qquad V_{TH} = V_{AB} = 20 - 0.7317$$

$$= \textbf{19.2683 V with A negative}$$

Fig. 2.2.3 (b)

Step 3 : Find R_{eq}, shorting the voltage sources.

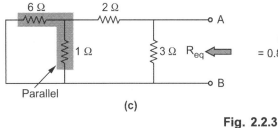

Fig. 2.2.3

$$\therefore \qquad R_{eq} = 3 \, \| \, 2.85714$$

$$= \textbf{1.4634 } \Omega$$

Step 4 : The Thevenin's equivalent is shown in the Fig. 2.2.3 (f).

Step 5 : The current through 10 Ω is,

$$I = \frac{V_{TH}}{R_{eq} + R_L} = \frac{19.2683}{1.4634 + 10}$$

$$= \textbf{1.6808 A} \uparrow$$

Fig. 2.2.3 (f)

Examples 2.2.2 *Determine current in 4 ohm resistance using Thevenin's theorem in the following circuit :*

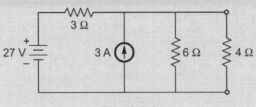

Fig. 2.2.4

2009-10, Marks 10

Solution : Step 1 : Remove the $4\,\Omega$ resistance.

Step 2 : Calculate the open circuit voltage V_{TH}.

From branch CD,

$$3 = I_2 - I_1 \qquad \dots (2.2.3)$$

Apply KVL to outer supermesh,

$$-3I_1 - 6I_2 + 27 = 0$$

i.e. $3I_1 + 6I_2 = 27$ ...(2.2.4)

Solving equation (2.2.3) and equation (2.2.4), $I_1 = 1\,A$, $I_2 = 4\,A$

$\therefore$ $V_{TH} = V_{AB} = 6\,I_2 = 6 \times 4 =$ **24 V with A positive**.

Step 3 : Calculate R_{eq}.

$\therefore$ $R_{eq} = 3 \parallel 6 = \dfrac{3 \times 6}{3 + 6}$

$$= 2\,\Omega$$

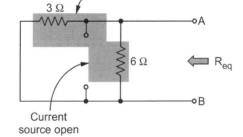

Fig. 2.2.4 (a)

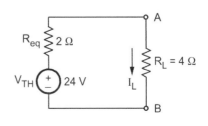

Step 4 : The Thevenin's equivalent is shown in the Fig. 2.2.4 (c).

Fig. 2.2.4 (b)

Step 5 : Hence current through $4\,\Omega$ is,

$$I_L = \dfrac{V_{TH}}{R_L + R_{eq}}$$

$$= \dfrac{24}{2 + 4} = \textbf{4 A} \downarrow$$

Fig. 2.2.4 (c)

Examples 2.2.3 *Calculate current in a 1000 Ω resistor connected between terminals A and B, as shown in the below Fig. 2.2.5 with the help of Thevenin's theorem.*

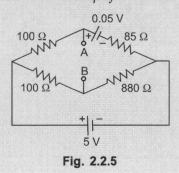

Fig. 2.2.5

2012-13, Marks 5

Solution : Step 1 : Branch AB is removed.

Step 2 : Find Thevenin's voltage $V_{TH} = V_{AB}$.

Applying KVL to FCADEF,

$-100I_1 - 0.05 - 85I_1 + 5 = 0$

∴ $I_1 = 0.02675$ A

Applying KVL to FCBDEF,

$-100I_2 - 880I_2 + 5 = 0$

∴ $I_2 = 0.005102$ A

Tracing path ACB and showing the drops as shown in the Fig. 2.2.5 (b) we get,

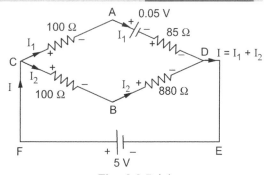

Fig. 2.2.5 (a)

(b)

Fig. 2.2.5 (b)

$$V_{AB} = 2.675 - 0.5102 = \textbf{2.1648 V with A negative} = V_{TH}$$

Step 3 : Find R_{eq}, shorting the voltage sources

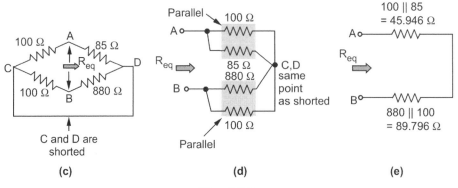

(c)   **(d)**   **(e)**

Fig. 2.2.5

∴ $R_{eq} = 45.946 + 89.796 = \textbf{135.7419 Ω}$

Step 4 : Thevenin's equivalent is shown in the Fig. 2.2.5 (f).

Step 5 : $I_L = \dfrac{V_{TH}}{R_L + R_{eq}}$

$= \dfrac{2.1648}{1000 + 135.7419} = \mathbf{1.906\ mA} \uparrow$

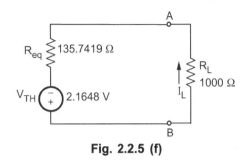

Fig. 2.2.5 (f)

Examples 2.2.4 *Find the Thevenin's equivalent, of the network shown below, between terminal 'a' and 'b'.*

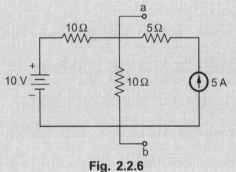

Fig. 2.2.6 `2004-05`

Solution : Step 1 : The branch a - b is already open

Step 2 : Calculte $V_{ab} = V_{TH}$

Apply KVL to the loop,

$- 10\ I_1 - 10\ I_1 - 10 \times 5 + 10 = 0$

$\therefore\quad I_1 = -2\ A$

So drop across centre 10 Ω is,

$V_{10\ \Omega} = 10\ I_1 + 5 \times 10$

$= -20 + 50 = 30\ V$

$\therefore\quad V_{ab} = V_{TH}$

$= $ Drop across centre $10\ \Omega$

$= \mathbf{30\ V}$

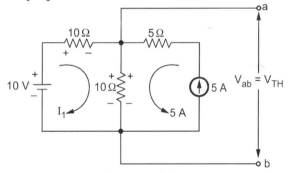

Fig. 2.2.6 (a)

Step 3 : To find R_{eq}

As 5 Ω is open, no current flows through it and the resistance is redundant

$\therefore\ R_{eq} = R_{ab} = 10 \parallel 10 = \mathbf{5\ \Omega}$

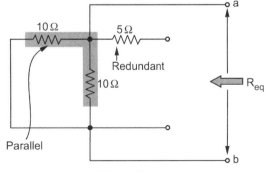

Fig. 2.2.6 (b)

Step 4 : Thevenin's equivalent
across a - b is shown in the
Fig. 2.2.6 (c).

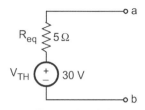

Fig. 2.2.6 (c)

Examples 2.2.5 *Find Thevenin's equivalent circuit across A-B shown in Fig. 2.2.7.*

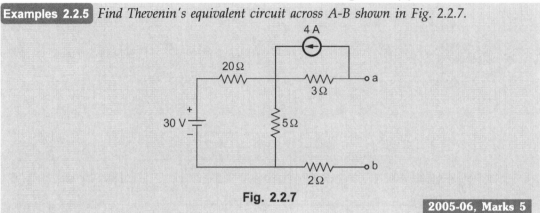

Fig. 2.2.7

2005-06, Marks 5

Solution : Step 1 : a - b is open

Step 2 : Calculate $V_{ab} = V_{TH}$

Converting 4 A current source to voltage
source we get the circuit as shown in the
Fig. 2.2.7 (a). As a - b terminals are open, no
current flows through $3\,\Omega$ and $2\,\Omega$
resistances hence voltage drop across them
is zero.

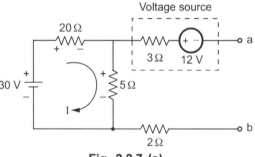

Fig. 2.2.7 (a)

$$\therefore \; - 20\,I - 5I + 30 = 0 \qquad \text{i.e.} \quad I = \frac{30}{25} = 1.2 \text{ A}$$

$$\therefore \text{Drop across } 5\,\Omega = 5I = 5 \times 1.2 = 6 \text{ V}$$

Tracing the path from a to b through $5\,\Omega$
as shown in the Fig. 2.2.7 (b),

$$\therefore \qquad V_{ab} = -12 + 6 = -6 \text{ V}$$

$$\therefore \qquad V_{TH} = \textbf{6 V with a negative w.r.t. b}$$

Fig. 2.2.7 (b)

Step 3 : To find R_{eq}

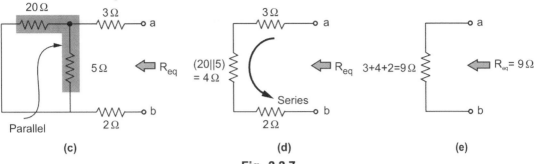

(c)   (d)   (e)

Fig. 2.2.7

Step 4 : Thevenin's equivalent is shown in the Fig. 2.2.7 (f)

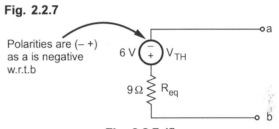

Polarities are (– +) as a is negative w.r.t.b

Fig. 2.2.7 (f)

Examples 2.2.6 *Determine the current flowing through 5 Ω resistor in the network shown using Thevenin's theorem.*

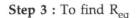

Fig. 2.2.8   **2002-03, Marks 5**

Solution : Step 1 : Remove 5 Ω resistance.

Step 2 : Find V_{TH}.

From branch A-B,

$$I_2 = 6 \text{ A}$$

Apply KVL to the loop,

$$-4 I_1 - 2 I_1 + 2 I_2 + 15 = 0$$

i.e. $$I_1 = 4.5 \text{ A}$$

Tracing path from C to D through 2 Ω,

∴ $$V_{CD} = V_{TH} = 3 \text{ V}$$

With D positive w.r.t. C

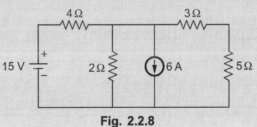

Fig. 2.2.8 (a)

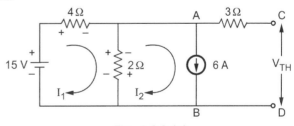

As no current through 3Ω

Fig. 2.2.8 (b)

Step 3 : Find R_{eq}, replace voltage source by short and current by open.

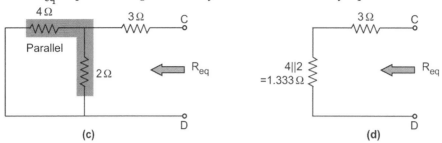

Fig. 2.2.8

$$\therefore \qquad R_{eq} = 3 + 1.333 = \mathbf{4.333} \ \Omega$$

Step 4 : Thevenin's equivalent is shown in the Fig. 2.2.8 (e).

$$\therefore \qquad I = \frac{3}{4.33 + 5}$$

$$= \mathbf{0.3214 \ A} \uparrow$$

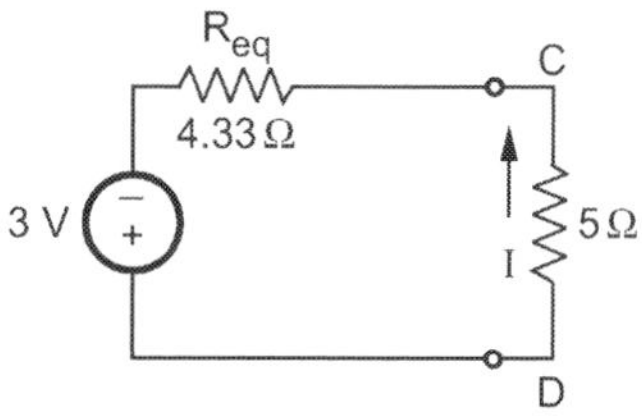

Fig. 2.2.8 (e)

Examples 2.2.7 *The resistances of the various arms of a Wheatstone bridge are shown in Fig. 2.2.9. The battery has an e.m.f. of 2 volts and negligible internal resistance. Using Thevenin's theorem, determine the value and direction of the current in the galvanometer circuit B-D.*

2001-02, Marks 10

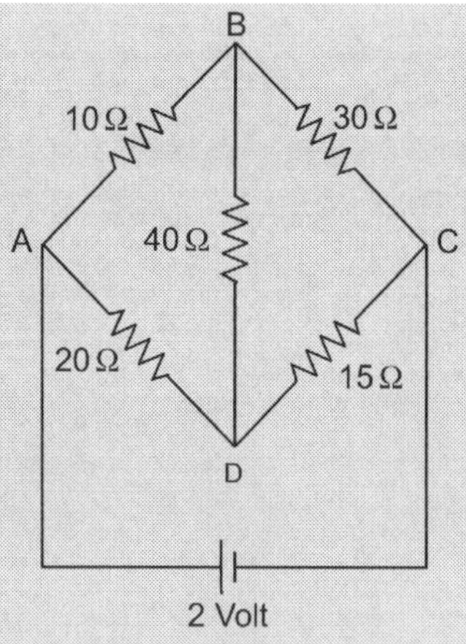

Fig. 2.2.9

Solution : Refer example 2.2.3 and verify the answer as **11.464 mA** ↓.

Examples 2.2.8 *Find the current I using Thevenin's theorem for the circuit shown in the Fig. 2.2.10.*

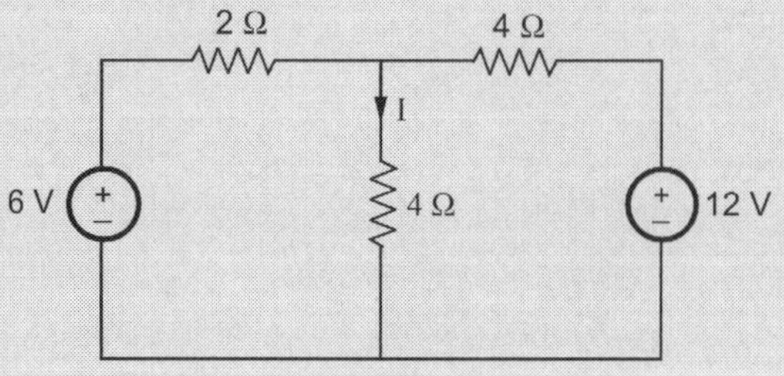

Fig. 2.2.10

2006-07, Marks 5

Solution : Step 1 : Remove the branch of 4 Ω.

Step 2 : Calculate $V_{TH} = V_{AB}$

Applying KVL,

$-4 I_x - 2 I_x - 6 + 12 = 0$

∴ $I_x = 1$ A

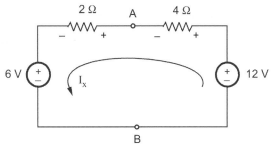

Fig. 2.2.10 (a)

Trace the path from A to B as shown in the Fig. 2.2.10 (b).

∴ $V_{AB} = 8$ V

∴ $V_{TH} = V_{AB} = \mathbf{8}$ **V**

Fig. 2.2.10 (b)

Step 3 : Calculate R_{eq}.

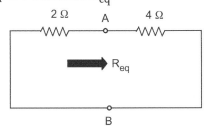 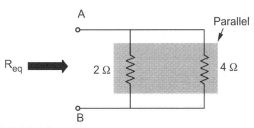

Fig. 2.2.10 (c)

∴ $R_{eq} = 2 \parallel 4 = \dfrac{2 \times 4}{2 + 4} = \mathbf{1.333}\ \Omega$

Step 4 : The Thevenin's equivalent is shown in the Fig. 2.2.10 (d).

Step 5 : Hence the current I is,

$$I = \frac{V_{TH}}{R_{eq} + R_L} = \frac{8}{1.333 + 4} = \mathbf{1.5\ A} \downarrow$$

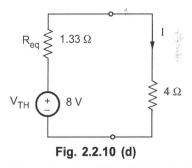

Fig. 2.2.10 (d)

Examples 2.2.9 *Find V_{TH} and R_{TH} for a circuit shown in Fig. 2.2.11 by Thevenin's theorem.*

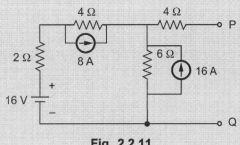

Fig. 2.2.11

2006-07, Marks 5

Solution : Step 1 : The branch PQ is open.

Step 2 : Calculate $V_{TH} = V_{PQ}$

Convert the current sources to the voltage sources.

Applying KVL to the loop.

$+ 4 \, I + 32 + 6 \, I - 96 + 16 + 2 \, I = 0$

$12 \, I = 48$

$I = 4 \, A$

Trace the path from P to Q as shown in the Fig. 2.2.11 (b).

$\therefore \qquad V_{PQ} = 96 - 24 = 72 \, \textbf{V} = \textbf{V}_{TH}$

Step 3 : Find R_{TH}, opening the current sources and shorting the voltage source.

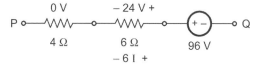

Fig. 2.2.11 (a)

Fig. 2.2.11 (b)

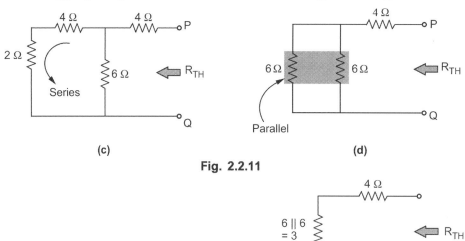

Fig. 2.2.11

$\therefore \qquad R_{TH} = 4 + 3 = 7 \, \Omega$

Fig. 2.2.11 (e)

1. *State Thevenin's theorem.*

   2010-11, Marks 5

2. *Find the current I_2, in Fig. 2.2.12, by application of Thevenin's theorem.*

[Ans. : 32.345 mA]

Fig. 2.2.12

3. For the network shown in the Fig. 2.2.13, find the current I_2 in the 3 ohm resistance, by applying Thevenin's theorem.

[Ans. : 0.0996 A ↓]

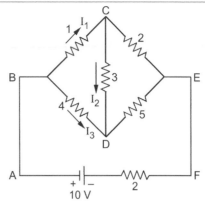

Fig. 2.2.13

4. Use Thevenin's theorem to find current in $1\,\Omega$ resistance for the circuit shown in Fig. 2.2.14.

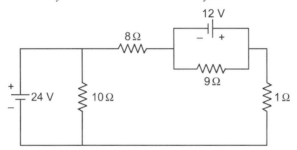

Fig. 2.2.14

[Ans. : 4 A ↓]

5. Apply Thevenin's theorem to calculate the current in $6\,\Omega$ resistance for the circuit shown in the Fig. 2.2.15. Also use superposition theorem to calculate the current in $10\,\Omega$ resistance.

[Ans. : 2.7027 A ↓, 2.7027 A →]

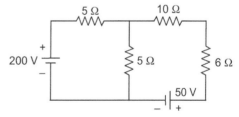

Fig. 2.2.15

6. Calculate current through $10\,\Omega$ resistance by
    i) Superposition theorem
    ii) Thevenin's theorem

[Ans. : 1.6208 A from A to B]

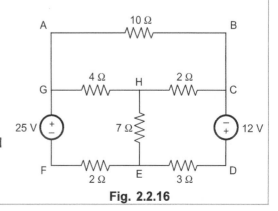

Fig. 2.2.16

7. *Estimate the power loss in the 8 Ω resistor using Thevenin's theorem.*

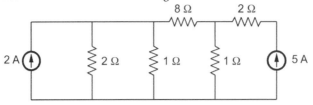

Fig. 2.2.17   **[Ans. : 1.151 W]**

8. *Find the current through 10 Ω resistor, using Thevenin's theorem.*

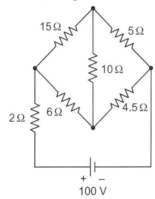

Fig. 2.2.18   **[Ans. : 0.8452 A ↑]**

9. *The network has following configuration, Arm AB = 10 Ω, Arm CD = 20 Ω, Arm BC = 30 Ω, Arm DA = 20 Ω, Arm DE = 5 Ω, Arm EC = 10 Ω and a galvanometer of 40 Ω is connected between B and E. Find by Thevenin's theorem, the current in the galvanometer if 2 V source is connected between A and C.*   **[Ans. : 20.56 mA]**

10. *In the circuit shown in the Fig. 2.2.19, calculate current through 1 Ω resistance connected between A-B, using Thevenin's theorem.*

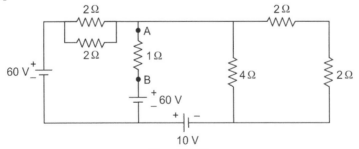

Fig. 2.2.19   **[Ans. : 14 A ↑]**

11. *Apply Thevenin's theorem to calculate current flowing in branch AB for the circuit shown in Fig. 2.2.20.*

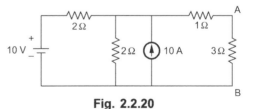

[Ans. : 3 A ↓]   **Fig. 2.2.20**

2.3 Norton's Theorem

2002-03, 2003-04, 2004-05, 2007-08, 2009-10, 2010-11, 2011-12

The Norton's theorem can be stated as below,

Statement : *Any combination of linear bilateral circuit elements and active sources, regardless of the connection or complexity, connected to a given load R_L, can be replaced by a simple two terminal network, consisting of a single current source of I_N amperes and a single impedance R_{eq} in parallel with it, across the two terminals of the load R_L. The I_N is the short circuit current flowing through the short circuited path, replaced instead of R_L. It is also called* **Norton's current**. *The R_{eq} is the equivalent impedance of the given network as viewed through the load terminals, with R_L removed and all the active sources are replaced by their internal impedances. If the internal impedances are unknown then the independent voltage sources must be replaced by short circuit while the independent current sources must be replaced by open circuit, while calculating R_{eq}.*

Key Point *Infact the calculation of R_{eq} and its value remains same, whether the theorem applied to the network is Thevenin or Norton, as long as terminals of interest remain same.*

2.3.1 Explanation of Norton's Theorem

Consider the network shown in the Fig. 2.3.1 (a). The terminals A-B are the load terminals where R_L is connected. According to the Norton's theorem, the network can be replaced by a current source I_N with equivalent resistance R_{eq} parallel with it, across the load terminals, as shown in the Fig. 2.3.1 (b).

Norton's equivalent
(b)

(a)

Fig. 2.3.1

For obtaining the current I_N, short the load terminals AB as shown in the Fig. 2.3.2 (a). Then find current I_N by using any of the network simplification techniques discussed earlier. This is Norton's current. While to calculate R_{eq} use

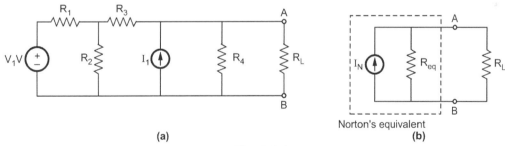

Fig. 2.3.2 (a)

same procedure as discussed earlier for Thevenin's theorem. For the convenience of reader circuit for calculation of R_{eq} is shown in the Fig. 2.3.2 (b).

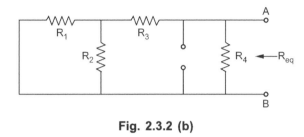

Fig. 2.3.2 (b)

This theorem is called **dual of the Thevenin's theorem**. This is because, if the Thevenin's equivalent voltage source is converted to equivalent current source using source transformation, we get the Norton's equivalent. This is shown in the Fig. 2.3.2 (c).

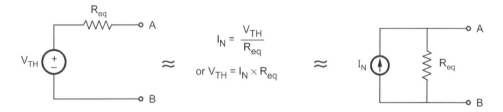

Fig. 2.3.2 (c)

2.3.2 Steps to Apply Norton's Theorem

Step 1 : Short the branch through which the current is to be calculated.

Step 2 : Obtain the current through this short circuited branch, using any of the network simplification techniques. This current is Norton's current I_N.

Step 3 : Calculate the equivalent resistance R_{eq}, as viewed through the terminals of interest, by removing the branch resistance and making all the independent sources inactive.

Step 4 : Draw the Norton's equivalent across the terminals of interest, showing a current source I_N with the resistance R_{eq} parallel with it.

Step 5 : Reconnect the branch resistance. Let it be R_L. Then using current division in parallel circuit of two resistances, current through the branch of interest can be obtained as,

$$I = I_N \times \frac{R_{eq}}{R_{eq} + R_L}$$

Example 2.3.1 *Replace the given network by Norton's equivalent across the terminals A-B.*

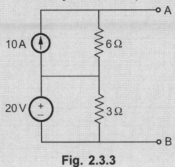

Fig. 2.3.3

Solution : **Step 1 :** Short the branch A-B.

Step 2 : Calculate the short circuit current using Kirchhoff's laws. As there is current source, **apply KVL to these loops only, which do not include current source**. The current source value is considered, for current distribution using KCL.

Loop C-A-B-E-C,

$+ 3I_1 + 6(10 - I_N) = 0$

∴ $3I_1 - 6 I_N = - 60$ ... (2.3.1)

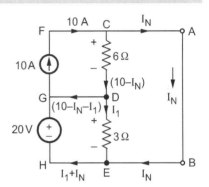

Fig. 2.3.3 (a)

Loop G-D-E-H-G,

$- 3I_1 + 20 = 0$

∴ $I_1 = \dfrac{20}{3} = 6.667 \text{ A}$ ... (2.3.2)

∴ $I_N = \mathbf{13.333 \text{ A}} \downarrow$

Fig. 2.3.3 (b)

Step 3 : To calculate R_{eq}, replace voltage source by short circuit and current source by open circuit.

Key Point *There is direct short circuit across 3 Ω resistance hence it becomes redundant from the circuit point of view.*

∴ $R_{eq} = \mathbf{6 \ \Omega}$

Step 4 : Norton's equivalent across
A-B is shown in the Fig. 2.3.3 (c).

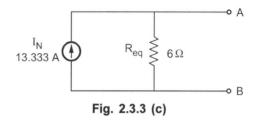

Fig. 2.3.3 (c)

Examples 2.3.2 *Determine current in 10 ohm resistance using Norton's theorem in the following network :*

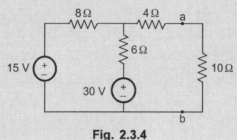

Fig. 2.3.4   2004-05, Marks 6

Solution : Step 1 : Short the branch a-b.

Step 2 : Calculate Norton's current I_N.

$$I_N = I_2$$

Apply KVL to the two loops,

$$-8 I_1 - 6 I_1 + 6 I_2 - 30 + 15 = 0$$

$$\therefore -14 I_1 + 6 I_2 = 15 \qquad \qquad ... (2.3.3)$$

$$-4 I_2 + 30 - 6 I_2 + 6 I_1 = 0$$

$$\therefore 6 I_1 - 10 I_2 = -30 \qquad \qquad ... (2.3.4)$$

Solving, $I_1 = 0.288$ A, $I_2 = 3.173$ A

$$\therefore \qquad I_N = I_2 = \textbf{3.173 A}$$

Fig. 2.3.4 (a)

Step 3 : To find R_{eq}

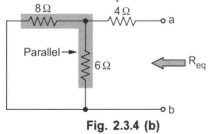

Fig. 2.3.4 (b)   **Fig. 2.3.4 (c)**

$$\therefore \qquad R_{eq} = 4 + 3.4285 = \textbf{7.4285}\ \Omega$$

Step 4 : Norton's equivalent is shown in the Fig. 2.3.4 (d).

$$I_L = I_N \times \frac{R_{eq}}{R_L + R_{eq}}$$

$$= 3.173 \times \frac{7.4285}{17.4285}$$

$$= \textbf{1.3524 A} \downarrow$$

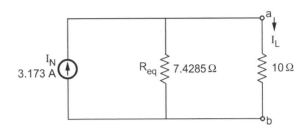

Fig. 2.3.4 (d)

Examples 2.3.3 *For the circuit of Fig. 2.3.5 below, obtain Norton current and equivalent resistance seen from 'a-b'.*

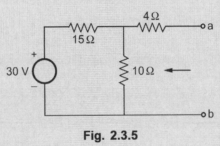

Fig. 2.3.5

2002-03

Solution : Step 1 : Short the terminals a - b

   Step 2 : Calculate I_N

   Applying KVL to the two loops,

$- 15\, I_1 - 10\, I_1 + 10\, I_2 + 30 = 0$

$\therefore \qquad\qquad - 25\, I_1 + 10\, I_2 = -30 \qquad ...(2.3.5)$

$\quad - 4\, I_2 - 10\, I_2 + 10\, I_1 = 0$

$\therefore \qquad\qquad 10\, I_1 - 14\, I_2 = 0 \qquad ...(2.3.6)$

Solving, $I_1 = 1.68$ A, $I_2 = 1.2$ A

But $I_N = I_2 = \textbf{1.2 A}$ ... Norton's current

Step 3 : Calculate R_{eq}

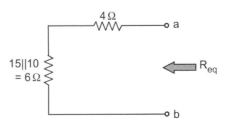

Fig. 2.3.5 (a)

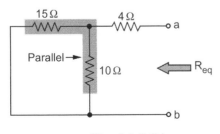

Fig. 2.3.5 (b)

Fig. 2.3.5 (c)

$$\therefore \qquad R_{eq} = 6 + 4 = 10\ \Omega$$

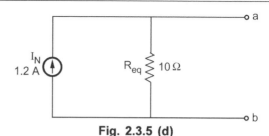

Fig. 2.3.5 (d)

Step 4 : Norton's equivalent is shown in the Fig. 2.3.5 (d).

Examples 2.3.4 *Draw the Norton's equivalent circuit across A-B, and determine current flowing through 12 Ω resistor for the network shown in Fig. 2.3.6.*

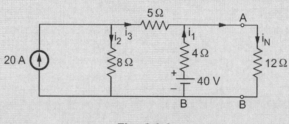

Fig. 2.3.6

2003-04, Marks 10

Solution : The current distribution is shown in the Fig. 2.3.6 (a).

Applying KCL at node C,

$$20 - i_2 - i_3 = 0$$

$$\therefore \qquad i_2 + i_3 = 20 \qquad \qquad ...(2.3.7)$$

At node E,

$$i_3 + i_1 - i_N = 0$$

$$\therefore \qquad i_N = i_1 + i_3 \qquad \qquad ...(2.3.8)$$

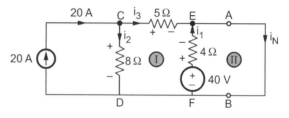

Fig. 2.3.6 (a)

Applying KVL to Loop I and II,

$$-5\ i_3 + 4\ i_1 - 40 + 8\ i_2 = 0 \quad \text{i.e. } 4\ i_1 + 8\ i_2 - 5\ i_3 = 40 \qquad ...(2.3.9)$$

$$+ 40 - 4\ i_1 = 0 \quad \text{i.e. } i_1 = 10\ A \qquad ...(2.3.10)$$

Using (2.3.7) and (2.3.8) in (2.3.9),

$$4 \times 10 + 8\ i_2 - 5\ (20 - i_2) = 40$$

$$\therefore \qquad i_2 = 7.6923\ A, \qquad i_3 = 12.3076\ A$$

$$\therefore \qquad i_N = 10 + 12.3076 = \mathbf{22.3076\ A} \qquad \qquad ... \text{From (2.3.8)}$$

To Find R_{eq} :

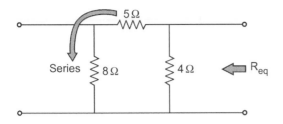

Fig. 2.3.6 (b)

Fig. 2.3.6 (c)

$\therefore$ $\quad R_{eq}$ = 13 || 4 = 3.0588 Ω

Norton's equivalent with R_L = 12 Ω
is shown in the Fig. 2.3.6 (d).

$\therefore$ $\quad I_L = i_N \times \dfrac{3.0588}{3.0588+12}$

$\quad$ = **4.532 A** $\downarrow$

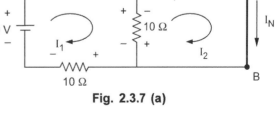

Fig. 2.3.6 (d)

Examples 2.3.5 *Determine the value of current through the 5 Ω resistance using Norton's theorem in the circuit shown in Fig. 2.3.7. State whether Superposition theorem can be applied for the circuit with reasons.*

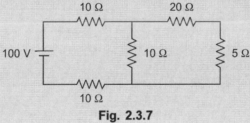

Fig. 2.3.7

2007-08, Marks 5

Solution : Step 1 : Short the 5 Ω branch

Step 2 : Calculate short circuit current I_N.

Applying KVL to the two loops,

$- 10\ I_1 - 10\ I_1 + 10\ I_2 - 10\ I_1 + 100 = 0$

i.e. $30\ I_1 - 10\ I_2$ = 100 $\quad$ ...(2.3.11)

$- 20\ I_2 - 10\ I_2 + 10\ I_1 = 0$

i.e. $10\ I_1 - 30\ I_2$ = 0 $\quad$ ...(2.3.12)

Fig. 2.3.7 (a)

Solving, I_1 = 3.75 A, I_2 = 1.25 A

∴ I_N = I_2 = **1.25 A**

Step 3 : Calculate R_{eq}, shorting voltage source

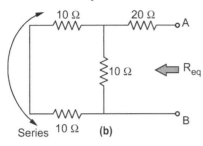 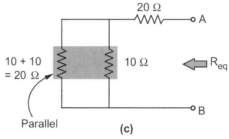

Fig. 2.3.7

∴ R_{eq} = 20 + 6.667

              = **26.6667 Ω**

Step 4 : The Norton's equivalent is shown in the Fig. 2.3.7 (e)

Step 5 : $I_L = I_N \times \dfrac{R_{eq}}{R_{eq} + R_L}$

∴ I_L = 1.25 × $\dfrac{26.667}{26.667 + 5}$ = **1.0526 A** ↓

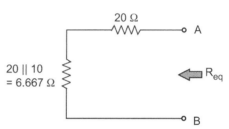

Fig. 2.3.7 (d)

As there is only one voltage source, Superposition theorem cannot be applied. It is applicable only for the circuits consisting more than one source.

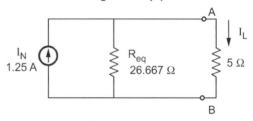

Fig. 2.3.7 (e)

Example 2.3.6 *Using Norton's theorem, find the current which would flow in a 25 Ω resistance connected between points 'A' and 'B'.*

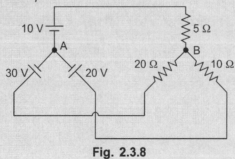

Fig. 2.3.8

Solution :

Step 1 : Short AB branch.

Step 2 : Find short circuit current $I_{SC} = I_N$.

Redrawing the given circuit as shown in the Fig. 2.3.8 (a).

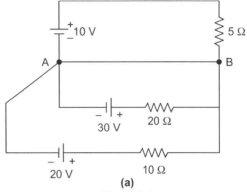

(a)

Fig. 2.3.8

Convert each voltage source to current source as shown in the Fig. 2.3.8 (b).

Due to short circuit, all resistances 5 Ω, 20 Ω and 10 Ω become redundant.

$\therefore \qquad I_N = 2 + 1.5 + 2 = \textbf{5.5 A}$

This flows from B to A.

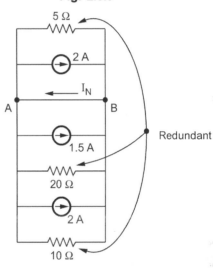

(b)

Fig. 2.3.8

Step 3 : Shorting the voltage sources, find R_{eq}.

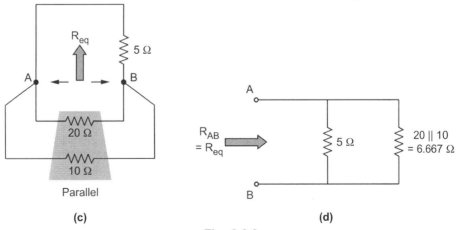

(c)   (d)

Fig. 2.3.8

$\therefore \qquad R_{eq} = 5 \parallel 6.667 = \textbf{2.8571 } \Omega$

Step 4 : The Norton's equivalent is shown in the Fig. 2.3.8 (e).

Step 5 :

$$I_L = \frac{I_N \times R_{eq}}{R_L + R_{eq}}$$

$$= \frac{5.5 \times 2.8571}{25 + 2.8571}$$

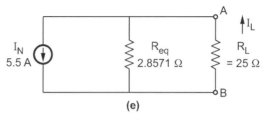

(e)

Fig. 2.3.8

$$= \textbf{0.5641 A from B to A}$$

Review Questions

1. *State Norton's theorem.* **2009-10, 2010-11, Marks 5**

2. *Explain the duality between Thevenin's and Norton's equivalent circuits.* **2011-12, Marks 5**

3. *Using Thevenin's theorem determine the current flowing through $2\,\Omega$ resistance in the network shown in Fig. 2.3.9. Verify the answer using Norton's theorem.*

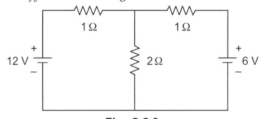

Fig. 2.3.9   [Ans. : 3.6 A ↓]

4. *Replace the given network by Norton's equivalent across the terminals A-B.*

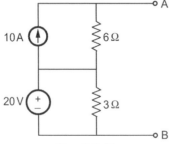

Fig. 2.3.10   [Ans. : $I_N = 13.33$ A, $R_{eq} = 6\,\Omega$]

5. *Find the current in $4\,\Omega$ resistance by Norton's theorem.*

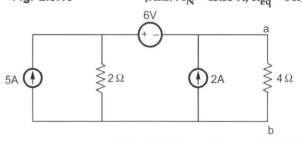

Fig. 2.3.11   [Ans. : 1.333 A ↓]

6. Find current through 8 Ω resistance by Norton's theorem.

[Ans. : 1.7954 A from A to B]

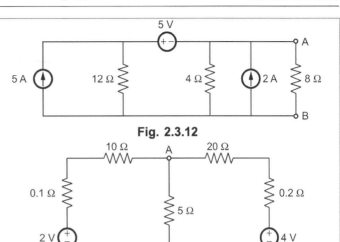

Fig. 2.3.12

7. Find the current through branch A-B by using
i) Thevenin's theorem
ii) Norton's theorem.

[Ans. : 0.2273 A from A to B]

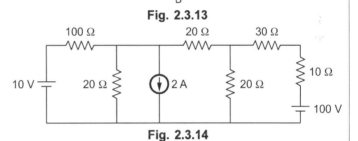

Fig. 2.3.13

8. Using Norton's theorem, find the current flowing through 100 Ω.

[Ans. : 0.2 A ↓]

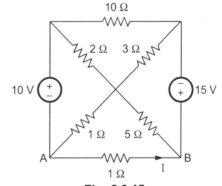

Fig. 2.3.14

9. Using Norton's theorem find I.

[Ans. : 5.0218 A]

Fig. 2.3.15

10. Find the Norton's equivalent circuit for the active linear network shown :

[Ans. : I_N = 2 A, R_{eq} = 16 Ω]

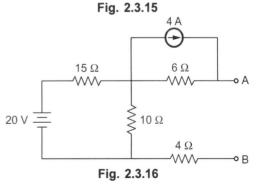

Fig. 2.3.16

2.4 Maximum Power Transfer Theorem

2000-01, 2002-03, 2003-04, 2006-07, 2007-08

Let us see the statement of the theorem.

Statement : *In an active resistive network, maximum power transfer to the load resistance takes place when the load resistance equals the equivalent resistance of the network as viewed from the terminals of the load.*

2.4.1 Proof of Maximum Power Transfer Theorem

Consider a d.c. source of voltage V volts and having internal resistance of r ohms connected to a variable load resistance R_L as shown in the Fig. 2.4.1 (a). The load current is I_L and is given by,

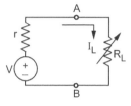

Fig. 2.4.1 (a)

$$I_L = \frac{V}{r + R_L}$$

The power consumed by the load resistance R_L, is

$$P = I_L^2 \; R_L = \left[\frac{V}{(r + R_L)} \right]^2 R_L$$

If R_L is changed, I_L is also going to change and at a particular value of R_L, power transferred to the load is maximum. Let us calculate value of R_L for which power transfer to load is maximum. To satisfy maximum power transfer we can write,

$$\frac{dP}{dR_L} = 0$$

$$\frac{dP}{dR_L} \left[\frac{V}{(r + R_L)} \right]^2 R_L = 0$$

$$\therefore \quad V^2 \frac{d}{dR_L} \left[\frac{R_L}{(r + R_L)^2} \right] = 0 \qquad \text{... As voltage is constant}$$

$$\therefore \quad (r + R_L)^2 \frac{d\,(R_L)}{dR_L} - R_L \frac{d}{dR_L} (r + R_L)^2 = 0$$

$$\therefore \quad (r + R_L)^2 \, (1) - R_L \, 2 \, (r + R_L) = 0$$

$$\therefore \quad (r + R_L - 2 \, R_L) = 0$$

$$\boxed{R_L = r}$$

Thus when load resistance is equal to the internal resistance of source the maximum power transfer takes place.

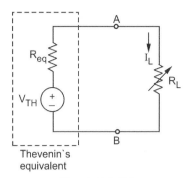

Now any complex network can be represented with a single voltage source of V_{TH} volts with equivalent resistance R_{eq} in series with it, using Thevenin's theorem across the load terminals. Thus the variable load resistance R_L, in such case must be equal to R_{eq} to have maximum power transfer to the load.

Thevenin's equivalent

Fig. 2.4.1 (b)

$\therefore$
$$\boxed{R_L = R_{eq}}$$
... For maximum power transfer

Let us calculate the magnitude of maximum power transfer. It can be obtained by substituting $R_L = R_{eq}$ in the expression of power.

$\therefore$
$$P_{max} = \left(\frac{V_{TH}}{R_{eq} + R_L}\right)^2 R_L \qquad \text{with } R_L = R_{eq}$$

$\therefore$
$$P_{max} = \frac{V_{TH}^2}{(2\,R_{eq})^2} \times R_{eq} = \frac{V_{TH}^2}{4\,R_{eq}} \quad \text{watts}$$

2.4.2 Steps to Apply Maximum Power Transfer Theorem

Step 1 : Calculate Thevenin's voltage V_{TH} or Norton's current I_N.

Step 2 : Calculate R_{eq} as viewed through the load terminals.

Step 3 : Draw Thevenin's equivalent or Norton's equivalent.

Step 4 : $R_L = R_{eq}$ gives the condition for maximum power transfer to load.

Step 5 : And maximum power is given by,

$$P_{max} = \frac{V_{TH}^2}{4\,R_{eq}}$$

Key Point *If in the problem only the value R_L for maximum power transfer is asked then only R_{eq} is to be calculated. In such case there is no need to calculate V_{TH} or I_N. These values are required only if magnitude of P_{max} is required.*

Examples 2.4.1 *Find the value of R_{AD} for maximum power transfer, in the circuit shown in the Fig. 2.4.2.*

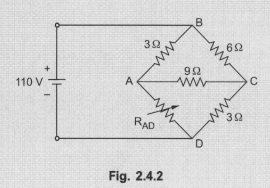

Fig. 2.4.2

Solution : As magnitude of P_{max} is not required, only R_{eq}, as seen through terminals AD is to be obtained with voltage source shorted.

As points B and D are directly connected, the circuit can be redrawn as shown in the Fig. 2.4.2 (b), showing B and D as a single point.

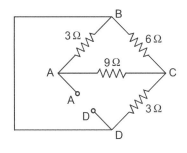

Fig. 2.4.2 (a)

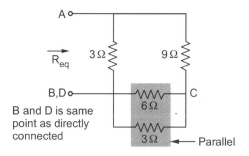

B and D is same
point as directly
connected

Fig. 2.4.2 (b)

$\therefore \qquad R_{eq} = (3) \parallel [9 + (6 \parallel 3)]$

$\qquad\qquad = (3) \parallel [9 + 2]$

$\qquad\qquad = (3) \parallel (11)$

$\qquad\qquad = \mathbf{2.3571 \ \Omega}$

For P_{max}, $R_{AD} = R_{eq} = \mathbf{2.3571 \ \Omega}$

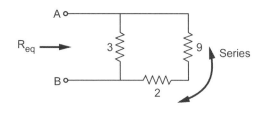

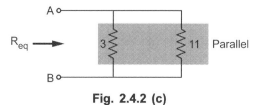

Fig. 2.4.2 (c)

Examples 2.4.2 *Find the magnitude of R_L for the maximum power transfer in the circuit shown in the Fig. 2.4.3. Also find out the maximum power.*

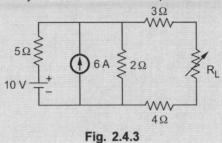

Fig. 2.4.3

Solution : **Step 1 :** Remove the load R_L.

Step 2 : Obtain V_{TH} or I_N by Kirchhoff's laws. Let us find I_N by shorting the load terminals.

Now $\qquad I_N = I_2$

Apply KVL to those loops which **do not consist current source**.

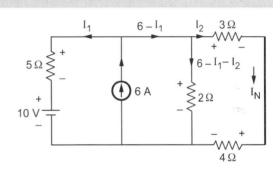

Fig. 2.4.3 (a)

$\therefore \ -2 (6 - I_1 - I_2) + 10 + 5 I_1 = 0$

$\therefore \qquad 7 I_1 + 2 I_2 = 2 \qquad\qquad \dots (2.4.1)$

$-3 I_2 - 4 I_2 + 2 (6 - I_1 - I_2) = 0$

$\therefore \ + 2 I_1 + 9 I_2 = + 12 \qquad\qquad \dots (2.4.2)$

Solving, $\quad I_N = I_2 = \dfrac{D_2}{D} = \dfrac{80}{59} = 1.3559$ A

Step 3 : Find R_{eq}, across load, opening current source and shorting voltage source.

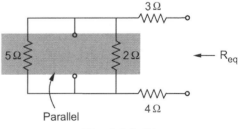

Fig. 2.4.3 (b)

$\therefore \qquad R_{eq} = 3 + (5 \parallel 2) + 4$

$\qquad\qquad = 3 + 1.4235 + 4$

$\qquad\qquad = 8.4235 \ \Omega$

Step 4 : For P_{max}, $R_L = R_{eq} = $ **8.4235 Ω**

And $\qquad V_{TH} = I_N \times R_{eq} = 1.3559 \times 8.4235 = 11.4216$ V

$\therefore \qquad P_{max} = \dfrac{V_{TH}^2}{4 R_{eq}} = \dfrac{(11.4216)^2}{4 \times 8.4235} = $ **3.8716 W**

Examples 2.4.3 *In the network shown in Fig. 2.4.4, find : i) The Norton equivalent circuit at terminal A - B. ii) The maximum power that can be provided to a resistance R connected to terminals A - B.*

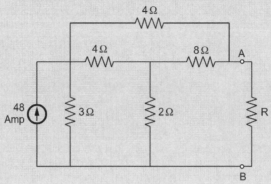

Fig. 2.4.4   2000-01, Marks 5

Solution : Step 1 : Short the terminals A - B

Step 2 : Calculate the short circuit current i.e. I_N.

Convert 4 Ω, 4 Ω, 8 Ω delta into star,

$$R_1 = \frac{4 \times 4}{4 + 4 + 8} = 1 \ \Omega$$

$$R_2 = R_3 = \frac{8 \times 4}{4 + 4 + 8} = 2 \ \Omega$$

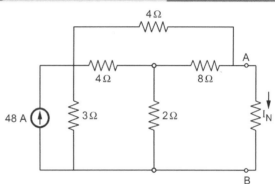

Fig. 2.4.4 (a)

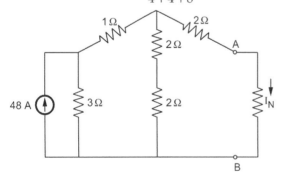

Fig. 2.4.4 (b)

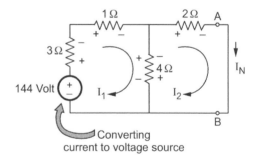

Converting current to voltage source

Fig. 2.4.4 (c)

Applying KVL to the two loops,

$- I_1 - 4 \ I_1 + 4 \ I_2 + 144 - 3 \ I_1 = 0$ i.e. $8 \ I_1 - 4 \ I_2 = 144$ ...(2.4.3)

$- 2 \ I_2 - 4 \ I_2 + 4 \ I_1 = 0$ i.e. $4 \ I_1 - 6 \ I_2 = 0$ ...(2.4.4)

Solving, $I_N = I_2 = \mathbf{18 \ A}$

Step 3 : To find R_{eq}, open the current source and use the circuit obtained after converting delta to star.

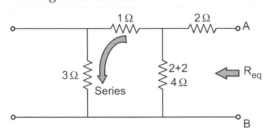

Fig. 2.4.4 (d)   **Fig. 2.4.4 (e)**

$$\therefore \quad R_{eq} = 2 + (4 \parallel 4) = 2 + \frac{4 \times 4}{4 + 4} = 2 + 2 = 4\,\Omega$$

Step 4 : The Norton's equivalent is as shown.

For maximum power transfer,

$$R = R_{eq} = 4\,\Omega$$

$$V_{TH} = I_N \times R_{eq} = 18 \times 4 = 72 \text{ V}$$

$$\therefore \quad P_{max} = \frac{V_{TH}^2}{4\,R_{eq}} = \frac{(72)^2}{4 \times 4} = 324 \text{ W}$$

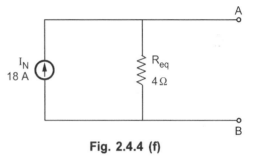

Fig. 2.4.4 (f)

Examples 2.4.4 *In the network shown in Fig. 2.4.5, determine : i) The value of load resistance R_L to given maximum power transfer and ii) The power delivered to the load.*

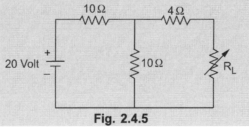

Fig. 2.4.5   **2002-03, Marks 5**

Solution : For P_{max}, $R_L = R_{eq}$

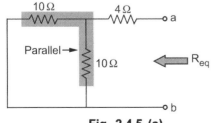

Fig. 2.4.5 (a)   **Fig. 2.4.5 (b)**

$$\therefore \quad R_L = R_{eq} = 9\,\Omega \quad \text{for } P_{max}$$

To find P_{max}, find Thevenin's voltage V_{TH}.

$$I = \frac{20}{10+10} = 1A$$

$\therefore$ $V_{TH} = V_{10\,\Omega} = I \times 10 = \mathbf{10\ V}$

$\therefore$ $P_{max} = \dfrac{V_{TH}^2}{4\,R_L} = \dfrac{(10)^2}{4\times 9} = \mathbf{2.778\ W}$

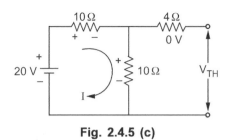

Fig. 2.4.5 (c)

Examples 2.4.5 *Find the value of resistance 'R' to have maximum power transfer in the circuit as shown in Fig. 2.4.6. Also obtain the amount of maximum power.*

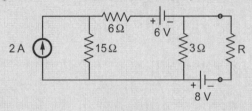

Fig. 2.4.6

2003-04, Marks 5

Solution : R for P_{max} means R_{eq},

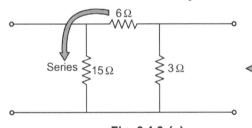

Fig. 2.4.6 (a)

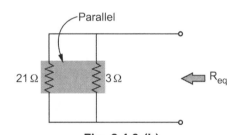

Fig. 2.4.6 (b)

$\therefore$ $R_{eq} = 21 \parallel 3 = \mathbf{2.625\ \Omega} = R$ ...for P_{max}

To find P_{max}, find V_{TH}

From branch C-D,

    $i_1 = 2\ A$

Then apply KVL to the remaining loop,

$-6\,i_2 - 6 - 3\,i_2 - 15\,i_2 + 15\,i_1 = 0$

$\therefore$ $i_2 = 1\ A$

So drop across $3\ \Omega$ is $3\,i_2 = 3\ V$. Trace the path A to B through $3\ \Omega$ as shown in the Fig. 2.4.6 (d).

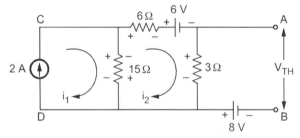

Fig. 2.4.6 (c)

Fig. 2.4.6 (d)

$$\therefore \qquad V_{AB} = 8 + 3 = \textbf{11 V} = V_{TH}$$

$$\therefore \qquad P_{max} = \frac{V_{TH}^2}{4\,R_{eq}} = \frac{(11)^2}{4 \times 2.625} = \textbf{11.5238 W}$$

Examples 2.4.6 *Using maximum power transfer theorem, find the value of the load resistance R_L for the maximum power flow through it in the network shown in the Fig. 2.4.7.*

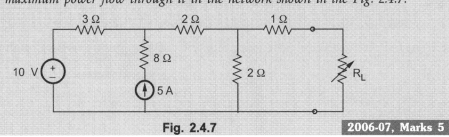

Fig. 2.4.7   2006-07, Marks 5

Solution : According to maximum power transfer theorem,

$$R_L = R_{eq} \qquad\qquad\qquad\qquad \text{...For } P_{max}$$

To find R_{eq}, remove R_L and replace voltage sources by short circuits while current sources by open circuits.

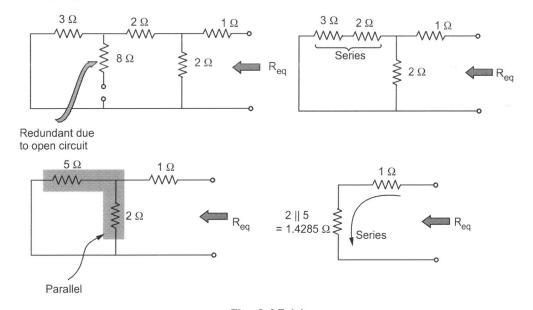

Fig. 2.4.7 (a)

$$\therefore \qquad R_{eq} = 1 + 1.4285 = 2.4285 \ \Omega$$

$$\therefore \qquad R_L = \textbf{2.4285} \ \Omega \qquad\qquad\qquad \text{... For maximum power transfer}$$

Examples 2.4.7 *In the network shown in Fig. 2.4.8 find i) The value of R_L for maximum power dissipation. ii) The value of the maximum power.*

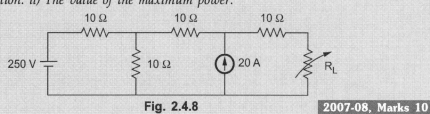

Fig. 2.4.8   2007-08, Marks 10

Solution : i) For getting R_L for P_{max}, replace voltage source by short circuit and current source by open circuit,

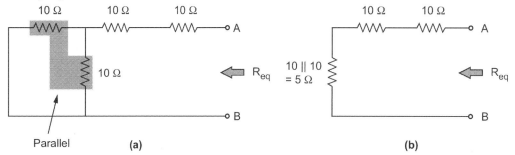

Parallel   (a)   (b)

Fig. 2.4.8

∴ $R_L = R_{eq} = 10 + 10 + 5 = \mathbf{25} \ \Omega$ ...For P_{max}

ii) To find P_{max}, calculate V_{TH}.

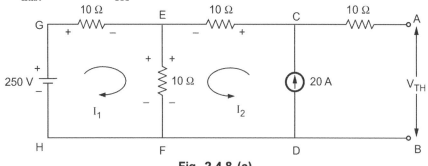

Fig. 2.4.8 (c)

From branch CD, $I_2 = 20$ A

Apply KVL to the first loop, $-10 I_1 - 10 I_1 - 10 I_2 + 250 = 0$

∴ $-20 I_1 - 10 \times 20 + 250 = 0$ i.e. $I_1 = 2.5$ A

Trace the path ACEGHFDB as shown in the Fig. 2.4.8 (d), for calculating $V_{AB} = V_{TH}$.

A $I = 0$ A   C I_2 E I_1 G   H   B
          10 Ω   10 Ω   10 Ω
          0 V   + 200 V −   − 25 V +   + 250 V −   0 V

Fig. 2.4.8 (d)

$\therefore$ $\quad\quad V_{AB} = + 200 + 250 - 25 = V_{TH} = 425 \text{ V}$ $\quad\quad\quad\quad$ ... A is + Ve

$\therefore$ $\quad\quad P_{max} = \dfrac{V_{TH}^2}{4\,R_L} = \dfrac{(425)^2}{4\times 25} = \mathbf{1806.25 \text{ W}}$

Review Questions

1. *State and prove maximum power transfer theorem.*

2. *Find the magnitude of R_L for the maximum power transfer in the circuit shown in the Fig. 2.4.9. Also find out the maximum power.*

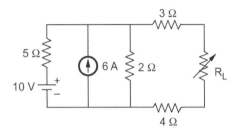

Fig. 2.4.9

[Ans. : 8.4235 Ω, 3.8716 W]

3. *Find the value R for maximum power to R and what is the value of maximum power ?*

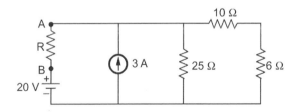

Fig. 2.4.10

[Ans. : 9.756 Ω, 2.202 W]

4. *Obtain the Thevenin's and Norton's equivalent of the network shown w.r.t terminals A and B. Also determine the value of load resistance to be connected between A-B to absorb maximum power. What is maximum power ?*

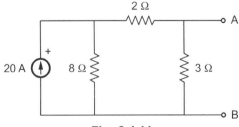

Fig. 2.4.11

[Ans. : 2.3077 Ω, 147.6928 W]

5. *Find R_{AB} for maximum power transfer. Also calculate maximum power.*

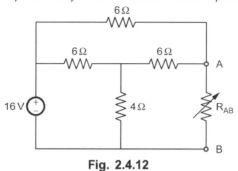

Fig. 2.4.12

[Ans. : $R_{AB} = 3.5 \Omega$ $P_{max} = 10.2857$ watts]

6. *Find R_L for maximum power transfer.*

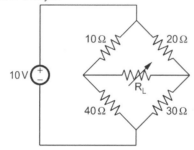

Fig. 2.4.13   [Ans. : $R_L = 20 \Omega$]

7. *Find R and power by maximum power transfer theorem.*

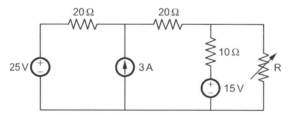

Fig. 2.4.14   [Ans. : $R = 8 \Omega$ $P_{max} = 26.28$ watts]

8. *Find the value of R_L for maximum power transfer and the magnitude of maximum power dissipated in the resistor R_L in the circuit shown in the Fig. 2.4.15.*

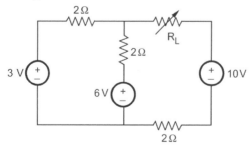

Fig. 2.4.15   [Ans. : 3Ω, 2.5208 W]

2.5 Short Answered and Objective Type Questions

Q.1   State the superposition theorem.

Ans. : In any multisource complex network consisting of linear bilateral elements, the voltage across or current through, any given element of the network is equal to the sum of the individual voltages or currents, produced independently across or in that element by each source acting independently, when all the remaining sources are replaced by their respective internal impedances.

Q.2   State the Thevenin's theorem.

Ans. : Any combination of linear bilateral circuit elements and active sources, regardless of the connection or complexity, connected to a given load Z_L, may be replaced by a simple two terminal network consisting of a single voltage source of V_{TH} volts and a single impedance Z_{eq} in series with the voltage source, across the two terminals of the load Z_L. The V_{TH} is the open circuit voltage measured at the two terminals of interest, with load impedance Z_L removed. This voltage is also called **Thevenin's equivalent voltage**. The Z_{eq} is the **equivalent impedance** of the given network as viewed through the terminals where Z_L is connected, with Z_L removed and all the active sources are replaced by their internal impedances. If the internal impedances are not known then **independent voltage sources** are to be replaced by the **short circuit** while the **independent current sources** must be replaced by **open circuit**.

Q.3   State the limitations of Thevenin's theorem.

Ans. :   Refer section 2.2.3.

Q.4   State Norton's theorem.

Ans. : Any combination of linear bilateral circuit elements and active sources, regardless of the connection or complexity, connected to a given load Z_L, can be replaced by a simple two terminal network, consisting of a single current source of I_N amperes and a single impedance Z_{eq} in parallel with it, across the two terminals of the load Z_L. The I_N is the short circuit current flowing through the short circuited path, replaced instead of Z_L. It is also called **Norton's current**. The Z_{eq} is the equivalent impedance of the given network as viewed through the load terminals, with Z_L removed and all the active sources are replaced by their internal impedances. If the internal impedances are unknown then the independent voltage sources must be replaced by short circuit while the independent current sources must be replaced by open circuit, while calculating Z_{eq}.

Q.5   State maximum power transfer theorem. State the expression for the maximum power.

Ans. : In an active network, maximum power transfer to the load takes place when the load impedance is the complex conjugate of an equivalent impedance of the network as viewed from the terminals of the load.

The maximum power is given by,

$$P_{max} = \frac{V_{TH}^2}{4\,R_L}$$

When V_{TH} = Thevenin's voltage as circuit is replaced by its Thevenin's equivalent

Q.6   Calculate the value of R_L, so that maximum power is transferred from battery. (Fig. 2.5.1)

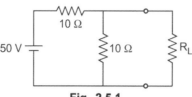

Fig. 2.5.1

Ans. :   For P_{max}, $R_L = R_{eq}$, shorting voltage source.

$\therefore$ $R_{eq} = \dfrac{10 \times 10}{10 + 10} = 5\ \Omega$

$\therefore$ $R_L = 5\ \Omega$ for P_{max}

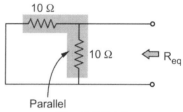

Fig. 2.5.1 (a)

Q.7   Find the maximum power that can be supplied to the load in the following circuit.

`2009-10, Marks 2`

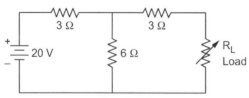

Fig. 2.5.2

Ans. :   **i) Calculate V_{TH} :**

$$I = \frac{20}{(3+6)} = 2.222\ A$$

$\therefore$ $V_{AB} = 0\,V + 6I = 13.333\ V$

$\therefore$ $V_{TH} = 13.333\ V$

$\therefore$ $R_{eq} = (3 \| 6) + 3 = 2 + 3$

        $= 5\ \Omega$

$\therefore$ $P_{max} = \dfrac{V_{TH}^2}{4\,R_{eq}} = \dfrac{(13.333)^2}{4 \times 5}$

        $= 8.88\ W$

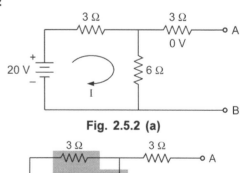

Fig. 2.5.2 (a)

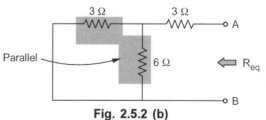

Fig. 2.5.2 (b)

Q.8 If internal resistance of voltage source is unknown, it is replaced by _____ while applying theorems.

a) open circuit   b) short circuit   c) delta circuit   d) none of these
                                                                    [Ans. : b]

Q.9 If internal resistance of current source is unknown it is replaced by _____ while applying theorems.

a) open circuit   b) short circuit   c) delta circuit   d) none of these
                                                                    [Ans. : a]

Q.10 The current through 5 Ω resistance due to 10 V source alone is _____ A in the circuit shown in the Fig. 2.5.3.

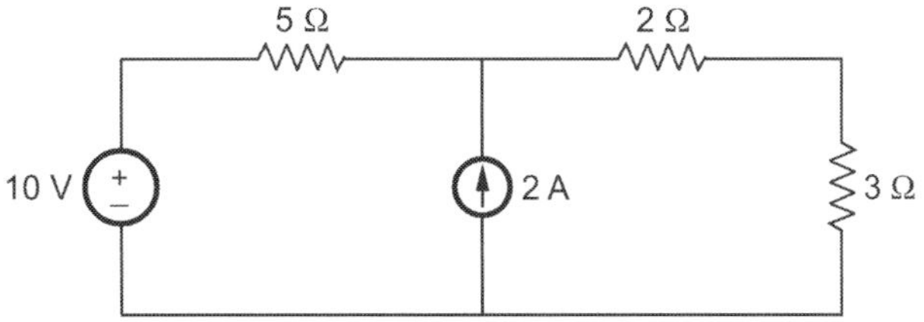

Fig. 2.5.3

a) 2 A   b) 3 A   c) 1 A   d) 4 A   **[Ans. : c]**

Q.11 The current through 5 Ω resistance due to 10 V source alone is _____ A in the circuit shown in the Fig. 2.5.4.

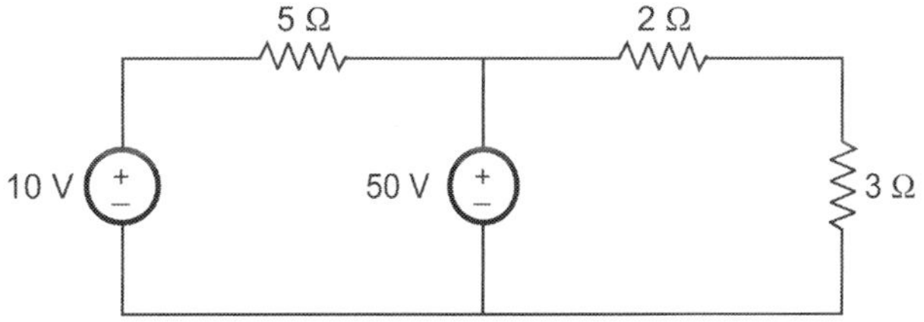

Fig. 2.5.4

a) 2   b) 3   c) 1   d) 4   **[Ans. : a]**

Q.12 While applying Thevenin's theorem, the load resistance must be _____.

a) shorted   b) removed   c) shunted   d) none of these
                                                                    [Ans. : b]

Q.13 The Thevenin's voltage across the terminals A-B shown in the Fig. 2.5.5 is _____ V.

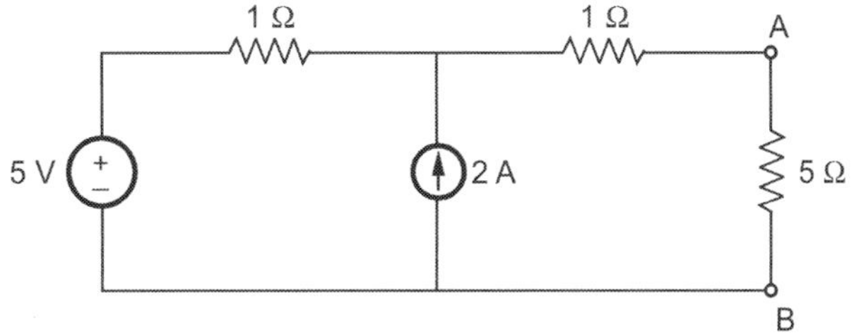

Fig. 2.5.5

a) 2   b) 3   c) 5   d) 7   **[Ans. : d]**

Q.14　The dual of Thevenin's theorem is _____ theorem.

a) superposition　　　b) maximum power transfer

c) Norton　　　　　　d) none of these　　　　　　　　　　**[Ans. : c]**

Q.15　The Thevenin's equivalent resistance for the network shown in the Fig. 2.5.6 is _____ Ω..

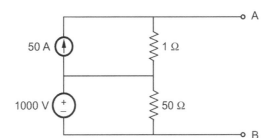

Fig. 2.5.6

a) 51　　　　　　b) 50　　　　　　c) 1　　　　　　d) none of these

　　　　　　　　　　　　　　　　　　　　　　　　　　　　　　　[Ans. : c]

Q.16　The Superposition theorem is used when the circuit consists of _____.

a) more than one energy sources　　　b) only one energy soruce

c) no energy source　　　　　　　　　d) none of these　　　　**[Ans. : a]**

Q.17　For maximum power transfer, the load resistance must be equal to _____ resistance of the network.

a) Norton's equivalent　　　　　　b) Thevenin's equivalent

c) short circuit　　　　　　　　　　d) open circuit　　　　　　**[Ans. : b]**

Q.18　A voltage source of 50 V having internal resistacne of 10 Ω will deliver maximum power when load resistance is equal to _____.

a) 5 Ω　　　　　b) 1 Ω　　　　　c) 10 Ω　　　　　d) 50 Ω　　**[Ans. : c]**

Q.19　The value of maximum power transferred to R_L in the circuit the shown in the Fig. 2.5.7 is _____.

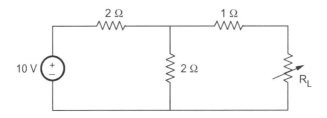

Fig. 2.5.7

a) 1.125 W　　　　b) 10 W　　　　c) 5 W　　　　d) 3.125 W

　　　　　　　　　　　　　　　　　　　　　　　　　　　　　　　[Ans. : d]

Q.20 The Thevenin's equivalent resistance across the terminals A-B of the circuit shown in the Fig. 2.5.8 is _____.

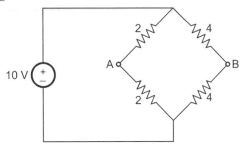

Fig. 2.5.8

a) 3 Ω   b) 2 Ω   c) 4 Ω   d) 6 Ω   **[Ans. : a]**

Q.21 The Norton's current if the load resistance is 10 Ω in the circuit shown in the Fig. 2.5.9 is _____.

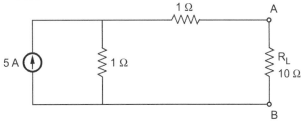

Fig. 2.5.9

a) 5 A   b) 2.5 A   c) 10 A   d) 15 A   **[Ans. : b]**

Q.22 If Thevenin's voltage of the circuit is 100 V and the Thevenin's resistance is 50 Ω then the Norton's current of the circuit is _____.

a) 1 A   b) 5 A   c) 2 A   d) 5000 A   **[Ans. : c]**

▢▢▢

Notes

3

Steady State Analysis of Single Phase A.C. Circuits

Syllabus

A.C. fundamentals : Sinusoidal, Square and triangular waveforms - Average and effective values, Form and peak factors, Concept of phasors, Phasor representation of sinusoidally varying voltage and current, Analysis of series, Parallel and series - parallel RLC circuits, Resonance in series and parallel circuits, Bandwidth and quality factor, Apparent, Active and reactive powers, Power factor.

Contents

3.1 Introduction

An electric supply used for domestic as well as commercial purposes is alternating in nature. Another type of an electric supply available has constant magnitude and direction.

Key Point *An alternating supply is the one which changes periodically both in magnitude and direction with respect to time and is called a.c. (alternating current) supply.*

An alternating current waveform is shown in the Fig. 3.1.1 (a).

Key Point *A supply which has constant magnitude and direction with respect to time is called d.c. (direct current) supply.*

A direct current waveform is shown in the Fig. 3.1.1 (b). Some quantities in practice may have variable magnitude but constant direction. Such a waveform is called **pulsating d.c.** and is shown in the Fig. 3.1.1 (c). The output of full wave rectifier is an example of pulsating d.c. waveform.

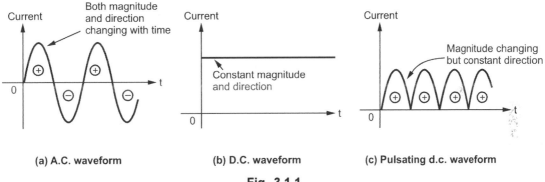

(a) A.C. waveform   (b) D.C. waveform   (c) Pulsating d.c. waveform

Fig. 3.1.1

3.1.1 Advantages of A.C.

The various advantages of a.c. are,

1. The voltages in a.c. system can be raised or lowered with the help of a device called transformer. In d.c. system, raising and lowering of voltages is not so easy.

2. As the voltages can be raised, electrical transmission at high voltages is possible. Now, higher the voltage, lesser is the current flowing through transmission line. Less the current, lesser are the copper losses and lesser is the conducting material required. This makes a.c. transmission always economical and efficient.

3. It is possible to build up high a.c. voltage with the help of high speed a.c. generators whose cost is very low.

4.   A.C. electrical motors are simple in construction, are cheaper and require less attention from maintenance point of view.

5.   Whenever it is necessary, a.c. supply can be easily converted to obtain d.c. supply.

Due to these advantages, a.c. is used extensively in practice and hence, it is necessary to study a.c. fundamentals.

3.1.2 Types of A.C. Waveforms

The waveform of alternating voltage or current is shown purely sinusoidal in the Fig. 3.1.1 (a). But, in practice, a quantity which undergoes variations in its instantaneous values, in magnitude as well as direction with respect to some zero reference is called an **alternating quantity.** The graph of such quantity against time is called its **waveform**. Various types of alternating waveforms other than sinusoidal are shown in the Fig. 3.1.2 (a), (b) and (c).

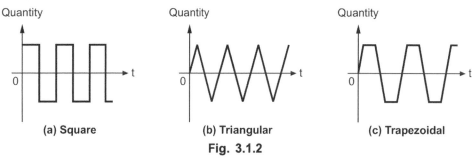

(a) Square   (b) Triangular   (c) Trapezoidal

Fig. 3.1.2

Out of all these types of alternating waveforms, purely sinusoidal waveform is preferred for a.c. system.

3.1.2.1 Advantages of Purely Sinusoidal Waveform

1)   Mathematically, it is very easy to write the equations for purely sinusoidal waveform.

2)   Any other type of complex waveform can be resolved into a series of sine or cosine waves of fundamental and higher frequencies. Sum of all these waves gives the original waveform.

3)   The sine and cosine waves are the only waves which can pass through linear circuits containing resistance, inductance and capacitance without distortion. In case of other waveforms, there is a possibility of distortion.

4)   The integration and derivative of a sinusoidal function is again a sinusoidal function. This makes the analysis of linear electrical networks with sinusoidal inputs, very easy.

1. *What is a.c. ? How it differs from d.c. ?*

2. *State the advantages of a.c.*

3. *State the advantages of sinusoidal alternating waveform.*

3.2 Generation of A.C. Voltage

The basic principle of an a.c. generation is the principle of electromagnetic induction. The sine wave is generated according to **Faraday's law of electromagnetic induction**.

Let us see how an alternator produces a sine wave, with the help of simplest form of an alternator called **single turn** or **single loop alternator.**

It consists of a permanent magnet having two poles. A single turn rectangular coil is kept in the vicinity of the permanent magnet.

The coil is made up of two conductors namely a-b and c-d. Such two conductors are connected at one end to form a coil.

The coil is so placed that it can be rotated about its own axis.

The remaining two ends C_1 and C_2 of the coil are connected to the rings mounted on the shaft called **slip rings.** Slip rings are also rotating members of the alternator.

The two brushes P and Q are resting on the slip rings. The **brushes are stationary** and just making contact with the slip rings. The overall construction is shown in the Fig. 3.2.1.

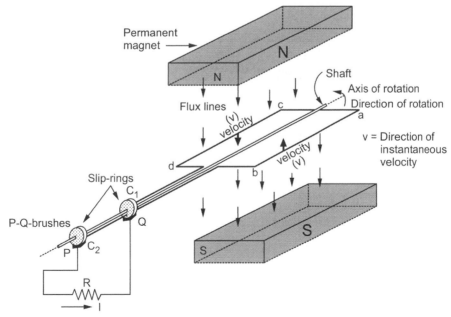

Fig. 3.2.1 Single turn alternator

Working : The coil is rotated in anticlockwise direction. While rotating, the conductors ab and cd cut the lines of flux of the permanent magnet. Due to Faraday's law of electromagnetic induction, an e.m.f. gets induced in the conductors. This e.m.f. drives a current through resistance R connected across the brushes P and Q. **The magnitude of the induced e.m.f. depends on the position of the coil in the magnetic field.**

Consider different instants and the different positions of the coil :

Instant 1 : Let the initial position of the coil be as shown in the Fig. 3.2.1. The plane of the coil is perpendicular to the direction of the magnetic field. The instantaneous component of velocity of conductors ab and cd, is parallel to the magnetic field as shown and there cannot be the cutting of the flux lines by the conductors. Hence, no e.m.f. will be generated in the conductors ab and cd. This shown in the Fig. 3.2.2 (a).

The angle θ is measured from plane of the magnetic flux.

Instant 2 : When the coil is rotated in anticlockwise direction through some angle θ, then the velocity will have two components $v \sin \theta$ perpendicular to flux lines and $v \cos \theta$ parallel to the flux lines. Due to $v \sin \theta$ component, there will be cutting of the flux and proportionally, there will be induced e.m.f. in the conductors ab and cd. This is shown in the Fig. 3.2.2 (b).

Instant 3 : As angle 'θ' increases, the component of velocity acting perpendicular to flux lines increases, hence induced e.m.f. also increases. At $\theta = 90°$, the plane of the coil is parallel to the plane of the magnetic field while the component of velocity cutting the lines of flux is at its maximum. **So, induced e.m.f. in this position, is at its maximum value.** This is shown in the Fig. 3.2.2 (c).

So, as θ increases from $0°$ to $90°$, e.m.f. induced in the conductors increases gradually from 0 to maximum value.

Instant 4 : As the coil continues to rotate further from $\theta = 90°$ to $180°$, the component of velocity, perpendicular to magnetic field starts decreasing, hence, gradually decreasing the magnitude of the induced e.m.f. This is shown in the Fig. 3.2.2 (d).

Instant 5 : In this position, the velocity component is fully parallel to the lines of flux similar to the instant 1. Hence, there is no cutting of flux and hence, no induced e.m.f. in both the conductors.

Instant 6 : As the coil rotates beyond $\theta = 180°$, the conductor ab uptil now cutting flux lines in one particular direction reverses the direction of cutting the flux lines. Similar is the behaviour of conductor cd. This change in direction of induced e.m.f. occurs because the direction of rotation of conductors ab and cd reverses with respect to the field as θ varies from $180°$ to $360°$. This process continues as coil rotates further.

So, as θ varies from $0°$ to $360°$, the e.m.f. in a conductor ab or cd varies in an alternating manner i.e. zero, increasing to achieve maximum in one direction, decreasing to zero, increasing to achieve maximum in other direction and again decreasing to zero. This set of variation repeats for every revolution as the conductors rotate in a circular motion with a certain speed.

This variation of e.m.f. in a conductor can be graphically represented as shown in the Fig. 3.2.2. From the waveform, it is clear that the waveform generated by the instantaneous values of the induced e.m.f. in any conductor (ab or cd) is **purely sinusoidal** in nature.

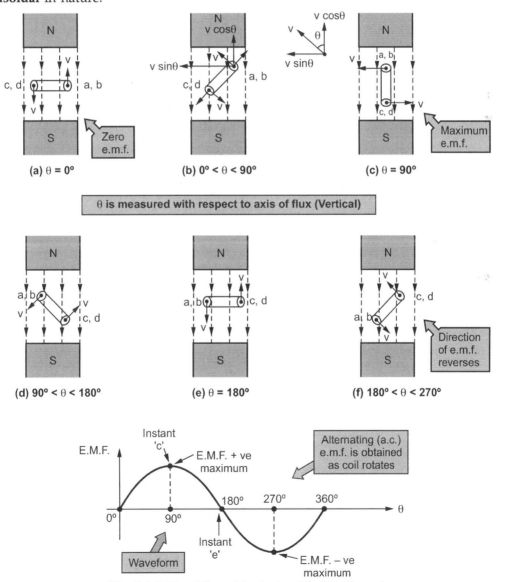

Fig. 3.2.2 The different instants of induced e.m.f.

The angle θ in radians and the angular velocity ω in radians/seconds of the coil are related to each other through time t by the equation,

$$\theta = \omega t \quad \text{radians}$$

Hence the waveform of alternating quantity can be shown with respect to time t rather than θ as ω is constant.

Review Question

> 1. *With a neat sketch briefly explain how an alternating voltage is produced when a coil is rotated in a magnetic field.*

3.3 Standard Definitions Related to Alternating Quantity

1. Instantaneous Value : The value of an alternating quantity at a particular instant is known as its **instantaneous value** e.g. e_1 and $-e_2$ are the instantaneous values of an alternating e.m.f. at the instants t_1 and t_2 respectively shown in the Fig. 3.3.1.

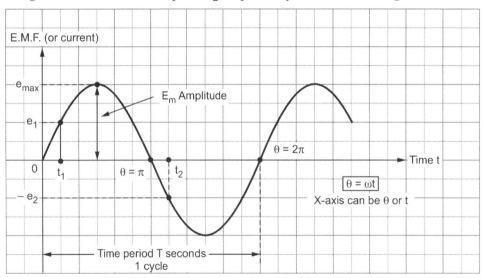

Fig. 3.3.1 Representation of an alternating quantity

2. Waveform : The graph of instantaneous values of an alternating quantity plotted against time is called its **waveform.**

3. Cycle : Each repetition of a set of positive and negative instantaneous values of the alternating quantity is called a **cycle.**

Such repetition occurs at regular interval of time. Such a waveform which exhibits variations that reoccur after a regular time interval is called **periodic waveform.**

A **cycle** can also be defined as that interval of time during which a complete set of non-repeating events or waveform variations occur (containing positive as well as negative loops). One such cycle of the alternating quantity is shown in the Fig. 3.3.1.

> One cycle corresponds to 2π radians or $360°$

4. Time Period (T) : The time taken by an alternating quantity to complete its one cycle is known as its **time period** denoted by **T** seconds. After every T seconds, the cycle of an alternating quantity repeats. This is shown in the Fig. 3.3.1.

5. Frequency (f) : The number of cycles completed by an alternating quantity per second is known as its **frequency.** It is denoted by **f** and it is measured in **cycles / second** which is known as **Hertz,** denoted as **Hz.**

As time period T is time for one cycle i.e. seconds/cycle and frequency is cycles/second, we can say that frequency is reciprocal of the time period.

$$f = \frac{1}{T} \quad Hz$$

As time period increases, frequency decreases while as time period decreases, frequency increases.

In our nation, standard frequency of alternating voltages and currents is 50 Hz.

6. Amplitude : The maximum value attained by an alternating quantity during positive or negative half cycle is called its **amplitude.** It is denoted as E_m or I_m.

Thus E_m is called peak value of the voltage while I_m is called peak value of the current.

7. Angular Frequency (ω) : It is the frequency expressed in electrical radians per second.

As one cycle of an alternating quantity corresponds to 2π radians, the angular frequency can be expressed as ($2\pi \times$ cycles/sec). It is denoted by 'ω' and its unit is radians/second. The relation between frequency ' f ' and angular frequency 'ω' is,

$$\omega = 2\pi f \quad radians/sec \quad or \quad \omega = \frac{2\pi}{T} \quad radians/sec$$

8. Peak to Peak Value : The value of an alternating quantity from its positive peak to negative peak is called its peak to peak value. It is denoted as I_{p-p} or V_{p-p}.

$$Amplitude = \frac{Peak \ to \ Peak \ Value}{2}$$

Review Question

1. *Sketch the sinusoidal alternating current waveform and define the following terms : instantaneous value, time period, frequency, amplitude, peak to peak value and cycle.*

3.4 Equation of an Alternating Quantity　　　2002-03

As the standard waveform of an alternating quantity is purely sinusoidal, the equation of an alternating voltage can be expressed as,

$$e = E_m \sin \theta \ \text{volts}$$

where　　E_m = Amplitude or maximum or peak value of the voltage.

　　　　　e = Instantaneous value of an alternating voltage

Similarly equation of an alternating current can be expressed as,

$$i = I_m \sin \theta$$

where　　I_m = Amplitude or maximum or peak value of the current.

　　　　　i = Instantaneous value of an alternating current

The equation can be expressed in various forms as :

Now,　　　$\theta = \omega t$ 　radians

∴　　　$e = E_m \sin (\omega t)$ 　　　　　　　　　　　　...(3.4.1)

But,　　　$\omega = 2 \pi f$ 　rad / sec.

∴　　　$e = E_m \sin (2 \pi f t)$ 　　　　　　　　　　　... (3.4.2)

But,　　　$f = \dfrac{1}{T}$ 　seconds

∴　　　$e = E_m \sin \left(\dfrac{2\pi}{T} t \right)$ 　　　　　　　　　... (3.4.3)

Important Note : *In all the above equations, the angle θ is expressed in **radians**. Hence, while calculating the instantaneous value of the e.m.f., it is necessary to calculate the sine of the angle expressed in radians.*

Example 3.4.1 *A sinusoidally varying alternating current of frequency 60 Hz has a maximum value of 15 amperes.*

i) Write down the equation for instantaneous value

ii) Find the value of current after $\dfrac{1}{200}$ second

iii) Find the time to reach 10 amperes for the first time, and

iv) Find its average value. 　　　　　　　　　　　2002-03, Marks 5

Solution : $I_m = 15$ A, $f = 60$ Hz

$$\omega = 2\pi f = 2\pi \times 60 = 377 \text{ rad/sec.}$$

i) $i = I_m \sin \omega t = \textbf{15 sin 377 t A}$

ii) $t = \left(\dfrac{1}{200}\right)$ sec.

∴ $i = 15 \sin\left(\dfrac{377}{200}\right) = \textbf{14.2656 A}$ ... use **radian** mode

iii) $i = 10$ A

∴ $10 = 15 \sin 377\ t$ i.e. $377\ t = \sin^{-1}\left(\dfrac{10}{15}\right)$ ... Use **radian** mode

∴ $t = \textbf{1.9356 ms}$

iv) $I_{av} = 0.637\ I_m = 0.637 \times 15 = \textbf{9.555 A}$

Example 3.4.2 *A sinusoidal voltage of 50 Hz has a maximum value of* $200\sqrt{2}$ *volts. At what time measured from a positive maximum value will the instantaneous voltage be equal to 141.4 volts ?*

Solution : $f = 50$ Hz, $V_m = 200\sqrt{2}$ V, $v_1 = 141.4$ V

The equation of the voltage is,

$$v = V_m \sin(2\pi f t) = 200\sqrt{2}\ \sin(2\pi \times 50\ t) \text{ V}$$

For $v = v_1$, $141.4 = 200\sqrt{2}\ \sin(2\pi \times 50 \times t_1)$

∴ $t_1 = 1.666 \times 10^{-3}$ sec.   ... Use **radian mode** for $\sin^{-1}$

But this time is measured from $t = 0$. At positive maximum, time is $\dfrac{T}{4} = \dfrac{1}{4f} = 5 \times 10^{-3}$ sec . So $t = t_1 = 1.666 \times 10^{-3}$ sec is before positive maximum.

From Fig. 3.4.1

$t_m - t_1 = 5 \times 10^{-3} - 1.666 \times 10^{-3}$

$ = \textbf{3.314} \times \textbf{10}^{-3}$ **sec.**

As the waveform is symmetrical, at the time of 3.314×10^{-3} sec. **measured after positive maximum** value, the instantaneous voltage will be again 141.4 V.

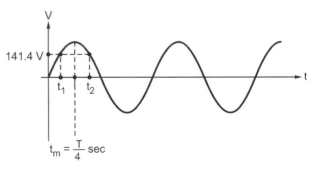

Fig. 3.4.1

Review Questions

1. *State the equation of an alternating quantity. State its various forms.*

2. *An alternating current varying sinusoidally with a frequency of 50 Hz has a r.m.s. value of current of 20 Amp. At what time, measured from negative maximum value, instantaneous current will be* $10\sqrt{2}$ *Amp. ?*
   [Ans. : 6.666 ms]

3. *An alternating current is given by i = 14.14 sin 377 t.*
   Find i) R.M.S. value of current, ii) Frequency, iii) Instantaneous value of current, when t = 3 ms and iv) Time taken by current to reach 10 amp for 1st time after passing through zero.
   [Ans. : i) 10 A, ii) 60 Hz, iii) 12.794 A, iv) 2.083 ms]

4. *A sinusoidal wave of frequency 50 Hz has its maximum value of 9.2 Amps. What will be its value at a) 0.002 sec after the wave pass through zero in positive direction. b) 0.0045 sec after the wave passes through positive maximum. Show the values of current in a neat sketch of the waveform.*
   [Ans. : 5.407 A, 1.4391 A]

3.5 Effective Value or R.M.S. Value

An alternating current varies from instant to instant, while the direct current is constant, with respect to time.

For the comparison of the two, a common effect to both the type of currents can be considered. Such an effect is heat produced by the two currents flowing through the resistance. The heating effect can be used to compare the alternating and direct current. From this, r.m.s. value of an alternating current can be defined as,

> The *effective or r.m.s. value* of an alternating current is given by that steady current (D.C.) which, when flowing through a given circuit for a given time, produces the same amount of heat as produced by the alternating current, which when flowing through the same circuit for the same time.

3.5.1 Analytical Method of Obtaining R.M.S. Value

Steps to find r.m.s. value of an a.c. quantity :

1. Write the equation of an a.c. quantity. Observe its behaviour during various time intervals.

2. Find square of the a.c. quantity from its equation.

3. Find average value of square of an alternating quantity as,

$$\text{Average} = \frac{\text{Area of curve over one cycle of squared waveform}}{\text{Length of the cycle}}$$

4. Find square root of average value which gives r.m.s. value of an alternating quantity.

Consider sinusoidally varying alternating current and square of this current as shown in the Fig. 3.5.1.

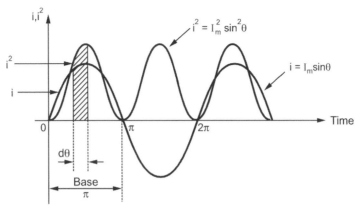

Fig. 3.5.1 Waveform of current and square of the current

Step 1 :   The current $i = I_m \sin \theta$

Step 2 : Square of current $i^2 = I_m^2 \sin^2 \theta$

The area of curve over half a cycle can be calculated by considering an interval $d\theta$ as shown.

Area of square curve over half cycle $= \int_0^\pi i^2 \, d\theta$ and length of the base is π .

Step 3 :   ∴Average value of square of the current over half cycle

$$= \frac{\text{Area of curve over half cycle}}{\text{Length of base over half cycle}} = \frac{\int_0^\pi i^2 \, d\theta}{\pi} = \frac{1}{\pi}\int_0^\pi i^2 \, d\theta = \frac{1}{\pi}\int_0^\pi I_m^2 \sin^2 \theta \, d\theta$$

$$= \frac{I_m^2}{\pi}\left[\int_0^\pi \frac{1-\cos 2\theta}{2}\right] d\theta = \frac{I_m^2}{2\pi}\left[\theta - \frac{\sin 2\theta}{2}\right]_0^\pi = \frac{I_m^2}{2\pi}[\,\pi\,] = \frac{I_m^2}{2}$$

Step 4 : Root mean square value i.e. r.m.s. value can be calculated as,

$$I_{r.m.s.} = \sqrt{\text{Mean or average of square of current}} = \sqrt{\frac{I_m^2}{2}} = \frac{I_m}{\sqrt{2}}$$

∴ $I_{r.m.s.} = 0.707 \, I_m$

The r.m.s. value of the sinusoidal alternating current is 0.707 times the maximum or peak value or amplitude of that alternating current.

> *The **instantaneous** values are denoted by **small** letters like i, e etc. while **r.m.s.** values are represented by **capital** letters like I, E etc.*

The above result is also applicable to **sinusoidal** alternating voltages.

∴ $V_{r.m.s.} = 0.707\ V_m$

3.5.2 Importance of R.M.S. Value

1. In case of alternating quantities, the r.m.s. values are used for specifying magnitudes of alternating quantities. The given values such as 230 V, 110 V are r.m.s. values of alternating quantities unless and otherwise specified to be other than r.m.s.

> In practice, everywhere, r.m.s. values are used to analyze alternating quantities.

2. The ammeters and voltmeters record the r.m.s. values of current and voltage respectively.

3. The heat produced due to a.c. is proportional to square of the r.m.s. value of the current.

Review Questions

> 1. *Define r.m.s. value of an alternating quantity. Obtain the relation between r.m.s. value and the maximum value of an alternating quantity.*
> 2. *State the practical significance of r.m.s. value.*

3.6 Average Value

The **average value** of an alternating quantity is defined as that value which is obtained by averaging all the instantaneous values over a period of half cycle.

> **For a symmetrical a.c., the average value over a complete cycle is zero** *as both positive and negative half cycles are exactly identical. Hence, the average value is defined for half cycle only.*

Average value can also be expressed by that steady current which transfers across any circuit, the same amount of charge as is transferred by that alternating current during the same time.

3.6.1 Analytical Method of Obtaining Average Value

Consider sinusoidally varying current, $I = I_m \sin \theta$

Consider the elementary interval of instant 'dθ' as shown in the Fig. 3.6.1. The average instantaneous value of current in this interval is say, 'i' as shown.

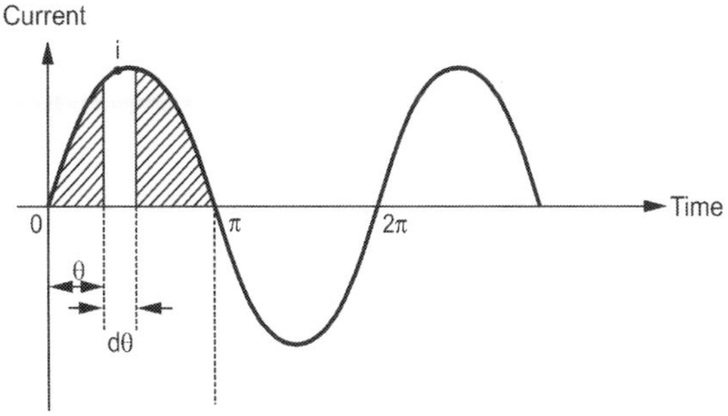

The average value can be obtained by taking ratio of area under curve over **half cycle** to length of the base for half cycle.

Fig. 3.6.1 Average value of an alternating current

$$\therefore \quad \boxed{I_{av} = \frac{\text{Area under curve for half cycle}}{\text{Length of base over half cycle}}}$$

$$I_{av} = \frac{\int_0^\pi i \, d\theta}{\pi} = \frac{1}{\pi}\int_0^\pi i \, d\theta$$

$$= \frac{1}{\pi}\int_0^\pi I_m \sin\theta \, d\theta = \frac{I_m}{\pi}\int_0^\pi \sin\theta = \frac{I_m}{\pi}[-\cos\theta]_0^\pi$$

$$= \frac{I_m}{\pi}[-\cos\pi + \cos 0] = \frac{I_m}{\pi}[2] = \frac{2 I_m}{\pi} = 0.637\, I_m$$

For a purely sinusoidal waveform, the average value is expressed in terms of its maximum value as,

$$\therefore \quad \boxed{I_{av} = 0.637\, I_m \quad \text{and} \quad V_{av} = 0.637\, V_m}$$

3.6.2 Importance of Average Value

1. The average value is used for applications like battery charging.

2. The charge transferred in capacitor circuits is measured using average values.

3. The average values of voltages and currents play an important role in analysis of the rectifier circuits.

4. The average value is indicated by d.c. ammeters and voltmeters.

5. The average value of purely sinusoidal waveform is always zero.

Review Questions

1. *Define average value of an alternating quantity. Obtain the relation between average value and the maximum value of an alternating quantity.*

2. *State the importance of average value.*

3.7 Form Factor (K_f)

The form factor of an alternating quantity is defined as the ratio of r.m.s. value to the average value,

Form factor,
$$K_f = \frac{\text{R.M.S. value}}{\text{Average value}}$$

The form factor for sinusoidal alternating currents or voltages can be obtained as,

$$K_f = \frac{0.707\ I_m}{0.637\ I_m} = \mathbf{1.11} \quad \text{for sinusoidally varying quantity}$$

Review Question

1. *Define form factor.*

3.8 Crest or Peak Factor (K_p)

2002-03, 2003-04, 2004-05, 2005-06, 2007-08, 2012-13

The peak factor of an alternating quantity is defined as ratio of maximum value to the r.m.s. value.

Peak factor
$$K_p = \frac{\text{Maximum value}}{\text{R.M.S. value}}$$

The peak factor for sinusoidally varying alternating currents and voltages can be obtained as,

$$K_p = \frac{I_m}{0.707\ I_m} = \mathbf{1.414} \quad \text{for sinusoidal waveform}$$

Example 3.8.1 *Calculate the r.m.s. value, average value, form factor, peak factor of a periodic current having following values for equal time intervals changing suddenly from one value to next as 0, 2, 4, 6, 8, 10, 8, 6, 4, 2, 0, –2, –4, –6, –8, –10, –8, ...*

Solution : The waveform can be represented as shown in the Fig. 3.8.1. (See Fig. 3.8.1 on next page)

The average value of the current is given by,

$$\text{Average value} = \frac{0+2+4+6+8+10+8+6+4+2}{10} = \mathbf{5\ A}$$

$$\text{The r.m.s. value of the current} = \sqrt{\frac{0^2 +2^2 +4^2 +6^2 +8^2 +10^2 +8^2 +6^2 +4^2 +2^2}{10}}$$

$$= \mathbf{5.8309\ A}$$

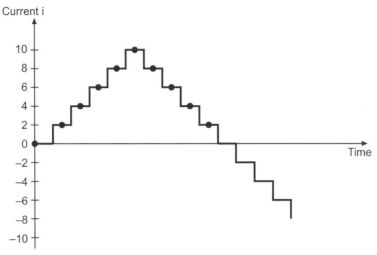

Fig. 3.8.1

$$\text{Form factor} \quad K_f = \frac{\text{r.m.s.}}{\text{average}} = \frac{5.8309}{5} = \mathbf{1.1661}$$

$$\text{Peak factor} \quad K_p = \frac{\text{maximum}}{\text{r.m.s.}} = \frac{10}{5.8309} = \mathbf{1.715}$$

Example 3.8.2 *An alternating voltage is v = 100 sin 100 t ; find*
i) Amplitude   ii) Time period and frequency   iii) Angular velocity
iv) Form factor   v) Crest factor.   **2002-03, 2005-06, 2007-08, Marks 5**

Solution : v = 100 sin 100 t

Comparing with, $v = V_m \sin \omega t$

i) Amplitude, $V_m = 100$ V

ii) $\omega = 100$ rad/sec But $\omega = 2\pi f$ i.e. $100 = 2\pi \times f$

∴   f = **15.9154 Hz**   ...Frequency

∴ $T = \dfrac{1}{f} = \mathbf{0.0628}$ **sec**   ... Time period

iii) $\omega = \mathbf{100}$ **rad/sec**   ...Angular frequency

iv) $K_f = \dfrac{\text{r.m.s.}}{\text{Average}} = \dfrac{(V_m / \sqrt{2})}{0.637\, V_m} = \mathbf{1.11}$

v) $K_p = \dfrac{\text{Maximum}}{\text{r.m.s.}} = \dfrac{V_m}{\left(\dfrac{V_m}{\sqrt{2}}\right)} = \sqrt{2} = \mathbf{1.414}$

Example 3.8.3 *Find the r.m.s. value, average value and form factor of the voltage waveform shown in figure.*   **2002-03, Marks 10**

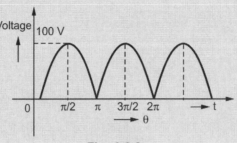

Fig. 3.8.2

Solution : Consider first cycle of the waveform,

$$I_{r.m.s.} = \sqrt{\frac{\text{Area of square curve over a cycle}}{\text{Length of base over a cycle}}} = \sqrt{\frac{\int_0^\pi i^2(\theta)\,d\theta}{\pi}}$$

$$i(\theta) = I_m \sin\theta = 100\sin\theta$$

$$i^2(\theta) = (100)^2 \sin^2\theta = (100)^2 \frac{[1-\cos 2\theta]}{2}$$

$$\therefore \int_0^\pi i^2(\theta)\,d\theta = \frac{(100)^2}{2}\int_0^\pi (1-\cos 2\theta)\,d\theta = \frac{(100)^2}{2}\left\{[\theta]_0^\pi - \left[\frac{\sin 2\theta}{2}\right]_0^\pi\right\} = \frac{(100)^2}{2}\times\pi$$

$$\therefore I_{r.m.s.} = \sqrt{\frac{\frac{(100)^2}{2}\times\pi}{\pi}} = \frac{(100)}{\sqrt{2}} = \textbf{70.7106 A}$$

$$I_{av} = \frac{\text{Area of curve over a cycle}}{\text{Length of base over a cycle}} = \frac{\int_0^\pi i(\theta)d(\theta)}{\pi}$$

$$\therefore \int_0^\pi i(\theta)d(\theta) = \int_0^\pi 100\sin(\theta)d(\theta) = 100[-\cos\theta]_0^\pi = 100\,[-\cos\pi - (-\cos 0)]$$

$$= 100\times[1+1] = 200$$

$$\therefore I_{av} = \frac{200}{\pi} = \textbf{63.6619 A}$$

$$K_f = \frac{I_{r.m.s.}}{I_{av}} = \frac{70.7106}{63.6619} = \textbf{1.11}$$

Example 3.8.4 *Calculate the average value, effective value and form factor of the output voltage wave of a half wave rectifier as shown in the Fig. 3.8.3.*   **2003-04, Marks 10**

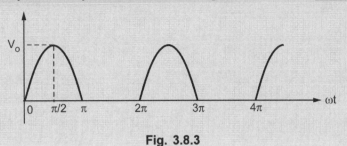

Fig. 3.8.3

Solution : i) Average value

$$V_{av} = \frac{\text{Area under 1 cycle}}{\text{base}} = \frac{\int_0^{2\pi} v(\theta)\, d\theta}{2\pi}$$

Now

$$v(\theta) = V_o \sin\theta \qquad \text{for} \qquad 0 < \theta < \pi$$
$$= 0 \qquad \text{for} \qquad \pi < \theta < 2\pi$$

$$\therefore \qquad V_{av} = \frac{\int_0^\pi V_o \sin\theta\, d\theta + 0}{2\pi} = \frac{V_o[-\cos\theta]_0^\pi}{2\pi} = \frac{V_o[-\cos\pi - (-\cos 0)]}{2\pi}$$

$$= \frac{V_o \times 2}{2\pi} = \frac{V_o}{\pi}$$

ii) Effective value i.e. r.m.s.

$$V_{r.m.s.} = \sqrt{\frac{\text{Area under squared 1 cycle}}{\text{base}}} = \sqrt{\frac{\int_0^{2\pi} v^2(\theta)\, d\theta}{2\pi}}$$

$$= \sqrt{\frac{\int_0^\pi V_o^2 \sin^2\theta\, d\theta}{2\pi}} = \frac{1}{\sqrt{2\pi}}\sqrt{\int_0^\pi V_o^2\left[\frac{1-\cos 2\theta}{2}\right]d\theta}$$

$$= \frac{V_o}{\sqrt{2\pi}}\sqrt{\frac{1}{2}\left\{[\theta]_0^\pi - \left[\frac{\sin 2\theta}{2}\right]_0^\pi\right\}} = \frac{V_o}{\sqrt{2\pi \times \sqrt{2}}}\sqrt{\pi - [0-0]} = \frac{V_o}{2\sqrt{\pi}} \times \sqrt{\pi} = \frac{V_o}{2}$$

$$\therefore \qquad K_f = \text{Form factor} = \frac{V_{r.m.s.}}{V_{av}} = \frac{\dfrac{V_o}{2}}{\dfrac{V_o}{\pi}} = \frac{\pi}{2} = \mathbf{1.57}$$

Example 3.8.5 *Determine the form factor of a voltage waveform in the Fig. 3.8.4.*

2004-05, Marks 10

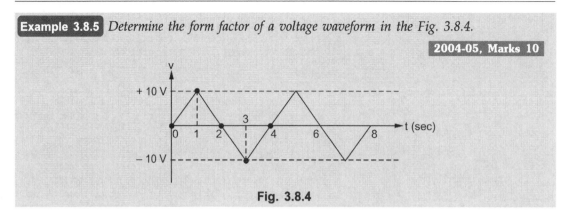

Fig. 3.8.4

Solution : For symmetric waveform, only half cycle is considered, to obtain the average value.

$$V_{av} = \frac{\text{Area under curve for half cycle}}{\text{base of half cycle}} = \frac{\frac{1}{2} \times 2 \times 10}{2} = \frac{20}{4} = 5 \text{ V}$$

$$V_{r.m.s.} = \sqrt{\frac{\text{Area of squared waveform for a cycle}}{\text{base of the cycle}}}$$

$$= \sqrt{\frac{\int_0^4 v^2(t)\,dt}{4}} = \frac{1}{2}\sqrt{2 \times \int_0^2 v^2(t)dt} = \frac{1}{\sqrt{2}}\sqrt{\int_0^2 v^2(t)dt}$$

For line AB, $v(t) = mt$.

$$m = \frac{y_2 - y_1}{x_2 - x_1} = \frac{10 - 0}{1 - 0} = 10$$

$\therefore \qquad v(t) = 10\,t$

For line BC, $v(t) = mt + C$

$$m = \frac{y_2 - y_1}{x_2 - x_1} = \frac{0 - 10}{2 - 1} = -10$$

And for point (2, 0), $\quad 0 = -10 \times 2 + C$ i.e. $C = 20$

$\therefore \qquad v(t) = -10\,t + 20$

$$\therefore \quad \int_0^2 v^2(t)dt = \int_0^1 (10t)^2\,dt + \int_1^2 (-10t+20)^2\,dt = \int_0^1 100\,t^2\,dt + \int_1^2 [100t^2 - 400t + 400]dt$$

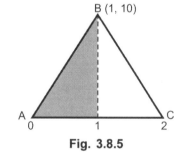

Fig. 3.8.5

$$= \left[\frac{100\,t^3}{3}\right]_0^1 + \left[\frac{100t^3}{3} - \frac{400t^2}{2} + 400t\right]_1^2$$

$$= \frac{100}{3} + \frac{100}{3}(2^3 - 1^3) - 200(2^2 - 1^2) + 400 \times (2-1) = 66.6667$$

$$\therefore \quad V_{r.m.s.} = \frac{1}{\sqrt{2}} \times \sqrt{66.667} = 5.773 \text{ V}$$

$$\therefore \quad K_f = \text{form factor} = \frac{r.m.s.}{\text{average}} = \frac{5.773}{5} = \textbf{1.154}$$

Example 3.8.6 *Find the form factor of a square wave.*   **2012-13, Marks 2**

Solution : A square wave is shown in the Fig. 3.8.6.

$$V_{av} = \frac{\int_0^\pi v(t)\,d\theta}{\pi} = \frac{\int_0^\pi A\,d\theta}{\pi}$$

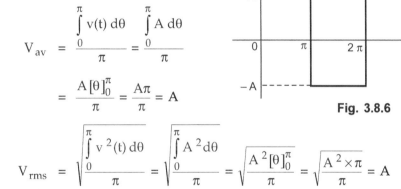

$$= \frac{A[\theta]_0^\pi}{\pi} = \frac{A\pi}{\pi} = A$$

Fig. 3.8.6

$$V_{rms} = \sqrt{\frac{\int_0^\pi v^2(t)\,d\theta}{\pi}} = \sqrt{\frac{\int_0^\pi A^2\,d\theta}{\pi}} = \sqrt{\frac{A^2[\theta]_0^\pi}{\pi}} = \sqrt{\frac{A^2 \times \pi}{\pi}} = A$$

$$\therefore \quad K_f = \frac{r.m.s.\ value}{\text{average value}} = \frac{A}{A} = 1$$

Example 3.8.7 *Calculate the average and effective values of the sawtooth waveform shown in Fig. 3.8.7. The voltage completes the cycle by falling back to zero instantaneously after regular interval of time.*

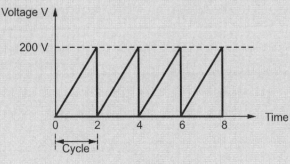

Fig. 3.8.7

Solution : Let us calculate equation for the instantaneous value of the voltage. The voltage increases linearly from 0 to 200 V in two seconds. So slope between 0 to 2 seconds is,

$$= \frac{200 - 0}{2} = 100$$

∴ Equation for the instantaneous value is,

$$v(t) = 100\,t$$

The average value $= \dfrac{\text{Area under curve}}{\text{Base}} = \displaystyle\int_0^2 \frac{(100\,t)\,dt}{2}$

$$= \frac{1}{2}\left[100\,\frac{t^2}{2}\right]_0^2 = 50 \times 2 = \textbf{100 volts}$$

The r.m.s. value = Root of the mean of square

$$= \sqrt{\frac{\displaystyle\int_0^2 (100\,t)^2\,dt}{2}} = \sqrt{\frac{\frac{1}{2}\times(100)^2 \times \left[\frac{t^3}{3}\right]_0^2}{2}}$$

$$= \sqrt{5000 \times \frac{8}{3}} = \textbf{115.47 volts}$$

Example 3.8.8 *A nonsinusoidal voltage has a form factor of 1.25 and crest factor of 1.63. If its average value is 50 V, calculate its i) r.m.s. value and ii) Maximum value.*

Solution : $K_f = 1.25$, $K_p = 1.63$, $V_{av} = 50$

$$K_f = \frac{\text{R.M.S.}}{\text{Average}} \quad \text{i.e.} \quad 1.25 = \frac{\text{R.M.S.}}{50} \quad \text{i.e.} \quad \text{R.M.S.} = \textbf{62.5 V}$$

$$K_P = \frac{\text{Max}}{\text{R.M.S.}} \quad \text{i.e.} \quad 1.63 = \frac{\text{Max}}{62.5} \quad \text{i.e.} \quad \text{Maximum} = \textbf{101.875 V}$$

Review Questions

1. Define peak factor.
2. For the waveform shown find the form factor.

[Ans. : 1.1546]

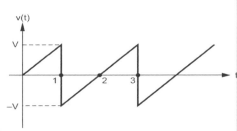

Fig. 3.8.8

3. *Find the form factor of the current waveform shown in the Fig. 3.8.9.*

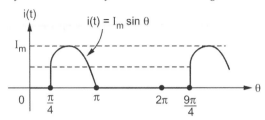

Fig. 3.8.9

[Ans. : 1.7545]

4. *Find the r.m.s. and average values of the following waveforms :*

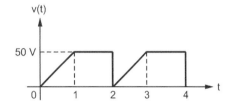

(a)

(b)

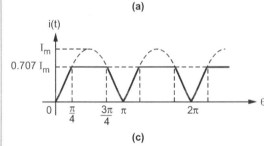

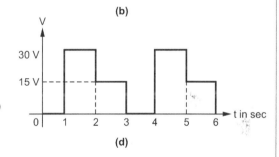

(c)

(d)

Fig. 3.8.10

[Ans. :   a) 5.773 V, 3.333 V   b) 40.8 V, 37.5 V

c) 0.584 I_m, 0.54 I_m d) 19.365 V, 15 V]

5. *Find the r.m.s. and average values of the current waveform shown.*

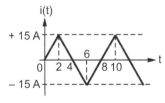

Fig. 3.8.11

[Ans. : 8.6602 A, 7.5 A]

6. *The equation of an alternating current is i = 62.35 sin(323t) A. Determine, i) maximum value*
ii) frequency iii) r.m.s. value iv) form factor.   2002-03, 2005-06

[Ans. : 62.35 A, 51.4 Hz, 44.09 A, 1.11]

3.9 R.M.S. Value of Combined Waveform

Consider a wire carrying simultaneously more than one alternating current of different magnitudes and frequencies alongwith certain d.c. current. It is required to calculate resultant **r.m.s. value** i.e. **effective value** of the current.

Let the wire carries three different currents as shown in the Fig. 3.9.1. It is required to obtain resultant $I_{r.m.s.}$ through the wire.

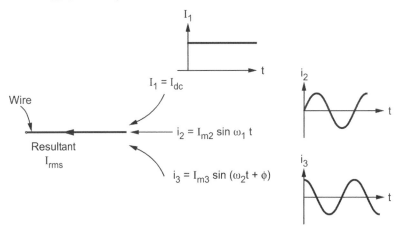

Fig. 3.9.1 Wire carrying 3 different currents simultaneously

Method : It is based on heating effect of various currents.

Let $I_{r.m.s.}$ = Resultant r.m.s. value of current

         R = Resistance of wire

         t = Time for which current is flowing

∴   H = Heat produced by resultant = $I_{r.m.s.}^2 \times R \times t$ ... (3.9.1)

This heat produced is sum of the heats produced by the individual current components flowing for the same time t.

$$H_1 = \text{Heat produced by d.c. component} = I_{dc}^2 \times R \times t$$

$$H_2 = \text{Heat produced by first a.c. component} = I_{r.m.s.2}^2 \times R \times t$$

$$= \left(\frac{I_{m2}}{\sqrt{2}}\right)^2 \times R \times t$$

$$H_3 = \text{Heat produced by second a.c. component} = I_{r.m.s.3}^2 \times R \times t$$

$$= \left(\frac{I_{m3}}{\sqrt{2}}\right)^2 \times R \times t$$

Note that for alternating currents $I_{r.m.s.} = I_m / \sqrt{2}$

Thus equating the total heat produced to sum of the individual heats produced,

$$H = H_1 + H_2 + H_3$$

$$\therefore \quad I_{r.m.s.}^2 Rt = I_{dc}^2 Rt + \left(\frac{I_{m2}}{\sqrt{2}}\right)^2 Rt + \left(\frac{I_{m3}}{\sqrt{2}}\right)^2 Rt$$

$$\therefore \quad I_{r.m.s.} = \sqrt{I_{dc}^2 + \left(\frac{I_{m2}}{\sqrt{2}}\right)^2 + \left(\frac{I_{m3}}{\sqrt{2}}\right)^2}$$

Key Point *The result can be extended to n number of current components flowing through the wire.*

If average value is to be calculated, it must be noted that average value of purely sinusoidal quantity over a cycle is zero. Hence average value of the resultant is the only d.c. component flowing through the wire.

$$\therefore \quad I_{av} = I_{dc}$$

Example 3.9.1 *Find the effective value of a resultant current in a wire which carries simultaneously a direct current of 10 A and alternating current given by,*
$i = 12 \sin \omega t + 6 \sin (3\omega t - \pi/6) + 4 \sin(5\omega t + \pi/3)$.

Solution : The **effective** value means **r.m.s.** value. It is based on the heating effect of the currents.

$$I_{dc} = 10 \text{ A}, \ I_{m1} = 12 \text{ A}, \ I_{m2} = 6 \text{ A}, \ I_{m3} = 4 \text{ A},$$

Let, $I_{r.m.s.}$ = Resultant r.m.s. value, R = Resistance of wire.

Equating heat produced in time t due to resultant to the sum of individual heats produced by various components.

$$\therefore \quad I_{r.m.s.}^2 \times R \times t = I_{dc}^2 \times R \times t + \left(\frac{I_{m1}}{\sqrt{2}}\right)^2 \times R \times t + \left(\frac{I_{m2}}{\sqrt{2}}\right)^2 \times R \times t + \left(\frac{I_{m3}}{\sqrt{2}}\right)^2 \times R \times t$$

Note that heat produced $= (\text{r.m.s. value})^2 \times R \times t$

and r.m.s. of a.c. $= \dfrac{I_m}{\sqrt{2}}$

$$\therefore \qquad I^2_{\text{r.m.s.}} = 10^2 + \left(\frac{12}{\sqrt{2}}\right)^2 + \left(\frac{6}{\sqrt{2}}\right)^2 + \left(\frac{4}{\sqrt{2}}\right)^2 = 198$$

$$\therefore \qquad I_{\text{r.m.s.}} = \mathbf{14.0712 \ A} \qquad\qquad \text{...Effective value of the resultant}$$

Review Question

> 1. *How to obtain effective value if multiple alternating currents are flowing through a conductor ?*

3.10 Phasor Representation of an Alternating Quantity   `2010-11`

The sinusoidally varying alternating quantity can be represented graphically by a straight line with an arrow in the phasor representation method.

The length of the line represents the magnitude of the quantity and arrow indicates its direction. This is similar to a vector representation. Such a line is called a **phasor.**

> The phasors are assumed to be rotated in anticlockwise direction with a constant speed ω rad/sec.

One complete cycle of a sine wave is represented by one complete rotation of a phasor. The anticlockwise direction of rotation is purely a conventional direction which has been universally adopted.

Consider a phasor, rotating in anticlockwise direction, with uniform angular velocity, with its starting position 'a' as shown in the Fig. 3.10.1.

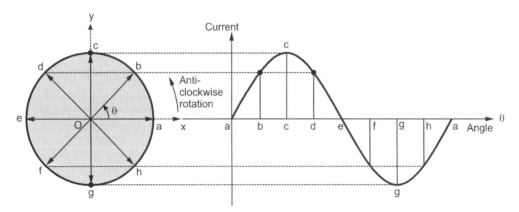

Fig. 3.10.1 Phasor representation of an alternating quantity

If the projections of this phasor on Y-axis are plotted against the angle turned through 'θ', (or time as θ = ω t), we get a sine waveform.

Consider the various positions shown in the Fig. 3.10.1.

1. At point 'a', the Y-axis projection is zero. The instantaneous value of the current is also zero.

2. At point 'b', the Y-axis projection is [l(Ob) sin θ]. The length of the phasor is equal to the maximum value of an alternating quantity. So, instantaneous value of the current at this position is i = I_m sin θ, represented in the waveform.

3. At point 'c', the Y-axis projection 'Oc' represents entire length of the phasor i.e. instantaneous value equal to the maximum value of current I_m.

4. Similarly, at point d, the Y-axis projection becomes I_m sin θ which is the instantaneous value of the current at that instant.

5. At point 'e', the Y-axis projection is zero and instantaneous value of the current is zero at this instant.

6. Similarly, at points f, g, h the Y-axis projections give us instantaneous values of the current at the respective instants and when plotted, give us negative half cycle of the alternating quantity.

Thus, if the length of the phasor is taken equal to the maximum value of the alternating quantity, then its rotation in space at any instant is such that the length of its projection on the Y-axis gives the instantaneous value of the alternating quantity at that particular instant.

The angular velocity 'ω' in an anticlockwise direction of the phasor should be such that it completes one revolution in the same time as taken by the alternating quantity to complete one cycle i.e. θ = ω t, where ω = 2π f rad/sec.

> **Points to Remember :**
>
> i) In practice, the alternating quantities are represented by their r.m.s. values. Hence, the length of the phasor represents r.m.s. value of the alternating quantity. In such case, projection on Y-axis does not give directly the instantaneous value but as $I_m = \sqrt{2}\,I_{r.m.s.}$, the projection on Y-axis must be multiplied by $\sqrt{2}$ to get an instantaneous value of that alternating quantity.
>
> ii) Phasors are always assumed to be rotated in **anticlockwise** direction.
>
> iii) Two alternating quantities of same frequencies can be represented on same phasor diagram.

Review Questions

1. *What is phasor ? How a rotating phasor represents an alternating quantity ?*

2. *Explain the phasor representation of sinusoidal quantities.*   **2010-11, Marks 5**

3.11 Concept of Phase and Phase Difference   2001-02

In the analysis of alternating quantities, it is necessary to know the position of the phasor representing that alternating quantity at a particular instant. It is represented in terms of angle θ in radians or degrees, measured from certain reference.

> **Phase :** The phase of an alternating quantity at any instant is the angle φ (in radians or degrees) traveled by the phasor representing that alternating quantity upto the instant of consideration, measured from the reference.

Let X-axis be the reference axis. So, phase of the alternating current shown in the Fig. 3.11.1 at the instant A is φ = 0°. While the phase of the current at the instant B is the angle φ through which the phasor has traveled, measured from the reference axis i.e. X-axis. In general, the phase φ of an alternating quantity varies from φ = 0 to 2 π radians or   φ = 0° to 360°.

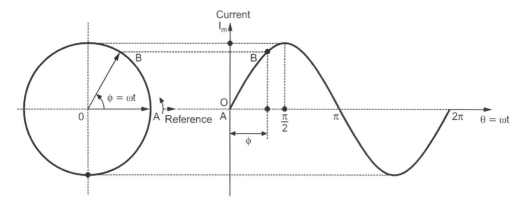

Fig. 3.11.1 Concept of phase

In terms of phase, the equation of an alternating quantity can be modified as,

> $e = E_m \sin(\omega t \pm \phi)$ where φ = Phase of the alternating quantity

Let us consider three cases;

Case 1 : φ = 0° :

When phase of an alternating quantity is zero, it is standard pure sinusoidal quantity having instantaneous value zero at t = 0. This is shown in the Fig. 3.11.2 (a).

Case 2 : Positive phase φ :

When phase of an alternating quantity is positive it means that quantity has **some positive instantaneous value at t = 0.** This is shown in the Fig. 3.11.2 (b).

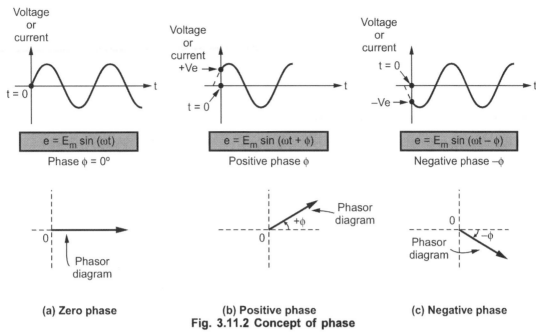

(a) Zero phase   (b) Positive phase   (c) Negative phase

Fig. 3.11.2 Concept of phase

Case 3 : Negative phase ϕ :

When phase of an alternating quantity is negative it means that quantity has **some negative instantaneous value at t = 0**. This is shown in the Fig. 3.11.2 (c).

1. The **phase** is measured with respect to **reference direction** i.e. positive X-axis direction.

2. The **phase** measured in **anticlockwise** direction is **positive** while the **phase** measured in **clockwise** direction is **negative**.

The **difference between the phases of the two alternating quantities is called the phase difference** which is nothing but the angle difference between the two phasors representing the two alternating quantities.

1. Zero Phase Difference : Consider the two alternating quantities having same frequency f Hz having different maximum values.

$$e \; = \; E_m \sin (\omega t) \quad \text{and} \quad i = I_m \sin (\omega t) \qquad \text{where} \quad E_m > I_m$$

The phasor representation and waveforms of both the quantities are shown in the Fig. 3.11.3. So, at any instant, we can say that the phase of voltage e will be same as phase of i. The difference between the phases of the two quantities is zero at any instant.

*When such **phase difference** between the two alternating quantities is **zero**, the two quantities are said to be **in phase**.*

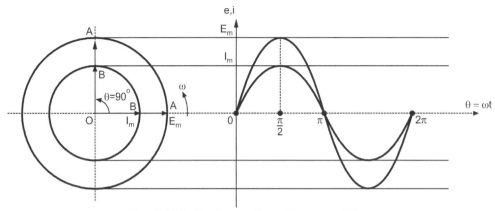

Fig. 3.11.3 In phase alternating quantities

In the a.c. analysis, it is not necessary that all the alternating quantities must be always in phase. It is possible that if one is achieving its zero value and at the same instant the other is having some negative value or positive value then such two quantities are said to have **phase difference** between them.

2. Lagging Phase Difference :   Consider an e.m.f. having maximum value E_m and current having maximum value I_m.

Now, when e.m.f. 'e' is at its zero value, the current 'i' has some negative value as shown in the Fig. 3.11.4. Thus, there exists a phase difference ϕ between the two phasors.

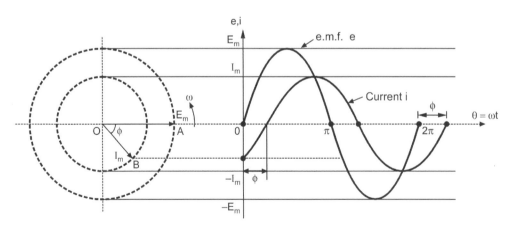

Fig. 3.11.4 Concept of phase difference (Lag)

Now, as the two are rotating in anticlockwise direction, we can say that current is falling back with respect to voltage, at all the instants by angle ϕ. This is called **lagging phase difference.** The current i is said to lag the voltage e by angle ϕ. The current i achieves its maximum and zero values, ϕ angle later than the corresponding maximum and zero values of voltage.

The equations of the two quantities are written as,

$e = E_m \sin \omega t$ and $i = I_m \sin(\omega t - \phi)$ and   'i' is said to lag 'e' by angle ϕ.

3. Leading Phase Difference :

It is possible in practice that the current 'i' may have some positive value when voltage 'e' is zero. This is shown in the Fig. 3.11.5. It can be seen that there exists a phase difference of ϕ angle between the two. But in this case, current 'i' is ahead of voltage 'e', as both are rotating in anticlockwise direction with same speed. Thus, current is said to be leading with respect to voltage and the phase difference is called **leading phase difference.**

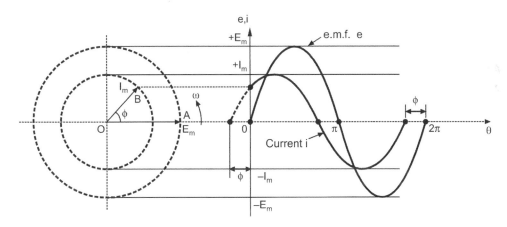

Fig. 3.11.5 Concept of phase difference (Lead)

At all instants, current i is going to remain ahead of voltage 'e' by angle 'ϕ'. The equations of such two quantities are written as

$e = E_m \sin \omega t$ and $i = I_m \sin(\omega t + \phi)$ and   'i' is said to lead 'e' by angle ϕ.

3.11.1 Phasor Diagram

The diagram in which different alternating quantities of the same frequency, sinusoidal in nature are represented by individual phasors indicating exact phase interrelationships is known as **phasor diagram.**

All phasors have a particular fixed position with respect to each other.

Phasor diagram can be considered as a still picture of these phasors at a particular instant.

Example 3.11.1 *Two sinusoidal currents are given by, $i_1 = 10 \sin(\omega t + \pi/3)$ and $i_2 = 15 \sin(\omega t - \pi/4)$. Calculate the phase difference between them in degrees.*

Solution : The phase of current i_1 is $\pi/3$ radians i.e. $60°$ while the phase of the current i_2 is $-\pi/4$ radians i.e. $-45°$. This is shown in the Fig. 3.11.6.

Hence the phase difference between the two is,

$$\phi = \theta_1 - \theta_2 = 60° - (-45°) = 105°$$

And i_2 lags i_1.

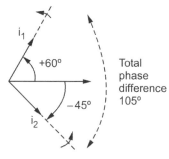

Fig. 3.11.6

Example 3.11.2 *In a certain circuit supplied from 50 Hz mains, the potential difference has a maximum value of 500 volt and the current has a maximum value of 10 Amp. At the instant t = 0, the instantaneous values of potential difference and current are 400 volt and 4 Amp respectively both increasing in positive direction. State expressions for instantaneous values of potential difference and current at time 't'. Calculate the instantaneous values at time t = 0.015 second. Find phase angle between potential difference and current.*   **2001-02, Marks 10**

Solution : $f = 50$ Hz, $V_m = 500$ V, $I_m = 10$ A

It is given that $t = 0$, $v = 400$ V and not zero hence it has phase ϕ_1. So its equation is,

$$v = V_m \sin(\omega t + \phi_1) \quad \text{and at } t = 0, \quad 400 = 500 \sin(0 + \phi_1)$$

$$\therefore \qquad \phi_1 = \sin^{-1}\left(\frac{4}{5}\right) = 53.13° = \textbf{0.9272 rad}$$

$$\therefore \qquad v = 500 \sin(2\pi ft + \phi_1) = \textbf{500 sin(100 } \pi \textbf{ t + 0.9272)V}$$

While at $t = 0$, $i = 4$ A hence it has phase ϕ_2. So its equation is $\quad i = I_m \sin(\omega t + \phi_2)$

So at $t = 0$, $\quad 4 = 10 \sin(0 + \phi_2) \quad$ i.e. $\quad \phi_2 = \sin^{-1}\left(\frac{4}{10}\right) = 23.5781° = \textbf{0.4115 rad}$

$$\therefore \quad i = 10 \sin(2\pi ft + \phi_2) \quad \text{i.e.} \quad \textbf{i = 10 sin(100 } \pi \textbf{ t + 0.4115) A}$$

At $t = 0.015$ sec, $v = 500 \sin(100\pi \times 0.015 + 0.9272) = \textbf{- 300.038 V}$ **...Use radian mode**

$$i = 10 \sin(100\pi \times 0.015 + 0.4115) = \textbf{- 9.1652 A}$$

The phasor diagram is shown in the Fig. 3.11.7.

Phase difference i.e. phase angle between

V and I $\quad = 53.13° - 23.5781°$

$$= \textbf{29.5515°, I lags V}$$

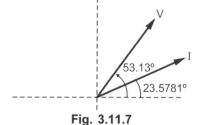

Fig. 3.11.7

Review Questions

1. *Explain the concept of phase and phase difference in alternating quantities.*

2. *Two sinusoidal sources of e.m.f. have r.m.s. values E_1 and E_2 and a phase difference α. When connected in series, the resultant voltage is 41.1 V.*
   When one of the source is reversed, the resultant e.m.f. is 17.52 V. When phase displacement is made zero, the resultant e.m.f. is 42.5 V. Calculate E_1, E_2 and α.
   [Ans. : E_1 = 28.14 V and E_2 = 14.35 V, E_1 = 14.35 V and E_2 = 28.14 V, 31.11°]

3. *At t = 0, the instantaneous value of a 60-Hz sinusoidal current is + 5 ampere and increases in magnitude further. Its r.m.s. value is 10-A.*
   i) Write the expression for its instantaneous value.
   ii) Find the current at t = 0.01 and t = 0.015 second.
   iii) Sketch the waveform indicating these values.
   [Ans. : $14.1421 \sin(120\pi t + 0.3613)$ A, – 11.8202 A, – 3.7214 A]

3.12 Addition and Subtraction of Alternating Quantities

2001-02, 2003-04, 2005-06, 2009-10

It is often required in a.c. analysis to add or subtract the two or more alternating quantities with same frequency but different amplitudes and phases. This is called **vector addition** or **subtraction** of the alternating quantities. The vector addition is possible by analytical method or graphical method.

3.12.1 Graphical Method

In this method, **the phasor diagram is required to be plotted to the scale**. Choose certain reference phasor and draw it along positive X direction. At that instant, the remaining phasors to be added having their own phases. Draw these remaining phasors one after the another, considering their individual phases appropriately. Join the last

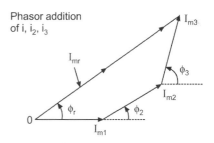

Fig. 3.12.1 Phasor addition

point with the origin to complete the vector polygon. The length of this phasor from origin to last point represents maximum or r.m.s. value of the resultant quantity and angle made by this phasor with respect to reference is the phase of the resultant quantity. This is shown in the Fig. 3.12.1.

For analytical method, it is necessary to study the mathematical representation of phasor.

3.12.2 Mathematical Representation of Phasor

Mathematically phasors are represented using two co-ordinate systems called i) polar co-ordinate system and ii) Rectangular co-ordinate system.

3.12.2.1 Polar Co-ordinate System

Consider an alternating current given by, $i = I_m \sin(\omega t + \phi)$

Thus its maximum value is I_m and phase is $+\phi$. The phase ϕ is always measured with respect to positive X-axis direction.

While representing this phasor by polar system, it is represented as $r \angle \phi$.

$r = I_m$ and ϕ is angle with respect to $+$ ve X-axis.

So draw a line at an angle ϕ measured with respect to $+$ ve X-axis from the origin. And measure a distance equal to $r = I_m$ on it.

The line OA represents polar representation of phasor. This is shown in the Fig. 3.12.2.

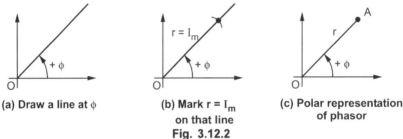

(a) Draw a line at ϕ　　(b) Mark $r = I_m$ on that line　　(c) Polar representation of phasor

Fig. 3.12.2

The angle ϕ can be positive or negative.

The **positive** ϕ is measured in **anticlockwise** direction while the **negative** ϕ is measured in **clockwise** direction.

While r is always positive and called **magnitude** of the phasor. The angle ϕ is called **phase** of that phasor.

Thus mathematically the polar representation of a phasor is,

> Polar representation $= r \angle \pm \phi$

Practically instead of $r = I_m$, r.m.s. value is used as the magnitude r.

The polar form of an alternating quantity can be easily obtained from its instantaneous equation directly.

> If $e = E_m \sin(\omega t \pm \phi)$ then polar form is,
>
> $E = E \angle \pm \phi$ where E is r.m.s. value $= \dfrac{E_m}{\sqrt{2}}$.

Key Point *The r.m.s. value of an alternating quantity exists in its polar form and not in rectangular form.* **Thus to find r.m.s. value of an alternating quantity express it in polar form.**

3.12.2.2 Rectangular Co-ordinate System

Mathematically an alternating quantity can be divided into two components, X-component and Y-component.

If an alternating current is $i = I_m \sin(\omega t + \phi)$ then,

X-component $= I_m \cos \phi$ and   Y-component $= I_m \sin \phi$

Thus to represent the phasor, travel ($I_m \cos\phi$) in +X direction then travel ($I_m \sin\phi$) in +Y direction. Joining final point to origin gives the required phasor OA as shown in the Fig. 3.12.3.

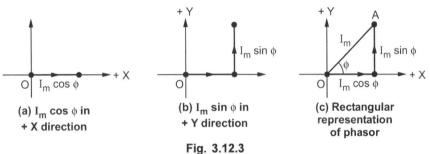

(a) $I_m \cos \phi$ in + X direction

(b) $I_m \sin \phi$ in + Y direction

(c) Rectangular representation of phasor

Fig. 3.12.3

The X and Y components can be positive or negative. To indicate that X and Y components are perpendicular to each other, the operator 'j' is used in mathematical representation of phasor in rectangular co-ordinate system.

Mathematically operator $j = \sqrt{-1}$ which indicates $90°$ anticlockwise rotation of the phasor.

Thus mathematically the rectangular representation of a phasor is,

Rectangular representation $= \pm X \pm j\, Y$

Practically instead of maximum value, r.m.s. value is used to find X and Y components.

3.12.2.3 Polar to Rectangular Conversion

Let a phasor is represented in polar form as shown in the Fig. 3.12.4.

It is necessary to find X and Y components in terms of r and ϕ.

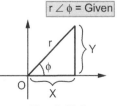

$r \angle \phi$ = Given

Fig. 3.12.4

From the Fig. 3.12.4,

X component = r cos ϕ and Y component = r sin ϕ

$\therefore$ | Rectangular representation = r cos ϕ + j r sin ϕ |

3.12.2.4 Rectangular to Polar Conversion

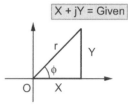

Let a phasor is represented in rectangular form X + j Y, as shown in the Fig. 3.12.5.

It is necessary to find r and ϕ in terms of X and Y.

From the Fig. 3.12.5,

$$r = \sqrt{X^2 + Y^2} \quad \text{and} \quad \phi = \tan^{-1} \frac{Y}{X}$$

Fig. 3.12.5

$\therefore$ | Polar representation = r $\angle \phi = \sqrt{X^2 + Y^2} \angle \tan^{-1} \frac{Y}{X}$ |

The polar form always gives r.m.s. value of an alternating quantity.

Important Note : To obtain polar form from the instantaneous equation, express the given equation in sine form instead of cosine form.

If, e = E_m cos ($\omega t \pm \phi$) then express it as,

e = E_m sin ($\omega t + 90° \pm \phi$)

$\therefore$ Phase of alternating quantity = 90° $\pm \phi$.

Instead of using above relations, use the polar to rectangular (P $\rightarrow$ R) and rectangular to polar (R $\rightarrow$ P) functions available on calculator for the required conversions.

Example 3.12.1 *Write the polar form of the voltage given by,*

V = 100 sin (100 π t + π / 6) V

Obtain its rectangular form.

Solution : V_m = 100 V and $\phi = +\frac{\pi}{6}$ rad = + 30°, $V_{r.m.s.} = \frac{V_m}{\sqrt{2}}$ = 70.7106 V

$\therefore$ In polar form = **70.7106** $\angle$ **+ 30° V**

$\therefore$ Rectangular form = **61.2371 + j 35.3553 V**

Key Point *The r.m.s. vlaue of an alternating quantity exists in its polar form and not in rectangular form.* **Thus to find r.m.s. value of an alternating quantity express it in polar form.**

Example 3.12.2 *A voltage is defined as* $- E_m \cos \omega t$. *Express it in polar form.*

Solution : To express a voltage in polar form express it in the form, $e = E_m \sin \omega t$

Now $\qquad e = - E_m \cos \omega t = - E_m \sin \left(\omega t + \dfrac{\pi}{2} \right)$ $\qquad\qquad$ as $\sin \left(\omega t + \dfrac{\pi}{2} \right) = \cos \omega t$

$\qquad\qquad\quad = E_m \sin \left(\omega t + \dfrac{3\pi}{2} \right)$ $\qquad\qquad$ as $\sin (\pi + \theta) = - \sin \theta$

Now it can be expressed in polar form as,

$$e = E_m \angle + \dfrac{3\pi}{2} \text{ rad} = E_m \angle + 270° \text{ V}$$

But $+ 270°$ phase is nothing but $- 90°$

$\therefore \qquad\qquad e = \mathbf{E_m} \angle - \mathbf{90° \ V}$

3.12.3 Analytical Method

> For addition and substraction of phasors, use rectangular representation of phasors.

While in addition of phasors, their X components get added and Y components get added.

While in substraction of phasors their X components get substracted and Y components get substracted.

If $\qquad \overline{P} = a_1 + jb_1 \quad$ and $\quad \overline{Q} = a_2 + jb_2 \quad$ then

$\overline{P} + \overline{Q} = (a_1 + a_2) + j(b_1 + b_2), \quad \overline{P} - \overline{Q} = (a_1 - a_2) + j(b_1 - b_2)$

The result finally can be expressed in polar form, if required.

Example 3.12.3 *The instantaneous values of two alternating voltages are represented by* $v_1 = 60 \sin \theta$ *and* $v_2 = 40 \sin (\theta - \pi/3)$. *Derive an expressions for the instantaneous values of i) the sum and ii) the difference of these voltages.* **2001-02, Marks 5**

Solution : Use **rectangular form** for addition and subtraction.

$$v_1 = 60 \sin \theta = 60 \angle 0° \text{ V} = 60 + j0 \text{ V}$$

$$v_2 = 40 \sin\left(\theta - \frac{\pi}{3}\right) = 40 \angle -\frac{\pi}{3} V = 40 \angle -60° \, V = 20 - j\,34.64 \, V$$

i) $\quad \overline{V}_1 + \overline{V}_2 = 60 + j0 + 20 - j34.64 = 80 - j34.64 \, V = \mathbf{87.177 \angle -23.41° \, V}$

$\therefore \quad \left(\overline{V}_1 + \overline{V}_2\right) = \mathbf{87.177 \sin(\theta - 23.41°) V}$

ii) $\quad \overline{V}_1 - \overline{V}_2 = 60 + j0 - 20 + j\,34.64 = 40 + j\,34.64 \, V = \mathbf{52.914 \angle 40.892° \, V}$

$\therefore \quad \left(\overline{V}_1 - \overline{V}_2\right) = \mathbf{52.914 \sin(\theta + 40.892°) \, V}$

Example 3.12.4 *Two a.c. voltages are represented by - $v_1(t) = 30 \sin(314t+45°)$, $v_2(t) = 60 \sin(314t+60°)$. Calculate the resultant voltage v(t) and express in the form $v(t) = V_m \sin(314t + \phi)$.* **2003-04, Marks 5**

Solution : Comparing given equations with $V_m \sin(\omega t + \phi)$,

For $v_1(t)$, $V_{m1} = 30$ and $\phi_1 = 45°$

For $v_2(t)$, $V_{m2} = 60$ and $\phi_2 = 60°$

$\therefore \qquad V_1 = V_{r.m.s.1} \angle \phi_1 = \dfrac{30}{\sqrt{2}} \angle 45° \, V = 15 + j\,15 \, V$

and $\qquad V_2 = V_{r.m.s.2} \angle \phi_2 = \dfrac{60}{\sqrt{2}} \angle 60° \, V = 21.2132 + j\,36.7423 \, V$

For addition, use rectangular co-ordinates,

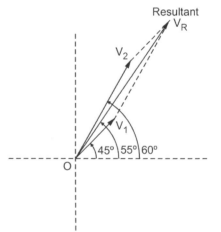

$\therefore \qquad \overline{V}_R = \overline{V}_1 + \overline{V}_2$

$\qquad\qquad = (15 + 21.2132) + j\,(15 + 36.7423)$

$\qquad\qquad = (36.2132 + j\,51.7423) \, V$

$\qquad\qquad = 63.1558 \angle 55° \, V$

$\therefore \quad V_{R \,(maximum)} = \sqrt{2} \times V_{R(r.m.s.)}$

$\qquad\qquad = \sqrt{2} \times 63.1558 = 89.3157$

Thus the resultant voltage is,

$\qquad \mathbf{v(t) = 89.3157 \sin(314\,t + 55°) \, V}$

Fig. 3.12.6

Example 3.12.5 *Draw a phasor diagram showing the following voltages :*

$\left.\begin{array}{l} v_1 = 100 \sin 500\,t, \ v_2 = 200 \sin(500\,t + \pi/3) \\ v_3 = -50 \cos 500\,t, \ v_4 = 150 \sin(500\,t - \pi/4) \end{array}\right]$ *Find r.m.s. value of resultant voltage.*

2005-06, Marks 5

Solution :

	V_m	$V_{r.m.s.} = \dfrac{V_m}{\sqrt{2}}$	Phase	Polar form	Rectangular form
$v_1 = 100 \sin (500\, t)$	100	70.7106	$0°$	$70.7106\angle 0°$	$70.7106 + j\, 0$
$v_2 = 200 \sin\left(500t + \dfrac{\pi}{3}\right)$	200	141.421	$60°$	$141.421\angle 60°$	$70.7105 + j122.474$
$v_3 = -50\cos (500\, t)$ $= -50 \sin (500\, t + 90°)$ $= 50 \sin (500\, t - 90°)$	50	35.3553	$-90°$	$35.3553\angle -90°$	$0 - j\, 35.3553$
$v_4 = 150 \sin\left(500\, t - \dfrac{\pi}{4}\right)$	150	106.066	$-45°$	$106.066\angle -45°$	$75 - j\, 75$

The phasor diagram is shown in the Fig. 3.12.7.

$$\overline{V}_R = \overline{V}_1 + \overline{V}_2 + \overline{V}_3 + \overline{V}_4$$

... Use rectangular form

$$= 216.4212 + j\, 12.1184 \ V$$

... Resultant

$$= \mathbf{216.76 \angle 3.205° \ V}$$

Thus r.m.s. value of the resultant is **216.76 V**.

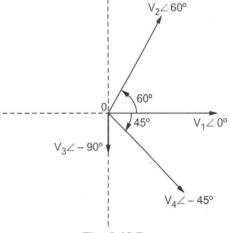

Fig. 3.12.7

Example 3.12.6 *Three voltages represented by the following equations, $e_1 = 15\sin\omega t$, $e_2 = 5\sin(\omega t + \pi/6)$; $e_3 = 10\cos\omega t$ together in an a.c. circuit. Represent these voltages by phasor and calculate an expression for the resultant voltage. Check the result so obtained graphically.*   **2009-10, Marks 10**

Solution : $e_1 = 15\sin\omega t$, $e_2 = 5\sin\left(\omega t + \dfrac{\pi}{6}\right)$, $e_3 = 10\cos\omega t$

$\therefore \qquad e_1 = 15\angle 0° = 15 + j\, 0 \ V, \qquad e_2 = 5\angle\dfrac{\pi}{6} = 5\angle 30° = 4.33 + j\, 2.5 \ V$

$\qquad\qquad e_3 = 10\cos\omega t = 10\sin\left(\omega t + \dfrac{\pi}{2}\right) \quad$ i.e. $\quad e_3 = 10\angle 90° = 0 + j10 \ V$

$\therefore \quad e_1 + e_2 + e_3 = 19.33 + j12.5 \ V = 23.019\angle 32.88° \ V$

$\therefore \qquad\qquad e_R = \mathbf{23.019 \sin (\omega t + 32.88°) \ V}$ ...Resultant

Graphical solution : Choose scale as 1 unit = 2 V. Represent each phasor and add them as shown in the Fig. 3.12.8.

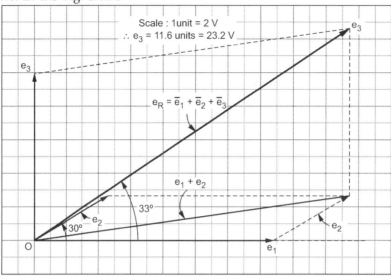

Fig. 3.12.8

Graphically, $e_R = 23.2\angle 33° \text{ V}$ i.e. $e_R = \textbf{23.2 sin } (\omega t + 33°) \textbf{ V}$

Thus the results obtained analytically and graphically match with each other.

1. *Explain the addition and substraction of two phasors.*

2. *Explain the mathematical representation of phasors.*

3. *Add the two given voltages and find the R.M.S. value and phase of the resultant.*

   $v_1(t) = 141.42 \sin (100\pi t) \text{ V}, v_2(t) = 282.842 \sin \left(100\pi t - \dfrac{\pi}{4} \right) \text{ V. Draw the phasor diagram.}$

   [Ans. : 279.79 V, –30.36°]

4. *Four wires p, q, r, s are connected to a common point. The currents in lines p, q and r are*

   $6 \sin \left(\omega t + \dfrac{\pi}{6} \right); 5 \cos \left(\omega t + \dfrac{\pi}{3} \right) \text{ and } \cos \left(\omega t + \dfrac{\pi}{3} \right)$ *respectively. Find the current in wire 's'.*
   [Ans. : 7.211 sin (ωt – 76.102°) A]

5. *Find the resultant of three voltages given by* $v_1 = 10 \sin \omega t,$
   $v_2 = 20 \sin(\omega t - \pi/4) \text{ and } v_3 = 30 \cos(\omega t + \pi/6)$
   [Ans. : 14.9575 ∠52.3239° V, 14.9575 sin(ωt + 52.3239°)V]

6. *Find the resultant of the three voltages* e_1, e_2 *and* e_3 *where,*

   $e_1 = 20 \sin (\omega t), \quad e_2 = 30 \sin \left(\omega t - \dfrac{\pi}{4} \right) \text{ and } e_3 = \cos \left(\omega t + \dfrac{\pi}{6} \right)$

   [Ans. : 25.1058 sin (ωt + 32.33°) V]

7. *The two voltages having r.m.s. values of 100 V and 120 V have a phase difference of 45°. Find the r.m.s. value of resultant sum and its phase.* **[Ans. : 203.3975 V, – 24.65°]**

3.13 Multiplication and Division of Phasors   2009-10

For multiplication and division of phasors, use **polar** representation of phasors.

If $\overline{P} = a_1 + jb_1$ and $\overline{Q} = a_2 + jb_2$ then convert them to polar form.

$\therefore \qquad \overline{P} = \sqrt{a_1^2 + b_1^2} \angle \phi_1 \quad$ and $\quad \overline{Q} = \sqrt{a_2^2 + b_2^2} \angle \phi_2$

$$\overline{P} \times \overline{Q} = |\overline{P}||\overline{Q}| \angle \phi_1 + \phi_2 = \left[\sqrt{a_1^2 + b_1^2} \times \sqrt{a_2^2 + b_2^2} \right] \angle \phi_1 + \phi_2$$

$$\frac{\overline{P}}{\overline{Q}} = \frac{|\overline{P}|}{|\overline{Q}|} \angle \phi_1 - \phi_2 = \frac{\sqrt{a_1^2 + b_1^2}}{\sqrt{a_2^2 + b_2^2}} \angle \phi_1 - \phi_2$$

In multiplication, magnitudes get multiplied and angles get added. In division, magnitudes get divided and angles get subtracted.

Remember

For **addition and subtraction**, use the **rectangular co-ordinate system.**

For **multiplication and division**, use the **polar co-ordinate system.**

Example 3.13.1 *If A = 4 + j 7; B = 8 + j 9 and C = 5 – j 6 then calculate*

i) $\dfrac{A+B}{C}$ *ii)* $\dfrac{A \times B}{C}$ *iii)* $\dfrac{A+B}{B+C}$ *iv)* $\dfrac{B-C}{A}$

Solution : $A = 4 + j\,7 = 8.062 \angle 60.255°, \quad B = 8 + j9 = 12.041 \angle 8.366°$

$\qquad\qquad\quad C = 5 - j\,6 = 7.8102 \angle -50.194°$

i) $\qquad \dfrac{A+B}{C} = \dfrac{4 + j7 + 8 + j9}{7.8102 \angle -50.194°} = \dfrac{12 + j16}{7.8102 \angle -50.194°} = \dfrac{20 \angle 53.13°}{7.8102 \angle -50.194°}$

$\qquad\qquad\quad = 2.5607 \angle 103.324° = -0.5901 + j\,2.4917$

ii) $\qquad \dfrac{A \times B}{C} = \dfrac{8.062 \angle 60.255° \times 12.041 \angle 48.366°}{7.8102 \angle -50.194°} = \dfrac{97.0745 \angle 108.621°}{7.8102 \angle -50.194°}$

$\qquad\qquad\quad = 12.4291 \angle 158.815° = -11.5891 + j4.\,4916$

iii) $\qquad \dfrac{A+B}{B+C} = \dfrac{20 \angle 53.13°}{8 + j9 + 5 - j6} = \dfrac{20 \angle 53.13°}{13 + j3} \qquad$ ...Using A+B calculated in (i)

$\qquad\qquad\quad = \dfrac{20 \angle 53.13°}{13.341 \angle 2.99°} = 1.499 \angle 40.14° = 1.1459 + j\,0.966$

iv) $\dfrac{B-C}{A} = \dfrac{(8 + j\,9) - (5 - j\,6)}{8.062 \angle 60.255^\circ} = \dfrac{3 + j5}{8.062 \angle 60.255^\circ} = \dfrac{15.297 \angle 78.69^\circ}{8.062 \angle 60.255^\circ}$

$$= 1.8974 \angle 18.435^\circ = 1.8 + j0.6$$

Review Question

1. *For the two phasors* $A = a_1 + j\,b_1$ *and* $B = a_2 + j\,b_2$, *obtain their multiplication and division using polar form of representation.* **2009-10, Marks 5**

3.14 A.C. through Pure Resistance

2002-03

Consider a simple circuit consisting of a pure resistance 'R' ohms connected across a voltage $v = V_m \sin \omega t$.

The circuit is shown in the Fig. 3.14.1.

According to Ohm's law, we can find the equation for the current i as,

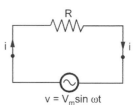

Fig. 3.14.1 Pure resistive circuit

$$i = \frac{v}{R} = \frac{V_m \sin \omega t}{R} \quad \text{i.e.} \quad i = \left(\frac{V_m}{R}\right) \sin (\omega t)$$

This is the equation giving instantaneous value of the current.

Comparing this with standard equation, $i = I_m \sin (\omega t + \phi)$

$$I_m = \frac{V_m}{R} \quad \text{and} \quad \phi = 0^\circ$$

So, maximum value of alternating current, i is $I_m = \dfrac{V_m}{R}$ while as $\phi = 0$, it indicates that it is in phase with the voltage applied.

In purely resistive circuit, the current and the voltage applied are in phase with each other.

The waveforms of voltage and current and the corresponding phasor diagram is shown in the Fig. 3.14.2 (a) and (b).

In the phasor diagram, the phasors are drawn in phase and there is no phase difference in between them. Phasors represent the **r.m.s. values** of alternating quantities.

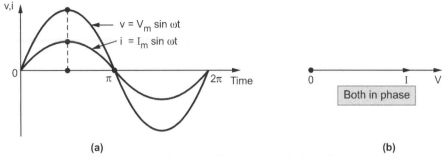

(a)   (b)

Fig. 3.14.2 A.C. through purely resistive circuit

3.14.1 Power

The instantaneous power in a.c. circuits can be obtained by taking product of the instantaneous values of current and voltage.

$$P = v \times i = V_m \sin(\omega t) \times I_m \sin \omega t = V_m I_m \sin^2(\omega t) = \frac{V_m I_m}{2} (1 - \cos 2\,\omega\,t)$$

∴
$$P = \frac{V_m I_m}{2} - \frac{V_m I_m}{2} \cos (2\,\omega\,t)$$

From the above equation, it is clear that the instantaneous power consists of two components,

1)   Constant power component $\left(\dfrac{V_m I_m}{2} \right)$

2)   Fluctuating component $\left[\dfrac{V_m I_m}{2} \cos(2\omega t) \right]$ having frequency, double the frequency of the applied voltage.

The average value of the fluctuating cosine component of double frequency is zero, over one complete cycle.

So, average power consumption over one cycle is equal to the constant power component i.e. $\dfrac{V_m I_m}{2}$ which is half of the peak power $V_m I_m$.

∴
$$P_{av} = \frac{V_m I_m}{2} = \frac{V_m}{\sqrt{2}} \cdot \frac{I_m}{\sqrt{2}}$$

∴
$$P_{av} = V_{r.m.s.} \times I_{r.m.s.} \text{ watts}$$

Generally, r.m.s. values are indicated by capital letters.

∴
$$P_{av} = V \times I \quad \text{watts} = I^2 R \quad \text{watts}$$

The Fig. 3.14.3 shows the waveforms of voltage, current and power.

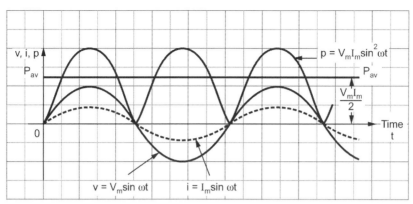

Fig. 3.14.3 v, i and p for purely resistive circuit

Example 3.14.1 *A 100 ohm resistance is carrying a sinusoidal current given by 3 cos ωt. Determine; (i) instantaneous power taken by resistance, (ii) average power.*

2002-03, Marks 5

Solution : $R = 100 \ \Omega$, $i = 3 \cos \omega t$

Now $\qquad i = 3 \cos \omega t = 3 \sin (\omega t + 90°)$

$\therefore \qquad v = iR = 300 \sin (\omega t + 90°)$

i) $\therefore \qquad p = vi = 3 \sin (\omega t + 90°) \times 300 \sin (\omega t + 90°)$

$\qquad\qquad = 900 \sin^2 (\omega t + 90°) = \mathbf{900 \cos^2 (\omega t) \ W}$

ii) $\qquad P_{av} = V_{r.m.s.} \ I_{r.m.s.} \cos \phi \quad$ and $\quad I_m = 3 \ A, \ V_m = 300 \ V, \ \phi = 0°$

$\therefore \qquad P_{av} = \dfrac{3}{\sqrt{2}} \times \dfrac{300}{\sqrt{2}} \times 1 = \mathbf{450 \ W}$

Review Questions

1. *With the help of phasor diagram and waveform comment on the phase realtion between voltage and current in purely resistive circuit.*

2. *Derive an expression for the instantaneous power in a pure resistor energised by sinusoidal voltage.*

3.15 A.C. through Pure Inductance

Consider a simple circuit consisting of a pure inductance of L henries, connected across a voltage given by the equation, $v = V_m \sin \omega t$.

The circuit is shown in the Fig. 3.15.1.

Pure inductance has zero ohmic resistance. Its internal resistance is zero. The coil has pure inductance of L henries (H).

When alternating current 'i' flows through inductance 'L', it sets up an alternating magnetic field around the inductance.

L

$\longleftarrow e$

i $\qquad\qquad\qquad$ i

$v = V_m \sin \omega t$

Fig. 3.15.1 Purely inductive circuit

This changing flux links the coil and due to self inductance, e.m.f. gets induced in the coil. This e.m.f. opposes the applied voltage.

The self induced e.m.f. in the coil is given by, $e = -L\dfrac{di}{dt}$.

At all instants, applied voltage, V is equal and opposite to the self induced e.m.f., e

$$\therefore \qquad v = -e = -\left(-L\dfrac{di}{dt}\right)$$

$$\therefore \qquad v = L\dfrac{di}{dt} \quad \text{i.e.} \quad V_m \sin \omega t = L\dfrac{di}{dt} \quad \text{i.e.} \quad di = \dfrac{V_m}{L}\sin \omega t \, dt$$

$$\therefore \qquad i = \int di = \int \dfrac{V_m}{L}\sin \omega t \, dt = \dfrac{V_m}{L}\left(\dfrac{-\cos \omega t}{\omega}\right)$$

$$= -\dfrac{V_m}{\omega L}\sin\left(\dfrac{\pi}{2}-\omega t\right) \text{ as } \cos \omega t = \sin\left(\dfrac{\pi}{2}-\omega t\right)$$

$$\therefore \qquad i = \dfrac{V_m}{\omega L}\sin\left(\omega t - \dfrac{\pi}{2}\right) \text{ as } \sin\left(\dfrac{\pi}{2}-\omega t\right) = -\sin\left(\omega t - \dfrac{\pi}{2}\right)$$

$$\therefore \qquad \boxed{i = I_m \sin\left(\omega t - \dfrac{\pi}{2}\right) \text{ where } I_m = \dfrac{V_m}{\omega L} = \dfrac{V_m}{X_L} \text{ and } X_L = \omega L = 2\pi f L \ \Omega}$$

The above equation clearly shows that the current is purely sinusoidal and having phase angle of $-\dfrac{\pi}{2}$ radians i.e. $-90°$. This means that **the current lags voltage applied by 90°**.

The negative sign indicates lagging nature of the current.

The Fig. 3.15.2 shows the waveforms and the corresponding phasor diagram.

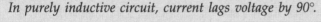

In purely inductive circuit, current lags voltage by 90°.

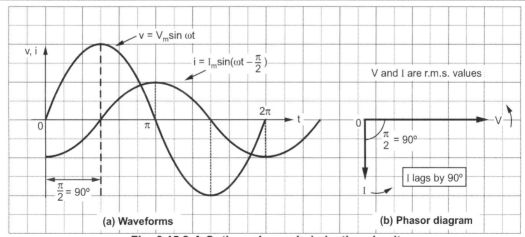

(a) Waveforms   (b) Phasor diagram
Fig. 3.15.2 A.C. through purely inductive circuit

3.15.1 Concept of Inductive Reactance

It is shown that,

$$X_L = \omega L = 2 \pi f L \ \Omega$$

The term, X_L, is called **Inductive Reactance** and is measured in **ohms.**

The **inductive reactance** is defined as the opposition offered by the inductance of a circuit to the flow of an alternating sinusoidal current.

It is measured in ohms and it depends on the frequency of the applied voltage.

The inductive reactance is directly proportional to the frequency for constant L.

$$X_L \propto f, \quad \text{for constant L}$$

So, graph of X_L Vs f is a straight line passing through the origin as shown in the Fig. 3.15.3.

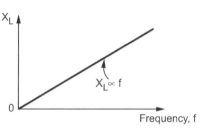

Fig. 3.15.3 X_L Vs f

If frequency is zero, which is so for d.c. voltage, the inductive reactance is zero. Therefore, it is said that the inductance offers zero reactance for the d.c. or steady current.

3.15.2 Power

The expression for the instantaneous power can be obtained by taking the product of instantaneous voltage and current.

$$\therefore \quad p = v \times i = V_m \sin \omega t \times I_m \sin \left(\omega t - \frac{\pi}{2} \right)$$

$$= - V_m I_m \sin (\omega t) \cos (\omega t) \quad \text{as } \sin \left(\omega t - \frac{\pi}{2} \right) = - \cos \omega t$$

$$\therefore \quad p = - \frac{V_m I_m}{2} \sin (2 \omega t) \quad \text{as } 2 \sin \omega t \cos \omega t = \sin 2\omega t$$

This power curve is a sine curve of frequency double than that of applied voltage.

The average value of sine curve over a complete cycle is always zero.

$$P_{av} = \int_0^{2\pi} - \frac{V_m I_m}{2} \sin(2\omega t) \ d(\omega t) = 0$$

The Fig. 3.15.4 shows voltage, current and power waveforms.

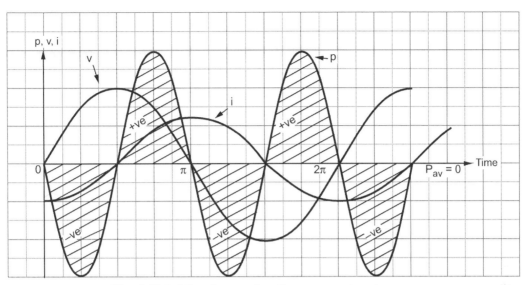

Fig. 3.15.4 Waveforms of voltage, current and power

It can be observed from it that when power curve is positive, energy gets stored in the magnetic field established due to the increasing current while during negative power curve, this power is returned back to the supply. The areas of positive loop and negative loop are exactly same and hence, **average power consumption is zero.**

Pure inductance never consumes power.

The average energy stored in an inductor is given by $E = \dfrac{1}{2} L I^2$ joules.

Review Questions

1. *Show graphical representation of voltage, current and power when a.c. sinusoidal voltage starting at t = 0 rising in positive direction is applied to pure inductance.*
2. *Prove that in a purely inductive circuit the current lags voltage by 90°.*
3. *Explain the concept of inductive reactance. How it depends on the frequency ?*
4. *Show that the average power consumed by pure inductor is zero.*

3.16 A.C. through Pure Capacitance

Consider a simple circuit consisting of a pure capacitor of C– farads, connected across a voltage given by the equation, $v = V_m \sin \omega t$. The circuit is shown in the Fig. 3.16.1.

The current i charges the capacitor C. The instantaneous charge 'q' on the plates of the capacitor is given by,

$$q = C v = C V_m \sin \omega t$$

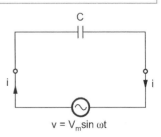

Fig. 3.16.1 Purely capacitive circuit

Current is rate of flow of charge.

$$i = \frac{dq}{dt} = \frac{d}{dt}(C\,V_m\,\sin\omega t) = C\,V_m\,\frac{d}{dt}(\sin\omega t) = C\,V_m\,\omega\,\cos\omega t$$

$\therefore \qquad i = \dfrac{V_m}{\left(\dfrac{1}{\omega C}\right)}\sin\left(\omega t + \dfrac{\pi}{2}\right) = I_m\,\sin\left(\omega t + \dfrac{\pi}{2}\right)$

where $\qquad \boxed{I_m = \dfrac{V_m}{X_C} \quad\text{and}\quad X_C = \dfrac{1}{\omega C} = \dfrac{1}{2\pi f C}\ \Omega}$

The above equation clearly shows that the current is purely sinusoidal and having phase angle of $+\dfrac{\pi}{2}$ radians i.e. $+ 90°$.

This means **current leads voltage applied by 90°**. The positive sign indicates leading nature of the current.

The Fig. 3.16.2 shows waveforms of voltage and current and the corresponding phasor diagram.

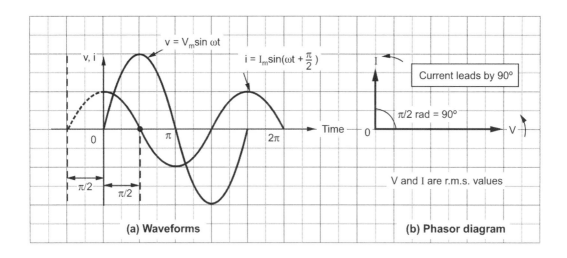

Fig. 3.16.2 A.C. through purely capacitive circuit

The current waveform starts earlier by 90° in comparison with voltage waveform. When voltage is zero, the current has positive maximum value.

In purely capacitive circuit, current leads voltage by 90°.

3.16.1 Concept of Capacitive Reactance

It is shown that, $X_C = \dfrac{1}{\omega C} = \dfrac{1}{2\pi f C}$ Ω

The term X_C is called **capacitive reactance** and is measured in ohms.

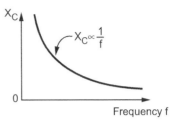

The **capacitive reactance** is defined as the opposition offered by the capacitance of a circuit to the flow of an alternating sinusoidal current.

X_C is measured in ohms and it depends on the frequency of the applied voltage.

Fig. 3.16.3 X_C Vs f

The capacitive reactance is inversely proportional to the frequency for constant capacitor C.

$$X_C \propto \dfrac{1}{f} \qquad \text{for constant C}$$

The graph of X_C Vs f is a rectangular hyperbola as shown in Fig. 3.16.3.

If the frequency is zero, which is so for d.c. voltage, the capacitive reactance is infinite. Therefore, it is said that the capacitance offers open circuit to the d.c. or it blocks d.c.

3.16.2 Power

The expression for the instantaneous power can be obtained by taking the product of instantaneous voltage and current.

$$p = v \times i = V_m \sin(\omega t) \times I_m \sin\left(\omega t + \dfrac{\pi}{2}\right)$$

$$= V_m I_m \sin(\omega t)\cos(\omega t) \qquad \text{as } \sin\left(\omega t + \dfrac{\pi}{2}\right) = \cos \omega t$$

∴ $\boxed{p = \dfrac{V_m I_m}{2} \sin(2\omega t)}$ as $2\sin \omega t \cos \omega t = \sin 2\omega t$

Thus, power curve is a sine wave of frequency double that of applied voltage.

The average value of sine curve over a complete cycle is always zero.

$$P_{av} = \int\limits_{0}^{2\pi} \dfrac{V_m I_m}{2} \sin(2\omega t)\, d(\omega t) = 0$$

The Fig. 3.16.4 shows waveforms of current, voltage and power.

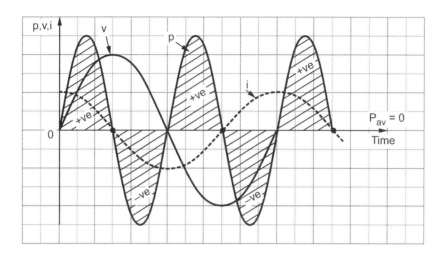

Fig. 3.16.4 Waveforms of voltage, current and power

It can be observed from the figure that when power curve is positive, in practice, an electrostatic energy gets stored in the capacitor during its charging while the negative power curve represents that the energy stored is returned back to the supply during its discharging.

The areas of positive and negative loops are exactly the same and hence, **average power consumption is zero.**

> Pure capacitance never consumes power.

The average energy stored in a capacitor is given by, $E = \dfrac{1}{2} C V^2$ joules.

Example 3.16.1 *A voltage v = 141 sin {314 t + π / 3} is applied to*
i) Resistor of 20 ohms   ii) Inductance of 0.1 henry   iii) Capacitance of 100 μF.
Find in each case r.m.s. value of current and power dissipated.
Draw the phasor diagram in each case.

Solution : Comparing given voltage with $v = V_m \sin(\omega t + \theta)$ we get,

$$V_m = 141 \text{ V and hence } V = V_{r.m.s.} = \frac{V_m}{\sqrt{2}} = 99.702 \text{ V}$$

$$\omega = 314 \text{ and hence } f = \frac{\omega}{2\pi} = 50 \text{ Hz}, \quad \theta = \frac{\pi}{3} = 60°$$

Hence the polar form of applied voltage becomes,

$$V = 99.702 \angle 60° \text{ V}$$

Case 1 :   R = 20 Ω

$$I = \frac{V}{R} = \frac{99.702 \angle 60°}{20 \angle 0°} = 4.9851 \angle 60° \text{ A}$$

∴ $I_{r.m.s.}$ = **4.9851 A**

The phase of both V and I is same for pure resistive circuit. Both are in phase.

$$P = VI = 99.702 \times 4.9851 = \textbf{497.0244 W}$$

The phasor diagram is shown in the Fig. 3.16.5 (a).

Case 2 :   L = 0.1 H

∴ $X_L = \omega L = 314 \times 0.1 = 31.4 \ \Omega$

∴ $I = \frac{|V|}{X_L} = \frac{99.702}{31.4} = \textbf{3.1752 A}$

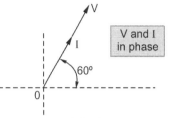

Fig. 3.16.5 (a)

This is r.m.s. value of current. It has to lag the applied voltage by 90° in case of pure inductor.

Hence phasor diagram is shown in the Fig. 3.16.5 (b).

The individual phase of I is – 30°.

In polar form I can be represented as $3.1752 \angle - 30° \text{ A}$.

Pure inductor never consumes power so **power dissipated is zero**.

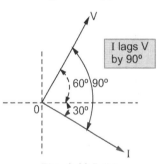

Fig. 3.16.5 (b)

Case 3 :   C = 100 μF

∴ $X_C = \frac{1}{\omega C} = \frac{1}{314 \times 100 \times 10^{-6}} = 31.8471 \ \Omega$

∴ $I = \frac{|V|}{X_C} = \frac{99.702}{31.8471} = \textbf{3.1306 A}$

This is r.m.s. value of current.

It has to lead the applied voltage by 90° in case of pure capacitor.

Hence phasor diagram is shown in the Fig. 3.16.5 (c).

The individual phase of I is 150°. In polar form I can be represented as $3.1306 \angle + 150°$. A Pure capacitor never consumes power and hence **power dissipated is zero**.

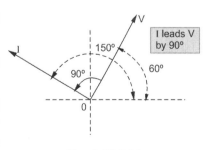

Fig. 3.16.5 (c)

Example 3.16.2 *The current drawn by a pure capacitor of 20 μF is 1.382 A from 220 V a.c. supply. What is the supply frequency ?*

Solution : $C = 20\ \mu F$, $I = 1.382\ A$, $V = 220\ V$

$$X_C = \frac{V}{I} = \frac{220}{1.382} = 159.1895\ \Omega$$

But $X_C = \dfrac{1}{2\pi f C}$ i.e. $f = \dfrac{1}{2\pi C\,X_C}$

∴ $f = \dfrac{1}{2\pi \times 20 \times 10^{-6} \times 159.1895} = 49.99 \approx \mathbf{50\ Hz}$ ...Supply frequency

Review Questions

1. Show that the current through purely capacitive circuit leads the applied voltage by 90°.
2. Explain the concept of inductive reactance. How it depends on the frequency ?
3. Show that the average power consumed by pure capacitor is zero.
4. Derive the expression for the instantaneous power in a pure capacitor energised by sinusiodal voltage. Draw the wave shapes of current, voltage and power.
5. A 50 Hz, alternating voltage of 150 V (r.m.s.) is applied independently to (1) Resistance of 10 Ω (2) Inductance of 0.2 H (3) Capacitance of 50 μF. Find the expression for the instantaneous current in each case. Draw the phasor diagram in each case.

   [Ans. : i) 21.213 sin 100πt A ii) 3.37 sin $\left(100\pi t - \dfrac{\pi}{2}\right)$ A iii) 3.33 sin sin $\left(100\pi t + \dfrac{\pi}{2}\right)$ A]

3.17 Impedance

The opposition offered by an electric circuit to the flow of an alternating current is called an impedance. It is denoted by Z. It is the ratio of an alternating voltage to an alternating current through the circuit.

Impedance is complex and is expressed in polar or rectangular form.

For pure resistance voltage and current are in phase hence impedance does not introduce any phase angle. So impedance of a pure resistance can be expressed in polar and rectangular form as,

$$Z = R + j0 = R\angle 0°\ \text{ohms}$$

For a pure inductance, the current lags voltage by 90° hence the inductive reactance X_L produces a phase lag of 90°.

For a pure inductance, if voltage is $V \angle 0°$ then current is $I \angle -90°$ hence its impedance in polar and rectangular form is given by,

$$Z = \frac{V \angle 0°}{I \angle -90°} = \frac{V}{I} \angle 90° = X_L \angle 90° = 0 + j X_L \text{ ohms}$$

For a pure capacitance, the current leads voltage by 90° hence the capacitive reactance X_C produces a phase lead of 90°.

For a pure capacitance, if voltage is $V \angle 0°$ then current is $I \angle +90°$ hence its impedance is given by,

$$Z = \frac{V \angle 0°}{I \angle +90°} = \frac{V}{I} \angle -90° = X_C \angle -90° = 0 - j X_C \text{ ohms}$$

Review Question

1. *Define impedance.*

3.18 A.C. through Series R-L Circuit 　2001-02, 2002-03, 2003-04, 2004-05, 2005-06, 2006-07, 2008-09, 2011-12

Consider a circuit consisting of pure resistance R ohms connected in series with a pure inductance of L henries as shown in the Fig. 3.18.1 (a).

The series combination is connected across a.c. supply given by $v = V_m \sin \omega t$.

Circuit draws a current I then there are two voltage drops,

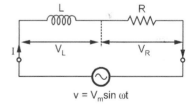

Fig. 3.18.1 (a) Series R-L circuit

a) Drop across pure resistance, $V_R = I \times R$

b) Drop across pure inductance, $V_L = I \times X_L$

where $X_L = 2 \pi f L$

　　　　　I = R.M.S. value of current drawn

　　V_R, V_L = R.M.S. values of the voltage drops.

The Kirchhoff's voltage law can be applied to the a.c. circuit but important point to remember is that the **addition of voltages is a phasor (vector) addition and no longer algebraic as in case of d.c.**

∴　　　　　$\overline{V} = \overline{V_R} + \overline{V_L} = \overline{I}R + \overline{I}X_L$　　　　　　(Phasor addition)

For series a.c. circuits, generally, current is taken as the reference phasor as it is common to both the elements.

Following are the **steps to draw the phasor diagram :**

1) Take current as a reference phasor.

2) In case of resistance, voltage and current are in phase, so V_R will be along current phasor.

3) In case of inductance, current lags voltage by 90°. But, as current is reference, V_L must be shown leading with respect to current by 90°.

4) The supply voltage being vector sum of these two vectors V_L and V_R obtained by law of parallelogram.

The phasor diagram and the voltage triangle is shown in the Fig. 3.18.1 (b) and (c).

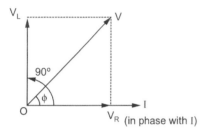

Fig. 3.18.1 (b) Phasor diagram   **Fig. 3.18.1 (c) Voltage triangle**

From the voltage triangle, we can write,

$$V = \sqrt{(V_R)^2 + (V_L)^2} = \sqrt{(IR)^2 + (I \times X_L)^2} = I\sqrt{(R)^2 + (X_L)^2}$$

$\therefore$ $V = I\,Z$ i.e. $Z = \dfrac{V}{I}$

Where $\boxed{Z = \sqrt{(R)^2 + (X_L)^2} \text{ (magnitude)}}$ ... Impedance of the circuit.

The impedance Z is measured in ohms.

3.18.1 Impedance

Impedance is defined as the opposition of circuit to flow of alternating current. It is denoted by Z and its unit is ohms.

For the R-L series circuit, it can be observed from the phasor diagram that the current lags behind the applied voltage by an angle ϕ. From the voltage triangle,

we can write,

$$\tan\phi = \frac{V_L}{V_R} = \frac{X_L}{R}, \quad \cos\phi = \frac{V_R}{V} = \frac{R}{Z}, \quad \sin\phi = \frac{V_L}{V} = \frac{X_L}{Z}$$

If all the sides of the voltage triangle are divided by current, we get a triangle called **impedance triangle** as shown in the Fig. 3.18.2.

Sides of this triangle are resistance R, inductive reactance X_L and an impedance Z.

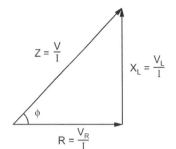

Fig. 3.18.2 Impedance triangle

From this impedance triangle, we can see that,

X component of $Z = R = Z \cos \phi$

Y component of $Z = X_L = Z \sin \phi$

In rectangular form the impedance is denoted as,

$$Z = R + j X_L \ \Omega$$

While in polar form, it is denoted as,

$$Z = |Z| \angle \phi \ \Omega$$
$$\text{where} |Z| = \sqrt{R^2 + X_L^2}, \quad \phi = \tan^{-1}\left[\frac{X_L}{R}\right]$$

Thus ϕ is positive for inductive impedance.

3.18.2 Power and Power Triangle

The expression for the current in the series R-L circuit is,

$i = I_m \sin (\omega t - \phi)$ as current lags voltage.

The power is product of instantaneous values of voltage and current,

$\therefore$ 　　　$p = v \times i = V_m \sin \omega t \times I_m \sin (\omega t - \phi) = V_m I_m [\sin (\omega t) \cdot \sin (\omega t - \phi)]$

$$= V_m I_m \left[\frac{\cos(\phi) - \cos(2\omega t - \phi)}{2}\right] = \frac{V_m I_m}{2} \cos \phi - \frac{V_m I_m}{2} \cos (2 \omega t - \phi)$$

The second term is cosine term whose average value over a cycle is zero. Hence, average power consumed is,

$$P_{av} = \frac{V_m I_m}{2} \cos \phi = \frac{V_m}{\sqrt{2}} \cdot \frac{I_m}{\sqrt{2}} \cos \phi$$

$\therefore$ 　　　$\boxed{P = V I \cos \phi \quad \text{watts}}$ 　　　where V and I are r.m.s. values

If we multiply voltage equation by current I, we get the power equation.

$$\overline{V I} = \overline{V_R I} + \overline{V_L I} \ \text{ i.e. } \overline{V I} = \overline{V \cos\phi I} + \overline{V \sin\phi I}$$

From this equation, power triangle can be obtained as shown in the Fig. 3.18.3.

So, three sides of this triangle are,

   1) VI   2) VI cos ϕ 3) VI sin ϕ

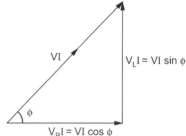

Fig. 3.18.3 Power triangle

1. Real or True or Active Power (P) :

It is defined as the product of the applied voltage and the active component of the current.

It is real component of the apparent power. It is measured in unit watts (W) or kilowatts (kW).

$$P = V I \cos \phi \quad \text{watts}$$

2. Apparent Power (S) :

It is defined as the product of r.m.s. value of voltage (V) and current (I). It is denoted by S.

∴ $$S = VI \text{ VA}$$

It is measured in unit volt-amp (VA) or kilo volt-amp (kVA).

3. Reactive Power (Q) :

It is defined as product of the applied voltage and the reactive component of the current.

It is also defined as imaginary component of the apparent power.

It is represented by 'Q' and it is measured in unit volt-amp reactive (VAR) or kilovolt-amp reactive (kVAR).

$$Q = V I \sin \phi \quad \text{VAR}$$

3.18.3 Power Factor (cos ϕ)

It is defined as factor by which the apparent power must be multiplied in order to obtain the true power.

It is the ratio of true power to apparent power.

$$\text{Power factor} = \frac{\text{True Power}}{\text{Apparent Power}} = \frac{V I \cos \phi}{V I} = \cos \phi$$

It is the factor which decides the true power consumption in the circuit.

The numerical value of cosine of the phase angle between the applied voltage and the current drawn from the supply voltage gives the power factor.

It cannot be greater than 1.

It is also defined as the ratio of resistance to the impedance.

$$\cos \phi = \frac{R}{Z}$$

The nature of power factor is always determined by position of current with respect to the voltage.

If current lags voltage power factor is said to be lagging. If current leads voltage power factor is said to be leading.

So, for pure inductance, the power factor is cos (90°) i.e. zero lagging while for pure capacitance, the power factor is cos (90°) i.e. zero but leading. For purely resistive circuit voltage and current are in phase i.e. $\phi = 0$. Therefore, power factor is cos (0°) = 1. Such circuit is called unity power factor circuit.

Power factor = cos ϕ where ϕ is the angle between supply voltage and current.

Nature of power factor always tells position of current with respect to voltage.

Example 3.18.1 *If load draws a current of 10 ampere at 0.8 p.f. lagging, when connected to 100 volt supply, calculate the values of real, reactive and apparent powers. Also find out the resistance of the load.*　　　　**2011-12, Marks 5**

Solution : I = 10 A, cos ϕ = 0.8 lag　　i.e.　ϕ = – 36.869°, V = 100 $\angle 0°$ V

Real power　= VI cos ϕ = 100 × 10 × 0.8 = **800 W**

Reactive power　= VI sin ϕ = 100 × 10 × 0.6 = **600 VAR**

Apparent power = VI = 100 × 10 = **1000 VA**

$$Z = \frac{V}{I} = \frac{100\angle 0°}{10\angle -36.869°} = 10 \angle 36.869° \ \Omega = 8 + j\,6 \ \Omega$$

Comparing with R + j X_L, R = **8 Ω of load.**

Example 3.18.2 *Given v = 200 sin 377 t V and i = 8 sin (377t – 30°) A for an a.c. circuit. Determine : a) The power factor b) True power c) Apparent power d) Reactive power.*　　　**2008-09, Marks 5**

Solution :　　　v = 200 sin 377 t V,　i = 8 sin (377 t – 30°) A

∴　　　　　　V_m = 200 V　and　I_m = 8 A

$\therefore$ $V_{r.m.s.} = \dfrac{200}{\sqrt{2}} = 141.4213$ V   and $I_{r.m.s.} = \dfrac{8}{\sqrt{2}} = 5.6568$ A

$\phi_1 = $ Phase of V $= 0°$ and $\phi_2 = $ Phase of I $= -30°$

$\therefore$ $V = 141.4213 \angle 0°$ and $I = 5.6568 \angle -30°$ A

The phasor diagram is as shown in the figure.

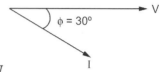

a)   Power factor $= \cos \phi$

                    $= \cos(30°) = \mathbf{0.866}$ **lagging**

b)   Apparent power $=$ VI $= \mathbf{800 \ VA}$

c)   True power $=$ VI $\cos \phi = 800 \times 0.866 = \mathbf{692.8 \ W}$

d)   Reactive power $=$ VI $\sin \phi = 800 \times \sin(30°) = \mathbf{400 \ VAR}$

Example 3.18.3 *A load having impedance of $1 + j1 \ \Omega$ is connected to an a.c. voltage represented as $v = 20\sqrt{2} \cos(\omega t + 10°)$ volt. i) Find the current in load, expressed in the form of $i = I_m \sin(\omega t + \phi)$ A. i) Find real power consumed by the load.*

2004-05, Marks 5

Solution : $Z = 1 + j1 \ \Omega = 1.4142 \angle 45° \Omega$

i) Comparing voltage with $V_m \sin(\omega t + \phi_1)$, $V_m = 20\sqrt{2}$ V

and $\cos(\omega t + 10°) = \sin(\omega t + 90° + 10°)$ i.e. $\phi_1 = 100°$

$\therefore$ $V = \dfrac{V_m}{\sqrt{2}} \angle \phi_1 = \dfrac{20\sqrt{2}}{\sqrt{2}} \angle 100° = 20 \angle 100°$ V

$\therefore$ $I = \dfrac{V}{Z} = \dfrac{20 \angle 100°}{1.4142 \angle 45°} = 14.142 \angle 55°$ A, $I_m =$

$\sqrt{2} \times 14.142 = 20$ A

$\therefore$ $i(t) = I_m \sin(\omega t + \phi_2) = \mathbf{20 \sin(\omega t + 55°) \ A}$ $\dots \phi_2 = 55°$

ii) $P = $ VI $\cos\phi = 20 \times 14.142 \times \cos(45°)$

           $= \mathbf{200 \ W}$

Fig. 3.18.4

Example 3.18.4 *An alternating voltage is given by the expression $v = 40 \sin(50 \pi t)$ is applied to a series R-L circuit, where resistance is of $2 \ \Omega$ and inductance is of 0.4 H. Find out the expression for the instantaneous current.*

Solution :

Given that, $v = 40 \sin(50 \pi t)$ i.e. $\omega = 50 \pi$ rad/sec

           $\omega = 2\pi f$ i.e. $f = 25$ Hz

i.e. $X_L = 2\pi f L = 62.8318 \ \Omega$ and $R = 2 \ \Omega$ given

$$Z = R + j X_L = 2 + j \; 62.8318 \; \Omega$$

$$= 62.8636 \angle 88.17° \; \Omega$$

$$\therefore \quad I_m = \frac{V_m}{Z} = \frac{40 \angle 0°}{62.8636 \angle 88.17°} = 0.6362 \angle -88.17° A \qquad \text{...As V is reference}$$

$$\therefore \quad i = I_m \sin (\omega t - \phi) = \textbf{0.6362 sin (50 } \pi t - \textbf{88.17°) A}$$

... Equation for instantaneous current

Example 3.18.5 *A coil connected to 100 V d.c. supply draws 10 amp. and the same coil when connected 100 V, a.c. voltage of frequency 50 Hz draws 5 amp. Calculate the parameters of the coil and power factor.*   **2003-04, Marks 10**

Solution : For d.c., the frequency f = 0

$$\therefore \quad X_L = 2\pi f L = 0 \; \Omega \text{ for d.c.}$$

$$\therefore \quad I = \frac{100}{r} = 10 \text{ A}$$

$$\therefore \quad r = \frac{100}{10} = 10 \; \Omega \qquad \text{... Resistance of coil}$$

$$Z = r + j X_L = 10 + j X_L$$

$$\therefore \quad |Z| = \sqrt{10^2 + X_L^2}$$

$$\therefore \quad |I| = \frac{V}{|Z|} \quad \text{i.e.} \quad 5 = \frac{100}{\sqrt{10^2 + X_L^2}}$$

$$\therefore \quad \sqrt{10^2 + X_L^2} = 20$$

$$\therefore \quad X_L^2 = 300 \quad \text{i.e.} \quad X_L = 17.3205 \; \Omega$$

$$\therefore \quad L = \frac{17.3205}{2\pi f} = \textbf{55.1328 mH}$$

$$\therefore \text{ Power factor} = \frac{r}{Z} = \frac{10}{\sqrt{10^2 + (17.3205)^2}} = \textbf{0.5 lagging}$$

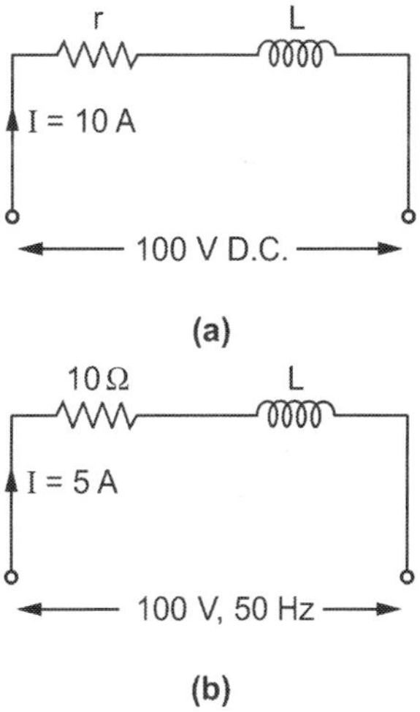

(a)

(b)

Fig. 3.18.5

Example 3.18.6 *A two-element series circuit is connected across an a.c. source* $v = 300 \cos(314t + 20°)$ *Volts. The current drawn in 15 cos (314 t − 10°) amp. Determine the circuit impedance magnitude and phase angle. What is the average power drawn?*   **2002-03, Marks 10**

Solution : $v = 300 \cos(314t + 20°) = 300 \sin(314t + 20° + 90°)$

$= 300 \sin(314t + 110°)$ V

$i = 15 \cos(314t - 10°) = 15 \sin(314t - 10° + 90°)$

$= 15 \sin(314t + 80°)$ A

∴ $V = \dfrac{300}{\sqrt{2}} \angle 110°$ V $= 212.132 \angle 110°$ V

$\cdots V_{r.m.s.} \angle \phi_1^\circ$

and $I = \dfrac{15}{\sqrt{2}} \angle 80°$ A $= 10.606 \angle 80°$ A

$\cdots I_{r.m.s.} \angle \phi_2^\circ$

∴ $Z = \dfrac{V}{I} = \dfrac{212.132 \angle 110°}{10.606 \angle 80°} = \mathbf{20 \angle 30°}$ Ω

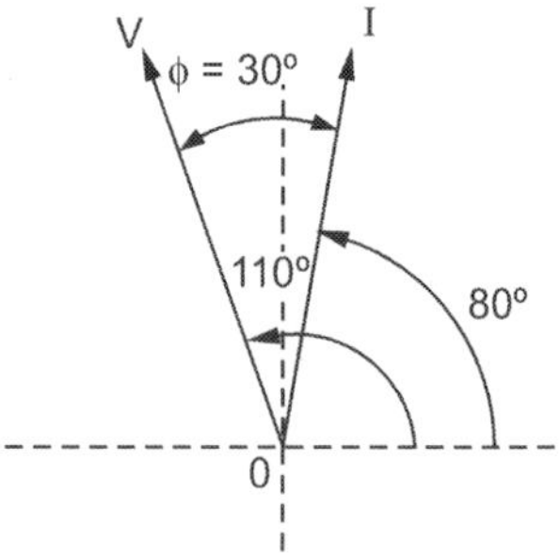

Fig. 3.18.6

$P_{av} = VI \cos\phi = 212.32 \times 10.606 \times \cos(30°) = \mathbf{1950.173\ W}$

Example 3.18.7 *A non-inductive resistance of 10 ohms is connected in series with an inductive coil across 200 V, 50 Hz a.c. supply. The current drawn by the series combination is 10 amperes. The resistance of the coil is 2 ohms. Determine i) Inductance of the coil, ii) Power factor iii) Voltage across the coil.* **2004-05, Marks 5**

Solution : $Z_T = (R + r) + j X_L = 12 + j X_L$ Ω

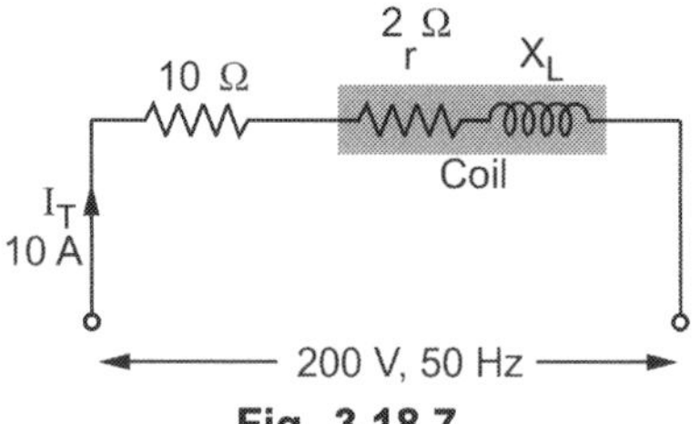

∴ $|Z_T| = \sqrt{12^2 + X_L^2}$

$|I_T| = 10$ A

$|I_T| = \dfrac{V}{|Z_T|}$

Fig. 3.18.7

i.e. $10 = \dfrac{200}{\sqrt{12^2 + X_L^2}}$ i.e. $12^2 + X_L^2 = (200/10)^2$

∴ $X_L^2 = 256$ i.e. $X_L = 16$ Ω

i) $L = \dfrac{X_L}{2\pi f} = \dfrac{16}{2\pi \times 50} = \mathbf{0.0509\ H}$

ii) $\cos\phi = \dfrac{(R+r)}{|Z_T|} = \dfrac{12}{\sqrt{12^2 + X_L^2}} = \dfrac{12}{20} = \mathbf{0.6\ lagging}$

iii) $V_L = I_T \times Z_{coil}$

Now $Z_{coil} = r + j X_L = 2 + j 16 \ \Omega = 16.1245 \angle 82.875° \ \Omega$

∴ $V_L = I_T \times |Z_{coil}| = 10 \times 16.1245 = \mathbf{161.245 \ V}$ ... Voltage across coil

Example 3.18.8 *A 120 V, 60 W lamp is to be operated on 220 V, 50 Hz supply mains, In order that lamp should operate on correct voltage, calculate value of : i) non inductive resistance ii) pure inductance.*   **2005-06, Marks 10**

Solution : Note that lamp is purely resistive.

i) Non inductive resistance

$$I = \frac{P_{lamp}}{V_{lamp}} = \frac{60}{120} = 0.5 \ A$$

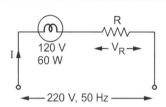

Fig. 3.18.8 (a)

∴ $V_R = I \times R$

But $V = V_{lamp} + V_R$

∴ $V_R = 220 - 120 = 100 \ V$

∴ $R = \frac{V_R}{I} = \frac{100}{0.5} = \mathbf{200 \ \Omega}$

... Both resistive

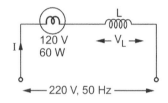

ii) Pure inductance

$$|I| = \frac{P_{lamp}}{V_{lamp}} = 0.5 \ A$$

Now current I lags V_L by 90° as shown in the Fig. 3.18.8 (c).

$$\overline{V} = \overline{V}_L + \overline{V}_{lamp}$$

∴ $|V| = \sqrt{V_L^2 + V_{lamp}^2}$

∴ $220 = \sqrt{V_L^2 + (120)^2}$

∴ $|V_L| = 184.3908 \ V$

But $|V_L| = I X_L = 0.5 X_L$

∴ $X_L = \frac{184.3908}{0.5} = 368.7818 \ \Omega$

∴ $L = \frac{X_L}{2\pi f} = \mathbf{1.1738 \ H}$

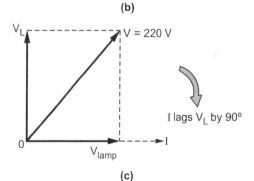

(c)

Fig. 3.18.8

Example 3.18.9 *The voltage and current through a circuit element are :*
$v = 50 \sin (314 t + 55°)$ *volts* $i = 10 \sin (314 t + 325°)$ *amperes. Find the value of power drawn by the element.* **2006-07, Marks 5**

Solution : Comparing the given equations with,

$$v = V_m \sin (\omega t + \phi_1) \text{ and } i = I_m \sin (\omega t + \phi_2)$$

$$V_m = 50 \quad \text{i.e.} \quad V = \frac{V_m}{\sqrt{2}} = \frac{50}{\sqrt{2}} = 35.3553 \text{ V (r.m.s.)}$$

$$I_m = 10 \quad \text{i.e.} \quad I = \frac{I_m}{\sqrt{2}} = \frac{10}{\sqrt{2}} = 7.071 \text{ V (r.m.s.)}$$

$$\omega = 314 \text{ and /sec} \quad \text{i.e.} \quad f = \frac{\omega}{2\pi} \frac{314}{2\pi} = 50 \text{ Hz}$$

The voltage has phase $\phi_1 = 55°$ while the current has phase $\phi_2 = 325°$.

$$\therefore \qquad V = 35.3553 \angle 55° \text{ V}$$

$$\therefore \qquad I = 7.071 \angle 325° \text{ A}$$

The phasors are shown in the Fig. 3.18.9.

The power factor angle ϕ is the angle between V and I i.e. $\phi = 55 + 35 = 90°$

$$\therefore \qquad P = VI \cos \phi = 35.3553 \times 7.071 \times \cos 90°$$

$$= \mathbf{0 \ W}$$

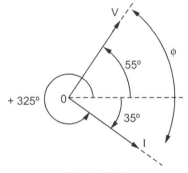

Fig. 3.18.9

... Power drawn by the element

Review Questions

1. *Explain the behaviour of series R-L circuit. Draw its phasor diagram.*
2. *Show that current lags behind the voltage in series R-L circuit.*
3. *Derive the impedance of a series R-L circuit.*
4. *Derive the expression for the instantaneous power in a series R-L circuit.*
5. *Draw the power triangle and define active power, reactive power and apparent power. State their units.*
6. *A voltage $e = 200 \sin 100 \pi t$ is applied to a load having $R = 200 \ \Omega$ in series with $L = 638 \ mH$ Estimate :-*
   i) Expression for current in $i = I_m \sin (\omega t \pm \phi)$ form ii) Power consumed by the load
   iii) Reactive power of the load iv) voltage across R and L.
   [Ans. : i) 0.7071 sin (100 πt − 45.06°) A, ii) 50 W, iii) 50 VAR iv) 100V, 100.21 V]

7. *A heater operates at 100 V, 50 Hz and takes current of 8 A and consumes 1200 W power. A choke coil is having ratio of reactance to resistance as 10, is connected in series with the heater. The series combination is connected across 230 V, 50 Hz a.c. supply. Calculate the*

i) Resistance of choke coil   *ii) Reactance of choke coil*

iii) Power consumed by choke coil   *iv) Total power consumed.*

[Ans. : i) 2.4552 Ω, ii) 24.552 Ω, iii) 157.13 W, iv) 957.1328 W]

8. *When connected to a 230 V, 50 Hz single phase supply, coil takes 10 kVA and 8 kVAR. For this coil, calculate :*   *i) Resistance* *ii) Inductance of coil and iii) Power consumed.*

[Ans. : i) 4.232 Ω, ii) 13.4708 mH, iii) 6 kW]

9. *A coil draws 5 amps when connected to 100 volts 50 Hz supply. The resistance of the coil is 5 Ω determine i) Inductance of the coil   ii) Real power, reactive power, apparent power for the coil.*

[Ans. : i) 61.64 mH, ii) 125 W, 484.1229 VAR, 500 VA]

10. *When an inductive coil is connected to a d.c. supply at 240 volt, the current in it is 16 amp. When the same coil is connected to an a.c. supply at 240 volt, 50 Hz, the current is 12.27 amp. Calculate 1) Resistance, 2) Impedance, 3) Reactance 4) Inductance of the coil.*

[Ans. : 1) 15 Ω, 2) 19.56 Ω, 3) 12.5536 Ω, 4) 0.04 H]

11. *A series RL circuit takes 400 W at a power factor of 0.8 from a 120 V, 50 Hz supply. Calculate the values of R and L.*   **[Ans. : 23.04 Ω, 0.055 H]**

12. *A resistance and an inductance are connected in series across a voltage : v = 283 sin 314 t. The current expression is found to be $4 \sin \left(314t - \dfrac{\pi}{4} \right)$. Find the values of resistance, inductance and power factor.*

2001-02

[Ans. : 50.028 Ω, 0.159 H, 0.707 lag]

13. *A 120 V, 100 W lamp is to be connected to a 220 V, 50 Hz a.c. supply. What value of pure inductance should be connected in series in order that lamp is run on the rated voltage?*

[Ans. : 0.7043 H]

3.19 A.C. through Series R-C Circuit   **2001-02, 2003-04, 2004-05**

Consider a circuit consisting of pure resistance R-ohms and connected in series with a pure capacitor of C-farads as shown in the Fig. 3.19.1.

The series combination is connected across a.c. supply, $v = V_m \sin \omega t$

Circuit draws a current I, then there are two voltage drops,

a) Drop across pure resistance $V_R = I \times R$

b) Drop across pure capacitance $V_C = I \times X_C$

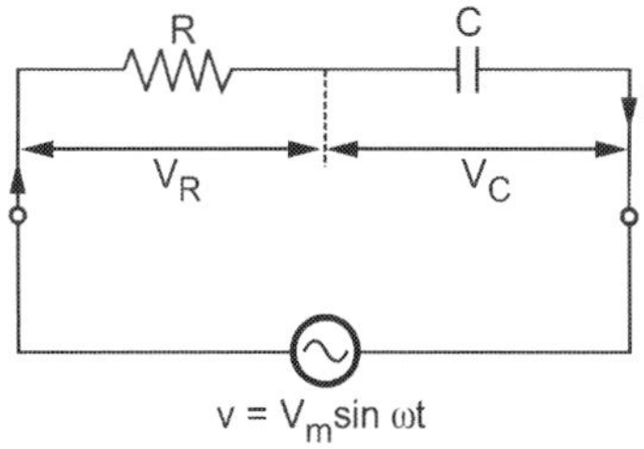

Fig. 3.19.1 Series R-C circuit

where $X_C = \dfrac{1}{2 \pi f C}$ and I, V_R, V_C are the r.m.s. values

The Kirchhoff's voltage law can be applied to get,

$$V = \overline{V}_R + \overline{V}_C = \overline{I}R + \overline{I}X_C \qquad \text{... (Phasor addition)}$$

Let us draw the phasor diagram. Current I is taken as reference as it is common to both the elements.

Following are the **steps to draw the phasor diagram :**

1) Take current as reference phasor.

2) In case of resistance, voltage and current are in phase. So, V_R will be along current phasor.

3) In case of pure capacitance, current leads voltage by 90° i.e. voltage lags current by 90° so V_C is shown downwards i.e. lagging current by 90°.

4) The supply voltage being vector sum of these two voltages V_C and V_R obtained by completing parallelogram.

The phasor diagram and voltage triangle are shown in the Fig. 3.19.2.

It can be seen from the phasor diagram that the current leads the voltage by angle ϕ which is decided by the circuit components R and C.

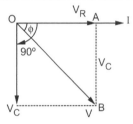

(a) Phasor diagram

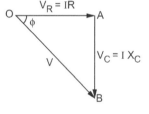

(b) Voltage triangle

Fig. 3.19.2

3.19.1 Impedance

From the voltage triangles,

$$V = \sqrt{(V_R)^2 + (V_C)^2} = \sqrt{(IR)^2 + (IX_C)^2} = I\sqrt{(R)^2 + (X_C)^2}$$

∴ $V = IZ$

where $Z = \sqrt{(R)^2 + (X_C)^2}$ (magnitude)   is the impedance of the circuit.

Similar to R-L series circuit, in this case also, the impedance is nothing but opposition to the flow of alternating current.

It is measured in ohms given by $Z = \sqrt{(R)^2 + (X_C)^2}$ where $X_C = \dfrac{1}{2\pi f C}$ Ω called **capacitive reactance**.

In R-C series circuit, current leads voltage by angle ϕ or supply voltage V lags current I by angle ϕ as shown in the phasor diagram in Fig. 3.19.2 (a).

From voltage triangle, we can write,

$$\tan \phi = \frac{V_C}{V_R} = \frac{X_C}{R}, \qquad \cos \phi = \frac{V_R}{V} = \frac{R}{Z}, \qquad \sin \phi = \frac{V_C}{V} = \frac{X_C}{Z}$$

If all the sides of the voltage triangle are divided by the current, we get a triangle called **impedance triangle.** It is shown in the Fig. 3.19.3.

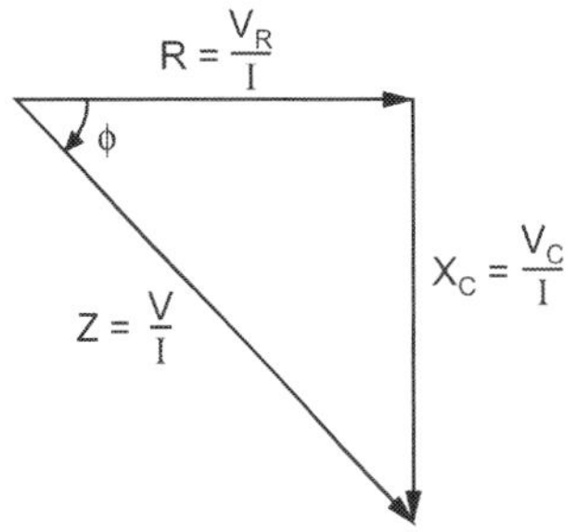

Two sides of the triangle are 'R' and 'X_C' and the third side is impedance 'Z'.

X component of $Z = R = Z \cos \phi$

Y component of $Z = X_C = Z \sin \phi$

But, as direction of the X_C is the negative Y direction, the rectangular form of the impedance is denoted as,

$$Z = R - j X_C \ \Omega$$

Fig. 3.19.3 Impedance triangle

While in polar form, it is denoted as,

$$Z = R - j X_C = |Z| \angle -\phi$$

$$\text{where} \ |Z| = \sqrt{R^2 + X_C^2}, \ \phi = \tan^{-1}\left[\frac{-X_C}{R}\right]$$

Thus ϕ is negative for capacitive impedance.

3.19.2 Power and Power Triangle

The current leads voltage by angle ϕ, hence its expression is,

$$i = I_m \sin (\omega t + \phi) \ \text{as current leads voltage}$$

The power is the product of instantaneous values of voltage and current.

$\therefore \qquad p = v \times i = V_m \sin \omega t \times I_m \sin (\omega t + \phi)$

$$= V_m I_m [\sin (\omega t) \cdot \sin (\omega t + \phi)] = V_m I_m \left[\frac{\cos(-\phi) - \cos(2\omega t + \phi)}{2}\right]$$

$$= \frac{V_m I_m \cos\phi}{2} - \frac{V_m I_m}{2} \cos (2 \omega t + \phi) \qquad\qquad \text{as} \cos (- \phi) = \cos \phi$$

The second term is cosine term whose average value over a cycle is zero. Hence, average power consumed by the circuit is,

$$P_{av} = \frac{V_m I_m}{2} \cos\phi = \frac{V_m}{\sqrt{2}} \cdot \frac{I_m}{\sqrt{2}} \cos\phi$$

∴ $P = V I \cos\phi$ watts   where V and I are r.m.s. values

If we multiply voltage equation by current I, we get the power equation,

$$\overline{VI} = \overline{V_R I} + \overline{V_C I} = \overline{VI\cos\phi} + \overline{VI\sin\phi}$$

Hence, the power triangle can be shown as in the Fig. 3.19.4.

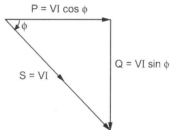

Thus, the various powers are,

Fig. 3.19.4 Power triangle

Apparent power,	S = V I	VA
True or average power,	P = V I cos φ	W
Reactive power,	Q = V I sin φ	VAR

For any single phase a.c. circuit, the average power is given by,
        P = V I cos φ   watts   where **V, I are r.m.s. values**
        cos φ = Power factor of circuit

cos φ is **lagging** for **inductive** circuit and cos φ is **leading** for **capacitive** circuit.

Example 3.19.1 *A resistance of 120 ohms and a capacitive reactance of 250 ohms are connected in series across a A.C. voltage source. If a current of 0.9 A is flowing in the circuit find out (i) power factor, (ii) supply voltage (iii) voltages across resistance and capacitance (iv) Active power and reactive power.*

Solution : The circuit is shown in the Fig. 3.19.5.

    R = 120 Ω, X_C = 250 Ω, I = 0.9 A

    $Z = R - j X_C = 120 - j250 \ \Omega = 277.308 \ \angle - 64.358°$

Take current as reference.

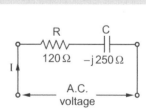

Fig. 3.19.5

∴ $I = 0.9 \ \angle 0° \ A$

i) Power factor $\cos\phi = \cos(-64.358°) = \textbf{0.4327 leading}$

ii) Supply voltage $V = I \times Z = [0.9 \ \angle 0°] \times [277.308 \ \angle - 64.358°]$

∴ $V = \textbf{249.5772} \ \angle \textbf{- 64.358° V}$

iii) $V_R = I \times R = 0.9 \times 120 =$ **108 V** (magnitude)

$V_C = I \times X_C = 0.9 \times 250 =$ **225 V** (magnitude)

iv)   P = active power = V I cos ϕ = 249.5772 × 0.9 × 0.4327 = **97.1928 W**

Q = reactive power = VI sin ϕ = 249.5772 × 0.9 × sin (− 64.358°) = **− 202.498 VAR**

The negative sign indicates leading nature of reactive volt-amperes.

Example 3.19.2 *The voltage applied to a circuit is v = 100 sin (ωt + 30°) and the current flowing in the circuit is i = 15 sin (ωt + 60°). Determine the impedance, resistance, reactance, power and the power factor of the circuit.*   **2003-04, Marks 5**

Solution : From the given equations of v(t) and i(t).

$$V = V_{r.m.s.} \angle \phi_1 = \frac{V_m}{\sqrt{2}} \angle \phi_1 = \frac{100}{\sqrt{2}} \angle 30° \text{ A}$$

$$I = I_{r.m.s.} \angle \phi_2 = \frac{I_m}{\sqrt{2}} \angle \phi_2 = \frac{15}{\sqrt{2}} \angle 60° \text{ A}$$

$$Z = \frac{V}{I} = \frac{\frac{100}{\sqrt{2}} \angle 30°}{\frac{15}{\sqrt{2}} \angle 60°} = 6.667 \angle -30° \ \Omega$$

$$= 5.7738 - j\ 3.333 \ \Omega = R - jX_C$$

∴   R = **5.7738 Ω**

X_C = **3.333 Ω**

∴ $P = VI \cos \phi = \frac{100}{\sqrt{2}} \times \frac{15}{\sqrt{2}} \cos(-30°)$

$= $ **649.52 W**

$\cos \phi = \cos (-30°) =$ **0.866 leading**

Example 3.19.3 *A metal filament lamp, rated at 750 W, 100 V is to be connected in series with a capacitance across a 230 V, 50 Hz supply. Calculate the value of capacitance required. Draw the phasor diagram.*   **2001-02, Marks 5**

Solution : $I = \dfrac{P}{V_{lamp}} = \dfrac{750}{100} = 7.5 \text{ A}$

From the Fig. 3.19.6 (b)

$$V = \sqrt{V_C^2 + V_{lamp}^2}$$

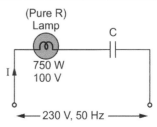

Fig. 3.19.6 (a)

$\therefore$ $\qquad$ $230 = \sqrt{V_C^2 + (100)^2}$

$\therefore$ $\qquad$ $V_C = 207.1231$ V

$\therefore$ $\qquad$ $X_C = \dfrac{V_C}{I} = \dfrac{207.1231}{7.5}$

$\qquad\qquad = 27.6164\ \Omega = \dfrac{1}{2\pi fC}$

$\therefore$ $\qquad$ $C = \dfrac{1}{2\pi \times 50 \times 27.6164}$

$\qquad\qquad = $ **115.261 μF**

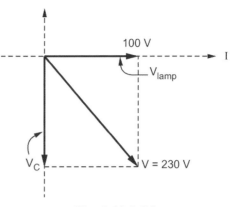

Fig. 3.19.6 (b)

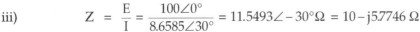

Example 3.19.4 *A voltage wave e(t) = 141.4 sin (120 t) produces a current,*
i(t) = 14.14 sin (120 t) + 7.07 cos (120t+30°) in a circuit. Determine, i) the resultant
time expression of the current, ii) the power factor and power delivered by the source.
iii) values of R and C of the circuit. **2001-02, 2004-05, Marks 10**

Solution : i) $i(t) = 14.14 \sin 120\,t + 7.07 \cos(120t + 30°)$

$\qquad\qquad = 14.14 \sin 120\,t + 7.07[\cos 120\,t \cos 30° - \sin 120\,t \sin 30°]$

$\qquad\qquad = 10.605 \sin 120\,t + 6.1228 \cos 120\,t = A \sin(120t + \phi)$

$\qquad\qquad = A \sin 120\,t \cos\phi + A \cos 120\,t \sin\phi$

Comparing $A \cos\phi = 10.605$, $A \sin\phi = 6.1228$

$\therefore$ $\qquad$ $(A \sin\phi)^2 + (A \cos\phi)^2 = A^2 = (10.605)^2 + (6.1228)^2$

$\therefore$ $\qquad$ $A = 12.245$ and $\tan\phi = \dfrac{6.1228}{10.605}$ i.e. $\phi = 30°$

$\therefore$ Resultant current is, $i(t) = $ **12.245 sin (120 t + 30°) A**

ii) $\qquad$ $E_m = 141.4$ V and phase $0°$ from given equation of e(t).

$\therefore$ $\qquad$ $E = \dfrac{141.4}{\sqrt{2}} \angle 0°$ V $= 100\angle 0°$ V, $I = \dfrac{12.245}{\sqrt{2}} \angle 30° = 8.6585\angle 30°$ A

$\therefore$ $\qquad\qquad$ Power factor angle $= \phi = E\,\hat{}\,I = 30°$

$\therefore$ Power factor $= \cos\phi = $ **0.866 leading**

$\therefore$ $\qquad$ $P = EI\cos\phi = 100 \times 8.6585 \times \cos 30° = $ **749.85 W**

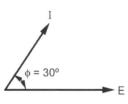

iii) $\qquad$ $Z = \dfrac{E}{I} = \dfrac{100\angle 0°}{8.6585\angle 30°} = 11.5493\angle -30°\ \Omega = 10 - j5.7746\ \Omega$

Comparing with, $Z = R - jX_C$

$R = 10 \ \Omega$, $X_C = 5.7746 = \dfrac{1}{2\pi f C} = \dfrac{1}{\omega C}$ and $\omega = 120 \ \text{rad/s}$ from given equations

$\therefore \qquad C = \dfrac{1}{120 \times 5.7746} = \textbf{1.4431 mF}$

Note that $e(t) = E_m \sin \omega t = 141.4 \sin(120t)$ V hence $\omega = 120$.

Review Questions

1. *For a.c. circuit consisting of R and C, draw the phasor diagram and show that the current leads the voltage.*

2. *Define impedance of a series R-C circuit.*

3. *Obtain the expression of power for series R-C circuit.*

4. *A current of average value 18.019 A is flowing in a circuit to which a voltage of peak value 141.42 V is applied. Determine - i) $Z_1 = R \pm jX$ ii) Power*

   Given : V lags I by $\dfrac{\pi}{6}$ radians.   **[Ans. : i) 4.3301 – j 2.5 Ω, ii) 1732.0508 W]**

5. *The waveforms of the voltage and current of a circuit are given by,*

   e = 120 sin (314 t) and i = 10 sin (314 t + π/6)

   Calculate the values of the resistance, capacitance which are connected in series to form the circuit. Also draw waveforms for current, voltage and phasor diagram. Calculate power consumed by the circuit.   **[Ans. : 10.393 Ω, 530.45 µF, 519.52 W]**

6. *A 230 V, 50 Hz voltage is applied first to resistor of value 100 Ω and then to a capacitor of 100 µF. Obtain the expressions for the instantaneous currents for both the cases and draw the phasor diagram.*   **[Ans. : 3.2526 sin (100 π t) A, 10.2185 sin(100 π t + 90°) A]**

7. *A series circuit of R = 10 Ω and $X_C = 15 \ \Omega$ has an applied phasor voltage V = 50 $\angle - 90°$ V r.m.s. Find the real power, reactive power, complete power and power factor.*

   [Ans. : 76.93 W, 115.3846 VAR, 138.675 VA, 0.5547 leading]

8. *A series R-C circuit with R = 20 Ω and C = 127 µF has 160 V, 50 Hz supply connectd to it, Find the impedance, current, power factor and power.*

   [Ans. : 32.064$\angle$ – 51.41° Ω, 5$\angle$51.41°A, 0.6237 leading, 500 W]

3.20 A.C. through Series R-L-C Circuit   2002-03, 2006-07, 2009-10, 2010-11

Consider a circuit consisting of resistance R ohms pure inductance L henries and capacitance C farads connected in series with each other across a.c. supply. The circuit is shown in the Fig. 3.20.1.

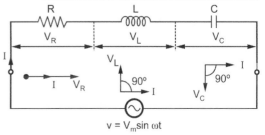

Fig. 3.20.1 R-L-C series circuit

The a.c. supply is given by,

$$v = V_m \sin \omega t$$

The circuit draws a current I.

Due to current I, there are different voltage drops across R, L and C which are given by,

a) Drop across resistance R is $V_R = I\,R$

b) Drop across inductance L is $V_L = I\,X_L$

c) Drop across capacitance C is $V_C = I\,X_C$

The values of I, V_R, V_L and V_C are r.m.s. values

The characteristics of three drops are,

a) V_R in phase with I   b) V_L leads I by 90°   c) V_C lags I by 90°

According to Kirchhoff's laws, we can write,

$$\overline{V} = \overline{V_R} + \overline{V_L} + \overline{V_C} \qquad \text{... Phasor addition}$$

Current I is taken as reference as it is common to all the elements.

Following are the steps to draw the phasor diagram :

1) Take current as reference.   2) V_R is in phase with I.

3) V_L leads current I by 90°.   4) V_C lags current I by 90°.

5) Obtain the resultant of V_L and V_C. Both V_L and V_C are in phase opposition.

6) Add that with V_R by law of parallelogram to get the supply voltage.

The phasor diagram depends on the conditions of the magnitudes of V_L and V_C which ultimately depends on the values of X_L and X_C.

Let us consider the different cases.

3.20.1 $X_L > X_C$

When $X_L > X_C$, obviously, $I X_L$ i.e. V_L is greater than $I X_C$ i.e. V_C.

So, resultant of V_L and V_C will be directed towards V_L. Current I will lag the resultant of the voltages V_L and V_C i.e. $(V_L - V_C)$.

The circuit is said to be **inductive** in nature.

The phasor sum of V_R and $(V_L - V_C)$ gives the resultant supply voltage, V. This is shown in the Fig. 3.20.2.

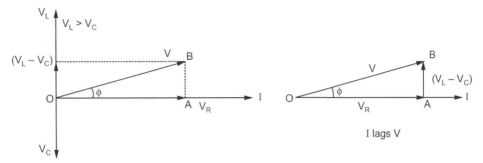

Fig. 3.20.2 Phasor diagram and voltage triangle for $X_L > X_C$

From the voltage triangle, $V = \sqrt{(V_R)^2 + (V_L - V_C)^2} = \sqrt{(I\,R)^2 + (I\,X_L - I\,X_C)^2}$

$$= I \sqrt{(R)^2 + (X_L - X_C)^2} = I\,Z$$

where $Z = \sqrt{(R)^2 + (X_L - X_C)^2}$

So, if $v = V_m \sin \omega t$, then $i = I_m \sin (\omega t - \phi)$ as current **lags** voltage by angle ϕ .

`3.20.2` $X_L < X_C$

When $X_L < X_C$, obviously, $I\,X_L$ i.e. V_L is less than $I\,X_C$ i.e. V_C. So, the resultant of V_L and V_C will be directed towards V_C. Current I will lead $(V_C - V_L)$.

The circuit is said to be **capacitive** in nature. The phasor sum of V_R and $(V_C - V_L)$ gives the resultant supply voltage V. This is shown in the Fig. 3.20.3.

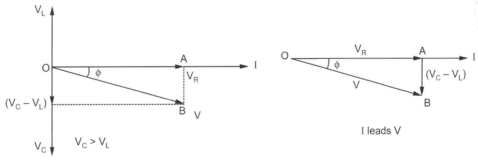

Fig. 3.20.3 Phasor diagram and voltage triangle for $X_L < X_C$

`3.20.3` $X_L = X_C$

When $X_L = X_C$, obviously, $V_L = V_C$. So, V_L and V_C will cancel each other and their resultant is zero.

So, $V_R = V$ in such case and overall circuit is purely resistive in nature. The phasor diagram is shown in the Fig. 3.20.4.

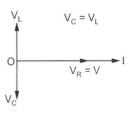

Fig. 3.20.4 Phasor diagram for $X_L = X_C$

From phasor diagram,

$$V = V_R = I R = I Z$$

Where $\quad Z = R$

The circuit is purely resistive with **unity power factor.**

3.20.4 Impedance

In general, for RLC series circuit impedance is given by,

$$Z = R + j X \quad \text{where} \quad X = X_L - X_C = \text{Total reactance of circuit}$$

If $\quad X_L > X_C,$ X is positive and circuit is inductive.

If $\quad X_L < X_C,$ X is negative and circuit is capacitive.

If $\quad X_L = X_C,$ X is zero and circuit is purely resistive.

$$\tan \phi = \left[\frac{X_L - X_C}{R} \right], \quad \cos \phi = \frac{R}{Z} \quad \text{and} \quad Z = \sqrt{R^2 + (X_L - X_C)^2}$$

3.20.5 Impedance Triangle

The impedance is expressed as,

$$Z = R + j X \quad \text{where} \quad X = X_L - X_C$$

For $X_L > X_C,$ ϕ is positive and the impedance triangle is as shown in the Fig. 3.20.5 (a).

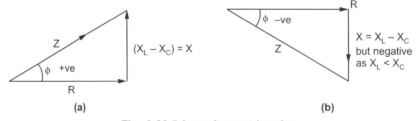

(a)   (b)

Fig. 3.20.5 Impedance triangles

For $X_L < X_C,$ $X_L - X_C$ is negative, so ϕ is negative and the impedance triangle is as shown in Fig. 3.20.5 (b).

In both the cases, $R = Z \cos \phi \quad$ and $\quad X = Z \sin \phi$

3.20.6 Power and Power Triangle

The average power consumed by the circuit is,

$$P_{av} = \text{Average power consumed by R} + \text{Average power}$$

$$\text{consumed by L} + \text{Average power consumed by C}$$

But, pure L and C never consume any power.

$\therefore$ $\qquad$ P_{av} = Power taken by R = I^2R = I (IR) = I V_R

But, $\qquad$ V_R = V cos ϕ in both the cases

$\therefore$ $\qquad$ P = V I cos ϕ $\quad$ W

Thus, for any condition, $X_L > X_C$ or $X_L < X_C$, in general power can be expressed as,

$$\boxed{P = V\,I\,\cos\phi \quad \text{watts}}$$

where magnitude of current is given by,

$$I = \frac{V}{|Z|} = \frac{V}{\sqrt{R^2 + (X_L - X_C)^2}} \qquad \text{(only magnitude)}$$

While ϕ is decided by the total impedance of the circuit.

Sr. No.	Circuit	Impedance (Z)		ϕ	p.f. cos ϕ	Remark
		Polar	Rectangular			
1.	Pure R	$R \angle 0° \; \Omega$	$R + j\,0 \; \Omega$	$0°$	1	Unity p.f.
2.	Pure L	$X_L \angle 90° \; \Omega$	$0 + j\,X_L \; \Omega$	$90°$	0	Zero lagging
3.	Pure C	$X_C \angle -90° \; \Omega$	$0 - j\,X_C \; \Omega$	$-90°$	0	Zero leading
4.	Series RL	$|Z| \angle + \phi° \; \Omega$	$R + j\,X_L \; \Omega$	$0° \angle \phi \angle 90°$	cos ϕ	Lagging
5.	Series RC	$|Z| \angle - \phi° \; \Omega$	$R - j\,X_C \; \Omega$	$-90° \angle \phi \angle 0°$	cos ϕ	Leading
6.	Series RLC	$|Z| \angle \pm \phi° \; \Omega$	$R + j\,X \; \Omega$ $X = X_L - X_C$	ϕ	cos ϕ	$X_L > X_C$ Lagging $X_L < X_C$ Leading $X_L = X_C$ Unity

Table 3.20.1 Summary of R, L and C circuits

Example 3.20.1 *A series RLC circuit is composed of 100 ohms resistance, 1.0 H inductance and 5 μF capacitance. A voltage, v(t) = 141.4 cos 377 t volts is applied to the circuit. Determine the current and voltages V_R, V_L and V_C.*

Solution : v(t) = 141.4 cos (377 t) V = 141.4 sin (377 t + 90°) V = V_m sin (ωt + θ) V

$\therefore$ $\qquad$ V_m = 141.4 V

and $\quad\omega = 377$ rad/sec

$\therefore\quad V = $ r.m.s. value $= \dfrac{V_m}{\sqrt{2}} = \dfrac{141.4}{\sqrt{2}}$

$\qquad = 99.984 \approx 100$ V

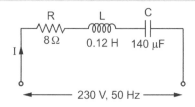

Thus the polar form of the voltage is,

$\qquad V = 100 \angle 90°$ V

$\qquad Z_L = 0 + j X_L = 0 + j\,\omega\,L = 0 + j\,377\ \Omega = 377 \angle 90°\,\Omega$

Now $\quad Z_C = 0 - j X_C = 0 - j\left(\dfrac{1}{\omega C}\right) = 0 - j\left(\dfrac{1}{377\times5\times10^{-6}}\right)$

$\qquad = 0 - j\,530.5039\ \Omega = 530.5039 \angle -90°\ \Omega$

$\therefore\quad Z_T = $ Total impedance $= R + Z_L + Z_C$

$\qquad = 100 + j\,377 - j\,530.5039\ \Omega = 100 - j\,153.5039\ \Omega$

$\qquad = 183.2032 \angle -56.9177°\ \Omega$

$\therefore\quad I = \dfrac{V}{Z_T} = \dfrac{100 \angle 90°}{183.2032 \angle -56.9177°} = \mathbf{0.5458 \angle 146.9177°\,A}$

$\therefore\quad V_R = I \times R = 0.5458 \angle 146.9177° \times 100 \angle 0° = \mathbf{54.58 \angle 146.9177°\,V}$

$\qquad V_L = I \times Z_L = 0.5458 \angle 146.9177° \times 377 \angle 90° = \mathbf{205.7666 \angle 236.9177°\,V}$

$\qquad V_C = I \times Z_C = 0.5458 \angle 146.9177° \times 530.5039 \angle -90° = \mathbf{289.549 \angle 56.9177°\,V}$

$\therefore\quad |V_R| = \mathbf{54.58\ V},\ |V_L| = \mathbf{205.7666\ V},\ |V_C| = \mathbf{289.549\ V}$

Example 3.20.2 *A coil of resistance 8 Ω and inductance 0.12 henry is connected in series with a condenser of capacitance 140 microfarads across a 230 volts, 50 Hz supply. Determine : i) Impedance of the entire circuit, ii) Current flowing through the condenser, iii) Power factor of the circuit, iv) Voltage across the condenser.* **2002-03, Marks 10**

Solution : $\quad X_L = 2\pi f\,L = 2\pi \times 50 \times 0.12 = 37.7\ \Omega$

$\qquad X_C = \dfrac{1}{2\pi f C} = \dfrac{1}{2\pi \times 50 \times 140 \times 10^{-6}}$

$\qquad = 22.7364\ \Omega$

i) $\qquad Z = R + jX_L - jX_C = 8 + j\,14.9636\ \Omega = \mathbf{16.9678 \angle 61.869°\ \Omega}$

ii) $\qquad I = \dfrac{V}{Z} = \dfrac{230 \angle 0°}{16.9678 \angle 61.869°} = \mathbf{13.555 \angle -61.869°\ A}$

Current **13.555 A** is same in magnitude through capacitor as series circuit.

iii) $\cos \phi$ = $\cos (- 61.869°) = $ **0.4715 lagging**

iv) V_C = $I X_C = 13.555 \times 22.7364 = $ **308.1919 V**   ... In magnitude

---

Example 3.20.3 *The voltage and current of an R-L-C series circuit are :*
v = 141.4 sin (314t + 45°) V and i = 28.28 sin (314t – 15°) A. Find :
i) r.m.s. V, I ii) Power factor iii) Power consumption
iv) Time period v) Resistance in a circuit.   **2006-07, Marks 10**

Solution : Comparing given equation with $v = V_m \sin (\omega t + \phi_1)$

          V_m = 141.4 V, $\phi_1 = + 45°$, $\omega = 314$ rad/sec

Similarly, I_m = 28.28 A, $\phi_2 = - 15°$, $\omega = 314$ rad/sec

i) $V_{r.m.s.}$ = $\dfrac{V_m}{\sqrt 2} = \dfrac{141.4}{\sqrt 2} = $ **100 V** = V

          $I_{r.m.s.}$ = $\dfrac{I_m}{\sqrt 2} = \dfrac{28.28}{\sqrt 2} = $ **20 A** = I

ii) The phasor diagram is shown in the Fig. 3.20.8.

          ϕ = Angle between V and I

∴ ϕ = $45° + 15° = 60°$

∴ $\cos \phi$ = Power factor = $\cos 60°$

          = **0.5 lagging**

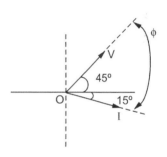

Fig. 3.20.8

Current lags voltage by angle ϕ .

iii)   P = $VI \cos \phi = 100 \times 20 \times 0.5 = $ **1000 W**

iv) ω = $2 \pi f = \dfrac{2\pi}{T}$ i.e. $T = \dfrac{2\pi}{\omega} = \dfrac{2\pi}{314} = $ **0.02 sec**

v)   Z = $\dfrac{V}{I} = \dfrac{100\angle 45°}{20\angle -15°} = 5 \angle 60° \ \Omega = 2.5 + j \ 4.3301 \ \Omega = R + j \ X \ \Omega$

∴   R = **2.5 Ω**   ...Resistance in a circuit

Example 3.20.4 *A coil having a resistance of 6 ohm and an inductance of 0.0255 H is connected across a 230 V, 50 Hz a.c. supply. Calculate i) Current ii) Power factor iii) Active power iv) Reactive power v) Apparent power vi) It is desired to improve power factor to 0.8. What value of capacitance to be connected in series R and what is reduction in reactive power?*   **2009-10, Marks 10**

Solution : The circuit is shown in the Fig. 3.20.9.

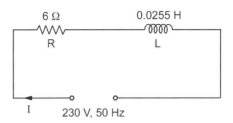

Fig. 3.20.9

i) $\qquad X_L = 2\pi f L = 2\pi \times 50 \times 0.0255 \approx 8\ \Omega$

$\therefore \qquad Z = R + jX_L = 6 + j8\ \Omega$

$\qquad\qquad = 10\angle 53.168^\circ\ \Omega$

$\therefore \qquad I = \dfrac{V}{Z} = \dfrac{230\angle 0^\circ}{10\angle 53.168^\circ}$

$\qquad\qquad = \mathbf{23\angle -53.168^\circ\,A}$

Assuming voltage reference.

ii) Power factor $= \cos\phi = \cos(-53.168^\circ) = \mathbf{0.6\ lagging}$.

iii) Active power : $P_{active} = VI\cos\phi = 230 \times 23 \times 0.6 = \mathbf{3174\ W}$

iv) Reactive power : $Q_{reactive} = VI\sin\phi = 230 \times 23 \times \sin(+53.168^\circ)$

$$= + \mathbf{4232\ VAR}$$

v) Apparent power : $S_{apparent} = V\,I = 230 \times 23 = \mathbf{5285.331\ VA}$.

vi) The capacitor C is connected in series with R.

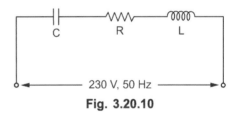

Fig. 3.20.10

$\therefore \qquad Z = R + j(X_L - X_C)$

$\therefore \qquad \cos\phi = \dfrac{R}{Z} = \dfrac{R}{\sqrt{R^2 + (X_L - X_C)^2}}$

Now $\cos\phi = 0.8$, $R = 6\ \Omega$, $X_L = 8.01106\ \Omega$.

$\therefore \qquad 0.8 = \dfrac{6}{\sqrt{6^2 + (8.01106 - X_C)^2}}$

Solving, $\quad X_C = 3.51106 = \dfrac{1}{2\pi f C}$ i.e. $C = \mathbf{906.5919\ \mu F}$

$\therefore \qquad Z = 6 + j(8.01106 - 3.5116) = 6 + j4.5\ \Omega = 7.5\angle 36.869^\circ\ \Omega$

$\therefore \qquad I = \dfrac{V}{Z} = \dfrac{230\angle 0^\circ}{7.5\angle 36.869^\circ} = 30.667\angle -36.869^\circ\ A$

$\therefore \qquad Q_{reactive} = VI\sin\phi = 230 \times 30.667 \times \sin(-36.869^\circ) = -\,\mathbf{4232.046\ VAR}$

The reactive power remains same as before.

Example 3.20.5 *Find the values of R and C so that $V_x = 3\ V_y$ while V_x and V_y are in quadrature. Find the phase relation between V and $V_x , V_y , I.$*

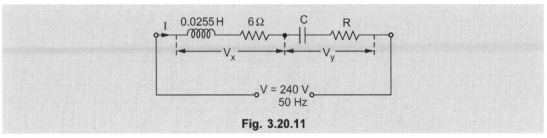

Fig. 3.20.11

Solution : Let $\quad Z_1 = R_1 + j\,X_1 \quad$ where $R_1 = 6\ \Omega$ and $L_1 = 0.0255$ H

$\therefore \qquad X_1 = 2\,\pi\,f\,L_1 = 2\,\pi \times 50 \times 0.0255 = 8.011\ \Omega$

$\therefore \qquad Z_1 = 6 + j\,8.011 = 10\ \angle\,53.16°\ \Omega$

Now $\qquad |V_x| = |I\,Z_1|$ and $|V_y| = |I\,Z_2|$

Where $\qquad Z_2 = R - j\,X_2 \quad$ Where X_2 is capacitive.

But $\qquad V_x = 3\,V_y$

$\therefore \qquad |I\,Z_1| = |3\,I\,Z_2|$

$\therefore \qquad |Z_1| = 3\,|Z_2|$

$\therefore \qquad 10 = 3\,|Z_2|$

$\therefore \qquad |Z_2| = 3.333\ \Omega = \sqrt{R^2 + X_2^2} \qquad\qquad\qquad …\ (3.20.1)$

Let current I is reference with angle $0°$.

$\therefore \qquad V_x = I\,Z_1 = I\ \angle\,0° \cdot 10\ \angle\,53.16° = 10\ I\ \angle\,53.16°\ V \qquad …\ (3.20.2)$

So phase of V_x is $+\,53.16°$.

While V_x and V_y are in quadrature i.e. at $90°$ w.r.t. each other.

The phasor diagram is shown in the Fig. 3.20.11 (a).

So phase of V_y is $-\,36.84°$.

$$V_y = I\,Z_2$$

$\therefore \qquad V_y \angle -36.84° = I\ \angle\,0° \cdot Z_2 \angle\,\phi_2° \qquad …\ (3.20.3)$

$\therefore \qquad \phi_2 = -\,36.84°$ … Equating phase angles

So impedance Z_2 can be represented as,

$$Z_2 = Z_2|\ \angle\,\phi_2 = 3.333\ \angle -36.84°\ \Omega$$

$$= 2.667 - j\,1.998\ \Omega$$

$\therefore \qquad R = \textbf{2.667}\ \Omega \quad$ and $\quad X_C = 1.998\ \Omega$

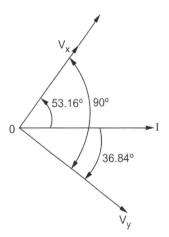

Fig. 3.20.11 (a)

$$\therefore \quad X_C = \frac{1}{2\pi f C} = 1.998$$

$$\therefore \quad C = \mathbf{1593.14 \ \mu F}$$

Now
$$Z_T = Z_1 + Z_2$$
$$= 6 + j\,8.011 + 2.667 - j\,1.998$$
$$= 8.667 + j\,6.013 \ \Omega$$
$$= 10.548 \ \angle + 34.75^\circ \ \Omega$$

Now
$$V = I\,Z_T = I \angle 0^\circ \times 10.548 \ \angle + 34.75^\circ$$
$$= 10.548\,I \angle + 34.75^\circ$$

Fig. 3.20.11 (b)

Thus phase of V is + 34.75° as shown in the Fig. 3.20.11 (b).

Thus V_x leads V by 53.16 − 34.75 = **18.41°**

V_y lags V by 34.75 + 36.84 = **71.59°**

I lags V by **34.75°**

Review Questions

1. *Derive an expression for impedance, phase angle and power for series R-L-C circuit energised by sinusoidal voltage.*

2. *For a R-L-C series circuit discuss the nature of the power factor for*
   i) $X_L > X_C$ *ii)* $X_L < X_C$ *iii)* $X_L = X_C$

3. *A circuit having a resistance of 12 Ω, in inductance of 0.15 H and a capacitance of 100 μF in series is connected across a 100 V, 50 Hz supply. Calculate the impedance, current, the phase difference between the current and supply voltage.*
   [Ans. : Z = 19.4389 ∠51.8795° Ω, I = 5.1443 ∠− 51.8795°A, cos φ = 0.6173 lagging]

4. *A circuit consists of a resistance of 10 Ω, an inductance of 16 mH and a capacitance of 150 μF connected in series. A supply of 100 V at 50 Hz is given to the circuit. Find the current, power factor and power consumed by the circuit. Draw the vector diagram.*
   [Ans. : cos φ = 0.5254 leading, P = 276.045 W]

5. *A series circuit having pure resistance of 40 ohms, pure inductance of 50.07 mH and a capacitor is connected across a 400 V, 50 Hz, A.C. supply. This R, L, C combination draws a current of 10 A. Calculate (i) Power factor of the circuit and (ii) Capacitor value.* [Ans. : i) 1, ii) 2.023 × 10⁻⁴ F]

6. *Two impedances, Z_1 = (100 + j 0) ohm and Z_2 = (R + jX) ohm are in series. An a.c. voltage of 400 V, 50 Hz is applied across the series combination. The voltage drops across the two impedances are 200 V and 300 V respectively. Sketch a neat connection diagram and phasor diagram and find the current and power consumed by Z_2.* [Ans. : I = 2 ∠− 46.567° A, P₂ = 150.025 W]

7. *An e.m.f. given by v = 100 sin π t is impressed across a circuit consists of resistance of 40 Ω in series with 100 μF capacitor and 0.25 H inductor.*

   Determine - i) R.M.S. value of current ii) Power consumed iii) Power factor.

   [Ans. : i) 1.1498A ii) 52.8837 W, iii) 0.6504 lagging]

8. *A series circuit consists of resistance of 10 ohm, an inductance of $\frac{200}{\pi}$ mH and capacitance of $\frac{1000}{\pi}$ μF. Calculate (1) Current flowing in the circuit if supply voltage is 200 V, 50 Hz (2) p.f. of the circuit, (3) Power drawn from the supply. Also draw the phasor diagram.*

   [Ans. : 1) 14.1421 $\angle$ – 45° A, 2) 2000 W, 3) 0.7071 lagging]

9. *Two impedances Z_1 = 40 $\angle$ 30° ohm and Z_2 = 30 $\angle$ 60° ohm are connected in series across single phase, 230 V, 50 Hz supply. Calculate the 1) Current drawn, 2) p.f. and 3) Power consumed by the circuit.* **[Ans. : 1) 3.399 $\angle$ – 42.807° A, 2) 0.7336 lagging, 3) 573.5064 W]**

10. *A pure resistance R, a choke coil and a pure capacitor of 15.91 μF are connected in series across a supply of V volts and carry current of 0.25 Amp. The voltage across choke is 40 volts, the voltage across capacitor is 50 volt and voltage across resistance is 20 volt. The voltage across combination of R and choke coil is 45 volts. Calculate,*

    i) Supply voltage   ii) Frequency   iii) Power loss in choke coil. **[Ans. : 28.268 V, 50 Hz, 1.5625 W]**

11. *Discuss the response of RLC series circuit to sinusoidal input.* **2010-11, Marks 5**

3.21 Resonance in Series R-L-C Circuit   **2001-02, 2005-06, 2006-07, 2009-10, 2010-11, 2011-12, 2012-13**

We know that both X_L and X_C are the functions of frequency f. When f is varied both X_L and X_C also get varied. At a certain frequency, X_L becomes equal to X_C. Such a condition when $X_L = X_C$ for a certain frequency is called **series resonance**. At resonance the reactive part in the impedance of RLC series circuit is zero. The frequency at which the resonance occurs is called **resonant frequency** denoted as ω_r rad/sec or f_r Hz.

3.21.1 Characteristics of Series Resonance

In a series resonance, the voltage applied is constant and frequency is variable. Hence following parameters of series RLC circuit get affected due to change in frequency :

1) X_L 2) X_C 3) Total reactance X 4) Impedance Z 5) I 6) cos φ

As $X_L = 2 \pi f L$, as frequency is changed from 0 to ∞, X_L increases linearly and graph of X_L against f is straight line passing through origin.

As $X_C = \frac{1}{2\pi f C}$, as frequency is changed from 0 to ∞, X_C reduces and the graph of X_C against f is rectangular hyperbola. Mathematically sign of X_C is opposite to X_L hence graph of X_L Vs f is shown in the first quadrant while X_C Vs f is shown in the third quadrant.

At $f = f_r$, the value of $X_L = X_C$ at this frequency.

As $X = X_L - X_C$, the graph of X against f is shown in the Fig. 3.21.1.

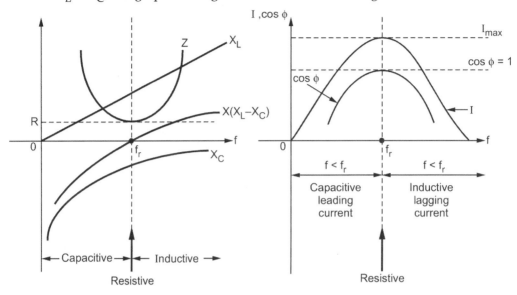

Fig. 3.21.1 Characteristics of series resonance

For $f < f_r$, the $X_C > X_L$ and net reactance X is **capacitive** while for $f > f_r$, the $X_L > X_C$ and net reactance X is **inductive**.

Now $Z = R + j X = R + j (X_L - X_C)$ but at $f = f_r$, $X_L = X_C$ and $X = 0$ hence the net impedance $Z = R$ which is purely resistive. So **impedance** is **minimum** and **purely resistive** at series resonance. The graph of Z against f is also shown in the Fig. 3.21.1.

Key Point *As impedance is minimum, the* **current** $I = V/Z$ *is* **maximum** *at series resonance.*

Now power factor $\cos \phi = R/Z$ and at $f = f_r$ as $Z = R$, the **power factor** is **unity** and at its **maximum** at series resonance. For $f < f_r$ it is **leading** in nature while for $f > f_r$ it is **lagging** in nature.

3.21.2 Expression for Resonant Frequency

Let f_r be the resonant frequency in Hz at which,

$$X_L = X_C \quad \text{i.e.} \quad 2\pi f_r L = \frac{1}{2\pi f_r C} \qquad \text{... Series resonance}$$

$$\therefore \qquad (f_r)^2 = \frac{1}{4\pi^2 LC} \quad \text{i.e.} \quad \boxed{f_r = \frac{1}{2\pi\sqrt{LC}} \quad \text{Hz}}$$

$$\boxed{\omega_r = \frac{1}{\sqrt{LC}} \quad \text{rad/sec}}$$

3.21.3 Bandwidth of Series R-L-C Circuit

At series resonance, current is maximum and impedance Z is minimum. Now power consumed in a circuit is proportional to square of the current as $P = I^2 R$. So at series resonance as current is maximum, power is also at its maximum i.e. P_m. The Fig. 3.21.2 shows the graph of current and power against frequency.

It can be observed that at two frequencies f_1 and f_2 the power is half of its maximum value. These frequencies are called **half power frequencies**.

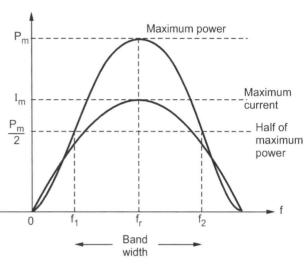

Fig. 3.21.2 Bandwidth

Definition of Bandwidth :

The difference between the half power frequencies f_1 and f_2 at which power is half of its maximum is called bandwidth of the series R-L-C circuit.

$\therefore$
$$ \text{B.W.} = f_2 - f_1 $$

In the bandwidth, the power is more than half the maximum value. The bandwidth decides the selectivity. The **selectivity** is defined as the ratio of the resonant frequency to the bandwidth.

$$ \text{Selectivity} = \frac{f_r}{\text{B.W.}} $$

Key Point *Thus if the bandwidth is more, the selectivity of the circuit is less.*

Out of the two half power frequencies, the frequency f_2 is called **upper cut-off frequency** while the frequency f_1 is called **lower cut-off frequency**.

3.21.4 Expressions for Lower and Upper Cut-off Frequencies

The current in a series RLC circuit is given by the equation,

$$ I = \frac{V}{Z} \quad \text{but } Z = R + j (X_L - X_C) $$

$$\therefore \qquad I = \frac{V}{\sqrt{R^2 + (X_L - X_C)^2}} = \frac{V}{\sqrt{R^2 + \left(\omega L - \dfrac{1}{\omega C}\right)^2}} \qquad \dots (3.21.1)$$

At resonance, $I_m = \dfrac{V}{R}$ (maximum value) and $P_m = I_m^2 R$ ... (3.21.2)

At half power point, $\quad P = \dfrac{P_m}{2} = \dfrac{I_m^2}{2} R = \left(\dfrac{I_m}{\sqrt{2}}\right)^2 R$

$$\therefore \qquad I = \frac{I_m}{\sqrt{2}} \qquad \text{at half power frequency}$$

Equating equations (3.21.1) and (3.21.2),

$$\frac{V}{\sqrt{R^2 + \left(\omega L - \dfrac{1}{\omega C}\right)^2}} = \frac{V}{\sqrt{2} \cdot R} \quad \text{i.e.} \quad \sqrt{R^2 + \left(\omega L - \dfrac{1}{\omega C}\right)^2} = \sqrt{2}\ R$$

$$\therefore \qquad R^2 + \left(\omega L - \frac{1}{\omega C}\right)^2 = 2\ R^2 \quad \text{i.e.} \quad \left(\omega L - \frac{1}{\omega C}\right)^2 = R^2$$

$$\therefore \qquad \omega L - \frac{1}{\omega C} = \pm\ R \qquad \dots (3.21.3)$$

From the equation (3.21.3) we can find two values of half power frequencies which are ω_1 and ω_2 corresponding to f_1 and f_2.

$$\therefore \qquad \omega_2 L - \frac{1}{\omega_2 C} = +\ R \quad \text{and} \quad \omega_1 L - \frac{1}{\omega_1 C} = -\ R \qquad \dots (3.21.4)$$

Adding, $\qquad (\omega_1 + \omega_2)\ L - \left(\dfrac{1}{\omega_1} + \dfrac{1}{\omega_2}\right) \dfrac{1}{C} = 0$

$$\therefore \qquad (\omega_1 + \omega_2)\ L = \frac{(\omega_1 + \omega_2)}{\omega_1 \omega_2} \cdot \frac{1}{C} \quad \text{i.e.} \quad \omega_1\ \omega_2 = \frac{1}{LC} \qquad \dots (3.21.5)$$

but $\quad \omega_r = \dfrac{1}{\sqrt{LC}} \quad$ hence $\quad \boxed{\omega_1\ \omega_2 = (\omega_r)^2 \ \text{i.e.} \ f_1 f_2 = (f_r)^2} \qquad \dots (3.21.6)$

The equation (3.21.6) shows that **the resonant frequency is the geometric mean of the two half power frequencies**.

$$\therefore \qquad \boxed{f_r = \sqrt{f_1\ f_2}} \qquad \dots (3.21.7)$$

Subtracting equations (3.21.4),

$$(\omega_2 - \omega_1)\, L - \left(\frac{1}{\omega_1} - \frac{1}{\omega_2}\right)\frac{1}{C} = 2R$$

$$\therefore \qquad (\omega_2 - \omega_1) + \frac{(\omega_2 - \omega_1)}{\omega_1\,\omega_2} \cdot \frac{1}{LC} = \frac{2R}{L} \qquad\qquad \text{... Dividing both sides by L}$$

$$\therefore \qquad (\omega_2 - \omega_1) + (\omega_2 - \omega_1) = \frac{2R}{L} \qquad\qquad \text{... as } \frac{1}{\omega_1\omega_2} = LC$$

$$\therefore \qquad (\omega_2 - \omega_1) = \frac{R}{L} \quad \text{i.e.} \quad f_2 - f_1 = \frac{R}{2\pi L} \qquad\qquad \text{... (3.21.8)}$$

Thus $\boxed{\text{B.W.} = \dfrac{R}{2\pi L}}$

The bandwidth is also denoted as,

B.W. = $2\,\Delta f$ where

$\boxed{\Delta f = \dfrac{R}{4\pi L}}$ as shown in the Fig. 3.21.3

From Fig. 3.21.3 we can write,

$\boxed{f_1 = f_r - \Delta f}$

and $\boxed{f_2 = f_r + \Delta f}$

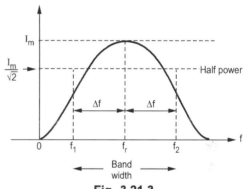

Fig. 3.21.3

3.21.5 Quality Factor

The quality factor of R-L-C series circuit is the voltage magnification in the circuit at resonance.

$$\text{Voltage magnification} = \frac{\text{Voltage across L or C}}{\text{Supply voltage}}$$

Now $\qquad V_L = $ Voltage across L $= I_m\, X_L = I_m\, \omega_r\, L$ at resonance

and $\qquad I_m = \dfrac{V}{R}$ at resonance

$\therefore \qquad V_L = \dfrac{V\omega_r L}{R}$ at resonance

$\therefore$ Voltage magnification $= \dfrac{\dfrac{V\omega_r L}{R}}{V} = \dfrac{\omega_r L}{R}$

This is nothing but quality factor Q.

$\therefore$ $\boxed{Q = \dfrac{\omega_r L}{R}}$ but $\omega_r = \dfrac{1}{\sqrt{LC}}$ $\therefore$ $\boxed{Q = \dfrac{1}{R}\sqrt{\dfrac{L}{C}}}$

and $\boxed{Q = \dfrac{\omega_r}{B.W.}}$ as B.W.$= (\omega_2 - \omega_1) = \dfrac{R}{L}$

The **significance of quality factor** can be stated as,

1. It indicates the selectivity or sharpness of the tuning of a series circuit.

2. It gives the correct indication of the selectivity of such series R-L-C circuit which are used in many radio circuits.

Key Point *At the resonant frequency, the impedance is minimum and hence the circuit is known as **acceptor circuit** at resonance.*

The various applications of series resonant circuits are,

1. tuning circuits in t.v. receivers

2. as a wave trap

3. inverters

Example 3.21.1 *A RLC series circuit with a resistance of 10 Ω, impedance of 0.2 H and a capacitance of 40 μF is supplied with a 100 V supply at variable frequency. Find the following w.r.t the series resonant circuit :- i) the frequency at resonance ii) the current iii) power iv) power factor v) voltage across R, L, C at that time vi) quality factor of the circuit vii) half power points viii) phasor diagram.*

Solution : The given values are, R = 10 Ω, L = 0.2 H, C = 40 μF and V = 100 V

i) $f_r = \dfrac{1}{2\pi\sqrt{LC}} = \dfrac{1}{2\pi\sqrt{0.2\times 40\times 10^{-6}}} = \mathbf{56.2697\ Hz}$

ii) $I_m = \dfrac{V}{R} = \dfrac{100}{10} = \mathbf{10\ A}$ ... Current is maximum at resonance

iii) $P_m = I_m^2 R = (10)^2 \times 10 = \mathbf{1000\ W}$

iv) Power factor is **unity**, as impedance is **purely resistive** at resonance

v) $V_R = I_m R = 10 \times 10 = \textbf{100 V}$

$X_L = 2\pi f_r L = 2\pi \times 56.2697 \times 0.2 = 70.7105 \ \Omega$

∴ $V_L = I_m X_L = 10 \times 70.7105 = \textbf{707.105 V}$

and $X_C = \dfrac{1}{2\pi f_r C} = \dfrac{1}{2\pi \times 56.2697 \times 40 \times 10^{-6}} = 70.7105 \ \Omega$

∴ $\boxed{V_C = I_m X_C = \textbf{707.105 V}}$

Thus $V_L = V_C$ at resonance

vi) $Q = \dfrac{\omega_r L}{R} = \dfrac{2\pi f_r L}{R} = \textbf{7.071}$

vii) $\Delta f = \dfrac{R}{4\pi L} = \dfrac{10}{4\pi \times 0.2} = 3.9788$

∴ $f_1 = f_r - \Delta f = 56.2697 - 3.9788$

        $= \textbf{52.2909 Hz}$

and $f_2 = f_r + \Delta f = 56.2697 + 3.9788$

        $= \textbf{60.2485 Hz}$

viii)   B.W. $= f_2 - f_1 = 60.2485 - 52.2909$

        $= \textbf{7.9576 Hz}$

The phasor diagram is shown in the Fig. 3.21.4.

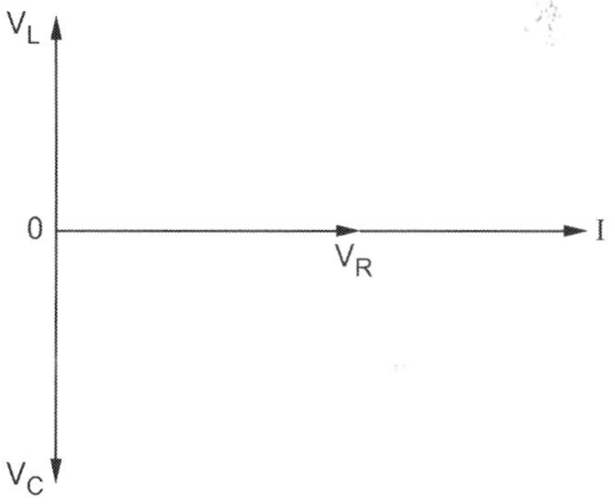

Fig. 3.21.4

Example 3.21.2 *A series R-L-C circuit has R = 10 Ω, L = 0.1 H and C = 8 μF. Determine: (i) resonant frequency, (ii) Q-factor of the circuit at resonance, (iii) the half power frequencies.*   **2005-06, Marks 5**

Solution :

i) $f_r = \dfrac{1}{2\pi\sqrt{LC}} = \dfrac{1}{2\pi\sqrt{0.1 \times 8 \times 10^{-6}}} = \textbf{177.9406 Hz}$

ii) $Q = \dfrac{1}{R}\sqrt{\dfrac{L}{C}} = \dfrac{1}{10}\sqrt{\dfrac{0.1}{8 \times 10^{-6}}} = \textbf{11.18}$

iii) $\Delta f = \dfrac{R}{4\pi L} = \dfrac{10}{4\pi \times 0.1} = 7.9577$

∴ $f_1 = f_r - \Delta f = 177.9406 - 7.9577 = \textbf{169.9829 Hz}$

∴ $f_2 = f_r + \Delta f = 177.9406 + 7.9577 = \textbf{185.8983 Hz}$

Example 3.21.3 *A circuit consists of resistance of 4 Ω, and inductance of 0.5 H and a variable capacitance in series across a 100 V, 500 Hz supply. Calculate, i) the value of capacitance to produce resonance ii) the voltage across the capacitance and iii) the Q-factor of the circuit.*   **2001-02, Marks 5**

Solution :

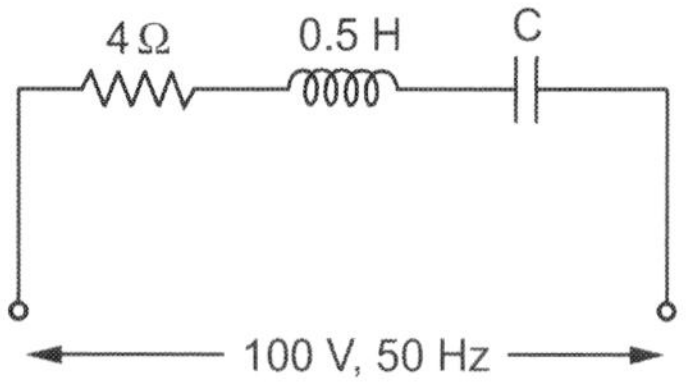

i) $X_L = X_C$ for resonance

$X_L = 2\pi\, fL = 2\pi \times 50 \times 0.5 = 157.0796\ \Omega$

∴ $X_C = \dfrac{1}{2\pi fC} = 157.0796$

∴ $C = \dfrac{1}{2\pi \times 50 \times 157.0796} = \mathbf{20.2642\ \mu F}$

ii) At resonance, $\;I = \dfrac{V}{R} = \dfrac{100}{4} = 25\ A$

∴ $V_C = I \times X_C = 25 \times 157.0796 = \mathbf{3927\ V}$

iii) $Q = \dfrac{\omega L}{R} = \dfrac{2\pi \times 50 \times 0.5}{4} = \mathbf{39.27}$

Fig. 3.21.5

4 Ω   0.5 H   C

100 V, 50 Hz

Example 3.21.4 *A 20 Ω resistor is connected in series with an inductor and a capacitor, across a variable frequency 25 V supply. When the frequency is 400 Hz, the current is at its maximum value of 0.5 A and the potential difference across the capacitor is 150 V, calculate the resistance and inductance of the inductor.*   **2001-02, Marks 5**

Solution : Let r = resistance of the inductor.

At resonance, $V_L = V_C = 150\ V$ given

          $I_{max} = 0.5\ A,\ \ Z = R + r$ ... At resonance

∴ $I_{max} = \dfrac{V}{R+r}\ $ i.e. $\ 0.5 = \dfrac{25}{20+r}$

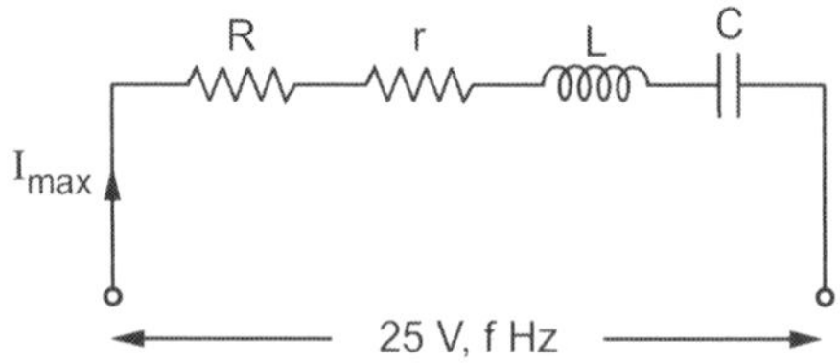

∴ $r = \mathbf{30\ \Omega}$

Now $V_C = I_{max}\, X_C$

∴ $150 = 0.5 \times \dfrac{1}{2\pi fC}\quad$ where f = 400 Hz

∴ $C = \dfrac{0.5}{2\pi \times 400 \times 150} = \mathbf{1.3263\ \mu F}$

And $V_L = I_{max} X_L = I_{max}\,(2\pi f\, L)\quad$ i.e. $\quad 150 = 0.5 \times 2\pi \times 400 \times L$

∴ $L = \mathbf{0.1193\ H}$

Fig. 3.21.6

R   r   L   C

I_{max}

25 V, f Hz

Example 3.21.5 *A coil of resistance 40 Ω and inductance 0.75 H are in a series circuit. The resonant frequency is 55 Hz. If supply is 250 V, 50 Hz find (i) line current (ii) power factor (iii) power consumed.*   **2006-07, Marks 10**

Solution : The circuit is shown in the Fig. 3.21.7.

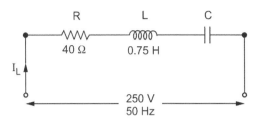

$$f_r = 55 \text{ Hz given}$$

At resonance, $X_L = X_C$

i.e.

$$f_r = \frac{1}{2\pi\sqrt{LC}}$$

Fig. 3.21.7

∴

$$55 = \frac{1}{2\pi\sqrt{0.75 \times C}} \quad \text{i.e. } 299.2768 = \frac{1}{\sqrt{C}}$$

∴

$$C = 11.1648 \ \mu\text{F}$$

Now the circuit is excited by 250 V, 50 Hz supply.

∴

$$X_L = 2\pi f L = 2\pi \times 50 \times 0.75 = 235.6194 \ \Omega$$

$$X_C = \frac{1}{2\pi f C} = \frac{1}{2\pi \times 50 \times 11.1648 \times 10^{-6}} = 285.1012 \ \Omega$$

∴

$$Z = R + jX_L - jX_C = 40 - j49.4818 = 63.6274 \angle -51.04° \Omega$$

Let supply voltage be reference i.e. $V = 250 \angle 0°$ V

∴

$$I = \frac{V}{Z} = \frac{250\angle 0°}{63.6274 \angle -51.04°} = \mathbf{3.9291 \ \angle + 51.04° \ A} \qquad \text{... Line current}$$

$$\cos\phi = \cos(51.04°) = \mathbf{0.6287 \ leading} \qquad \text{... Power factor}$$

$$P = VI\cos\phi = 250 \times 3.9291 \times 0.6287 = \mathbf{617.6326 \ W} \qquad \text{... Power}$$

Example 3.21.6 *Voltage across R, L, C connected in series are 5, 8 and 10 volts respectively. Calculate the value of supply voltage at 50 Hz. Also find the frequency at which this circuit would resonate.*   **2011-12, Marks 10**

Solution : The circuit is shown in the Fig. 3.21.8.

$$|V_R| = IR = 5 \text{ V}, \ |V_L| = I X_L = 8 \text{ V},$$
$$|V_C| = I X_C = 10 \text{ V}$$

Let current be reference, $I \angle 0°$ A,

∴

$$\overline{V}_R = I \angle 0° \times R \angle 0° = I R \angle 0°$$

$$= 5 \angle 0° \text{ V} = 5 + j0 \text{ V}$$

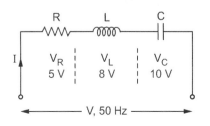

Fig. 3.21.8

$\therefore$ $\quad\overline{V}_L$ $= I\angle0° \times X_L \angle90° = I\,X_L\,\angle90°$

$\qquad\qquad = 8\,\angle90°\,V = 0 + j8\,V$

$\therefore$ $\quad\overline{V}_C$ $= I\angle0° \times X_C \angle-90° = I\,X_C\,\angle-90° = 10\,\angle-90°\,V = 0 - j\,10\,V$

$\therefore$ $\quad\overline{V}$ $= \overline{V}_R + \overline{V}_L + \overline{V}_C = 5 + j0 + 0 + j8 + 0 - j10\,V$

$\qquad\qquad = 5 - j2\,V = 5.3851\,\angle-21.8°\,V$

$\therefore$ Supply voltage = **5.3851 V**

$\qquad\qquad Z = R + j\,X_L - j\,X_C$ as $V_C > V_L$, $X_C > X_L$

$\therefore$ $\qquad Z = R - j\,(X_C - X_L)\,\Omega = |Z|\,\angle\phi\,\Omega$

$\qquad\qquad \phi = 21.8°$ and $\tan\phi = \dfrac{X_C - X_L}{R} = 0.4$

$\therefore$ $\quad X_C - X_L = 0.4\,R$ ... (3.21.9)

$\quad IR = 5,\qquad I\,X_L = 8,\qquad I\,X_C = 10$

$\therefore$ $\qquad\qquad I = \dfrac{5}{R}$ i.e. $X_L = \dfrac{8\,R}{5}$ and $X_C = 2\,R$ ... (3.21.10)

$\quad$ Using in equation (3.21.9), $2\,R - \dfrac{8\,R}{5} = 0.4\,R$ i.e. $R = 1\,\Omega$

$\therefore$ $\qquad X_C = 2\,\Omega$ and $X_L = 1.6\,\Omega$ ... At f = 50 Hz

$\therefore$ $\qquad C = \dfrac{1}{2\,\pi\,f\,X_C} = 1.5915\,mF$ and $L = \dfrac{1.6}{2\,\pi\times50} = 5.093\,mH$

$\therefore$ $\qquad f_r = \dfrac{1}{2\pi\sqrt{LC}} = \dfrac{1}{2\pi\sqrt{5.093\times10^{-3}\times1.5915\times10^{-3}}} = $ **55.9026 Hz**

Example 3.21.7 *A series RLC circuit consisting of a resistance of 20 Ω, inductance 0.2 H and capacitance of 150 μF is connected across a 230 V, 50 Hz source. Calculate :*
i) the impedance ii) the current iii) power factor iv) the frequency of supply to be adjusted to make power factor unity.   2001-02, 2012-13, Marks 10

Solution : The cicruit is shown in the Fig. 3.21.9.

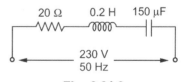

Fig. 3.21.9

i) $\qquad X_L = 2\pi f L = 62.831\,\Omega$

$\qquad\qquad X_C = \dfrac{1}{2\pi f C} = 21.22\,\Omega$

$\therefore$ $\qquad Z = R + j X_L - j X_C = 20 + j62.831 - j21.22\,\Omega$

$\qquad\qquad = 20 + j41.6103\,\Omega = 46.1672\angle64.328°\Omega$

ii) $$I = \frac{V}{Z} = \frac{230\angle 0^\circ}{46.1672\angle 64.328^\circ} = 4.9818\angle -64.328^\circ \text{ A}$$

iii) $$\cos\phi = \cos(-64.328^\circ) = \mathbf{0.4332 \text{ lag}}$$

iv) For unity power factor, there must be resonance.

$$\therefore \quad f_r = \frac{1}{2\pi\sqrt{LC}} = \frac{1}{2\pi\sqrt{0.2\times 150\times 10^{-6}}} = \mathbf{29.0575 \text{ Hz}}$$

Review Questions

1. *Derive the condition of resonance for RLC series circuit.*   **2010-11, Marks 5**

2. *Explain bandwidth and quality factor.*   **2010-11, Marks 5**

3. *Deduce the formula for the half power frequencies for a series RLC circuit under resonance. Why are they called half power frequencies ?*   **2011-12, Marks 5**

4. *State the applications of series resonance.*   **2009-10, Marks 2**

5. *Draw the resonance graph for the following :*
   a) X_L *ii) R   iii) Z   iv) cos ϕ v) I*

6. *Impedance of a circuit is observed to be capacitive and decreasing from 1 Hz to 100 Hz. Beyond 100 Hz, impedance starts increasing. Find the values of the circuit elements if power drawn by the circuit is 100 W, at 100 Hz, when the current is 1 A power factor of the circuit is 0.707 at 70 Hz.*
   (Ans. : R = 100 Ω, L = 0.2186 H, C = 11.585 μF)

7. *A series resonant circuit has in an impedance of 500 Ω at resonant frequency and the cut off frequencies are 10 kHz and 100 Hz. Determine :*
   i) Resonant frequency ii) Value of R, L and C
   iii) Quality factor at resonant frequency   **(Ans. : 5050 Hz, R = 500 Ω, L = 8.03 mH, C = 0.123 μF, Q = 0.509)**

8. *A voltage of 25 V is applied to a series RLC circuit. The voltage across capacitor is observed to be 500 V at the time of resonance. The bandwidth of the circuit is 500 rad/s and the impedance of the circuit at resonance is 14.142 Ω, calculate : i) Resonating frequency   ii) Lower and upper cut off frequencies iii) Values of R, L and C.*
   (Ans. : 1.596 kHz, 1.636 kHz, 1.556 kHz, R = 14.142 Ω, L = 28.2 mH, C = 0.3525 μF)

3.22 A.C. Parallel Circuit   **2000-01, 2001-02, 2002-03, 2003-04, 2004-05, 2006-07, 2007-08, 2008-09, 2009-10, 2011-12, 2012-13**

A parallel circuit is one in which two or more impedances are connected in parallel across the supply voltage.

Each impedance may be a separate series circuit. Each impedance is called branch of the parallel circuit.

The Fig. 3.22.1 shows a parallel circuit consisting of three impedances connected in parallel across an a.c. supply of V volts.

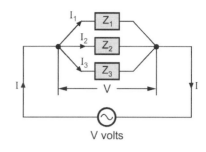

> The voltage across all the impedances is same as supply voltage of V volts.

The current taken by each impedance is different.

Fig. 3.22.1 A.C. parallel circuit

Applying Kirchhoff's law, $\bar{I} = \bar{I}_1 + \bar{I}_2 + \bar{I}_3$ ... (Phasor addition)

$$\therefore \qquad \frac{\bar{V}}{\bar{Z}} = \frac{\bar{V}}{\bar{Z}_1} + \frac{\bar{V}}{\bar{Z}_2} + \frac{\bar{V}}{\bar{Z}_3}$$

$$\therefore \qquad \frac{1}{\bar{Z}} = \frac{1}{\bar{Z}_1} + \frac{1}{\bar{Z}_2} + \frac{1}{\bar{Z}_3} \quad \text{where Z is called \textbf{equivalent impedance.}}$$

This result is applicable for 'n' such impedances connected in parallel.

Following are the steps to solve parallel a.c. circuit :

1) The currents in the individual branches are to be calculated by using the relation

$$\bar{I}_1 = \frac{\bar{V}}{\bar{Z}_1}, \quad \bar{I}_2 = \frac{\bar{V}}{\bar{Z}_2}, \dots, \quad \bar{I}_n = \frac{\bar{V}}{\bar{Z}_n}$$

While the individual phase angles can be calculated by the relation,

$$\tan\phi_1 = \frac{X_1}{R_1}, \quad \tan\phi_2 = \frac{X_2}{R_2}, \quad \dots, \quad \tan\phi_n = \frac{X_n}{R_n}$$

2) Voltage must be taken as reference phasor as it is common to all branches.

3) Represent all the currents on the phasor diagram and add them graphically or mathematically by expressing them in **rectangular form**. This is the resultant current drawn from the supply.

4) The phase angle of resultant current I is power factor angle. Cosine of this angle is the power factor of the circuit.

3.22.1 Concept of Admittance

Admittance is defined as the reciprocal of the impedance. It is denoted by Y and is measured in unit **siemens** or **mho**.

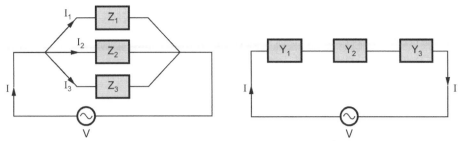

Fig. 3.22.2 Equivalent parallel circuit using admittances

Now, current equation for the circuit shown in the Fig. 3.22.2 is,

$$\overline{I} = \overline{I_1} + \overline{I_2} + \overline{I_3}$$

$$\overline{I} = \overline{V} \times \left(\frac{1}{Z_1}\right) + \overline{V} \times \left(\frac{1}{Z_2}\right) + \overline{V} \times \left(\frac{1}{Z_3}\right)$$

$$\overline{VY} = \overline{VY_1} + \overline{VY_2} + \overline{VY_3}$$

∴ $\overline{Y} = \overline{Y_1} + \overline{Y_2} + \overline{Y_3}$ where **Y** is the **total admittance** of circuit.

The three impedances connected in parallel can be replaced by an equivalent circuit, where three admittances are connected in series, as shown in the Fig. 3.22.2.

3.22.2 Components of Admittance

Consider an impedance given as, Z = R ± j X

Positive sign for inductive and negative sign for capacitive circuit.

Admittance $Y = \dfrac{1}{Z} = \dfrac{1}{R \pm j X}$

Rationalising the above expression,

$$Y = \frac{R \mp j X}{(R \pm j X)(R \mp j X)} = \frac{R \mp j X}{R^2 + X^2}$$

$$= \left(\frac{R}{R^2 + X^2}\right) \mp j \left(\frac{X}{R^2 + X^2}\right) = \frac{R}{Z^2} \mp j \frac{X}{Z^2}$$

∴

$$Y = G \mp j B, \quad |Y| = \sqrt{G^2 + B^2}, \quad \phi = \tan^{-1}\frac{B}{G}$$

In the above expression,

$$G = \text{Conductance} = \frac{R}{Z^2}, \quad B = \text{Susceptance} = \frac{X}{Z^2}$$

Conductance (G) :

It is defined as the ratio of the resistance to the square of the impedance. It is measured in the unit **siemens.**

Susceptance (B) :

It is defined as the ratio of the reactance to the square of the impedance. It is measured in the unit **siemens.**

> The susceptance is said to be inductive (B_L) if its sign is negative. The susceptance is said to be capacitive (B_C) if its sign is positive.

Note *The sign convention for the reactance and the susceptance are opposite to each other.*

3.22.3 Admittance Triangles

The sides of the triangle representing the conductance, susceptance and admittance of the circuit, it is known as **admittance triangle.** The Fig. 3.22.3 shows such admittance triangles.

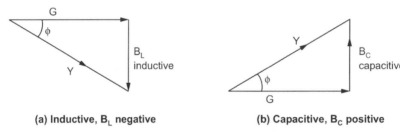

(a) Inductive, B_L negative   (b) Capacitive, B_C positive

Fig. 3.22.3 Admittance triangles

3.22.4 Admittance Method to Solve Parallel Circuit

The various steps to solve the parallel circuit by admittance method are,

Step 1 : Calculate the admittance of each branch from the respective impedance.

$$Y_1 = \frac{1}{Z_1}, \ Y_2 = \frac{1}{Z_2}, \ Y_3 = \frac{1}{Z_3} \ \text{......}$$

Step 2 : Convert all the admittances to the respective rectangular form.

Step 3 : Calculate the equivalent admittance of the circuit by adding the individual admittances of the branches.

$$Y_{eq} = Y_1 + Y_2 + Y_3 ..... = G_{eq} + B_{eq}$$

Step 4 : The total current drawn from the supply is then given by,

$$I_T = V \times Y_{eq}$$

Step 5 : The individual branch currents can be obtained as,

$$I_1 = V \times Y_1, \ I_2 = V \times Y_2, \ I_3 = V \times Y_3 \ \text{......}$$

It can be crosschecked that the vector addition of all the above currents gives the total current calculated in step 4.

Step 6 :   The angle between V and I_T is the power factor angle ϕ. The cosine of this angle is the power factor of the circuit. The power factor of the circuit can also be obtained as,

$$\cos \phi \;=\; \frac{G_{eq}}{Y_{eq}}$$

The nature of the power factor is to be decided from the sign of B_{eq}. If it is negative power factor is lagging while if it is positive the power factor is leading.

Step 7 :   Voltage must be taken as reference phasor as it is common to all branches to draw the phasor diagram.

3.22.5 Two Impedances in Parallel

If there are two impedances connected in parallel and if I_T is the total current, then current division rule can be applied to find individual branch currents.

$$\bar{I}_1 = \bar{I}_T \times \frac{\overline{Z_2}}{Z_1 + Z_2} \qquad \text{and} \qquad \bar{I}_2 = \bar{I}_T \times \frac{\overline{Z_1}}{Z_1 + Z_2}$$

Example 3.22.1 *For the circuit shown in the Fig. 3.22.4, find the current and power drawn from the source.*   **2003-04, Marks 5**

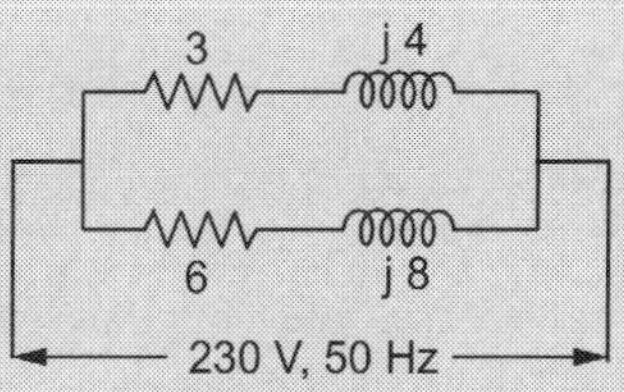

Fig. 3.22.4

Solution : $Z_1 = 3 + j\,4\,\Omega = 5 \angle 53.13°\,\Omega$, $Z_2 = 6 + j\,8\,\Omega = 10 \angle 53.13°\,\Omega$

$$\therefore \qquad I_1 = \frac{V}{Z_1} = \frac{230 \angle 0°}{5 \angle 53.13°} = 46 \angle -53.13°\ A = 27.6 - j\,36.8\ A$$

and $\qquad I_2 = \dfrac{V}{Z_2} = \dfrac{230 \angle 0°}{10 \angle 53.13°} = 23 \angle -53.13°\ A = 13.8 - j\,18.4\ A$

$$\therefore \qquad \bar{I}_T = \bar{I}_1 + \bar{I}_2 = 27.6 - j\,36.8 + 13.8 - j\,18.4$$

$$= 41.4 - j\,55.2\ A = 69 \angle -53.13°A \qquad \text{... Current from supply}$$

$$\therefore \qquad P = V\,I_T \cos \phi_T = 230 \times 69 \times \cos(-53.13°) = \mathbf{9522.022\ W}$$

or $\qquad P = \left|I_1\right|^2 \times R_1 + \left|I_2\right|^2 R_2 = 46^2 \times 3 + 23^2 \times 6 = \mathbf{9522\ W}$

Example 3.22.2 *The following Fig. 3.225 shows as series - parallel circuit. Find :*
i) Admittance of each parallel branch ii) Total circuit impedance iii) Total power supplied
by the source.   **2004-05, Marks 5**

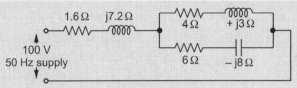

Fig. 3.22.5

Solution :

$$Z_1 = 1.6 + j\,7.2\ \Omega = 7.3756 \angle 77.4711°\ \Omega$$

$$Z_2 = 4 + j3\ \Omega = 5 \angle 36.8698°\ \Omega$$

$$Z_2 = 6 - j8\ \Omega = 10 \angle -53.13°\ \Omega$$

i) $$Y_2 = \frac{1}{Z_2} = \frac{1}{5\angle 36.8698°} = 0.2\angle -36.8698°\ \mho = \textbf{0.16 - j 0.12}\ \mho$$

$$Y_3 = \frac{1}{Z_3} = \frac{1}{10\angle -53.13°} = 0.1\angle 53.13°\ \mho = \textbf{0.06 + j 0.08}\ \mho$$

∴ $$Y_2 + Y_3 = 0.16 - j0.12 + 0.06 + j0.08 = 0.22 - j\,0.04\ \mho = 0.2236 \angle -10.3°\ \mho$$

ii) $$Z_2 \| Z_3 = \frac{1}{Y_2 + Y_3} = \frac{1}{0.2236\angle -10.3°} = 4.4722 \angle 10.3°\ \Omega = 4.4 + j\,0.8\ \Omega$$

∴ $$Z_T = Z_1 + (Z_2 \| Z_3) = 1.6 + j\,7.2 + 4.4 + j\,0.8 = \textbf{6 + j 8}\ \Omega$$

$$= \textbf{10} \angle\ \textbf{53.13°} \Omega$$

iii) $$P_T = V\,I_T \cos \phi_T \text{ where } I_T = \frac{V}{Z_T} = \frac{100\angle 0°}{10 \angle 53.13°} = 10\angle -53.13°\ A$$

∴ $$P_T = 100\times 10\times \cos(+53.13°) = \textbf{600 W}$$

Example 3.22.3 *The following circuit figure shows a parallel R-L arrangement connected*
across 200 volts, 50 Hz, a.c. supply. Calculate - i) the current drawn from the supply,
ii) apparent power, iii) real power and iv) reactive power.

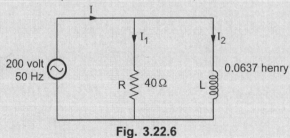

Fig. 3.22.6

Solution : L = 0.0637 H, f = 50 Hz, V = 200 V.

$$X_L = 2\pi fL = 2\pi \times 50 \times 0.0637 = 20.0119 \ \Omega$$

$$I_1 = \frac{V}{R} = \frac{200\angle 0°}{40\angle 0°} = 5\angle 0° \text{ A} = 5 + j\,0 \text{ A}$$

$$I_2 = \frac{V}{jX_L} = \frac{200\angle 0°}{20.0119\angle 90°} = 10 \angle - 90° \text{ A} = 0 - j\,10 \text{ A}$$

i) $\overline{I} = \overline{I}_1 + \overline{I}_2 = 5 + j0 + 0 - j10 = \mathbf{5 - j\,10 \text{ A}} = \mathbf{11.1803} \ \angle - \mathbf{63.434°A}$

ii) $S = VI = 200 \times 11.1803 = \mathbf{2236.06 \text{ VA}}$ ... Apparent power

iii) $P = VI \cos \phi = 2236.06 \times \cos (+ 63.434°) = \mathbf{1000 \text{ W}}$ ... Real power

iv) $Q = VI \sin \phi = 2236.06 \times \sin (+ 63.434°) = \mathbf{+ 2000 \text{ VAR}}$ ... Reactive power

$$\boxed{\text{Complex power} = P + j\,Q = 1000 + j\,2000}$$

Example 3.22.4 *In the circuit shown in Fig. 3.22.7, the reactance of capacitor C_1 is 4 ohms, the reactance of capacitor C_2 is 8 ohm and the reactance of L is 8 ohms. A sinusoidal voltage of 120 V is applied to the circuit. Find*

i) current in each branch

ii) voltage V_{ab} and V_{bc}

iii) power loss in the circuit.

2001-02, Marks 10

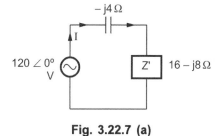

Fig. 3.22.7

Solution : $(4 + j8) \ \Omega$ is in parallel with $-j8 \ \Omega$.

$$\therefore \ \ Z' = \frac{(4 + j8) \times (-j8)}{4 + j8 - j8} = 16 - j8 \ \Omega$$

$$I = \frac{120\angle 0°}{-j4 + 16 - j8} = \frac{120\angle 0°}{16 - j12}$$

$$= \frac{120\angle 0°}{20\angle - 36.869°} = \mathbf{6\angle +36.869° A}$$

Using current distribution rule,

$$I_1 = I \times \frac{4 + j8}{(4 + j8 - j8)} = \frac{6\angle + 36.869° \times 8.944\angle 63.43°}{4} = \mathbf{13.416 \ \angle \ 10.29°A}$$

$$I_2 = I \times \frac{- j8}{(4 + j8 - j8)} = \frac{6\angle + 36.869° \times 8\angle - 90°}{4} = \mathbf{12\angle - 53.131°A}$$

Fig. 3.22.7 (a)

$$V_{ab} = I \times -j4 = 6\angle 36.869° \times 4\angle -90° = \mathbf{24\angle -53.131° \ V}$$

$$V_{bc} = I_1 \times -j8 = 13.416\angle 100.29° \times 8\angle -90° = \mathbf{107.328\angle 10.29° \ V}$$

Pure L and C do not consume power hence only 4 Ω resistance consumes power.

$$\therefore \quad P = |I_2|^2 \times R = (12)^2 \times 4 = \mathbf{576 \ W}$$

or $$\quad P = V \ I \cos \phi = 120 \times 6 \times \cos(36.869°) = \mathbf{576 \ W}$$

Example 3.22.5 *An inductive coil of (6 + j8) ohms impedance is connected to 100 V, 50 Hz a.c. supply. It is desired to improve power factor of supply current to 0.8 lagging by connecting a capacitor i) in series of the coil, ii) in parallel of the coil. Determine value of capacitance in each case.*　　　　**2000-01, Marks 10**

Solution : Case i) Capacitor in series

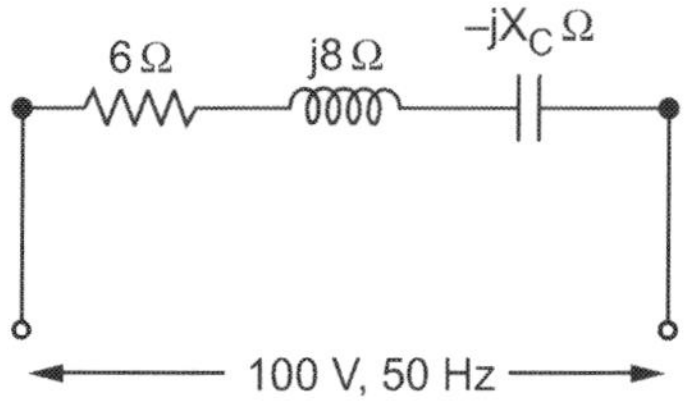

$$Z = 6 + j(8 - X_C)$$

$$\cos \phi = \frac{R}{Z} = \frac{6}{\sqrt{6^2 + (8 - X_C)^2}} \quad \text{... Power factor}$$

$$\therefore \quad 0.8 = \frac{6}{\sqrt{6^2 + (8 - X_C)^2}}$$

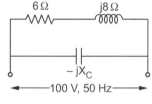

Fig. 3.22.8

$$\therefore 36 + (8 - X_C)^2 = 56.25 \quad \text{i.e.} \quad 8 - X_C = \sqrt{20.25}$$

$$\therefore \quad X_C = 3.5 = \frac{1}{2\pi f C} \quad \text{i.e.} \quad C = \frac{1}{2\pi \times 50 \times 3.5} = \mathbf{9.095 \times 10^{-4} \ F}$$

Case ii) Capacitor in parallel

$$\therefore \quad Z_T = (6 + j8) \| (-jX_C)$$

$$= \frac{[10 \angle 53.13°] [X_C \angle -90°]}{6 + j(8 - X_C)}$$

$$= \frac{10 X_C [-36.86°]}{6 + j(8 - X_C)}$$

Fig. 3.22.9

Note : $\angle x + jy = \tan^{-1} \dfrac{y}{x}$

$$\therefore \quad \phi = \angle Z_T = -36.86° - \tan^{-1} \frac{(8 - X_C)}{6}$$

But $$\quad \phi = \cos^{-1} 0.8 = 36.86°$$ 　　　　.... +ve as lagging

$\therefore \qquad 36.86° = -36.86° - \tan^{-1}\dfrac{(8-X_C)}{6}$

$\therefore \quad \tan[73.72°] = -\left(\dfrac{8-X_C}{6}\right) \quad$ i.e. $-20.545 = 8 - X_C$

$\therefore \qquad X_C = 28.545 = \dfrac{1}{2\pi fC} \quad$ i.e. $\quad C = \dfrac{1}{2\pi \times 50 \times 28545} = 1.1151 \times 10^{-4}$ **F**

Example 3.22.6 *In a circuit, shown in Fig. 3.22.10, U = 100 sin 3t is applied. Find :*
i) Currents I_1 and I_2 with their phase angles. ii) Total current I iii) Phase angle ϕ of current I. **2006-07, Marks 10**

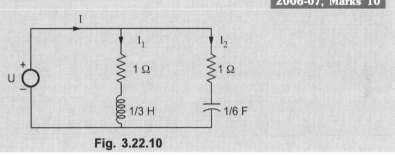

Fig. 3.22.10

Solution : $U = 100 \sin 3\,t = V_m \sin \omega t$

$\therefore \qquad V_m = 100 \text{ V}, \quad V = \dfrac{V_m}{\sqrt{2}} = 70.7106 \text{ V}, \quad \phi = 0°, \quad \omega = 3 \text{ rad/sec}$

$Z_1 = 1 + j\,X_L = 1 + j\,\omega\,L$

$\quad = 1 + j\dfrac{1}{3} \times 3 = 1 + j\,1\ \Omega$

$\quad = 1.4142 \angle 45°\ \Omega$

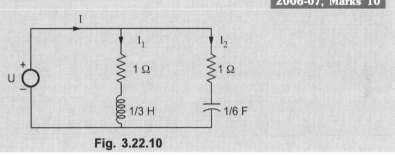

Fig. 3.22.10 (a)

$Z_2 = 1 - j\,X_C = 1 - j\left(\dfrac{1}{\omega C}\right)$

$\quad = 1 - j\left(\dfrac{1}{3 \times \dfrac{1}{6}}\right) = 1 - j\,2\ \Omega$

$\quad = 2.236 \angle - 63.43°\ \Omega$

i) $\qquad I_1 = \dfrac{U}{Z_1} = \dfrac{70.7106 \angle 0°}{1.4142 \angle 45°} = 50 \angle - 45° \text{ A} = \mathbf{35.35 - j\ 35.35\ A}$

$\qquad I_2 = \dfrac{U}{Z_2} = \dfrac{70.7106 \angle 0°}{2.236 \angle - 63.43°} = 31.623 \angle 63.43° \text{ A} = \mathbf{14.144 + j\ 28.283\ A}$

ii) $\qquad \bar{I} = \bar{I}_1 + \bar{I}_2 = 35.35 - j\ 35.35 + 14.144 + j\ 28.283$

$$= 49.4975 - j\ 7.067\ A$$

$$= \mathbf{50\ \angle -8.125^\circ\ A}$$

Fig. 3.22.10 (b)

iii) The phasor diagram is shown in the Fig. 3.22.10 (b).

∴ $\phi = \mathbf{8.125^\circ\ lagging}$

Example 3.22.7 *Determine the following in the circuit shown in Fig. 3.22.11.*

i) The current phasors I, I_1 and I_2.

ii) Active power dissipated in the three resistive branches.

iii) Power factor of the circuit.   **2007-08, Marks 10**

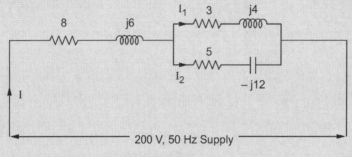

Fig. 3.22.11

Solution : Let $Z_1 = 3 + j\ 4\ \Omega = 5\ \angle 53.13^\circ\ \Omega$, $Z_2 = 5 - j\ 12\ \Omega = 13\ \angle -67.38^\circ\ \Omega$

$$Z_3 = 8 + j\ 6\ \Omega = 10\ \angle 36.86^\circ\ \Omega$$

The impedances Z_1 and Z_2 are in parallel.

$$Z_1 \parallel Z_2 = \frac{Z_1 Z_2}{Z_1 + Z_2} = \frac{5\ \angle 53.13^\circ \times 13\ \angle -67.38^\circ}{3 + j\ 4 + 5 - j\ 12} = \frac{65\ \angle -14.25^\circ}{8 - j8}$$

$$= \frac{65\ \angle -14.25^\circ}{11.313 \angle -45^\circ} = 5.745\ \angle 30.75^\circ\ \Omega = 4.937 + j\ 2.937\ \Omega$$

$$Z_T = Z_3 + [Z_1 \parallel Z_2] = 8 + j\ 6 + 4.937 + j\ 2.937$$

$$= 12.937 + j\ 8.937\ \Omega = 15.7237\ \angle 34.63^\circ\ \Omega$$

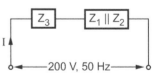

Fig. 3.22.11 (a)

Assuming voltage as reference,

i) $I = \dfrac{V}{Z_T} = \dfrac{200\angle 0^\circ}{15.7237\ \angle 34.63^\circ} = \mathbf{12.7196\ \angle -34.63^\circ\ A}$

Using current division rule,

$$I_1 = I \times \frac{Z_2}{Z_1 + Z_2} = \frac{12.7196\ \angle -34.63^\circ \times 13\ \angle -67.38^\circ}{11.313\ \angle -45^\circ} = \mathbf{14.616\ \angle -57.01^\circ\ A}$$

$$I_2 = I \times \frac{Z_1}{Z_1 + Z_2} = \frac{12.7196 \angle -34.63° \times 5 \angle 53.13°}{11.313 \angle -45°} = \mathbf{5.6216 \angle 63.5° \ A}$$

ii)   Active power dissipated in three branches,

$$P_1 \text{ in branch } Z_1 = |I_1|^2 \times 3 = 14.616^2 \times 3 = \mathbf{640.882 \ W}$$

$$P_2 \text{ in branch } Z_2 = |I_2|^2 \times 13 = 5.6216^2 \times 5 = \mathbf{158.0119 \ W}$$

$$P_3 \text{ in branch } Z_3 = |I|^2 \times 8 = 12.7196^2 \times 8 = \mathbf{1294.305 \ W}$$

iii)   Power factor = $\cos \phi$ = $\cos (- 34.63°)$ = **0.8228 lagging**

Example 3.22.8 *A 46 mH inductive coil has a resistance of 10 Ω.*
  a) How much current will it draw if connected across a 100 V, 60 Hz source ?
  b) Determine the value of the capacitance that must be connected across the
  coil to make the power factor of the overall circuit unity.   **2008-09, Marks 5**

Solution : L = 46 mH, R = 10 Ω, V= 100 V,   f = 60 Hz

a) $X_L = 2 \pi f L = 2 \pi \times 60 \times 46 \times 10^{-3} = 17.3416 \ \Omega$

$\therefore$ $Z = R + j X_L = 10 + j17.3416 \ \Omega = 20.0182 \angle 60.03° \ \Omega$

$\therefore$ $I = \dfrac{V}{Z} = \dfrac{100 \angle 0°}{20.0182 \angle 60.03°} = 4.999 \angle - 60.03° \ A$

$\therefore$ Current drawn by the coil $\approx$ **5 A**

b) Let C be the capacitor connected across the coil.

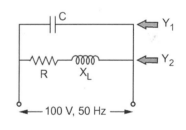

Fig. 3.22.12

$$Y_1 = \frac{1}{Z_1} = \frac{1}{-jX_C} = j \frac{1}{X_C} \quad ....\frac{1}{j} = -j$$

$$Y_2 = \frac{1}{Z_2} = \frac{1}{20.0182 \angle 60.03°} = 0.04995 \angle -60.03°$$

$$= 0.02495 - j \, 0.04327 \text{ mho}$$

$\therefore$ $Y_{eq} = Y_1 + Y_2 = 0.02495 - j \, 0.04327 + j \dfrac{1}{X_C}$

$$= 0.02495 + j \left[\frac{1}{X_C} - 0.04327 \right]$$

$\therefore$ The overall power factor must be unity i.e. the **imaginary term of Y_{eq} must be zero.**

$\therefore$ $\dfrac{1}{X_C} - 0.04327 = 0$ i.e. $X_C = 23.1107 \ \Omega$

But $X_C = \dfrac{1}{2\pi f C}$ i.e. $23.1107 = \dfrac{1}{2\pi \times 60 \times C}$

        $C = $ **114.777 μF**

Example 3.22.9 *Two impedances $Z_1 = (10 + j15)$ ohms and $Z_2 = (6 - j8)$ ohms are connected in parallel. The total current supplied is 15 A. What is the power taken by each impedance?*   **2002-03, 2009-10, Marks 5**

Solution : $Z_1 = 10 + j15\ \Omega$, $Z_2 = 6 - j8\ \Omega$

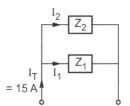

Fig. 3.22.13

Let I_T be reference i.e. $15\angle 0°$ A. By current distribution rule,

$$I_1 = I_T \times \dfrac{Z_2}{Z_1 + Z_2} = 15\angle 0° \times \dfrac{(6 - j8)}{(16 + j7)}$$

$$= \dfrac{15\angle 0° \times 10\angle -53.13°}{17.4642 \angle 23.629°} = 8.5889\angle -76.759°\ A$$

$$\bar{I}_2 = \bar{I}_T - \bar{I}_1 = (15 + j0) - (8.5889 \angle -76.759°)$$

$$= (15 + j0) - (1.9672 - j8.36) = 13.0328 + j8.36$$

$$= 15.4836\angle 32.37°\ A$$

∴   Power taken by $Z_1 = (I_1)^2 \times R_1 = (8.5889)^2 \times 10 =$ **737.692 W**

∴   Power taken by $Z_2 = (I_2^2) \times R_2 = (15.4836)^2 \times 6 =$ **1438.4512 W**

Note that, power gets consumed by the resistive part of the impedance only.

Example 3.22.10 *The two branches of a parallel circuit draw current I_1 and I_2 such that $I_1 = 10\sqrt{2} \sin \omega t$ and $I_2 = 5\sqrt{2} \sin(\omega t - 60°)$. What is the total current drawn by them ?*   **2011-12, Marks 5**

Solution : Comparing current with $I = I_m \sin (\omega t \pm \phi)$,

$I_{m1} = 10\sqrt{2}$ A, $\phi_1 = 0°$, $I_{m2} = 5\sqrt{2}$ A, $\phi_2 = -60°$

∴ $I_1(\text{R.M.S.}) = \dfrac{I_{m1}}{\sqrt{2}} = 10$ A   i.e. $\bar{I}_1 = 10 \angle 0°$ A $= 10 + j0$ A

∴ $I_2(\text{R.M.S.}) = \dfrac{I_{m2}}{\sqrt{2}} = 5$ A   i.e. $\bar{I}_2 = 5 \angle -60°$ A $= 2.5 - j\,4.3301$ A

    $\bar{I}_T = \bar{I}_1 + \bar{I}_2 = 10 + j0 + 2.5 - j\,4.3301 = 12.5 - j\,4.3301$ A $=$ **13.228 $\angle$ –19.106° A**

∴ $I_{TM} = \sqrt{2} \times I_T = \sqrt{2} \times 13.228 = 18.707$ A, $\phi_T = -19.106°$

∴ $I_T =$ **18.707 sin (ωt – 19.106°) A**   ... Equation form

Example 3.22.11 *Obtain the power factor of a two branch parallel circuit where the first branch has $\overline{Z}_1 = (2 + j4)\ \Omega$ and second $\overline{Z}_2 = (6 + j0)\ \Omega$. To what value must the 6 Ω resistor be changed to result in the overall power factor 0.9 lagging ?* **2012-13, Marks 10**

Solution : $Z_1 = 2 + j4\ \Omega = 4.472\angle63.435°\ \Omega$

$$Z_2 = 6 + j0\ \Omega = 6\angle0°\ \Omega$$

Z_1 and Z_2 are in parallel hence,

$$Z_{eq} = \frac{Z_1 Z_2}{Z_1 + Z_2} = \frac{4.472\angle63.435° \times 6\angle0°}{2 + j4 + 6 + j0} = \frac{26.832\ \angle63.435°}{8.9442\ \angle26.565°}$$

$$= 3\angle36.87°\ \Omega = 2.4 + j1.8\ \Omega$$

$\therefore$ Power factor $= \cos\phi = \dfrac{R}{Z} = \dfrac{2.4}{3} = \textbf{0.8 lagging}$

New power factor is 0.9.

Let new $\quad Z_2 = R_2 + j0 = R_2\angle0°\ \Omega$

$\therefore \qquad Z_{eq} = \dfrac{4.472\angle63.435° \times R_2\angle0°}{(2 + j4 + R_2 + j0)} = \dfrac{4.472\,R_2\angle63.435°}{(2 + R_2) + j4}$

$$= \frac{4.472\,R_2\angle63.435°}{\sqrt{(2 + R_2)^2 + 4^2}\ \angle\tan^{-1}\left(\dfrac{4}{2 + R_2}\right)} = |Z_{eq}|\angle\phi_{eq}$$

$\therefore \qquad \phi_{eq} = 63.435° - \tan^{-1}\left(\dfrac{4}{2 + R_2}\right) \quad$ but $\quad \phi_{eq} = \cos^{-1} 0.9$

$\therefore \qquad 25.841° = 63.435° - \tan^{-1}\left(\dfrac{4}{2 + R_2}\right) \quad$ i.e. $\quad \tan^{-1}\left(\dfrac{4}{2 + R_2}\right) = 37.593°$

$\therefore \qquad \dfrac{4}{2 + R_2} = \tan(37.593°) \quad$ i.e. $\quad R_2 = \textbf{3.1954}\ \Omega$

Review Questions

1. Define admittance, susceptance and conductance.

2. Define susceptance and conductance. State their units.

3. What is admittance triangle ?

4. Explain the admittance method to solve parallel a.c. circuit.

5. Two impedance $Z_1 = 5 - j\,13.1\ \Omega$ and $Z_1 = 8.57 + j\,6.42\ \Omega$ are connected in parallel across a voltage of $(100 + j200)$ volts.

   Estimate :- i) Branch currents in complex form ii) Total power consumed,

   Draw a neat phasor diagram showing voltage, branch currents and all phase angles.

   [Ans. : $I_1 = -10.782 + j\,11.75$ A, $I_2 = 18.668 + j\,9.3483$ A, $I_T = 22.5239\ \angle\,69.5°$ A, $\phi_T = 6.075°$ leading, $P_T = 5008.212$ W

6. *Two admittances, $Y_1 = (0.167 - j0.167)$ siemen, and $Y_2 = (0.1 + j\,0.05)$ siemen are connected in parallel across a 100 V, 50-Hz single-phase supply. Find the current in each branch and the total current. Also find the power-factor of the combination. Sketch a neat phasor diagram.*

    [Ans. : 16.7 – j 16.7 A, 10 + j 5 A, $I_T = 29.15 \angle - 23.66°$ A, p.f.= 0.9159 lagging]

7. *A parallel circuit of 25 Ω resistor, 64 mH inductor and 80 μF capacitor connected across a 110 V, 50 Hz, single phase supply, is shown in Fig. 3.22.14. Calculate the current in individual element, the total current drawn from the supply and the overall p.f. of the circuit. Draw a neat phasor diagram showing $\overline{V}, \overline{I}_R, \overline{I}_L, \overline{I}_C$ and $\overline{I}$.*

    [Ans. : $I_R = 4.4 \angle 0°$ A, $I_L = 5.47 \angle - 90°$ A, $I_C = 2.76 \angle 90°$ A, p.f. = 0.851 lagging, $\overline{I} = 5.1676 \angle - 31.62°$ A]

    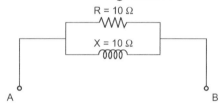

    Fig. 3.22.14

8. *A circuit is shown in Fig. 3.22.15. Draw its equivalent admittance circuit. Also calculate admittance, conductance and susceptance.*

    [Ans. : G = 0.1, B = 0.05, Y = 0.1118 siemens]

    R = 10 Ω
    X = 10 Ω
    A   B

    Fig. 3.22.15

9. *An a.c. circuit connected across 200 V, 50 Hz supply has two parallel branches A and B. Branch A draws a current of 4 A at 0.8 lagging power factor; while the total current drawn by the parallel combination is 5 A at unity power factor. Find (i) Current and power-factor of branch B and (ii) Admittances of branch A, branch B and the parallel combination, both in polar form and rectangular form.*

    [Ans. : i) 0.6 lagging, ii) 0.016 + j 0.012 mho, 0.009 – j 0.012 mho, 0.025 $\angle$ 0° mho]

10. *For the circuit shown in Fig. 3.22.16, find the current supplied by the source. Use complex number method and sketch its phasor diagram. Also, find currents I_1 and I_2.*

    10 Ω   (–)j12 Ω
    4 Ω   j6 Ω
    A   B   C
    6 Ω   j10 Ω
    V = (200+j0) V

    Fig. 3.22.16

    [Ans. : $I_1 = 8.3 \angle 34.659°$, $I_2 = 11.1163 \angle - 74.571°$]

11. *Two admittances, $Y_1 = (0.167 - j0.167)$ siemen, and $Y_2 = (0.1 + j\,0.05)$ siemen are connected in parallel across a 100 V, 50-Hz single-phase supply. Find the current in each branch and the total current. Also find the power-factor of the combination. Sketch a neat phasor diagram.*

    [Ans. : $I_1 = 16.699 - j\,16.699$ A, $I_2 = 10 + j\,5$ A, $I_T = 29.15 \angle - 23.66°$ A, p.f. = 0.9159 lagging.]

3.23 Resonance in Parallel Circuit   2000-01, 2004-05, 2005-06, 2009-10

Similar to a series a.c. circuit, there can be a resonance in parallel a.c. circuit. When the power factor of a parallel a.c. circuit is unity i.e. the voltage and total current are in phase at a particular frequency then the parallel circuit is said to be at **resonance**. The frequency at which the parallel resonance occurs is called **resonant frequency** denoted as f_r Hz.

3.23.1 Characteristics of Parallel Resonance

Consider a practical parallel circuit used for the parallel resonance as shown in the Fig. 3.23.1.

The one branch consists of resistance R in series with inductor L. So it is series R-L circuit with impedance Z_L. The other branch is pure capacitive with a capacitor C. Both the branches are connected in parallel across a variable frequency constant voltage source.

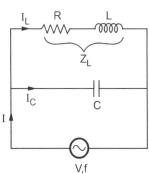

Fig. 3.23.1 Practical parallel circuit

The current drawn by inductive branch is I_L while drawn by capacitive branch is I_C.

$$I_L = \frac{V}{Z_L} \quad \text{where } Z_L = R + j\,X_L$$

and

$$I_C = \frac{V}{X_C} \quad \text{where } X_C = \frac{1}{2\pi f\,C}$$

The current I_L lags voltage V by angle ϕ_L which is decided by R and X_L while the current I_C leads voltage V by 90°. The total current I is phasor addition of I_L and I_C. The phasor diagram is shown in the Fig. 3.23.2.

For the parallel resonance V and I must be in phase. To achieve this unity p.f. condition,

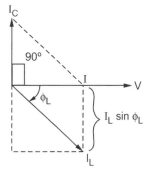

Fig. 3.23.2

$$I = I_L \cos \phi_L$$

and

$$I_C = I_L \sin \phi_L$$

From the impedance triangle of R-L series circuit we can write,

$$\tan \phi_L = \frac{X_L}{R}, \ \cos \phi_L = \frac{R}{Z_L}, \ \sin \phi_L = \frac{X_L}{Z_L}$$

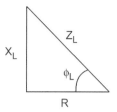

As frequency is increased, $X_L = 2\pi \, fL$ increases due to which $Z_L = \sqrt{R^2 + X_L^2}$ also

Fig. 3.23.3 Impedance triangle

increases. Hence $\cos \phi_L$ decreases and $\sin \phi_L$ increases. As Z_L increases, the current I_L also decreases.

At resonance $f = f_r$ and $I_L \cos \phi_L$ is at its minimum. Thus at resonance **current is minimum** while the total **impedance** of the circuit is **maximum**. As admittance is reciprocal of impedance, as frequency is changed, **admittance** decreases and is **minimum** at resonance. The three curves are shown in the Fig. 3.23.4 (a), (b) and (c).

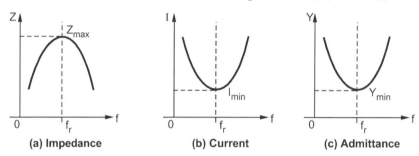

(a) Impedance   (b) Current   (c) Admittance

Fig. 3.23.4 Characteristics of parallel resonance

3.23.2 Expression for Resonant Frequency

At resonance $I_C = I_L \sin \phi_L$

$$\therefore \qquad \frac{V}{X_C} = \frac{V}{Z_L} \cdot \frac{X_L}{Z_L} = \frac{V \, X_L}{Z_L^2} \quad \text{i.e.} \quad Z_L^2 = X_L \, X_C$$

$$\therefore \quad R^2 + (2\pi f_r \, L)^2 = (2\pi f_r \, L) \times \frac{1}{2\pi f_r \, C} \quad \text{as } f = f_r$$

$$\therefore \quad R^2 + (2\pi f_r \, L)^2 = \frac{L}{C} \quad \text{i.e.} \quad (2\pi f_r \, L)^2 = \frac{L}{C} - R^2$$

$$\therefore \qquad (2\pi f_r)^2 = \frac{1}{LC} - \frac{R^2}{L^2}$$

$$\therefore \qquad \boxed{f_r = \frac{1}{2\pi}\sqrt{\frac{1}{LC} - \frac{R^2}{L^2}}}$$

Thus if R is very small compared to L and C, $\dfrac{R^2}{L^2} << \dfrac{1}{LC}$

$\therefore$ $$f_r = \dfrac{1}{2\pi\sqrt{LC}}$$ ... As that for series resonance

Key Point *The net susceptance of the whole circuit is zero at resonance.*

3.23.3 Dynamic Impedance at Resonance

The impedance offered by the parallel circuit at resonance is called **dynamic impedance** denoted as Z_D. This is maximum at resonance. As current drawn at resonance is minimum, the parallel circuit at resonance is called **rejector circuit**. This indicates that it rejects the unwanted frequencies and hence it is used as filter in radio receiver.

From $I_C = I_L \sin\phi_L$ we have seen that,

$$Z_L^2 = \dfrac{L}{C}$$

while $I = I_L \cos\phi_L = \dfrac{V}{Z_L}\cdot\dfrac{R}{Z_L} = \dfrac{VR}{Z_L^2} = \dfrac{VR}{\dfrac{L}{C}} = \dfrac{V}{(L/RC)}$

$\therefore$ $I = \dfrac{V}{Z_D}$ where $Z_D = \dfrac{L}{RC} = $ Dynamic impedance

3.23.4 Quality Factor of Parallel Circuit

The parallel circuit is used to magnify the current and hence known as current resonance circuit.

The quality factor of the parallel circuit is defined as the current magnification in the circuit at resonance.

The current magnification is defined as,

$$\text{Current magnification} = \dfrac{\text{current in the inductive branch}}{\text{current in supply at resonance}} = \dfrac{I_L}{I}$$

$$= \dfrac{\dfrac{V}{Z_L}}{\dfrac{V}{Z_D}} = \dfrac{Z_D}{Z_L}$$

$$= \frac{\dfrac{L}{RC}}{\sqrt{\dfrac{L}{C}}} = \frac{1}{R}\sqrt{\frac{L}{C}} \quad \text{as } Z_L = \sqrt{X_L X_C} = \sqrt{\frac{L}{C}}$$

This is nothing but the quality factor at resonance.

$\therefore$

$$Q = \frac{1}{R}\sqrt{\frac{L}{C}}$$

The various applications of parallel resonant circuit are,

1. In R.F. oscillators

2. Complex communication circuits

3. For impedance transformation

4. In filters

Example 3.23.1 *An inductive coil of resistance 10 Ω and inductance 0.1 henrys is connected in parallel with a 150 µF capacitor to a variable frequency, 200 V supply. Find the resonant frequency at which the total current taken from the supply is in phase with the supply voltage. Also find the value of this current. Draw the phasor diagram.*

Solution : The circuit is shown in the Fig. 3.23.5.

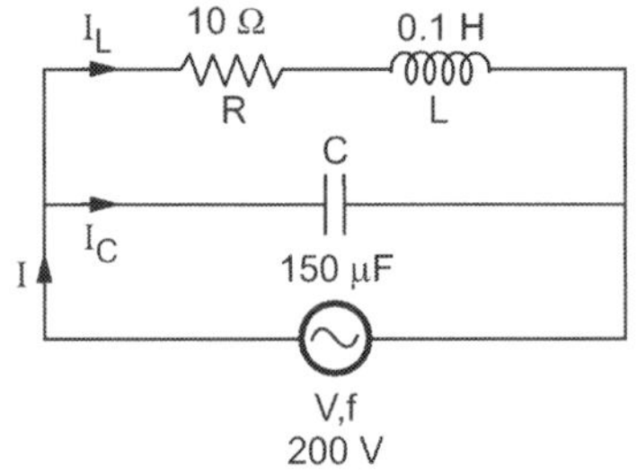

The resonant frequency is,

$$f_r = \frac{1}{2\pi}\sqrt{\frac{1}{LC} - \frac{R^2}{L^2}}$$

$$= \frac{1}{2\pi}\sqrt{\frac{1}{0.1 \times 150 \times 10^{-6}} - \frac{(10)^2}{(0.1)^2}}$$

$$= \mathbf{37.8865 \ \ Hz}$$

Fig. 3.23.5

Now

$$Z_L = R + j\, X_L = 10 + j\ (2\pi f_r\, L)$$

$$= 10 + j\ 23.805 = 25.82 \angle 67.21° \ \Omega$$

$\therefore$

$$I_L = \frac{V}{Z_L} = \frac{200\angle 0°}{25.82\angle 67.21°} = \mathbf{7.7459 \angle - 67.21° \ A}$$

and

$$I_C = \frac{V}{X_C} = \frac{200\angle 0°}{\dfrac{1}{2\pi f_r\, C}\angle -90°} = \frac{200\angle 0°}{28\angle -90°} = \mathbf{7.143 \angle + 90° \ A}$$

where

$$Z_C = 0 - j\, X_C = 0 - j\ 28 = 28 \angle \ - 90° \ \Omega$$

$$\therefore \quad Z_T = \frac{Z_C \, Z_L}{Z_C + Z_L} = \frac{28 \angle -90° \times 25.82 \angle 67.21°}{0 - j\,28 + 10 + j\,23.805}$$

$$= \frac{722.96 \angle -22.79°}{10 - j\,4.195} = \frac{722.96 \angle -22.79}{10.844 \angle -22.79}$$

$$= 66.67 \ \Omega \ \text{pure resistive}$$

$$\therefore \quad Z_T = Z_D = \frac{L}{C\,R} = \frac{0.1}{150 \times 10^{-6} \times 10}$$

$$= 66.67 \ \Omega$$

$$\therefore \quad I = \frac{V}{Z_D} = \frac{200}{66.67} = \mathbf{3 \ A}$$

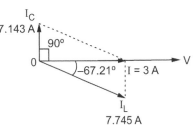

Fig. 3.23.6

The phasor diagram is shown in the Fig. 3.23.6.

Example 3.23.2 *A series a.c. circuit has resistance of 15 Ω and inductive reactance of 10 Ω. Calculate the value of a capacitor which is connected across this series combination so that system has unity power factor. The frequency of a.c. supply is 50 Hz.* **2005-06, Marks 5**

Solution : This is parallel resonance with $f_r = 50$ Hz

$$f_r = \frac{1}{2\pi} \sqrt{\frac{1}{LC} - \frac{R^2}{L^2}}$$

$$\therefore \quad L = \frac{X_L}{2\pi f_r} = \frac{10}{2\pi \times 50} = 0.03183 \ H$$

$$\therefore \quad 50 = \frac{1}{2\pi} \sqrt{\frac{1}{0.03183\,C} - \frac{15^2}{0.03183^2}}$$

$$\therefore \quad C = \mathbf{97.94 \ \mu F}$$

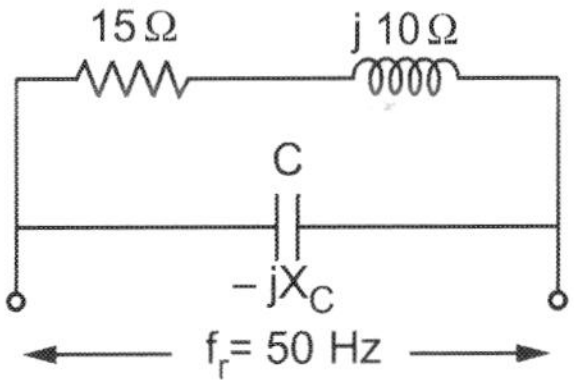

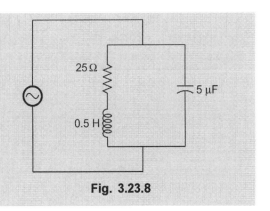

Fig. 3.23.7

Example 3.23.3 *For the circuit shown below, determine : i) Resonant frequency, ii) Total impedance of the circuit at resonance iii) Bandwidth iv) Quality factor.* **2004-05, Marks 5**

Fig. 3.23.8

Solution : i) The circuit shows parallel resonant circuit. The resonant frequency for such circuit is,

$$ f_r \; = \; \frac{1}{2\pi\sqrt{LC}} = \frac{1}{2\pi\sqrt{0.5\times5\times10^{-6}}} = \textbf{100.658 Hz} $$

ii) At resonance, $\; Z_D = \dfrac{L}{RC} = \dfrac{0.5}{25\times5\times10^{-6}} = \textbf{4000}\ \Omega$

iii)   Bandwidth $\; = \; \dfrac{\omega_r}{Q} \;$ and $\; Q = \dfrac{\omega_r L}{R}$

∴   Bandwidth $\; = \; \dfrac{R}{L} = \dfrac{25}{0.5} = \textbf{50 Hz}$

iv) $Q \; = \; \dfrac{\omega_r L}{R} = \dfrac{2\pi\times100.658\times0.5}{25} = \textbf{12.6491}$

Example 3.23.4 *In the circuit shown in the Fig. 3.23.9, find the value of R such that the impedance of whole circuit should be independent of the frequency of supply. If V = 200 V, L = 0.16 H and C= 100 μF, calculate the power loss in the circuit.*   **2000-01, Marks 10**

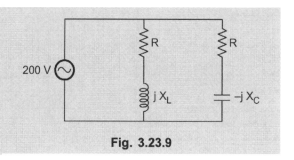

Fig. 3.23.9

Solution : $Z_1 = R + jX_L,\ Z_2 = R - jX_C$

∴ $Z_T = \dfrac{Z_1 Z_2}{Z_1 + Z_2} = \dfrac{(R+jX_L)(R-jX_C)}{2R+j(X_L-X_C)} = \dfrac{R^2 + jR(X_L - X_C) + X_L X_C}{2R + j(X_L - X_C)}$

Rationalize to separate real and imaginary parts,

∴ $Z_T \; = \; \dfrac{[R^2 + jR(X_L - X_C) + X_L X_C\ ]\ [2R - j(X_L - X_C)]}{[2R + j(X_L - X_C)]\ [2R - j(X_L - X_C)]}$

$$ = \; \frac{2R^3 + j2R^2(X_L - X_C) + 2RX_L X_C - jR^2(X_L - X_C) + R(X_L - X_C)^2 - jX_L X_C[X_L - X_C]}{\{(2R)^2 - [j(X_L - X_C)]^2\}} $$

$$ = \; \frac{2R^3 + 2RX_L X_C + R(X_L - X_C)^2 + j\,(X_L - X_C)\,[R^2 - X_L X_C]}{[4R^2 + (X_L - X_C)]^2} \qquad \dots (3.23.1) $$

For making Z_T independent of frequency, imaginary part must be zero. As $(X_L - X_C)$ can not be zero,

$$ R^2 - X_L X_C \; = \; 0 \quad \text{i.e.} \quad R^2 = X_L X_C = 2\pi fL \times \frac{1}{2\pi f C} $$

$$\therefore \qquad \boxed{R = \sqrt{\frac{L}{C}}} \quad \text{i.e. } R = \sqrt{\frac{0.16}{100 \times 10^{-6}}} = \mathbf{40 \ \Omega}$$

Using $X_L X_C = R^2$ in equation (3.23.1), $Z_T = R = 40 \ \Omega$

$$\therefore \qquad P = \left(\frac{V^2}{R}\right) = \frac{200^2}{40} = \mathbf{1000 \ W}$$

Review Questions

1. *Explain the parallel resonance and draw the graphs of Z, I and Y against the frequency.*

   2009-10, Marks 5

2. *Show that the condition for parallel resonance is same as that for series resonance. State the applications of parallel resonance.*

   2009-10, Marks 5

3. *A coil 20 Ω resistance has an inductance of 0.2 H connected in parallel with a condenser of 100 μF capacitance. Calculate the frequency at which this circuit will have a non inductive resistance. Find the value of R.*   **(Ans. : 31.83 Hz, 100 Ω)**

4. *A series circuit consisting of a 12 Ω resistance, 0.3 henry inductance and a variable capacitor is connected across 100 V, 50 Hz a.c. supply. The capacitance value is adjusted to obtain maximum current. Find this capacitance value and the power drawn by the circuit under this condition.*

   Now, the supply frequency is raised to 60 Hz, the voltage remaining same at 100 V. Find the value of capacitor C_1 to be connected across the above series circuit, so that current drawn from supply is the minimum.   **(Ans. : C = 33.77 μF, P = 833.33 W, C' = 68.4896 μF)**

3.24 Comparison of Resonant Circuits

Sr. No.	Parameter	Series Resonant	Parallel Resonant
1.	Circuit		
2.	Type of circuit	Purely resistive	Purely resistive
3.	Power factor	Unity	Unity
4.	Impedance	Minimum Z = R	Dynamic but maximum $Z_D = \dfrac{L}{RC}$

5.	Frequency	$f_r = \dfrac{1}{2\pi\sqrt{LC}}$	$f_r = \dfrac{1}{2\pi\sqrt{LC}}$
6.	Current	Maximum $I = \dfrac{V}{R}$	Minimum $I = \dfrac{V}{Z_D}$
7.	Magnification	Voltage magnification	Current magnification
8.	Quality factor	$Q = \dfrac{\omega_r L}{R} = \dfrac{\omega_r}{B.W.}$	$Q = \dfrac{1}{R}\sqrt{\dfrac{L}{C}}$
9.	Nature	Acceptor	Rejector
10.	Practical use	Radio circuits sharpness of tunning circuit	Impedance for matching, tuning, as a filter
11.	Current waveform		

Review Question

1. *Compare series and parallel resonating circuits.*

3.25 Short Answered and Objective Type Questions

Q.1 The dimension of $\dfrac{L}{CR}$ is _____.

2012-13

(Ans. : ohms)

Q.2 The maximum and minimum value of power factor can be _____.

2012-13

(Ans. : 1 and zero)

Q.3 A voltage source of 100 V has internal impedance 2 Ω and supplies a load having that same impedance. The power absorbed by the load is _____.

2008-09

Ans. : $P_{max} = \dfrac{V_{TH}^2}{4\,RL} = \dfrac{(100)^2}{4 \times 2} =$ **1250 W**

Q.4 The instantaneous voltage and current for an ac circuit are $v = 155.6 \sin 377\, t$ V, $i = 7.07 \sin (377t - 36.87°)$ A. Represent these in a phasor diagram.   **2008-09**

Ans. : The phasor diagram is as shown.

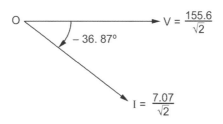

Q.5 A sinusoidal current having r.m.s. value of $8\angle 0°$ A is added to another sinusoidal current of rms value $6\angle 90° A$. The r.m.s. value of the resultant current is _____.   **2009-10**

Ans. : The two currents are shown in the Fig. 3.25.1.

$$\therefore \qquad I_R = \sqrt{6^2 + 8^2} = \textbf{10 A}$$

This is r.m.s. value of the resultant.

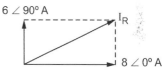

Fig. 3.25.1

Q.6 A series R-L-C circuit with R = 10 Ω, L = 0.02 H, C = 2 μF is connected to 100 V variable frequency source. Find the frequency for which the current is maximum.   **2003-04**

Ans. : For current to be maximum, $X_L = X_C$.

$$\therefore \qquad 2\pi f L = \frac{1}{2\pi f C} \quad \text{i.e} \quad f = \frac{1}{2\pi\sqrt{LC}}$$

$$\therefore \qquad f = \frac{1}{2\pi\sqrt{0.02 \times 2 \times 10^{-6}}} = \textbf{795.7747 Hz}$$

Q.7 If the bandwidth of a resonant circuit is 10 kHz and lower half power frequency is 120 kHz. Find out the value of the upper half power frequency and the quality factor of the circuit.   **2003-04**

Ans. :

$$\text{B.W.} = f_2 - f_1$$
$$\therefore \qquad 10 = f_2 - 120$$
$$\therefore \qquad f_2 = \textbf{130 kHz}$$

... Upper half power frequency

$$Q = \frac{\omega_r}{\text{B. W.}}$$

where $\omega_r = 2\pi f_r = 2\pi\sqrt{f_1 f_2}$

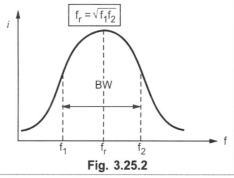

Fig. 3.25.2

$$\therefore \quad Q = \frac{2\pi\sqrt{120\times10^3 \times 130\times10^3}}{10\times10^3} = \mathbf{78.4769}$$

Q.8 In an a.c. circuit, the current is given by - $i = 22 \sin\left(314\,t - \frac{\pi}{6}\right)$ A. If the voltage of the circuit is the reference quantity, determine - i) power factor   ii) r.m.s. value of the current iii) frequency of the current   2001-02

Ans. :   Comparing the given equation with,

$$i = I_m \sin(\omega t - \phi)$$

i) $$\phi = \frac{\pi}{6} \text{ lagging as negative}$$

$\therefore \quad \cos\phi = \cos\frac{\pi}{6} = \mathbf{0.866\ lag}$ ... Power factor

ii) $$I_{r.m.s.} = \frac{I_m}{\sqrt{2}} = \frac{22}{\sqrt{2}} = \mathbf{15.5563\ A}$$

iii) $$\omega = 314 = 2\pi f$$

$\therefore \quad f = \frac{314}{2\pi} = \mathbf{50\ Hz}$ ... Frequency

Q.9 If impedance is given as $Z = 20 \angle 30° \Omega$, find its components. Assume $f = 50$ Hz.

Ans. : $Z = 20 \angle 30° \Omega = 17.3205 + j\,10 \Omega = R + j\,X\ \Omega$

Hence the resistance is $17.3205\ \Omega$ while the reactive component is $10\ \Omega$. As X is positive, it is inductive in nature. Hence $X_L = 10\ \Omega$. But $X_L = 2\pi\,fL$ hence $L = 31.83$ mH.

Q.10 If impedance is given as $Z = 20 \angle 30° \Omega$, find corresponding admittance and its components. Assume $f = 50$ Hz.

Ans. :

$$Y = \frac{1}{Z} = \frac{1}{20 \angle 30°} = 0.05 \angle -30° \text{ mho} = 0.0433 - j\,0.025 \text{ mho}$$

$$= G - j\,B \text{ mho}$$

Hence the conductance is 0.0433 mho while inductive susceptance is 0.025 mho.

Q.11 A circuit consists of $R = 5\ \Omega$ and $L = 20$ mH connected in series and supplied with an a.c. voltage of 100 V at 50 Hz. Find the current through the circuit.

Ans. :

$$X_L = 2\pi\,fL = 2\pi \times 50 \times 20\times10^{-3} = 6.283\ \Omega$$

$$Z = R + j X = 5 + j 6.283 \ \Omega = 8.029 \ \angle 51.48° \ \Omega$$

$$I = \frac{V}{Z} = \frac{100 \angle 0°}{8.029 \angle 51.48°} = 12.454 \ \angle -51.48° \ \Omega \qquad \text{... Current}$$

Q.12 Draw suitable waveforms to show the following :
$v = V_m \sin \omega t$; $i = I_m \sin (\omega t + \theta)$
Label the quantities suitably. **(Refer section 3.11)**   `2011-12`

Q.13 For a series RLC circuit draw the phasor diagram and show the power factor angle in that. Assume the circuit draws inductive current. **(Refer section 3.20)**
`2011-12`

Q.14 Give the relationship between quality factor, resonant frequency and bandwidth for a series RLC circuit. **(Refer section 3.21)**   `2011-12`

Q.15 Which of the following conditions is common to both series and parallel resonance?

`2009-10`

a) Current is maximum   b) Power is low

c) Impedance is minimum   d) Power factor is unity   **(Ans. : d)**

Q.16 Pure inductive circuit : _____ .   `2009-10`
a) Consumes some power on average
b) Does not consume power
c) Take power from the line during some part of the cycle and then returns back during other part of cycle
d) None of these   **(Ans. : b)**

Q.17 Power factor of the following circuit will be zero : _____ .   `2009-10`
a) Resistive   b) Inductive   c) Capacitive   d) Both (ii) and (iii)
(Ans. : d)

Q.18 At resonance power factor of series R-L-C circuit would be : _____ .   `2009-10`
a) 0   b) 1   c) –1   d) 1.1   **(Ans. : b)**

Q.19 The form factor of sinusoidal alternating current is : _____ .   `2009-10`
a) 1   b) 0   c) 1.11   d) 1.15   **(Ans. : c)**

Q.20 The main advantages of a.c. is, _____.

a) A.C. motors are expensive
b) The a.c. voltages can be raised or lowered
c) A.C. transmission is very costly
d) None of the above   **(Ans. : b)**

Q.21 The main advantage of purely sinusoidal waveform is, _____.

a) It is the only alternating waveform
b) It is the only standard waveform

c) Any other waveform can be resolved into series of sinusoidal waveforms of different frequencies

d) It produces distorted waveforms when applied   **(Ans. : c)**

Q.22 The generation of a.c. is according to, _____.

a) Faraday's law   b) Thevenin's theorem

c) Ohm's law   d) Kirchhoff's law   **(Ans. : a)**

Q.23 The time taken by an alternating quantity to complete one cycle is called _____.

a) frequency   b) speed   c) waveform   d) time period
                                                                    (Ans. : d)

Q.24 The unit of frequency is, _____.

a) rad/sec   b) seconds   c) hertz   d) volts   **(Ans. : c)**

Q.25 The relation between f and ω is, _____.

a) $f = \dfrac{1}{\omega}$ b) $\omega = \dfrac{2\pi}{f}$ c) $\omega = 2\pi f$ d) $\omega = \dfrac{1}{f}$
                                                                    (Ans. : c)

Q.26 The equation of an alternating quantity is v = 282.84 sin 100 π t then its r.m.s. value is, _____.

a) 200   b) $200\sqrt{2}$ c) 141.421   d) 400   **(Ans. : a)**

Q.27 The equation of an alternating current is given by, i = 14.1421 sin 100 π t then the time taken by it to complete three cycles is, _____.

a) 0.02 sec   b) 0.06 sec   c) 0.08 sec   d) 0.01 sec **(Ans. : b)**

Q.28 An instantaneous value of an alternating current having r.m.s. value of 7.071 A at 120° is, _____.

a) 4.33 A   b) 6.123 A   c) 8.66 A   d) 3.061 A **(Ans. : c)**

Q.29 An instantaneous value of an alternating voltage having 50 Hz frequency and maximum value of 100 V at 0.01 sec is, _____.

a) 100 V   b) 100 $\sqrt{2}$ V   c) $\dfrac{100}{\sqrt{2}}$ V   d) 0 V
                                                                    (Ans. : d)

Q.30 A sinusoidal voltage has a magnitude of 200 V at 150° then its maximum value is, _____.

a) 100 V   b) 400 V   c) 200 V   d) 300 V   **(Ans. : b)**

Q.31 An alternating current is given by i = 20 sin 100 π t. The time taken by the current to achieve – 20 A second time, measuring from t = 0 is, _____.

a) 0.035 sec   b) 0.015 sec   c) 0.02 sec   d) 0.07 sec **(Ans. : a)**

Q.32 The concept of effective value is based on, _____.

    a) photoelectric effect   b) heating effect

    c) friction   d) none of the above   **(Ans. : b)**

Q.33 The form factor of purely sinusoidal waveform is, _____.

    a) 1.11   b) 1.21   c) 1.414   d) $\sqrt{2}$ **(Ans. : a)**

Q.34 The peak factor of purely sinusoidal waveform is, _____.

    a) 1.11   b) 1.21   c) 1.414   d) $\sqrt{2}$ **(Ans. : c)**

Q.35 A wire carries 5 A d.c. and alternating current of 15 sin ωt A then the effective value of the resultant current is, _____.

    a) 5 A   b) $15\sqrt{2}$ A   c) 20 A   d) 11.72 A **(Ans. : d)**

Q.36 Maximum transmission voltage in India is, _____.

    a) 220 kV   b) 400 kV   c) 765 kV   d) 1200 kV **(Ans. : b)**

Q.37 An alternating current is 14.142 sin (100 π t − 30°) A and an alternating voltage is 282.842 sin (100 π t + $\dfrac{\pi}{4}$) V then the phase difference between V and I is, _____.

    a) 75°   b) 30°   c) $\dfrac{\pi}{4}$ rad   d) 15°   **(Ans. : a)**

Q.38 The average value of sinusoidally varying voltage is _____ than its r.m.s. value.

    a) more   b) less   c) same as   d) none of the above   **(Ans. : b)**

Q.39 For addition and subtraction, a.c. quantity is expressed in _____ system.

    a) spherical   b) cylindrical   c) rectangular   d) polar   **(Ans. : c)**

Q.40 For multiplication and division, a.c. quantity is expressed in _____ system.

    a) cylindrical   b) spherical   c) rectangular   d) polar   **(Ans. : d)**

Q.41 Which of the following wave has least value of peak factor ?

    a) Sine wave   b) Square wave

    c) Triangular wave   d) Full wave rectified sine wave. **(Ans. : b)**

Q.42 The voltage of domestic a.c. supply is 230 V. This value represents, _____.

    a) peak value   b) average value   c) r.m.s. value   d) mean value   **(Ans. : c)**

Q.43 If two sinusoidal quantities are in phase quadrature then the phase difference between them is, _____.

    a) 45°   b) zero   c) 180°   d) 90°   **(Ans. : d)**

Q.44 The phasor rotates in _____ direction.

a) anticlockwise   b) clockwise   c) circular   d) none of the above

(Ans. : a)

Q.45 If $i_1 = A \sin (\omega t)$ and $i_2 = B \sin (\omega t + 30°)$ then, _____.

a) i_1 leads i_2 by 30°   b) i_1 and i_2 are in phase
c) i_2 leads i_1 by 30°   d) None of the above   **(Ans. : c)**

Q.46 The negative maximum of a cosine wave occurs at, _____.

a) 45°   b) 90°   c) 180°   d) 270°   **(Ans. : c)**

Q.47 A 100 W, 200 V bulb takes the r.m.s. current of _____ A from 200 V, 50 Hz a.c. supply.

a) 1 A   b) 0.5 A   c) $\dfrac{0.5}{\sqrt{2}}$ A   d) 0.7071 A

(Ans. : b)

Q.48 The domestics appliances are connected in _____ with the supply.

a) series   b) parallel   c) series-parallel   d) none of these

(Ans. : b)

Q.49 An electric lamp of 100 W will consume 1.5 units in _____ hours.

a) 10   b) 15   c) 20   d) 30   **(Ans. : a)**

Q.50 The voltmeter in a.c. circuit always measures _____ values.

a) average   b) maximum   c) r.m.s.   d) none of these

(Ans. : c)

Q.51 The r.m.s. value of an alternating current is $\dfrac{10}{\sqrt{2}}$ A then its peak to peak value is, _____.

a) 10 A   b) 30 A   c) 5 A   d) 20 A   **(Ans. : d)**

Q.52 The unit of measurement of electric energy is, _____.

a) watt   b) watt-hour   c) watt-sec   d) kilowatt **(Ans. : b)**

Q.53 For a pure resistive circuit, the voltage and current relation is, _____.

a) in phase   b) voltage leads current
c) voltage lags current   d) none of the above .   **(Ans. : a)**

Q.54 The average power consumption in a pure resistance is, _____.

a) $V_{r.m.s.} \, I_m$ b) $V_{r.m.s.} \, I_{r.m.s.}^2$ c) $I_m^2 R$ d) $\dfrac{V_m I_m}{2}$

(Ans. : d)

Q.55 In a pure inductor, the current _____ voltage by 90°

a) leads   b) lags   c) in phase   d) none of the above

(Ans. : b)

Q.56 In a pure capacitor, the voltage _____ current by 90°

a) leads   b) in phase   c) lags   d) none of the above
                                                                        (Ans. : c)

Q.57 The inductive reactance of an inductor L is given by, _____.

a) ωL b) $\dfrac{L}{f}$ c) fL   d) $\dfrac{2\pi L}{f}$ **(Ans. : a)**

Q.58 The average power consumption in a pure inductor is, _____.

a) maximum   b) minimum   c) zero   d) infinite **(Ans. : c)**

Q.59 The capacitive reactance of a capacitor C is given by, _____.

a) $\dfrac{1}{fC}$ b) $\dfrac{1}{2\pi\omega C}$ c) $\dfrac{2\pi\omega}{C}$ d) $\dfrac{1}{2\pi fC}$ **(Ans. : d)**

Q.60 The average power consumption in a pure capacitor is, _____.

a) zero   b) infinite   c) negative   d) none of the above
        (Ans. : a)

Q.61 The impedance of the series R-L circuit is, _____.

a) $R - jX_L$ b) $R + jX_L$ c) $X_L + jR$ d) none of these
        (Ans. : b)

Q.62 The power factor for the series R-L circuit is, _____.

a) zero   b) unity   c) lagging   d) leading **(Ans. : c)**

Q.63 The phase difference between V and I for the series R-L circuit _____ as X_L increases.

a) decreases   b) remains constant   c) increases   d) none of these
        (Ans. : c)

Q.64 The apparent power in single phase a.c. circuit is given by, _____.

a) VI cos φ   b) VI sin φ   c) IZ   d) VI   **(Ans. : d)**

Q.65 The true power in single phase a.c. circuit is given by, _____.

a) VI cos φ   b) VI sin φ   c) IZ   d) VI   **(Ans. : a)**

Q.66 The power factor of d.c. circuit is, _____.

a) lagging   b) unity   c) zero   d) leading **(Ans. : b)**

Q.67 A series R-L circuit of $6 + j8\ \Omega$ carries a current of 5 A then its power consumption is, _____.

a) zero   b) 30 W   c) 150 W   d) 40 W   **(Ans. : c)**

Q.68 The impedance of the series R-C circuit is, _____.

a) $R + jX_C$ b) $X_C - jR$ c) $R + j\,2\pi fC$ d) $R + \dfrac{X_C}{j}$ **(Ans. : d)**

Q.69   The power factor for the series R-C circuit is, _____.

a) zero   b) unity   c) leading   d) lagging (**Ans. : c**)

Q.70   The power consumption of series R-C circuit _____ if X_C increases.

a) remains same   b) decreases   c) increases   d) none of these
                                                                                           (**Ans. : a**)

Q.71   A series R-C circuit of $6 - j8\ \Omega$ carries a current of 10 A then its power consumption is, _____.

a) 60 W   b) 600 W   c) 100 W   d) 80 W   (**Ans. : b**)

Q.72   As the power factor angle increases, _____.

a) the active power increases   b) the reactive power decreases
c) the active power decreases   d) the apparent power increases (**Ans. : c**)

Q.73   If the active and reactive power components of a circuit are equal then the power factor angle is, _____.

a) 30°   b) 0°   c) 90°   d) 45°   (**Ans. : d**)

Q.74   The capacitive reactance of a 20 µF capacitor is 7.9577 Ω at a frequency of......

a) 1 kHz   c) 50 Hz   d) 2 kHz   d) 60 Hz   (**Ans. : a**)

Q.75   The relation between frequency and capacitive reactance is, _____.

a) square   b) direct   c) inverse   d) linear   (**Ans. : c**)

Q.76   For improving power factor, the resistance in the circuit must be _____.

a) decreased   b) increased   c) kept same   d) removed
                                                                                           (**Ans. : b**)

Q.77   The series R-L-C circuit will have lagging power factor if X_L is _____ X_C.

a) less than   b) greater than   c) same as   d) none of these
                                                                                           (**Ans. : b**)

Q.78   The power consumption of R-L-C series circuit is, _____.

a) VI   b) $\dfrac{V}{Z}$ c) I^2R d) I^2V
                                                                                           (**Ans. : c**)

Q.79   If the total current drawn by the circuit is 20 A and a component in phase with the voltage is 15 A then the power factor of the circuit is, _____.

a) 0.8   b) 0.65   c) 0.55   d) 0.75   (**Ans. : d**)

Q.80   At a series resonance, current is _____.

a) minimum   b) maximum   c) zero   d) none of these
                                                                                           (**Ans. : b**)

Q.81 At a series resonance, the power factor of the circuit is _____.

a) unity   b) zero   c) lagging   d) leading **(Ans. : a)**

Q.82 In a series R-L-C circuit, if operating frequency is less than the resonant frequency the current drawn is _____.

a) zero   b) lagging   c) leading   d) unity   **(Ans. : c)**

Q.83 The resonant frequency is the _____ of the two half power frequencies.

a) product   b) division   c) square root   d) geometric mean
(Ans. : d)

Q.84 The quality factor of a series R-L-C circuit indicates, _____.

a) rejection capacity b) selectivity   c) bandwidth   d) none of these
(Ans. : b)

Q.85 A series R-L-C circuit has L = 10 mH and c = 100 μF while R = 1 Ω then its quality factor is, _____.

a) 10   b) 100   c) 0.1   d) 1000   **(Ans. : a)**

Q.86 The admittance is _____ the impedance.

a) equal to   b) square of   c) reciprocal of   d) none of these
(Ans. : c)

Q.87 The admittance of series R-L circuit is given by, _____.

a) G + jB   b) B − jG   c) B + jG   d) G − jB **(Ans. : d)**

Q.88 The unit of admittance is _____.

a) mho   b) ohm   c) watt   d) ampere **(Ans. : a)**

Q.89 The net susceptance of a parallel resonating circuit is _____.

a) maximum   b) zero   c) unity   d) negative
(Ans. : b)

Q.90 The current magnification is achieved in _____.

a) series resonating circuit   b) series R-L-C circuit
c) parallel resonating circuit   c) none of these   **(Ans. : c)**

Q.91 If the voltage across R is 25 V and across C is 100 V in a series R-C circuit then the supply voltage is _____.

a) 125 V   b) 25 V   c) 100 V   d) 103.077 V
(Ans. : d)

Q.92 The instantaneous voltage and current for a.c. circuit are, v = 100 sin 377 t V and $i = 25 \sin\left(377t - \dfrac{\pi}{3}\right)$ A then the power consumption of the circuit is, _____.

a) 125 W   b) 625 W   c) 225 W   d) 526 W **(Ans. : b)**

Q.93 A series R-L-C circuit consists of R = 8 Ω and L = 20 mH and its resonating frequency is 1 kHz then its capacitive reactance at the resonance is, _____.

a) 125.663 Ω b) 166.253 Ω c) 8 Ω d) none of these

(Ans. : a)

Q.94 The power factor of the circuit shown in the Fig. 3.25.3 is _____.

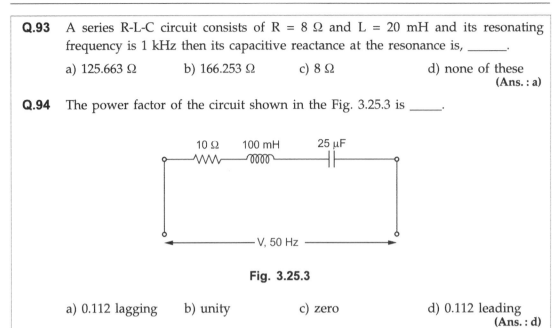

Fig. 3.25.3

a) 0.112 lagging   b) unity   c) zero   d) 0.112 leading

(Ans. : d)

4 Three Phase A.C. Circuits

Syllabus

Three phase system - Its necessity and advantages, Star and delta connections, Balanced supply and balanced load, Line and phase voltage / current relations, Three-phase power and its measurement (Simple numerical problems), Causes and problems of low power factor, Concept of power factor improvement (Simple numerical problems).

Contents

4.1 Introduction
2009-10

There are certain loads which require polyphase supply. **Phase** means **branch, circuit** or **winding** while **poly** means **many**. So such applications need a supply having many a.c. voltages present in it simultaneously. Such a system is called **polyphase system**.

To develop polyphase system, the armature winding in a generator is divided into number of phases required.

In each section, a separate a.c. voltage gets induced. So there are many independent a.c. voltages present equal to number of phases of winding.

The various phases of winding are arranged in such a manner that the magnitudes and frequencies of all these voltages is same but they have definite phase difference with respect to each other.

The phase difference depends on number of phases in which winding is divided. For example, if winding is divided into 'n' phases then 'n' separate a.c. voltages will be available having same magnitude and frequency but they will have a phase difference of (360°/n) with respect to each other.

Thus in a three phase supply system, there are three voltages with a same magnitude and freuqency but having a phase difference of 360°/3 = 120° between them. Such a supply system is called **three phase system**.

In practice a three phase system is found to be more economical and it has certain advantages over other polyphase systems. Hence three phase system is very popularly used everywhere in practice.

4.1.1 Advantages of Three Phase System

A three phase system has following advantages over single phase system :

1) The output of three phase machine is always greater than single phase machine of same size, approximately 1.5 times. So for a given size and voltage a three phase alternator occupies less space and has less cost too than single phase having same rating.

2) For a transmission and distribution, three phase system needs less copper or less conducting material than single phase system for given volt amperes and voltage rating so transmission becomes very much economical.

3) It is possible to produce rotating magnetic field with stationary coils by using three phase system. Hence three phase motors are self starting.

4) In single phase system, the instantaneous power is a function of time and hence fluctuates w.r.t. time. This fluctuating power causes considerable vibrations in

single phase motors. Hence performance of single phase motors is poor. While instantaneous power in symmetrical three phase system is constant.

5)   Three phase system give steady output.

6)   Single phase supply can be obtained from three phase but three phase cannot be obtained from single phase.

7)   Power factor of single phase motor is poor than three phase motors of same rating.

8)   For converting machines like rectifiers, the d.c. output voltage becomes smoother if number of phases are increased.

But it is found that optimum number of phases required to get all above said advantages is three. Hence three phase system is accepted as standard system throughout the world.

Review Question

| 1. What is three phase system ? Explain its advantages. | 2009-10, Marks 5 |

4.2 Generation of Three Phase Voltage System

It is already discussed that alternator consisting of one group of coils on armature produces one alternating voltage. But if armature coils are divided into three groups such that they are **displaced by the angle** $120°$ from each other, three separate alternating voltages get developed.

Consider armature of alternator divided into three groups as shown in the Fig. 4.2.1. The coils are named as R_1-R_2, Y_1-Y_2 and B_1-B_2 and mounted on same shaft.

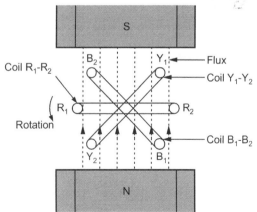

The ends of each coil are brought out through the slipring and brush arrangement to collect the induced e.m.f.

Let e_R, e_Y and e_B be the three independent voltages induced in coils R_1-R_2, Y_1-Y_2 and B_1-B_2 respectively. All are alternating voltages having same

Fig. 4.2.1 Generation of 3 phase

magnitude and frequency as they are rotated at uniform speed.

All of them will be displaced from one other by $120°$.

Suppose e_R is assumed to be the reference and is zero for the instant shown in the Fig. 4.2.2. At the same instant e_Y will be displaced by 120° from e_R and will follow e_R while e_B will be displaced by 120° from e_Y and will follow e_Y i.e. if e_R is reference then e_Y will attain its maximum and minimum position 120° later than e_R and e_B will attain its maximum and minimum position 120° later than e_Y i.e.

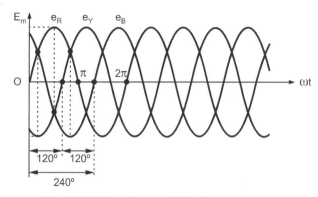

Fig. 4.2.2 Waveforms of 3 phase voltages

120°+120° = 240° later with respect to e_R. All coils together represent three phase supply system. The waveforms are shown in the Fig. 4.2.2.

The equations for the induced voltages are :

$$e_R = E_m \sin(\omega t)$$
$$e_Y = E_m \sin(\omega t - 120°)$$
$$e_B = E_m \sin(\omega t - 240°) = E_m \sin(\omega t + 120°)$$

The phasor diagram of these voltages can be shown as in the Fig. 4.2.3.

As phasors rotate in anticlockwise direction, we can say that e_Y lags e_R by 120° and e_B lags e_Y by 120°.

If we add three voltages vectorially, it can be observed that the **sum of the three voltages at any instant is zero**.

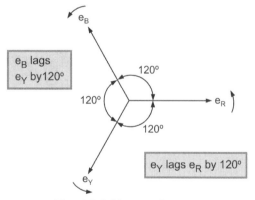

e_B lags e_Y by 120°

e_Y lags e_R by 120°

Fig. 4.2.3 Phasor diagram

Mathematically this can be shown as :

$$e_R + e_Y + e_B = E_m \sin\omega t + E_m \sin(\omega t - 120°) + E_m \sin(\omega t + 120°)$$

$$= E_m [\sin \omega t + \sin \omega t \cos 120° - \cos \omega t \sin 120° + \sin \omega t \cos 120° + \cos \omega t \sin 120°]$$

$$= E_m [\sin \omega t + 2 \sin \omega t \cos 120°] = E_m \left[\sin \omega t + 2 \sin \omega t \left(\frac{-1}{2} \right) \right] = 0$$

∴　　　　$$\bar{e}_R + \bar{e}_Y + \bar{e}_B = 0$$

> The phasor addition of all the phase voltages at any instant in three phase system is always zero.

Review Questions

> 1. State the principle of 3 phase e.m.f. generation and state the equations of all the three phase voltages. Represent them in graphical form.
> 2. Show that the sum of the instantaneous values of the voltages in a three phase system is always zero.

4.3 Important Definitions Related to Three Phase System   2009-10

1) Symmetrical system : It is possible in polyphase system that magnitudes of different alternating voltages are different. But a three phase system in which the three voltages are of same magnitude and frequency and displaced from each other by 120° phase angle is defined as **symmetrical system**.

2) Phase sequence : The sequence in which the voltages in three phases reach their maximum positive values is called **phase sequence**. Generally the phase sequence is R-Y-B.

> The phase sequence is important in determining direction of rotation of a.c. motors, parallel operation of alternators etc.

There are two possible phase sequences which are RYB and RBY. The phase sequence of a three phase system can be changed by interchanging any two terminals out of R, Y and B. If three phase supply is given to a three phase motor with a phase sequence of RYB then by interchanging any two terminals of RYB the phase sequence can be reversed. Due to this the direction of motor gets reversed.

Review Questions

> 1. Define symmetrical three phase system.
> 2. What is the meaning of phase sequence ? How it can be changed ?   2009-10, Marks 5

4.4 Three Phase Supply Connections

In single phase system, two wires are sufficient for transmitting voltage to the load i.e. phase and neutral. But in case of three phase system, two ends of each phase i.e. $R_1 - R_2$, $Y_1 - Y_2$, and $B_1 - B_2$ are available to supply voltage to the load.

If all the six terminals are used independently to supply voltage to load as shown in the Fig. 4.4.1, then total six wires will be required and it will be very much costly.

To reduce the cost by reducing the number of windings, the three windings are interconnected in a particular fashion. This gives different three phase connections.

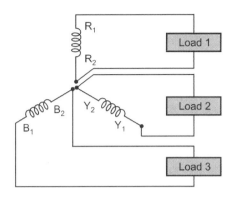

Fig. 4.4.1 Three phase connections

4.4.1 Star Connection

The star connection is formed by connecting starting **or** terminating ends of all the three windings together. The ends R_1-Y_1-B_1 are connected or ends R_2-Y_2-B_2 are connected together. This common point is called **Neutral Point**. The remaining three ends are brought out for connection purpose. These ends are generally referred as R-Y-B, to which load is to be connected.

The star connection is shown in the Fig. 4.4.2.

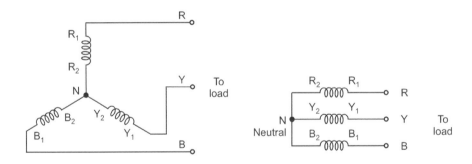

Fig. 4.4.2 Star connection

4.4.2 Delta Connection

The delta is formed by connecting one end of winding to starting end of other and connections are continued to form a closed loop. The supply terminals are taken out from the three junction points. Delta connection always forms a closed loop.

The delta connection is shown in the Fig. 4.4.3.

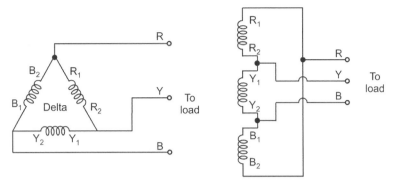

Fig. 4.4.3 Delta connection

4.4.3 Concept of Line Voltages and Line Currents

The potential difference between any two lines of supply is called **line voltage** and current passing through any line is called **line current**.

Consider a star connected system as shown in the Fig. 4.4.4.

Line voltages are denoted by V_L. These are V_{RY}, V_{YB} and V_{BR}.

Line currents are denoted by I_L. These are I_R, I_Y and I_B.

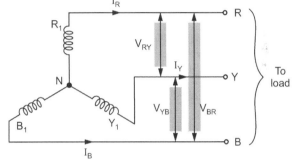

Fig. 4.4.4 Star connection

Similarly for delta connected system we can show the line voltages and line currents as in the Fig. 4.4.5.

Line voltages V_L are V_{RY}, V_{BR}, V_{YB}.

While Line currents I_L are I_R, I_Y and I_B.

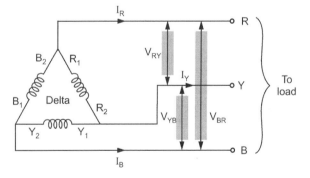

Fig. 4.4.5 Delta connection

4.4.4 Concept of Phase Voltages and Phase Currents

To define the phase voltages and phase currents let us see the connections of the three phase load to the supply lines.

The load can be connected in two ways, i) Star connection, ii) Delta connection

The **three phase load** is nothing but three different impedances connected together in star or delta fashion

i) Star connected load :   There are three different impedances and are connected such that one end of each is connected together and other three are connected to supply terminalis R-Y-B. This is shown in the Fig. 4.4.6.

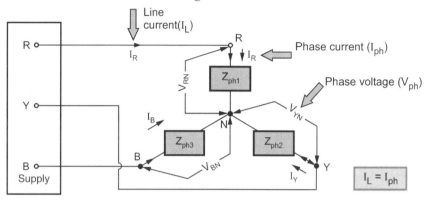

Fig. 4.4.6 Star connected load

The voltage across any branch of the three phase load i.e. across Z_{ph1}, Z_{ph2} or Z_{ph3} is called **phase voltage** and current passing through any branch of the three phase load is called **phase current.**

In the diagram shown in the Fig. 4.4.6 V_{RN}, V_{YN} and V_{BN} are phase voltages while I_R, I_Y and I_B as shown in the Fig. 4.4.6 are phase currents. The phase voltages are denoted as V_{ph} while the phase currents are denoted as I_{ph}. Generally suffix N is not indicated for phase voltages in star connected load. So $V_{ph} = V_R = V_Y = V_B$

It can be seen from the Fig. 4.4.6 that, $I_{ph} = I_R = I_Y = I_B$

But same are the currents flowing through the three lines also and hence defined as line currents. Thus we can conclude that for star connection $I_L = I_{ph}$.

$$I_L = I_{ph} \quad \text{(For star connection)}$$

ii) Delta connected load :   If the three impedances Z_{ph1}, Z_{ph2} and Z_{ph3} are connected such that starting end of one is connected to terminating end of other, to form a closed loop it is called delta connection of load. The junction points are connected to supply terminalis R-Y-B. This is shown in the Fig. 4.4.7.

The current I_{RY}, I_{YB} and I_{BR} flowing through the various branches of the load are **phase currents**. The lines currents are I_R, I_Y, I_B flowing through supply lines. Thus in delta connection of load, line and phase currents are different.

In the Fig. 4.4.7, the voltage across Z_{ph1} is V_{RY}, across Z_{ph2} is V_{YB} and across Z_{ph3} is V_{BR} and all are phase voltages.

$$V_{ph} = V_{RY} = V_{YB} = V_{BR}$$

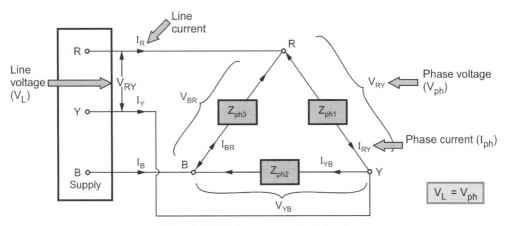

Fig. 4.4.7 Delta connected load

But as per definition of line voltages, same are the voltages across supply lines also. Thus it can be concluded that in delta connection $V_L = V_{ph}$.

$$V_L = V_{ph} \quad \text{For delta connection}$$

4.4.5 Balanced Load

The load is said to be balanced when **magnitudes** of all the impedances Z_{ph1}, Z_{ph2} and Z_{ph3} are **equal** and the **phase angles** of all of them are **equal** and of **same nature** either all inductive or all capacitive or all resistive.

> In such case all phase voltages have equal magnitudes and are displaced from each other by 120° while all phase currents also have equal magnitudes and are displaced from each other by 120°.
>
> The same is true for all the line voltages and line currents.

The load is said to be unbalanced when **magnitudes** of all the impedances Z_{ph1}, Z_{ph2} and Z_{ph3} are **unequal** and the **phase angles** of all of them are **unequal**. In such a case the phase voltages are unequal and not displaced from each other by 120°. Same is true for phase currents.

Review Questions

1. *Explain the star connection of a three phase system.*
2. *Explain the delta connection of a three phase system.*
3. *Explain the concept of line voltages and line currents.*
4. *Explain the concept of phase voltages and phase currents.*
5. *Describe the meaning of three phase unbalanced load and balanced load ?*

4.5 Relations for Star Connected Load   2006-07, 2008-09, 2010-11, 2012-13

Consider the balanced star connected load as shown in the Fig. 4.5.1.

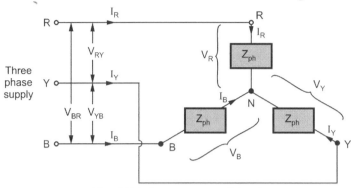

Fig. 4.5.1 Star connected load

Line voltages, $V_L = V_{RY} = V_{YB} = V_{BR}$ and   Line currents, $I_L = I_R = I_Y = I_B$

Phase voltages, $V_{ph} = V_R = V_Y = V_B$ and   Phase currents, $I_{ph} = I_R = I_Y = I_B$

As seen earlier, $I_L = I_{ph}$ for star connected load.

To derive relation between V_L and V_{ph}, consider line voltage V_{RY}. From the Fig. 4.5.1 we can write,

$$\overline{V}_{RY} = \overline{V}_{RN} + \overline{V}_{NY} \text{ But } \overline{V}_{NY} = -\overline{V}_{YN}, \text{ Hence } \overline{V}_{RY} = \overline{V}_R - \overline{V}_Y \qquad \dots (4.5.1)$$

Similarly, $\overline{V}_{YB} = \overline{V}_{YN} + \overline{V}_{NB} = \overline{V}_{YN} - \overline{V}_{BN} = \overline{V}_Y - \overline{V}_B$ $\qquad \dots (4.5.2)$

and $\overline{V}_{BR} = \overline{V}_B - \overline{V}_R$ $\qquad\qquad\qquad\qquad\qquad \dots (4.5.3)$

The three phase voltage are displaced by 120° from each other.

The phasor diagram to get V_{RY} is shown in the Fig. 4.5.2. The V_Y is reversed to get $-V_Y$ and then it is added to V_R to get V_{RY}.

The perpendicular is drawn from point A on vector OB representing V_L.

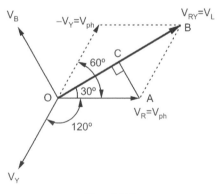

Fig. 4.5.2

In triangle OAB, the sides OA and AB are same as phase voltages. Hence OB bisects angle between V_R and $-V_Y$.

$\therefore$ $\angle$ BOA = 30°

And perpendicular AC bisects the vector OB.

$\therefore$ $OC = CB = \dfrac{V_L}{2}$

From triangle OAB, $\quad \cos 30° = \dfrac{OC}{OA} = \dfrac{(V_{RY}/2)}{V_R}$ i.e. $\dfrac{\sqrt{3}}{2} = \dfrac{(V_L/2)}{V_{ph}}$

$\therefore$ $V_L = \sqrt{3}\ V_{ph}$ **for star connection and** $I_L = I_{ph}$

Thus line voltage is $\sqrt{3}$ times the phase voltage in star connection.

The lagging or leading nature of current depends on per phase impedance. If Z_{ph} is inductive i.e. $R + j\ X_L$ then current I_{ph} lags V_{ph} by angle ϕ where ϕ is $\tan^{-1}(X_L/R)$. If Z_{ph} is capacitive i.e. $R - j\ X_C$ then I_{ph} leads V_{ph} by angle ϕ. If Z_{ph} is resistive i.e. $R + j\ 0$ then I_{ph} is in phase with V_{ph}.

Remember that $\mathbf{Z_{ph}}$ relates $\mathbf{I_{ph}}$ and $\mathbf{V_{ph}}$ hence angle ϕ is always between $\mathbf{I_{ph}}$ and $\mathbf{V_{ph}}$ and not between the line values.

And $\quad\quad \left| Z_{ph} \right| = \dfrac{\left| V_{ph} \right|}{\left| I_{ph} \right|}$

Key Point *The line values do not decide the impedance angle or power factor angle.*

The complete phasor diagram for lagging power factor load is shown in the Fig. 4.5.3.

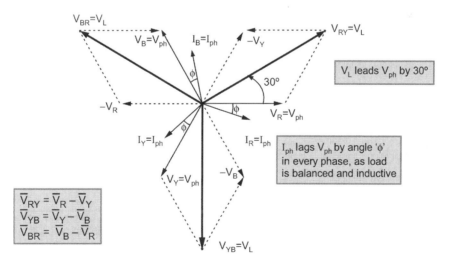

Fig. 4.5.3 Star and lagging p.f. load

$Z_{ph} = R_{ph} + j\ X_{Lph} = \left| Z_{ph} \right| \angle \phi \ \ \Omega$

Each I_{ph} lags corresponding V_{ph} by angle ϕ.

All line voltages are also displaced by $120°$ from each other.

Every line voltage leads the respective phase voltage by 30°.

For star connection, to draw phasor diagram, use

$$\overline{V}_{RY} = \overline{V}_R - \overline{V}_Y, \ \overline{V}_{YB} = \overline{V}_Y - \overline{V}_B \ \text{ and } \ \overline{V}_{BR} = \overline{V}_B - \overline{V}_R$$

Power : The power consumed in each phase is single phase power given by,

$$P_{ph} = V_{ph} \ I_{ph} \ \cos\phi$$

For balanced load, all phase powers are equal. Hence total three phase power consumed is,

$$P = 3P_{ph} = 3 \ V_{ph} \ I_{ph} \ \cos\phi \ = 3 \ \frac{V_L}{\sqrt{3}} I_L \ \cos\phi$$

$$\therefore \qquad \boxed{P = \sqrt{3} \ V_L I_L \cos\phi}$$

4.5.1 Steps to Solve Problems on Three Phase Systems

While solving three phase problems :

1) Given supply voltages are always line voltages.

2) Determine phase voltage depending on whether load is star or delta connected.

3) Then determine phase current,

$$I_{ph} = \frac{V_{ph}}{Z_{ph}}$$

4) Determine line current depending on whether load is star or delta connected.

5) ϕ is angle between V_{ph} and I_{ph}. Value can be obtained from given Z_{ph}.

6) The total power consumed is $\sqrt{3} \ V_L I_L \cos\phi$.

Examples 4.5.1 *Three inductive coils each having resistance of 16 ohm and reactance of 12 ohm are connected in star across a 400 V, three-phase 50 Hz supply. Calculate :*
i) Line voltage, ii) Phase voltage, iii) Line current, iv) Phase current, v) Power factor, vi) Power absorbed Draw phasor diagram.

Solution : $R_{ph} = 16 \ \Omega$, $X_L = 12 \ \Omega$ per ph, Star connection $V_L = 400$ V

$\therefore \qquad Z_{ph} = R_{ph} + j \ X_L = 16 + j \ 12 \ \Omega = 20 \ \angle + 36.86° \ \Omega$

Using rectangular to polar conversion on calculator.

i) Line voltage $\qquad V_L = \mathbf{400\ V}$

ii) Phase voltage $\qquad V_{ph} = \dfrac{V_L}{\sqrt{3}} = \dfrac{400}{\sqrt{3}} = \mathbf{230.94\ V}$

For star connection, $\qquad V_L = \sqrt{3}\ V_{ph}$

iii) $\qquad I_{ph} = \dfrac{V_{ph}}{Z_{ph}} = \dfrac{230.94}{20} = \mathbf{11.547\ A}$

For star connection, $\qquad I_L = I_{ph}$

$\therefore \qquad$ Line current $= \mathbf{11.547\ A}$

iv) $\qquad$ Phase current $= \mathbf{11.547\ A}$

v) Power factor $\qquad \cos\phi = \dfrac{R_{ph}}{Z_{ph}} = \dfrac{16}{20} = \mathbf{0.8\ lagging}$

As coil is inductive, the nature of the power factor is lagging.

vi) Power absorbed $\qquad P = \sqrt{3}\ V_L\ I_L\ \cos\phi = \sqrt{3}\times400\times11.547\times0.8 = \mathbf{6400\ W}$

The phasor diagram is as shown in the Fig. 4.5.3 with $\phi = 36.867°$.

Examples 4.5.2 *A 3 phase, 400 V supply is connected to a 3 phase star connected balanced load. The line current is 20 A and the power consumed by the load is 12 kW. Calculate the impedance of the load, phase current and power factor.*   **2006-07, Marks 5**

Solution : $V_L = 400$ V, Star, $I_L = 20$ A, $P = 12$ kW

$$P = \sqrt{3}\ V_L\ I_L\ \cos\phi \quad \text{i.e.} \quad 12\times10^3 = \sqrt{3}\times400\times20\times\cos\phi$$

$\therefore \qquad \cos\phi = \dfrac{12\times10^3}{\sqrt{3}\times400\times20} = \mathbf{0.866} \qquad\qquad$ ... Power factor

$\therefore \qquad \phi = 30°$

$\qquad V_{ph} = \dfrac{V_L}{\sqrt{3}} = \dfrac{400}{\sqrt{3}} = 230.9401\ V \qquad\qquad$ ... Star

$\qquad I_{ph} = I_L = \mathbf{20\ A} \qquad\qquad$ ... Phase current

$\therefore \qquad \left|Z_{ph}\right| = \dfrac{V_{ph}}{I_{ph}} = \dfrac{230.9401}{20} = 11.547\ \Omega/ph$

Assuming lagging power factor load, ϕ is positive.

$$\therefore \quad Z_{ph} = |Z_{ph}| \angle + \phi = 11.547 \angle 30° \ \Omega$$

$$= 10 + j\ 5.7735\ \Omega \qquad \text{... Load impedance}$$

Examples 4.5.3 *A balanced Y-connected load is connected from symmetrical 3 - φ, 400 V supply system. The current in each phase is 30 A with lagging power factor at 30°. Find :*
i) Impedance in each phase ii) Total power drawn iii) Draw phasor diagrams.

2006-07, Marks 10

Solution : $V_L = 400$ V, $I_{ph} = 30$ A, $\phi = 30°$ lagging, star

$$V_{ph} = \frac{V_L}{\sqrt{3}} = \frac{400}{\sqrt{3}} = 230.94 \text{ A}$$

Let V_{ph} be the reference phasor i.e. $V_{ph} = 230.94 \angle 0°$ V

$$I_{ph} = 30 \angle -30° \text{ A} \qquad \text{... Negative } \phi \text{ as lagging}$$

i) $$Z_{ph} = \frac{V_{ph}}{I_{ph}} = \frac{230.94\angle 0°}{30\angle -30°} = 7.698 \angle 30° \ \Omega$$

ii) $$P = \sqrt{3}\ V_L I_L \cos\phi$$

Where $$I_L = I_{ph} = 30 \text{ A}$$

$$\therefore \quad P = \sqrt{3} \times 400 \times 30 \times \cos(30°) = 18000 \text{ W}$$

iii) The phasor diagram is,

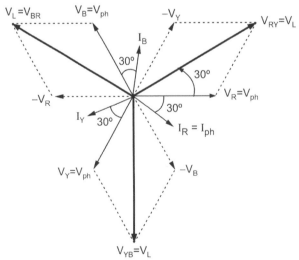

Fig. 4.5.4

Example 4.5.4 *For the circuit shown below, calculate the line current, the power and the power factor. The value of R, L and C in each phase are 10 Ω, 1 H and 100 μF.*

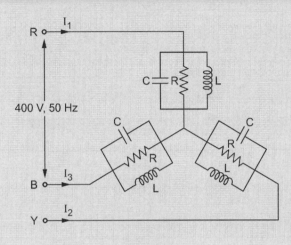

Fig. 4.5.5

Solution : $R = 10\ \Omega$, $L = 1\ H$, $C = 100\ \mu F$, $f = 50\ Hz$, $V_L = 400\ V$

$$X_L = 2\pi f L = 314.159\ \Omega, \quad X_C = \frac{1}{2\pi f C} = 31.8309\ \Omega$$

Z_{ph} is the parallel combination of R, L and C.

$\therefore \qquad Y_1 = \dfrac{1}{R\angle 0^\circ} = \dfrac{1}{10\angle 0^\circ}, 0.1 \angle 0^\circ = 0.1 + j\,0\ \mho$

$\therefore \qquad Y_2 = \dfrac{1}{X_L \angle 90^\circ} = \dfrac{1}{314.159\angle 90^\circ} = 3.183 \times 10^{-3} \angle -90^\circ = 0 - j\,3.183 \times 10^{-3}\ \mho$

$\qquad\qquad Y_3 = \dfrac{1}{X_C \angle -90^\circ} = \dfrac{1}{31.8309 \angle -90^\circ}$

$\qquad\qquad\quad = 0.03141 \angle +90^\circ = 0 + j\,0.03141\ \mho$

$\therefore \qquad Y_{eq} = Y_1 + Y_2 + Y_3 = 0.1 + j\,0.028227 = 0.1039 \angle 15.76^\circ\ \mho$

$\therefore \qquad Z_{ph} = \dfrac{1}{Y_{eq}} = \dfrac{1}{0.1039\angle 15.76^\circ} = 9.6246 \angle -15.76^\circ\ \Omega$

$\qquad\qquad V_{ph} = \dfrac{V_L}{\sqrt{3}} = \dfrac{400}{\sqrt{3}} = 230.94\ V \qquad\qquad\qquad$ ... Star connection

$\therefore \qquad I_{ph} = \dfrac{V_{ph}}{Z_{ph}} = \dfrac{230.94 \angle 0^\circ}{9.6246 \angle -15.76^\circ} = \mathbf{24 \angle 15.76^\circ\,A} \qquad\qquad$ ... Current

$\therefore \qquad I_L = I_{ph} = \mathbf{24 \angle 15.76^\circ\,A}$ and $\phi = 15.76^\circ$ leading

$\therefore \qquad P = \sqrt{3} V_L I_L \cos\phi = \sqrt{3} \times 400 \times 24 \times \cos(15.76^\circ) = \mathbf{16.0026 \ kW}$

$\therefore$ Power factor $= \cos\phi = \cos(15.76^\circ) = \mathbf{0.9624 \ leading}$

Example 4.5.5 *A balanced 3-phase star-connected load of 18 kW taking a leading current of 60 amperes when connected across a 3-phase 440 V, 50 Hz supply. Find the values and nature of load.* **2008-09, 2012-13, Marks 5**

Solution : $P = 18$ kW, $I_L = 60$ A, $V_L = 440$ V, star, leading p.f.

$$P = \sqrt{3} V_L I_L \cos\phi \quad \text{i.e.} \quad 18 \times 10^3 = \sqrt{3} \times 440 \times 60 \times \cos\phi$$

$\therefore \qquad \cos\phi = 0.3936 \quad \text{i.e.} \quad \phi = -66.8183^\circ \qquad\qquad \text{... -ve as leading}$

$|V_{ph}| = \dfrac{V_L}{\sqrt{3}} = 254.034$ V, $\quad |I_{ph}| = |I_L| = 60$ A $\qquad\qquad$ ... star load

$\therefore \qquad |Z_{ph}| = \dfrac{|V_{ph}|}{|I_{ph}|} = \dfrac{254.034}{60} = 4.2339 \ \Omega$

$\therefore \qquad Z_{ph} = |Z_{ph}|\angle\phi = 4.2339\angle - 66.8183^\circ \ \Omega$

$\qquad\qquad = 1.667 - j3.892 \ \Omega = R - jX_C$

$\therefore \qquad R_{ph} = \mathbf{1.667 \ \Omega}, \quad X_{Cph} = \dfrac{1}{2\pi f C_{ph}} = 3.892$

$\therefore \qquad C_{ph} = \dfrac{1}{2\pi \times 50 \times 3.892} = \mathbf{0.8178 \ mF}, \ \mathbf{Capacitive \ load.}$

Example 4.5.6 *A 3-phase voltage source has a phase voltage of 120 V and supplies star connected load having impedance 36 + j 48 Ω per phase. Calculate : a) The line voltage b) The line current c) The power factor d) The total 3-phase power supplied to the load.* **2008-09, Marks 10**

Solution : $V_{ph} = 120$ V, $\quad Z_{ph} = 36 + j48 \ \Omega$, Star connection

$$Z_{ph} = 36 + j48 \ \Omega = 60 \angle 53.1301^\circ \ \Omega$$

Assume phase voltage as reference,

$\therefore \qquad I_{ph} = \dfrac{V_{ph}}{Z_{ph}} = \dfrac{120\angle 0^\circ}{60\angle 53.1301^\circ} = 2 \angle - 53.1301^\circ \ A$

a) $\qquad V_L = \sqrt{3} \ V_{ph} = \sqrt{3} \times 120 = \mathbf{207.846 \ V}$

b) $\qquad I_L = I_{ph} = \mathbf{2 \ A}$

c) $\qquad \cos\phi = \cos(-53.1301^\circ) = \mathbf{0.6 \ lagging}$

d) $\qquad P = \sqrt{3} V_L I_L \cos\phi = \sqrt{3} \times 207.846 \times 2 \times 0.6 = \mathbf{432 \ W}$

Review Questions

1. Derive the relation between line and phase quantities in a three phase star connected circuit. Derive the expression for the power.   **2010-11, Marks 5**

2. A star connected load consists of $6\,\Omega$ resistance in series with an $8\,\Omega$ inductive reactance in each phase. A supply voltage of 440 V at 50 Hz is applied to the load. Find the line current, power factor and power consumed by the load .   **[Ans. : 25.4034 A, 0.6 lagging, 11.616 kW]**

3. A balanced star connected load of $(8 + j6)\,\Omega$ is connected to a 3 phase, 230 V supply. Find the line current, power factor, power, reactive voltamperes and total voltamperes.   **[Ans. : 13.279 A, 4232 W, 3174 VAR, 5290 VA]**

4. A 3-phase, Y connected supply with a phase voltage of 230 V is supplying a balanced Δ load. The load draws 15 kW at 0.8 p.f. lagging. Find the line currents and the current in each phase of the load. What is load impedance per phase ?   **[Ans. : 27.1739 A, 8.464 $\angle$ 36.86° Ω = 6.772 + j 5.077 Ω Per phase]**

5. A balanced star connected load of $(8 + j6)\,\Omega$ per phase is connected to a three phase, 230 V supply. Find the line current, power factor, power, reactive voltampere and total voltampere.   **[Ans. : 13.279 Amp, 4231.98 W, 3173.98 VAR, 5289.97 VA]**

6. Calculate the active and reactive components of each phase of Y connected 10 kV, 3 ϕ alternator supplying 5 MW at 0.8 p.f. If the total current remains the same, when load p.f. is raised to 0.9, calculate the new output and its active and reactive components per phase.   **[Ans. : 360.844 A, 1.666 MW, 1.25 MVAR, 5.625 MW, 1.875 MW, 0.9081 MVAR]**

7. A symmetrical 3 phase, 400 volt system supplies a balanced load of 0.8 lagging power factor and connected in star. If the line current is 34.64 Amp, find
   i) Impedance   ii) Resistance and reactance per phase
   iii) Total power and   iv) Total reactive voltamperes.   **[Ans. : 19.1999 kW, 14.399 kVAR]**

8. A balanced three-phase star connected load of 100 kW takes a leading current of 80 Amp, when connected across $3 - \phi$, 1100 volt, 50 Hz supply. Find the value of resistance/phase and capacitance/phase of load and p.f. of load. If the same load is connected in delta, calculate power consumed.   **[Ans. : 0.656 leading, 300 kW]**

9. Three similar choke coils are connected in star to a three phase supply. If the line current is 15 A, the total power consumed is 11 kW, and the volt ampere input is 15 kVA, find the line and phase voltages, the VAR input and the reactance and resistance of each coil.
   If these coils are now connected in delta calculate phase and line currents, active and reactive power.   **(Ans. : 10.197 kVAR, 30.592 kVAR)**

4.6 Relations for Delta Connected Load   **2000-01, 2001-02, 2011-12**

Consider the balanced delta connected load as shown in the Fig. 4.6.1.

Line voltages $V_L = V_{RY} = V_{YB} = V_{BR}$

Line currents $I_L = I_R = I_Y = I_B$

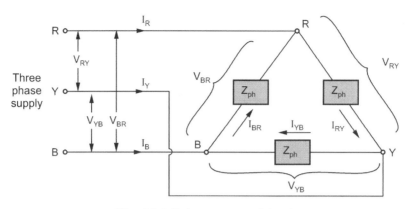

Fig. 4.6.1 Delta connected load

Phase voltages $\qquad\qquad\qquad V_{ph} = V_{RY} = V_{YB} = V_{BR}$

Phase currents $\qquad\qquad\qquad I_{ph} = I_{RY} = I_{YB} = I_{BR}$

As seen earlier, $V_{ph} = V_L$ for delta connected load. To derive the relation between I_L and I_{ph}, apply the KCL at the node R of the load shown in the Fig. 4.6.1.

$$\sum I_{entering} = \sum I_{leaving} \text{ at node R}$$

$\therefore \qquad \bar{I}_R + \bar{I}_{BR} = \bar{I}_{RY}$

$\therefore \qquad\quad \bar{I}_R = \bar{I}_{RY} - \bar{I}_{BR} \qquad\qquad\qquad\qquad\qquad\qquad\qquad ...(4.6.1)$

Applying KCL at node Y and B, we can write equations for line currents I_Y and I_B as,

$\bar{I}_Y = \bar{I}_{YB} - \bar{I}_{RY} \qquad\qquad ...(4.6.2)$

$\bar{I}_B = \bar{I}_{BR} - \bar{I}_{YB} \qquad\qquad ...(4.6.3)$

The phasor diagram to obtain line current I_R by carrying out vector subtraction of phase currents I_{RY} and I_{YB} is shown in the Fig. 4.6.2.

The three phase currents are displaced from each other by 120°.

I_{BR} is reversed to get $-I_{BR}$ and then added to I_{RY} to get I_R.

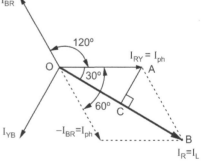

Fig. 4.6.2

The perpendicular AC drawn on vector OB, bisects the vector OB which represents I_L. Similarly OB bisects angle between $-I_{YB}$ and I_{RY} which is 60°.

$\therefore \qquad \angle\, BOA = 30° \qquad \text{and} \qquad OC = CB = \dfrac{I_L}{2}$

From triangle OAB,

$$\cos 30° = \frac{OC}{OA} = \frac{I_R/2}{I_{RY}} \qquad \text{i.e.} \qquad \frac{\sqrt{3}}{2} = \frac{I_L/2}{I_{ph}}$$

$$\therefore \qquad \mathbf{I_L = \sqrt{3}\ I_{ph}} \quad \text{and} \quad \mathbf{V_{ph} = V_L} \qquad\qquad \textbf{... for delta connection}$$

Thus line current is $\sqrt{3}$ times the phase current in delta connection.

Again Z_{ph} decides whether I_{ph} has to lag, lead or remain in phase with V_{ph}. **Angle between V_{ph} and I_{ph} is ϕ .**

Thus for delta connection, to draw phasor diagram, use

$$\bar{I}_R = \bar{I}_{RY} - \bar{I}_{BR}, \quad \bar{I}_Y = \bar{I}_{YB} - \bar{I}_{RY} \quad \text{and} \quad \bar{I}_B = \bar{I}_{BR} - \bar{I}_{YB}$$

The complete phasor diagram for $\cos\phi$ lagging power factor load is shown in the Fig. 4.6.3.

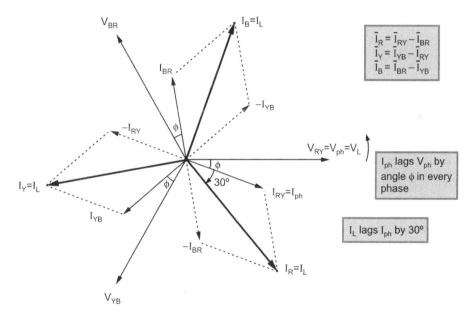

Fig. 4.6.3

$$Z_{ph} = R_{ph} + j\ X_{Lph} = \left| Z_{ph} \right| \angle \phi\ \Omega$$

Each I_{ph} lags respective V_{ph} by angle ϕ

Every line current lags the respective phase current by 30°.

Power : Power consumed in each phase is single phase power given by,

$$P_{ph} = V_{ph}\, I_{ph}\, \cos\phi$$

Total power $\quad P = 3\,P_{ph} = 3\,V_{ph}I_{ph}\cos\phi = 3\,V_L\,\dfrac{I_L}{\sqrt{3}}\cos\phi = \sqrt{3}\,V_L I_L \cos\phi$

> The expression for power is same but values of line currents are different in star and delta connected load which must be correctly determined to obtain power.

Example 4.6.1 *Three identical coils, each having resistance of 15 Ω and inductance of 0.03 H are connected in delta across a three-phase, 400 V, 50 Hz supply. Calculate : i) The phase current, ii) The line current, iii) The total power consumed, iv) p.f. and p.f. angle. Draw a neat phasor diagram.*

Solution : $R_{ph} = 15\ \Omega$, $L_{ph} = 0.03$ H

$\therefore\qquad X_{Lph} = \pi f L = 2\,\pi\times 50\times 0.03 = 9.425\ \Omega$

$\therefore\qquad Z_{ph} = R_{ph} + j\,X_{Lph} = 17.72\ \angle + 32.14^\circ\ \Omega = 15 + j\,9.425\ \Omega$

As connection is delta, $\qquad V_L = V_{ph}\quad$ and $\quad I_L = \sqrt{3}\,I_{ph},\ V_L = 400$ V

i) Phase current : $\qquad\qquad I_{ph} = \dfrac{V_{ph}}{Z_{ph}} = \dfrac{400}{17.72} = \mathbf{22.58\ A}$

ii) Line current : $\qquad\qquad I_L = \sqrt{3}\,I_{ph} = \sqrt{3}\times 22.58 = \mathbf{39.11\ A}$

ii) Total power consumed : $\qquad P = \sqrt{3}\,V_L\,I_L\,\cos\phi = \sqrt{3}\times 400\times 39.11\times\cos(32.14)$

$$= \mathbf{22.943\ kW}$$

iv) p.f. and p.f. angle : p.f. angle $= 32.14^\circ$

and $\qquad$ p.f. $= \cos(32.14) = \mathbf{0.8468\ lagging}$

The phasor diagram is as shown in the Fig. 4.6.3 with $\phi = 32.14^\circ$.

Example 4.6.2 *Prove that a three phase balanced load draws three times as much power when connected in delta, as it would draw when connected in star.*

Solution : Let load is three phase balanced with per phase impedance of $Z_{ph}\ \Omega$. Let V_L be the line voltage available which remains same whether load is connected in star or delta. What changes is the phase voltage and hence phase and line current values depending on star and delta connection of the load.

Case 1 : Star connection of load

$\therefore\qquad V_{ph1} = \dfrac{V_L}{\sqrt{3}} =$ Phase voltage for star connection

$$\therefore \qquad I_{ph1} = \frac{V_{ph1}}{Z_{ph}} \quad \text{and} \quad I_{L1} = I_{ph1} = \frac{V_{ph1}}{Z_{ph}} \qquad \text{... star connection}$$

$\cos \phi$ depends on components of Z_{ph} and remains same for any connection of the load.

$$\therefore \qquad P_{star} = \sqrt{3}\, V_L\, I_{L1} \cos \phi = \sqrt{3} \times V_L \times \frac{V_{ph1}}{Z_{ph}} \cos \phi \qquad \text{... } V_L \text{ is constant.}$$

$$= \sqrt{3}\, V_L \times \frac{(V_L / \sqrt{3})}{Z_{ph}} \cos \phi \qquad \text{... As } V_{ph1} = V_L / \sqrt{3}$$

$$= \frac{V_L^{\,2}}{Z_{ph}} \cos \phi \quad \text{watts}$$

Case 2 : Delta connection of load

$$V_{ph2} = V_L = \text{Phase voltage for delta connection}$$

$$\therefore \qquad I_{ph2} = \frac{V_{ph2}}{Z_{ph}} = \frac{V_L}{Z_{ph}} \quad \text{and} \quad I_{L2} = \sqrt{3}\, I_{ph2} = \frac{\sqrt{3}\, V_L}{Z_{ph}} \qquad \text{... Delta connection}$$

$\cos \phi$ remains same for both star and delta connection.

$$\therefore \qquad P_{delta} = \sqrt{3}\, V_L\, I_{L2} \cos \phi \qquad \text{... } V_L \text{ is constant}$$

$$= \sqrt{3}\, V_L \times \frac{\sqrt{3}\, V_L}{Z_{ph}} \cos \phi \qquad \text{... As } I_{L2} = \sqrt{3}\, V_L / Z_{ph}$$

$$= 3\, \frac{V_L^{\,2}}{Z_{ph}} \cos \phi = 3\, P_{star} \qquad \text{... Proved}$$

Key Point *Thus three phase balanced load draws three times as much power when connected in delta, as it would draw when connected in star.*

Example 4.6.3 *Three identical coils connected in delta across 400 V, 50 Hz, 3-phase a.c. supply, take a line current of 17.32 A at a power factor of 0.8 lagging. Calculate - i) the phase current ii) the resistance and inductance of each coil iii) the power drawn by each coil.*   **2000-01, Marks 5**

Solution :

i) For delta, $I_{ph} = \dfrac{I_L}{\sqrt{3}} = \dfrac{17.32}{\sqrt{3}} = \mathbf{10\ A}$

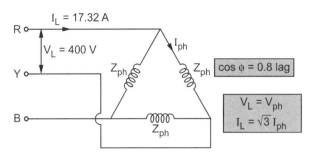

Fig. 4.6.4

ii) $|Z_{ph}| = \dfrac{V_{ph}}{I_{ph}} = \dfrac{400}{10} = 40 \ \Omega$ $\ldots V_L = V_{ph}$ for delta

and $\phi = \cos^{-1} 0.8 = 36.869°$ $\ldots$Positive as lagging

$\therefore$ $Z_{ph} = 40 \angle 36.869° \ \Omega = 32 + j\ 24 \ \Omega = R + j\ X_L \ \Omega$

$\therefore$ $R = \mathbf{32} \ \mathbf{\Omega}$ and $X_L = 24 \ \Omega = 2\pi f\ L$

$\therefore$ $L = \dfrac{24}{2\pi \times 50} = \mathbf{76.3943 \ mH}$

iii) $P_{ph} = V_{ph}\ I_{ph} \cos\phi = 400 \times 10 \times 0.8 = \mathbf{3200 \ W}$

Example 4.6.4 *Each phase of a delta connected load has a resistance of 25 Ω, an inductance of 0.15 H and a capacitance of 120 µF. The load is connected across a 400 V, 50 Hz, 3-phase supply. Determine the line current, active power and reactive volt-ampere.*

2001-02, Marks 5

Solution : $V_L = 400$ V, f = 50 Hz, R = 25 Ω, L = 0.15 H, C = 120 µF

$\therefore$ $X_L = 2\pi f L = 2\pi \times 50 \times 0.15 = 47.1238 \ \Omega$

       $X_C = \dfrac{1}{2\pi f C} = \dfrac{1}{2\pi \times 50 \times 120 \times 10^{-6}} = 26.5258 \ \Omega$

$\therefore$ $Z_{Ph} = R + j\ X_L - j\ X_C = 25 + j\ 20.598 \ \Omega = 32.3925 \angle 39.48° \ \Omega$

       $V_{ph} = V_L = 400$ V $\ldots$Delta connected

$\therefore$ $I_{ph} = \dfrac{V_{ph}}{Z_{ph}} = \dfrac{400 \angle 0°}{32.3925 \angle 39.48°} = 12.3485 \angle \mathbf{-39.48°}$ **A**

$\therefore$ $I_L = \sqrt{3}\ I_{ph} = \sqrt{3} \times 12.3485 = \mathbf{21.3882 \ A}$

       $P_T = \sqrt{3}\ V_L\ I_L \cos\phi = \sqrt{3} \times 400 \times 21.3882 \times \cos(39.48°) = \mathbf{11.6 \ kW}$

       $Q_T = \sqrt{3}\ V_L\ I_L \sin\phi = \sqrt{3} \times 400 \times 21.3882 \times \sin(39.48°) = \mathbf{9.4215 \ kVAR}$

Example 4.6.5 *Three identical resistors of 20 Ω each are connected in star to a 415 V, 50 Hz, 3 φ supply . Calculate, i) The total power consumed. ii) The total power consumed, if they are connected in delta. iii) The power consumed, if one of the resistors is opened.*

2001-02, Marks 10

Solution :

i) V_L = 415 V,

$$V_{ph} = \frac{V_L}{\sqrt{3}} = \frac{415}{\sqrt{3}} = 239.6 \text{ V}$$

$$I_{ph} = \frac{V_{ph}}{R} = \frac{239.6}{20} = 11.98 \text{ A} = I_L$$

As load is pure resistive, cos φ = 1

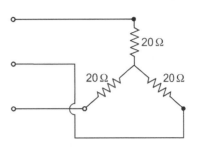

Fig. 4.6.5 (a)

∴ $\qquad P = \sqrt{3} V_L I_L \cos \phi = \sqrt{3} \times 415 \times 11.98 \times 1 = \mathbf{8611.25 \ W}$

ii) $V_L = V_{ph} = 415$ V

∴ $I_{ph} = \dfrac{V_{ph}}{R} = \dfrac{415}{20} = 20.75$ A

∴ $I_L = \sqrt{3} I_{ph} = 35.94$ A

∴ $P = \sqrt{3} V_L I_L \cos \phi$

$\qquad = \sqrt{3} \times 415 \times 35.94 \times 1$

$\qquad = \mathbf{25833.711 \ W}$

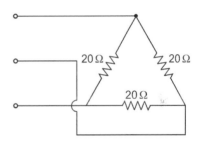

Fig. 4.6.5 (b)

iii) One resistance open in star

$$I = \frac{415}{40}$$

$\qquad = 10.375$ A

∴ $P = 2 I^2 R$

∴ $\qquad = 2 \times (10.375)^2 \times 20$

$\qquad = \mathbf{4305.625 \ W}$

Fig. 4.6.5 (c)

One resistance open in delta.

Across each 20 Ω, V_L = 415 V appears.

$$\therefore \quad I = \frac{V_L}{R} = \frac{415}{20} = 20.75 \text{ A}$$

$$\therefore \quad P = 2 \times I^2 \times R = 2 \times (20.75)^2 \times 20$$

$$= \mathbf{17222.5 \ W}$$

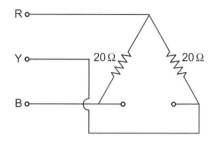

Fig. 4.6.5 (d)

Example 4.6.6 *Find the current in phase R in the following circuit.*

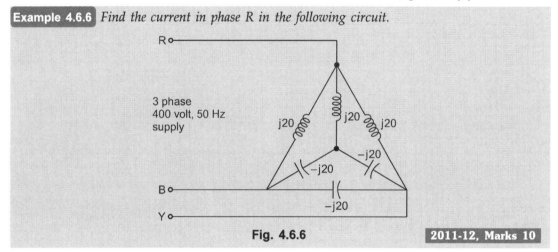

Fig. 4.6.6   **2011-12, Marks 10**

Solution : Convert the inner star to delta

$$\therefore \quad Z_1 = j\,20 - j\,20 + \frac{(j\,20)(-j\,20)}{(-j\,20)} = j\,20 \ \Omega$$

$$\therefore \quad Z_2 = -\,j\,20 - j\,20 + \frac{(-j\,20)(-j\,20)}{(j\,20)} = -\,j\,20 \ \Omega$$

$$\therefore \quad Z_3 = j\,20 - j\,20 + \frac{(j\,20)(-j\,20)}{(-j\,20)} = j\,20 \ \Omega$$

Fig. 4.6.6 (a)

Hence the load reduces as shown in the Fig. 4.6.6 (b).

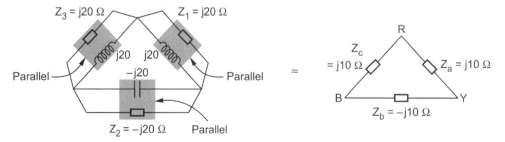

Fig. 4.6.6 (b)

Let V_{RY} be the reference hence $V_{RY} = 400 \angle 0°$ V

$V_{YB} = 400 \angle -120°$ V, $V_{BR} = 400 \angle +120°$ V,

$$\therefore \quad \bar{I}_{RY} = \frac{\bar{V}_{RY}}{Z_a} = \frac{400\angle 0°}{j\,10} = \frac{400\angle 0°}{10\angle 90°} = 40\angle -90° \text{ A} = 0 - j\,40 \text{ A}$$

$$\therefore \quad \bar{I}_{YB} = \frac{\bar{V}_{YB}}{Z_b} = \frac{400\angle -120°}{-j\,10} = \frac{400\angle -120°}{10\angle -90°} = 40\angle -30° \text{ A} = 34.641 - j\,20 \text{ A}$$

$$\therefore \quad \bar{I}_{BR} = \frac{\bar{V}_{BR}}{Z_c} = \frac{400\angle +120°}{j\,10} = \frac{400\angle +120°}{10\angle 90°} = 40\angle +30° \text{ A} = 34.641 + j\,20 \text{ A}$$

$$\therefore \quad \bar{I}_R = \bar{I}_{RY} - \bar{I}_{BR} = (0 - j\,40) - (34.641 + j\,20)$$

$$= -\,34.641 - j\,60 \text{ A} = 69.282 \angle -120° \text{ A}$$

$\therefore$ Current in phase R = **69.282 A**

Review Questions

1. *Derive the relationship between line and phase values of current for balanced delta connected load with the help of phasor diagram.*

2. *Three identical coils, each having resistance of 10 Ω and inductance of 0.03 H are connected in delta across a three phase, 400 V, 50 Hz supply. Calculate :*
   i) The phase current, ii) The line current,
   iii) The total power consumed,
   iv) p.f. and p.f. angle. Draw a neat phasor diagram.
   [Ans. : 29.1089 A, 50.4181 A, 25.42 kW, 0.7277 lagging]

3. *Three 100 Ω resistors are connected in i) Star and ii) Delta across a 415 V, 50 Hz, 3-phase supply. Calculate the line and phase currents and the power consumed in each case.*
   [Ans. : 2.396A, 2.396 A, 1722.2474 W, 4.15 A, 7.188 A, 5166.7422 W]

4. *A three phase load of three equal impedances connected in delta across a balanced 400 V supply takes a line current of 10 A a power factor of 0.7 lagging. Calculate from the first principles :*
   i) The phase current   ii) The total power   iii) The total reactive kVA.
   If the windings are connected in star, what will be the new value of phase current and the total power ? **[Ans. : 5.7735 A, 4849.7422 W, 4947.7267 VAR , 4.94772 kVAR, 3.3333 A, 1616.5645 W]**

5. *Three equal impedances each of 10 $\angle$ 60° ohms are connected in star across 3-phase, 400 volts 50 Hz supply. Calculate*
   i) Line voltage and phase voltage   ii) Line current and phase current
   iii) Power factor and active power consumed
   iv) If the same three impedances are connected in delta to the same source of supply what is the active power consumed ?
   [Ans. : 400 V, 230.94 V, 23.094 A, 23.094 A, 0.5 lagging, 8000 W, 400 V, 40 A, 40 $\sqrt{3}$ A, 24000 W]

6. *A series combination of 3 ohms resistance and a 796.18 µF capacitor in each branch forms a three phase 'star' connected balanced load which is connected to a 415 V, 3 phase, 50 Hz, a.c. supply. Calculate*

    i) The power consumed and

    ii) Current drawn by the load. If the same load is now connected as a 'delta', determine

    i) The power consumed and

    ii) Current drawn from the supply.   **[Ans. : 20667.05 W, 143.7602 A, 62001 W]**

7. *A balanced delta-connected load of impedance* $60\angle30°$ *ohm per phase is connected to a 3-phase supply of 400 V, phase sequence A-B-C.*

    Find :

    i) The phase and line values of current

    ii) Total power and reactive voltampere, and iii) The phase angle of line current I_A *with respect ot line voltage* V_{AB}, *drawing a sketch of the relevant phasors.*

    [Ans. : 6.667 $\angle$**–30°A, 11.547 A, 6928.2 W, 4000 VAR]**

8. *Three identical coils connected in delta across 400 V, 50 Hz, 3-phase a.c. supply, take a line current of 17.32 A at a power factor of 0.8 lagging. Calculate -*

    i) the phase current

    ii) the resistance and inductance of each coil

    iii) the power drawn by each coil   **[Ans. : 10 A, 76.3943 mH, 3200 W]**

4.7 Power Triangle for Three Phase Load

Total apparent power	S = 3 × Apparent power per phase
∴	$S = 3\ V_{ph}I_{ph} = 3\ \dfrac{V_L}{\sqrt{3}}I_L = 3\ V_L\dfrac{I_L}{\sqrt{3}}$
∴	$S = \sqrt{3}\ V_L I_L$ volt-amperes (VA) or kVA
Total active power	$P = \sqrt{3}\ V_L I_L \cos\phi$ watts (W) or kW
Total reactive power	$Q = \sqrt{3}\ V_L I_L \sin\phi$ reactive volt amperes (VAR) or kVAR

Hence power triangle is as shown in the Fig. 4.7.1.

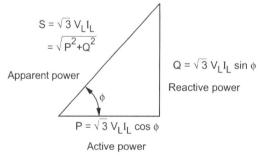

Fig. 4.7.1 Power triangle

Example 4.7.1   *Two balanced 3 -ph loads are connected in parallel to a 415 V, 3-ph, 50 Hz a.c. supply. The loads are :-*

*Load "A" : draws 10 A at 0.8 lag p.f., **star** connected.*

Load "B" : has R = 6 Ω and C = 198 micro-farads per phase, delta connected.

Estimate :- i) Total line current,   ii) Total power consumed,

iii) Impedance of load "A" in complex form , iv) Power factor of load "B" and its nature.

Solution :   The loads are shown in the Fig. 4.7.2. (a)

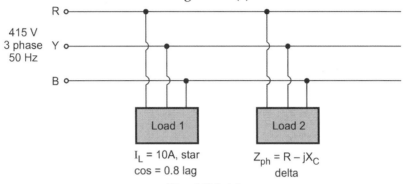

Fig. 4.7.2 (a)

$$V_L = 415 \text{ V}$$

For load 1 : $V_{ph} = V_L / \sqrt{3} = 239.6 \text{ V}$

$$I_L = I_{ph} = 10A, \cos \phi = 0.8 \text{ lag}$$

$$P_1 = \sqrt{3} \, V_L \, I_L \, \cos \phi$$

$$= \sqrt{3} \times 415 \times 10 \times 0.8$$

$$= 5750.408 \text{ W}$$

$$Q_1 = \sqrt{3} \, V_L \, I_L \, \sin \phi$$

$$= \sqrt{3} \times 415 \times 10 \times 0.6$$

$$= 4312.8065 \text{ VAR}$$

For load 2 : $Z_{ph} = R_{ph} - j \, X_{Cph}$

$$X_C = \frac{1}{2 \pi f C} = \frac{1}{2\pi \times 50 \times 198 \times 10^{-6}}$$

$$= 16.076 \, \Omega$$

∴ $Z_{ph} = 6 - j \, 16.076 \, \Omega = 17.159 \angle -69.53° \, \Omega$

$$V_{ph} = V_L = 415 \text{ V} \hspace{3cm} \text{... delta connection}$$

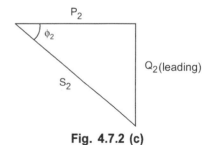

Fig. 4.7.2 (b)

Fig. 4.7.2 (c)

$\therefore$ $\qquad I_{ph} = \dfrac{V_{ph}}{Z_{ph}} = \dfrac{415}{17.159} = 24.1855$ A

$\therefore$ $\qquad I_L = \sqrt{3}\, I_{ph} = \sqrt{3} \times 24.1855 = 41.89$ A

$\therefore$ $\qquad P_2 = \sqrt{3}\, V_L\, I_L \cos\phi = \sqrt{3} \times 415 \times 41.89 \times \cos(-69.53°)$

$\qquad\qquad = 10515.405$ W

and $\qquad Q_2 = \sqrt{3}\, V_L\, I_L \sin\phi = \sqrt{3} \times 415 \times 41.89 \times \sin(-69.53°)$

$\qquad\qquad = -28209.257$ VAR $\qquad\qquad$ ... – ve as leading

$\therefore$ $\qquad P_T = P_1 + P_2 = 16265.813$ W

$\qquad\quad Q_T = Q_1 + Q_2$

$\qquad\qquad = 4312.8065 - 28209.257$

$\qquad\qquad = -23896.4505$ VAR $\qquad$ ... Leading

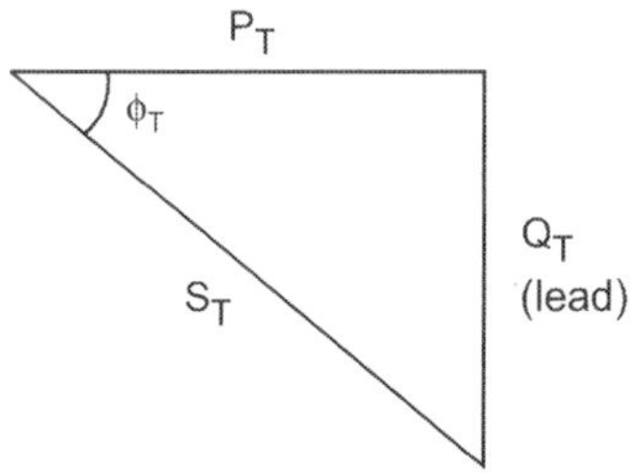

$\qquad \tan\phi_T = \dfrac{Q_T}{P_T} = \dfrac{23896.4505}{16265.813} = 1.4699$

Fig. 4.7.2 (d)

$\therefore$ $\qquad \phi_T = 55.77°$ $\qquad$ i.e. $\qquad \cos\phi_T = 0.5624$ leading

i) $\qquad$ Total power consumed = P_T = **16265.813 W**

ii) $\qquad\qquad\qquad\qquad P_T = \sqrt{3}\, V_L\, I_L \cos\phi_T$

$\therefore$ $\qquad\qquad 16265.813 = \sqrt{3} \times 415 \times I_L \times 0.5624$

$\therefore$ $\qquad\qquad\qquad\qquad I_L = $ **40.23 A** $\qquad\qquad$ ...Total line current

iii) $\qquad\qquad Z_{ph1} = \dfrac{V_{ph}}{I_{ph}} = \dfrac{239.6}{10} = 23.96$ A and $\phi_1 = \cos^{-1} 0.8 = 36.86°$

$\qquad\qquad Z_{ph1} = $ **23.96 $\angle +36.86°\,\Omega$**

iv) p.f. of load B= $\cos(-69.53) = $ **0.3497 leading**

Example 4.7.2 *Three pure elements are connected in star, draw x kVAR. What will be the value of elements that will draw the same kVAR when connected in delta across the same supply .*

Solution : Let reactance of pure element be X_1 per phase.

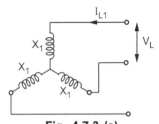

Fig. 4.7.3 (a)

Case 1 : Star connection

$$V_{ph1} = \frac{V_L}{\sqrt{3}}, \quad I_{ph1} = \frac{V_{ph1}}{X_1} = I_{L1} \text{ (magnitude)}$$

$$\therefore \quad kVAR_1 = \sqrt{3}\, V_L\, I_{L1}\, \sin\phi = \sqrt{3}\, V_L\, \frac{V_{ph1}}{X_1} \qquad \dots \sin\phi = 1, \phi = 90°$$

$$= \sqrt{3}\, V_L\, \frac{V_L}{\sqrt{3}\, X_1} = \frac{V_L^2}{X_1} \qquad \dots(4.7.1)$$

Case 2 : Delta connection

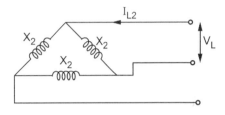

Fig. 4.7.3 (b)

$$V_L = V_{ph2}, \quad I_{ph2} = \frac{V_{ph2}}{X_2}$$

$$I_{L2} = \sqrt{3}\, I_{ph2} = \frac{\sqrt{3}\, V_{ph2}}{X_2} \text{ (magnitude)}$$

$$kVAR_2 = \sqrt{3}\, V_L\, I_{L2}\, \sin\phi = \sqrt{3}\, V_L \times \sqrt{3}\, \frac{V_{ph2}}{X_2} \qquad \dots V_{ph2} = V_L$$

$$= \frac{\sqrt{3}\, V_L\, \sqrt{3}\, V_L}{X_2} = 3\, \frac{V_L^2}{X_2} \qquad \dots(4.7.2)$$

For same kVAR, equate equations (4.7.1) and (4.7.2),

$$\therefore \qquad \frac{V_L^2}{X_1} = \frac{3\, V_L^2}{X_2} \quad \text{i.e.} \quad \boxed{X_2 = 3\, X_1}$$

Review Question

   1. Explain the power triangle for the three phase load.

4.8 Three Phase Power Measurement

    In three phase circuits whether load is star connected or delta connected, total three phase power is given by $\sqrt{3}\, V_L I_L \cos\phi$.

    The ϕ is the angle between $\mathbf{V}_{ph}$ and $\mathbf{I}_{ph}$.

In practice, the problems in measuring three phase power occur as power factor cos ϕ for different types of loads may not be known to us.

Not only this but power factor of induction motor, synchronous motor may vary depending on different load conditions. It is very difficult to notice such on line changes in the value of power factor and then using it to calculate the power.

Hence it is absolute necessity to use some device which will sense the power factor and will give the wattage reading directly.

Such a device which senses voltage, current and (power factor) angle between voltage and current to give power reading in watts directly is called **wattmeter**.

4.9 Wattmeter

It is a device which gives power reading, when connected in single phase or three phase system, directly in watts.

It consists of two coils.

i) Current coil : This senses the current and always to be connected in series with the load. Similar to ammeter, the resistance of this coil is as small as possible and hence its cross-sectional area is large and it has less number of turns.

ii) Voltage coil : This is also called **pressure coil**. This senses the voltage and always to be connected across the supply terminals. Similar to voltmeter, the resistance of this coil is very large and hence its cross-sectional area is small and it has large number of turns.

> It is important to note that wattmeter senses the angle between current phasor which is sensed by its current coil and voltage phasor which is sensed by its voltage coil.

It will not read phase angle 'ϕ' all the time. It depends on how we connect its current and voltage coils in the system.

> As 'ϕ' is the angle between V_{ph} and I_{ph}, if wattmeter has to sense this, its current coil must carry phase current I_{ph} and its voltage coil must sense phase voltage V_{ph}.

In general if I_c is the current through its current coil (may be phase or line depends on its connection) and V_{pc} is voltage across its pressure coil (may be phase or line depends on its connection) then wattmeter reading is,

$$W = V_{pc} \times I_c \times \cos \left(I_c{}^\wedge V_{pc} \right) \quad \text{watts}$$

Angle between V_{pc} and I_c is to be decided from the phasor diagram.

If $I_c = I_{ph}$ and $V_{pc} = V_{ph}$ then $I_c \hat{\,} V_{pc} = I_{ph} \hat{\,} V_{ph} = \phi$ and then only wattmeter reads per phase power which is $V_{ph} I_{ph} \cos \phi$.

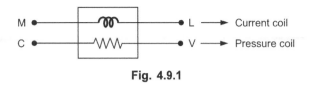

Fig. 4.9.1

A wattmeter can be represented symbolically as shown in Fig. 4.9.1.

The terminologies used to denote current and pressure coil are,

M = From mains, L = To load = For current coil

C = Common,   V = Voltage = For voltage coil

The terminals M and C are generally connected together.

To sense the phase voltage by pressure coil and the phase current by the current coil, it must be connected as shown in the Fig. 4.9.2 (a) and (b).

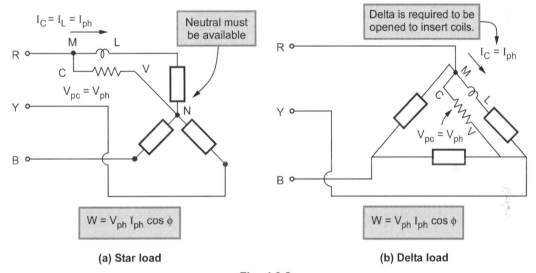

(a) Star load   (b) Delta load

Fig. 4.9.2

But connecting wattmeter to measure phase power is not always possible because many times neutral point of star connected load is not available. Similarly in delta connected load it is necessary to open delta load to insert current coil of the wattmeter, which is not practicable.

Hence the best method of measuring power whether load is star or delta connected, balanced or unbalanced, neutral is available or not is, using only two wattmeters which is called Two Wattmeter Method.

Review Question

1. *Explain the wattmeter connections. When wattmeter reads phase power ? Why two wattmeter method is necessary ?*

4.10 Two Wattmeter Method   2004-05, 2009-10, 2011-12

The current coils of the two wattmeters are connected in any two lines while the voltage coil of each wattmeter is connected between its own current coil terminal and the line without a current coil.

For example, the current coils are inserted in the lines R and Y then the pressure coils are connected between R - B for one wattmeter and Y- B for other wattmeter, as shown in the Fig. 4.10.1

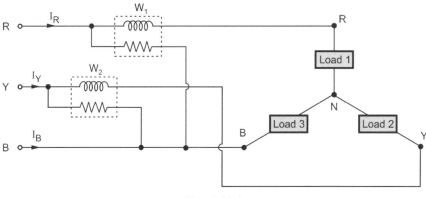

Fig. 4.10.1

The connections are same for star or delta connected load.

It can be shown that when two wattmeters are connected in this way, the algebraic sum of the two wattmeter readings gives the total power dissipated in the three phase circuit.

If W_1 and W_2 are the two wattmeter readings then total power

$$W = W_1 + W_2 = \text{Three phase power} = \sqrt{3}\, V_L I_L \cos\phi$$

Proof of Two Wattmeter Method for Star Connected Load :

Consider star connected load and two wattmeters connected as shown in the Fig. 4.10.1

Let us consider the r.m.s. values of the currents and voltages to prove that sum of two wattmeter gives total power consumed by three phase load.

$$W_1 = I_R \times V_{RB} \times \cos\left(I_R{}^{\wedge}V_{RB}\right) \quad \text{and}$$

$$W_2 = I_Y \times V_{YB} \times \cos\left(I_Y{}^{\wedge}V_{YB}\right)$$

To find angle between (I_R and V_{RB}) and (I_Y and V_{YB}) let us draw phasor diagram. (Assuming load p.f. be $\cos\phi$ lagging)

$$\overline{V}_{RB} = \overline{V}_R - \overline{V}_B$$

and $\quad \overline{V}_{YB} = \overline{V}_Y - \overline{V}_B$

$$V_R {}^\wedge I_R = \phi \quad \text{and} \quad V_Y {}^\wedge I_Y = \phi$$

$$V_R = V_Y = V_B = V_{ph}$$

and $\quad V_{RB} = V_{YB} = V_L$

$$I_R = I_Y = I_L = I_{ph} \ \text{(star)}$$

From Fig. 4.10.2, $\quad I_R {}^\wedge V_{RB} = 30 - \phi$

and $\quad I_Y {}^\wedge V_{YB} = 30 + \phi$

$\therefore \qquad W_1 = I_R V_{RB} \cos(30-\phi)$

$\therefore \qquad \boxed{W_1 = V_L I_L \cos(30-\phi)}$

and $\qquad W_2 = I_Y V_{YB} \cos(30+\phi)$

$\boxed{W_2 = V_L I_L \ \cos(30+\phi)}$

$\therefore \quad W_1 + W_2 = V_L I_L \left[\cos(30-\phi) + \cos(30+\phi)\right]$

$\qquad\qquad = V_L I_L [\cos 30 \cos\phi + \sin 30 \sin\phi + \cos 30 \cos\phi - \sin 30 \sin\phi]$

$\qquad\qquad = 2 \ V_L I_L \ \cos 30 \cos\phi \ = 2 V_L I_L \dfrac{\sqrt{3}}{2} \cos\phi$

$\therefore \quad \boxed{W_1 + W_2 = \sqrt{3} \ V_L \ I_L \ \cos\phi \ = \text{Total 3 phase power}}$

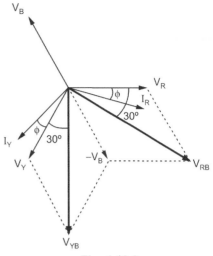

Fig. 4.10.2

Proof of Two Wattmeter Method for Delta Connected Load :

Consider delta connected balanced load, as shown in the Fig. 4.10.3.

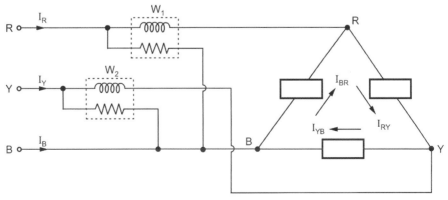

Fig. 4.10.3

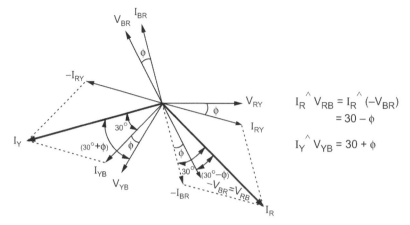

$$I_R {}^\wedge V_{RB} = I_R {}^\wedge (-V_{BR})$$
$$= 30 - \phi$$
$$I_Y {}^\wedge V_{YB} = 30 + \phi$$

Fig. 4.10.4 Delta connected load, lagging p.f

For W_1, $I_c = I_R$ and $V_{pc} = V_{RB}$

and W_2, $I_c = I_Y$ and $V_{pc} = V_{YB}$

$\therefore$ $W_1 = I_R V_{RB} \cos\left(I_R{}^\wedge V_{RB}\right)$ and $W_2 = I_Y V_{YB} \cos\left(I_Y{}^\wedge V_{YB}\right)$

To find $I_R{}^\wedge V_{RB}$ and $I_Y{}^\wedge V_{YB}$ let us draw phasor diagram. Assume load having $\cos\phi$ lagging p.f.

$$V_{RB} = V_{YB} = V_{phase} = V_{line} \text{ (Delta)} \quad \text{and} \quad I_R = I_Y = I_{line}$$

$$\bar{I}_R = \bar{I}_{RY} - \bar{I}_{BR} \quad \text{and} \quad \bar{I}_Y = \bar{I}_{YB} - \bar{I}_{RY}$$

$\therefore$ $W_1 = I_R V_{RB} \cos(30-\phi) = I_L V_L \cos(30-\phi)$

            $W_2 = I_Y V_{YB} \cos(30+\phi) = I_L V_L \cos(30+\phi)$

$\therefore$ $W_1 + W_2 = V_L I_L [\cos(30-\phi) + \cos(30+\phi)] = \sqrt{3} V_L I_L \cos\phi$

$\therefore$ $\boxed{W_1 + W_2 = \text{Total power consumed by three phase load.}}$

It can be observed that whether load is star of delta, the expressions for W_1 and W_2 remain same.

For load having leading power factor, I_{ph} will lead V_{ph} by angle ϕ and hence W_1 reading and W_2 reading will get interchanged as $30 - \phi$ will become $30 + \phi$ and viceversa.

In case of leading power factor loads , readings of W_1 and W_2 are interchanged compared to lagging power factor load.

For **star or delta lagging p.f. load**, $W_1 = V_L I_L \cos(30-\phi)$ and $W_2 = V_L I_L \cos(30+\phi)$

For **star or delta leading p.f. load**, $W_1 = V_L I_L \cos(30+\phi)$ and $W_2 = V_L I_L \cos(30-\phi)$

For **star or delta unity p.f. load**, $\cos\phi = 1$ and $\phi = 0°$, $W_1 = W_2 = V_L I_L \cos 30°$

Example 4.10.1 *Two wattmeters are connected to measure the input of a 15 H.P., 50 Hz, 3-phase induction motor at full-load. The full-load efficiency and p.f. are 0.9 and 0.8 lagging respectively. Find the readings of the two wattmeters.*

Solution : P_{out} = 15 H.P., $\eta = 0.9$, $\cos\phi = 0.8$

Now   % η = $\dfrac{P_{out}}{P_{in}} \times 100$

∴ $0.9 = \dfrac{15 \times 735.5}{P_{in}}$ as 1 H.P. = 735.5 watts

∴ P_{in} = 12258.33 W

But $P_{in} = \sqrt{3} \, V_L I_L \cos\phi$

∴ $12258.33 = \sqrt{3} \, V_L I_L \times 0.8$

∴ $V_L I_L$ = 8846.9 and $\phi = \cos^{-1} 0.8 = 36.86°$

∴ $W_1 = V_L I_L \cos(30-\phi) = 8846.69 \cos(30-36.86) =$ **8783.1737 watts**

and $W_2 = V_L I_L \cos(30+\phi) = 8846.69 \cos(30+36.86) =$ **3476.569 watts**

Example 4.10.2 *3 ϕ, 220 V, 50 Hz, 11.2 kW induction motor has full load efficiency of 88 % and draws a line current of 38 amp. Under full load, when connected to 3 ϕ, 220 V supply find the reading on two wattmeter connected in the circuit to measure the input to the motor. Determine also p.f. at which motor is operating.*

Solution : I_L = 38 A,   % η = 88 %, P_{out} = 11.2 kW, V_L = 220 V

∴ $P_{in} = \dfrac{P_{out}}{\eta} = \dfrac{11.2 \times 10^3}{0.88} = 12727.2727$ W

     $V_L I_L$ = 220 × 38 = 8360

Now $P_{in} = \sqrt{3} \, V_L I_L \cos\phi$ i.e. $\cos\phi$ = 0.8789

∴ ϕ = 28.483°

∴ $W_1 = V_L I_L \cos(30-\phi) = 8360 \times \cos(30 - 28.483) =$ **8357.069 W**

∴ $W_2 = V_L I_L \cos(30+\phi) = 8360 \times \cos(30 + 28.483) =$ **4370.202 W**

     The power factor = $\cos\phi$ = **0.8789 lagging**.

Example 4.10.3 *Calculate the reading of each wattmeter in the circuit shown below. The load impedance* $Z_{ph} = 40 \angle -30°$ *Ω.*

`2004-05, Marks 10`

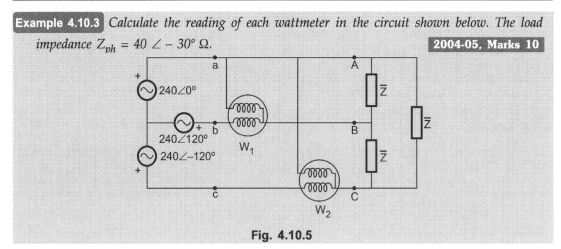

Fig. 4.10.5

Solution : For W_1, $V_{pc} = V_{BA}$, $I_{pc} = I_B$

For W_2, $V_{pc} = V_{CA}$, $I_{pc} = I_C$

The load is delta connected with $Z_{ph} = 40 \angle -30°$ Ω. Thus each phase current leads phase voltage by 30° as Z_{ph} is capacitive (ϕ is negative). The phasor diagram is shown in the Fig. 4.10.5 (a).

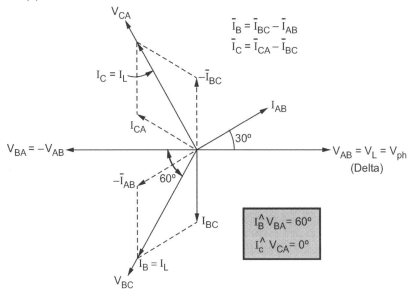

Fig. 4.10.5 (a)

$$|I_{ph}| = \frac{V_{ph}}{Z_{ph}} = \frac{240}{40} = 6 \text{ A}$$

$\therefore$ $I_L = \sqrt{3}\, I_{ph} = \sqrt{3} \times 6 = 10.3923$ A

$\therefore$ $I_L = I_B = I_C = 10.3923$ A   and $V_{BA} = V_{CA} = 240$ V

$$\therefore \quad W_1 = V_{pc} I_{pc} \cos (V_{pc} \wedge I_{pc}) = 240 \times 10.3923 \times \cos (60°) = \textbf{1247.076 W}$$

$$W_2 = V_{pc} I_{pc} \cos (V_{pc} \wedge I_{pc}) = 240 \times 10.3923 \times \cos (0°) = \textbf{2494.152 W}$$

Check : $\quad W_1 + W_2 = \sqrt{3} \ V_L \ I_L \cos \phi = \sqrt{3} \times 240 \times 10.3923 \times \cos (30°) = \textbf{3741.22 W}$

Example 4.10.4 *A star connected three phase load has a resistance of 8 ohms and an inductive reactance of 6 ohms in each phase. It is fed from a 400 V, three phase balanced supply. Determine line current, power factor, active and reactive powers. Draw phasor diagram showing phase and line voltages and currents. If power measurement is made using two wattmeter method, what will be readings of both wattmeters ?* **2004-05, Marks 10**

Solution : $\quad Z_{ph} = 8 + j6 \ \Omega = 10 \ \angle \ 36.86° \ \Omega$, Star, $V_L = 400$ V

$$V_{ph} = \frac{V_L}{\sqrt{3}} = \frac{400}{\sqrt{3}} = 230.9401 \text{ V} \qquad \qquad \qquad \text{...Star}$$

$$\therefore \quad I_{ph} = \frac{V_{ph} \angle 0°}{Z_{ph}} = \frac{230.9401 \angle 0°}{10 \angle 36.86°} = 23.094 \ \angle - 36.86° \text{ A}$$

$$\therefore \quad I_L = I_{ph} = \textbf{23.094 A}$$

Each I_{ph} lags the respective V_{ph} by 36.86°.

$$\therefore \quad \cos \phi = \cos (36.86°) = \textbf{0.8 lagging}$$

$$P = \sqrt{3} \ V_L \ I_L \cos \phi = \sqrt{3} \times 400 \times 23.094 \times 0.8 = \textbf{12800 W}$$

$$Q = \sqrt{3} \ V_L \ I_L \sin \phi = \sqrt{3} \times 400 \times 23.094 \times 0.6 = \textbf{9600 VAR}$$

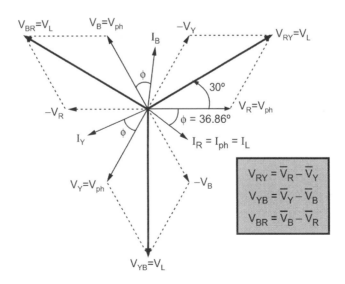

Fig. 4.10.6

$$W_1 = V_L I_L \cos(30 - \phi) = 400 \times 23.094 \times \cos(30 - 36.86°) = \textbf{9171.4677 W}$$

$$W_2 = V_L I_L \cos(30 + \phi) = 400 \times 23.094 \times \cos(30 + 36.86°) = \textbf{3630.1844 W}$$

Check : $W_1 + W_2 = P = $ Active power.

Review Questions

1. *Show that the two wattmeters are sufficient to measure the power in a three phase circuit.*

   2009-10, 2011-12, Marks 5

2. *2 wattmeters are connected to measure the input to a 3 φ, 20 H.P., 50 Hz induction motor which works at a full load efficiency of 90 % and a power factor of 0.85. Find the readings of the 2 wattmeters.*   **[Ans. : 11096.323 W, 5248.179 W]**

3. *Three similar choking coils each having resistance 10 Ω and reactance 10 Ω are connected in star across a 440 V, 3 phase supply. Find line current and reading of each of two wattmeters connected to measure power.*   **[Ans. : 17.9605, 7.6333 kW, 2.0453 kW, 9.6787 kW]**

4.11 Power Factor Calculation by Two Wattmeter Method

2000-01, 2001-02, 2009-10

In case of balanced load, the p.f. can be calculated from W_1 and W_2 readings.

For balanced, lagging p.f. load, $W_1 = V_L I_L \cos(30 - \phi)$ and $W_2 = V_L I_L \cos(30 + \phi)$

$$W_1 + W_2 = \sqrt{3} V_L I_L \cos\phi \qquad \qquad \dots(4.11.1)$$

$$
\begin{aligned}
W_1 - W_2 &= V_L I_L [\cos(30 - \phi) - \cos(30 + \phi)] \\
&= V_L I_L [\cos 30 \cos\phi + \sin 30 \sin\phi - \cos 30 \cos\phi + \sin 30 \sin\phi] \\
&= V_L I_L [2 \sin 30 \sin\phi] = V_L I_L \left[2 \times \frac{1}{2} \times \sin\phi \right]
\end{aligned}
$$

$\therefore$ $W_1 - W_2 = V_L I_L \sin(\phi)$ $\dots(4.11.2)$

Taking ratio of equations (4.11.1) and (4.11.2),

$$\frac{W_1 - W_2}{W_1 + W_2} = \frac{V_L I_L \sin\phi}{\sqrt{3} V_L I_L \cos\phi} = \frac{\tan\phi}{\sqrt{3}} \qquad \text{i.e.} \quad \tan\phi = \frac{\sqrt{3}(W_1 - W_2)}{(W_1 + W_2)}$$

$\therefore$ $\phi = \tan^{-1}\left[\dfrac{\sqrt{3}(W_1 - W_2)}{(W_1 + W_2)} \right]$

$\therefore$ $\boxed{\text{p.f. } \cos\phi = \cos\left\{ \tan^{-1}\left[\dfrac{\sqrt{3}(W_1 - W_2)}{(W_1 + W_2)} \right] \right\}}$

For **leading p.f.** we get **tan φ negative**. But cosine of negative angle is positive.

> **The power factor cos ϕ is always positive but its nature must be determined by observing sign of tan ϕ.**

Example 4.11.1 *For a certain load, one of the wattmeter read 20 kW and the other 5 kW after the voltage circuit of this wattmeter has been reversed. Calculate the power and the power factor of the load.*   **2001-02, Marks 5**

Solution : $W_1 = 20$ kW, $W_2 = -5$ kW, Negative as terminals reversed.

$\therefore$ $\qquad P_T = W_1 + W_2 = 20 - 5 = \textbf{15 kW}$ ...Power

$$\cos \phi = \cos \left\{ \tan^{-1} \left[\frac{\sqrt{3}(W_1 - W_2)}{(W_1 + W_2)} \right] \right\} = \cos \left\{ \tan^{-1} \left[\frac{\sqrt{3}(25)}{(15)} \right] \right\}$$

$\qquad\qquad = \cos (70.8933°) = \textbf{0.3273}$ ...Power factor

Example 4.11.2 *A 3-phase balanced load connected across a 3-phase, 400 V a.c. supply draws a line current of 10 A. Two wattmeters are used to measure input power. The ratio of two wattmeter reading is 2 : 1. Find reading of two wattmeters.*   **2000-01, Marks 5**

Solution : $I_L = 10$ A, $V_L = 400$ V, $W_1 = 2 W_2$

$$\cos \phi = \cos \left\{ \tan^{-1} \left[\frac{\sqrt{3}(W_1 - W_2)}{(W_1 + W_2)} \right] \right\} = \cos \left\{ \tan^{-1} \left[\frac{\sqrt{3}(2W_2 - W_2)}{(2W_2 + W_2)} \right] \right\}$$

$$= \cos \left\{ \tan^{-1} \frac{1}{\sqrt{3}} \right\} = \cos (30°) = 0.866$$

$\therefore \qquad\qquad \phi = 30°$

$\therefore \qquad\quad W_1 = V_L I_L \cos (30 - \phi) = 400 \cos (0°) = \textbf{4000 W}$

$\therefore \qquad\quad W_2 = V_L I_L \cos (30 + \phi) = 400 \cos (60°) = \textbf{2000 W}$

Example 4.11.3 *A balanced star connected inducive load is connected to a 400 V, 50 Hz a.c. supply. Two wattmeters used to measure supply power indicate 8000 W and 4000 W respectively. Determine i) Line current ii) Impedance of each phase iii) Resistance and inductance of each phase.*   **2009-10, Marks 5**

Solution : $V_L = 400$ V,   f = 50 Hz, star, $W_1 = 8000$ W, $W_2 = 4000$ W

$$W = W_1 + W_2 = 12000 \text{ W} = \sqrt{3} V_L I_L \cos\phi$$

$$\cos \phi = \cos \left\{ \tan^{-1} \left[\frac{\sqrt{3}(W_1 - W_2)}{(W_1 + W_2)} \right] \right\} = \cos \left\{ \tan^{-1} \left[\frac{\sqrt{3} \times 4000}{12000} \right] \right\} = 0.86602 \text{ lag}$$

i) Line current :

$$12000 = \sqrt{3} \times 400 \times I_L \times 0.86602 \quad \text{i.e.} \quad I_L = \textbf{20 A}$$

ii) Impedance of each phase :

For star, $\quad V_{ph} = \dfrac{V_L}{\sqrt{3}} = \dfrac{400}{\sqrt{3}} = 230.9401 \text{ V},$

$$I_{ph} = I_L = 20 \text{ A}$$

$$\therefore \quad \left| Z_{ph} \right| = \dfrac{V_{ph}}{I_{ph}} = \dfrac{230.9401}{20} = 11.547 \ \Omega, \quad \phi = \cos^{-1} 0.86602 = 30°$$

$$\therefore \quad Z_{ph} = \textbf{11.547} \angle 30°\,\Omega = 10 + j5.7735 \ \Omega.$$

iii) Resistance and inductance of each phase :

$$Z_{ph} = R_{ph} + j\, X_{Lph} = 10 + j\, 5.7735$$

$$\therefore \quad R_{ph} = 10 \ \Omega, \quad X_{Lph} = 5.7735 = 2\pi f\, L_{ph} \quad \text{i.e.} \quad L_{ph} = \dfrac{5.7735}{2\pi \times 50} = \textbf{0.01837 H}$$

Review Questions

> 1. *How power factor can be obtained from two wattmeter readings ?*
>
> 2. *A balanced three phase star connected load draws power from 440 V supply. The two wattmeters connected indicate* $W_1 = 5$ *kW and* $W_2 = 1.2$ *kW. Calculate power, power factor and current in the circuit.*   **(Ans. : 6.2 kW, 0.68561 lag, 11.866 A)**

4.12 Effect of P.F. on Wattmeter Readings   `2009-10`

For a lagging p.f. $\quad W_1 = V_L I_L \cos(30 - \phi) \quad$ and $\quad W_2 = V_L I_L \cos(30 + \phi)$

Consider different cases,

Case i) $\quad \cos\phi = 0 \quad \phi = 90°$

$$\therefore \ W_1 = V_L I_L \cos(30 - 90) = +\frac{1}{2} V_L I_L \quad \text{and} \quad W_2 = V_L I_L \cos(30 + 90) = -\frac{1}{2} V_L I_L$$

i.e. $\quad W_1 + W_2 = 0$

$$\left| W_1 \right| = \left| W_2 \right| \qquad \text{but} \quad W_2 = -W_1$$

> **Note** *Wattmeter can not show negative reading as it has only positive scale. Indication of negative reading is that pointer tries to deflect in negative direction i.e. to the left of zero. In such case, reading can be converted to positive by interchanging either pressure coil connections i.e. (C ↔ V) or by interchanging current coil connections (M ↔ L). This is shown in the Fig. 4.12.1.*

Remember that interchanging connections of both the coils will have no effect on the wattmeter reading.

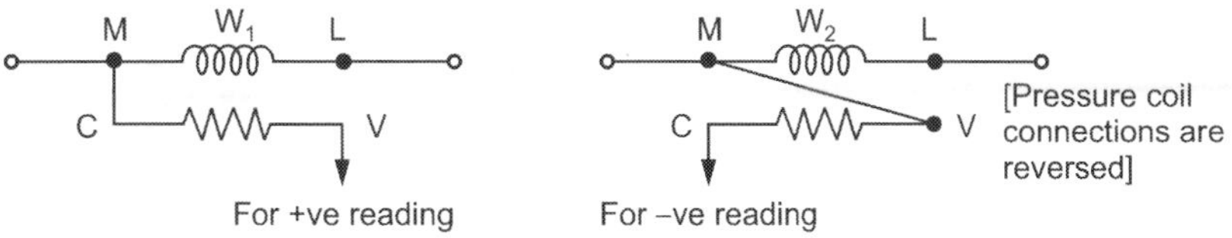

Fig. 4.12.1 Negative reading on wattmeter

> Such a reading obtained by interchanging connections of either of the two coils will be positive on wattmeter but must be taken as negative for calculations.

Case ii) $\cos \phi = 0.5$, $\phi = 60°$

$\therefore$ $W_1 = V_L I_L \cos(30-60) = V_L I_L \cos 30$ and $W_2 = V_L I_L \cos(30+60) = 0$

$\therefore$ $$W_1 + W_2 = W_1 = \text{Total power.}$$

One wattmeter shows zero reading for $\cos \phi = 0.5$.

For all power factors between 0 to 0.5 W_2 shows negative and W_1 shows positive, **for lagging p.f.**

Case iii) $\cos \phi = 1$, $\phi = 0°$

$\therefore$ $W_1 = V_L I_L \cos(30+0) = V_L I_L \cos 30$ and $W_2 = V_L I_L \cos(30-0) = V_L I_L \cos 30$

Both W_1 and W_2 are equal and positive.

For all power factors between 0.5 to 1 both wattmeter gives +ve reading.

In short, the result can be summarised as,

Range of p.f.	Range of 'ϕ'	W_1 sign	W_2 sign	Remark
$\cos \phi = 0$	$\phi = 90°$	positive	negative	$|W_1| = |W_2|$
$0 \angle \cos \phi \angle 0.5$	$90° \angle \phi \angle 60°$	positive	negative	
$\cos \phi = 0.5$	$\phi = 60°$	positive	0	
$0.5 \angle \cos \phi \angle 1$	$60° \angle \phi \angle 0°$	positive	positive	
$\cos \phi = 1$	$\phi = 0°$	positive	positive	$W_1 = W_2$

Table 4.12.1

The Table 4.12.1 is applicable for lagging power factors but same table is applicable for leading power factors by interchanging columns of W_1 and W_2.

Example 4.12.1 *Estimate the power factor in each of the following cases of two wattmeter method of measuring three phase power;*

i) *Wattmeter readings are equal*

ii) *Wattmeter readings are equal and opposite*

iii) *Wattmeter readings are in the ratio 1:2.*

iv) *One wattmeter reads zero.*

Solution : If is known that the p.f. from 2 wattmeter method is,

$$\cos\phi \ = \ \cos\left\{\tan^{-1}\left[\frac{\sqrt{3}(W_1 - W_2)}{(W_1 + W_2)}\right]\right\}$$

Case 1 : $W_1 \ = \ W_2$

∴ $\cos\phi \ = \ \cos\left\{\tan^{-1}(0)\right\} = \ \cos\{90^\circ\} = \mathbf{1}$ ... $W_1 - W_2 = 0$

Case 2 : $W_1 \ = \ -W_2$

∴ $\cos\phi \ = \ \cos\left\{\tan^{1}(\infty)\right\} = \cos\{90^\circ\} = \mathbf{0}$ ... $W_1 + W_2 = 0$

Case 3 : $W_2 \ = \ 2W_1$

∴ $\cos\phi \ = \ \cos\left\{\tan^{-1}\left[\frac{\sqrt{3}(W_1 - 2W_1)}{3W_1}\right]\right\} = \ \cos\left\{\tan^{-1}\left(-\frac{1}{\sqrt{3}}\right)\right\}$

$$= \ \cos\{(-30^\circ)\} = \mathbf{0.866}$$

Case 4 : $W_2 \ = \ 0$

∴ $\cos\phi \ = \ \cos\left\{\tan^{-1}\left[\frac{\sqrt{3}W_1}{W_1}\right]\right\} = \cos(60^\circ) = \mathbf{0.5}$

Example 4.12.2 *Two wattmeters connected to measure the input to balanced three-phase circuit indicates 2500 and 500 W, respectively. Find the total power supplied, and the power factor of the circuit*

i) When both readings are positive and

ii) When the latter reading is obtained after reversing the connections to the current coil.

Solution : $W_1 = 2500$ W, $W_2 = 500$ W

Case 1 : Both positive

∴ $\cos\phi \ = \ \cos\left\{\tan^{-1}\left[\frac{\sqrt{3}(W_1 - W_2)}{(W_1 + W_2)}\right]\right\} = \mathbf{0.6546}$

$$P_T \ = \ W_1 + W_2 = \mathbf{3000 \ W}$$

Case 2 : W_2 is negative i.e. $W_2 = -500$ W

$$\therefore \qquad \cos \phi = \cos \left\{ \tan^{-1} \left[\frac{\sqrt{3}\,(2500-(-500))}{(2500-500)} \right] \right\} = \mathbf{0.3592}$$

$$P_T = W_1 + W_2 = 2500 - 500 = \mathbf{2000\ W}$$

Review Questions

1. Discuss the effect of variation of power factor on wattmeter readings.

2. The power flowing in a 3ϕ, 3-wire balanced load system is measured by two wattmeter method. The reading in wattmeter A is 750 watts and wattmeter B is 1500 watts. What is the power factor of the system and load current per phase ?   **[Ans. : 0.866 leading]**

3. Three similar impedances are connected in delta across a 3ϕ supply. The two wattmeters connected to measure the input power indicate 12 kW and 7 kW. Calculate : i) Power input   ii) Power factor of the load.   **[Ans. : 0.9099, 19 kW]**

4. Power is measured in a 3 phase balanced load using two wattmeters. The line voltage is 400 V. The load and its p.f. is so adjusted that the line current is always 10 A. Find the reading of the wattmeters when the p.f. is

   i) unity ii) 0.866 iii) 0.5 and iv) zero.
   [Ans. : 3464.1 W, 4000 W, 2000 W, 3464.1 W, 0 W, 2000 W, – 2000 W]

5. Explain the significance of i) equal wattmeter readings   ii) zero reading on one wattmeter, in two wattmeter method.   **2009-10, Marks 5**

4.13 Reactive Volt-Amperes by Two Wattmeter Method

We have seen that, $W_1 - W_2 = V_L\, I_L \sin \phi$

The total reactive volt-amperes for a 3 phase circuit is given by,

$$Q = \sqrt{3}\,V_L\, I_L\ \sin \phi\ = \sqrt{3}\,(W_1 - W_2) \quad \text{VAR}$$

Thus reactive volt-amperes of a 3 phase circuit can be obtained by multiplying the difference of two wattmeter readings by $\sqrt{3}$.

$$\boxed{Q = \text{Reactive power} = \sqrt{3}\,V_L\, I_L \sin \phi = \sqrt{3}\,(W_1 - W_2)} \quad \text{VAR or kVAR}$$

Review Question

How to find reactive volt-amperes by two wattmeter method ?

4.14 Advantages of Two Wattmeter Method

1.   The method is applicable for balanced as well as unbalanced loads.

2.   Neutral point for star connected load is not necessary to connect the wattmeters.

3.   The delta connected load, need not be opened for connecting the wattmeters.

4.   Only two wattmeters are sufficient to measure total 3 phase power.

5.   If the load is balanced not only the power but power factor also can be determined.

6.   Total reactive volt amperes can be obtained using two wattmeter readings for balanced loads.

Review Question

1. State the various advantages of two wattmeter method.

4.15 Disadvantages of Two Wattmeter Method

1.   Not applicable for three phase, 4 wire syste.

2.   The signs of W_1 and W_2 must be identified and noted down correctly otherwise it may lead to the wrong results.

Review Question

1. State the disadvantages of two wattmeter method.

4.16 Concept of Power Factor Improvement   2009-10, 2012-13

The electrical energy is exclusively generated and transmitted in the form of alternating current. And hence the question of power factor immediately arises. The low power factor is undesirable and for better engineering and economical conditions of supply system, it is necessary to have power factor as close as unity.

4.16.1 Power Factor

In a.c. circuits the cosine of angle between voltage and current is called **power factor**.

So power consumption in a.c. circuits is the product of voltage and the component of the current which is in phase with the voltage. So if current is lagging with respect to voltage by angle ϕ then active power consumption gets decided by the component Icos ϕ , which is in phase with the voltage, as shown in the Fig. 4.16.1.

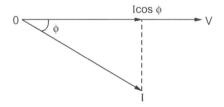

Fig. 4.16.1

So for single phase circuits, the active power is given by, $P = VI \cos \phi$ W.

While for three phase circuits, the active power is given by, $P = \sqrt{3}\, V_L \, I_L \cos \phi$ W.

In the three phase circuits, ϕ is the angle between phase voltage and the phase current. The power triangle for three phase circuit which is as shown in the Fig. 4.16.2.

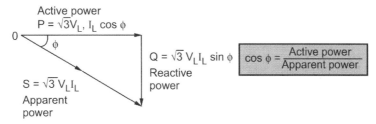

Fig. 4.16.2

So power factor can be defined as the ratio of active power to apparent power. If the lagging reactive power component is shown downwards then the leading reactive power component is shown upwards.

Key Point *So lagging reactive power tries to lower the power factor while the leading reactive power increases the power factor.*

Hence leading power factor loads is the key of power factor improvement.

Causes of low power factor : The main cause of low power factor is inductive loads. The inductive loads are the sources of large lagging reactive power. Such loads include,

    i) Transformers   ii) Induction motors (3 phase and single phase)   iii) Induction generators   iv) Domestic appliances and lighting load   v) High intensity discharge lighting.

All these loads constitute a major portion of the power consumption while leading power factor loads are very less in number. Hence the overall power factor is very low.

4.16.2 Disadvantages of Low Power Factor

We have seen that the single phase power is given by,

$$P = VI \cos \phi \quad \text{i.e.} \quad I = \frac{P}{V \cos \phi}$$

Now supply voltage is generally constant and hence for supplying fixed power to the load, the current is inversely proportional to the power factor $\cos \phi$.

So as power factor decreases, current drawn from the supply increases to supply the same load power. As against this if power factor is improved, the current drawn from the supply decreases.

Key Point *In general, lower is the power factor, higher is the load current and vice versa.*

Such higher current results into the following **disadvantages** :

i) The conductor size depends on the current. For higher current greater conductor size is required. This increases the cost.

ii)
$$\cos \phi = \frac{\text{Active Power}}{\text{Apparent Power}} = \frac{\text{kW}}{\text{kVA}}$$

Now kVA is nothing but the rating of various machines like alternators and transformers. For low power factor values, to supply fixed active power, large kVA rating alternators and transformers are required. This makes the equipments larger in size. This overall increases the cost of the system.

iii) Large current causes more copper losses (I^2R). This results into poor efficiency.

iv) Large current causes large voltage drop (IZ) in transmission lines, alternators and transformers. This reduces the voltage available at the supply end. This results into poor regulation of the various devices. To compensate such voltage drop, extra equipment is necessary, which further increases the cost.

Key Point *Thus for a given power, lower is the power factor, the greater is the cost of generation, transmission and distribution.*

Therefore supply authorities encourage the consumers to increase their power factor.

4.16.3 Power Factor Improvement

The low factor is mainly because of a.c. motors which are of induction type having low lagging power factor. Similarly lighting load, arc lamps, electric discharge lamps, industrial induction furnaces etc. also contribute to low power factor operation. To improve the power factor, it is necessary to connect some device which takes leading power to neutralize lagging effect. One of such devices is a capacitor which draws a leading current. Let us see the action of capacitor in a power factor improvement.

Consider a lagging power factor load as shown in the Fig. 4.16.3. The corresponding phasor diagram is shown in the Fig. 4.16.3 (b).

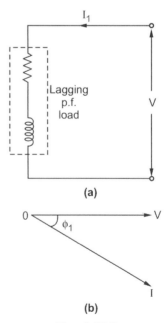

Fig. 4.16.3

Let I_1 be the current drawn at a lagging power factor angle of ϕ_1.

Now to improve the power factor, a capacitor is connected across the load as shown in the Fig. 4.16.4.

Now the capacitor takes a leading current I_2, which leads voltage V by an angle of 90° as shown in the Fig. 4.16.5 (a). Now this leading component of current I_2 tries to neutralize the lagging effect of I_1. Hence the resultant current becomes as shown in the Fig. 4.16.5 (b).

Now from the Fig. 4.16.5 (b), it can be seen that the effective power factor angle becomes ϕ which is less than ϕ_1. Hence cos ϕ is more than cos ϕ_1, thus there is improvement in the power factor of the system. Thus by connecting

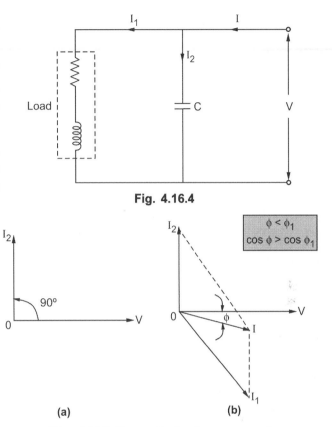

Fig. 4.16.4

Fig. 4.16.5 Power factor improvement

a leading power factor device, across the supply power factor can be improved which is advantageous from the supplier as well as consumer point of view.

4.16.4 Power Factor Improvement Devices

In practise, for power factor improvement special steps are taken by using special devices.

The devices generally used to improve the power factor are,

1. Bank of static capacitors, 2. Synchronous condensers, 3. Phase advancers

Example 4.16.1 *Three coils having resistance of 20 Ω and inductive reactance of 15 Ω are connected in Star to a 400 V, 50 Hz, 3 phase supply. Calculate the line current, the active power and power factor. If 3 capacitors each of same value are connected in Delta to the same supply so as to form a parallel circuit with above coils. Calculate i) The capacitance to obtain the resultant power factor of 0.95 lagging. ii) The line current taken by combined load.*

Solution : Given : 3 coils, $R = 20\ \Omega$, $X_L = 15\ \Omega$, Star connection, $V_L = 400$ V.

3 capacitors in delta connected to improve p.f. to 0.95 lag.

To find : I_L, active power and power factor of coils and value of capacitance in each phase, combined line current.

Load 1 : $Z_{ph} = 20 + j15 = 25\ \angle\ 36.86°$

star so $V_{ph} = \dfrac{V_L}{\sqrt{3}} = \dfrac{400}{\sqrt{3}} = 230.9401$ V

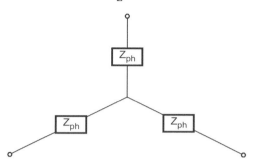

Fig. 4.16.6 (a)

$\therefore$ $\overline{I}_{ph} = \dfrac{\overline{V}_{ph}}{\overline{Z}_{ph}} = \dfrac{230.9401\angle 0°}{25\angle 36.86°}$

$\therefore$ $I_{ph} = 9.2376$ A at $(- 36.86)°$

Negative sign indicates power factor is lagging.

$\therefore$ $I_{ph} = I_L =$ **9.2376 A** and

Power factor $= \cos(- 36.86°) =$ **0.8 lagging**

Active power $= \sqrt{3}\ V_L\ I_L\ \sin\phi = \sqrt{3}\times 440\times 9.2376\times 0.8 =$ **5.1199 kW**

Reactive power $= \sqrt{3}\ V_L\ I_L\ \cos\phi =$ **3.8399 kVAR**

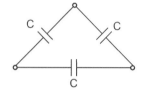

Now, Delta capacitances are connected.

Now $Z_{ph} = X_{Cph}$ as $R_{ph} = 0$ for capacitors

$\therefore$ Active power consumption $= 0$ W by capacitors $(\cos \phi = 0)$.

Total active power = Active power by coils

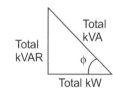

Fig. 4.16.6 (c)

$\therefore$ $P_T = 5.1199$ kW

Now new $\cos \phi = 0.95$ lag   i.e. $\phi = 18.1948$ $\therefore$ $\tan \phi = 0.3286$

$\tan \phi = \dfrac{kVAR}{kW}$

$\therefore$ Total kVAR $= (kW)_{total} \times \tan \phi$

$= 5.1199 \times 0.3286 = 1.682$ kVAR

$\therefore$ kVAR drawn by capacitor $= 1.682$ kVAR $- 3.83399$ kVAR $= -$ **2.1570 kVAR (leading)**

The negative sign indicates that capacitor kVAR are leading in nature.

Now for capacitor bank as delta connected,

$$V_L = V_{ph} = 400 \text{ V}, \qquad \sin\phi = 1, \qquad \cos\phi = 0$$

∴   kVAR of capacitors $= \sqrt{3}\, V_L\, I_L \sin\phi$ ... $\sin\phi = 1$

∴ $2.1570 \times 10^3 = \sqrt{3}\times 400\times I_L$ i.e. $I_L = \textbf{3.1134 A}$ ... For capacitors

∴ $I_{ph} = \dfrac{I_L}{\sqrt{3}} = 1.7975 \text{ A}$ ... Delta connected

∴ $X_{Cph} = \dfrac{V_{ph}}{I_{ph}} = \dfrac{400}{1.7975} = 222.524 \ \Omega$

∴ $C = \dfrac{1}{2\pi f \times X_C} = \textbf{14.3045 } \boldsymbol{\mu}\textbf{F}$

        Total kW $= 5.1199 \text{ kW} = \sqrt{3}\, V_L\, I_L \cos\phi$ where $\cos\phi = 0.95$

∴ $5.1199 \times 10^3 = \sqrt{3}\times 400\times I_L \times 0.95$

∴   Combined line current $= \textbf{7.7788 A}$ ... Total line current

Review Questions

1. *What is power factor ? What is its significance ? How will you obtain power factor from kVA triangle ?* **2009-10, Marks 5**

2. *What are the causes and problems of low power factor ? How power factor can be improved ?* **2012-13, Marks 5**

4.17 Short Answered and Objective Type Questions

Q.1   In two wattmeter method, if the reading are equal with opposite sign then the power factor of the load is _____ .   **2010-11**

(Ans. : zero)

Q.2   If W1, W2 and W3 are the readings of three wattmeters used to measure the power in 3-phase, 4-wire circuit, the total power of load circuit will be _____ .   **2008-09**

(Ans. : $W_1 + W_2 + W_3$)

Q.3   State any 4 advantages of three phase system.

Ans. :

1)   The output of three phase machine is always greater than single phase machine of same size, approximately 1.5 times.

2) For a transmission and distribution, three phase system needs less copper or less conducting material than single phase system for given volt amperes and voltage rating so transmission becomes very much economical.

3) It is possible to produce rotating magnetic field with stationary coils by using three phase system. Hence three phase motors are self starting.

4) In single phase system, the instantaneous power is a function of time and hence fluctuates w.r.t. time. This fluctuating power causes considerable vibrations in single phase motors. Hence performance of single phase motors is poor. While instantaneous power in symmetrical three phase system is constant.

5) Single phase supply can be obtained from three phase but three phase cannot be obtained from single phase.

6) Power factor of single phase motors is poor than three phase motors of same rating.

Q.4   Give the equations for the induced e.m.f.s in three phase voltage generation.

Ans. :   In three phase generation, the three voltages are displaced from each other by $120°$ and their equations can be expressed as,

$$e_R = E_m \sin(\omega t)$$

$$e_Y = E_m \sin(\omega t - 120°)$$

$$e_B = E_m \sin(\omega t - 240°) = E_m \sin(\omega t + 120°)$$

Q.5   Define symmetrical system and phase sequence for three phase supply system.

Ans. : 1) Symmetrical system :   A three phase system in which the three voltages are of same magnitude and frequency and displaced from each other by $120°$ phase angle is defined as **symmetrical system**.

2) Phase sequence : The sequence in which the voltages in three phases reach their maximum positive values is called **phase sequence**. Generally the phase sequence is R-Y-B.

Q.6   Which are the two possible three phase connections ? Show them with neat diagrams.

Ans. : The two possible three phase connections are star connection and delta connection.

These are shown in the Fig. 4.17.1 and 4.17.2.

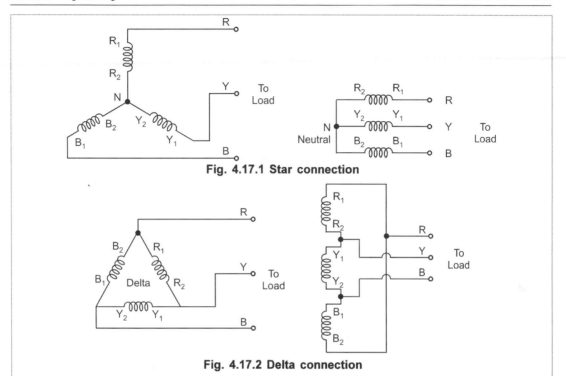

Fig. 4.17.1 Star connection

Fig. 4.17.2 Delta connection

Q.7 What is line voltage and line current ? Show them for star and delta connected systems.

Ans. : The potential difference between any two lines of supply is called **line voltage** and current passing through any line is called **line current**.

The Fig. 4.17.3 shows the lone voltages and line currents for the star connected system.

Line voltages are denoted by V_L. These are V_{RY}, V_{YB} and V_{BR}.

Line currents are denoted by I_L. These are I_R, I_Y and I_B.

Similarly for delta connected system we can show the line voltages and line currents as in the Fig. 4.17.4.

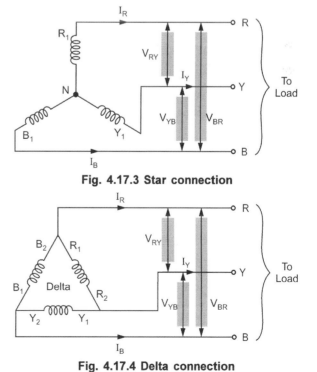

Fig. 4.17.3 Star connection

Fig. 4.17.4 Delta connection

Line voltages V_L are V_{RY}, V_{BR}, V_{YB}.

While line currents I_L are I_R, I_Y and I_B.

Q.8   State the relations for star and delta connected loads. Also state the expression for the power consumption.

Ans. :   For star connected load,

$\therefore$ $V_L = \sqrt{3}\ V_{ph}$ for star connection and $I_L = I_{ph}$

Thus line voltage is $\sqrt{3}$ times the phase voltage in star connection.

For delta connected load,

$$I_L = \sqrt{3}\ I_{ph} \quad \text{and} \quad V_{ph} = V_L \qquad \textbf{... for delta connection}$$

Thus line current is $\sqrt{3}$ times the phase current in delta connection. While the expression for the power consumption for both the type of loads remains same and given as,

$$P = \sqrt{3}\,V_L I_L \cos\phi$$

Q.9   Describe the meaning of three phase balanced load ?

Ans. :   The load is said to be balanced when **magnitudes** of all the impedances Z_{ph1}, Z_{ph2} and Z_{ph3} are **equal** and the **phase angles** of all of them are **equal** and of **same nature** either all inductive or all capacitive or all resistive.

> In such case all phase voltages have equal magnitudes and are displaced from each other by 120° while all phase currents also have equal magnitudes and are displaced from each other by 120° . The same is true for all the line voltages and line currents.

Q.10   State the expressions for the various powers in three phase circuit and draw the power triangle.

Ans. :   Total apparent power,

$S = \sqrt{3}\,V_L I_L$ volt-amperes (VA) or kVA

Total active power,

   $P = \sqrt{3}\,V_L I_L \cos\phi$ watts (W) or kW

Total reactive power,

   $Q = \sqrt{3}\,V_L I_L \sin\phi$ VAR or kVAR

Hence power triangle is as shown in the Fig. 4.17.5.

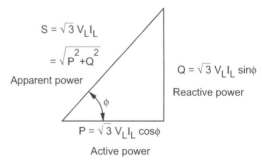

Fig. 4.17.5 Power triangle

Q.11 Which of the following formulae is used to express active power in a balanced three-phase circuit ? **2009-10**

a) $V_L I_L \cos\phi$ b) $\sqrt{3}V_L I_L \cos\phi$ c) $V_{ph} I_{ph} \cos\phi$ d) $\sqrt{3}V_{ph} I_{ph} \cos\phi$

(Ans. : b)

Q.12 The power measurement in balanced 3-phase circuit can be done by : _____ . **2009-10**

a) One wattmeter method only   b) Two wattmeters method by

b) Three wattmeter method only   d) Any one of the above   **(Ans. : d)**

Q.13 In a three phase balanced system, the voltages are displaced by an angle of ...... from each other.

a) 90°   b) 180°   c) 120°   d) 360°   **(Ans. : c)**

Q.14 The output of three phase machine is _____ the output of single phase machine of same size.

a) greater than   b) less than   c) same as   d) none of these

(Ans. : a)

Q.15 _____ cannot be produced using single phase supply.

a) Alternating magnetic field   b) Rotating magnetic field

c) Alternating flux   d) None of these   **(Ans. : b)**

Q.16 In a 6 phase supply system, the voltages are separated from each other by _____.

a) 120°   b) 90°   c) 180°   d) 60°   **(Ans. : d)**

Q.17 For the same rating, the size of a three phase machine is _____ that of single phase machine.

a) less than   b) more than   c) same as   d) none of these

(Ans. : a)

Q.18 For transmission of voltage, three phase system requires _____ copper than the single phase system.

a) less   b) more   c) same   d) none of these

(Ans. : a)

Q.19 For star connection, the line current is _____ that of phase current.

a) greater than   b) less than   c) same as   d) none of these

(Ans. : c)

Q.20 For star connection, the phase voltage is _____ times the line voltage.

a) $\sqrt{3}$ b) $\dfrac{1}{\sqrt{3}}$ c) $\sqrt{2}$ d) $\dfrac{1}{\sqrt{2}}$

(Ans. : b)

Q.21 The power factor angle is the angle between _____.

a) line voltage and phase current.

b) line voltage and line current.

c) phase voltage and line current.

d) phase voltage and phase current.

(Ans. : d)

Q.22 The line voltage V_{RY} is given by _____ in a star connected system.

a) $\overline{V}_R + \overline{V}_Y$ b) $\overline{V}_R - \overline{V}_Y$ c) $\dfrac{\overline{V}_R}{\overline{V}_Y}$ d) $\overline{V}_R \times \overline{V}_Y$

(Ans. : b)

Q.23 In star connection, the line voltage leads phase voltage by _____.

a) 120°   b) 180°   c) 60°   d) 30°   **(Ans. : d)**

Q.24 In delta connection, the relation between line current and phase current is _____.

a) $I_L = \dfrac{1}{\sqrt{3}} I_{ph}$ b) $I_L = \sqrt{3}\, I_{ph}$ c) $I_L = I_{ph}$ d) None of these

(Ans. : b)

Q.25 In delta connection, the relation between line voltage and phase voltage is _____.

a) $V_L = V_{ph}$ b) $V_L = \sqrt{3}\, V_{ph}$ c) $V_L = \dfrac{1}{\sqrt{3}} V_{ph}$ d) None of these

(Ans. : a)

Q.26 In delta connection shown in the Fig. 4.17.6 the line current I_R is given by _____.

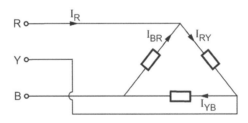

Fig. 4.17.6

a) $\overline{I}_{RY} - \overline{I}_{BR}$ b) $\overline{I}_{BR} - \overline{I}_{RY}$ c) $\overline{I}_{RY} + \overline{I}_{BR}$ d) none of these

(Ans. : a)

Q.27 The total apparent power in a three phase system is given by _____.

a) $V_L I_L$ b) $V_{ph} I_{ph}$ c) $\sqrt{3}\, V_L I_L$ d) $\sqrt{3}\, V_{ph} I_{ph}$

(Ans. : c)

Q.28 The total reactive volt-amperes in a three phase system are given by _____.

a) $\sqrt{3}\, V_L I_L$ b) $\sqrt{3}\, V_L I_L \cos\phi$ c) $V_L I_L$ d) $\sqrt{3}\, V_L I_L \sin\phi$

(Ans. : d)

Q.29 The wattmeter senses the angle between _____.

a) the phase voltage and phase current.
b) the line voltage and line current.
c) the current in current coil and voltage across pressure coil.
d) none of the above. **(Ans. : c)**

Q.30 For a wattmeter shown in the Fig. 4.17.7 its reading is _____.

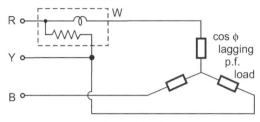

Fig. 4.17.7

a) $V_L I_L \sin \phi$ b) $V_L I_L \cos(30 + \phi)$
c) $V_L I_L \cos \phi$ d) $V_L I_L \cos(30 - \phi)$ **(Ans. : b)**

Q.31 For a wattmeter shown in the Fig. 4.17.8 its reading is _____.

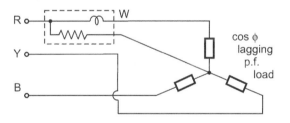

Fig. 4.17.8

a) $V_L I_L \cos \phi$ b) $V_L I_L \sin \phi$ c) $V_{ph} I_{ph} \cos \phi$ d) $V_{ph} I_{ph} \sin \phi$
     (Ans. : c)

Q.32 The algebraic addition of all the phase voltages at any instant in a three phase balanced system is always _____.

a) zero   b) one   c) infinite   d) none of these
     (Ans. : a)

Q.33 In a two wattmeter method, $W_1 = 4000$ W and $W_2 = 1000$ W, then the power factor of the circuit is _____.

a) 0.72   b) 0.69   c) 0.55   d) 0.51   **(Ans. : b)**

Q.34 If one of the two wattmeter reading is negative then the range of power factor is ____.

a) 0.5 to 1   b) 0.8 to 1   c) 0.5 to 0.75   d) 0 to 0.5 **(Ans. : d)**

Q.35 If the two wattmeters show equal reading, the power factor of the circuit is
_____.

a) zero   b) 0.5   c) unity   d) 0.866   **(Ans. : c)**

Q.36 The total reactive volt-amperes by two wattmeter readings is given by _____.

a) $W_1 - W_2$ b) $\sqrt{3} (W_1 - W_2)$ c) $W_1 + W_2$ d) $\sqrt{3} (W_1 + W_2)$

(Ans. : b)

Q.37 The cos ϕ can be expressed as _____.

a) $\dfrac{\text{Active power}}{\text{Apparent power}}$ b) $\dfrac{\text{Active power}}{\text{Reactive power}}$ c) $\dfrac{\text{Reactive power}}{\text{Apparent power}}$ d) None of these

(Ans. : a)

Q.38 The device used for the power factor improvement is _____.

a) Induction motor b) Alternator   c) Sychronous condenser d) Fan **(Ans. : c)**

Q.39 Which of the following apply to power in a purely reactive circuit ?

a) P = 0, Q = 0   b) P is maximum and Q = 0
b) P = 0 and Q is maximum   d) P and Q both are maximum   **(Ans. : c)**

Q.40 The direction of rotation of the three phase machines depends on _____.

a) line voltages   b) phase sequence
c) phase currents   d) phase voltages   **(Ans. : b)**

Q.41 In a star connected circuit, the load impedance per phase is 10 + j0 Ω while the
line voltage is 440 V then the two wattmeter readings are _____.

a) 9680 W, 2000 W   b) 10000 W, 1800 W
c) 9680 W, 3200 W   d) 16766.25 W, 16766.25 W   **(Ans. : d)**

Q.42 In a star connected system $V_R = 220 \angle 30°$ V and $V_Y = 220 \angle -90°$ V then the
line voltage $V_{RY} = $ _____V.

a) $381.05 + \angle 60°$ b) $381.051 + \angle -60°$ c) $381.051 \angle 90°$ d) $381.051 \angle 120°$

(Ans. : a)

❑❑❑

5 Measuring Instruments

Syllabus

Types of instruments, Construction and working principles of PMMC, and moving iron type voltmeters and ammeters, Single phase dynamometer wattmeter, Use of shunts and multipliers (Simple numerical problems on shunts and multipliers).

Contents

5.1 Introduction

The measurement of a given quantity is the result of comparison between the quantity to be measured and a definite standard. The instruments which are used for such measurements are called **measuring instruments**.

> The necessary requirements for any measuring instruments are :
>
> 1) With the introduction of the instrument in the circuit, the circuit conditions should not be altered. Thus the quantity to be measured should not get affected due to the instrument used.
>
> 2) The power consumed by the instruments for their operation should be as small as possible.

The instrument which measures the current flowing in the circuit is called **ammeter** while the instrument which measures the voltage across any two points of a circuit is called **voltmeter**. But there is no fundamental difference in the operating principle of analog voltmeter and ammeter.

The action of almost all the analog ammeters and voltmeters depends on the deflecting torque produced by an electric current. In ammeters such a torque is proportional to the current to be measured. In voltmeters this torque is decided by a current which is proportional to the voltage to be measured. Thus all the analog ammeters and voltmeters are basically current measuring devices.

The instruments which are used to measure the power are called **power meters** or **wattmeters**. The instrument which is used to measure electrical energy is called an **energy meter**.

Review Question

1. State the necessary requirements for any measuring instrument.

5.2 Classification of Measuring Instruments

Electrical measuring instruments are mainly classified as :

a) Indicating instruments : These instruments make use of a dial and pointer for showing or indicating magnitude of unknown quantity.

The examples are ammeter, voltmeter, wattmeter etc.

b) Recording instruments : These instruments give a continuous record of the given electrical quantity which is being measured over a specific period.

The examples are various types of recorders. In such recording instruments, the readings are recorded by drawing the graph. The pointer of such instruments is provided with a marker i.e. pen or pencil, which moves on graph paper as per the reading. The X-Y plotter is the best example of such an instrument.

c) Integrating instruments : These instruments measure the total quantity of electricity delivered over period of time.

For example a household energymeter registers number of revolutions made by the disc to give the total energy delivered, with the help of counting mechanism, consisting of dials and pointers.

Review Question

> 1. *Give the classification of measuring instruments.*

5.3 Essential Requirements of an Instrument

For satisfactory operation of any **indicating instrument,** following systems must be present in an instrument.

1) Deflecting system producing deflecting torque T_d

2) Controlling system producing controlling torque T_c

3) Damping system producing damping torque.

5.4 Deflecting System

In most of the measuring instruments the mechanical force proportional to the quantity to be measured is generated. This force or torque deflects the pointer. This is called deflecting torque. The system which produces such a deflecting torque is called **deflecting system** and the torque is denoted as T_d.

The deflecting torque overcomes,

1) The inertia of the moving system

2) The controlling torque provided by controlling system

3) The damping torque provided by damping system.

The deflecting system uses one of the following effects produced by current or voltage, to produce deflecting torque.

1) **Magnetic effect :** When a current carrying conductor is placed in uniform magnetic field, it experiences a force which causes to move it. This effect is mostly used in many instruments like moving iron attraction and repulsion type, permanent magnet moving coil instruments etc.

2) **Thermal effect :** The current to be measured is passed through a small element which heats it to cause rise in temperature which is converted to an e.m.f. by a thermocouple attached to it. This effect is used in various thermocouple instruments.

3) **Electrostatic effects :** When two plates are charged, there is a force exerted between them, which moves one of the plates. This effect is used in electrostatic instruments which are normally voltmeters.

4) **Induction effects :** When a non-magnetic conducting disc is placed in a magnetic field produced by electromagnets which are excited by alternating currents, an e.m.f. is induced in it. If a closed path is provided, there is a flow of current in the disc. The interaction between induced currents and the alternating magnetic fields exerts a force on the disc which causes to move it. This interaction is called an **induction effect**. This principle is mainly used in energymeters.

5) **Hall effect :** If a bar of semiconducting material is placed in uniform magnetic field and if the bar carries current, then an e.m.f. is produced between two edges of conductor. This effect is mainly used in flux-meters.

Review Question

1. State the various effects in measuring instruments used to produce necessary deflecting torque.

5.5 Controlling System

The controlling system should provide a force so that current or any other electrical quantity will produce deflection of the pointer proportional to its magnitude.

The important functions of this system are,

1) It produces a force equal and opposite to the deflecting force in order to make the deflection of pointer at a definite magnitude. If this system is absent, then the pointer will swing beyond its final steady position for the given magnitude and deflection will become indefinite.

2) It brings the moving system back to zero position when the force which causes the movement of the moving system is removed. It will never come back to its zero position in the absence of controlling system.

Controlling torque is generally provided by springs. Sometimes gravity control is also used.

5.5.1 Gravity Control

This type of control consists of a small weight attached to the moving system whose position is adjustable. This weight produces a controlling torque due to gravity. This weight is called **control weight**.

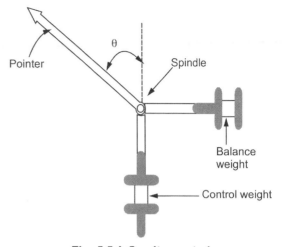

The Fig. 5.5.1 shows the gravity control system. At the zero position of the pointer, the controlling torque is zero. This position is shown as position A of the weight in the Fig. 5.5.2.

Fig. 5.5.1 Gravity control

If the system deflects, the weight position also changes, as shown in the Fig. 5.5.2.

The system deflects through an angle θ.

The control weight acts at a distance l from the center. The component $W \sin \theta$ of this weight tries to restore the pointer back to the zero position. This is nothing but the controlling torque T_c.

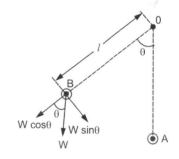

Thus, controlling torque

$$T_c = W \sin \theta \times l = K \sin \theta$$

where $K = W l$ = Gravity constant

Fig. 5.5.2

Now generally all meters are current sensing meters where, deflecting torque $T_d = K_t I$ where K_t = another constant.

In equilibrium position, $T_d = T_c$ i.e. $K_t I = K \sin \theta$

$\therefore$
$$\boxed{I \propto \sin \theta}$$

Thus the deflection is proportional to current i.e. quantity to be measured. But as it is a function of sin θ, the **scale for the instrument using gravity control is not uniform**.

Its **advantages** are :

1) Its performance is not time dependent.

2) It is simple and cheap.

3) The controlling torque can be varied by adjusting the position of the control weight.

4) Its performance is not temperature dependent.

Its **disadvantages** are :

1) The scale is nonuniform causing problems to record accurate readings.

2) The system must be used in vertical position only and must be properly levelled. Otherwise it may cause serious errors in the measurement.

3) As delicate and proper levelling required, in general it is not used for indicating instruments and portable instruments.

5.5.2 Spring Control

Two hair springs are attached to the moving system which exerts controlling torque. The arrangement of the springs is shown in the Fig. 5.5.3.

The springs are made up of non-magnetic materials like silicon bronze, hard rolled silver or copper, platinum silver and german silver.

For most of the instruments, phosphor bronze spiral springs are provided. Flat spiral springs are used in almost all indicating instruments.

The inner end of the spring is attached to the spindle while the outer end is attached to a lever or arm which is actuated by a set of

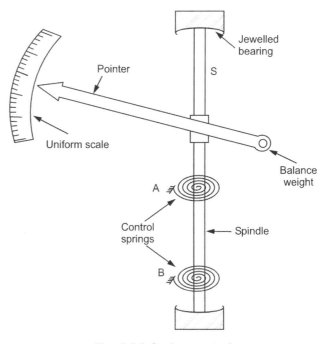

Fig. 5.5.3 Spring control

screw mounted at the front of the instrument. So zero setting can be easily done.

The controlling torque provided by the instrument is directly proportional to the angular deflection of the pointer.

The controlling torque produced by spiral spring is given by,

$$T_c = \frac{E\,b\,t^3}{12\,L}\,\theta = K_s\theta \qquad \text{where } K_s = \text{Spring constant} = \frac{E\,b\,t^3}{12\,L}$$

and   E = Young's modulus of spring material in N/m^2

t = Thickness in metres,   b = Depth in metres,   L = Length in metres

$\therefore$ $\qquad$ $T_c \propto \theta$

Now deflecting torque is proportional to current i.e. $T_d \propto I$

At equilibrium, $T_d = T_c$ hence,

$\therefore$ $\qquad$ $\boxed{I \propto \theta}$

Thus the deflection is proportional to the current. Hence the **scale of the instrument using spring control is uniform**.

To following requirements are essential for a spring used in spring control system,

1) The spring should be non-magnetic.

2) The spring should be free from mechanical stress.

3) The spring should have a small resistance, sufficient cross-sectional area.

4) It should have low resistance temperature co-efficient.

5.5.3 Comparison of Controlling Systems

Sr. No.	Gravity Control	Spring Control
1.	Adjustable small weight is used which produces the controlling torque.	Two hair springs are used which exert controlling torque.
2.	Controlling torque can be varied.	Controlling torque is fixed.
3.	The performance is not temperature dependent.	The performance is temperature dependent.
4.	The scale is nonuniform.	The scale is uniform.
5.	The controlling torque is proportional to $\sin \theta$.	The controlling torque is proportional to θ.
6.	The readings cannot be taken accurately.	The readings can be taken very accurately.
7.	The system must be used in vertical position only.	The system need not be necessarily in vertical position.
8.	Proper levelling is required as gravity control.	The levelling is not required.
9.	Simple, cheap but delicate.	Simple, rigid but costlier compared to gravity control.
10.	Rarely used for indicating and portable instruments.	Very popularly used in most of the instruments.

Review Questions

1. *Why controlling system is necessary in a measuring instrument ? How controlling torque is provided ?*

2. *Why scale of the gravity control is nonuniform ?*

3. *State the advantages and disadvantages of gravity control system.*

4. *Why the scale of the spring control is uniform ?*

5. *State the necessary requirements of springs used in spring control system.*

6. *Compare gravity control system with spring control system.*

5.6 Damping System   2010-11

The deflecting torque provides some deflection and controlling torque acts in the opposite direction to that of deflecting torque. So before coming to the rest, pointer always oscillates due to inertia, about the equilibrium position. So to bring the pointer to rest within short time, damping system is required.

The system should provide a damping torque only when the moving system is in motion.

Damping torque is proportional to velocity of the moving system but it does not depend on operating current. It must not affect controlling torque or increase the friction.

The quickness with which the moving system settles to the final steady position depends on relative damping.

If the moving system reaches to its final position rapidly but smoothly without oscillations, the instrument is said to be **critically damped.**

If the instrument is **under damped,** the moving system will oscillate about the final steady position with a decreasing amplitude and will take sometime to come to rest.

While the instrument is said to be **over damped** if the moving system moves slowly to its final steady position. In over damped case the response of the system is very slow and sluggish.

In practice slightly under damped systems are preferred.

The time response of damping system for various types of damping conditions is shown in the Fig. 5.6.1

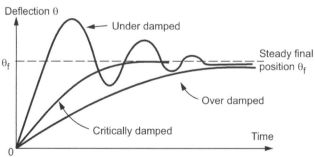

Fig. 5.6.1

The following methods are used to produce damping torque.

1) Air friction damping   2) Fluid friction damping   3) Eddy current damping

5.6.1 Air Friction Damping

This arrangement consists of a light aluminium piston which is attached to the moving system, as shown in the Fig. 5.6.2.

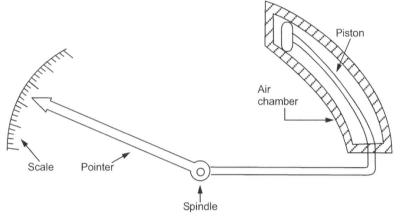

Fig. 5.6.2 Air friction damping

The piston moves in a fixed air chamber. It is close to one end. The piston reciprocates in the chamber when there are oscillations. When piston moves into the chamber, air inside is compressed and pressure of air developed due to friction opposes the motion of pointer. There is also opposition to motion of moving system when piston moves out of the chamber.

Thus the oscillations and the overshoot gets reduced due to and fro motion of the piston in the chamber, providing necessary damping torque.

5.6.2 Fluid Friction Damping

Fluid friction damping may be used in some instruments. The method is similar to air friction damping, only air is replaced by working fluid.

Damping force due to fluid is greater than that of air due to more viscosity. The disc is also called vane.

The arrangement is shown in the Fig. 5.6.3.

It consists of a vane attached to the spindle which is completely dipped in the oil. The frictional force between oil and the vane is used to produce the damping torque, which opposes the oscillating behaviour of the pointer.

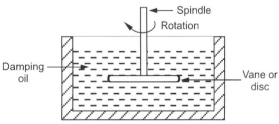

Fig. 5.6.3 Fluid friction damping

5.6.3 Eddy Current Damping

This is the most effective way of providing damping. It is based on the **Faraday's law** and **Lenz's law**.

When a conductor moves in a magnetic field cutting the flux, e.m.f. gets induced in it. And direction of this e.m.f. is so as to oppose the cause producing it according to Lenz's law.

In this method, an aluminium disc is connected to the spindle.

The arrangement of disc is such that when it rotates, it cuts the magnetic flux lines of a permanent magnet. The arrangement is shown in the Fig. 5.6.4

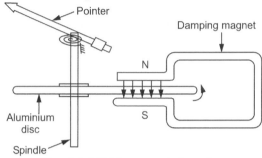

When the pointer oscillates, aluminium disc rotates under the influence of magnetic field of damping magnet. So disc cuts the flux which causes an induced e.m.f. in the disc.

Fig. 5.6.4 Eddy current damping

The disc is a closed path hence induced e.m.f. circulates current through the disc called **eddy current**. The direction of such eddy current is so as oppose the cause producing it. The cause is relative motion between disc and field.

Thus it produces an opposing torque so as to reduce the oscillations of pointer. This brings pointer to rest quickly.

This is most effective and efficient method of damping.

Review Questions

> 1. *Explain the necessity of damping system in a measuring instrument.*
>
> 2. *Explain in brief, the various methods used to provide damping torque.*
>
> 3. *What are the different torques required in an indicating instrument ?*   **2010-11, Marks 5**

5.7 Permanent Magnet Moving Coil Instruments (PMMC)   **2010-11**

The permanent magnet moving coil instruments are most accurate type for d.c. measurements. The action of these instruments is based on the motoring principle.

When a current carrying coil is placed in the magnetic field produced by permanent magnet, the coil experiences a force and moves. As the coil is moving and the magnet is permanent, the instrument is called permanent magnet moving coil instrument. This basic principle is called **D'Arsonval principle.** The amount of force experienced by the coil is proportional to the current passing through the coil.

The construction of a PMMC instrument is shown in the Fig. 5.7.1

The moving coil is either rectangular or circular in shape. It has number of turns of fine wire. The coil is suspended so that it is free to turn about its vertical axis. The coil is placed in uniform, horizontal and radial magnetic field of a permanent magnet in the shape of a horse-shoe. The iron core is

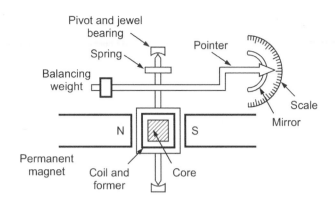

Fig. 5.7.1 Construction of PMMC instrument

spherical if coil is circular and is cylindrical if the coil is rectangular. Due to iron core, the deflecting torque increases, increasing the sensitivity of the instrument.

The controlling torque is provided by two phosphor bronze hair springs.

The damping torque is provided by eddy current damping. It is obtained by movement of the aluminium former, moving in the magnetic field of the permanent magnet.

The pointer is carried by the spindle and it moves over a graduated scale. The pointer has light weight so that it can deflect rapidly.

The mirror is placed below the pointer to get the accurate reading by removing the parallax. The weight of the instrument is normally counter balanced by the weights situated diametrically opposite and rigidly connected to it.

The scale markings of the basic d.c. PMMC instruments are usually linearly spaced as the deflecting torque and hence the pointer deflection are directly proportional to the current passing through the coil.

The top view of PMMC instrument is shown in the Fig. 5.7.2.

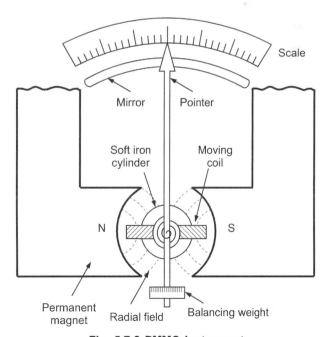

Fig. 5.7.2 PMMC instrument

5.7.1 Torque Equation

The equation for the developed torque can be obtained from the basic law of the electromagnetic torque. The deflecting toque is given by,

$$T_d \ = \ NBAI$$

where T_d = Deflecting torque in N-m,   B = Flux density in air gap, Wb/m^2

   N = Number of turns of the coil,   A = Effective coil area m^2

   I = Current in the moving coil, amperes

∴ T_d = GI   where G = NBA = Constant

The controlling torque is provided by the springs and is proportional to the angular deflection of the pointer.

   T_c = K θ   where T_c = Controlling torque

   K = Spring constant, Nm/rad or Nm/deg and θ = Angular deflection

For the final steady state position, $T_d = T_c$ i.e.   GI = K θ

∴
$$\theta \ = \ \left(\frac{G}{K}\right)I \quad or \quad I = \left(\frac{K}{G}\right)\theta$$

Key Point *Thus the deflection is directly proportional to the current passing through the coil. The pointer deflection can therefore be used to measure current.*

As the direction of the current through the coil changes, the direction of the deflection of the pointer also changes. Hence such instruments are well suited for the d.c. measurements.

The power requirement of PMMC instrument is very small, typically of the order of 25 µW to 200 µW. Accuracy is generally of the order of 2 to 5 % of the full scale reading.

5.7.2 Advantages and Disadvantages

The various **advantages of PMMC** instruments are,

1) It has uniform scale.

2) With a powerful magnet, its torque to weight ratio is very high. So operating current is small.

3) The sensitivity is high.

4) The eddy currents induced in the metallic former over which coil is wound, provide effective damping.

5) It consumes low power, of the order of 25 μW to 200 μW.

6) It has high accuracy.

7) Instrument is free from hysteresis error.

8) Extension of instrument range is possible.

9) Not affected by external magnetic fields called stray magnetic fields.

The various **disadvantages of PMMC** instruments are,

1) Suitable for d.c. measurements only.

2) Ageing of permanent magnet and the control springs introduces the errors.

3) The cost is high due to delicate construction and accurate machining.

4) The friction due to jewel-pivot suspension.

5.7.3 Errors in PMMC Instrument

The basic sources of errors in PMMC instruments are friction, temperature and aging of various parts. To reduce the frictional errors ratio of torque to weight is made very high.

The most serious errors are produced by the heat generated or by changes in the temperature. This changes the resistance of the working coil, causing large errors. In case of voltmeters, a large series resistance of very low temperature coefficient is used. This reduces the temperature errors.

The aging of permanent magnet and control springs also cause errors. The weakening of magnet and springs cause opposite errors. The weakening of magnet cause less deflection while weakening of the control springs cause large deflection, for a particular value of current. The proper use of material and preageing during manufacturing can reduce the errors due to weakening of the control springs.

Example 5.7.1 *A PMMC instrument has a coil of dimensions 10 mm × 8 mm. The flux density in the air gap is 0.15 Wb/m². If the coil is wound for 100 turns, carrying a current of 5 mA then calculate the deflecting torque. Calculate the deflection if the spring constant is 0.2×10^{-6} Nm/degree.*

Solution : The deflecting torque is given by,

$$T_d = NBAI = 100 \times 0.15 \times (A) \times 5 \times 10^{-3} \text{ Nm}, \quad K = 0.2 \times 10^{-6} \text{ Nm/degree}$$

Now $A = \text{Area} = 10 \times 8 = 80 \text{ mm}^2 = 80 \times 10^{-6} \text{m}^2$

∴ $T_d = 100 \times 0.15 \times 80 \times 10^{-6} \times 5 \times 10^{-3} = 6 \times 10^{-6} \text{ Nm}$

Now $\qquad T_d = T_c = K\theta \qquad$ i.e. $\qquad 6 \times 10^{-6} = 0.2 \times 10^{-6} \times \theta$

$\therefore \qquad \theta = \dfrac{6 \times 10^{-6}}{0.2 \times 10^{-6}} = \textbf{30 degrees}$

Review Questions

1. With the help of neat diagram explain the construction and working of PMMC type of instrument.
2. State the advantages and disadvantages of PMMC instrument.
3. Explain the possible errors in PMMC instrument.
4. Explain the PMMC instrument. Derive the expression for its deflecting torque.

2010-11, Marks 5

5.8 Moving Iron Instruments

2009-10, 2010-11

The moving iron instruments are classified as :

i) Moving iron attraction type instruments   and ii) Moving iron repulsion type instruments

5.8.1 Moving Iron Attraction Type Instruments

The basic working principle of these instruments is very simple that a soft iron piece if brought near the magnet gets attracted by the magnet.

The construction of the attraction type instrument is shown in the Fig. 5.8.1.

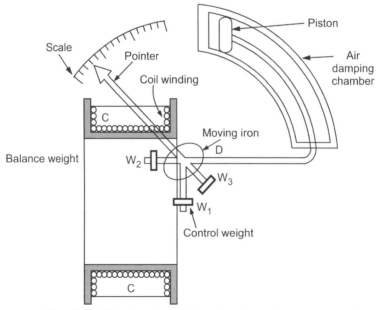

Fig. 5.8.1 Moving iron attraction type instrument

It consists of a fixed coil C and moving iron piece D. The coil is flat and has a narrow slot like opening. The moving iron is a flat disc which is eccentrically mounted on the spindle. The spindle is supported between the jewel bearings. The spindle carries a pointer which moves over a graduated scale. The number of turns of the fixed coil are dependent on the range of the instrument. For passing large current through the coil only few turns are required.

The controlling torque is provided by the springs but gravity control may also be used for vertically mounted panel type instruments.

The damping torque is provided by the air friction. A light aluminium piston is attached to the moving system. It moves in a fixed chamber. The chamber is closed at one end. It can also be provided with the help of vane attached to the moving system.

The operating magnetic field in moving iron instruments is very weak. Hence eddy current damping is not used since it requires a permanent magnet which would affect or distort the operating field.

5.8.2 Moving Iron Repulsion Type Instrument

These instruments have two vanes inside the coil, the one is fixed and other is movable. When the current flows in the coil, both the vanes are magnetised with like polarities induced on the same side. Hence due to the repulsion of like polarities, there is a force of repulsion between the two vanes causing the movement of the moving vane. The repulsion type instruments are the most commonly used instruments.

The two different designs of repulsion type instruments are :

i) Radial vane type   and   ii) Co-axial vane type

1. Radial Vane Repulsion Type Instrument

The Fig. 5.8.2 shows the radial vane repulsion type instrument. Out of the other moving iron mechanisms, this is the most sensitive and has most linear scale.

The two vanes are radial strips of iron. The fixed vane is attached to the coil. The movable vane is attached to the spindle and suspended in the induction field of the coil. The needle of the instrument is attached to this vane.

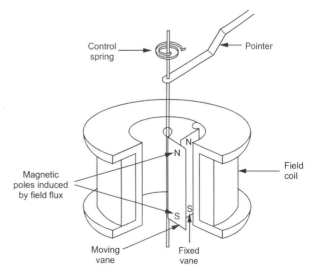

Fig. 5.8.2 Radial vane repulsion type instrument

Eventhough the current through the coil is alternating, there is always repulsion between the like poles of the fixed and the movable vane. Hence the deflection of the pointer is always in the same direction. The deflection is effectively proportional to the actual current and hence the scale is calibrated directly to read amperes or volts. The calibration is accurate only for the frequency for which it is designed because the impedance is different for different frequencies.

2. Concentric Vane Repulsion Type Instrument

The Fig. 5.8.3 shows the concentric vane repulsion type instrument.

The instrument has two concentric vanes. One is attached to the coil frame rigidly while the other can rotate coaxially inside the stationary vane.

Both the vanes are magnetised to the same polarity due to the current in the coil. Thus the movable vane rotates under the repulsive force. As the movable vane is attached to the pivoted shaft, the repulsion results in a rotation of the shaft. The pointer deflection is proportional to the

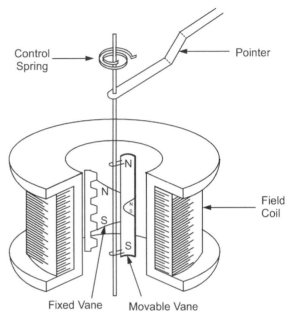

Fig. 5.8.3 Concentric vane repulsion type instrument

current in the coil. The concentric vane type instrument is moderately sensitive and the deflection is proportional to the square of the current through coil. Thus the instrument is said to have square law response. Thus the scale of the instrument is non-uniform in nature. Thus whatever may be the direction of the current in the coil, the deflection in the moving iron instruments is in the same direction. **Hence moving iron instruments can be used for both a.c. and d.c. measurements.**

5.8.3 Torque Equation of Moving Iron Instruments

Consider a small increment in current supplied to the coil of the instrument. Due to this current let $d\theta$ be the deflection under the deflecting torque T_d. Due to such deflection, some mechanical work will be done.

∴   Mechanical work = $T_d d\theta$

There will be a change in the energy stored in the magnetic field due to the change in inductance. This is because the vane tries to occupy the position of minimum reluctance hence the force is always in such a direction so as to increase the inductance of coil. The inductance is inversely proportional to the reluctance of the magnetic circuit of coil.

Let I = Initial current, L = Instrument inductance, θ = Deflection

dI = Increase in current, dθ = Change in deflection, dL = Change in inductance

In order to effect an increment dI in the current, there must be an increase in the applied voltage given by,

$$e \ = \ \frac{d(LI)}{dt} \ = I\frac{dL}{dt} + L\frac{dI}{dt} \qquad \text{as both I and L are changing.}$$

The electrical energy supplied is given by,

$$eIdt \ = \ \left(I\frac{dL}{dt} + L\frac{dI}{dt} \right)Idt = I^2\ dL + IL\ dI$$

The stored energy increases from $\frac{1}{2}LI^2$ to $\frac{1}{2}(L+dL)(I+dI)^2$.

Hence the change in the stored energy $= \frac{1}{2}(L+dL)(I+dI)^2 - \frac{1}{2}LI^2$

Neglecting higher order terms, this becomes, $IL\ dI + \frac{1}{2}I^2\ dL$

The energy supplied is nothing but increase in stored energy plus the energy required for mechanical work done.

$$\therefore \quad I^2 dL + IL\ dI \ = \ IL\ dI + \frac{1}{2}I^2\ dL + T_d \cdot d\theta$$

$$\therefore \qquad T_d \cdot d\theta \ = \ \frac{1}{2}I^2\ dL$$

$$\therefore \qquad \boxed{T_d \ = \ \frac{1}{2}I^2\frac{dL}{d\theta}}$$

While the controlling torque is given by,

$$\boxed{T_c \ = \ K\theta \quad \text{where } K = \text{Spring constant}}$$

$$\therefore \qquad \text{Under equilibrium} \quad T_c = T_d \qquad \text{i.e.} \qquad K\theta = \frac{1}{2}I^2\frac{dL}{d\theta}$$

$$\therefore \qquad \boxed{\theta = \frac{1}{2}\frac{I^2}{K}\frac{dL}{d\theta}}$$

Thus the deflection is proportional to the square of the current through the coil. And the instrument gives square law response.

5.8.4 Advantages and Disadvantages

The various **advantages** of moving iron instruments are,

1) The instruments can be used for both a.c. and d.c. measurements.

2) As the torque to weight ratio is high, errors due to the friction are very less.

3) A single type of moving element can cover the wide range hence these instruments are cheaper than other types of instruments.

4) There are no current carrying parts in the moving system hence these meters are extremely rugged and reliable.

5) These are capable of giving good accuracy. Modern moving iron instruments have a d.c. error of 2 % or less.

6) These can withstand large loads and are not damaged even under severe overload conditions.

7) The range of instruments can be extended.

The various **disadvantages** of moving iron instruments are,

1) The scale of the moving iron instruments is not uniform and is cramped at the lower end. Hence accurate readings are not possible at this end.

2) There are serious errors due to hysteresis, frequency changes and stray magnetic fields.

3) The increase in temperature increases the resistance of coil, decreases stiffness of the springs, decreases the permeability and hence affect the reading severely.

4) Due to the non linearity of B-H curve, the deflecting torque is not exactly proportional to the square of the current.

5) There is a difference between a.c. and d.c. calibrations on account of the effect of inductance of the meter. Hence these meters must always be calibrated at the frequency at which they are to be used. The usual commercial moving iron instrument may be used within its specified accuracy from 25 to 125 Hz frequency range.

6) Power consumption is on higher side.

5.8.5 Errors in Moving Iron Instruments

The various errors in the moving iron instruments are,

1) **Hysteresis errors :** Due to hysteresis effect, the flux density for the same current while ascending and descending values are different. So remedy for this is to use smaller iron parts which can demagnetise quickly or to work with lower flux densities.

2) **Temperature error :** The temperature error arises due to the effect of temperature on the temperature coefficient of the spring. Errors can cause due to self heating of the coil and due to which change in resistance of the coil. So coil and series resistance must have low temperature coefficient. Hence manganin is generally used for the series resistances.

3) **Stray magnetic field error :** The operating magnetic field in case of moving iron instruments is very low. Hence effect of external i.e. stray magnetic field can cause error. This effect depends on the direction of the stray magnetic field with respect to the operating field of the instrument.

4) **Frequency error :** These are related to a.c. operation of the instrument. The change in frequency affects the reactance of the working coil and also affects the magnitude of the eddy currents. This causes errors in the instrument.

5) **Eddy current error :** When instrument is used for a.c. measurements the eddy currents are produced in the iron parts of the instrument. The eddy current affects the instrument current causing the change in the deflecting torque. This produces the error in the meter reading. As eddy currents are frequency dependent, frequency changes cause eddy current error.

Example 5.8.1 *The inductance of a moving iron instrument is given by*

$$L = (12 + 6\,\theta - \theta^2)\,\mu H$$

where θ is the deflection in radians from zero position. The spring constant is $12 \times 10^{-6}\,Nm/radians$. Calculate the deflection for a current of 8 A.

Solution : The rate of change of inductance with deflection is,

$$\frac{dL}{d\theta} = \frac{d}{d\theta}(12 + 6\,\theta - \theta^2) = 6 - 2\theta \ \ \mu H/radians = (6 - 2\theta) \times 10^{-6} \ H/radians$$

From the torque equation, $\quad \theta = \dfrac{1}{2}\dfrac{I^2}{K}\dfrac{dL}{d\theta} = \dfrac{1}{2} \times \dfrac{(8)^2}{12 \times 10^{-6}} \times [6 - 2\theta] \times 10^{-6}$

∴ $\quad$ $0.375\,\theta = 6 - 2\,\theta \quad$ i.e. $\quad \theta = 2.526$ radians = **144.74°**

Review Questions

1. *Explain the principle of operation of attraction and repulsion type of moving iron instruments with neat sketches.*

2. *Derive the torque equation of moving iron instruments.*

3. *State the advantages and disadvantages of moving iron instruments.*

4. *Explain the various possible errors in the moving iron instruments. How are these minimised ?*

5. *The change of inductance for a moving iron ammeter is 3 µH/degree. The control spring constant is 5×10^{-7} Nm/degree. The maximum deflection of the pointer is 100°. Find the current corresponding to the maximum deflection.* **(Ans. : 5.7735 A)**

6. *Why moving iron type instrument is suitable for both a.c. and d.c. Also differentiate between moving iron and moving coil instruments.* **2009-10, Marks 5**

7. *Draw and explain the working of attraction type moving iron instrument.* **2010-11, Marks 5**

5.9 Dynamometer Type Wattmeter

The Fig. 5.9.1 shows the construction of the dynamometer type wattmeter.

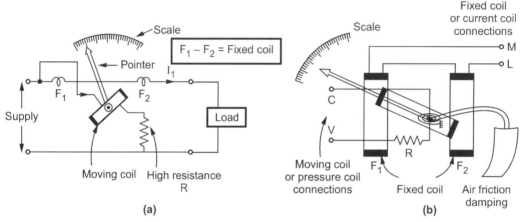

Fig. 5.9.1 Construction of dynamometer type wattmeter

It consists of a fixed coil. It is divided into two halves F_1 and F_2 positioned parallel to each other. The distance between them can be adjusted to provide uniform magnetic field required for the operation. These coils are air cored to avoid hysteresis losses. These are clamped in place against the coil supports made up of ceramic.

The moving coil is wound on a non-metallic former which is pivoted centrally between the fixed coils. It is made highly resistive by connecting high resistance in series with it.

A pointer is connected to the moving system madeup of aluminium.

The fixed coil is called a **current coil** as it is connected in series with the load to carry the current I_1 which is main current.

The moving coil is connected across the supply carrying current I_2 proportional to the voltage hence it is called **pressure coil** or **voltage coil**.

The controlling torque is provided by the springs.

The damping is provided by the air friction damping. The eddy current damping is not used as it may distort the operating magnetic field.

Working :   While operation, the wattmeter is connected in the circuit as shown in the Fig. 5.9.2.

When current passes through the fixed and moving coils, both coils produce the magnetic fields.

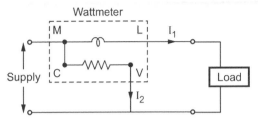

The field produced by fixed coil is proportional to the load current while the field produced by the moving coil is proportional to the voltage.

Fig. 5.9.2 Connections of wattmeter

As the deflecting torque is produced due to the interaction of these two fields, the deflection is proportional to the power supplied to the load.

Thus the wattmeter indicates the power consumption of the load.

It can be used for a.c. and d.c both.

D.C. working :   For the air cored fixed coils the flux density B is proportional to the current through the coils i.e. $B \propto I_1$.

While the current through pressure coil is proportional to the voltage i.e. $I_2 \propto V$.

The deflecting torque is due to the interaction of the two fluxes hence proportional to BI_2.

$T_d \propto B\, I_2 \propto I_1 V \propto$ POWER as the d.c. power is the product of voltage and current.

A.C. working :   In a.c. circuit the value of the instantaneous torque is proportional to the product of the instantaneous voltage (v) and the current (i).

Let ϕ is the power factor angle of the load then the voltage and current are given by,

$$v = V_m \sin \omega t \quad \text{and} \quad i = I_m \sin(\omega t - \phi)$$

Due to the inertia of the moving system, the deflection is proportional to the average value of the torque produced.

$T_d \propto$ average of (vi) $\propto$ average $[\ V_m \sin \omega t \times I_m \sin(\omega t - \phi)\ ] \propto [V\ I \cos \phi] \propto$ POWER

In a.c. operation, V and I are the r.m.s. values of the voltage and current respectively.

Due to spring control, these instruments have uniform scale and $\theta \propto$ POWER.

5.9.1 Torque Equation

Let I_c = Current through current coil   and I_{pc} = Current through pressure coil

R = Series resistance of pressure coil   and r_{pc} = Resistance of pressure coil

V = R.M.S. value of supply voltage   and I = R.M.S. value of current

According to theory of electrodynamic instruments,

$$T_i = i_1 \, i_2 \, \frac{dM}{d\theta} \qquad\qquad \dots (5.9.1)$$

Let $\qquad v = $ Instantaneous voltage $= V_m \sin \omega t = \sqrt{2} \, V \sin \omega t \qquad \dots (5.9.2)$

Due to high series resistance, pressure coil is treated to be purely resistive.

Key Point *The current I_{pc} is in phase with V as pressure coil is purely resistive.*

$$i_{pc} = \text{Instantaneous value} = \frac{v}{R_p} \text{ where } R_p = r_{pc} + R$$

$\therefore \qquad\qquad i_{pc} = \dfrac{\sqrt{2}\,V}{R_p} \sin \omega t = \sqrt{2} \, I_{pc} \sin \omega t \qquad\qquad \dots (5.9.3)$

If current coil current lags the voltage by angle ϕ then its instantaneous value is,

$$i_c = \sqrt{2} I_c \sin(\omega t - \phi) \qquad\qquad \dots (5.9.4)$$

Now $\qquad i_1 = i_c \quad$ and $\quad i_2 = i_{pc} \quad$ hence,

$$T_i = [\sqrt{2} I_{pc} \sin \omega t][\sqrt{2} I_c \sin(\omega t - \phi)]\frac{dM}{d\theta} = 2 I_c I_{pc} \sin(\omega t) \sin(\omega t - \phi)\frac{dM}{d\theta}$$

$\therefore \qquad\qquad T_i = I_c \, I_{pc}[\cos \phi - \cos(2\omega t - \phi)]\,\dfrac{dM}{d\theta} \qquad\qquad \dots (5.9.5)$

Key Point *Thus instantaneous torque has a component of power which varies as twice the frequency of current and voltage.*

$\therefore \qquad\qquad T_d = \text{Average deflecting torque} = \dfrac{1}{T}\displaystyle\int_0^T T_i \, d(\omega t)$

$$= \frac{1}{T}\int_0^T I_c I_{pc}\,[\cos\phi - \cos(2\omega t - \phi)]\frac{dM}{d\theta}\,d(\omega t) \ = I_c I_{pc}\cos\phi\,\frac{dM}{d\theta} \qquad \dots (5.9.6)$$

where $\qquad I_{pc} = \dfrac{V}{R_p}$

For a spring controlled wattmeter,

$$T_c = K\,\theta \qquad\qquad \dots (5.9.7)$$

But $\qquad T_d = T_c \qquad$ i.e. $\ I_c I_{pc} \cos\phi \, \dfrac{dM}{d\theta} = K\,\theta$

$$\therefore \quad \theta = \frac{1}{K} I_c\, I_{pc} \cos\phi\, \frac{dM}{d\theta} = K_1\, I_c\, I_{pc} \cos\phi \quad \text{where } K_1 = \frac{1}{K}\frac{dM}{d\theta} \qquad \dots (5.9.8)$$

$$\therefore \quad \theta = K_1\, I_c\, \frac{V}{R_p} \cos\phi = K_2\, P \qquad \dots (5.9.9)$$

where $\quad K_2 = \dfrac{K_1}{R_p} \quad$ and $\quad P = V\, I_c \cos\phi = \text{Power}$

$$\therefore \quad \theta \propto P \qquad \dots (5.9.10)$$

Key Point *Thus the wattmeter deflection when calibrated gives the power consumption of the circuit.*

5.9.2 Reading on Wattmeter

The Fig. 5.9.3 shows symbolic representation of wattmeter.

Thus if,

I_c = Current through current coil

V_{pc} = Voltage across pressure coil

Then wattmeter reading is,

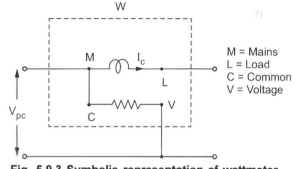

M = Mains
L = Load
C = Common
V = Voltage

Fig. 5.9.3 Symbolic representation of wattmeter

$$W = V_{pc}\, I_c \cos (V_{pc} \,{}^{\wedge} I_{pc})$$

5.9.3 Advantages and Disadvantages

The **advantages** of electrodynamometer type wattmeter are,

1) As the coils are air cored, these instruments are free from hysteresis and eddy current losses.

2) They have a precision grade accuracy.

3) These instruments can be used on both a.c. and d.c. They are also used as a transfer instruments.

4) Electrodynamometer voltmeters are very useful where accurate rms values of voltage, irrespective of waveforms, are required.

5) Free from hysteresis errors. 6) Low power consumption.   7) Light in weight.

The **disadvantages** of electrodynamometer type wattmeter are,

1) These instruments have a low sensitivity due to a low torque to weight ratio. Also it introduces increased frictional losses. To get accurate results, these errors must be minimized.

2) They are more expensive than other type of instruments.

3) These instruments are sensitive to overloads and mechanical impacts. Therefore care must be taken while handling them.

4) They have a non-uniform scale.

5) The operating current of these instruments is large due to the fact that they have weak magnetic field.

5.9.4 Errors in Electrodynamometer Instruments

The various errors in electrodynamometer instruments are,

1. **Torque to weight ratio :** The large number of turns of pressure coil increases weight of the coil. This makes the system heavy reducing torque to weight ratio. This can cause frictional errors in the reading.

2. **Frequency errors :** The changes in the frequency causes to change self inductances of moving coil and fixed coil. This causes the error in the reading. The frequency error can be reduced by having equal time constants for both fixed and moving coil circuits.

3. **Eddy current errors :** In metal parts of the instrument the eddy currents get produced. The eddy currents interact with the instrument current, to cause change in the deflecting torque, to cause error. Hence metal parts should be kept as minimum as possible. Also the resistivity of the metal parts used must be high, to reduce the eddy currents.

4. **Stray magnetic field error :** Similar to moving iron instruments the operating field in electrodynamometer instrument is very weak. Hence external magnetic field can interact with the operating field to cause change in the deflection, causing the error. To reduce the effect of stray magnetic field, the shields must be used for the instruments.

5. **Temperature error :** The temperature errors are caused due to the self heating of the coil, which causes change in the resistance of the coil. Thus temperature compensating resistors can be used in the precise instrument to eliminate the temperature errors.

Review Questions

1. *With the help of neat diagram explain the construction and principle of operation of dynamometer type wattmeter.*

2. *Derive the torque equation of electrodynamometer type wattmeter.*

3. *State the advantages and disadvantages of electrodynamometer type wattmeter.*

4. *Explain the various possible errors in electrodynamometer type wattmeter.*

5.10 Basic D.C. Ammeter   2002-03, 2011-12, 2012-13

The basic d.c. ammeter is nothing but a D'Arsonval galvanometer. The coil winding of a basic movement is very small and light and hence it can carry very small currents. So as mentioned earlier, for large currents, the major part of current is required to be bypassed using a resistance called **shunt**. It is shown in the Fig. 5.10.1.

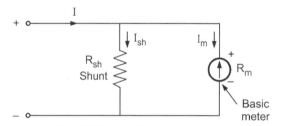

Fig. 5.10.1 Basic d.c. ammeter

The shunt resistance can be calculated as :

Let R_m = Internal resistance of coil, R_{sh} = Shunt resistance

I_m = Full scale deflection current, I_{sh} = Shunt current

I = Total current   i.e. $I = I_{sh} + I_m$

As the two resistances R_{sh} and R_m are in parallel, the voltage drop across them is same.

$\therefore$ $I_{sh} R_{sh} = I_m R_m$ i.e. $R_{sh} = \dfrac{I_m R_m}{I_{sh}}$ but $I_{sh} = I - I_m$

$\therefore$ $R_{sh} = \dfrac{I_m R_m}{(I - I_m)}$

$\therefore$ $\boxed{R_{sh} = \dfrac{R_m}{m - 1}}$ where $m = \dfrac{I}{I_m}$

The m is called **multiplying power** of the shunt and defined as the ratio of total current to the current through the coil. It can be expressed as,

$$m = \frac{I}{I_m} = 1 + \frac{R_m}{R_{sh}}$$

The shunt resistance may consist of a constant temperature resistance wire within the case of the meter or it may be external shunt having low resistance.

Thus to increase the range of ammeter 'm' times, the shunt resistance required is $1/(m-1)$ times the basic meter resistance. This is nothing but **extension of ranges of an ammeter.**

5.10.1 Requirements of a Shunt

1) The temperature coefficient of shunt and the meter should be low and should be as equal as possible.

2) The shunt resistances should be stable and constant with time.

3) The shunt resistances should not carry currents which will cause excessive temperature rise.

4) The type of material used to join the shunts should have low thermo dielectric voltage drop i.e. the soldering of joints should not cause a voltage drop.

5) Due to the soldering, the values of resistance should not be change.

6) The resistances should have low thermal electromotive force with copper.

The manganin is usually used for the shunts of d.c. instruments while the constantan is useful for the shunts of a.c. instruments.

Example 5.10.1 *A 2 mA meter with an internal resistance of 100 Ω is to be converted to 0-150 mA ammeter. Calculate the value of the shunt resistance required.*

Solution : $R_m = 100 \, \Omega$, $I_m = 2 \, mA$, $I = 150 \, mA$

$$R_{sh} = \frac{I_m \, R_m}{I - I_m} = \frac{2 \times 10^{-3} \times 100}{[150 \times 10^{-3} - 2 \times 10^{-3}]} = \mathbf{1.351 \, \Omega}$$

Example 5.10.2 *Two ammeters, one with a current scale of 10 A and resistance of 0.01 ohm and the other with a current scale of 15 A and resistance of 0.005 ohm are connected in parallel. What can be the maximum current carried by this parallel combination so that no meter reading goes out of the scale ?* **2002-03, Marks 5**

Solution :
$$I_1 = I_T \times \frac{0.005}{0.005 + 0.01}$$

$\therefore$
$$10 = I_T \times \frac{0.005}{0.005 + 0.01}$$

i.e. $\quad I_L = 30 \, A$

For this I_T, $\quad I_2 = I_T - I_1 = 30 - 10 = 20 \, A$

So **ammeter goes out of scale**

Now $\qquad I_2 = I_T \times \dfrac{0.01}{0.005+0.01}$ with $I_2 = 15$ A

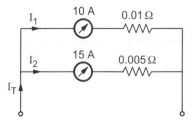

$\therefore \qquad I_T = \dfrac{15\times(0.005+0.01)}{0.01} = 22.5$ A

For this I_T, $\quad I_1 = I_T - I_2 = 22.5 - 15 = 7.5$ A

This I_1 is within range i.e. below 10 A

Fig. 5.10.2

Thus maximum current carried is **22.5 A**, so that no meter reading goes out of the scale.

Example 5.10.3 *An ammeter has internal resistance of 2 ohms and it is designed to measure 1 amp. current. What would you do to make this meter read 15 ampere current ?*

2011-12, Marks 5

Solution : $R_m = 2\ \Omega$, $I_m = 1$ A, $I = 15$ A

$$R_{sh} = \frac{I_m R_m}{I - I_m} = \frac{1\times 2}{15-1} = \textbf{0.1428}\ \boldsymbol{\Omega}$$

Connect $\mathbf{R_{sh}}$ **in shunt with the meter** to read 15 A current.

Example 5.10.4 *A moving coil instrument having a resistance of 50 Ω has a full-scale deflection of 1 mA. Calculate : i) Shunt resistance to convert the instrument into an ammeter of 2 A range. ii) Net resistance of the meter.*   **2012-13, Marks 10**

Solution : $R_m = 50\ \Omega$, $I_m = 1$ mA

i) $\qquad\qquad I = 2$ A

$$R_{sh} = \frac{I_m R_m}{I - I_m} = \frac{1\times 10^{-3}\times 50}{2 - 1\times 10^{-3}} = \textbf{0.02501}\ \boldsymbol{\Omega}$$

ii) Net resistance of the meter is parallel combination of R_{sh} and R_m.

$$\therefore \qquad R_{net} = \frac{50\times 0.02501}{50 + 0.02501} = \textbf{0.025}\ \boldsymbol{\Omega}$$

Review Question

> 1. *How range of measurement of basic d.c. ammeter can be extended using shunt ?*

5.11 Basic D.C. Voltmeter

The basic d.c. voltmeter is nothing but a PMMC D'Arsonoval galvanometer. The resistance is required to be connected in series with the basic meter to use it as a voltmeter. This series resistance is called a **multiplier**. The main function of the multiplier is to limit the current through the basic meter so that the meter current does not exceed the full scale deflection value. The voltmeter measures the voltage across the two points of a circuit or a voltage across a circuit component. The basic d.c. voltmeter is shown in the Fig. 5.11.1.

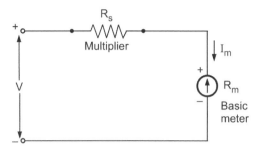

Fig. 5.11.1 Basic d.c. voltmeter

The voltmeter must be connected across the two points or a component, to measure the potential difference, with the proper polarity.

The multiplier resistance can be calculated as :

Let R_m = Internal resistance of meter, R_s = Series multiplier resistance

   I_m = Full scale deflection current,   V = Full range voltage to be measured

From Fig. 5.11.1, $\therefore V = I_m (R_m + R_s) = I_m R_m + I_m R_s$

$\therefore$ $I_m R_s = V - I_m R_m$

$\therefore$ $$R_s = \frac{V}{I_m} - R_m$$

The **multiplying factor** for multiplier is the ratio of full range voltage to be measured and the drop across the basic meter.

Let   v = Drop across the basic meter = $I_m R_m$

$\therefore$ m = Multiplying factor = $\dfrac{V}{v} = \dfrac{I_m (R_m + R_s)}{I_m R_m}$

$\therefore$ $$m = 1 + \frac{R_s}{R_m}$$

Hence multiplier resistance can also be expressed as, $R_s = (m - 1) R_m$.

Thus to increase the range of voltmeter 'm' times, the series resistance required is (m–1) times the basic meter resistance. This is nothing but **extension of ranges of a voltmeter**.

5.11.1 Requirements of a Multiplier

1) Their resistance should not change with time.

2) The change in their resistance with temperature should be small.

3) They should be non-inductively wound for a.c. meters.

Commonly used resistive materials for construction of multiplier are manganin and constantan.

Example 5.11.1 *A moving coil instrument gives a full scale deflection for a current of 20 mA with a potential difference of 200 mV across it. Calculate : i) Shunt required to use it as an ammeter to get a range of 0 - 200 A ii) Multiplier required to use it as a voltmeter of range 0 - 500 V.*

Solution : The meter current $\qquad I_m = 20$ mA

Drop across meter , $\qquad\qquad\qquad V_m = 200$ mV

Now $\qquad\qquad\qquad\qquad\qquad V_m = I_m R_m$

$\therefore \qquad\qquad\qquad\qquad 200 \text{ mV} = (20 \text{ mA}) R_m$

$\therefore \qquad\qquad\qquad\qquad\qquad R_m = 10 \ \Omega$

i) For using it as an ammeter, I = 200 A

$$R_{sh} = \frac{I_m R_m}{I - I_m} = \frac{20 \times 10^{-3} \times 10}{200 - 20 \times 10^{-3}} = \mathbf{0.001 \ \Omega}$$

This is the required shunt.

ii) For using it as a voltmeter,

$\qquad\qquad V = 500$ V

$\therefore \qquad R_s = \dfrac{V}{I_m} - R_m = \dfrac{500}{20 \times 10^{-3}} - 10 = \mathbf{24.99 \ k\Omega}$

This is the required multiplier.

Example 5.11.2 *A moving coil instrument has a resistance of 2 ohms and it reads upto 250 V when a resistance of 5000 ohms is connected in series with it. Find the current range of the instrument when it is used as an ammeter with the coil connected across a shunt resistance of 2 milli-ohms.* **2000-01, Marks 5**

Solution :

$$I_m = \text{full scale deflection current}$$

$$= \frac{250}{5000 + 2} = 49.98 \text{ mA}$$

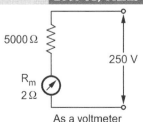

As a voltmeter

Fig. 5.11.2 (a)

For an ammeter,

$$I_{sh} R_{sh} = I_m R_m$$

$$I_{sh} = I - I_m$$

$$\therefore \quad (I - I_m) R_{sh} = I_m R_m$$

$$\therefore \quad (I - 49.98 \times 10^{-3}) \, 2 \times 10^{-3} = 49.98 \times 10^{-3} \times 2$$

$$\therefore \qquad I = \mathbf{50.02998 \ A}$$

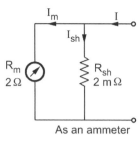

As an ammeter

Fig. 5.11.2 (b)

Example 5.11.3 *A moving coil milliammeter gives full scale deflection with 15 mA and has a resistance of 5 Ω. Calculate the resistance to be connected a) in parallel to enable the instrument to read up to 1 A, b) in series to enable it to read upto 10 V.*

2001-02, Marks 5

Solution : $I_m = 15$ mA, $R_m = 5 \ \Omega$

a) As ammeter with I = 1 A

$$I_m R_m = I_{sh} R_{sh}$$

and $\qquad I_{sh} = I - I_m$

$$\therefore 15 \times 10^{-3} \times 5 = (1 - 15 \times 10^{-3}) \, R_{sh}$$

$$\therefore \qquad R_{sh} = \mathbf{0.0761 \ \Omega} \qquad \text{...in parallel}$$

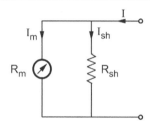

Fig. 5.11.3 (a)

b) As voltmeter with V = 10 V

$$V = I_m (R_s + R_m)$$

$$\therefore \qquad 10 = 15 \times 10^{-3} \, [R_s + 5]$$

$$\therefore \qquad R_s = \frac{10}{15 \times 10^{-3}} - 5 = \mathbf{661.667 \ \Omega}$$

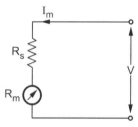

Fig. 5.11.3 (b)

... in series

Example 5.11.4 *A moving coil instrument gives a full-scale deflection of 20 mA when a potential difference of 50 mV is applied. Calculate the series resistance to measure 500 V on full scale.*

2003-04, Marks 5

Solution : $\qquad I_m = 20$ mA, $V = 500$ V, $V_m = 50$ mV

$$\therefore \qquad R_m = \frac{V_m}{I_m} = \frac{50 \times 10^{-3}}{20 \times 10^{-3}} = 2.5 \ \Omega$$

$$R_s = \frac{V_m}{I_m} - R_m = \frac{500}{20 \times 10^{-3}} - 2.5 = \mathbf{24997.5 \ \Omega}$$

Example 5.11.5 *A moving coil milliammeter having a resistance of 8 Ω gives full scale deflection when a current of 5 mA is passed through it. Explain how this instrument can be used for measurement of i) current up to 2 A ii) voltages up to 8 V.*

2009-10, Marks 5

Solution : $R_m = 8\ \Omega$, $I_m = 5$ mA.

i) As an ammeter with $I = 2$ A

$$R_{sh} = \frac{I_m R_m}{I - I_m} = \frac{5 \times 10^{-3} \times 8}{2 - 5 \times 10^{-3}} = \textbf{0.02}\ \Omega \text{ in shunt}$$

ii) As a voltmeter with $V = 8$ V

$$R_s = \frac{V}{I_m} - R_m = \frac{8}{5 \times 10^{-3}} - 8 = \textbf{1592}\ \Omega \text{ in series.}$$

Review Question

1. *How range of measurement of basic d.c. voltmeter can be extended using multiplier ?*

5.12 Comparison of Various Types of Instruments

The comparison of PMMC, moving iron and dynamometer type instruments is summarized in the Table 5.12.1.

Meter Type	Control	Damping	Suitability	Application
PMMC	Spring	Eddy current	D.C.	Widely used for d.c. current and voltage measurements in low and medium impedance circuits.
Moving iron	Spring or Gravity	Air friction	D.C. and A.C.	Used for rough indication of currents and voltages. Widely used for the indicator type instruments on panels.
Dynamometer	Spring	Air friction	D.C. and A.C.	Used mainly as wattmeter. Also may be used as ammeter or voltmeter. Widely used as a calibration instrument and as a transfer instrument.

Table 5.12.1

5.13 Short Answered and Objective Type Questions

Q.1 A moving coil ammeter has full scale deflection of 50 μA and a coil resistance of 100 Ω. The value of the shunt resistance required for the instrument to be converted to read a full - scale reading of 1 A will be _____ . **2008-09**

Ans. : $I_m = 50\ \mu A$, $R_m = 100\ \Omega$, $I = 1\ A$

$$R_{sh} = \frac{I_m\ R_m}{I - I_m} = \frac{50 \times 10^{-6} \times 100}{1 - 50 \times 10^{-6}} = \mathbf{0.005\ \Omega}.$$

Q.2 A moving coil instrument gives full scale deflection with 20 mA. The resistance of coil is 4 ohm. The value of series resistance needed for the instrument to read upto 30 V is _____. **2009-10**

Ans. : $I_m = 20\ mA$, $\qquad R_m = 4\ \Omega$, $\qquad V = 30\ V$

$$R_s = \frac{V}{I_m} - R_m = \frac{30}{20 \times 10^{-3}} - 4 = \mathbf{1496\ \Omega}.$$

Q.3 What is the major difference between PMMC type and dynamometer type of instruments ? **(Refer section 5.12)** **2011-12**

Q.4 State the necessary requirements of measuring instruments.

Ans. :

1) With the introduction of the instrument in the circuit, the circuit conditions should not be altered. Thus the quantity to be measured should not get affected due to the instrument used.

2) The power consumed by the instruments for their operation should be as small as possible.

Q.5 List any three types of indicating instruments.

Ans. : The instruments which make use of a dial and pointer for showing or indicating magnitude of unknown quantity are called indicating instruments. The examples are ammeter, voltmeter, wattmeter etc.

Q.6 What are the advantages of electromechanical measuring instruments ?

Ans. : The various advantages of electromechanical measuring instruments are simple in design, reliable, low in cost and work without any additional power supply.

Q.7 List the essential torques required in an indicating instruments.

Ans. : The three torques required in an indicating instruments are,

      1. Deflecting torque   2. Controlling torque   3. Damping torque

Q.8   List the various effects used to provide deflecting torque.

Ans. :   The various effects used to provide deflecting torque are,

1) Magnetic effect 2) Thermal effect   3) Electrostatic effects

4) Induction effects   5) Hall effect

Q.9   State the functions of controlling system.

Ans. :

1) It produces a force equal and opposite to the deflecting force in order to make the deflection of pointer at a definite magnitude. If this system is absent, then the pointer will swing beyond its final steady position for the given magnitude and deflection will become indefinite.

2) It brings the moving system back to zero position when the force which causes the movement of the moving system is removed. It will never come back to its zero position in the absence of controlling system.

Q.10   State the necessary requirements of springs used in spring control system.

Ans. :

1)   The spring should be non-magnetic.

2)   The spring should be free from mechanical stress.

3)   The spring should have a small resistance, sufficient cross-sectional area.

4)   It should have low resistance temperature co-efficient.

Q.11   List the various methods used to provide damping torque.

Ans. :   The various methods used to provide damping torque are,

1. Air friction damping   2. Fluid friction damping   3. Eddy current damping

Q.12   State the basic principle of PMMC instrument.

Ans. :   When a current carrying coil is placed in the magnetic field produced by permanent magnet, the coil experiences a force and moves.

Q.13   Why PMMC instruments cannot be used for a.c. measurements ?

Ans. :   If a.c. supply is given to PMMC instruments, an alternating torque will be developed. Due to moment of inertia of the moving system, the pointer will not follow the rapidly changing alternating torque and will fail to show any reading.

Q.14   State any four advantages of PMMC instrument.

Ans. :

1) It has uniform scale.

2) With a powerful magnet, its torque to weight ratio is very high. So operating current is small.

3) The sensitivity is high.

4) The eddy currents induced in the metallic former over which coil is wound, provide effective damping.

5) It has high accuracy.

Q.15 State the disadvantages of PMMC instrument.

Ans. :

1) Suitable for d.c. measurements only.

2) Ageing of permanent magnet and the control springs introduces the errors.

3) The cost is high due to delicate construction and accurate machining.

4) The friction due to jewel-pivot suspension.

Q.16 A 5 mA meter with an internal resistance of 50 Ω is to be converted to 0-100 mA ammeter. Calculate the value of the shunt resistance required.

Ans. : Given values are, $R_m = 50\ \Omega$, $I_m = 5$ mA, $I = 100$ mA

$$R_{sh} = \frac{I_m\ R_m}{I - I_m} = \frac{5\times10^{-3}\times50}{[100\times10^{-3} - 5\times10^{-3}]} = \mathbf{2.6315\ \Omega}$$

Q.17 State any four advantages of moving iron instruments.

Ans. :

1) The instruments can be used for both a.c. and d.c. measurements.

2) As the torque to weight ratio is high, errors due to the friction are very less.

3) A single type of moving element can cover the wide range hence these instruments are cheaper than other types of instruments.

4) There are no current carrying parts in the moving system hence these meters are extremely rugged and reliable.

Q.18 State the disadvantages of moving iron instruments.

Ans. :

1) The scale of the moving iron instruments is not uniform and is cramped at the lower end. Hence accurate readings are not possible at this end.

2) There are serious errors due to hysteresis, frequency changes and stray magnetic fields.

3) The increase in temperature increases the resistance of coil, decreases stiffness of the springs, decreases the permeability and hence affect the reading severely.

Q.19 A moving coil instrument gives a full scale deflection with a current of 80 µA, while the internal resistance of the meter is 250 Ω. It is to be used as a voltmeter to measure a voltage range of 0 - 50 V. Calculate the multiplier resistance needed.

Ans. : Given values are, $R_m = 250\ \Omega$, $I_m = 80\ \mu A$ and $V = 50\ V$

$$\text{Now} \quad R_s = \frac{V}{I_m} - R_m = \frac{50}{80 \times 10^{-6}} - 250 = \textbf{624.75 k}\boldsymbol{\Omega}$$

Q.20 What is accuracy and resolution of an instrument ?   `2010-11`

Ans. : Accuracy : It is the degree of closeness with which the instrument reading approaches the true value of the quantity to be measured. It is expressed as a percentage of full scale reading or as a percentage of true value.

Resolution : It is the smallest increment of quantity being measured which can be detected with certainity by an instrument. Thus the resolution means the smallest measurable input change.

Q.21 Enlist the types of moving iron instrument.   `2012-13`

Ans. : i) Attraction type   ii) Repulsion type

The repulsion type are further classified as,

a) Radial vane type   b) Concentric vane type.

Q.22 A voltmeter is _____ instrument.

     a) recording   b) indicating   c) integrating   d) none of these

                                                                        (Ans. : b)

Q.23 A X-Y plotter is _____ instrument.

     a) recording   b) indicating   c) integrating   d) none of these

                                                                         (Ans. : a)

Q.24 An energymeter is _____ instrument.

     a) recording   b) indicating   c) integrating   d) none of these

                                                                         (Ans. : c)

Q.25 In moving iron instrument _____ effect is used.

     a) thermal   b) photoelectric   c) electrostatic   d) magnetic

                                                                         (Ans. : d)

Q.26 Without _____ torque, pointer will swing beyond it's final position with indefinite deflection.

     a) controlling   b) deflecting   c) damping   d) none of these

                                                                         (Ans. : a)

Q.27 _____ is used to obtain the controlling torque.

     a) Air   b) Springs   c) Fluid   d) Magnets **(Ans. : b)**

Q.28 When pointer deflects and attains a final steady state position then _____.

a) only damping torque acts   b) only controlling torque acts

c) only deflecting torque acts   d) both controlling and deflecting torques act
(Ans. : d)

Q.29 If the pointer moves very slowly to its final position without oscillation, the system is said to be _____.

a) critically damped b) underdamped c) overdamped   d) none of these
(Ans. : c)

Q.30 In practice slightly _____ systems are preferred.

a) critically damped b) underdamped   c) overdamped   d) none of these
(Ans. : b)

Q.31 The damping force due to fluid is _____ that of air force.

a) greater than   b) less than   c) same as   d) none of these
(Ans. : a)

Q.32 In eddy current damping, the disc is made up of _____.

a) iron   b) copper   c) aluminium   d) nickel alloy
(Ans. : c)

Q.33 The basic principle of PMMC instrument is _____.

a) Generator principle   b) Induction principle

c) Hall effect principle   d) D'Arsonval principle   **(Ans. : d)**

Q.34 PMMC instruments can be used for _____.

a) A.C.   b) D.C.   c) A.C. and D.C.   d) None of these.
(Ans. : b)

Q.35 A PMMC instrument with a coil dimension 10 mm × 8 mm, Flux density of 0.8 T, 1000 turns carrying a current of 3 mA produces deflecting torque of _____.

a) 2.92×10^4 Nm   b) 1 mNm   c) 1.92×10^{-4} Nm   d) 0.92 Nm **(Ans. : c)**

Q.36 For a temperature compensation in PMMC instrument a resistor made up of _____ is used.

a) copper   b) copper+nickel   c) copper+iron   d) copper+manganin
(Ans. : d)

Q.37 The scale of moving iron instruments is nonuniform because _____.

a) they have square law response   b) they use spring control

c) they use eddy current damping   d) none of these   **(Ans. : a)**

Q.38 The moving iron instruments can be used for _____.

a) only A.C.   b) only D.C.   c) A.C. and D.C. both d) none of these.
(Ans. : c)

Q.39 A 5 mA meter with R_m of 150 Ω is to be converted to 0-200 mA ammeter, then the shunt required is _____.

a) 2.846 Ω b) 3.846 Ω c) 1.846 Ω d) 0.846 Ω **(Ans. : b)**

Q.40 The multiplying power of the shunt is expressed as _____.

a) II_m b) $\dfrac{I_m}{I}$ c) $\dfrac{I}{I_m}$ d) $\dfrac{I_m}{R_m}$ **(Ans. : c)**

Q.41 Shunts are usually made up of _____ for d.c. instruments.

a) manganin   b) copper   c) aluminium   d) silver   **(Ans. : a)**

Q.42 The multiplying factor for the multipliers is expressed as _____.

a) $1 + \dfrac{R_m}{R_s}$ b) $1 + \dfrac{R_s}{R_m}$ c) $\dfrac{R_s R_m + 1}{R_s}$ d) R_m **(Ans. : b)**

Q.43 If a multiplying power of an instrument is 500 and meter resistance is 500 Ω then the shunt multiplier resistance is _____.

a) 149.5 kΩ b) 49.5 kΩ c) 1 kΩ d) 249.5 kΩ **(Ans. : d)**

Q.44 _____ instrument is used as a calibration instrument.

a) Moving coil   b) Moving iron   c) Dynamometer   d) None of these

(Ans. : c)

Q.45 _____ instrument is mainly used as a wattmeter.

a) Dynamometer   b) Moving coil   c) Moving iron   d) None of these.

(Ans. : a)

Q.46 The material for shunt must have _____ temperature coefficient of resistance.

a) high   b) very low   c) negative   d) none of these.

(Ans. : b)

Q.47 _____ resistors are used for temperature compensation.

a) Shunt   b) Series   c) Swamping   d) None of these.

(Ans. : c)

Q.48 In the measuring instruments, under equilibrium condition, controlling torque (T_c) and deflecting torque (T_d) are _____ .

a) $T_c = T_d$ b) $T_c > T_d$ c) $T_c < T_d$ d) none of these

(Ans. : a)

Q.49 Without _____ torque, pointer will swing beyond it's final position with indefinite deflection.

a) controlling   b) deflecting   c) damping   d) none of these

(Ans. : a)

Q.50 _____ is used to obtain the controlling torque.

     a) Air   b) Springs   c) Fluid   d) Magnets **(Ans. : b)**

Q.51 When pointer deflects and attains a final steady state position then _____ .

     a) only damping torque acts   b) only controlling torque acts

     c) only deflecting torque acts   d) both controlling and deflecting
                                                torques act   **(Ans. : d)**

Q.52 The damping force due to fluid is _____ that of air force.

     a) greater than   b) less than   c) same as   d) none of these
                                                                      (Ans. : a)

Q.53 In eddy current damping, the disc is made up of _____ .

     a) iron   b) copper   c) aluminium   d) nickel alloy
                                                                    (Ans. : c)

Q.54 In a dynamometer wattmeter the fixed coil is _____ .

     a) current coil   b) potential coil

     c) current or potential coil   d) none of the above   **(Ans. : a)**

Q.55 An electrodynamometer type instrument can be employed for measurement of ,

     _____ .

     a) d.c. voltages   b) a.c. voltages

     c) d.c. as well as a.c. voltages

     d) d.c. voltages but for a.c. volatges, rectification is necessary   **(Ans. : c)**

Q.56 The dynamometer type wattmeter is used to measure _____ .

     a) only D.C. power   b) only AC power

     c) both D.C. and A.C. power   d) both active and reactive power
                                                                    (Ans. : c)

Q.57 The pointer in the dynamometer type wattmeter is made of _____.

     a) copper   b) aluminum   c) phosphor bronze   d) platinum
                                                                      (Ans. : b)

□□□

6

Introduction to Earthing and Electrical Safety

Syllabus

Need of earthing of equipment and devices, Important electrical safety issues.

Contents

6.1 Introduction

For all practical purposes, the earth's potential is taken zero. Almost all the machinery, electric poles, towers, neutral wires are connected to earth. The neutral wire of an a.c. supply and middle wire of three wire d.c. distribution system are always earthed.

The connection of electrical machinery to the general mass of earth, with a conducting material of very low resistance is called **earthing** or **grounding**.

Key Point *The earthing of electrical equipment bring the equipments to zero potential and avoid the shock to the operator, under any fault conditions.*

In India, three phase four wire distribution is generally preferred. The potential between any two phase (line voltage) is 400 V while between any one of the three phases and the neutral is 230 V. The single phase equipments are supplied with one phase called line and a neutral. The neutral wire is always grounded at the generating station. In an ungrounded supply system where neutral is not earthed, under a single earth fault any where in the system, the voltage of two healthy phases with respect to ground increases to $\sqrt{3}$ times the normal to phase voltage. Such an over voltage is harmful to the various electrical equipments. Hence all modern supply systems use grounded neutral.

The grounded neutral supply system has following advantages :

i)   It is very easy for earth fault protection.

ii) Spikes of over voltages are easily dissipated to the earth. Such spikes include the lightning and switching over voltages.

iii) Less stresses on insulation, if there is earth fault elsewhere.

Review Questions

1. *What is earthing ?*
2. *State the advantages of grounded neutral supply system.*

6.2 Necessity of Earthing

Consider a single phase machine which is not earthed. The windings and coils inside the frame of the machine carry the current. The potential between line and neutral is V volts. The resistance between the windings and the frame is say R_i called **insulation resistance**. And R_{body} be the **resistance of the body** of a person who happens to touch to the machine.

Neutral is generally earthed at supply system as shown in the Fig. 6.2.1.

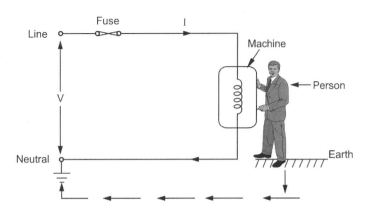

Fig. 6.2.1 Machine is not earthed

The equivalent electric circuit of the above condition can be shown as in the Fig. 6.2.2.

In the equivalent circuit we have,

I_m = Machine current

I_{body} = Current passing through the body of the person.

When a person, standing on the earth touches the machine, current I gets an alternative path through the body of the person to earth from the

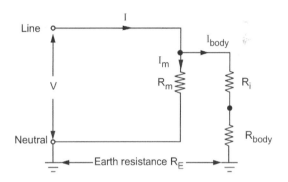

Fig. 6.2.2 Equivalent circuit

insulation resistance, finally to the neutral of the supply. From the equivalent circuit we can write,

$$I_{body} = \frac{V}{R_i + R_{body} + R_E} \qquad \ldots(6.2.1)$$

When the insulation of the machine is perfect, the insulation resistance is of the order of few mega ohms and practically can be considered as infinity.

So $\qquad R_i = \infty \qquad\qquad\qquad$ ... Insulation perfect

$\therefore \qquad I_{body} = \dfrac{V}{R_E + \infty + R_{body}} = 0 \qquad \ldots(6.2.2)$

So in normal operating conditions, there is no current passing through the body of the person and hence there is no danger of the shock.

But when the insulation becomes weak or defective or if one of the windings is touching to the frame directly due to some fault then R_i i.e. insulation resistance becomes almost zero. Now resistance of body and earth are not very high and hence I_{body} increases to such a high value that the person receives a fatal shock. Such a current is called a leakage current. Hence when the machine is not earthed, there is always a danger of the shock, under certain fault conditions.

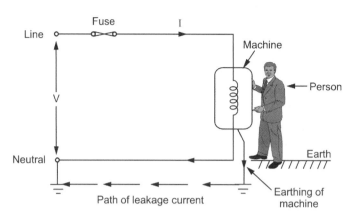

Fig. 6.2.3 Machine is earthed

Let us see now, what happens due to earthing. In case of earthing, the frame of the machine is earthed as shown in the Fig. 6.2.3.

The resistance of the path from frame to earth is very very low. When the person touches to the frame, and if there is a leakage due to fault condition, due to earthing a leakage current takes a low resistance path i.e. path from frame to earth, bypassing the person. So body of the person carries very low current which is not sufficient to cause any shock.

The equivalent circuit of the earthed condition is shown in the Fig. 6.2.4.

When there is a leakage current due to deterioration of an insulation R_i approaches to zero. So current is sufficiently high to cause a fatal shock. But at point E shown in the Fig. 6.2.4 the current I_T has two paths :

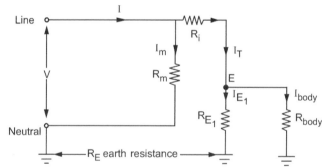

Fig. 6.2.4 Equivalent circuit when machine is earthed

i) One flowing through R_{body} through the person.

ii) Other through new earthing connection having resistance R_{E1}.

The current through the body of the person can be obtained by using the results of current division in a parallel combination.

$$I_{body} = I_T \times \frac{R_{E1}}{R_{body} + R_{E1}} \qquad\qquad ...(6.2.3)$$

Now R_{E1} is very very small about 5 while R_{body} under worst condition is 1000 Ω but generally higher than 1000 Ω. Hence current I_{body} is negligibly small compared to current I_{E1}. So entire leakage current I_T passes through the earthing contact bypassing the body of the person. The value of I_{body} is not sufficient to cause any shock to the person.

Not only this but the current I_T, is high due to which fuse blows off and thus it helps to isolate the machine from the electric supply.

6.2.1 Uses of Earthing

Apart from basic use of earthing discussed above, the other uses can be stated as

1)   To maintain the line voltage constant.

2)   To protect tall buildings and structures from atmospheric lightening strikes.

3)   To protect all the machines, fed from overhead lines, from atmospheric lightening.

4)   To serve as the return conductor for telephone and traction work. In such case, all the complications in laying a separate wire and the actual cost of the wire, is thus saved.

5)   To protect the human being from disability or death from shock in case the human body comes into the contact with the frame of any electrical machinery, appliance or component, which is electrically charged due to leakage current or fault.

Review Questions

> 1. *Explain the necessity of earthing.*
> 2. *State the uses of earthing.*

6.3 Methods of Earthing

Earthing is achieved by connecting the electrical appliances or components to earth by employing a good conductor called **'Earth Electrode'**. This ensures very low resistance path from appliance to the earth. The various methods of earthing are

  i)   Plate earthing

  ii) Pipe earthing

  iii) Earthing through water main

  iv) Horizontal strip earthing

  v)   Rod earthing

Let us discuss in detail, the two methods of earthing which are commonly used in practice.

6.3.1 Plate Earthing

The earth connection is provided with the help of copper plate or galvanized iron (G.I.) plate. The copper plate size is 60 cm × 60 cm × 3.18 mm while G.I. plate size is not less than 60 cm × 60 cm × 6.3 mm. The G.I. plates are commonly used now-a-days. The plate is embedded 3 meters (10 feet) into the ground. The plate is kept with its face vertical.

The plate is surrounded by the alternate layer of coke and salt for minimum thickness of about 15 cm. The earth wire is drawn through G.I. pipe and is perfectly bolted to the earth plate. The nuts and bolts must be of copper plate and must be of galvanized iron for G.I. plate.

The earth lead used must be G.I. wire or G.I. strip of sufficient cross-sectional area to carry the fault current safely. The earth wire is drawn through G.I. pipe of 19 mm diameter, at about 60 cm below the ground.

The G.I. pipe is fitted with a funnel on the top. In order to have an effective earthing, salt water is poured periodically through the funnel.

The earthing efficiency, increases with the increases of the plate area and depth of embedding. If the resistivity of the soil is high, then it is necessary to embed the plate vertically at a greater depth into the ground.

The only disadvantage of this method is that the discontinuity of the earth wire from the earthing plate below the earth can not be observed physically. This may cause misleading and may result into heavy losses under fault conditions.

The schematic arrangement of plate earthing is shown in the Fig. 6.3.1.

(See Fig. 6.3.1 on next page)

6.3.2 Pipe Earthing

In this method of earthing a G.I. pipe of 38 mm diameter and 2 meter (7 feet) length is embedded vertically into the ground. This pipe acts as an earth electrode. The depth depends on the condition of the soil.

The earth wires are fastened to the top section of the pipe above the ground level with nut and bolts.

The pit area around the pipe is filled with salt and coal mixture for improving the condition of the soil and earthing efficiency. The schematic arrangement of pipe earthing system is shown in the Fig. 6.3.2. (See Fig. 6.3.2 on page 6 - 8)

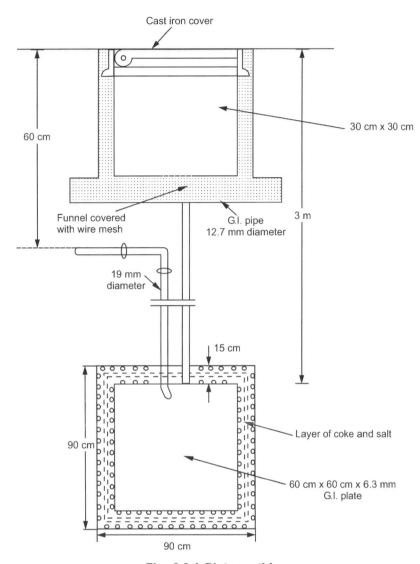

Fig. 6.3.1 Plate earthing

The contact surface of G.I. pipe with the soil is more as compared to the plate due to its circular section and hence can handle heavier leakage current for the same electrode size.

According to Indian standard, the pipe should be placed at a depth of 4.75 m. Impregnating the coke with salt decreases the earth resistance. Generally alternate layers of salt and coke are used for best results.

In summer season, soil becomes dry, in such case salt water is poured through the funnel connected to the main G.I. pipe through 19 mm diameter pipe. This keeps the soil wet.

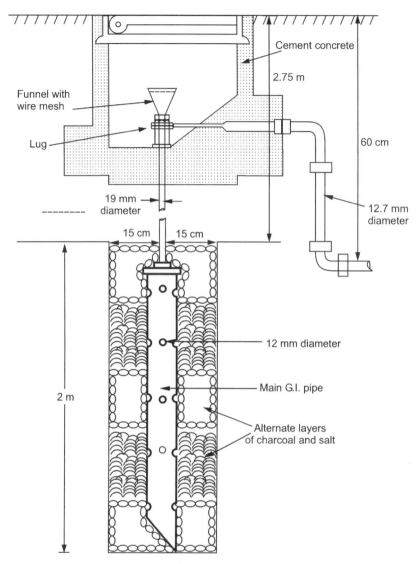

Fig. 6.3.2 Pipe earthing

The earth wires are connected to the G.I. pipe above the ground level and can be physically inspected from time to time. These connections can be checked for performing continuity tests. This is the important advantage of pipe earthing over the plate earthing. The earth lead used must be G.I. wire of sufficient cross-sectional area to carry fault current safely. It should not be less than electrical equivalent of copper conductor of 12.97 mm^2 cross-sectional area.

The only disadvantage of pipe earthing is that the embedded pipe length has to be increased sufficiently in case the soil specific resistivity is of high order. This increases the excavation work and hence increased cost. In ordinary soil condition the range of the earth resistance should be 2 to 5 ohms.

In the places where rocky soil earth bed exists, horizontal strip earthing is used. This is suitable as soil excavation required for plate or pipe earthing is difficult in such places. For such soils earth resistance is between 5 to 8 ohms.

Review Questions

1. *Explain plate earthing with the help of neat diagram.*
2. *Explain pipe earthing with the help of neat diagram.*

6.4 Safety Precautions

It is necessary to observe some safety precautions while using the electric supply to avoid the serious problems like shocks and fire hazards.

Some of the safety precautions are listed below :

1) Insulation of the conductors used must be proper and in good condition. If it is not so the current carried by the conductors may leak out. The person coming in contact with such faulty insulated conductors may receive a shock.

2) Megger tests should be conducted and insulation must be checked. With the help of megger all the tests discussed above must be performed, on the new wiring before starting use of it.

3) Earth connection should be always maintained in proper condition.

4) Make the mains supply switch off and remove the fuses before starting work with any installation.

5) Fuses must have correct ratings.

6) Use rubber soled shoes while working. Use some wooden supper under the feet. this removes the contact with the earth.

7) Use rubber gloves while touching any terminals or removing insulation layer from a conductor.

8) Use a line tester to check whether a 'live' terminal carries any current still better method is to use a test lamp.

9) Always use insulated screw drivers, pilers, line testers etc.

10) Never touch two different terminals at the same time.

11) Never remove the plug by pulling the wires connected to it.

12) The sockets should be fixed at a height beyond the reach of the children.

Review Question

1. *State the various safety precautions to be observed while using electric supply.*

6.5 Electric Shock

A sudden agitation of the nervous system of a body, due to the passage of an electric current is called an **electric shock**.

The factors affecting the severity of the shock are,

1. Magnitude of current passed through the body.

2. Path of the current passed through the body.

3. Time for which the current is passed through the body.

4. Frequency of the current.

5. Physical and psychological condition of the affected person.

The Table 6.5.1 shows an electric shock effect chart.

250 V supply current	Resistance of body	Condition of body	Effect due to shock
About 2.5 mA	10 - 600 kΩ	Dry skin	Mild shock
About 25 mA	1 kΩ	Wet skin	Strong painful shock, stoppage of breathing, possible death
More than 25 mA	Few hundred ohms	Wet skin making fair contact with earth	Ventricular fibrillation, stoppage of breathing, muscular contraction, death

Table 6.5.1

Key Point *Thus it is necessary to avoid the electric shocks.*

6.5.1 Elementary First Aid against Shock

The first aid can save the life and reduce severity of the accidents. Hence elementary first aid is important. The first aid against an electric shock involves following steps,

1. Do not panic.

2. Carry the affected person and lay him in a comfortable position and call the doctor immediately.

3. Look for stoppage of breathing.

4. Start giving him artificial respiration if breathing is stopped.

5. Never give anything to the person to drink when the person is unconscious.

6. The artificial respiration should be continued for longer time.

7. The burns caused due to electric flashes should be covered with sterile dressing and then bandaged.

8. Do not make crowd round and let patient get the fresh air.

Following Table gives the probable effects of shock under various operating conditions and voltages.

Sr. No.	Condition of Body	Body Resistance in ohms	100 V		500 V		10,000 V	
			Current (Amp)	Effect	Current (Amp)	Effect	Current (Amp)	Effect
1	Totally wet	1000	0.1	Slight burns. Death certain.	0.5	Burns. Death probable.	10	Severe burns but may survive.
2.	Dry	100000	0.001	No burns and very light shock.	0.005	Light shock with no burns.	0.1	Death sure but slight burns.
3.	Neither dry nor wet	5000	0.02	Painful shock but no injury or burns.	0.1	Death certain with slight burns.	2	Severe burns but may survive.

Review Questions

1. *What is electric shock ? Which factors affect the severity of the shock ?*
2. *Explain the elementary first aid against an electric shock.*

6.6 Safety Rules

Following are few of the safety rules must be observed while dealing with electricity.

1) All the electrical supply lines shall be sufficient in power and size and of sufficient mechanical strength for the work.

2) All electric supply lines, wires, fittings and apparatus at a consumer's premises should be in a safe condition and in all respects fit for supplying energy.

3) The underground cable must be properly insulated and protected under all the ordinary operating conditions.

4) A suitable earthed terminal should be provided by supplier on the consumer's premises.

5) The bare conductors, if any are ensured that they are inaccessible.

6) The conductor or apparatus, before handled by any person proper precaution is taken by earthing or suitable means to discharge electrically.

7) No person shall work on any live electric supply line or apparatus and no person shall assist such person.

8) Flexible cables shall not be used for portable or transportable motors, generators, transformers, rectifiers, electric drills, welding sets etc. unless they are heavily insulated and adequately protected from mechanical injury.

9) When a.c. and d.c. circuits are installed on the same supports they shall be so arranged and protected that they shall not come into contact with each other when live.

10) First aid boxes must be provided and maintained at generating stations and substations.

11) Fire buckets filled with clean dry sand and ready for immediate use for extinguishing fires.

12) Instructions in English, Hindi and any local languages for the restoration of person suffering from electric shock must be affixed in generating station and substation at a suitable place.

13) Each installation is periodically inspected and tested.

14) The neutral conductor of a three phase four wire system shall be earthed by not less than two separate and distinct connections with the earth both at generating station and at substation.

Review Question

1. *State the various safety rules to be observed while dealing with electricity.*

6.7 Short Answered and Objective Type Questions

Q.1   *A conductor used to connect electrical equipment to earth is called _____.*
                                        (Ans. : earth electrode)

Q.2   *In plate earthing, the plate is made up of _____.*   **(Ans. : copper or galvanized iron)**

Q.3   *The pit are a around the plate or pipe is filled with mixture of _____.*
                                        (Ans. : salt and coal)

Q.4   *State the various methods of earthing.*

Ans. : i) Plate earthing   ii) Pipe earthing   iii) Rod earthing   iv) Horizontal strip earthing v) Earthing through water main.

Q.5   *What is important advantage of pipe earthing over plate earthing ?*

Ans. : In pipe earthing, the earth wires are connected to pipe above the ground level and can be physically inspected from time to time. In plate earthing, the earthing wires are connected to plate below the ground hence can not be physically inspected. If earthing wires are disconnected, in plate earthing it can not be known easily and may lead to losses under fault conditions.

Q.6   State any four safety precautions to be taken while using electricity.
(Refer section 6.4)

Q.7   State the factors affecting electric shock. **(Refer section 6.5)**

Q.8   State any 4 uses of earthing. **(Refer section 6.2.1)**

Q.9   The earthing of electrical equipment brings the body of equipments to _____ voltage.

a) 100 V   b) 230 V   c) zero   d) infinite **(Ans. : c)**

Q.10   Under single earth fault, in ungrounded neutral system, the voltage of healthy phases increases by factor _____.

a) 2   b) $\sqrt{3}$ c) $\sqrt{2}$ d) 3   **(Ans. : b)**

Q.11   In plate earthing, the plate is embedded _____ feet into the ground.

a) 10   b) 50   c) 1   d) 22.5   **(Ans. : a)**

Q.12   According to Indian standard the pipe should be placed at a depth of _____ metres in pipe earthing.

a) 3   b) 10   c) 2   d) 4.75   **(Ans. : d)**

Q.13   A good earthing should provide _____ resistance in earthing path.

a) low   b) high   c) medium   d) none of these.
(Ans. : a)

Q.14   The earth wire should be _____ .

a) good conductor of electricity   b) mechanically strong
c) both (a) and (b)
d) mechanically strong but bad conductor of electricity.   **(Ans. : a)**

Q.15   The resistance of the earthing wire is _____.

a) very high   b) moderate   c) very small   d) none of these
(Ans. : c)

Q.16   The current causing an electric shock is called _____current.

a) skin   b) leakage   c) insulating   d) none of these
(Ans. : b)

Q.17   For the current levels of about _____, person with dry skin gets a mild shock.
a) 2.5 A   b) 1.5 mA   c) 100 mA   d) 2.5 mA **(Ans. : d)**

Q.18   Coke can be used as a sandwich between salt of an earthing system, to _____ .

a) by pass the current   b) avoid melting of the salt
c) improve conductivity   d) to hole moisture content.   **(Ans. : c)**

□□□

Notes

7 Magnetic Circuits

Syllabus

Magnetic circuit concepts, Analogy between electric and magnetic circuits, B-H curve, Hysteresis and eddy current losses, Mutual coupling with dot convention, Magnetic circuit calculations.

Contents

7.1 Magnet and its Properties

Magnet is a piece of solid body which possesses property of attracting iron and some other metal pieces.

i) When such a magnet is rolled into iron pieces it will be observed that iron pieces cling to it as shown in Fig. 7.1.1.

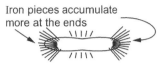

Iron pieces accumulate more at the ends

Fig. 7.1.1 Natural magnet

The maximum iron pieces accumulate at the two ends of the magnet while very few accumulate at the centre of the magnet.

The points at which the iron pieces accumulate maximum are called **Poles** of the magnet while imaginary line joining these poles is called **Axis** of the magnet.

ii) When such magnet is suspended freely by a piece of silk fibre, it turns and always adjusts itself in the direction of North and South of the earth.

The pole which adjusts itself in the direction of North is called North seeking or **North (N) pole**, while the pole which points in the direction of South is called South seeking or **South (S) pole**. Such freely suspended magnet is shown in the Fig. 7.1.2.

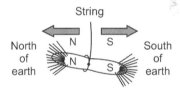

String

North of earth

South of earth

Fig. 7.1.2 Freely suspended

iii) When a magnet is placed near an iron or steel piece, its property of attraction gets transferred to iron or steel piece. Such transfer of property of attraction is also possible by actually rubbing the pole of magnet on an iron or steel piece. Such property is called **magnetic induction**.

iv) An ordinary piece of magnetic material when brought near to any pole N or S gets attracted towards the pole. But if another magnet is brought near the magnet such that two like poles ('N' and 'N' or 'S' and 'S'), it shows a repulsion in between them while if two unlike poles are brought near, it shows a force of attraction.

Key Point *Like poles repel each other and the unlike poles attract each other. Repulsion is the sure test of magnetism as ordinary piece of magnetic material always shows attraction towards both the poles.*

v) If the magnet is broken at any point, each piece behaves like an independent magnet with two poles to each, 'N' and 'S'.

vi) Some materials continues to show magnetism though magnetizing force is removed. They retain magnetism for some time. The power of retaining magnetism after the magnetizing force is removed is called **retentivity**. The time for which material retains such magnetism in absence of magnetizing force depends on its retentivity.

1. *State the various properties of a magnet.*

7.2 Laws of Magnetism

There are two fundamental laws of magnetism which are as follows :

Law 1 : It states that like magnetic poles repel and unlike poles attract each other.

Law 2 : This law is experimentally proved by Scientist Coulomb and hence also known as Coulomb's Law. It states that, the force (F) exerted by one pole on the other pole is,

a) Directly proportional to the product of the pole strengths,

b) Inversely proportional to the square of the distance between them, and

c) Nature of medium surrounding the poles.

Mathematically this law can be expressed as,

$$F \propto \frac{M_1 M_2}{d^2}$$

where M_1 and M_2 are pole strengths of the poles while d is distance between the poles.

$$\therefore \quad F = \frac{K M_1 M_2}{d^2} \quad \text{where K depends on the surroundings and called permeability}$$

Review Question

1. *State the laws of magnetism.*

7.3 Magnetic Field　　　　　2009-10

Magnet has its influence on the surrounding medium. The region around a magnet within which the influence of the magnet can be experienced is called **magnetic field**.

Existence of such field can be experienced with the help of compass needle, iron or pieces of metals or by bringing another magnet in vicinity of a magnet.

7.3.1 Magnetic Lines of Force

The magnetic field of magnet is represented by imaginary lines around it which are called **magnetic lines of force.** Note that these lines have no physical existence, these are purely imaginary and were introduced by **Michael Faraday** to get the visualization of distribution of such lines of force.

A line of force can be defined as, consider the isolated N pole (we cannot separate the pole but imagine to explain line of force) and it is allowed to move freely, in a magnetic field. Then path along which it moves is called **line of force**. Its direction always from N-pole towards S-pole. The lines of force for a bar magnet and U-shaped magnet are shown in the Fig. 7.3.1.

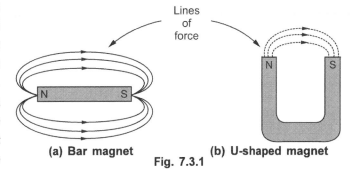

(a) Bar magnet   **(b) U-shaped magnet**

Fig. 7.3.1

7.3.2 Properties of Lines of Force

1) Lines of force are always originating on a N-pole and terminating on a S-pole, external to the magnet.

2) Each line forms a **closed loop** as shown in the Fig. 7.3.2.

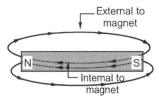

Fig. 7.3.2 Lines of force complete the closed path

Key Point *This means that a line emerging from N-pole, continues upto S-pole **external to the magnet** while it is assumed to continue from S-pole to N-pole **internal to the magnet** completing a closed loop. Such lines internal to the magnet are called as **lines of induction.***

3) Lines of force never intersect each other.

4) The lines of force, are like stretched rubberbands and always try to contract in length.

5) The lines of force, which are parallel and travelling in the same direction repel each other.

6) Magnetic lines of force always prefer a path offering least opposition.

Key Point *The opposition by the material to the flow of lines of force is called reluctance. Air has more reluctance while magnetic materials like iron, steel etc. have low reluctance. Thus magnetic lines of force can easily pass through iron or steel but cannot pass easily through the air.*

Review Question

1. *What are magnetic lines of force ? State its properties.*   **2009-10, Marks 3**

7.4 Magnetic Flux (ϕ)

The total number of lines of force existing in a particular magnetic field is called **magnetic flux**. Lines of force can be called **lines of magnetic flux**.

The flux is denoted by symbol (ϕ) and its unit is **weber** is denoted as **Wb**.

$\therefore$
$$1 \text{ weber} = 10^8 \text{ lines of force}$$

Review Question

1. Define magnetic flux and state its units.

7.5 Pole Strength

Every pole has a capacity to radiate or accept certain number of magnetic lines of force i.e. magnetic flux which is called its **strength**.

Pole strength is measurable quantity assigned to poles which depends on the force between the poles. If two poles are exerting equal force on one other, they are said to have equal pole strengths.

Unit of pole strength is **weber** as pole strength is directly related to flux i.e. lines of force.

Key Point *A unit pole may be defined as that pole which when placed from an identical pole at a distance of 1 metre in free space experiences a force of $\dfrac{10^7}{16\pi^2}$ newtons.*

So when we say Unit N-pole, it means a pole is having a pole strength of 1 weber.

Review Question

1. Define unit pole.

7.6 Magnetic Flux Density (B)   2009-10

It can be defined as 'The flux per unit area (a) in a plane at right angles to the flux is known as '**flux density**'. Mathematically,

$\therefore$
$$B = \frac{\phi}{a} \quad \frac{Wb}{m^2} \text{ or Tesla}$$

It is shown in the Fig. 7.6.1.

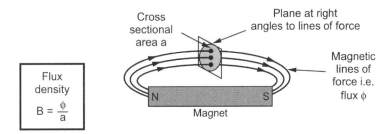

Fig. 7.6.1 Concept of magnetic flux density

Key Point *The unit of flux density is Wb/m², also called **tesla** denoted as **T**.*

Review Question

　　1. *Define magnetic flux density and state its unit.*　　　　　2009-10, Marks 3

7.7 Magnetic Field Strength (H)

This gives quantitative measure of strongness or weakness of the magnetic field. Note that pole strength and magnetic field strength are different.

The force experienced by a unit N-pole (i.e. N pole with 1 Wb of pole strength) when placed at any point in a magnetic field is known as **magnetic field strength** at that point.

It is denoted by H and its unit is **newtons per weber i.e. (N/Wb) or amperes per metre (A/m) or ampere turns per metre (AT/m).**

The mathematical expression for calculating magnetic field strength is,

$$\therefore \quad H = \frac{\text{Ampere turns}}{\text{Length}} = \frac{NI}{l} \ \text{AT} / m$$

Key Point *More the value of 'H', more stronger is the magnetic field. This is also called **magnetic field intensity**.*

Review Question

　　1. *Define magnetic field strength and state its units.*

7.8 Magnetic Effect of an Electric Current (Electromagnets)

When a coil or a conductor carries a current, it produces the magnetic flux around it. Then it starts behaving as a magnet. Such a current carrying coil or conductor is called an **electromagnet.** This is due to magnetic effect of an electric current.

If such a coil is wound around a piece of magnetic material like iron or steel and carries current then piece of material around which the coil is wound, starts behaving as a magnet, which is called an electromagnet.

The flux produced and the flux density can be controlled by controlling the magnitude the current.

The direction and shape of the magnetic field around the coil or conductor depends on the direction of current and shape of the conductor through which it is passing.

7.8.1 Magnetic Field due to Straight Conductor

When a straight conductor carries a current, it produces a magnetic field all along its length. The lines of force are in the form of concentric circles in the planes right angles to the conductor. This can be demonstrated by a small experiment.

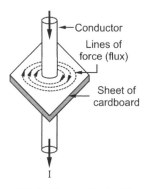

Consider a straight conductor carrying a current, passing through a sheet of cardboard as shown in the Fig. 7.8.1.

Sprinkle iron fillings on the cardboard. Small tapping on the cardboard causes the iron filling to set themselves, in the concentric circular pattern.

Fig. 7.8.1 Magnetic field due to a straight conductor

The direction of the magnetic flux can be determined by placing compass needle near the conductor. This direction depends on the direction of the current passing through the conductor.

For the current direction shown in the Fig. 7.8.1 i.e. from top to bottom the direction of flux is clockwise around the conductor.

Conventionally such current carrying conductor is represented by small circle, (top view of conductor shown in the Fig. 7.8.1). Then current through such conductor will either come out of paper or will go into the plane of the paper.

Key Point *When current is going **into the plane of the paper**, i.e. away from observer, it is represented by a 'cross', inside the circle indicating the conductors.*

The cross indicates rear view of feathered end of an arrow.

Key Point *The current flowing towards the observer i.e.* **coming out of the plane of the paper** *is represented by a 'dot' inside the circle.*

The dot indicates front view i.e. tip of an arrow. This is shown in the Fig. 7.8.2.

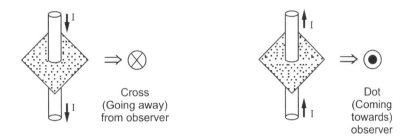

(a) **Current into the paper**   (b) **Current out of the paper**

Fig. 7.8.2 Cross and Dot convention

1) Right Hand Thumb Rule :

It states that, hold the current carrying conductor in the right hand such that the thumb pointing in the direction of current and parallel to the conductor, then curled fingers point in the direction of the magnetic field or flux around it.

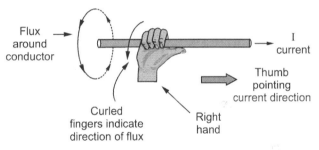

Fig. 7.8.3 Right hand thumb rule

The Fig. 7.8.3 explains the rule.

Let us apply this rule to the conductor passing through card sheet considered earlier. This can be explained by the Fig. 7.8.4.

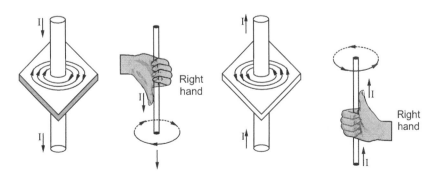

Fig. 7.8.4 Direction of magnetic lines by right hand thumb rule

Conventionally it is shown as in the Fig. 7.8.5.

(a) Clockwise   **(b) Anticlockwise**
Fig. 7.8.5 Representation of direction of flux

2) Corkscrew Rule :

Imagine a right handed screw to be along the conductor carrying current with its axis parallel to the conductor and tip pointing in the direction of the current flow.

Then the direction of the magnetic field is given by the direction in which the screw must be turned so as to advance in the direction of the current.

This is shown in the Fig. 7.8.6.

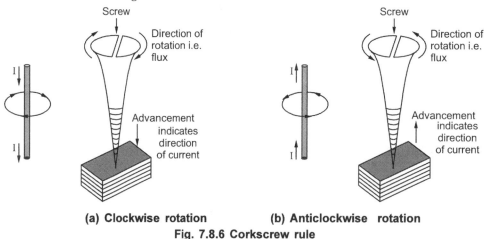

(a) Clockwise rotation   **(b) Anticlockwise rotation**
Fig. 7.8.6 Corkscrew rule

7.8.2 Magnetic Field due to Circular Conductor i.e. Solenoid

A **solenoid** is an arrangement in which long conductor is wound with number of turns close together to form a coil. The axial length of conductor is much more than the diameter of turns.

The part or element around which the conductor is wound is called as **core** of the solenoid. Core may be air or may be some magnetic material.

Solenoid with a steel or iron core in shown in Fig. 7.8.7 (a).

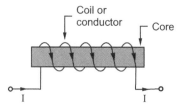

Fig. 7.8.7 (a) Solenoid

When such conductor is excited by the supply so that it carries a current then it produces a magnetic field which acts through the coil along its axis and also around the solenoid.

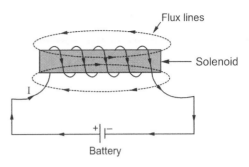

Fig. 7.8.7 (b) Flux around a solenoid

The pattern of the flux around the solenoid is shown in the Fig. 7.8.7 (b).

Instead of using a straight core to wound the conductor, a circular core also can be used to wound the conductor. In such case the resulting solenoid is called **Toroid**.

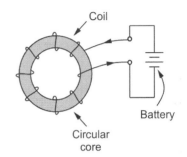

Fig. 7.8.8 Toroid

The rules to determine the direction of flux and poles of the magnet formed :

1) The right hand thumb rule :

Hold the solenoid in the right hand such that curled fingers point in the direction of the current through the curled conductor, then the outstretched thumb along the axis of the solenoid point to the **North pole** of the solenoid or point the direction of flux lines **inside the core.** This is shown in Fig. 7.8.9.

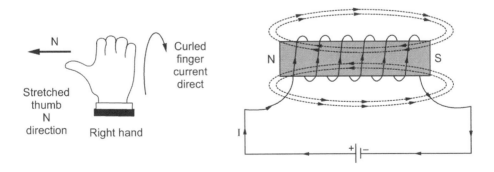

Fig. 7.8.9 Direction of flux around a solenoid

If the direction of winding or direction of current is reversed then the positions of N and S poles also get reversed.

In case of toroid, the core is circular and right hand thumb rule can be used as shown in the Fig. 7.8.10 (a) and (b).

In the Fig. 7.8.10 (a), corresponding to direction of winding, the flux set in the core is anticlockwise while in the Fig. 7.8.10 (b) due to direction of winding, the direction of flux set in the core is clockwise.

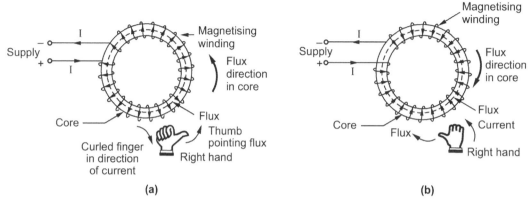

Fig. 7.8.10 Use of right hand thumb rule for toroid

The winding is also called **magnetising winding** or **magnetising coil** as it magnetises the core.

2) Corkscrew rule : If axis of the screw is placed along the axis of the solenoid and if screw is turned in the direction of the current, then it travels towards the **N-pole** or in the direction of the magnetic field **inside** the solenoid.

Review Questions

1. *What is electromagnet ?*
2. *Explain the magnetic field due to straight conductor. Explain the cross and dot convention.*
3. *Explain the right hand thumb rule and cork screw rule used to determine direction of flux around a conductor.*
4. *What is solenoid and toroid ? How to apply right hand thumb rule for the soenoids and toroids ?*

7.9 Permeability

The flow of flux produced by the magnet not only depends on the magnetic field strength but also related to the medium in which magnet is placed. The force exerted by one magnetic pole on other depends on the medium in which magnets are placed.

Key Point *The* **permeability** *is defined as the ability or ease with which the magnetic material forces the magnetic flux through a given medium.*

For any magnetic material, there are two permeabilities,

    i) Absolute permeability   ii) Relative permeability.

7.9.1 Absolute Permeability (μ)

The magnetic field strength (H) decides the flux density (B) to be produced by the magnet around it, in a given medium.

The ratio of magnetic flux density B in a particular medium (other than vacuum or air) to the magnetic field strength H producing that flux density is called **absolute permeability** of that medium.

It is denoted by μ and mathematically can be expressed as,

$$\therefore \qquad \mu = \frac{B}{H} \qquad \text{i.e.} \quad B = \mu H$$

The permeability is measured in units **henries per metre** denoted as **H/m**.

7.9.2 Permeability of Free Space or Vacuum (μ$_0$)

If the magnet is placed in a free space or vacuum or in air then the ratio of flux density B and magnetic field strength H is called **Permeability of free space** or **Vacuum** or **air**.

It is denoted as μ$_0$ and measured in **H/m**. It denotes the ease with which the magnetic flux permeates the free space or vacuum or air.

It is experimentally found that this μ$_0$ i.e. ratio of B and H in vacuum remains constant every where in the vacuum and its value is $4\pi \times 10^{-7}$ H/m.

$$\therefore \qquad \mu_0 = \frac{B}{H} \text{ in vacuum } = 4\pi \times 10^{-7} \text{ H/m}$$

Key Point *For a magnetic material, the absolute permeability μ is not constant. This is because B and H bears a nonlinear relation in case of magnetic materials. If magnetic field strength is increased, there is change in flux density B but not exactly proportional to the increase in H. **The ratio B to H is constant only for free space, vacuum or air .***

7.9.3 Relative Permeability (μ$_r$)

Generally the permeability of different magnetic materials is defined relative to the permeability of free space (μ$_0$).

The **relative permeability** is defined as the ratio of flux density produced in a medium (other than free space) to the flux density produced in free space, under the influence of same magnetic field strength and under identical conditions.

Thus if the magnetic field strength is H which is producing flux density B in the medium while flux density B$_0$ in free space then the relative permeability is defined as,

$$\therefore \quad \boxed{\mu_r = \frac{B}{B_0}} \quad \text{where H is same.}$$

It is dimensionless and has no units.

For free space, vacuum or air, $\mu_r = 1$

According to definition of absolute permeability we can write for given H,

$$\mu = \frac{B}{H} \quad \text{in medium} \quad ...(7.9.1) \quad \text{and} \quad \mu_0 = \frac{B_0}{H} \quad \text{in free space} \quad ...(7.9.2)$$

Dividing (7.9.1) and (7.9.2) , $\quad \frac{\mu}{\mu_0} = \frac{B}{B_0} \quad$ but $\quad \frac{B}{B_0} = \mu_r \quad$ i.e. $\quad \frac{\mu}{\mu_0} = \mu_r$

$$\therefore \quad \boxed{\mu = \mu_0 \mu_r \ \ H/m}$$

The relative permeability of metals like iron, steel varies from 100 to 100,000

Key Point *If we require maximum flux production for the lesser magnetic field strength then the value of the relative permeability of the core material should be as high as possible.*

Review Questions

1. *Define permeability.*
2. *Define absolute permeability. State its units.*
3. *Define permeablity of free space and state its units.*
4. *What is relative permeability ?*

7.10 Magnetomotive Force (M.M.F. or F)

The flow of electrons is current which is basically due to electromotive force (e.m.f.). Similarly the force behind the flow of flux or production of flux in a magnetic circuit is called magnetomotive force (m.m.f.) The m.m.f. determines the magnetic field strength. It is the driving force behind the magnetic circuit.

It is given by the product of the number of turns of the magnetizing coil and the current passing through it. Mathematically it can be expressed as,

$$\boxed{\text{m. m. f.} = N \, I \quad \text{ampere turns}}$$

where   N = Number of turns of magnetising coil   and   I = Current through coil

Its unit is **ampere turns (AT) or amperes (A)**. It is also defined as the work done in joules on a unit magnetic pole in taking it once round a closed magnetic circuit.

Review Question

> 1. *Explain the concept of magnetomotive force and state its units.*

7.11 Reluctance (S)

In an electric circuit, current flow is opposed by the resistance of the material, similarly there is opposition by the material to the flow of flux which is called **reluctance**

It is defined as the resistance offered by the material to the flow of magnetic flux through it. It is denoted by 'S'.

It is directly proportional to the length of the magnetic circuit while inversely proportional to the area of cross-section.

$$S \propto \frac{l}{a} \quad \text{where' } l \text{' in ' m ' while ' a ' in ' m}^2 \text{'}$$

$$\therefore \quad S = \frac{Kl}{a}$$

where $\quad$ K = Constant = Reciprocal of absolute permeability of material $= \dfrac{1}{\mu}$

$$\therefore \quad \boxed{S = \frac{l}{\mu a} = \frac{l}{\mu_0 \mu_r a} \quad A/Wb}$$

It is measured in **amperes per weber (A/Wb)** or **ampere-turns per weber (AT/Wb).**

As in the electric circuit the resistance is the ratio of e.m.f. and the current, in magnetic circuit the reluctance can be expressed as the ratio of magnetomotive force to the flux produced.

$$\therefore \quad \text{Reluctance} = \frac{m.m.f}{flux} \quad \text{i.e.} \quad \boxed{S = \frac{NI}{\phi} \quad AT/Wb \ \text{ or } \ A/Wb}$$

7.11.1 Permeance

The **permeance** of the magnetic circuit is defined as the reciprocal of the reluctance.

It is defined as the property of the magnetic circuit due to which it allows flow of the magnetic flux through it.

$$\therefore \quad \boxed{\text{Permeance} = \frac{1}{\text{Reluctance}}}$$

It is measured in **weber per amperes (Wb/A).**

Review Questions

1. *What is reluctance ? Obtain its expression and state its units.*
2. *Define permeance and state its units.*

7.12 Magnetic Circuits   2001-02, 2007-08

The **magnetic circuit** can be defined as, the closed path traced by the magnetic lines of force i.e. flux. Such a magnetic circuit is associated with different magnetic quantities as m.m.f., flux reluctance, permeability etc. Consider simple magnetic circuit shown in the Fig. 7.12.1 (a). This circuit consists of an iron core with cross-sectional area of 'a' m^2 with a mean length of 'l' m. (This is mean length of the magnetic path which flux is going to trace.)

A coil of N turns is wound on one of the sides of the square core which is excited by a supply. This supply drives a current I through the coil. This current carrying coil produces the flux (ϕ) which completes its path through the core as shown in the Fig. 7.12.1 (a).

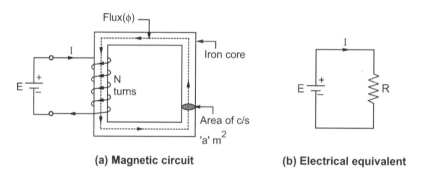

(a) Magnetic circuit   (b) Electrical equivalent

Fig. 7.12.1

This is analogous to simple electric circuit in which a supply i.e. e.m.f. of E volts drives a current I which completes its path through a closed conductor having resistance R. This analogous electrical circuit is shown in the Fig. 7.12.1 (b).

Relationship between m.m.f., flux and reluctance :

I = Current flowing through the coil, N = Number of turns, ϕ = Flux in webers

B = Flux density in the core, μ = Absolute permeability of the magnetic material

μ_r = Relative permeability of the magnetic material

Magnetic field strength inside the solenoid is given by,

$$H = \frac{NI}{l} \quad AT/m \qquad \qquad \dots (7.12.1)$$

Now flux density is, $\qquad B = \mu H = \dfrac{\mu_0 \mu_r N I}{l} \quad Wb/m^2 \qquad$ ... (7.12.2)

Now as area of cross-section is 'a ' m^2 , total flux in core is,

$$\phi = B a = \dfrac{\mu_0 \mu_r N I a}{l} \quad Wb \qquad \qquad ... (7.12.3)$$

Thus, $\qquad \boxed{\phi = \dfrac{NI}{\dfrac{l}{\mu_0 \mu_r a}} = \dfrac{m.m.f.}{reluctance}} \qquad$ where NI = Magnetomotive force m.m.f. in AT

$$S = \dfrac{l}{\mu_0 \mu_r a} = \text{Reluctance offered by the magnetic path.}$$

This expression of the flux is very much similar to expression for current in electric circuit.

Key Point *So current is analogous to the flux, e.m.f. is analogous to the m.m.f. and reluctance is analogous to the reluctance.*

Example 7.12.1 *A coil of 2000 turns is wound uniformly over a nonmagnetic ring of mean circumference of 80 cm and cross sectional area of 0.6 sq.cm. If the current through the coil is 2 A, calculate : i) Magnetising force   ii) Reluctance   iii) Total flux and iv) Flux density.*

Solution : $a = 0.6 \ cm^2 = 0.6 \times 10^{-4} \ m^2, \ l = 80 \ cm, \ N = 2000, \ I = 2 \ A, \ \mu_r = 1.$

i) Magnetising force, $\quad H = \dfrac{NI}{l} = \dfrac{2000 \times 2}{80 \times 10^{-2}} = \textbf{5000 AT/m}$

ii) Reluctance, $\quad S = \dfrac{l}{\mu_0 \mu_r a} = \dfrac{80 \times 10^{-2}}{4 \pi \times 10^{-7} \times 1 \times 0.6 \times 10^{-4}} = \textbf{1.061} \times \textbf{10}^{\textbf{10}} \ \textbf{AT / Wb}$

iii) Flux, $\qquad \phi = \dfrac{NI}{S} = \dfrac{2000 \times 2}{1.061 \times 10^{10}} = \textbf{0.377} \ \boldsymbol{\mu}\textbf{Wb}$

iv) Flux density, $B = \dfrac{\phi}{a} = \dfrac{0.377 \times 10^{-6}}{0.6 \times 10^{-4}} = \textbf{6.2833} \times \textbf{10}^{\textbf{-3}} \ \textbf{Wb/m}^{\textbf{2}}$

Example 7.12.2 *A coil of insulated wire of 500 turns and of resistance 4 Ω is closely wound on an iron ring. The ring has a mean diameter 0.25 m and a uniform cross sectional area of 700 mm^2. Calculate the total flux in the ring when a d.c. supply of 6 V is applied to the ends of the winding. Assume a relative permeability of 550.*   **2001-02, Marks 5**

Solution : $d_{mean} = 0.25$ m, $\mu_r = 550$

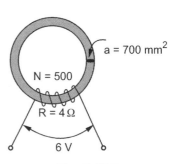

a = 700 mm²

N = 500

R = 4 Ω

6 V

Fig. 7.12.2

∴ $\quad l_i = \pi \times d_{mean} = 0.7854$ m

∴ $\quad S = \dfrac{l_i}{\mu_0 \mu_r a} = \dfrac{0.7854}{4\pi \times 10^{-7} \times 550 \times 700 \times 10^{-6}}$

$\quad\quad = 1.62338 \times 10^6$ AT/Wb

m.m.f. $= NI$ and $I = V/R = 6/4 = 1.5$ A

∴ $\quad$ m.m.f. $= 500 \times 1.5 = 750$ AT

∴ $\quad \phi = \dfrac{m.m.f.}{S} = \dfrac{750}{1.62338 \times 10^6} = \mathbf{462\ \mu Wb}$

Example 7.12.3 *A ring of ferromagnetic material has a circular cross-section. The inner diameter is 7.4 inch, the outer diameter is 9 inch and the thickness is 0.8 inch. There is a coil of 600 turns wound on the ring. When the coil carries a current of 2.5 A, the flux produced in the ring is 1.2×10^{-3} Wb. Find : i) Magnetic field intensity ii) Reluctance iii) Permeability.* **2007-08, Marks 10**

Solution : The ring is shown in the Fig. 7.12.3.

$\quad$ m.m.f. $= NI = 600 \times 2.5 = 1500$ AT

Mean diameter $= \dfrac{Outer + Inner}{2} = \dfrac{9 + 7.4}{2} = 8.2$ inch

$\boxed{1\ inch = 2.54\ cm}$

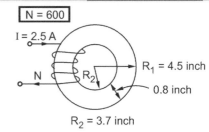

N = 600

I = 2.5 A

N

R_2

R_1 = 4.5 inch

0.8 inch

R_2 = 3.7 inch

Fig. 7.12.3

∴ $\quad$ Mean diameter $= 8.2 \times 2.54 = 20.828$ cm

∴ $\quad l =$ Iron length $= \pi \times$ (Mean diameter) $= 65.4331$ cm

Thickness $=$ Cross-sectional diameter $= 0.8 \times 2.54 = 2.032$ cm

∴ $\quad a = \dfrac{\pi}{4} \times d^2 = \dfrac{\pi}{4} \times (2.032)^2 = 3.2429$ cm²

i) $\quad H = \dfrac{NI}{l} = \dfrac{1500}{65.4331 \times 10^{-2}} = \mathbf{2292.4177\ AT/m}$

ii) $\quad S = \dfrac{l}{\mu_0 \mu_r a} = \dfrac{65.4331 \times 10^{-2}}{4\pi \times 10^{-7} \times \mu_r \times 3.2429 \times 10^{-4}} = \dfrac{1.60566 \times 10^9}{\mu_r}$ AT/Wb

iii) $\quad \phi = \dfrac{m.m.f.}{Reluctance} = \dfrac{NI}{S}$

∴ $\quad 1.2 \times 10^{-3} = \dfrac{1500}{\dfrac{1.60566 \times 10^9}{\mu_r}}$ $\quad$ i.e. $\quad \mu_r = \dfrac{1.2 \times 10^{-3} \times 1.60566 \times 10^9}{1500}$

∴ $\quad \mu_r = \mathbf{1284.529}$

Review Questions

1. *What is magnetic circuit ? Derive the relation between m.m.f., flux and reluctance from it.*

2. *A coil is wound uniformly with 300 turns over a steel of relative permiability 900, having a mean circumference of 40 mm and cross-sectional area of 50 mm^2. If a current of 5 A is passed through the coil, find i) m.m.f.   ii) reluctance of the ring and   iii) flux*
   [Ans. : 1500 AT, 70.7355×10^3 AT/Wb, 21.2057 mWb]

3. *An iron ring has its mean length of flux path as 60 cm and its cross-sectional areas as 15 cm^2. Its relative permeability is 500. Find the current required to be passed, through a coil of 300 turns wound uniformly around it, to produce a flux density of 1.2 tesla. What would be the flux density with the same current, if the iron ring is replaced by air-core ?*
   [Ans. : 3.8197 A, 2.4×10^{-3} T or Wb/m^2]

4. *An iron ring of 20 cm mean diameter and 10 cm^2 cross-section is magnetised by a coil of 500 turns. The current through the coil is 8 A. The relative permeability of iron is 500. Find the flux density inside the ring.*   **(Ans. : 4 Wb/m^2)**

7.13 Series Magnetic Circuits

In practice magnetic circuit may be composed of various materials of different permeabilities, of different lengths and of different cross-sectional areas. Such a circuit is called **composite** magnetic circuit. When such parts are connected one after the other the circuit is called **series magnetic circuit**.

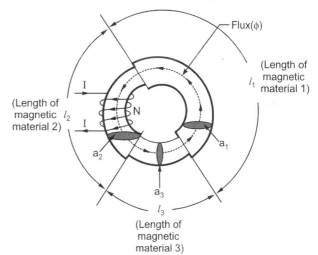

Consider a circular ring made up of different materials of lengths l_1, l_2 and l_3 and with cross-sectional areas a_1, a_2 and a_3 with absolute permeabilities μ_1, μ_2 and μ_3 as shown in the Fig. 7.13.1.

Let coil wound on ring has N turns carrying a current of I amperes.

The total m.m.f. available is = NI AT

Fig. 7.13.1 A series magnetic circuit

This will set the flux 'ϕ' which is same through all the three elements of the circuit.

This is similar to three resistances connected in series in electrical circuit and connected to e.m.f. carrying same current 'I' through all of them.

Its analogous electric circuit can be shown as in the Fig. 7.13.2.

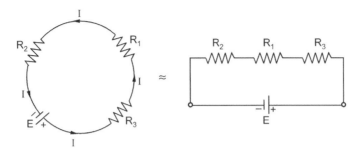

Fig. 7.13.2 Equivalent electrical circuit

The total resistance of the electric circuit is $R_1 + R_2 + R_3$. Similarly the total reluctance of the magnetic circuit is,

$$\text{Total } S_T = S_1 + S_2 + S_3 = \frac{l_1}{\mu_1 a_1} + \frac{l_2}{\mu_2 a_2} + \frac{l_3}{\mu_3 a_3}$$

$\therefore$ Total $\phi = \dfrac{\text{Total m.m.f.}}{\text{Total reluctance}} = \dfrac{NI}{S_T} = \dfrac{NI}{(S_1 + S_2 + S_3)}$

$\therefore$ $\quad NI = S_T \phi = (S_1 + S_2 + S_3) \phi$ $\quad$ i.e. $NI = S_1 \phi + S_2 \phi + S_3 \phi$

$\therefore$ Total (m.m.f.) $= (m.m.f.)_1 + (m.m.f.)_2 + (m.m.f.)_3$

The total m.m.f. also can be expressed as,

Total (m.m.f.) $= H_1 l_1 + H_2 l_2 + H_3 l_3$ where $H_1 = \dfrac{B_1}{\mu_1}$, $\quad H_2 = \dfrac{B_2}{\mu_2}$, $\quad H_3 = \dfrac{B_3}{\mu_3}$

So for a **series magnetic** circuit we can remember,

> 1) The magnetic flux through all the parts is same.
>
> 2) The equivalent reluctance is sum of the reluctances of different parts.
>
> 3) The resultant m.m.f. necessary is sum of the m.m.f.s in each individual part.

7.13.1 Series Circuit with Air Gap

The series magnetic circuit can also have a short air gap.

Key Point *This is possible because we have seen earlier that flux can pass through air also.*

Such air gap is not possible in case of electric circuit.

Consider a ring having mean length of iron part as 'l_i' as shown in the Fig. 7.13.3.

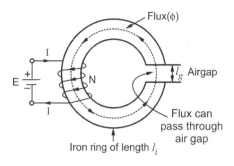

Total m.m.f = N I AT

Total reluctance $S_T = S_i + S_g$

where S_i = Reluctance of iron path

S_g = Reluctance of air gap

$$\therefore \quad S_i = \frac{l_i}{\mu\, a_i} \quad \text{and} \quad S_g = \frac{l_g}{\mu_0\, a_i}$$

Fig. 7.13.3 A ring with an air gap

Key Point *The absolute permeability of air* $\mu = \mu_0$ *as* $\mu_r = 1$ *for air.*

The cross-sectional area of air gap is assumed to be equal to area of the iron ring.

$$\therefore \quad S_T = \frac{l_i}{\mu\, a_i} + \frac{l_g}{\mu_0\, a_i} \quad \text{and} \quad \phi = \frac{\text{m.m.f.}}{\text{Reluctance}} = \frac{NI}{S_T}$$

or Total m.m.f. = m.m.f. for iron + m.m.f for air gap

$$\therefore \quad NI = S_i \phi + S_g \phi \quad \text{AT for ring.}$$

Example 7.13.1 *An iron ring of 8 cm. mean diameter is made up of round iron of diameter 1 cm and permeability of 900, has an air gap of 2 mm wide. It consists of winding with 400 turns carrying a current of 3.5 A. Determine, i) M.M.F. ii) Total reluctance iii) The flux iv) Flux density in ring.*

Solution : The ring and the winding is shown in the Fig. 7.13.4.

Diameter of ring d = 8 cm,

$\therefore$ length of iron = πd – length of air gap

$$l_i = \pi \times \left(8 \times 10^{-2}\right) - 2 \times 10^{-3}$$

$$= 0.2493 \text{ m.}$$

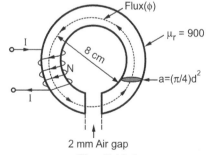

Fig. 7.13.4

Key Point *While calculating iron length, do not forget to subtract length of air gap from total mean length.*

l_g = Length of air gap

$$= 2 \text{ mm} = 2 \times 10^{-3} \text{ m}$$

$$\text{Diameter of iron} = 1 \text{ cm}$$

∴   Area of cross section, $a = \frac{\pi}{4}d^2 = \frac{\pi}{4}\left(1\times10^{-2}\right)^2 = 7.853\times10^{-5} \text{ m}^2$

Area of cross section of air gap and ring is to be assumed same.

i) Total m.m.f. produced $= N\,I = 400 \times 3.5 = \textbf{1400 AT}$ (ampere turns)

ii) Total reluctance $S_T = S_i + S_g$

$$S_i = \frac{l_i}{\mu_0\mu_r a} = \frac{0.2493}{4\pi\times10^{-7}\times900\times7.853\times10^{-5}} = 2806947.615 \text{ AT/Wb}$$

∴ $S_g = \frac{l_g}{\mu_0 a} = \frac{2\times10^{-3}}{4\pi\times10^{-7}\times7.853\times10^{-5}} = 20.2667\times10^6 \text{ AT/Wb}$ ... $\mu_r = 1$ for air

∴ $S_T = 2806947.615 + 20.2667\times10^6 = \textbf{23.0737}\times\textbf{10}^\textbf{6} \text{ \textbf{AT/Wb}}$

iii) $\phi = \frac{\text{m.m.f.}}{\text{reluctance}} = \frac{N\,I}{S_T} = \frac{1400}{23.0737\times10^6} = \textbf{6.067}\times\textbf{10}^{-\textbf{5}} \text{ \textbf{Wb}}$

iv) Flux density $= \frac{\phi}{a} = \frac{6.067\times10^{-5}}{7.853\times10^{-5}} = \textbf{0.7725 Wb / m}^\textbf{2}$

Example 7.13.2 *A wrought iron bar 30 cm long and 2 cm in diameter is bent into a circular shape as given in figure. It is then wound with 500 turns of wire. Calculate the current required to produce a flux of 0.5 mWb in magnetic circuit with an air gap of 1 mm :* μ_r *(iron)* $= 4000$ *(assume constant).*

2004-05, Marks 10

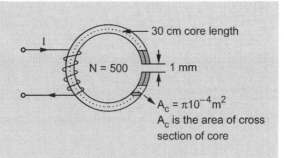

Fig. 7.13.5

Solution : $N = 500$, $\phi = 0.5$ mWb, $\mu_r = 4000$, diameter $= 2$ cm

$$A_c = \frac{\pi}{4} \times (\text{diameter})^2 = \frac{\pi}{4} \times 4 = \pi \text{ cm}^2 = \pi \times 10^{-4} \text{ m}^2$$

$$l_i = \text{Iron length} = 30 \text{ cm} - \text{Air gap} = 0.299 \text{ m}$$

$$l_g = \text{Air gap length} = 1 \text{ mm} = 1\times10^{-3} \text{ m}$$

∴ $S = S_i + S_g = \frac{l_i}{\mu_0\mu_r A_c} + \frac{l_g}{\mu_0 A_c} = \frac{1}{\mu_0 A_c}\left[\frac{l_i}{\mu_r} + l_g\right]$

$$= \frac{1}{4\pi \times 10^{-7} \times \pi \times 10^{-4}} \left[\frac{0.299}{4000} + 1 \times 10^{-3} \right] = 2.72237 \times 10^6 \ \text{AT/Wb}$$

$$\phi = \frac{\text{m.m.f.}}{\text{reluctance}} = \frac{NI}{S} \quad \text{i.e.} \quad 0.5 \times 10^{-3} = \frac{500I}{2.72237 \times 10^6}$$

∴ $I = \textbf{2.7223 A}$ ... Current required

Example 7.13.3 *A rectangular magnetic core shown in Fig. 7.13.6 has square cross-section of area 16 cm². An air gap of 2 mm is cut across one of its limbs. Find the exciting current needed in a coil having 1000 turns would on the core to create an air gap flux of 4 mWb. The relative permeability of the core is 2000.*   **2000-01, Marks 10**

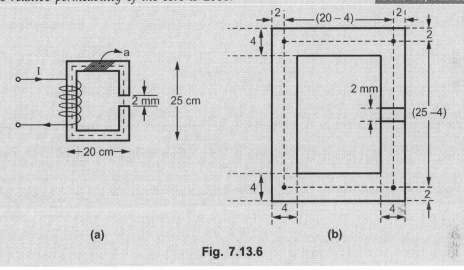

(a)   (b)

Fig. 7.13.6

Solution : $\phi = 4$ mWb, $N = 1000$, $\mu_r = 2000$, $a = 16$ cm², $l_g = 2$ mm

$$l_i = \text{Iron path} = \left\{ [20 - 4] \times 2 + [25 - 4] \times 2 - 2 \times 10^{-1} \right\} \text{cm} = 73.8 \text{ cm}$$

$$S_T = S_i + S_g = \frac{l_i}{\mu_0 \mu_r a} + \frac{l_g}{\mu_0 a} \qquad \qquad ... \mu_r = 1 \text{ for air gap}$$

$$= \frac{1}{4\pi \times 10^{-7} \times 16 \times 10^{-4}} \left[\frac{73.8 \times 10^{-2}}{2000} + \frac{2 \times 10^{-3}}{1} \right] = 1.1782 \times 10^6 \text{ AT/Wb}$$

$$\phi = \frac{\text{m.m.f.}}{S_T} = \frac{NI}{S_T} \quad \text{i.e.} \quad 4 \times 10^{-3} = \frac{1000 \times I}{1.1782 \times 10^6}$$

∴ $I = \textbf{4.713 A}$

Example 7.13.4 *An electromagnet has an air gap of 4 mm and flux density in the gap is 1.3 Wb/m². Determine the ampere turns for the gap.*   **2006-07, Marks 5**

Solution : l_g = 4 mm, B = 1.3 Wb/m^2

$$S_g = \frac{l_g}{\mu_0 a}$$ ... Reluctance of air gap

For air gap, μ_r = 1

$$\therefore \quad S_g = \frac{4\times10^{-3}}{4\pi\times10^{-7}\times a} = \frac{3183.0988}{a}$$

$$\therefore \quad \phi = \frac{m.m.f.}{S_g} = \frac{(NI)}{S_g} = \frac{(NI)}{\frac{3183.0988}{a}} = \frac{(NI)\times a}{3183.0988}$$

$$\therefore \quad \frac{\phi}{a} = \frac{(NI)}{3183.0988} \quad but \quad \frac{\phi}{a} = B = \text{Flux density}$$

$$\therefore \quad 1.3 = \frac{NI}{3183.0988} \quad i.e. \quad NI = \textbf{4138.028 AT} \quad ... \text{Required ampere-turns}$$

Example 7.13.5 *An electromagnet shown in Fig. 7.13.7 has c.s. area of 12 cm^2. Mean length of iron path is 50 cm, length of air gap is 0.4 cm. It is excited by two coils of 400 turns each at 1 A. μ_r for material is 1300. Calculate : i) Reluctance of magnetic circuit ii) Reluctance of air gap iii) Total reluctance iv) Total ϕ v) Flux density of air gap.*

2006-07, Marks 5

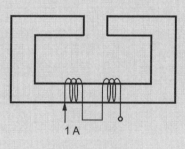

1 A

Fig. 7.13.7

Solution : a = 12 cm^2 = 12 × 10^{-4} m^2, l_i = 50 cm, l_g = 0.4 cm, μ_r = 1300

$$I = 1\ A, \quad N = 2\times400 = 800$$

$$m.m.f. = NI = 800\times1 = 800\ AT$$

i) $$S_i = \frac{l_i}{\mu_0\mu_r a} = \frac{50\times10^{-2}}{4\pi\times10^{-7}\times1300\times12\times10^{-4}} = \textbf{255.056}\times\textbf{10}^3\ \textbf{AT/Wb}$$

ii) $$S_g = \frac{l_g}{\mu_0 a} = \frac{0.4\times10^{-2}}{4\pi\times10^{-7}\times12\times10^{-4}}$$ ... μ_r = 1 for air

$$= \textbf{2.65258}\times\textbf{10}^6\ \textbf{AT/Wb}$$

iii) $S_T = S_i + S_g = 2.90763 \times 10^6$ **AT/Wb**

iv) $\phi_T = \dfrac{m.m.f.}{S_T} = \dfrac{800}{2.90763 \times 10^6} = 0.27513$ **mWb**

v) $B = \dfrac{\phi_T}{a} = \dfrac{0.27513 \times 10^{-3}}{12 \times 10^{-4}} = 0.2293$ **Wb/m²**

Example 7.13.6 *A ring is composed of three sections. The cross sectional area is 0.001 m² for each section. The mean arc lengths are, For part A = 0.3 m , For part B = 0.2 m and For part C = 0.1 m. An air-gap length of 0.1 mm is cut in the ring. The relative permeabilities for the sections A, B, C are 5000, 1000 and 10000 respectively. Flux in the air-gap is 7.5×10^{-4} Wb. Find i) mmf ii) Exciting current if the coil has 100 turns. iii) Reluctances of the sections.*

Solution : The ring is shown in the Fig. 7.13.8.

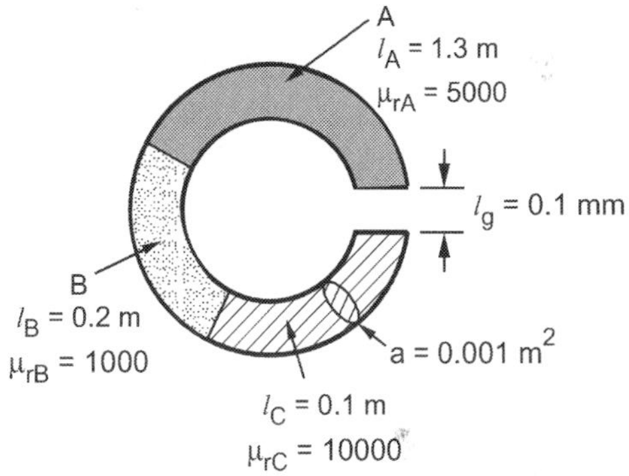

$$\phi_g = 7.5 \times 10^{-4} \text{ Wb}$$

$$N = 100$$

The given circuit is series circuit hence the flux ϕ remains same everywhere neglecting leakage. Hence B is also same.

Fig. 7.13.8

$$B = \dfrac{\phi}{a} = \dfrac{7.5 \times 10^{-4}}{0.001} = 0.75 \text{ Wb/m}^2$$

$$B = \mu_0 \mu_{rA} H_A = \mu_0 \mu_{rB} H_B = \mu_0 \mu_{rC} H_C = \mu_0 H_g$$

Note that $\mu_r = 1$ for the air gap and B is constant for the entire ring.

∴ $H_A = \dfrac{0.75}{4\pi \times 10^{-7} \times 5000} = 119.3662$ AT/m ,

$H_B = \dfrac{0.75}{4\pi \times 10^{-7} \times 1000} = 596.83103$ AT/m

∴ $H_C = \dfrac{0.75}{4\pi \times 10^{-7} \times 10000} = 59.6831$ AT/m, $H_g = \dfrac{0.75}{4\pi \times 10^{-7}} = 596831.0366$ AT/m

∴ Total m.m.f. = m.m.f for A + m.m.f for B + m.m.f for C + m.m.f. for air gap

$$= H_A \times l_A + H_B \times l_B + H_C \times l_C + H_g \times l_g$$

$$= 119.3662 \times 0.3 + 596.83103 \times 0.2 + 59.6831 \times 0.1 + 596831.0366 \times 0.1 \times 10^{-3}$$

$$= 35.8098 + 119.3662 + 5.96831 + 59.6831 = \textbf{220.8274 AT}$$

Total m.m.f. $= NI$ i.e. $220.8274 = 100\ I$

$\therefore$ $I = \mathbf{2.2082\ A}$ ... Exciting current

Reluctances of the sections are,

$$S_A = \frac{(\mathrm{m.m.f.})A}{\phi} = \mathbf{47746.48\ AT/Wb}, \qquad S_B = \frac{(\mathrm{m.m.f.})B}{\phi} = \mathbf{159154.9333\ AT/Wb}$$

$$S_C = \frac{(\mathrm{m.m.f.})C}{\phi} = \mathbf{7957.7466\ AT/Wb}, \qquad S_g = \frac{(\mathrm{m.m.f.})\mathrm{gap}}{\phi} = \mathbf{79577.4666\ AT/Wb}$$

Review Questions

1. Write a note on series magnetic circuit.

2. How to analyse the series magnetic circuit with air gap ?

3. An iron ring has circular cross-section 4 cm in radius and the average circumference of 100 cm. The ring is uniformly wound with a coil of 700 turns. Calculate,
   i) Current required to produce a flux of 2 mWb in the ring, if relative permeability of the iron is 900.
   ii) If a saw cut of 1mm wide is made in the ring, calculate the current which will give same flux as in part (i). Neglect leakage and fringing.   **[Ans. : 0.5025 A, 0.9545 A]**

4. An iron ring 8 cm mean diameter is made up of round iron of diameter 1 cm and permeability of 900, has an air gap of 2 mm wide. It consists of winding with 400 turns carrying a current of 3.5 A. Determine,
   i) m.m.f. ii) total reluctance iii) the flux iv) flux density in ring
   [Ans. : 1400 AT, 23.0737×10^6 AT / Wb, 6.067×10^{-5} Wb, 0.7725 Wb / m^2]

5. An iron ring has a mean diameter of 20 cm and a uniform circular cross section of 2.5232 cm diameter with a small brass piece fitted of 1 mm length. Three coils are wound on the ring as shown in the Fig. 7.13.9 and carry identical d.c. current of 2 A. If the relative permeability of iron is 800, estimate :- i) the magnetic flux produced in air-gap, ii) self-inductance of the arrangement. iii) net m.m.f. in the ring.   **[Ans. : 1500 AT, 5.282×10^{-4} Wb, 0.198 H]**

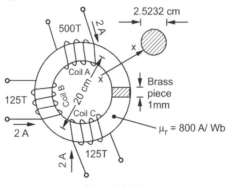

Fig. 7.13.9

6. *An iron ring of mean length 50 cm has air gap of 1 mm and a winding of 200 turns. If the relative permeability of iron is 300, find the flux density when a current of 1 amp flows through the coil.*　　　　　　　　　**[Ans. : 0.0943 Wb/m^2]**

7. *A ring shaped core is made up of two parts of same material. Part one is a magnetic path of length 25 cm and with cross sectional area 4 cm^2, whereas part two is of length 10 cm and cross sectional area of 6 cm^2. The flux density in part two is 1.5 Tesla. If the current through the coil, wound over core, is 0.5 amp., calculate the number of turns of coil. Assume μ_r is 1000 for material.*　　　　　　　　　**[Ans. : 1134]**

7.14 Parallel Magnetic Circuits

In case of electric circuits, resistances can be connected in parallel. Current through each of such resistances is different while voltage across all of them is same. Similarly different reluctances may be in parallel in case of magnetic circuits. A magnetic circuit which has more than one path for the flux is known as a **parallel magnetic circuit**.

Consider a magnetic circuit shown in the Fig. 7.14.1 (a). At point A the total flux ϕ, divides into two parts ϕ_1 and ϕ_2.

$$\therefore \qquad \phi = \phi_1 + \phi_2$$

The fluxes ϕ_1 and ϕ_2 have their paths completed through ABCD and AFED respectively.

This is similar to division of current in case of parallel connection of two resistances in an electric circuit. The analogous electric circuit is shown in the Fig. 7.14.1 (b).

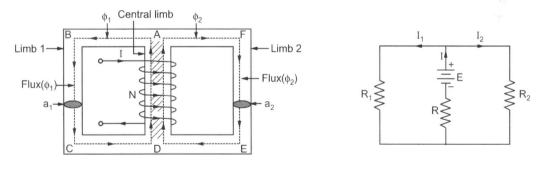

(a) Magnetic circuit　　　　　　　　　(b) Equivalent electrical circuit

Fig. 7.14.1 A parallel magnetic circuit

Mean length of path ABCD = l_1 m,　Mean length of the path AFED = l_2 m

Mean length of the path AD = l_c m,　Reluctance of the path ABCD = S_1

Reluctance of path AFED = S_2,　Reluctance of path AD = S_c

The total m.m.f. produced = N I　AT

$$\text{Flux} = \frac{\text{m.m.f.}}{\text{reluctance}} \quad \text{i.e.} \quad \text{m.m.f.} = \phi \times S$$

For path ABCDA, $NI = \phi_1 S_1 + \phi S_c$

For path AFEDA, $NI = \phi_2 S_2 + \phi S_c$

where $S_1 = \dfrac{l_1}{\mu a_1}, \quad S_2 = \dfrac{l_2}{\mu a_2} \text{ and } S_c = \dfrac{l_c}{\mu a_c}$

Generally $a_1 = a_2 = a_c = \text{Area of cross-section}$

For parallel circuit, $\text{Total m.m.f.} = \dfrac{\text{m.m.f. required}}{\text{by central limb}} + \dfrac{\text{m.m.f. required by}}{\textbf{any one} \text{ of outer limbs}}$

$$NI = (NI)_{AD} + (NI)_{ABCD} \textbf{ or } (NI)_{AFED}$$

$$NI = \phi S_c + [\phi_1 S_1 \textbf{ or } \phi_2 S_2]$$

As in the electric circuit e.m.f. across parallel branches is same, in the magnetic circuit the m.m.f. across parallel branches is same.

Thus same m.m.f. produces different fluxes in the two parallel branches. For such parallel branches,

$$\phi_1 S_1 = \phi_2 S_2$$

Hence while calculating total m.m.f., the m.m.f. of **only one** of the two parallel branches must be considered.

7.14.1 Parallel Magnetic Circuit with Air Gap

Consider a parallel magnetic circuit with air gap in the central limb as shown in the Fig. 7.14.2.

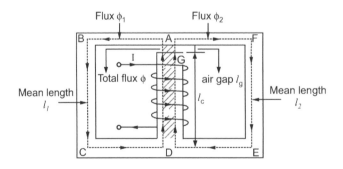

Fig. 7.14.2 Parallel circuit with air gap

The analysis of this circuit is exactly similar to the parallel circuit discussed above. The only change is the analysis of central limb. The central limb is series combination of iron path and air gap. The central limb is made up of,

path GD = Iron path = l_c, path GA = Air gap = l_g

The total flux produced is ϕ. It gets divided at A into ϕ_1 and ϕ_2.

$\therefore$ $\phi = \phi_1 + \phi_2$

The reluctance of central limb is now,

$$S_c = S_i + S_g = \frac{l_c}{\mu a_c} + \frac{l_g}{\mu_0 a_c}$$

Hence m.m.f. of central limb is now,

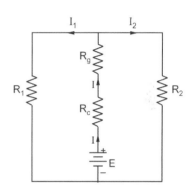

$$(\text{m.m.f.})_{AD} = (\text{m.m.f.})_{GD} + (\text{m.m.f.})_{GA}$$

Hence the total m.m.f. can be expressed as,

$$(NI)_{total} = (NI)_{GD} + (NI)_{GA} + (NI)_{ABCD} \text{ or } (NI)_{AFED}$$

Thus the electrical equivalent circuit for such case becomes as shown in the Fig. 7.14.3.

Similarly there may be air gaps in the side limbs but the method of analysis remains the same.

Fig. 7.14.3 Electrical equivalent circuit

> **Example 7.14.1** *A ring of cast steel has an external diameter of 25 cm and a square cross-section of 4 cm side. An ordinary steel bar 17 cm × 4 cm × 0.5 cm is fitted with negligible gap inside and across this ring. A coil of 500 turns and carrying a D.C. current of 1.5 A is placed on one half of the ring. Find the flux in the other half of the ring. Neglect leakage. Assume relative permeability of cast steel as 850 and that for ordinary steel as 700.*

Solution : The ring is shown in the Fig. 7.14.4 (a).

Inner diameter of ring = length of steel bar = 17 cm.

$\therefore$ Mean diameter of ring

$= \dfrac{\text{outer} + \text{inner}}{2} = \dfrac{25 + 17}{2} = 21$ cm

$\therefore$ Mean circumference

$= \pi \times 21 = 65.9734$ cm.

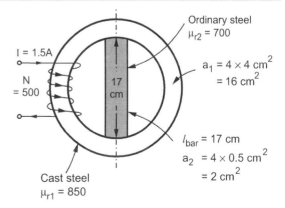

Fig. 7.14.4 (a)

∴ Length of half section of ring

$$= l_{i1} = \frac{65.9734}{2} = 32.9867 \text{ cm}$$

∴ Length of other section of ring

$$= l'_{i1} = l_{i1} = 32.9867 \text{ cm}$$

This is a parallel magnetic circuit as shown in the Fig. 7.14.4 (b).

∴ Total m.m.f. = NI = 500×1.5 = 750 AT

Now $\phi_T = \phi_1 + \phi_2$

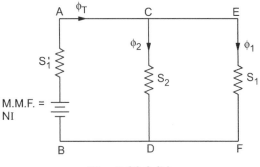

Fig. 7.14.4 (b)

> **Key Point** *M.M.F across CD and EF is same as both are in parallel.*

∴ Total m.m.f = m.m.f. for path AB + m.m.f. for path CD **or** path EF.

    m.m.f. for path AB = $\phi_T \times S'_1$ while   m.m.f. for path CD = $\phi_2 \times S_2 = \phi_1 \times S_1$

∴ Total m.m.f. = $\phi_T \times S'_1 + \phi_1 \times S_1$

$$S_1 = \frac{l_{i1}}{\mu_0 \mu_{r1} a_1} = \frac{32.9867 \times 10^{-2}}{4\pi \times 10^{-7} \times 850 \times 16 \times 10^{-4}} = 193.0145 \times 10^3 \text{ AT/Wb}$$

$$S'_1 = \frac{l'_{i1}}{\mu_0 \mu_{r1} a_1} \text{ but } l'_{i1} = l_{i1} \text{ hence } S'_1 = 193.0145 \times 10^3 \text{ AT/Wb}$$

∴ Total m.m.f. = $(\phi_1 + \phi_T) 193.0145 \times 10^3$ ... (2.13.6)

But $\phi_2 S_2 = \phi_1 S_1$ and $S_2 = \dfrac{l_{bar}}{\mu_0 \mu_{r2} a_2}$

∴ $S_2 = \dfrac{17 \times 10^{-2}}{4\pi \times 10^{-7} \times 700 \times 2 \times 10^{-4}} = 966.297 \times 10^3 \text{ AT/Wb}$

∴ $\phi_2 \times 966.297 \times 10^3 = \phi_1 \times 193.0145 \times 10^3$ i.e. $\phi_2 = 0.19974 \phi_1$ ... (2.13.7)

But $\phi_T = \phi_1 + \phi_2$ hence using in (2.13.6),

Total m.m.f. = $(\phi_1 + \phi_1 + \phi_2) \times 193.0145 \times 10^3$ i.e. $750 = (2\phi_1 + 0.19974 \phi_1) \times 193.0145 \times 10^3$

∴ $\phi_1 = $ **1.7664 mWb**   **... Flux through other half of ring**

Review Questions

1. *Explain the analysis of parallel magnetic circuit.*
2. *A cast steel structure is made of a rod of square section 2.5 cm ×2.5 cm as shown in the Fig. 7.14.5. What is the current that should be passed in a 500 turn coil on the left limb so that a*

flux of 2.5 mWb is made to pass in the right limb. Assume permeability as 750 and neglect leakage.

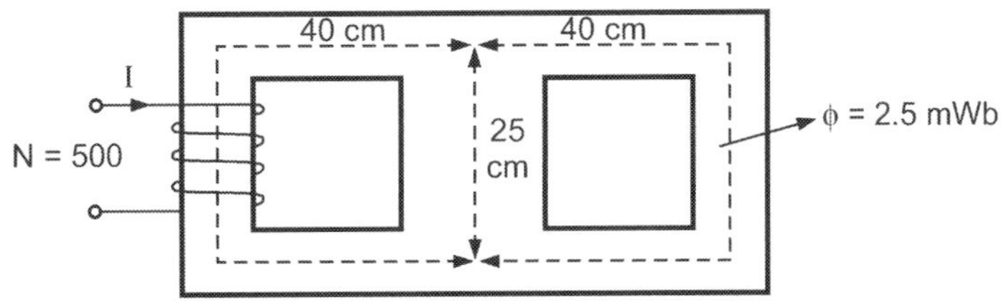

Fig. 7.14.5

[Ans. : 12.223 A]

7.15 Kirchhoff's Laws for Magnetic Circuit

Similar to the electrical circuit Kirchhoff's laws can be used to analyse complex magnetic circuit. The laws can be stated as below :

7.15.1 Kirchhoff's Flux Law

The total magnetic flux arriving at any junction in a magnetic circuit is equal to the total magnetic flux leaving that junction.

At a junction, $\qquad \sum \phi = 0$

7.15.2 Kirchhoff's M.M.F. Law

The resultant m.m.f. around a closed magnetic circuit is equal to the algebraic sum of the products of the flux and the reluctance of each part of the closed circuit i.e. for a closed magnetic circuit.

$$\sum m.m.f. = \sum \phi S$$

As $\qquad \phi \times S =$ flux $\times$ reluctance $=$ m.m.f.

M.M.F. also can be calculated as $H \times l$ where H is field strength and 'l' is mean length

$\therefore \qquad$ m.m.f. $= Hl$

Alternatively the same law can be stated as :

The resultant m.m.f. around any closed loop of a magnetic circuit is equal to the algebraic sum of the products of the magnetic field strength and the length of each part of the circuit i.e. for a closed magnetic circuit

$$\sum m.m.f. = \sum H.l$$

Review Question

> 1. State Kirchhoff's laws for magnetic circuit.

7.16 Comparison of Magnetic and Electric Circuits

Similarities between electric and magnetic circuits are listed below :

Sr. No.	Electric Circuit	Magnetic Circuit
1.	Path traced by the current is called electric circuit.	Path traced by the magnetic flux is defined as magnetic circuit.
2.	E.M.F. is the driving force in electric circuit, the unit is **volts.**	M.M.F. is the driving force in the magnetic circuit, the unit of which is **ampere turns.**
3.	There is current I in the electric circuit measured in amperes.	There is flux ϕ in the magnetic circuit measured in webers.
4.	The flow of electrons decides the current in conductor.	The number of magnetic lines of force decides the flux.
5.	Resistance oppose the flow of the current. Unit is ohm.	Reluctance is opposed by magnetic path to the flux. Unit is ampere turn/weber.
6.	$R = \rho \dfrac{l}{a}$. Directly proportional to l. Inversely proportional to 'a'. Depends on nature of material.	$S = \dfrac{l}{\mu_0 \mu_r a}$. Directly proportional to l. Inversely proportional to $\mu = \mu_0 \mu_r$. Inversely proportional to area 'a'.
7.	The current $I = \dfrac{\text{e.m.f.}}{\text{resistance}}$	The flux $\phi = \dfrac{\text{m.m.f.}}{\text{reluctance}}$
8.	The current density $\delta = \dfrac{I}{a} \ A/m^2$	The flux density $B = \dfrac{\phi}{a} \ Wb/m^2$
9.	Conductivity is reciprocal of the resistivity. Conductance $= \dfrac{1}{R}$	Permeance is reciprocal of the reluctance. Permeance $= \dfrac{1}{S}$
10.	Kirchhoff's current and voltage law is applicable to the electric circuit.	Kirchhoff's m.m.f. law and flux law is applicable to the magnetic circuit.

- There are few dissimilarities between the two which are listed below :

Sr. No.	Electric Circuit	Magnetic Circuit
1.	In the electric circuit the current actually flows i.e. there is movement of electrons.	Due to m.m.f. flux gets established and does not flow in the sense in which current flows.

2.	There are many materials which can be used as insulators i.e. air, P.V.C., synthetic resin etc, from which current cannot pass.	There is no magnetic insulator as flux can pass through all the materials, even through the air as well.
3.	Energy must be supplied to the electric circuit to maintain the flow of current.	Energy is required to create the magnetic flux, but is not required to maintain it.
4.	The resistance and the conductivity are independent of current density (δ) under constant temperature. But may change due to the temperature.	The reluctance, permeance and permeability are dependent on the flux density.
5.	Electric lines of flux are not closed. They start from positive charge and end on negative charge.	Magnetic lines of flux are closed lines. They flow from N pole to S pole externally while S pole to N pole internally.
6.	There is continuous consumption of electrical energy.	Energy is required to create the magnetic flux and not to maintain it.

Review Question

> 1. *Compare electric and magnetic circuits clearly stating similarities and dissimilarities between them.*

7.17 Magnetic Leakage and Fringing

Most of the applications which are using magnetic effects of an electric current, are using flux in air gap for their operation. Such devices are generators, motors, measuring instruments like ammeter, voltmeter etc. Such devices consist of magnetic circuit with an air gap and flux in air gap is used to produce the required effect. Such flux which is available in air gap and is utilised to produce the desired effect is called **useful flux** denoted by ϕ_u. It is expected that whatever is the flux produced by the magnetizing coil, it should complete its path through the iron and air gap. So all the flux will be available in air gap.

In actual practice it is not possible to have entire flux available in air gap. This is because, we have already seen that there is no perfect insulator for the flux. So part of the flux completes its path through the air or medium in which coil and magnetic circuit is placed.

Key Point *Such flux which leaks and completes its path through surrounding air or medium instead of the desired path is called the leakage flux.*

The Fig. 7.17.1 shows the useful and leakage flux.

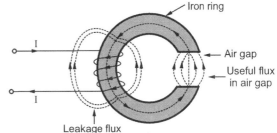

Fig. 7.17.1 Leakage and useful flux

7.17.1 Leakage Coefficient or Hopkinson's Coefficient

The ratio of the total flux (ϕ_T) to the useful flux (ϕ_u) is defined as the **leakage coefficient** of **Hopkinson's coefficient** or **leakage factor** of that magnetic circuit. It is denoted by λ.

$$\therefore \qquad \lambda = \frac{\text{Total flux}}{\text{Useful flux}} = \frac{\phi_T}{\phi_u}$$

The value of 'λ' is always greater than 1 as ϕ_T is always more than ϕ_u. It generally varies between 1.1 and 1.25. Ideally its value should be 1.

7.17.2 Magnetic Fringing

When flux enters into the air gap, it passes through the air gap in terms of parallel flux lines. There exists a force of repulsion between the magnetic lines of force which are parallel and having same direction.

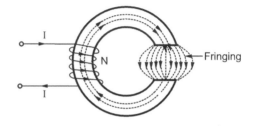

Fig. 7.17.2 Magnetic fringing

Due to this repulsive force there is tendency of the magnetic flux to bulge out (spread out) at the edge of the air gap. This tendency of flux to bulge out at the edges of the air gap is called **magnetic fringing**.

It has following two effects :

1) It increases the effective cross-sectional area of the air gap.

2) It reduces the flux density in the air gap.

So leakage, fringing and reluctance, in practice should be as small as possible.

Key Point *This is possible by choosing good magnetic material and making the air gap as narrow as possible.*

Example 7.17.1 *A soft iron ring of 20 cm mean diameter and circular cross-section of 4 cm diameter is wound with a magnetising coil. A current of 5 A flowing in the coil produces flux of 2.5 mWb in the air gap which is 2.2 mm wide. Taking relative permeability to be 1000 at this flux density and allowing for a leakage coefficient of 1.2, find the number of the turns on the coil.*

Solution : d_{mean} = 20 cm, d = 4 cm, I = 5 A, ϕ_g= 2.5 mWb, l_g = 2.2 mm, λ = 1.2

$$\therefore \qquad \text{mean length } l = \pi \times d_{mean} = \pi \times 20 \times 10^{-2} = 0.6283 \text{ m}$$

Cross section diameter = 4 cm

$\therefore$
$$a = \frac{\pi}{4}d^2 = \frac{\pi}{4}\times(4)^2 = 12.566 \text{ cm}^2 = 12.566 \times 10^{-4} \text{ m}^2$$

$$l_g = \text{length of air gap} = 2.2 \text{ mm} = 2.2 \times 10^{-3} \text{ m}$$

$\therefore$
$$l_i = \text{length of iron path} = l - l_g = 0.6261 \text{ m}$$

Now
$$\lambda = \frac{\text{total flux}}{\text{air gap flux}} = \frac{\phi}{\phi_g} \text{ i.e. } 1.2 = \frac{\phi}{2.5\times10^{-3}}$$

$\therefore$
$$\phi = 3 \times 10^{-3} \text{ Wb.}$$

The total reluctance of the magnetic circuit,

$$S = S_i + S_g$$

Now
$$S_i = \frac{l_i}{\mu_0\mu_r a} = \frac{0.6261}{4\pi\times10^{-7}\times1000\times12.566\times10^{-4}} = 396494.15 \text{ AT/Wb}$$

While
$$S_g = \frac{l_g}{\mu_0 a} = \frac{2.2\times10^{-3}}{4\pi\times10^{-7}\times12.566\times10^{-4}} = 1393207.4 \text{ AT/Wb}$$

Now
$$\phi = \frac{\text{m.m.f.}}{\text{reluctance}} = \frac{NI}{S_i + S_g}$$

$$\phi_g = \frac{\text{m.m.f. for air gap}}{S_g} \text{ i.e. } 2.5\times10^{-3} = \frac{\text{m.m.f. for air gap}}{1393207.4}$$

$\therefore$ m.m.f. for air gap = 3483.01

$$\phi = \frac{\text{m.m.f. for iron}}{S_i} \text{ i.e. } 3\times10^{-3} = \frac{\text{m.m.f. for iron}}{396494.15}$$

$\therefore$ m.m.f. for iron = 1189.4825

Hence the total m.m.f. can be obtained as :

Total = m.m.f. for air gap + m.m.f. for iron

$\therefore$ m.m.f. = 3483.01 + 1189.48 = **4672.501** AT/Wb

Now   m.m.f. = $N \times I$ i.e. $4672.501 = N \times 5$

$\therefore$
$$N = \frac{4672.501}{5} = \textbf{934.5}$$

Hence the number of turns on the coil required is approximately **935**.

Review Questions

1. *Write a note on magnetic leakage and fringing.*

2. *Define leakage coefficient and state its importance.*

3. *A cast iron ring of 40 cm mean length and circular cross section of 5 cm diameter is wound with a coil. The coil carries a current of 3 A and produces a flux of 3 mWb in the air gap. The length of the air gap is 2 mm. The relative permeability of the cast iron is 800. The leakage coefficient is 1.2. Calculate number of turns of the coil.*   **[Ans. : 702 turns]**

7.18 Force on a Current Carrying Conductor in a Magnetic Field

2009-10

When a current carrying conductor is placed in a magnetic field, it produces its own flux around it. There is a flux of magnetic field in which it is placed. These two fluxes interact with each other so as to exert a force on a conductor.

7.18.1 Magnitude of Force Experienced by the Conductor

The magnitude of the force experienced by the conductor depends on the following factors,

1) Flux density (B) of the magnetic field in which the conductor is placed measured in Wb/m^2 i.e. Tesla.

2) Magnitude of the current I passing through the conductor in Amperes.

3) Active length 'l' of the conductor in metres.

The **active length** of the conductor is that part of the conductor which is actually under the influence of magnetic field.

If the conductor is at right angles to the magnetic field as shown in Fig. 7.18.1 (a) then force F is given by,

$$F = BIl \text{ Newtons}$$

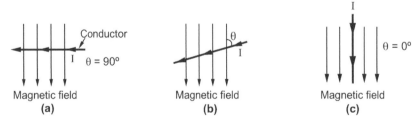

Fig. 7.18.1 Force on a current carrying conductor

But if the conductor is not exactly at right angles, but inclined at angle θ degrees with respect to axis of magnetic field as shown in the Fig. 7.18.1 (b) then force F is given by,

$$F = B\,I\,l\sin\theta \ \ \text{Newtons}$$

As shown in the Fig. 7.18.1 (c), if conductor is kept along the lines of magnetic field then θ = 0° and as sin 0° = 0, the force experienced by the conductor is also zero.

Key Point *The direction of such force can be reversed either by changing the direction of current or by changing the direction of the flux lines in which it is kept.*

7.18.2 Fleming's Left Hand Rule

The direction of the force experienced by the current carrying conductor placed in magnetic field can be determined by a rule called **'Fleming's Left Hand Rule'**. The rule states that, 'Outstretch the three fingers of the left hand namely the first finger, middle finger and thumb such that they are mutually perpendicular to each other. Now point the first finger in the direction of magnetic field and the middle finger in the direction of the current then the thumb gives the direction of the force experienced by the conductor'.

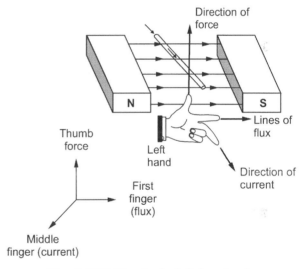

Fig. 7.18.2 Fleming's left hand rule

The rule is explained in the diagrammatic form in the Fig. 7.18.2.

Review Questions

1. *State and explain Fleming's left hand rule.*   **2009-10, Marks 5**

2. *Why current carrying conductor placed in a magnetic field experiences a force ? What is its magnitude ? How its direction can be changed ?*

7.19 Introduction to Electromagnetic Induction

The phenomenon by which e.m.f. is obtained from flux is called **electromagnetic induction**.

E.M.F. can be induced in a coil by moving a coil in the fixed magnetic field or keeping the coil fixed in a moving magnetic field, by creating relative motion between flux and coil.

If there is **change of flux lines with respect to conductor** i.e. there is cutting of the flux lines by the conductor then e.m.f. gets induced in that conductor.

This phenomenon of cutting of flux lines by the conductor to get the induced e.m.f. in the conductor or coil is called electromagnetic induction.

Review Question

1. *What is electromagnetic induction ?*

7.20 Faraday's Experiment

Scientist Faraday conducted an experiment to get understanding of electromagnetic induction.

The setup for the Faraday's experiment is shown in the Fig. 7.20.1. There is a fixed permanent magnet and moving coil or a conductor.

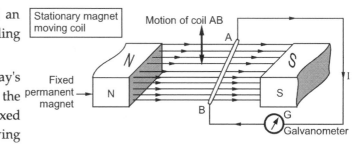

Fig. 7.20.1 Faraday's experiment

The coil AB is moved in a magnetic flux so that there is relative motion between constant flux and moving coil. Then the galvanometer connected to the coil showed deflection, indicating that there is induced e.m.f. in the coil.

Similarly if coil is kept fixed and magnetic flux is moved to create relative motion between the coil and the flux then also galvanometer deflects indicating presence of an induced e.m.f.

Thus, to have induced e.m.f. there must exist,

1) A coil or conductor

2) A magnetic field (permanent magnet or electromagnet)

3) Relative motion between conductor and magnetic flux (achieved by moving conductor with respect to flux or moving with respect to conductor.)

Key Point *The e.m.f. exists as long as relative motion persists.*

7.21 Faraday's Laws of Electromagnetic Induction

1. First Law : Whenever the number of magnetic lines of force (flux) linking with a coil or circuit changes, an e.m.f. gets induced in that coil or circuit.

2. Second Law : The magnitude of the induced e.m.f. is directly proportional to the rate of change of flux linkages (flux × turns of coil).

> **Flux linkages = Flux × Number of turns of coil**

Consider a coil having N turns. The initial flux linking with a coil is ϕ_1.

∴　　　　　　　Initial flux linkages $= N\phi_1$

In time interval dt, the flux linking with the coil changes from ϕ_1 to ϕ_2.

∴　　　　　　　Final flux linkages $= N\phi_2$

∴　　Rate of change of flux linkages $= \dfrac{N\phi_2 - N\phi_1}{dt}$

Now as per the first law, e.m.f. will get induced in the coil and as per second law the magnitude of e.m.f. is proportional to the rate of change of flux linkages.

∴　　　　$e \propto \dfrac{N\phi_2 - N\phi_1}{dt}$　　i.e.　　$e = K \times \dfrac{N\phi_2 - N\phi_1}{dt}$

∴　　　　$e = N\dfrac{d\phi}{dt}$　　$(d\phi = \phi_2 - \phi_1)$

With K as unity to get units of e as volts, $d\phi$ is change in flux, dt is change in time hence $(d\phi/dt)$ is rate of change of flux.

As per Lenz's law, the induced e.m.f. sets up a current in such a direction so as to oppose the very cause producing it. Mathematically this opposition is expressed by a negative sign.

Thus such an induced e.m.f. is mathematically expressed alongwith its sign as,

> $e = -N\dfrac{d\phi}{dt}$　volts

Example 7.21.1 *An electromagnet is wound with 800 turns. Find the value of average e.m.f. induced and current through coil, if it is moved to that magnetic field is changed from 1 mWb to 0.25 mWb in 0.2 sec. The resistance of the coil is 500 Ω.*

Solution :　　N = 800, $\phi_2 = 0.25$ mWb, $\phi_1 = 1$ mWb, t = 0.2 sec., R = 500 Ω

$$\text{Induced e.m.f } e = -N\frac{d\phi}{dt} = -800\left[\frac{\phi_2 - \phi_1}{dt}\right] = -\left[\frac{0.25 \times 10^{-3} - 1 \times 10^{-3}}{0.2}\right] = 3 \text{ volts}$$

∴　　Current $I = \dfrac{\text{e.m.f.}}{R} = \dfrac{3}{500} = 6 \times 10^{-3}$ A $= \textbf{6 mA}$

Review Questions

1. *State and explain the Faraday's laws of electromagnetic induction.*

2. *A coil of 1000 turns produces a flux of 1 mWb when carries certain current. If this flux is reversed in time of 0.1 sec, find the average value of e.m.f. induced in the coil.*   **(Ans. : 20 V)**

7.22 Nature of the Induced E.M.F.

E.M.F. gets induced in a conductor, whenever there exists change in flux with that conductor, according to Faraday's Law. Such change in flux can be brought about by different methods.

Depending upon the nature of methods, the induced e.m.f. is classified as,

1) Dynamically induced e.m.f.   and

2) Statically induced e.m.f.

7.23 Dynamically Induced E.M.F.   2001-02, 2002-03, 2004-05, 2009-10

The change in the flux linking with a coil, conductor or circuit can be brought about by its motion relative to magnetic field. This is possible by moving flux with respect to coil conductor or circuit or it is possible by moving conductor, coil, circuit with respect to stationary magnetic flux.

Key Point *Such an induced e.m.f. which is due to **physical movement** of coil, conductor with respect to flux or movement of magnet with respect to stationary coil, conductor is called dynamically induced e.m.f. or motional induced e.m.f.*

7.23.1 Magnitude of Dynamically Induced E.M.F.

If the plane of the motion of the conductor is parallel to the plane of the flux, there is no cutting of flux and there can not be induced e.m.f. in a conductor. This is shown in the Fig. 7.23.1 (a).

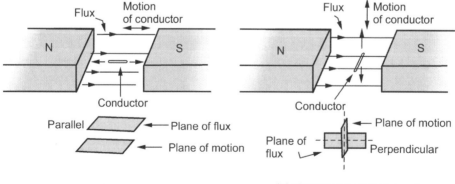

(a) No induced e.m.f.   (b) Maximum induced e.m.f.

Fig. 7.23.1

If the plane of the motion of the conductor is perpendicular to the plane of the flux then entire length of conductor cuts the flux and maximum possible e.m.f. gets induced in a conductor. This is shown in the Fig. 7.23.1 (b).

Consider a conductor moving with velocity v m/s such that its plane of motion or direction of velocity is perpendicular to the direction of flux lines as shown in Fig. 7.23.2 (a).

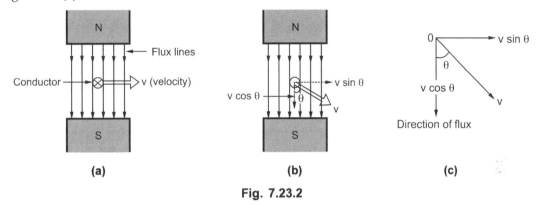

Fig. 7.23.2

B = Flux density in Wb/m^2,   v = Velocity in m/sec., l = Active length of conductor in metres

(This is the length of conductor which is actually responsible for cutting of flux lines.)

Let this conductor is moved through distance dx in a small time interval dt, then

$$\text{Area swept by conductor} \ = \ l \times dx \quad m^2$$

∴   Flux cut by conductor = Flux density × Area swept

$$d\phi \ = \ B \times l \times dx \ \ Wb$$

According to Faraday's law, magnitude of induced e.m.f. is proportional to the rate of change of flux.

∴ $e \ = \ \dfrac{\text{Flux cut}}{\text{Time}} \ = \ \dfrac{d\phi}{dt} \ = \ \dfrac{B\,l\,\,dx}{dt}$ [Here N = 1 as single conductor]

But $\dfrac{dx}{dt}$ = Rate of change of displacement = Velocity of the conductor = v

∴ $\boxed{e = B\,l\,v \quad \text{volts}}$

This is the induced e.m.f. when plane of motion is exactly perpendicular to the plane of flux. This is maximum possible e.m.f. as plane of motion is at right angles to plane of the flux.

But if conductor is moving with a velocity v but at a certain angle θ measured with respect to direction of the field (plane of the flux) as shown in the Fig. 7.23.2 (b) then component of velocity which is v sin θ is perpendicular to the direction of flux and hence responsible for the induced e.m.f.. The other component v cos θ is parallel to the plane of the flux and hence will not contribute to the dynamically induced e.m.f.

Under this condition, magnitude of induced e.m.f. is given by,

$$e = B\,l\,v\,\sin\theta \text{ volts} \quad \textbf{where } \theta \textbf{ is measured with respect to plane of the flux.}$$

7.23.2 Direction of Dynamically Induced E.M.F.

The direction of induced e.m.f. can be decided by using two rules.

7.23.2.1 Fleming's Right Hand Rule

The Fleming's Right Hand Rule is to be used to get direction of induced e.m.f. when conductor is moving in a magnetic field.

According to Fleming's right hand rule, outstretch the three fingers of right hand namely the thumb, fore finger and the middle finger, perpendicular to each other. Arrange the right hand so that first finger point in the direction of flux lines (from N to S) and thumb in the direction of motion of conductor with respect to the flux then the middle finger will point in the direction of the induced e.m.f. (or current).

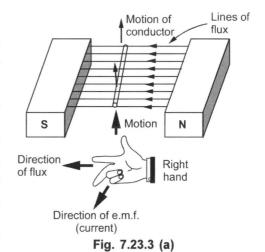

Fig. 7.23.3 (a)

Consider the conductor moving in a magnetic field as shown in the Fig. 7.23.3 (a). It can be verified using Fleming's right hand rule that the direction of the current due to the induced e.m.f. is coming out. Symbolically this is shown in the Fig. 7.23.3 (b).

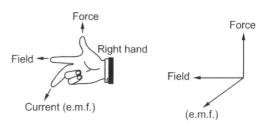

Fig. 7.23.3 (b)

> **Key Point** *In practice though magnet is moved keeping the conductor stationary, while application of rule, thumb should point in the direction of relative motion of **conductor with respect to flux**, assuming the flux stationary.*

This rule mainly gives direction of current which induced e.m.f. in conductor will set up when closed path is provided to it.

7.23.2.2 Lenz's Law

This rule is based on the principles derived by German Physicist Heinrich Lenz.

The Lenz's Law states that, **'The direction of an induced e.m.f. produced by the electromagnetic induction is such that it sets up a current which always opposes the cause that is responsible for inducing the e.m.f.'**

In short the induced e.m.f. always opposes the cause producing it, which is represented by a negative sign, mathematically in its expression.

$$\therefore \quad e = -N\frac{d\phi}{dt}$$

The explanation can be given as below :

Consider a solenoid as shown in the Fig. 7.23.4. Let a bar magnet is moved towards coil such that N-pole of magnet is facing a coil which will circulate the current through the coil.

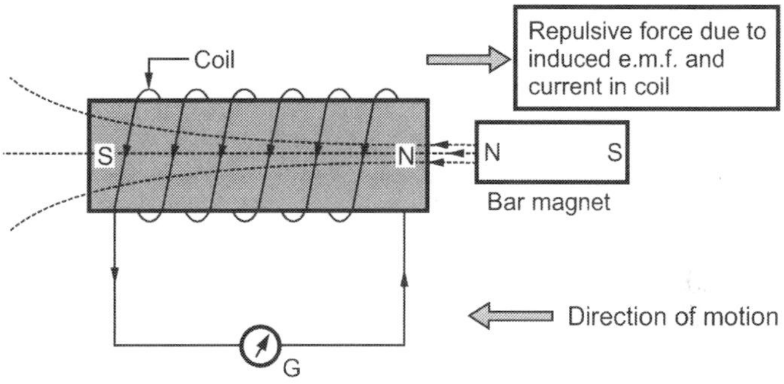

Fig. 7.23.4 Lenz's law

According to Lenz's Law, the direction of current due to induced e.m.f. is so as to oppose the cause. The cause is motion of bar magnet towards coil. So e.m.f. will set up a current through coil in such a way that the end of solenoid facing bar magnet will become N-pole. Hence two like poles will face each other experiencing force of repulsion which is opposite to the motion of bar magnet as shown in the Fig. 7.23.5.

If the same bar magnet is moved away from the coil, then induced e.m.f. will set up a current in the direction which will cause, the end of solenoid facing bar magnet to behave as S-pole. Because of this two unlike poles face each other and there will be force of attraction which is opposite to direction of magnet.

The Lenz's law can be summarized as,

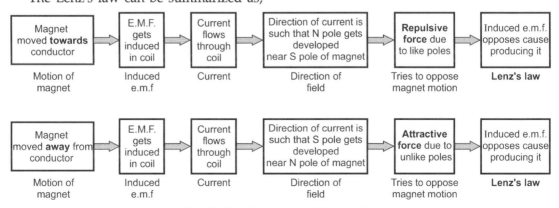

Fig. 7.23.5 Concept of Lenz's law

Review Questions

1. What is dynamically induced e.m.f. ? Derive the expression for its magnitude.

   2001-02, Marks 5

2. State and explain Fleming's right hand rule.   **2004-05, 2009-10, Marks 4**

3. State and explain Lenz's law.   **2002-03, 2009-10, Marks 10**

7.24 Statically Induced E.M.F.

*The change in flux lines with respect to coil can be achieved without physically moving the coil or the magnet. Such induced e.m.f. in a coil which is without physical movement of coil or a magnet is called **statically induced e.m.f.***

To have an induced e.m.f. there must be change in flux associated with a coil. Such a change in flux can be achieved without any physical movement by increasing and decreasing the current producing the flux rapidly, with time.

Let current through the coil of an electromagnet producing the flux be an alternating one. Such alternating current means **it changes its magnitude periodically with time**. This produces the flux which is also alternating i.e. changing with time.

If this alternating flux comes in contact with another coil, there exists $d\phi/dt$ associated with the coil placed in the vicinity of an electromagnet. According to Faraday's law, this is responsible for producing an e.m.f. in the coil. This is called statically induced e.m.f.

It can be noted that there is no physical movement of magnet or conductor, it is the alternating supply which is responsible for such an induced e.m.f.

The statically induced e.m.f. is used in transformers and coupled coils.

The statically induced e.m.f. is further classified as,

1) Self induced e.m.f. and 2) Mutually induced e.m.f.

Review Question

1. What is statically induced e.m.f. ?

7.25 Self Induced E.M.F.   **2008-09**

Consider a coil having 'N' turns and carrying current 'I' when switch 'S' is in closed position. The current magnitude can be varied with the help of variable resistance connected in series with battery, coil and switch as shown in the Fig. 7.25.1.

The flux produced by the coil links with the coil itself. The total flux linkages of coil will be Nϕ Wb-turns. Now if the current 'I' is changed with the help of variable resistance, then flux produced will also change, due to which flux linkages will also change.

Hence according to Faraday's law, due to rate of change of flux linkages there will be induced e.m.f. in the coil. So without physically moving coil or flux there is induced e.m.f. in the coil. The phenomenon is called **self induction**.

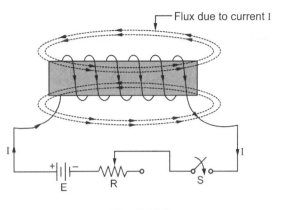

Fig. 7.25.1

The e.m.f. induced in a coil due to the change of its own flux linked with it is called **self induced e.m.f.**

Key Point *The self induced e.m.f. lasts till the current in the coil is changing. The direction of such induced e.m.f. can be obtained by Lenz's law.*

7.25.1 Self Inductance

According to Lenz's law the direction of this induced e.m.f. will be so as to oppose the cause producing it. The cause is the current I hence the self induced e.m.f. will try to set up a current which is in opposite direction to that of current I. **So any change in current through coil is opposed by the coil.**

This property of the coil which opposes any change in the current passing through it is called **Self Inductance or Only Inductance**.

It is analogous to electrical inertia or electromagnetic inertia.

7.25.2 Magnitude of Self Induced E.M.F.

From the Faraday's Law of electromagnetic induction, self induced e.m.f. can be expressed as

$$e = -N\frac{d\phi}{dt}$$

Negative sign indicates that direction of this e.m.f. is opposing change in current due to which it exists.

The flux can be expressed as,

$$\phi = (\text{Flux / Ampere})\times\text{Ampere} = \frac{\phi}{I}\times I$$

For a circuit, as long as permeability 'μ' is constant, ratio of flux to current (i.e. B/H) remains constant.

$\therefore$ Rate of change of flux $= \dfrac{\phi}{I} \times$ Rate of change of current

$\therefore \qquad \dfrac{d\phi}{dt} = \dfrac{\phi}{I} \cdot \dfrac{dI}{dt}$

$\qquad e = -N.\dfrac{\phi}{I} \cdot \dfrac{dI}{dt} = -\left(\dfrac{N\phi}{I}\right)\dfrac{dI}{dt}$

The constant $\dfrac{N\phi}{I}$ is called **coefficient of self inductance and denoted by 'L'.**

$\therefore \qquad \boxed{L = \dfrac{N\phi}{I}}$

It can be defined as flux linkages per ampere current in it. Its unit is **Henry (H).**

A circuit possesses **a self inductance of 1 H** when a current of 1 A through it produces flux linkages of 1 Wb-turn in it.

$\therefore \qquad \boxed{e = -L\dfrac{dI}{dt} \quad \text{volts}}$

From this equation, the unit Henry of self inductance can be defined as below,

Key Point *A circuit possesses an inductance of 1 H when a current through coil is changing uniformly at the rate of one ampere per second inducing an opposing e.m.f. 1 volt in it.*

The coefficient of self inductance is also defined as the e.m.f. induced in volts when the current in the circuit changes uniformly at the rate of one ampere per second.

7.25.3 Expressions for Coefficient of Self Inductance (L)

$\qquad L = \dfrac{N\phi}{I} \qquad\qquad\qquad\qquad\qquad \text{... (7.25.1)}$

But $\qquad \phi = \dfrac{\text{m.m.f.}}{\text{reluctance}} = \dfrac{N\,I}{S} \quad \text{i.e.} \quad L = \dfrac{N \cdot NI}{I \cdot S}$

$\therefore \qquad \boxed{L = \dfrac{N^2}{S} \quad \text{Henries}} \qquad\qquad\qquad \text{... (7.25.2)}$

Now $\qquad S = \dfrac{l}{\mu\,a} \quad \text{hence} \quad L = \dfrac{N^2}{\left(\dfrac{l}{\mu\,a}\right)}$

$\therefore$

$$\boxed{L = \frac{N^2 \mu a}{l} = \frac{N^2 \mu_0 \mu_r a}{l} \quad \text{Henries}}$$
... (7.25.3)

where l = Length of magnetic circuit

         a = Area of cross-section of magnetic circuit through which flux is passing.

7.25.4 Factors Affecting Self Inductance of a Coil

Now as defined in last section,

$$L = \frac{N^2 \mu_0 \mu_r a}{l}$$

We can define factors on which self inductance of a coil depends as,

1) It is directly proportional to the square of number of turns of a coil. This means for same length, if number of turns are more then self inductance of coil will be more.

2) It is directly proportional to the cross-sectional area of the magnetic circuit.

3) It is inversely proportional to the length of the magnetic circuit.

4) It is directly proportional to the relative permeability of the core. So for iron and other magnetic materials inductance is high as their relative permeabilities are high.

5) For air cored or non magnetic cored magnetic circuits, $\mu_r = 1$ and constant, hence self inductance coefficient is also small and always constant.

   As against this for magnetic materials, as current i.e. magnetic field strength H (NI/l) is changed, μ_r also changes. Due to this change in current, cause change in value of self inductance. So for magnetic materials it is not constant but varies with current.

Key Point *For magnetic materials, L changes as the current I.*

6) Since the relative permeability of iron varies with respect to flux density, the coefficient of self inductance varies with respect to flux density.

7) If the conductor is bent back on itself, then magnetic fields produced by current through it will be opposite to each other and hence will neutralize each other. Hence **inductance will be zero** under such condition.

Example 7.25.1 *A coil is wound uniformly on an iron core. The relative permeability of the iron is 1400. The length of the magnetic circuit is 70 cm. The cross-sectional area of the core is 5 cm². The coil has 1000 turns. Calculate, i) Reluctance of magnetic circuit ii) Inductance of coil in Henries.   iii) E.M.F. induced in coil if a current of 10 A is uniformly reversed in 0.2 seconds.*

Solution : $\mu_r = 1400$, $L = 70$ cm $= 0.7$ m, $N = 1000$

$$A = 5 \text{ cm}^2 = 5 \times 10^{-4} \text{ m}^2, \quad \mu_0 = 4\pi \times 10^{-7}$$

i) $$S = \frac{l}{\mu_0 \mu_r a} = \frac{0.7}{4\pi \times 10^{-7} \times 1400 \times 5 \times 10^{-4}} = 7.957 \times 10^5 \quad \text{AT/Wb}$$

ii) $$L = \frac{N^2}{S} = \frac{(1000)^2}{7.957 \times 10^5} = \mathbf{1.2566} \text{ H}$$

iii) A current of +10 A is made –10 A in 0.2 sec.   ... current is reversed

$\therefore$ $$\frac{dI}{dt} = \frac{-10 - 10}{0.2} = -100$$

$$e = -L\frac{dI}{dt} = -1.2566 \times (-100) = \mathbf{125.66} \text{ volts.}$$

Again it is positive indicating that this e.m.f. opposes the reversal i.e. decrease of current from +10 towards –10 A.

Example 7.25.2 *The core of a magnetic circuit is of mean length 40 cm and uniform cross-sectional area 4 cm². The relative permeability of the core material is 1000. An air gap of 1 mm is cut in the core, and 1000 turns are wound on the core. Determine the inductance of the coil if fringing is negligible.*   **2008-09, Marks 5**

Solution : $l = 40$ cm, $a = 4$ cm², $\mu_r = 1000$, $l_g = 1$ mm, $N = 1000$

$$l_i = l - l_g = 40 \times 10^{-2} - 1 \times 10^{-3} = 0.399 \text{ m}$$

$$S_i = \frac{l_i}{\mu_0 \mu_r a} = \frac{0.399}{1000 \times 4\pi \times 10^{-7} \times 4 \times 10^{-4}} = 793.7852 \times 10^3 \text{ AT/Wb}$$

$$S_g = \frac{l_g}{\mu_0 a} = \frac{1 \times 10^{-3}}{4\pi \times 10^{-7} \times 4 \times 10^{-4}} = 1.9894 \times 10^6 \text{ AT/Wb}$$

$\therefore$ $$S = S_i + S_g = 2.78322 \times 10^6 \text{ AT/Wb}$$

$\therefore$ $$L = \frac{N^2}{S} = \frac{(1000)^2}{2.78322 \times 10^6} = \mathbf{0.3593} \text{ H}$$

Review Questions

1. *Explain the phenomenon of self induced e.m.f. ?*

2. *Define self inductance.*

3. *Derive the expression for the self induced e.m.f. and state its unit.*

4. *Derive the equation* $L = \dfrac{N^2}{S}$ *where L is the self inductance of coil having N turns and S is the reluctance of the magnetic circuit.*

5. *State the various expressions for the coefficient of self inductance.*

6. *State the various factors affecting the self inductance of the coil.*

7. *Find the inductance of a coil of 200 turns wound on a paper core tube of 25 cm length and 5 cm radius.* **[Ans. : 1.579 mH]**

8. *If a coil has 500 turns is linked with a flux of 50 mWb, when carrying a current of 125 A. Calculate the inductance of the coil. If this current is reduced to zero uniformly in 0.1 sec, calculate the self induced e.m.f. in the coil.* **[Ans. : 250 volts]**

7.26 Mutually Induced E.M.F.

If the flux produced by one coil is getting linked with another coil and due to change in this flux produced by first coil, there is induced e.m.f. in the second coil, then such an e.m.f. is called **mutually induced e.m.f.**

Consider two coils which are placed adjacent to each other as shown in the Fig. 7.26.1. The coil A has N_1 turns while coil B has N_2 number of turns. The coil A has switch S, variable resistance R and battery of 'E' volts in series with it. A galvanometer is connected across coil B to sense induced e.m.f. and current because of it.

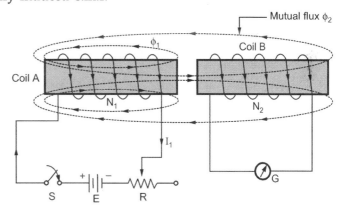

Fig. 7.26.1 Mutually induced e.m.f.

Current through coil A is I_1 producing flux ϕ_1. Part of this flux will link with coil B i.e. will complete its path through coil B as shown in the Fig. 7.26.1. This is the mutual flux ϕ_2.

Now if current through coil A is changed by means of variable resistance R, then flux ϕ_1 changes. Due to this, flux associated with coil B, which is mutual flux ϕ_2 also changes. Due to Faraday's law there will be induced e.m.f. in coil B which will set up a current through coil B, which will be detected by galvanometer G.

Key Point *Any change in current through coil A produces e.m.f. in coil B, this phenomenon is called mutual induction and e.m.f. is called mutually induced e.m.f.*

7.26.1 **Magnitude of Mutually Induced E.M.F.**

Let N_1 = Number of turns of coil A, N_2 = Number of turns of coil B

I_1 = Current flowing through coil A

ϕ_1 = Flux produced due to current I_1 in webers

ϕ_2 = Flux linking with coil B

According to Faraday's law, the induced e.m.f. in coil B is,

$$e_2 = -N_2 \frac{d\phi_2}{dt}$$

Negative sign indicates that this e.m.f. will set up a current which will oppose the change of flux linking with it.

Now $\quad \phi_2 = \dfrac{\phi_2}{I_1} \times I_1$

If permeability of the surroundings is assumed constant then $\phi_2 \propto I_1$ and hence ϕ_2 / I_1 is constant.

$\therefore$ Rate of change of $\phi_2 = \dfrac{\phi_2}{I_1} \times$ Rate of change of current I_1

$\therefore \qquad \dfrac{d\phi_2}{dt} = \dfrac{\phi_2}{I_1} \cdot \dfrac{dI_1}{dt}$

$\therefore \qquad e_2 = -N_2 \cdot \dfrac{\phi_2}{I_1} \cdot \dfrac{dI_1}{dt} = -\left(\dfrac{N_2 \phi_2}{I_1} \right) \dfrac{dI_1}{dt}$

Here $\left(\dfrac{N_2 \phi_2}{I_1} \right)$ is called coefficient of mutual inductance denoted by M.

$\therefore \qquad \boxed{e_2 = -M \dfrac{dI_1}{dt} \qquad \text{volts}}$

Coefficient of mutual inductance is defined as the property by which e.m.f. gets induced in the second coil because of change in current through first coil.

Coefficient of mutual inductance is also called mutual inductance. It is measured in Henries.

7.26.2 Definitions of Mutual Inductance and its Unit

1. The coefficient of mutual inductance is defined as the flux linkages of the coil per ampere current in other coil.

2. It can also be defined as equal to e.m.f. induced in volts in one coil when current in other coil changes uniformly at a rate of one ampere per second.

Similarly its unit can be defined as follows :

1. Two coils which are magnetically coupled are said to have mutual inductance of one Henry when a current of one ampere flowing through one coil produces a flux linkage of one weber turn in the other coil.

2. Two coils which are magnetically coupled are said to have mutual inductance of one Henry when a current changing uniformly at the rate of one ampere per second in one coil, induces as e.m.f. of one volt in the other coil.

7.26.3 Expressions of the Mutual Inductance (M)

1)
$$M = \frac{N_2 \phi_2}{I_1}$$

2) ϕ_2 is the part of the flux ϕ_1 produced due to I_1. Let K_1 be the fraction of ϕ_1 which is linking with coil B.

∴
$$\phi_2 = K_1 \phi_1$$

$$M = \frac{N_2 K_1 \phi_1}{I_1}$$

3) The flux ϕ_1 can be expressed as,

$$\phi_1 = \frac{m.m.f.}{reluctance} = \frac{N_1 I_1}{S}$$

∴
$$M = \frac{N_2 K_1}{I_1}\left(\frac{N_1 I_1}{S}\right) = \frac{K_1 N_1 N_2}{S}$$

If all the flux produced by coil A links with coil B then $K_1 = 1$.

$$M = \frac{N_1 N_2}{S}$$

4) Now $\quad S = \dfrac{l}{\mu a} \quad$ and $\quad K_1 = 1$

Then
$$M = \frac{N_1 N_2}{\left(\dfrac{l}{\mu a}\right)} = \frac{N_1 N_2 \, a \, \mu}{l} = \frac{N_1 N_2 \, a \, \mu_0 \mu_r}{l}$$

5) If second coil carries current I_2, producing flux ϕ_2, the part of which links with coil A i.e. ϕ_1 then,

$$\phi_1 = K_2\phi_2 \quad \text{and} \quad M = \frac{N_1\phi_1}{I_2} \quad \text{i.e.} \quad M = \frac{N_1 K_2\phi_2}{I_2}$$

Now $\quad \phi_2 = \dfrac{N_2 I_2}{S} \quad$ i.e. $\quad M = \dfrac{N_1 K_2 N_2 I_2}{I_2 S}$

$\therefore \qquad \boxed{M = \dfrac{K_2 N_1 N_2}{S}}$

If entire flux produced by coil B_2 links with coil 1, $K_2 = 1$ hence,

$$\boxed{M = \frac{N_1 N_2}{S}}$$

7.26.4 Coefficient of Coupling or Magnetic Coupling Coefficient

We know that, $\quad M = \dfrac{N_2 K_1\phi_1}{I_1} \quad$ and $\quad M = \dfrac{N_1 K_2\phi_2}{I_2}$

Multiplying the two expressions of M,

$$M \times M = \frac{N_2 K_1\phi_1}{I_1} \times \frac{N_1 K_2\phi_2}{I_2}$$

$\therefore \qquad M^2 = K_1 K_2 \left(\dfrac{N_1\phi_1}{I_1}\right)\left(\dfrac{N_2\phi_2}{I_2}\right)$

but $\quad \dfrac{N_1\phi_1}{I_1} = $ Self inductance of coil 1 = L_1

$\dfrac{N_2\phi_2}{I_2} = $ Self inductance of coil 2 = L_2

$\therefore \qquad M^2 = K_1 K_2 L_1 L_2$

$$M = \sqrt{K_1 K_2} \cdot \sqrt{L_1 L_2} = K\sqrt{L_1 L_2} \quad \text{where} \quad \boxed{K = \sqrt{K_1 K_2}}$$

The K is called **coefficient of coupling**.

If entire flux produced by one coil links with other then $K = K_1 = K_2 = 1$ and maximum mutual inductance existing between the coil is $M = K\sqrt{L_1 L_2}$.

This gives an idea about magnetic coupling between the two coils. When entire flux produced by one coil links with other, this coefficient is maximum i.e. Unity.

It can be defined as the ratio of the actual mutual inductance present between the two coils to the maximum possible value of the mutual inductance.

The expression for K is,

$$K = \frac{M}{\sqrt{L_1 L_2}}$$

Key Point *When K = 1 coils are said to be* **tightly coupled** *and if K is a fraction the coils are said to be* **loosely coupled**.

Example 7.26.1 *The coils A and B in a magnetic circuit have 700 and 600 turns respectively. A current of 10 A in coil A produces a flux of 0.04 Wb. If the co-efficient of coupling is 0.2.*
Calculate : i) Self-inductance of the coil A when B is open circuit   ii) Flux linkage with the coil B.   iii) Mutual inductance iv) E.m.f. induced in the coil B when the flux linking with it changes from zero to full value in 0.02 s.

Solution : $N_A = 700$, $N_B = 600$, $I_A = 10$ A, $\phi_A = 0.04$ Wb, $K = 0.2$

1) $\quad L_A = \dfrac{N_A \phi_A}{I_A} = \dfrac{700 \times 0.04}{10} = \textbf{2.8 H}$

2) $\quad \phi_B = K \phi_A = 0.2 \times 0.04 = \textbf{8} \times \textbf{10}^{-3}$ **Wb**

3) $\quad M = \dfrac{N_B \phi_B}{I_A} = \dfrac{600 \times 8 \times 10^{-3}}{10} = \textbf{0.48 H}$

4) $\quad e_B = -N_B \dfrac{d\phi_B}{dt}$ where $d\phi_B = [8 \times 10^{-3} - 0]$, $dt = 0.02$ s

$\therefore \quad e_B = -\dfrac{600 \times [8 \times 10^{-3} - 0]}{0.02} = \textbf{- 240 V}$

The negative sign indicates that, the induced e.m.f. opposes the increase in the flux from zero to full value.

Example 7.26.2 *Two coils A and B are placed such that 40 % of flux produced by coil A links with coil B. The coils A and B have 2000 and 1000 turns respectively. A current of 2.5 A in coil A produces a flux of 0.035 mWb in coil B. For the above coil combination, find out i) M, the mutual inductance and ii) the coefficient of coupling K_A, K_B and K iii) Self inductances L_A and L_B.*

Solution : $N_A = 2000$, $N_B = 1000$, $K_A = 0.4$, $\phi_B = 0.4\ \phi_A$

$I_A = 2.5$ A and $\phi_B = 0.035$ mWb

i) Mutual inductance, $M = \dfrac{N_B\,\phi_B}{I_A} = \dfrac{1000 \times 0.035 \times 10^{-3}}{2.5} = \textbf{0.014 H}$

ii) $\phi_B = 0.035$ mWb and $\phi_B = 0.4\ \phi_A$

∴ $\phi_A = \dfrac{\phi_B}{0.4} = \dfrac{0.035}{0.4} = 0.0875$ mWb

∴ $L_A = \dfrac{N_A\,\phi_A}{I_A} = \dfrac{2000 \times 0.0875 \times 10^{-3}}{2.5}$

∴ $L_A = \textbf{0.07 H}$

Assuming that same current in coil B produces 0.035 mWb in coil B.

∴ $L_B = \dfrac{N_B\,\phi_B}{I_B} = \dfrac{1000 \times 0.035 \times 10^{-3}}{2.5} = \textbf{0.014 H}$

iii) $M = \dfrac{N_A\,\phi_A}{I_B}$ $M = \dfrac{N_A\,K_B\,\phi_B}{I_B}$

∴ $0.014 = \dfrac{2000 \times K_B \times 0.035 \times 10^{-3}}{2.5}$

∴ $K_B = \textbf{0.5}$

$\phi_B = K_A\,\phi_A$ and it is given that 40 % of ϕ_A links with coil B,

∴ $K_A = \textbf{0.4}$

$K = \sqrt{K_A K_B} = \sqrt{0.4 \times 0.5} = \textbf{0.4472}$

Review Questions

1. Explain the phenomenon of mutually induced e.m.f.

2. Define mutual inductance and state its unit. Derive the expression for mutual inductance.

3. Derive the expression for the magnitude of mutually induced e.m.f.

4. State the various expressions for the mutual inducatnce.

5. Define coefficient of coupling and obtain the relation between self inductances, mutual inductance and coefficient of coupling.

6. Two coils A and B are kept in parallel planes, such that 70 % of the flux produced by coil A links with coil B. Coil A has 10,000 turns. Coil B has 12,000 turns. A current of 4 A in coil A produces a flux of 0.04 mWb while a current of 4 A in coil B produces a flux of 0.08 mWb.

Calculate, i) Self inductances L_A and L_B ii) Mutual inductance M iii) Coupling coefficient.

[Ans. : 0.1 H, 0.24 H, 0.084 H, 0.5422]

7. *Two coils having 3000 and 2000 turns are wound on a magnetic ring. 60 % of flux produced in first coil links with the second coil. A current of 3 A produces flux of 0.5 mWb in the first coil and 0.3 mWb in the second coil. Determine the mutual inductance and coefficient of coupling.*

[Ans. : 0.2 H, 0.6324]

8. *Two identical coils P and Q, each with 1500 turns, are placed in parallel planes near to each other, so that 70 % of the flux produced by current in coil P links with coil Q. If a current of 4 A is passed through any one coil, it produces a flux of 0.04 mWb linking with itself. Find the self inductances of the two coils, the mutual inductance and coefficient of coupling between them.*

[Ans. : 15 mH, 15 mH, 10.5 mH, 0.7]

7.27 Dot Convention

The sign of mutually induced voltage depends on direction of winding of the coils. But it is very inconvenient to supply the information about winding direction of the coils. Hence dot conventions are used for purpose of indicating direction of winding. The dot conventions are interpreted as below :

1. If a positive current enters into the dots of both the coils or out of dots of both the coils, then mutually induced voltages for both the coils add to the self induced voltages hence mutually induced voltages will have same polarity as that of self induced voltages.

2. If a positive current enter into (or out of) the dot in one coil and in other coil current flows out of (or into) the dot, then the mutually induced voltages will have polarity opposite to that of self induced voltages.

The dot conventions can be interpreted in simple words as follows :

1. **If a current enters a dot in one coil, then mutually induced voltage in other coil is positive at the dotted end.**

2. **If a current leaves a dot in one coil, then mutually induced voltage in other coil is negative at the dotted end.**

Consider a magnetically coupled circuit with dots placed as shown in the Fig. 7.27.1 (a). Both the currents, i_1 and i_2 are entering the dotted terminals. Hence according to the dot convention, the mutually induced e.m.f. in both the coils has the polarity same as self induced e.m.f. in respective coil. The equivalent circuit is as shown in the Fig. 7.27.1 (b). Applying KVL, the network equations of the equivalent circuit can be written as :

$$v_1 = L_1 \frac{di_1}{dt} + M \frac{di_2}{dt}$$

... (7.27.1)

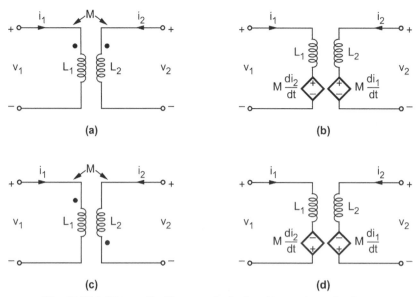

Fig. 7.27.1 Magnetically coupled circuits and equivalent circuits with different dot conventions

$$v_2 = L_2 \frac{di_2}{dt} + M \frac{di_1}{dt}$$

... (7.27.2)

Now consider magnetically coupled circuit as shown in the Fig. 7.27.1 (c) with dot placed at lower terminal of coil L_2. Hence current i_1 enters through dotted terminal of L_1 while current i_2 leaves through dotted terminal of L_2. So according to dot convention, the polarity of mutually induced e.m.f. in L_1 due to i_2 in L_2 will be opposite to that of self induced e.m.f. in coil L_1. Also the polarity of mutually induced e.m.f. in coil L_2 due to the current i_1 in coil L_1 will be opposite to that of self induced e.m.f. in coil L_2. The equivalent circuit is as shown in the Fig. 7.27.1 (d). By using KVL, the network equations can be written as,

$$v_1 = L_1 \frac{di_1}{dt} - M \frac{di_2}{dt}$$

... (7.27.3)

$$v_2 = L_2 \frac{di_2}{dt} - M \frac{di_1}{dt}$$

... (7.27.4)

Review Question

1. *Explain the dot convention used for the mututally coupled coils.*

7.28 B-H Curve or Magnetization Curve   `2004-05`

We have already seen that magnetic field strength H is $\dfrac{NI}{l}$. As current in coil changes, magnetic field strength also changes. Due to this flux produced and hence the flux density also changes.

Key Point *The graph between the flux density (B) and the magnetic field strength (H) for the magnetic material is called as its magnetization curve or B-H curve.*

Let us obtain the B-H curve experimentally for a magnetic material. The arrangement required is shown in the Fig. 7.28.1.

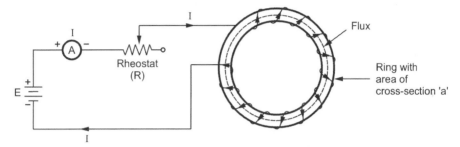

Fig. 7.28.1 Experimental set up to obtain B-H curve

The ring specimen as a mean length of 'l' metres with a cross-sectional area of 'a' square metres. Coil is wound for 'N' turns carrying a current 'I' which can be varied by changing the variable resistance 'R' connected in series. Ammeter is connected to measure the current. For measurement of flux produced, fluxmeter can be used which is not shown in the Fig. 7.28.1.

So H can be calculated as $\dfrac{NI}{l}$ while B can be calculated as $\dfrac{\phi}{a}$ for various values of current and plotted.

With the help of resistance R, I can be changed from zero to maximum possible value.

The B-H curve takes the following form, as shown in the Fig. 7.28.2.

The graph can be analysed as below :

i) **Initial portion** : Near the origin for low values of 'H', the flux density does not increase rapidly. This is represented by curve OA. The point A is called as **instep**.

ii) **Middle portion** : In this portion as 'H' increases, the flux density B increases

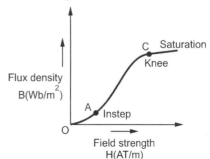

Fig. 7.28.2 B-H curve

rapidly. This is almost straight line curve. At point 'C' it starts bending again. The point 'C' where this portion bends is called as **knee point**.

iii) **Saturation portion** : After the knee point, rate of increase in 'B' reduces drastically. Finally the curve becomes parallel to 'X' axis indicating that any increase in 'H' hereafter is not going to cause any change in 'B'. The ring is said to be **saturated** and region as **saturation region**.

Review Question

1. *Draw and explain B-H curve for a magnetic material.*   **2004-05, Marks 5**

7.29 Magnetic Hysteresis and Hysteresis Loop   **2009-10, 2011-12**

Instead of plotting B-H curve only for increase in current if plotted for one complete cycle of magnetization (increase in current) and demagnetization (decrease in current) then it is called **hysteresis curve or hysteresis loop**.

Consider a circuit consisting of a battery 'E', an ammeter, variable resistance R and reversible switch shown in the Fig. 7.29.1.

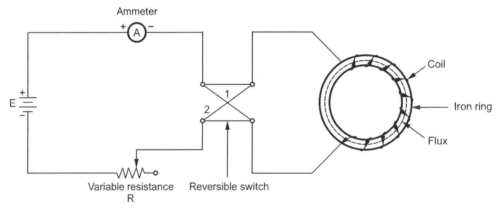

Fig. 7.29.1 Experimental set up to obtain hysteresis loop

7.29.1 Steps in Obtaining Hysteresis Loop

i) Initially variable resistance is kept maximum so current through the circuit is very low. The field strength $H = \dfrac{NI}{l}$ is also very low. So as current is increased, for low values of field strengths, flux density do not increase rapidly. But after the knee point flux density increases rapidly upto certain point. This point is called **point of saturation**. There-after any change in current do not have an effect on the flux density. This is the initial part of hysteresis loop.

ii) After the saturation point, now current is again reduced to zero. Due to this field strength also reduces to zero. But it is observed that flux density do not trace the same curve back but falls back as compared to previous magnetization curve. This phenomenon of falling back of flux density while demagnetization cycle is called **hysteresis**. Hence due to this effect, when current becomes exactly zero, there remains some magnetism associated with a coil and hence the flux density. The core does not get completely demagnetized though current through coil becomes zero. This value of flux density when exciting current through the coil and magnetic field strength is reduced to zero is called **residual flux density or remanent flux density**. This is also called **residual magnetism** of the core. The magnitude of this residual flux or magnetism depends on the nature of the material of the core. And this property of the material is called **retentivity**.

iii) But now if it is required to demagnetize the core entirely then it is necessary to reverse the direction of the current through the coil. This is possible with the help of the intermediate switch.

Key Point *The value of magnetic field strength required to wipe out the residual flux density is called the* ***coercive force****. It is measured interms of coercivity.*

iv) If now this reversed current is increased, core will get saturated but in opposite direction. At this point flux density is maximum but with opposite direction.

v) If this current is reduced to zero, again core shows a hysteresis property and does not get fully demagnetized. It shows same value of residual magnetism but with opposite direction.

vi) If current is reversed again, then for a certain magnitude of field strength, complete demagnetization of the core is possible.

vii) And if it is increased further, then saturation in the original direction is achieved completing one cycle of magnetization and demagnetization.

The curve plotted for such one cycle turns out to be a closed loop which is called hysteresis loop. Its nature is shown in the Fig. 7.29.2.

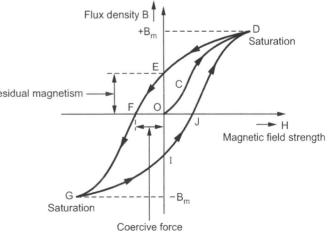

Fig. 7.29.2 Hysteresis loop

Parts of Curve	Represents What ?
O-C-D :	Region corresponding to normal magnetization curve increased form 'O' to 'I_{max}' corresponding to 'B_m'. Maximum flux density is $+ B_m$.
D-E :	Current reduced to zero, but core cannot be completely demagnetized. O-E represents residual magnetism and residual flux density, denoted by $+ B_r$.
E-F :	Current is reversed and increased in reversed direction to get complete demagnetization of the core. O-F represent coercive force required to completely wipe out $+ B_r$.
F-G :	Current is increased in reversed direction till saturation in opposite direction is achieved. Maximum flux density same but with opposite direction i.e. $- B_m$.
G-I :	Current is reduced to zero but again flux density lags and core cannot be completely demagnetized. O-I represents residual flux density in other direction i.e. $- B_r$.
I-J :	Current is again reversed and increased till complete demagnetization is achieved.
J-D :	Current is again increased in original direction till saturation is reached. Corresponding flux density is again $+ B_m$.

As seen from the loop 'O-C-D-E-F-G-I-J-D' shown in the Fig. 7.29.2, the flux density B always lags behind the values of magnetic field strength H. When H is zero, corresponding flux density is $+ B_r$. This effect is known as **hysteresis**.

Key Point *Higher the value of retentivity, higher the value of the power of the magnetic material to retain its magnetism. For high retentivity, higher is the coercive force required.*

It can be measured in terms **coercivity** of the material.

7.29.2 Practical use of Hysteresis Loop

The hysteresis loss is undesirable as it produces heat which increases temperature and also reduces the efficiency.

In machines where the frequency of the magnetization and demagnetization cycle is more, such hysteresis loss is bound to be more.

So selection of the magnetic material in such machines based on the hysteresis loss. Less the hysteresis loop area for the material, less is the hysteresis loss.

Key Point *So generally material with less hysteresis loop area of preferred for different machines like transformer cores, alternating current machines, telephones.*

Shapes of hysteresis loops for different materials are shown in the Fig. 7.29.3.

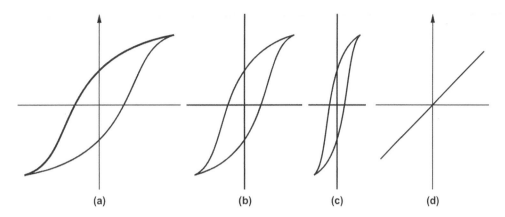

(a)   (b)   (c)   (d)

Fig. 7.29.3 Practical importance of hysterisis loop

The Fig. 7.29.3 (a) shows loop of hard steel, which is magnetic material.

The Fig. 7.29.3 (b) shows loop of cast steel.

The Fig. 7.29.3 (c) shows loop of permalloy (Alloy of nickel and iron) i.e. ferromagnetic materials.

The Fig. 7.29.3 (d) shows loop for air or non magnetic material.

The materials iron, nickel, cobalt and some of their alloys and compounds show a strong tendency to move from weaker to stronger portion of a non-uniform magnetic field. Such substances are called **ferromagnetic materials.**

The hysteresis loss is proportional to the area of the hysteresis loop. For ferromagnetic materials the hysteresis loop area is less as shown in the Fig. 7.29.3 (c) thus hysteresis loss is less in such materials.

In nonmagnetic materials, the hysteresis loop is straight line having zero area hence hysteresis loss is also zero in such materials.

Review Questions

1. *Draw and explain hysteresis loop. What is its significance ?*   **2009-10, Marks 5**

2. *What is hysteresis loop ? What is meant by saturation, coercive force and residual magnetism ? Show them in the diagram.*   **2011-12, Marks 5**

7.30 Hysteresis Loss   **2010-11**

According to the molecular theory of magnetism groups of molecules acts like elementary magnets, which are magnetized to saturation. This magnetism is developed because of the magnetic effect of electron spins, which are known as '**domains**'.

When the material is unmagnetized, the axis of the different domains are in various direction. Thus the resultant magnetic effect is zero.

When the external magnetomotive force is applied the axes of the various domains are oriented. The axes coincide with the direction of the magnetomotive force. Hence the resultant of individual magnetic effects is a strong magnetic field.

When a magnetic material is subjected to repeated cycles of magnetization and demagnetization, it results into disturbance in the alignment of the various domain. Now energy gets stored when magnetic field is established and energy is returned when field collapses. But due to hysteresis, all the energy is never returned though field completely collapses. This loss of energy appears as heat in the magnetic material. This is called as **hysteresis loss**. So disturbance in the alignment of the various domains causes hysteresis loss to take place. This hysteresis loss is undesirable and may cause undesirable high temperature rise due to heat produced. Due to such loss overall efficiency also reduces.

Such hysteresis loss depends on the following factors.

1. The hysteresis loss is directly proportional to the area under the hysteresis curve i.e. area of the hysteresis loop.

2. It is directly proportional to frequency i.e. number of cycles of magnetization per second.

3. It is directly proportional to volume of the material. It can be shown that quantitatively the hysteresis loss in joules per unit volume of the material in one cycle is equal to the area of the hysteresis loop.

In practice the hysteresis loss is calculated with reasonable accuracy by experimentally determined mathematical expression devised by **Steinmetz**, which is as follows.

$$\text{Hysteresis loss} = K_h \, (B_m)^{1.6} \, f \times \text{volume} \quad \text{watts}$$

where K_h = Characteristic constant of the material

B_m = Maximum flux density

f = Frequency in cycles per second

Review Question

1. *Explain the hysteresis loss.*   **2010-11, Marks 5**

7.31 Eddy Current Loss

2006-07, 2010-11

Consider a coil wound on a core. If this coil carries an alternating current i.e. current whose magnitude varies with respect to time, then flux produced by it is also of alternating nature. So core is under the influence of the changing flux and under such condition according to the Faraday's law of electromagnetic induction, e.m.f. gets induced in the core. Now if core is solid, then such induced e.m.f. circulates currents through the core. Such currents in the core which are due to induced e.m.f. in the core are called as eddy currents. Due to such currents there is power loss (I^2R) in the core. Such loss is called as **eddy current loss**. This loss, similar to hysteresis loss, reduces the efficiency. For solid core with less resistance, eddy currents are always very high.

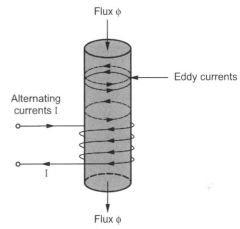

Fig. 7.31.1 Eddy currents

The Fig. 7.31.1 shows a core carrying the eddy currents.

Eddy current loss depends on the various factors which are

    i) Nature of the material

    ii) Maximum flux density

    iii) Frequency

    iv) Thickness of laminations used to construct to core

    v) Volume of magnetic material.

It has been found that loss can be considerably reduced by selecting high resistivity magnetic material like silicon. Most popular method used to reduce eddy current loss is to use laminated construction to construct the core. Core is constructed by stacking thin pieces known as laminations as shown in the Fig. 7.31.2. The laminations are insulated from each other by thin layers of insulating material like varnish, paper, mica. This restricts the paths of eddy currents, to respective laminations only. So area through which currents flow decreases, increasing the resistance and magnitude of currents gets reduced considerably.

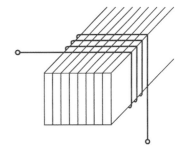

Fig. 7.31.2 Laminated core

The loss may also be reduced by grinding the ferromagnetic material to a powder and mixing it with a binder that effectively insulates the particles one from other. This mixture is then formed under pressure into the desired shape and heat treated. Magnetic cores for use in communication equipment are frequently made by this process.

This loss is quantified by using the expression,

$$\text{Eddy current loss} = K_e \, (B_m)^2 \, f^2 \, t^2 \times \text{volume} \quad \text{watts}$$

K_e = A characteristic constant of material, B_m = Maximum flux density,

f = Frequency, t = Thickness of the lamination

Review Question

1. *Explain the eddy current loss.* **2006-07, 2010-11, Marks 5**

7.32 Short Answered and Objective Type Questions

Q.1 Show the residual magnetism in a B-H curve. **(Refer section 7.28)** **2011-12**

Q.2 The magnetic effect of an electric current is discovered by,

a) Ampere   b) Ohms   c) Oersted   d) Faraday **(Ans.: c)**

Q.3 A freely suspended magnet adjusts itself in the _____ direction.

a) East-West   b) North-South   c) None of these   d) Vertical **(Ans.: b)**

Q.4 The region around the magnet in which magnetic influence can be experienced is called _____.

a) flux   b) line of force   c) strength   d) magnetic field **(Ans.: d)**

Q.5 The direction of flux internal to the magnet is from _____.

a) N-pole to S-pole b) S-pole to N-pole

c) Circular   d) None of the above   **(Ans.: b)**

Q.6 1 weber = _____ lines of force

a) 10^8 b) 10^6 c) 10^3 d) 10^{-8} **(Ans.: a)**

Q.7 The unit of flux density is _____.

a) weber   b) AT   c) tesla   d) None of these **(Ans.: c)**

Q.8 The magnetic field strength H is given by _____.

a) $\dfrac{Nl}{I}$ b) $\dfrac{Il}{N}$ c) $\dfrac{NI}{l}$ d) N I l **(Ans.: c)**

Q.9 The unit of magnetic field strength H is _____.

a) weber   b) AT   c) tesla   d) AT/m   **(Ans. : d)**

Q.10 The direction of magnetic field due to straight current carrying conductor is given by _____.

a) Fleming's left hand rule   b) Right hand thumb rule
c) Fleming's right hand rule   d) None of the above   **(Ans. : b)**

Q.11 The unit of permeability is _____.

a) H/m   b) Hm   c) weber   d) tesla   **(Ans. : a)**

Q.12 Higher value of μ_r means _____.

a) Difficult to pass the flux, through the material

b) Easy to pass the flux, through the material

c) None of these   **(Ans. : b)**

Q.13 For a magnetic material, the value of μ_r is _____.

a) low   b) zero   c) high   d) one   **(Ans. : c)**

Q.14 For free space, the value of μ_r is _____.

a) low   b) zero   c) high   d) one   **(Ans. : d)**

Q.15 The S.I. unit of reluctance is _____.

a) AT/Wb   b) AT   c) AT/m   d) Wb/AT **(Ans. : a)**

Q.16 The _____ is reciprocal of the reluctance.

a) permeability   b) permeance   c) susceptance   d) resistance
     (Ans. : b)

Q.17 A magnetic circuit has a reluctance of 1×10^5 AT/Wb and m.m.f. is produced by coil having 100 turns, carrying current of 5 A then the flux produced is _____ Wb.

a) 5   b) 0.2×10^{-3} c) 5×10^{-3} d) 0.2   **(Ans. : c)**

Q.18 A magnetic circuit has μ_r = 1000 and length of 50 cm with cross-sectional area of 4 cm². The amperes required through a coil of 1000 turns to produce the flux of 2 mWb are _____ A.

a) 3.98   b) 5.28   c) 4.989   d) 1.989   **(Ans. : d)**

Q.19 The reluctance is _____ to the relative permeability of the magnetic circuit.

a) inversely proportional   b) directly proportional
c) not dependent   d) none of the above   **(Ans. : a)**

Q.20 The reluctance in a magnetic circuit is analogous to _____ in an electric circuit.

a) voltage   b) current   c) resistance   d) e.m.f.   **(Ans. : c)**

Q.21 The e.m.f. is obtained from the magnetic flux by _____.

a) ampere   b) faraday   c) oersted   d) ohms   **(Ans. : b)**

Q.22 A coil of 2000 turns, produces a flux of 1 mWb. The flux is reversed in 0.1 sec then e.m.f. induced is _____V.

a) – 40   b) 20   c) 40   d) 60   **(Ans. : c)**

Q.23 When e.m.f. is induced due to physical movement of the coil then it is called _____.

a) statically induced e.m.f.   b) forcefully induced e.m.f.

c) dynamically induced e.m.f.   d) magnetically induced e.m.f.   **(Ans. : c)**

Q.24 The dynamically induced e.m.f. can be found in _____.

a) generator   b) transformer   c) bulb   d) none of these
                                                                            (Ans. : a)

Q.25 Direction of dynamically induced e.m.f. is given by _____.

a) fleming's left hand rule   b) fleming's right hand rule

c) end rule   d) corkscrew rule   **(Ans. : b)**

Q.26 According to _____ the induced e.m.f. opposes the cause producing it.

a) Ohm's law   b) Faraday's law   c) Kirchhoff's law   d) Lenz's law
                                                                            (Ans. : d)

Q.27 The magnitude of force experienced by a current carrying conductor is given by, _____.

a) $B \phi l$ b) $B I l$ c) $\dfrac{NI}{l}$ d) $\dfrac{BI}{l}$
                                                                            (Ans. : b)

Q.28 When the conductor and lines of flux are parallel then the force experienced by the conductor is, _____.

a) zero   b) maximum   c) small   d) unity   **(Ans. : a)**

Q.29 The self inductance L is given by, _____.

a) $N \phi I$ b) $\dfrac{NI}{\phi}$ c) $\dfrac{N\phi}{I}$ d) $\dfrac{I}{N\phi}$
                                                                            (Ans. : c)

Q.30 The self inductance L is _____ number of turns.

a) directly proportional to square of

b) inversely proportional to square of

c) directly proportional to

d) none of the above   **(Ans. : a)**

Q.31 A current of 20 A is reversed in 0.1 sec through an inductor of 1 H then e.m.f. induced is _____ volts.

a) 200   b) – 200   c) – 400   d) 400   **(Ans. : d)**

Q.32 If the entire flux produced by one coil links with the other then its coefficient of coupling is _____.

a) zero   b) unity   c) very high   d) 0.5   **(Ans. : b)**

Q.33 If K = 1 then the coils are said to be _____.

a) loosely coupled   b) decoupled   c) tightly coupled   d) none of these
                                                                        (Ans. : c)

Q.34 The unit of coefficient of coupling is _____.

a) amperes   b) AT/Wb   c) unitless   d) H/m   **(Ans. : c)**

Q.35 The slope of B-H curve at various points decide the value of _____.

a) relative permeability   b) flux

c) flux density   d) permeance   **(Ans. : a)**

Q.36 The value of magnetic field strength required to wipe out the residual flux is called _____.

a) electromotive force   b) magnetomotive force

c) residual force   d) coercive force   **(Ans. : d)**

Q.37 Lesser the hysteresis loss if _____ is the hysteresis loop area.

a) higher   b) lesser   c) very high   d) none of these
                                                                        (Ans. : b)

Q.38 For _____ of the following material, the hysteresis loop is a straight line.

a) air   b) steel   c) cast steel   d) alloy   **(Ans. : a)**

Q.39 Using the B-H curve, the m.m.f. of _____ is obtained.

a) iron path   b) air gap

c) both iron path and air gap   d) none of the above   **(Ans. : a)**

Q.40 The saturation is not possible in case of _____.

a) silicon steel   b) iron   c) cast steel   d) air   **(Ans. : d)**

Q.41 *The area under the B-H curve represents _____.*

a) eddy current loss   b) power loss   c) hysteresis loss   d) core loss
                                                                        (Ans. : c)

Q.42 If the permeability of a magnetic material is $4\pi \times 10^{-4}$ then its relative permeability is _____.

a) $4\pi \times 10^{-7}$ b) 10000   c) 100   d) 1000   **(Ans. : d)**

Q.43 The Hopkinson's coefficient is defined as _____.

  a) $\phi_T \times \phi_u$ b) $\dfrac{\phi_T}{\phi_u}$ c) $\dfrac{\phi_T}{\phi_g}$ d) none of these

                                                                     (Ans. : b)

Q.44 The ideal value of leakage coefficient is _____.

  a) zero   b) infinite   c) one   d) none of these

                                                                      (Ans. : c)

Q.45 The tendency of flux to bulge out at the edges of the air gap is called _____.

  a) magnetic leakage   b) hysteresis

  c) residual flux   d) magnetic fringing   **(Ans. : d)**

Q.46 The flux completing the path through air instead of the desired path is called _____.

  a) leakage flux   b) residual flux   c) coercive flux   d) none of these

                                                                      (Ans. : a)

Q.47 The eddy current loss is _____ frequency.

  a) proportional to   b) reciprocal of

  c) proportional to square of   d) none of these   **(Ans. : c)**

Q.48 The eddy current loss can be minimized by _____.

  a) selecting material with low hysteresis loop area

  b) using laminated construction

  c) using air gaps

  d) none of the above   **(Ans. : b)**

Q.49 When the current carrying conductor and lines of flux are parallel then the force experienced by the conductor is _____.

  a) zero   b) maximum   c) small   d) unity   **(Ans. : a)**

Q.50 Direction of the force experienced by a current carrying conductor in a magnetic field is given by _____ .

  a) Fleming's left hand rule   b) Fleming's right hand rule

  c) End rule   d) Corkscrew rule   **(Ans. : a)**

Q.51 A conductor of length 30 cm carrying a current of 7 A is placed in a uniform magnetic field of flux density 1.10 tesla, making an angle of 60° with respect to the plane of the flux then the force experienced by the conductor is _____ N.

  a) 2.31   b) 2   c) 2.1   d) 2.3   **(Ans. : b)**

Q.52 The e.m.f. induced in a coil of N turns is _____ .

  a) $N\dfrac{d\phi}{dt}$ b) $N\dfrac{d\phi}{di}$ c) $-N\dfrac{d\phi}{dt}$ d) $L\dfrac{d\phi}{di}$ **(Ans. : c)**

Q.53 A coil of 2000 turns, produces a flux of 1 mWb. The flux is reversed in 0.1 sec then e.m.f. induced is _____ V.

a) 40   b) 20   c) – 40   d) 60   **(Ans. : a)**

Q.54 Direction of dynamically induced e.m.f. is given by _____.

a) Fleming's left hand rule   b) Fleming's right hand rule

c) End rule   d) Corkscrew rule   **(Ans. : b)**

Q.55 The magnitude of dynamically induced e.m.f. is given by _____.

a) B l I sin θ   b) B l v sin θ   c) $\dfrac{Bl \sin \theta}{v}$ d) none of these

(Ans. : b)

Q.56 Induced e.m.f. in a conductor is maximum when the plane of rotation of conductor is at _____ with respect to the plane of the flux.

a) 60°   b) 90°   c) 30°   d) 0°   **(Ans. : b)**

Q.57 A conductor of length 40 cm is made to move with constant velocity of 10 m/s perpendicular to the magnetic field of flux density 1.2 tesla then the induced e.m.f. in the conductor is _____ V.

a) 4.8   b) 0   c) 4   d) 0.48   **(Ans. : a)**

Q.58 Induced e.m.f. in a conductor of length 0.5 m, when moved in a magnetic field of flux density 1.05 tesla with a velocity 5 m/s is observed to be 1.856 V then the angle between plane of motion and plane of the flux is _____.

a) 60°   b) 90°   c) 0°   d) 45°   **(Ans. : d)**

Q.59 The self inductance L is given by _____.

a) N φI   b) $\dfrac{NI}{\phi}$ c) $\dfrac{N\phi}{I}$ d) $\dfrac{I}{N\phi}$

(Ans. : c)

Q.60 An e.m.f. of 7.2 volts is induced in a coil of 6 mH. Then the rate of change of current is _____.

a) 12 A/s   b) 120 A/s   c) 1200 A/s   d) 12000 A/s.

(Ans. : c)

Q.61 If the entire flux produced by one coil links with the other then its coefficient of coupling is _____.

a) zero   b) unity   c) very high   d) 0.5   **(Ans. : b)**

Q.62 The unit of coefficient of coupling is _____ .

a) amperes   b) AT/Wb   c) unitless   d) H/m   **(Ans. : c)**

Q.63 Two coils have self inductances of 100 μH and 250 μH and coefficient of coupling is 0.253 then their mutual inductance is _____.

a) 400 μH   b) 158.11 μH   c) 40 μH   d) 40 mH   **(Ans. : c)**

Q.64 The mutual inductance between coils A and B is 5 µH and the current of 2 A in coil A is reversed in 0.5 seconds then average e.m.f. induced in coil B is _____ V.

a) 40 µV   b) 40 mV   c) 10 µV   d) 10 mV **(Ans. : a)**

Q.65 A conductor of length 20 cm carrying a current of 10 A is placed in a uniform magnetic field of flux density 1.15 tesla, perpendicular to the lines of flux then the force experienced by the conductor is _____ N.

a) 11.5   b) 23   c) 3.2   d) 2.3   **(Ans. : d)**

Q.66 A conductor experiences a force of 0.3125 N when placed in a magnetic field of flux density 1.25 tesla. The length of the conductor is 10 cm and it carries a current of 5 A then its angle with respect to the plane of the flux is _____.

a) 60°   b) 90°   c) 30°   d) 0°   **(Ans. : c)**

Q.67 A 0.1 A of current reverses in 0.2 seconds then the rate of change of current is _____ A/sec.

a) 1   b) – 1   c) 2   d) 0.5   **(Ans. : b)**

Q.68 The coupling between two magnetically coupled coils is said to be the ideal if the coefficient of coupling is _____.   **2009-10**

a) zero   b) 0.5   c) 0.75   d) 1   **(Ans. : d)**

❑❑❑

8 Single Phase Transformer

Syllabus

Principle of operation, Construction, E.M.F. equation, Equivalent circuit, Power losses, Efficiency (Simple numerical problems), Introduction to auto transformer.

Contents

8.1 Introduction

Alternating voltages can be raised or lowered as per the requirements in the different stages of electrical network as generation, transmission, distribution and utilization. This is possible with a static device called **transformer.**

We can define transformer as below :

The transformer is a static piece of apparatus by means of which an electrical power is transformed from one alternating current circuit to another with the desired change in voltage and current, without any change in the frequency.

Thus the transformer is used to increase or decrease the voltage as per the requirement.

The use of transformers in a.c. transmission system is shown in the Fig. 8.1.1.

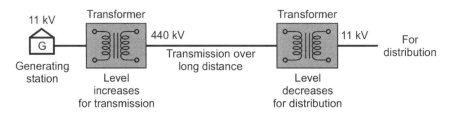

Fig. 8.1.1 Use of transformers in transmission system

Review Question

1. *What is transformer ? What are its functions ? Mention its application in a.c. transmission.*

8.2 Principle of Working   2005-06, 2012-13

The transformer works on the principle of **mutual induction** which states that **when two coils are inductively coupled and if current in one coil is changed uniformly then an e.m.f. gets induced in the other coil**. This e.m.f. can drive a current, when a closed path is provided to it. In its elementary form, it consists of two inductive coils which are electrically separated but linked through a common magnetic circuit. The two coils have high mutual inductance. The basic transformer is shown in the Fig. 8.2.1. (See Fig. 8.2.1 on next page)

One of the two coils is connected to a source of alternating voltage. This coil in which electrical energy is fed with the help of source is called **primary winding (P)**. The other winding is connected to load. The electrical energy transformed to this winding is drawn out to the load. This winding is called **secondary winding (S)**. The primary winding has N_1 number of turns while the secondary winding has N_2 number of turns. Symbolically the transformer is indicated as shown in the Fig. 8.2.2.

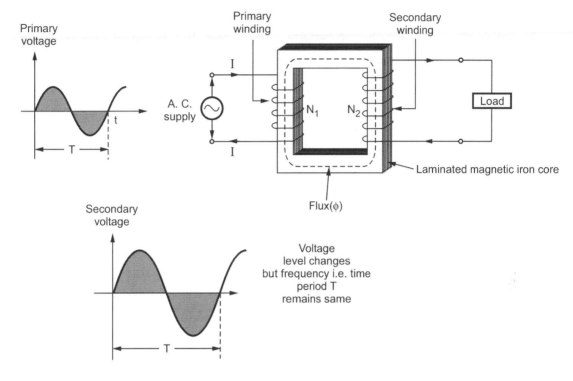

Voltage level changes but frequency i.e. time period T remains same

Fig. 8.2.1 Basic transformer

When primary winding is excited by an alternating voltage, it circulates an alternating current. This current produces an alternating flux (ϕ) which completes its path through common magnetic core as shown dotted in the Fig. 8.2.1. Thus an alternating, flux links with the secondary winding. As the flux is alternating, according to

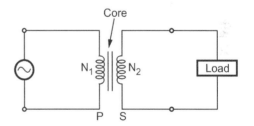

Fig. 8.2.2 Symbolic representation

Faraday's law of an electromagnetic induction, mutually induced e.m.f. gets developed in the secondary winding. If now load is connected to the secondary winding, this e.m.f. drives a current through it.

Thus though there is no electrical contact between the two windings, an electrical energy gets transferred from primary to the secondary.

Key Point *The frequency of the mutually induced e.m.f. is same as that of the alternating source which is supplying energy to the primary winding.*

8.2.1 Can D.C. Supply be used for Transformers ?

The transformer works on the principle of mutual induction, for which current in one coil must change uniformly. If d.c. supply is given, the current will not change due to constant supply and transformer will not work.

Practically winding resistance is very small. For d.c., the inductive reactance X_L is zero as d.c. has no frequency. So total impedance of winding is very low for d.c. Thus winding will draw very high current if d.c. supply is given to it. This may cause the burning of windings due to extra heat generated and may cause permanent damage to the transformer.

There can be saturation of the core due to which transformer draws very large current from the supply when connected to d.c.

Thus d.c. supply should not be connected to the transformers.

Review Questions

1.	*Explain the working principle of transformer.*	**2005-06, Marks 5**
2.	*What happens if d.c. supply is given to transformer ?*	**2012-13, Marks 2**

8.3 Parts of Transformer

The various parts of transformer are,

1. Core : It is made up of high grade silicon steel laminations. Its function is to carry the flux, providing low reluctance to it. Generally 'L' shaped or 'I' shaped laminations are used as shown in the Fig. 8.3.1.

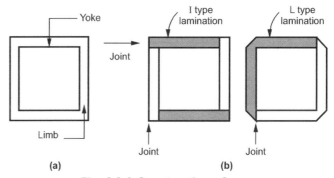

Fig. 8.3.1 Construction of core

2. **Limb** : It is vertical portion of the core and its function is to carry the windings.

3. **Yoke** : The top and bottom horizontal portion of the core is called **yoke.** Its function is to carry the flux produced by one winding to reach to the other winding and provide the low reluctance path to the flux.

4. **Windings** : The coils used are wound on the limbs and are insulated from each other. The function of the windings is to carry the current and produce the flux necessary for the functioning of the transformer.

5. **Conservator** : The oil in the transformer expands when temperature inside the transformer increases due to heat while it contracts when the temperature decreases. The function of the conservator is to take up the expansion and contraction of the oil without allowing it to come in contact with the ambient air.

6. **Breather :** Smaller transformers are not fully filled with oil and some space remains between oil level and tank. The tank is connected to atmosphere by vent pipe. When oil expands air goes out while when oil contracts the air is taken in. The breather is a device which extracts the moisture from the air when the air is taken in and does not allow oil to come in contact with the moisture. The breathers contain the silica gel crystals which immediately absorb the atmospheric moisture.

7. **Explosion vent :** It is a bent pipe fitted on the main tank which acts as a relief valve. It uses nonmetallic diaphragm which bursts when pressure inside the transformer becomes excessive which releases the pressure and protects the transformer.

8. **Buchholz relay :** It is a safety gas operated relay connected to transformer. When the fault gets developed inside the transformer, the gases are released. The Buchholz relay is operated with these gases and trips the circuit breaker to protect the device.

Review Question

> 1. *What are the main parts of transformer ? State the function of each part.*

8.4 Construction of Transformer   `2002-03`

The various types based on the construction of single phase transformers are,

     1. Core type   and   2. Shell type

1. Core type transformer : It has a single magnetic circuit. The core is rectangular having two limbs. The winding encircles the core.

The Fig. 8.4.1 (a) shows the schematic representation of the core type transformer while the Fig. 8.4.1 (b) shows the view of actual construction of the core type transformer.

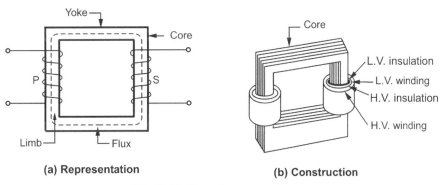

(a) Representation   (b) Construction

Fig. 8.4.1 Core type transformer

The coils used are of cylindrical type, wound in helical layers with different layers insulated from each other by paper or mica.

Both the coils are placed on both the limbs. The low voltage coil is placed inside near the core while high voltage coil surrounds the low voltage coil.

Core is made up of large number of thin laminations.

As the windings are uniformly distributed over the two limbs, the natural cooling is more effective.

The coils can be easily removed by removing the laminations of the top yoke, for maintenance.

2. Shell type transformer : It has a double magnetic circuit. The core has three limbs.

Both the windings are placed on the central limb. The core encircles most part of the windings.

The coils used are generally multilayer disc type or sandwich coils.

The core is laminated. While arranging the laminations of the core, the care is taken that all the joints at alternate layers are staggered. This is done to avoid narrow air gap at the joint, right through the cross-section of the core.

Generally for very high voltage transformers, the shell type construction is preferred.

As the windings are surrounded by the core, the natural cooling does not exist.

For removing any winding for maintenance, large number of laminations are required to be removed.

The Fig. 8.4.2 (a) shows the schematic representation while the Fig. 8.4.2 (b) shows the outway view of the construction of the shell type transformer.

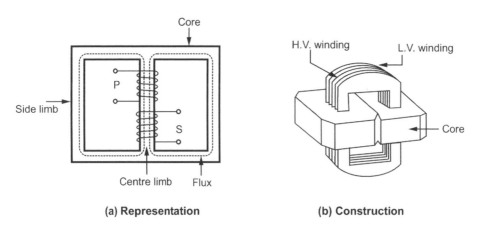

(a) Representation   (b) Construction

Fig. 8.4.2 Shell type transformer

8.4.1 Comparison of Core and Shell Type Constructions

The comparison of core type and shell type transformers is given in the Table 8.4.1.

Sr. No.	Core type	Shell type
1.	The winding encircles the core.	The core encircles most part of the windings.
2.	The cylindrical type of coils are used.	Generally, multilayer disc type or sandwich coils are used.
3.	As windings are distributed, the natural cooling is more effective.	As windings are surrounded by the core, the natural cooling does not exist.
4.	The coils can be easily removed from maintenance point of view.	For removing any winding for the maintenance, large number of laminations are required to be removed. This is difficult.
5.	The construction is preferred for low voltage transformers.	The construction is used for very high voltage transformers.
6.	It has a single magnetic circuit.	It has a double magnetic circuit.
7.	In a single phase type, the core has two limbs.	In a single phase type, the core has three limbs.

Table 8.4.1

Review Questions

1. *With neat sketch explain the constructional details of core and shell type transformers.*
2. *Compare core type and shell type transformers.*   **2002-03, Marks 5**

8.5 E.M.F. Equation of a Transformer   **2009-10**

When the primary winding is excited by an alternating voltage V_1, it circulates alternating current, producing an alternating flux ϕ.

The primary winding has N_1 number of turns. The alternating flux ϕ linking with the primary winding itself induces an e.m.f. in it denoted as E_1.

The flux links with secondary winding through the common magnetic core. It produces induced e.m.f. E_2 in the secondary winding. This is mutually induced e.m.f.

The primary winding is excited by purely sinusoidal alternating voltage. Hence the flux produced is also sinusoidal in nature having maximum value of ϕ_m as shown in the Fig. 8.5.1.

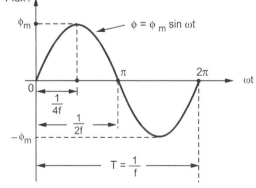

Fig. 8.5.1 Sinusoidal flux

The various quantities which affect the magnitude of the induced e.m.f. are :

ϕ = Flux   and ϕ_m = Maximum value of flux

N_1 = Number of primary winding turns N_2 = Number of secondary winding turns

f = Frequency of the supply voltage

E_1 = R.M.S. value of the primary induced e.m.f.

E_2 = R.M.S. value of the secondary induced e.m.f.

From Faraday's law of electromagnetic induction the average e.m.f. induced in each turn is proportional to the average rate of change of flux.

$\therefore$ Average e.m.f. per turn = Average rate of change of flux = $\dfrac{d\phi}{dt}$

Now, $\dfrac{d\phi}{dt} = \dfrac{\text{Change in flux}}{\text{Time required for change in flux}}$

Consider the $1/4^{\text{th}}$ cycle of the flux as shown in the Fig. 8.5.1. Complete cycle gets completed in 1/f seconds. In $1/4^{\text{th}}$ time period, the change in flux is from 0 to ϕ_m.

$\therefore$ $\dfrac{d\phi}{dt} = \dfrac{\phi_m - 0}{\left(\dfrac{1}{4f}\right)} = 4\,f\,\phi_m$ Wb/sec   as dt for $1/4^{\text{th}}$ time period is 1/4f seconds

$\therefore$ **Average e.m.f. per turn** $= 4\,f\,\phi_m$ volts

As ϕ is sinusoidal, the induced e.m.f. in each turn of both the windings is also sinusoidal in nature.

For sinusoidal quantity,   Form Factor $= \dfrac{\text{R.M.S. value}}{\text{Average value}} = 1.11$

$\therefore$ R.M.S. value = $1.11 \times$ Average value

$\therefore$ R.M.S. value of induced e.m.f. per turn $= 1.11 \times 4\,f\,\phi_m = 4.44\,f\,\phi_m$

There are N_1 number of primary turns hence the R.M.S. value of induced e.m.f. of primary denoted as E_1 is,

$E_1 = N_1 \times 4.44\,f\,\phi_m$ volts

While as there are N_2 number of secondary turns the R.M.S. value of induced e.m.f. of secondary denoted E_2 is,

$E_2 = N_2 \times 4.44\,f\,\phi_m$ volts

The expressions of E_1 and E_2 are called e.m.f. equations of a transformer.

$$E_1 = 4.44 \, f \, \phi_m \, N_1 \text{ volts} \qquad \qquad \dots (8.5.1)$$

$$E_2 = 4.44 \, f \, \phi_m \, N_2 \text{ volts} \qquad \qquad \dots (8.5.2)$$

8.5.1 Concept of Ideal Transformer

A transformer is said to be ideal if it satisfies following properties :

i) It has no losses.

ii) Its windings have zero resistance.

iii) Leakage flux is zero i.e. 100 % flux produced by primary links with the secondary.

iv) Permeability of core is so high that negligible current is required to establish the flux in it.

8.5.2 Ratios of a Transformer

Consider a transformer shown in Fig. 8.5.2 indicating various voltages and currents.

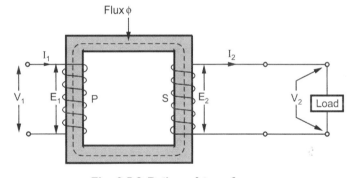

Fig. 8.5.2 Ratios of transformer

1. Voltage ratio

We know from the e.m.f. equations,

$$E_1 = 4.44 \, f \, \phi_m \, N_1 \quad \text{and}$$

$$E_2 = 4.44 \, f \, \phi_m \, N_2$$

Taking ratio of the two equations we get,

$$\frac{E_2}{E_1} = \frac{N_2}{N_1} = K$$

This ratio of secondary induced e.m.f. to primary induced e.m.f. is known as voltage transformation ratio denoted as K.

Thus, $\qquad$ $E_2 = K \, E_1 \qquad \text{where} \quad K = \dfrac{N_2}{N_1}$

1. If $N_2 > N_1$ i.e. $K > 1$, we get $E_2 > E_1$ then the transformer is called **step-up transformer**.

2. If $N_2 < N_1$ i.e. $K < 1$, we get $E_2 < E_1$ then the transformer is called **step-down transformer**.

3. If $N_2 = N_1$ i.e. $K = 1$, we get $E_2 = E_1$ then the transformer is called **isolation transformer** or **1 : 1 transformer**.

2. Current ratio

For an ideal transformer there are no losses. Hence the product of primary voltage V_1 and primary current I_1, is same as the product of secondary voltage V_2 and the secondary current I_2.

So $V_1 I_1$ = Input VA   and $V_2 I_2$ = Output VA

For an ideal transformer, $V_1 I_1 = V_2 I_2$

$\therefore$

$$\frac{V_2}{V_1} = \frac{I_1}{I_2} = K$$

Hence the currents are in the inverse ratio of the voltage transformation ratio.

8.5.3 Volt-Ampere Rating

When electrical power is transferred from primary winding to secondary there are few power losses in between. These power losses appear in the form of heat which increase the temperature of the device.

This temperature must be maintained below certain limiting value as it is always harmful from insulation point of view.

The copper loss (I^2R) in the transformer depends on the current 'I' through the winding while the iron or core loss depends on the voltage 'V' as frequency of operation is constant.

None of these losses depend on the power factor ($\cos \phi$) of the load. Hence losses decide the temperature rise and hence the rating of the transformer.

As losses depend on V and I only, the rating of the transformer is specified as a product of these two parameters $V \times I$. Hence the transformer rating is specified as the product of voltage and current are called **VA rating.**

On both sides, primary and secondary VA rating remains same. This rating is generally expressed in kVA (kilo volt amperes rating).

$$\text{kVA rating of a transformer} = \frac{V_1 I_1}{1000} = \frac{V_2 I_2}{1000} \qquad \text{... 1000 to express in kVA}$$

8.5.4 Full Load Currents

If V_1 and V_2 are the terminal voltages of primary and secondary then from specified kVA rating we can decide full load currents of primary and secondary, I_1 and I_2.

This is the **safe maximum current limit** which may carry, keeping temperature rise below its limiting value.

$$I_1 \text{ full load} = \frac{\text{kVA rating} \times 1000}{V_1}$$

$$I_2 \text{ full load} = \frac{\text{kVA rating} \times 1000}{V_2}$$

... (1000 to convert kVA to VA)

These values indicate, how much maximum load can be connected to a given transformer of a specified kVA rating.

The full load primary and secondary currents indicate the safe maximum values of currents which transformer windings can carry.

Example 8.5.1 *A single-phase, 50 Hz transformer has 80 turns on the primary winding and 400 turns on the secondary winding. The net cross-sectional area of the core is 200 cm^2. If the primary winding is connected to a 240 V, 50 Hz supply, determine : i) The e.m.f. induced in the secondary winding. ii) The maximum value of the flux density in the core.*

Solution : $N_1 = 80$, $f = 50$ Hz, $N_2 = 400$, $a = 200$ $cm^2 = 200 \times 10^{-4}$ m^2, $E_1 = 240$ V

$$K = \frac{N_2}{N_1} = \frac{400}{80} = \frac{5}{1} = \frac{E_2}{E_1}$$

$\therefore$ $E_2 = 5 \times 240 = \textbf{1200 V}$

Now $E_1 = 4.44 \, f \, \phi_m \, N_1$ i.e. $240 = 4.44 \times 50 \times \phi_m \times 80$

$\therefore$ $\phi_m = \dfrac{240}{4.44 \times 50 \times 80} = 0.01351$ Wb

$\therefore$ $B_m = \dfrac{\phi_m}{a} = \dfrac{0.01351}{200 \times 10^{-4}} = \textbf{0.6756 Wb/m}^2$

Example 8.5.2 *For a single phase transformer having primary and secondary turns of 440 and 880 respectively, determine the transformer kVA rating if half load secondary current is 7.5 A and maximum value of core flux is 2.25 mWb.*

Solution : $N_1 = 440$, $N_2 = 880$, $(I_2)_{H.L.} = 7.5$ A,

$\phi_m = 2.25$ mWb, $E_2 = 4.44 \, \phi_m \, f \, N_2$ ... Assume $f = 50$ Hz

$\therefore$ $\qquad$ $E_2 = 4.44 \times 2.25 \times 10^{-3} \times 50 \times 880 = 439.56 \text{ V}$

$$(I_2)_{\text{F.L.}} = \frac{\text{kVA rating}}{E_2}$$

$$(I_2)_{\text{H.L.}} = \frac{1}{2}(I_2)_{\text{F.L.}} \quad \text{i.e.} \quad (I_2)_{\text{H.L.}} = \frac{1}{2} \times \frac{\text{kVA rating}}{E_2} \quad \text{i.e.} \quad 7.5 = \frac{1}{2} \times \frac{\text{kVA rating}}{439.56}$$

$\therefore$ $\quad$ kVA rating $= 2 \times 7.5 \times 439.56 \times 10^{-3} = \textbf{6.5934 kVA}$ $\qquad\qquad$ ... $(10^{-3}$ for kVA)

Review Questions

1. *Derive the e.m.f. equation of a single phase transformer.* **2009-10, Marks 5**

2. *What is ideal transformer ?*

3. *Explain the various transformation ratios of a transformer.*

4. *What are the assumptions for an ideal transformer ?*

5. *What is volt-ampere rating of a transformer ? Why is it specified in volt-ampere and not in watts ?*

6. *How to obtain full load currents of a transformer from its rating ?*

7. *A 250 kVA, 11000/415 V, 50 Hz single phase transformer has 80 turns on the secondary. Calculate : i) The rated primary and secondary currents. ii) The number of primary turns.*
   $\qquad$ *iii) The maximum value of flux.* $\qquad\qquad$ *iv) Voltage induced per turn.*
   $\qquad\qquad\qquad$ **[Ans. : 22.7272 A, 602.4096 A, 2122, 23.3671 mWb, 5.1875 V/turn]**

8. *A 1 ϕ transformer has 1000 turns on its primary and 400 turns on the secondary side. An a.c. voltage of 1250 V, 50 Hz is applied to its primary side, with the secondary open circuited. Calculate : i) The secondary e.m.f. ii) Maximum value of flux density, given that the effective cross-sectional area of core is 60 cm^2.* $\qquad$ **[Ans. : 500 V, 0.9384 Wb$/$m^2]**

8.6 Ideal Transformer on No Load

Consider an ideal transformer on no load as shown in the Fig. 8.6.1. The supply voltage is V_1 and as it is an no load the secondary current $I_2 = 0$.

The primary draws a current I_1 which is just necessary to produce flux in the core. As it is magnetizing the core, it is called **magnetizing current** denoted as I_m.

As the transformer is ideal, the winding resistance is zero and it is purely inductive in nature.

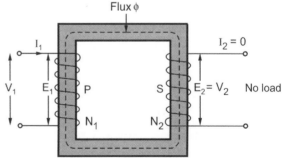

Fig. 8.6.1 Ideal transformer on no load

The magnetizing current I_m is very small and lags V_1 by 90° as the winding is purely inductive. This I_m produces an alternating flux ϕ which is in phase with I_m.

The flux links with both the winding producing the induced e.m.f.s E_1 and E_2, in the primary and secondary windings respectively.

According to Lenz's law, the induced e.m.f. opposes the cause producing it which is supply voltage V_1. Hence E_1 is in antiphase with V_1 but equal in magnitude.

The induced E_2 also opposes V_1 hence in antiphase with V_1 but its magnitude depends on N_2. Thus E_1 and E_2 are in phase.

The phasor diagram for the ideal transformer on no load is shown in the Fig. 8.6.2.

It can be seen that flux ϕ is reference.

I_m produces ϕ hence in phase with ϕ. V_1 leads I_m by 90° as winding is purely inductive so current has to lag voltage by 90°.

E_1 and E_2 are in phase and both opposing supply voltage V_1.

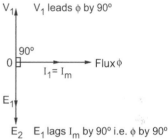

Fig. 8.6.2 Phasor diagram for ideal transformer on no load

Review Question

> *1. Explain the operation of an ideal transformer on no load.*

8.7 Practical Transformer on No Load   2003-04, 2004-05, 2009-10

Actually in practical transformer iron core causes hysteresis and eddy current losses as it is subjected to alternating flux.

Practically, primary winding has certain resistance hence there are small primary copper loss present.

Thus the primary current under no load condition has to supply the iron losses i.e. hysteresis loss and eddy current loss and a small amount of primary copper loss. This current is denoted as I_0.

Now the no load input current I_0 has two components :

1. A purely reactive component I_m called magnetizing component of no load current required to produce the flux. This is also called **wattless component**.

2. An active component I_c which supplies total losses under no load condition called **power component** of no load current. This is also called **wattful component** or **core loss component** of I_0.

The total no load current I_0 is the vector addition of I_m and I_c.

$$\boxed{\bar{I}_0 = \bar{I}_m + \bar{I}_c} \qquad \qquad \ldots (8.7.1)$$

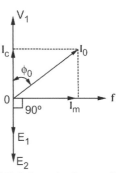

Fig. 8.7.1 Practical transformer on no load

In practical transformer, due to winding resistance, no load current I_0 is no longer at $90°$ with respect to V_1. But it lags V_1 by angle ϕ_0 which is less than $90°$. Thus $\cos \phi_0$ is called **no load power factor** of practical transformer.

The phasor diagram is shown in the Fig. 8.7.1.

It can be seen that the two components of I_0 are,

$$\boxed{I_m = I_0 \sin \phi_0, \text{ magnetizing component lagging } V_1 \text{ exactly by } 90°} \qquad \ldots (8.7.2)$$

$$\boxed{I_c = I_0 \cos \phi_0, \quad \text{core loss component which is in phase with } V_1} \qquad \ldots (8.7.3)$$

The magnitude of the no load current is given by,

$$\boxed{I_0 = \sqrt{I_m^2 + I_c^2}} \qquad \qquad \ldots (8.7.4)$$

while $\qquad \phi_0 =$ No load primary power factor angle

The total power input on no load is denoted as W_0 and is given by,

$$\boxed{W_0 = V_1 I_0 \cos \phi_0 = V_1 I_c} \qquad \qquad \ldots (8.7.5)$$

It may be noted that the current I_0 is very small, about 3 to 5 % of the full load rated current. Hence the primary copper loss is negligibly small.

Hence power input W_0 on no load always represents the iron losses, as copper loss is negligibly small. **The iron losses are denoted as P_i and are constant for all load conditions.**

$\therefore \qquad \boxed{W_0 = V_1 I_0 \cos \phi_0 = P_i = \text{Iron loss}} \qquad \qquad \ldots (8.7.6)$

Example 8.7.1 *A 25 kVA, 3300 / 230 V, 50 Hz, 1-phase transformer draws no load current of 15 A when excited on load voltage side and consumes 350 watts. Calculate two components of current.* **2003-04, Marks 5**

Solution : $\qquad W_0 = 350$ W, $\quad I_0 = 15$ A, $\quad V_0 = 230$ V

$\therefore \qquad \cos \phi_0 = \dfrac{W_0}{V_0 I_0} = \dfrac{350}{15 \times 230} = 0.1014$ lag, $\sin \phi_0 = 0.9948$

$\therefore \qquad I_c =$ Active component $= I_0 \cos \phi_0 =$ **1.521 A**

$\qquad \quad I_m =$ Magnetising component $= I_0 \sin \phi_0 =$ **14.922 A**

Review Question

> 1. *Draw and explain the no load phasor diagram of transformer.*   **2004-05, 2009-10, Marks 5**

8.8 Transformer on Load (M.M.F. Balancing on Load)   **2000-01, 2009-10**

When the transformer is loaded, the current I_2 flows through the secondary winding. The magnitude and phase of I_2 is determined by the load.

If load is inductive, I_2 lags V_2. If load is capacitive, I_2 leads V_2 while for resistive load, I_2 is in phase with V_2.

There exists a secondary m.m.f. $N_2 I_2$ due to which secondary current sets up its own flux ϕ_2.

This flux opposes the main flux ϕ which is produced in the core due to magnetizing component of no load current. Hence the m.m.f. $N_2 I_2$ is called **demagnetizing ampere-turns**. This is shown in the Fig. 8.8.1 (a).

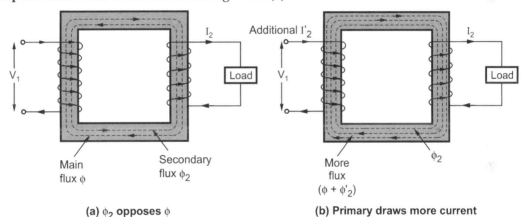

(a) ϕ_2 opposes ϕ (b) Primary draws more current

Fig. 8.8.1 Transformer on load

The flux ϕ_2 momentarily reduces the main flux ϕ, due to which the primary induced e.m.f. E_1 also reduces. Hence the vector difference $\overline{V}_1 - \overline{E}_1$ increases due to which **primary draws more current from the supply.**

This additional current drawn by primary is due to the load hence called load component of primary current denoted as I_2' as shown in the Fig. 8.8.1 (b).

This current I_2' is in antiphase with I_2. The current I_2' sets up its own flux ϕ_2' which opposes the flux ϕ_2 and helps the main flux ϕ. This flux ϕ_2' neutralizes the flux ϕ_2 produced by I_2. The m.m.f. i.e. ampere turns $N_1 I_2'$ balances the ampere turns $N_2 I_2$. Hence the net flux in the core is again maintained at constant level.

> Thus for any load condition, no load to full load the flux in the core is practically constant.

> The load component current I_2' always neutralizes the changes in the load. As practically flux in core is constant, the core loss is also constant for all the loads. Hence the transformer is called **constant flux machine**.

As the ampere turns are balanced we can write,

$$N_2 I_2 = N_1 I_2' \qquad \text{i.e.} \qquad I_2' = \frac{N_2}{N_1} I_2 = K I_2 \qquad \qquad \dots (8.8.1)$$

Thus when transformer is loaded, the primary current I_1 has two components :

1. The no load current I_0 which lags V_1 by angle ϕ_0. It has two components I_m and I_c.

2. The load component I_2' which is in antiphase with I_2. And phase of I_2 is decided by the load.

Hence primary current I_1 is vector sum of I_0 and I_2'.

$$\therefore \qquad \boxed{\bar{I}_1 = \bar{I}_0 + \bar{I}_2'} \qquad \qquad \dots (8.8.2)$$

The phasor diagram of transformer on load for $\cos\phi_2$ lagging power factor load is shown in the Fig. 8.8.2. The winding resistances and reactances are neglected hence $E_2 = V_2$. The current I_2 lags V_2 by ϕ_2. The current $I_2' = K I_2$ is in antiphase with I_2. The vactor sum of I_2' and I_0 is primary current I_1 and $\cos\phi_1$ is primary power factor.

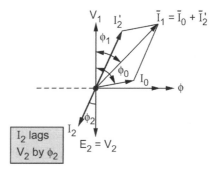

Fig. 8.8.2 Phasor diagram for inductive load

Similarly phasor diagram for unity power factor and leading power factor loads can be drawn. The current I_2 will be in phase with V_2 for unity power factor while I_2 will lead V_2 by ϕ_2 for leading power factor load.

Example 8.8.1 *A single phase 440 V/110 V transformer takes a no load current of 4 A at 0.2 power factor. If the secondary supplies a current of 100 A at a power factor of 0.8 lagging. Determine i) The current taken by the primary winding. ii) The magnetizing reactance and resistance representing core losses.*   **2000-01, Marks 5**

Solution : $I_0 = 4$ A, $\cos\phi_0 = 0.2$ lag, $I_2 = 100$ A, $\cos\phi_2 = 0.8$ lag

$$\bar{I}_1 = \bar{I}_2' + \bar{I}_0$$

$$K = \frac{V_2}{V_1} = \frac{110}{440} = 0.25$$

$$\therefore \qquad \bar{I}_2' = K\,I_2 = 25\ A$$

$$I_c = I_0 \cos\phi_0 = 4 \times 0.2 = 0.8\ A$$

(y-component)

$$I_m = I_0 \sin\phi_0 = 3.9191\ A$$

(x-component)

$$I_2' \cos\phi_2 = 25 \times 0.8 = 20\ A$$

(y-component)

$$I_2' \sin\phi_2 = 25 \times 0.6 = 15\ A$$

(x-component)

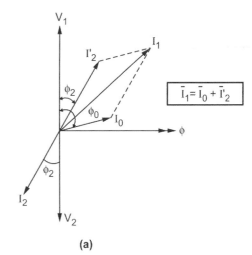

$$\boxed{\bar{I}_1 = \bar{I}_0 + \bar{I}_2'}$$

(a)

Hence the y and x components of current I_1 are,

$$I_{1y} = 20 + 0.8 = 20.8\ A$$

$$I_{1x} = 15 + 3.9191 = 18.9191\ A$$

$$\therefore \qquad I_1 = \sqrt{I_{1y}^2 + I_{1x}^2} = \mathbf{28.1171\ A}$$

$$X_0 = \frac{V_1}{I_m} = \frac{440}{3.9191} = \mathbf{112.2706\ \Omega}$$

$$R_0 = \frac{V_1}{I_c} = \frac{440}{0.8} = \mathbf{550\ \Omega}$$

$$\cos\phi_1 = \frac{I_{1x}}{I_1} = \frac{18.9191}{28.1171} = \mathbf{0.6728\ lag}$$

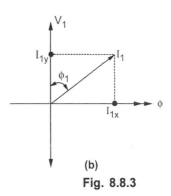

(b)

Fig. 8.8.3

Note that ϕ_1 is measured with respect to V_1 which is along y-axis.

Example 8.8.2 *A transformer has a primary winding of 600 turns and a secondary winding of 150 turns. When the load current on the secondary is 60 A at 0.8 power factor lagging, the primary current is 20 A at 0.707 power factor lagging. Determine the no-load current of the transformer and its phase with respect to the voltage.*

2009-10, Marks 5

Solution : Refer example 8.8.1 for the procedure. Find x and y components of I_1 and I_2'.

Then $\bar{I}_0 = \bar{I}_1 - \bar{I}_2'$.

Verify the answer : x component of $I_0 = 5.14\ A$, y component of $I_0 = 2.14\ A$,

$I_0 = \mathbf{5.567\ A}$, $\cos\phi_0 = \mathbf{0.3843\ lag}$

Review Question

> 1. *Why there is inrush of primary current when transformer secondary is loaded ?*

8.9 Equivalent Resistance of Transformer

Let R_1 = Primary winding resistance in ohms

           R_2 = Secondary winding resistance in ohms

The resistance of the two windings can be transferred to any one side either primary or secondary without affecting the performance of the transformer.

The total copper loss due to both the resistances can be obtained as,

$$\text{Total copper loss} = I_1^2\, R_1 + I_2^2\, R_2 = I_1^2 \left[R_1 + \frac{I_2^2}{I_1^2} R_2 \right] = I_1^2 \left[R_1 + \frac{1}{K^2} R_2 \right] \left(\frac{I_2}{I_1} = \frac{1}{K} \right) \dots (8.9.1)$$

Now the expression (8.9.1) indicates that the total copper loss can be expressed as $I_1^2\, R_1 + I_1^2 \cdot \frac{R_2}{K^2}$. This means $\frac{R_2}{K^2}$ is the resistance value of R_2 shifted to primary side which causes same copper loss with I_1 as R_2 causes with I_2.

This value of resistance R_2/K^2 which is the value of R_2 referred to primary is called **equivalent resistance of secondary referred to primary**. It is denoted as R_2'.

$\therefore$ $$R_2' = \frac{R_2}{K^2}$$ $\dots (8.9.2)$

Hence the **total resistance referred to primary** is the addition of R_1 and R_2' called equivalent resistance of transformer referred to primary and denoted as R_{1e}.

$\therefore$ $$R_{1e} = R_1 + R_2' = R_1 + \frac{R_2}{K^2}$$ $\dots (8.9.3)$

Similarly the **equivalent resistance of primary referred to secondary is**,

$\therefore$ $R_1' = K^2\, R_1$ $\dots (8.9.4)$

Hence the total resistance referred to secondary is the addition of R_2 and R_1' called **equivalent resistance of transformer referred to secondary** and denoted as R_{2e}.

$\therefore$ $$R_{2e} = R_2 + R_1' = R_2 + K^2\, R_1$$ $\dots (8.9.5)$

> **High voltage side** $\rightarrow$ **Low current side** $\rightarrow$ **High resistance side**
>
> **Low voltage side** $\rightarrow$ **High current side** $\rightarrow$ **Low resistance side**

1. *How to calculate equivalent resistance referred to primary and secondary in a transformer ?*

8.10 Magnetic Leakage in a Transformer

In practice the part of the primary flux as well as the secondary flux completes the path through air and links with the respecting winding only. Such a flux is called **leakage flux**.

Thus there are two leakage fluxes present as shown in the Fig. 8.10.1.

The flux ϕ_{L1} is the primary leakage flux which is produced due to primary current I_1. It is in phase with I_1 and links with primary only.

The flux ϕ_{L2} is the secondary leakage flux which is produced due to current I_2. It is in phase with I_2 and links with the secondary winding only.

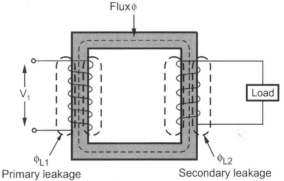

Fig. 8.10.1 Leakage fluxes

Due to leakage flux ϕ_{L1} there is self induced e.m.f. e_{L1} in primary. While due to leakage flux ϕ_{L2} there is self induced e.m.f. e_{L2} in secondary. The primary voltage V_1 has to overcome this voltage e_{L1} to produce E_1 while induced e.m.f. E_2 has to overcome e_{L2} to produce terminal voltage V_2.

Thus the self induced e.m.f.s are treated as the voltage drops across the fictitious reactances placed in series with the windings. These reactances are called leakage reactances of the winding.

So, X_1 = Leakage reactance of primary winding.

and X_2 = Leakage reactance of secondary winding.

Leakage fluxes link with the respective windings only and not to both the windings. To reduce the leakage, as mentioned, in the construction both the winding's are placed on same limb rather than on separate limbs.

8.10.1 Equivalent Leakage Reactance

Similar to the resistances, the leakage reactances also can be transferred from primary to secondary or viceversa. The relation through K^2 remains same for the transfer of reactances as it is studied earlier for the resistances.

Let X_1 is leakage reactance of primary and X_2 is leakage reactance of secondary.

Then the total leakage reactance referred to primary is X_{1e} given by,

$$X_{1e} = X_1 + X_2' \quad \text{where} \quad X_2' = \frac{X_2}{K^2}$$

While the total leakage reactance referred to secondary is X_{2e} given by,

$$X_{2e} = X_2 + X_1' \quad \text{where} \quad X_1' = K^2 X_1$$

$$\dots K = \frac{N_2}{N_1}$$

Review Question

1. *Explain the magnetic leakage and its effect in a transformer.*

8.11 Equivalent Impedance
`2004-05`

The transformer primary has resistance R_1 and reactance X_1. While the transformer secondary has resistance R_2 and reactance X_2.

Thus we can say that the total impedance of primary winding is Z_1 which is,

$$Z_1 = R_1 + j X_1 \, \Omega \qquad \dots (8.11.1)$$

And the total impedance of the secondary winding is Z_2 which is ,

$$Z_2 = R_2 + j X_2 \, \Omega \qquad \dots (8.11.2)$$

Let $\quad Z_{1e}$ = Total equivalent impedance referred to primary then,

$$Z_{1e} = R_{1e} + j X_{1e}$$

$$\therefore \quad Z_{1e} = Z_1 + Z_2' = Z_1 + \frac{Z_2}{K^2} \qquad \dots (8.11.3)$$

Similarly Z_{2e} = Total equivalent impedance referred to secondary then,

$$Z_{2e} = R_{2e} + j X_{2e}$$

$$\therefore \quad Z_{2e} = Z_2 + Z_1' = Z_2 + K^2 Z_1 \qquad \dots (8.11.4)$$

The magnitudes of Z_{1e} and Z_{2e} are,

$$Z_{1e} = \sqrt{R_{1e}^2 + X_{1e}^2} \quad \text{and} \quad Z_{2e} = \sqrt{R_{2e}^2 + X_{2e}^2} \qquad \dots (8.11.5)$$

It can be noted that,

$$Z_{2e} = K^2 Z_{1e} \quad \text{and} \quad Z_{1e} = \frac{Z_{2e}}{K^2} \qquad \dots (8.11.6)$$

> **High voltage side → Low current side → High impedance side**
>
> **Low voltage side → High current side → Low impedance side**

Example 8.11.1 *A 30 kVA, 2000/200 V, single phase, 50 Hz transformer has a primary resistance of 3.5 ohms and reactance of 4.5 ohms. The secondary resistance and reactance are 0.015 ohms and 0.02 ohms respectively. Find i) Equivalent resistance, reactance and impedance referred to the primary side ii) Total copper losses in the transformer.*

2004-05, Marks 5

Solution : $R_1 = 3.5\ \Omega$, $R_2 = 0.015\ \Omega$, $X_1 = 4.5\ \Omega$, $X_2 = 0.02\ \Omega$

$$K = \frac{V_2}{V_1} = \frac{200}{2000} = 0.1$$

i)
$$R_{1e} = R_1 + R_2' = R_1 + \frac{R_2}{K^2} = 3.5 + \frac{0.015}{(0.1)^2} = \mathbf{5\ \Omega}$$

$$X_{1e} = X_1 + X_2' = X_1 + \frac{X_2}{K^2} = 4.5 + \frac{0.02}{(0.1)^2} = \mathbf{6.5\ \Omega}$$

$$Z_{1e} = \sqrt{R_{1e}^2 + X_{1e}^2} = \mathbf{8.2\ \Omega}$$

ii)
$$(I_1)_{FL} = \frac{VA}{V_1} = \frac{30 \times 10^3}{2000} = \mathbf{15\ A}$$

∴
$$(P_{cu})_{total} = (I_1)_{FL}^2\, R_{1e} = 15^2 \times 5 = \mathbf{1125\ W}$$

Review Question

> 1. *A 15 kVA, 2200/110 V transformer has $R_1 = 1.75\ \Omega$, $R_2 = 0.0045\ \Omega$. The leakage reactances are $X_1 = 2.6\ \Omega$ and $X_2 = 0.0075\ \Omega$. Calculate,*
>   *a) Equivalent resistance referred to primary   b) Equivalent resistance referred to secondary*
>   *c) Equivalent reactance referred to primary   d) Equivalent reactance referred to secondary*
>   *e) Equivalent impedance referred to primary   f) Equivalent impedance referred to secondary*
>   *g) Total copper loss.*   **(Ans. : $R_{2e} = 0.00887\ \Omega$, $X_{2e} = 0.014\ \Omega$, Copper loss = 458.419 W)**

8.12 Phasor Diagrams for Transformer on Load   **2002-03, 2009-10**

Consider a transformer supplying the load as shown in the Fig. 8.12.1.

The various transformer parameters are,

R_1 = Primary winding resistance, X_1 = Primary leakage reactance

R_2 = Secondary winding resistance, X_2 = Secondary leakage reactance

Z_L = Load impedance, I_1 = Primary current

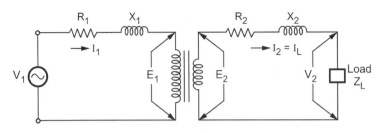

Fig. 8.12.1

$$I_2 = \text{Secondary current} = I_L = \text{Load current}$$

Now $\qquad \bar{I}_1 = \bar{I}_0 + \bar{I}_2'$

where $\qquad I_0 = \text{No load current}$

$\qquad I_2' = \text{Load component of current decided by the load} = K\,I_2$

The primary voltage V_1 has now three components,

1. $-E_1$, the induced e.m.f. which opposes V_1.

2. $I_1 R_1$, the drop across the resistance, in phase with I_1.

3. $I_1 X_1$, the drop across the reactance, leading I_1 by $90°$.

$\therefore \qquad \overline{V}_1 = -\overline{E}_1 + \overline{I_1 R_1} + \overline{I_1 X_1} = -\overline{E}_1 + \bar{I}_1\,(R_1 + j\,X_1)$ ... Phasor sum

$$\boxed{\overline{V}_1 = -\overline{E}_1 + \overline{I_1 Z_1}}$$

The secondary induced e.m.f. E_2 has also three components,

1. V_2, the terminal voltage across the load.

2. $I_2 R_2$, the drop across the resistance, in phase with I_2.

3. $I_2 X_2$, the drop across the reactance, leading I_2 by $90°$.

$\therefore \qquad \overline{E}_2 = \overline{V}_2 + \overline{I_2 R_2} + \overline{I_2 X_2}$ ... Phasor sum

$\therefore \qquad \overline{V}_2 = \overline{E}_2 - \bar{I}_2\,(R_2 + j\,X_2) = \boxed{\overline{E}_2 - \overline{I_2 Z_2}}$

The phasor diagram for the transformer on load depends on the nature of the load power factor. Let us consider the various cases of the load power factor.

8.12.1 Unity Power Factor Load, $\cos \phi_2 = 1$

As load power factor is unity, the voltage V_2 and I_2 are in phase.

Steps to draw the phasor diagram are,

1. Consider flux ϕ as reference.   2. E_1 lags ϕ by $90°$. Reverse E_1 to get $-E_1$.

3. E_1 and E_2 are in phase.   4. Assume V_2 in a particular direction.

5. I_2 is in phase with V_2.   6. Add $I_2 R_2$ and $I_2 X_2$ to V_2 to get E_2.

7. Reverse I_2 to get I_2'.   8. Add I_0 and I_2' to get I_1.

9. Add $I_1 R_1$ and $I_1 X_1$ to $- E_1$ to get V_1.

Angle between V_1 and I_1 is ϕ_1 and $\cos \phi_1$ is primary power factor. Remember that $I_1 X_1$ leads I_1 direction by $90°$ and $I_2 X_2$ leads I_2 by $90°$ as current through inductance lags voltage across inductance by $90°$. The phasor diagram is shown in the Fig. 8.12.2.

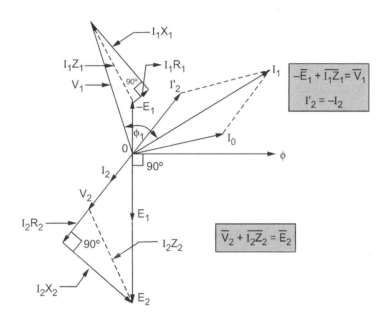

Fig. 8.12.2 Phasor diagram for unity power factor load

8.12.2 Lagging Power Factor Load, cos ϕ_2

As load power factor is lagging $\cos \phi_2$, the current I_2 lags V_2 by angle ϕ_2. So only change in drawing the phasor diagram is to draw I_2 lagging V_2 by ϕ_2 in step 5 discussed earlier. Accordingly directions of $I_2 R_2$, $I_2 X_2$, I_2', I_1, $I_1 R_1$ and $I_1 X_1$ will change. Remember that whatever may be the power factor of load, $I_2 X_2$ leads I_2 by $90°$ and $I_1 X_1$ leads I_1 by $90°$. The complete phasor diagram is shown in the Fig. 8.12.3.

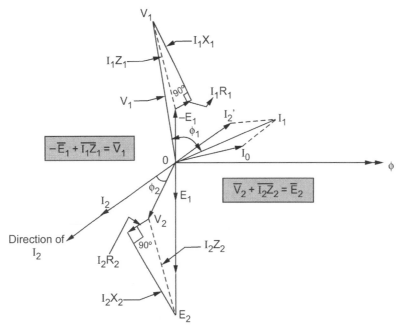

Fig. 8.12.3 Phasor diagram for lagging power factor load

8.12.3 Leading Power Factor Load, cos ϕ_2

As load power factor is leading, the current I_2 leads V_2 by angle ϕ_2. So the change is to draw I_2 leading V_2 by angle ϕ_2. All other steps remain same as before. The complete phasor diagram is shown in the Fig. 8.12.4.

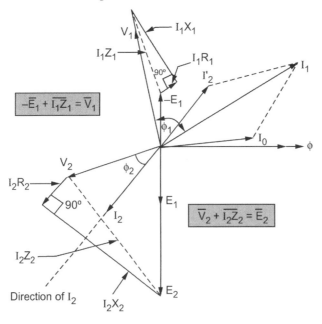

Fig. 8.12.4 Phasor diagram for leading power factor load

Review Question

> 1. *Draw and explain the full load phasor diagrams of single phase transformer for lagging, leading and unity power factor loads.*　　　　**2002-03, 2009-10, Marks 5**

8.13 Equivalent Circuit of Transformer　　　　　　　**2008-09**

The term equivalent circuit of a machine means the combination of fixed and variable resistances and reactances, which exactly simulates performance and working of the machine.

For a transformer, no load primary current I_0 has two components,

$$I_m = I_0 \sin \phi_0 = \text{Magnetising component}$$

$$I_c = I_0 \cos \phi_0 = \text{Active component}$$

I_m produces the flux and is assumed to flow through reactance X_0 called no load reactance while I_c is active component representing core losses hence is assumed to flow through the resistance R_0. Hence equivalent circuit on no load can be shown as in the Fig. 8.13.1. This circuit consisting of R_0 and X_0 in parallel is called **exciting circuit**. From the equivalent circuit we can write,

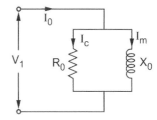

Fig. 8.13.1 No load equivalent circuit

$$R_0 = \frac{V_1}{I_c} \quad \text{and} \quad X_0 = \frac{V_1}{I_m}$$

When the load is connected to the transformer then secondary current I_2 flows. This causes voltage drop across R_2 and X_2. Due to I_2, primary draws an additional current

$I_2' = I_2 / K$. Now I_1 is the phasor addition of I_0 and I_2'. This I_1 causes the voltage drop across primary resistance R_1 and reactance X_1.

Hence the equivalent circuit can be shown as in the Fig. 8.13.2.

But in the equivalent circuit, windings are not shown and it is further simplified by transferring all the values to the primary or secondary. This makes the transformer calculations much easy.

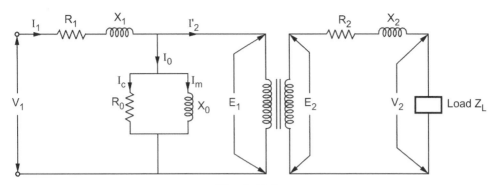

Fig. 8.13.2

So transferring secondary parameters to primary we get,

$$R_2' = \frac{R_2}{K^2}, \qquad X_2' = \frac{X_2}{K^2}, \qquad Z_2' = \frac{Z_2}{K^2}$$

while $E_2' = \dfrac{E_2}{K}, \qquad I_2' = KI_2 \quad \text{where} \quad K = \dfrac{N_2}{N_1}$

While transferring the values remember the rule that

> Low voltage winding $\rightarrow$ High current $\rightarrow$ Low impedance
>
> High voltage winding $\rightarrow$ Low current $\rightarrow$ High impedance

Thus the exact equivalent circuit referred to primary can be shown as in the Fig. 8.13.3.

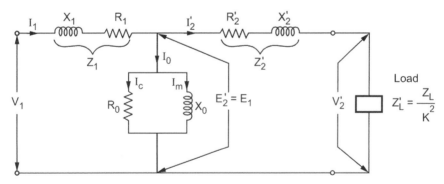

Fig. 8.13.3 Exact equivalent circuit referred to primary

Similarly all the primary value can be referred to secondary and we can obtain the equivalent circuit referred to secondary.

$$R_1' = K^2 R_1, \qquad X_1' = K^2 X_1, \qquad Z_1' = K^2 Z_1$$

$$E_1' = K E_1, \qquad I_1' = \frac{I_1}{K}, \qquad I_0' = \frac{I_0}{K}$$

Similarly the exciting circuit parameters also gets transferred to secondary as R_0' and X_0'. The circuit is shown in the Fig. 8.13.4.

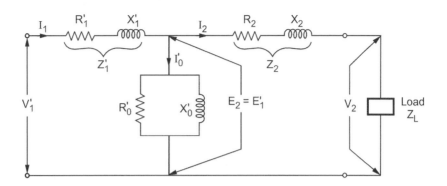

Fig. 8.13.4 Exact equivalent circuit referred to secondary

Now as long as no load branch i.e. exciting branch is in between Z_1 and Z_2', the impedances cannot be combined. So further simplification of the circuit can be done. Such circuit is called approximate equivalent circuit.

8.13.1 Approximate Equivalent Circuit

To get approximate equivalent circuit, shift the no load branch containing R_0 and X_0 to the left of R_1 and X_1. By doing this we are creating an error that the drop across R_1 and X_1 due to I_0 is neglected. Hence such an equivalent circuit is called **approximate equivalent circuit.**

So approximate equivalent circuit referred to primary can be as shown in the Fig. 8.13.5.

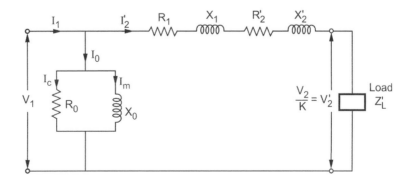

Fig. 8.13.5 Approximate equivalent circuit referred to primary

In this circuit now R_1 and R'_2 can be combined to get equivalent resistance referred to primary R_{1e} as discussed earlier. Similarly X_1 and X'_2 can be combined to get X_{1e}. And equivalent circuit can be simplified as shown in the Fig. 8.13.6.

In the similar fashion, the approximate equivalent circuit referred to secondary also can be obtained.

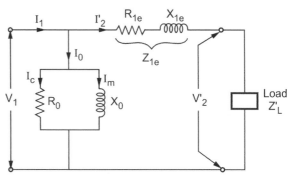

Fig. 8.13.6

Example 8.13.1 *The ohmic values of the circuit parameters of a transformer, having a turns ratio of 5, are $R_1 = 0.5\ \Omega$, $R_2 = 0.021\ \Omega$, $X_1 = 3.2\ \Omega$, $X_2 = 0.12\ \Omega$, $R_c = 350\ \Omega$, and $X_m = 98\ \Omega$ referred to primary. Draw the approximate equivalent circuits of the transformer referred to secondary. Show the numerical values of the circuit parameters.* **2008-09, Marks 10**

Solution : $R_1 = 0.5\ \Omega$, $R_2 = 0.021\ \Omega$, $X_1 = 3.2\ \Omega$, $X_2 = 0.12\ \Omega$, $R_c = 350\ \Omega$, $X_m = 98\ \Omega$.

Turns ratio $= \dfrac{N_1}{N_2} = \dfrac{5}{1}$ i.e. $K = \dfrac{N_2}{N_1} = \dfrac{1}{5} = 0.2$

∴ $R_{2e} = R_2 + K^2 R_1 = 0.021 + (0.2)^2 \times 0.5 = 0.041\ \Omega$

∴ $X_{2e} = X_2 + K^2 X_1 = 0.12 + (0.2)^2 \times 3.2 = 0.248\ \Omega$

∴ $R'_c = K^2 R_c = (0.2)^2 \times 350 = 14\ \Omega$ and $X'_m = K^2 X_m = (0.2)^2 \times 98 = 3.92\ \Omega$

The approximate equivalent circuit referred to secondary is as shown in the Fig. 8.13.7.

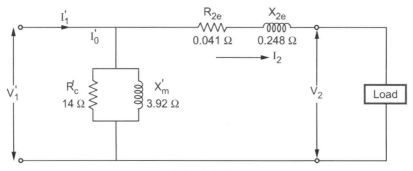

Fig. 8.13.7

Review Question

1. *Derive and explain the equivalent circuit of a transformer.*

8.14 Voltage Regulation of Transformer   2001-02, 2005-06

Because of the voltage drop across the primary and secondary impedances it is observed that the secondary terminal voltage drops from its no load value (E_2) to load value (V_2) as load and load current increases.

This decrease in the secondary terminal voltage expressed as a fraction of the no load secondary terminal voltage is called regulation of a transformer.

Let E_2 = Secondary terminal voltage **on no load**

            V_2 = Secondary terminal voltage **on given load**

Then mathematically voltage regulation at given load can be expressed as,

$$\% \text{ voltage regulation} = \frac{E_2 - V_2}{V_2} \times 100$$

The ratio ($E_2 - V_2$ / V_2) is called **per unit regulation.**

The secondary terminal voltage does not depend only on the magnitude of the load current but also on the nature of the power factor of the load. If V_2 is determined for full load and specified power factor condition the regulation is called full load regulation.

As load current I_L increases, the voltage drops tend to increase and V_2 drops more and more. In case of lagging power factor $V_2 < E_2$ and we get positive voltage regulation, while for leading power factor $E_2 < V_2$ and we get negative voltage regulation. This is shown in the Fig. 8.14.1.

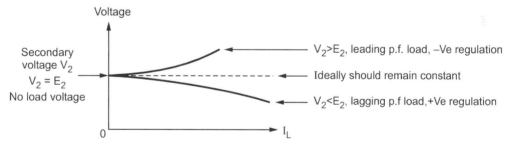

Fig. 8.14.1 Regulation Characteristics

Key Point *The voltage drop should be as small as possible hence less the regulation better is the performance of a transformer.*

8.14.1 Expression for Voltage Regulation

Mathematically percentage voltage regulation is defined as,

$$\% R = \frac{E_2 - V_2}{V_2} \times 100 = \frac{\text{Total voltage drop}}{V_2} \times 100$$

The total voltage drop depends on the nature of the power factor of the load.

Case I : Lagging power factor load

It is known that when the transformer is loaded, there are voltage drops across resistance and inductance. Hence the no load voltage E_2 is given by,

$$\overline{E}_2 = \overline{V}_2 + \overline{I_2 R_{2e}} + \overline{I_2 X_{2e}}$$

For lagging p.f. load, I_2 lags V_2 by $\phi._2$. Take V_2 as a reference phasor. The drop $I_2 R_{2e}$ is in the direction of I_2 while $I_2 X_{2e}$ is at $90°$ to I_2 R_{2e} such that I_2 lags by $90°$.

The phasor diagram is shown in the Fig. 8.14.2.

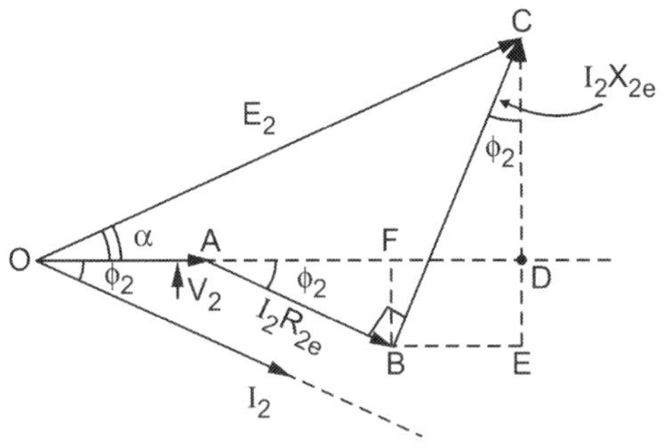

Fig. 8.14.2

$$OA = V_2$$

$$AF = AB \cos \phi_2 = I_2 R_{2e} \cos \phi_2$$

$$BE = FD = BC \sin \phi_2 = I_2 X_{2e} \sin \phi_2$$

$$\therefore \quad OD = OA + AF + FD$$

$$= V_2 + I_2 R_{2e} \cos \phi_2 + I_2 X_{2e} \sin \phi_2$$

$$CE = BC \cos \phi_2 = I_2 X_{2e} \cos \phi_2$$

$$DE = AB \sin \phi_2 = I_2 R_{2e} \sin \phi_2$$

$$\therefore \quad CD = CE - DE = I_2 X_{2e} \cos\phi_2 - I_2 R_{2e} \sin\phi_2$$

$\therefore$ Approximately $CE \approx DE$ i.e. $CD \approx 0$ as angle α is practically small.

$$\therefore \quad (OC)^2 = (OD)^2 + (CD)^2 = (OD)^2$$

$$\therefore \quad E_2 = V_2 + I_2 R_{2e} \cos \phi_2 + I_2 X_{2e} \sin \phi_2$$

$\therefore$ Approximate voltage drop $= E_2 - V_2 = I_2 R_{2e} \cos \phi_2 + I_2 X_{2e} \sin \phi_2$

$$\therefore \quad \% R = \frac{E_2 - V_2}{V_2} \times 100 = \frac{I_2 [R_{2e} \cos \phi_2 + X_{2e} \sin \phi_2]}{V_2} \times 100$$

Case II : Leading power factor load

The current I_2 leads V_2 by ϕ_2 and the phasor diagram is as shown in the Fig. 8.14.3.

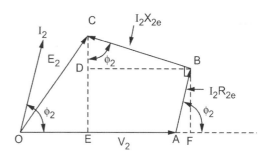

$OA = V_2$

$AF = AB \cos \phi_2 = I_2 R_{2e} \cos \phi_2$

$BD = BC \sin \phi_2 = I_2 X_{2e} \sin \phi_2 = EF$

$OE = OA + AF - EF$

$\quad = V_2 + I_2 R_{2e} \cos \phi_2 - I_2 X_{2e} \sin \phi_2$

Fig. 8.14.3

$CE = CD + DE = I_2 X_{2e} \cos \phi_2 + I_2 R_{2e} \sin \phi_2$

But practically CE can be assumed zero i.e. CE $\approx$ 0.

$\therefore \qquad (OC)^2 = (OE)^2 + (CE)^2 \approx (OE)^2$

$\therefore \qquad E_2 = V_2 + I_2 R_{2e} \cos \phi_2 - I_2 X_{2e} \sin \phi_2$

$\therefore \qquad \boxed{\text{Approximate voltage drop} = E_2 - V_2 = I_2 R_{2e} \cos \phi_2 - I_2 X_{2e} \sin \phi_2}$

$\therefore \qquad \boxed{\% \; R = \dfrac{E_2 - V_2}{V_2} \times 100 = \dfrac{I_2 [R_{2e} \cos \phi_2 - X_{2e} \sin \phi_2]}{V_2} \times 100}$

If all the values are transferred to primary, we get,

$\therefore \qquad \boxed{\% \; R = \dfrac{I_1 [R_{1e} \cos \phi_2 - X_{1e} \sin \phi_2]}{V_1} \times 100} \qquad\qquad \text{... Referred to primary}$

Thus generalised expression for regulation is,

$\therefore \qquad \boxed{\begin{aligned} \% \; R = \dfrac{I_2 [R_{2e} \cos \phi \pm X_{2e} \sin \phi]}{V_2} \times 100 = \dfrac{I_1 [R_{1e} \cos \phi \pm X_{1e} \sin \phi]}{V_1} \times 100 \\[2mm] \textbf{+ ve sign for lagging power factor load, } \textbf{- ve sign for leading power factor load} \end{aligned}}$

Key Point *If I_2 or I_1 in above expression is full load current it gives full load regulation.*

8.14.2 Constants of a Transformer

From the regulation expression we can define constants of a transformer.

$$\% \; R = \frac{I_2 R_{2e} \cos \phi \pm I_2 X_{2e} \sin \phi}{E_2} \times 100$$

$$= \left\{ \left(\frac{I_2\,R_{2e}}{E_2} \right) \cos\phi \pm \left(\frac{I_2\,X_{2e}}{E_2} \right) \sin\phi \right\} \times 100$$

The ratio $\frac{I_2\,R_{2e}}{E_2}$ or $\frac{I_1\,R_{1e}}{E_1}$ is called **per unit resistive drop** and denoted as V_R.

$$\therefore \quad V_R = \text{per unit resistive drop} = \frac{I_2\,R_{2e}}{E_2} = \frac{I_1\,R_{1e}}{E_1}$$

The ratio $\frac{I_2\,X_{2e}}{E_2}$ or $\frac{I_1\,X_{1e}}{E_1}$ is called **per unit reactive drop** and is denoted as V_X.

$$\therefore \quad V_X = \text{per unit reactive drop} = \frac{I_2\,X_{2e}}{E_2} = \frac{I_1\,X_{1e}}{E_1}$$

The terms V_R and V_X are called **constants of a transformer** because for the rated output I_2, E_2, R_{1e}, X_{1e}, R_{2e}, X_{2e} are constants. The regulation can be expressed interms of V_R and V_X as,

$$\therefore \quad \% R = [V_R \cos\phi \pm V_X \sin\phi] \times 100$$

On no load condition, $E_2 = V_2$ and $E_1 = V_1$

where V_1 and V_2 are the given voltage ratings of a transformer. Hence V_R and V_X can be expressed as,

$$\therefore \quad V_R = \frac{I_{2e}\,R_{2e}}{V_2} = \frac{I_{1e}\,R_{1e}}{V_1} \quad \text{and} \quad V_X = \frac{I_{2e}\,X_{2e}}{V_2} = \frac{I_{1e}\,X_{1e}}{V_1}$$

where V_1 and V_2 are no load primary and secondary voltages.

V_R and V_X can be represented on percentage basis as,

$$\therefore \quad \text{Percentage resistive drop} = V_R \times 100$$
$$\text{Percentage reactive drop} = V_X \times 100$$

Key Point *Note that V_R and V_X are also called per unit resistance and reactance respectively.*

Example 8.14.1 *A 250/125 V, 5 kVA single phase transformer has primary resistance of 0.2 Ω and reactance of 0.75 Ω. The secondary resistance is 0.05 Ω and reactance of 0.2 Ω. i) Determine its regulation while supplying full load on 0.8 leading p.f. ii) The secondary terminal voltage on full load and 0.8 leading p.f.*

Solution : The given values are,

$$R_1 = 0.2 \ \Omega, \ X_1 = 0.75 \ \Omega, \ R_2 = 0.05 \ \Omega, \ X_2 = 0.2 \ \Omega, \ \cos\phi = 0.8 \text{ leading}$$

$$K = \frac{E_2}{E_1} = \frac{125}{250} = \frac{1}{2} = 0.5$$

$$(I_2) \ \text{F.L.} = \frac{kVA}{V_2} = \frac{5 \times 10^3}{125} = 40 \text{ A} \qquad \qquad \dots \text{ Full load}$$

$$R_{2e} = R_2 + K^2 R_1 = 0.05 + (0.5)^2 \times 0.2 = 0.1 \ \Omega$$

$$X_{2e} = X_2 + K^2 X_1 = 0.2 + (0.5)^2 \times 0.75 = 0.3875 \ \Omega$$

i) Regulation on full load, $\cos\phi = 0.8$ leading

$$\therefore \quad \% \ R = \frac{I_2 [R_{2e} \cos\phi - X_{2e} \sin\phi]}{V_2} \times 100 = \frac{40[0.1 \times 0.8 - 0.3875 \times 0.6]}{125} \times 100 = -\mathbf{4.88 \ \%}$$

ii) For secondary terminal voltage,

Voltage drop $= I_2 R_{2e} \cos\phi - I_2 X_{2e} \sin\phi = 40 [0.1 \times 0.8 - 0.3875 \times 0.6] = -6.1$ V

Now $\quad E_2 = V_2 + \text{voltage drop}$

$\therefore \qquad V_2 = E_2 - \text{voltage drop} = 125 - (-6.1) = \mathbf{131.1 \ V}$

It can be seen that for leading p.f., $E_2 < V_2$.

Example 8.14.2 *A 10 kVA, 1-phase transformer with 2000/400 V at no load, has resistance and leakage reactance of primary winding of 5.5 Ω and 12 Ω respectively, the corresponding values of secondary winding being 0.2 Ω and 0.45 Ω. Determine the value of secondary voltage at full load, 0.8 power factor lagging, when the primary applied voltage is 2000 V.* **2001-02, Marks 5**

Solution : Refer example 8.14.1 for the procedure and verify the answer as **377.65 V.** As p.f. is lagging $V_2 < E_2$.

Example 8.14.3 *Calculate the voltage regulation of transformer in which ohmic drop is 1 % and reactance drop 5 % of the voltage at the following power factor i) 0.8 lagging ii) 0.8 leading.* **2005-06, Marks 5**

Solution : For a transformer,

$$\% \text{ Ohmic drop} = \% \ V_R = \frac{I_1 R_{1e}}{V_1} \times 100 = \frac{I_2 R_{2e}}{V_2} \times 100$$

$$\% \text{ Reactance drop} = \% \ V_X = \frac{I_1 X_{1e}}{V_1} \times 100 = \frac{I_2 X_{2e}}{V_2} \times 100$$

$$\% \ R = \frac{I_1 [R_{1e} \cos\phi \pm X_{1e} \sin\phi]}{V_1} \times 100 = V_R \cos\phi \pm V_X \sin\phi$$

i) $\cos \phi = 0.8$ lagging

                % R $= 1 \times 0.8 + 5 \times 0.6 = $ **3.8 %**

ii) $\cos \phi = 0.8$ leading

                % R $= 1 \times 0.8 - 5 \times 0.6 = $ **– 2.2 %**

Review Questions

1. *What is regulation of transformer ? State its significance.*

2. *Derive the expression for voltage regulation of a transformer on lagging and leading power factor loads.*

3. *A 20 kVA, 2000/200 V single phase transformer has the following parameters. H.V. winding : $R_1 = 3\,\Omega$, $X_1 = 5.3\,\Omega$, L.V. winding : $R_2 = 0.05\,\Omega$, $X_2 = 0.1\,\Omega$. Find the voltage regulation at, i) Power factor 0.8 lagging ii) UPF iii) 0.707 power factor leading.*

   (Ans. : 7.79 %, 4 %, –2.5805 % Use $\cos\phi = 1$, $\sin\phi = 0$ for unity power factor)

8.15 Losses in a Transformer   `2009-10`

In a transformer, there exists two types of losses.

i)   The core gets subjected to an alternating flux, causing **core losses**.

ii)   The windings carry currents when transformer is loaded, causing **copper losses**.

1. Core or Iron losses

Due to alternating flux set up in the magnetic core of the transformer, it undergoes a cycle of magnetisation and demagnetisation. Due to hysteresis effect there is loss of energy in this process which is called hysteresis loss.

It is given by, $$\text{Hysteresis loss} = K_h\, B_m^{1.67}\, f\, v \quad \text{watts}$$

K_h = Hysteresis constant depends on material   and B_m = Maximum flux density

f = Frequency   and v = Volume of the core.

The induced e.m.f. in the core tries to set up eddy currents in the core and hence responsible for the eddy current losses. The eddy current loss is given by,

$$\text{Eddy current loss} = K_e\, B_m^2\, f^2 t^2 \ \text{watts/unit volume}$$

where K_e = Eddy current constant   and t = Thickness of the core.

As seen earlier, the flux in the core is almost constant as supply voltage V_1 at rated frequency f is always constant. Hence, the flux density B_m in the core and hence both hysteresis and eddy current losses are constants at all the loads. Hence the core or iron losses are also called **constant losses**. The iron losses are denoted as P_i.

The iron losses are minimized by using high grade core material like silicon steel having very low hysteresis loop and by manufacturing the core in the form of laminations.

2. Copper losses

The copper losses are due to the power wasted in the form of I^2R loss due to the resistances of the primary and secondary windings. The copper loss depends on the magnitude of the currents flowing through the windings.

Total Cu loss $= I_1^2\,R_1 + I_2^2\,R_2 \quad = I_1^2\,(R_1 + R_2') = I_2^2\,(R_2 + R_1') \ = I_1^2\,R_{1e} = I_2^2\,R_{2e}$.

The copper losses are denoted as P_{Cu}. If the current through the windings is full load current, we get copper losses at full load. If the load on transformer is half then we get copper losses at half load which are less than full load copper losses. Thus copper losses are called **variable losses**.

Copper losses are proportional to the square of the current and square of the kVA rating as voltage is constant.

So,

$$P_{Cu} \;\propto\; I^2 \propto (kVA)^2$$

Thus for a transformer,

$$\text{Total losses} = \text{Iron losses} + \text{Copper losses} = P_i + P_{Cu}$$

The copper losses are kept minimum by designing the windings with low resistance values.

Review Questions

1. *Explain the various losses in a transformer and how to minimize them ? On what factors they depend ? Give the equations for these losses.*
2. *How eddy current losses and hysteresis losses occur ? How frequency affects these losses in transformer ?* **2009-10, Marks 5**

8.16 Efficiency of a Transformer 2003-04, 2007-08, 2010-11, 2011-12, 2012-13

Due to the losses in a transformer, the output power of a transformer is less than the input power supplied.

$\therefore$ Power output $=$ Power input $-$ Total losses

$\therefore$ Power input $=$ Power output $+$ Total losses $=$ Power output $+ P_i + P_{Cu}$.

The efficiency of any device is defined as the ratio of the power output to power input. So for a transformer the efficiency can be expressed as,

$$\eta = \frac{\text{Power output}}{\text{Power input}} = \frac{\text{Power output}}{\text{Power output} + P_i + P_{Cu}}$$

Now power output $= V_2\, I_2\, \cos\phi$ where $\cos\phi$ = Load power factor.

The transformer supplies full load of current I_2 and with terminal voltage V_2.

$$P_{Cu} = \text{Copper losses on full load} = I_2^2\, R_{2e}$$

$\therefore$
$$\eta = \frac{V_2\, I_2\, \cos\phi_2}{V_2\, I_2\, \cos\phi_2 + P_i + P_{Cu}}$$

But $V_2\, I_2$ = VA rating of a transformer

$\therefore$
$$\% \eta = \frac{(\text{VA rating}) \times \cos\phi}{(\text{VA rating}) \times \cos\phi + P_i + P_{Cu}} \times 100$$

This is full load percentage efficiency with I_2 = Full load secondary current.

But if the transformer is subjected to fractional load then using the appropriate values of various quantities, the efficiency can be obtained.

Let n = Fraction by which load is less than full load $= \dfrac{\text{Actual load}}{\text{Full load}}$

For example, if transformer is subjected to half load then, $n = \dfrac{\text{Half load}}{\text{Full load}} = \dfrac{(1/2)}{1} = 0.5$

When load changes, the load current changes by same proportion.

$\therefore$ New $I_2 = n\, (I_2)\text{F.L.}$

Similarly the output $V_2 I_2 \cos\phi_2$ also reduces by the same fraction. Thus fraction of VA rating is available at the output.

Similarly as copper losses are proportional to square of current then,

New $P_{Cu} = n^2\, (P_{Cu})\text{F.L.}$

The copper losses get reduced by n^2 while iron losses remain same.

In general for fractional load the efficiency is given by,

$$\% \eta = \frac{n\,(\text{VA rating})\cos\phi}{n\,(\text{VA rating})\cos\phi + P_i + n^2(P_{Cu})\, \text{F. L.}} \times 100$$

where n = **Fraction by which load is less than full load.**

For all types of load power factors lagging, leading and unity the efficiency expression does not change and remains same.

8.16.1 Condition for Maximum Efficiency

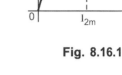

Fig. 8.16.1

The load current at which the efficiency attains maximum value is denoted as I_{2m} and maximum efficiency is denoted as η_{max}.

The efficiency is a function of load i.e. load current I_2 assuming $\cos \phi_2$ constant. The secondary terminal voltage V_2 is also assumed constant.

The graph of efficiency against load current is shown in the Fig. 8.16.1.

So for maximum efficiency,

$$\frac{d\eta}{dI_2} = 0 \qquad \text{while} \qquad \eta = \frac{V_2 \, I_2 \, \cos\phi_2}{V_2 \, I_2 \, \cos\phi_2 + P_i + I_2^2 \, R_{2e}}$$

$$\therefore \qquad \frac{d\eta}{dI_2} = \frac{d}{dI_2}\left[\frac{V_2 \, I_2 \, \cos\phi_2}{V_2 \, I_2 \, \cos\phi_2 + P_i + I_2^2 \, R_{2e}}\right] = 0$$

$$\therefore \; (V_2 \, I_2 \, \cos\phi_2 + P_i + I_2^2 \, R_{2e})\,(V_2 \cos\phi_2) - (V_2 \, I_2 \, \cos\phi_2)\,(V_2 \cos\phi_2 + 2I_2 \, R_{2e}) = 0$$

Cancelling $(V_2 \cos\phi_2)$ from both the terms we get,

$$V_2 \, I_2 \, \cos\phi_2 + P_i + I_2^2 \, R_{2e} - V_2 \, I_2 \, \cos\phi_2 - 2\,I_2^2 \, R_{2e} = 0 \qquad \text{i.e.} \qquad P_i - I_2^2 \, R_{2e} = 0$$

$$\therefore \qquad \boxed{P_i = I_2^2 \, R_{2e} = P_{Cu}}$$

So condition to achieve maximum efficiency is that,

$$\boxed{\text{Copper losses = Iron losses} \qquad \text{i.e.} \quad P_i = P_{Cu}}$$

8.16.2 Load Current I_{2m} at Maximum Efficiency

For η_{max}, $\; I_2^2 \, R_{2e} = P_i \qquad$ but $I_2 = I_{2m} \qquad$ i.e. $\qquad I_{2m}^2 \, R_{2e} = P_i$

$$\therefore \qquad I_{2m} = \sqrt{\frac{P_i}{R_{2e}}} \qquad\qquad\qquad \text{... This is the load current at } \eta_{max}$$

Let (I_2)F.L. = Full load current,

$$\therefore \qquad \frac{I_{2m}}{(I_2)F.L.} = \frac{1}{(I_2)F.L.}\sqrt{\frac{P_i}{R_{2e}}} \quad \text{i.e.} \quad \frac{I_{2m}}{(I_2)F.L.} = \sqrt{\frac{P_i}{[(I_2)F.L.]^2\,R_{2e}}} = \sqrt{\frac{P_i}{(P_{Cu})F.L.}}$$

$$\therefore \qquad \boxed{I_{2m} = (I_2)F.L.\sqrt{\frac{P_i}{(P_{Cu})F.L.}}}$$

This is the load current at η_{max} interms of full load current.

8.16.3 kVA Supplied at Maximum Efficiency

For constant V_2 the kVA supplied is function of load current.

$$\therefore \qquad \boxed{\text{kVA at } \eta_{max} = I_{2m}\,V_2 = V_2\,(I_2)F.L. \times \sqrt{\frac{P_i}{(P_{Cu})F.L.}} = (\text{kVA rating}) \times \sqrt{\frac{P_i}{(P_{Cu})F.L.}}}$$

Substituting condition for η_{max} in the expression of efficiency, we can write expression for η_{max} as,

$$\boxed{\% \; \eta_{max} = \frac{V_2\,I_{2m}\,\cos\phi}{V_2\,I_{2m}\,\cos\phi + 2\,P_i} \times 100 \qquad \text{as } P_{Cu} = P_i}$$

Example 8.16.1 *A 4 kVA, 200/400 V, 50 Hz, single phase transformer has equivalent resistance referred to primary as 0.15 Ω. Calculate, i) The total copper losses on full load ii) The efficiency while supplying full load at 0.9 p.f. lagging   iii) The efficiency while supplying half load at 0.8 p.f. leading. Assume total iron losses equal to 60 W.*

Solution : The given values are,

$$V_1 = 200\text{ V}, \; V_2 = 400\text{ V}, \; S = 4\text{ kVA}, \; R_{1e} = 0.15\ \Omega, \; P_i = 60\text{ W}$$

$$K = \frac{400}{200} = 2$$

$$\therefore \qquad R_{2e} = K^2\,R_{1e} = (2)^2 \times 0.15 = 0.6\ \Omega$$

$$(I_2)\text{ F.L.} = \frac{\text{kVA}}{V_2} = \frac{4 \times 10^3}{400} = 10\text{ A}$$

i) Total copper losses on full load,

$$(P_{cu})\text{ F.L.} = [(I_2)\text{ F.L.}]^2\,R_{2e} = (10)^2 \times 0.6 = \mathbf{60\ W}$$

ii) $\cos\phi = 0.9$ lagging and full load

$$\therefore \qquad \% \; \eta = \frac{\text{VA rating }\cos\phi}{\text{VA rating }\cos\phi + P_i + (P_{cu})\text{ F.L.}} \times 100$$

$$\therefore \qquad \eta = \frac{4\times10^3\times0.9}{4\times10^3\times0.9+60+60}\times100 = \mathbf{96.77 \ \%}$$

iii) $\cos\phi = 0.8$ leading, half load

As half load, $n = 0.5$

$$(P_{cu})H.L. = n^2\times(P_{cu})F.L. = (0.5)^2\times60 = \mathbf{15 \ W}$$

$$\therefore \qquad \% \ \eta = \frac{n\times(VA \ rating)\cos\phi}{n\times(VA \ rating)\cos\phi + P_i + (P_{cu})H.L.}\times100$$

$$= \frac{0.5\times4\times10^3\times0.8}{0.5\times4\times10^3\times0.8+60+15}\times100 = \mathbf{95.52 \ \%}$$

Example 8.16.2 *A 250 / 500 volts, single-phase transformer gave the following test results - Short circuit test : 20 volts, 12 A, 100 watts (L.V. short-circuited) Open circuit test : 250 volts, 1 A, 80 watts (Low voltage side) Determine the efficiency of the transformer when the output is 12 amp., 500 volts at 0.85 power factor lagging.* **2003-04, Marks 5**

Solution : From S.C. test, we get copper losses hence,

$$P_{cu} = \text{Copper losses} = 100 \ W \ at \ 12 \ A$$

From O.C. test, $P_i = $ Iron losses $= 80$ W

$$\therefore \qquad \% \ \eta = \frac{VA \cos\phi}{VA \cos\phi + P_i + P_{cu}}\times100 = \frac{500\times12\times0.85}{500\times12\times0.85+80+100}\times100 = \mathbf{96.59 \ \%}$$

Example 8.16.3 *The efficiency of a 400 kVA, single phase transformer is 98.77 % at full load 0.8 power factor and 99.13 % at half full load unity power factor. Find : i) Iron losses at full and half full loads ii) Cu losses at full and half full loads.* **2007-08, Marks 10**

Solution : 400 kVA, $\eta_{FL} = 98.77$ %, $\cos\phi = 0.8$, $\eta_{HL} = 99.13$ %, $\cos\phi = 1$

$$\% \ \eta_{FL} = \frac{VA \cos\phi}{VA \cos\phi + P_i + P_{cu}(F.L.)}\times100$$

$$\therefore \qquad 0.9877 = \frac{400\times10^3\times0.8}{400\times10^3\times0.8+P_i+P_{cu}(F.L.)}$$

$$\therefore \ P_i + P_{cu}(F.L.) = 3985.01569 \qquad\qquad \text{...(8.16.1)}$$

$$\% \ \eta_{HL} = \frac{n \ VA \cos\phi}{n \ VA \cos\phi + P_i + n^2 \ P_{cu}(F.L.)}\times100 \qquad \text{where } n = 0.5$$

$$\therefore \qquad 0.9913 = \frac{0.5\times400\times10^3\times1}{0.5\times400\times10^3\times1+P_i+(0.5)^2 \ P_{cu}(F.L.)}$$

$$\therefore \qquad P_i + 0.25 \ P_{cu}(F.L.) = 1755.27085 \qquad\qquad \text{...(8.16.2)}$$

Subtracting equation (8.16.2) from (8.16.1)

$0.75\, P_{cu}$ (F.L.) $=\ 2229.74483$ i.e. P_{cu} (F.L.) $= 2972.9931$ W

$\therefore$ $P_i\ =\ 1012.0225$ W

i) Iron losses remain same on full load and half load which are P_i = **1012.0225 W**

ii) Copper losses on full load = P_{cu} (F.L.) = **2972.9931 W**

iii) Copper losses on half load = $(0.5)^2\, P_{cu}$ (F.L.) = **743.2482 W**

Example 8.16.4 *A 250 kVA single phase transformer has iron loss of 1.8 kW. The full load copper loss is 2000 watts. Calculate, i) Efficiency at full load, 0.8 lagging p.f.   ii) kVA supplied at maximum efficiency iii) Maximum efficiency at 0.8 lagging p.f.*

Solution : The given values are, $P_i = 1800$ W, (P_{cu})F.L. $= 2000$ W

i) $\% \ \eta\ =\ \dfrac{(\text{VA rating})\ \cos\phi}{(\text{VA rating})\ \cos\phi + P_i + (P_{cu})\,\text{F.L.}} \times 100$

$=\ \dfrac{250\times10^3\times0.8}{250\times10^3\times0.8+1800+2000}\times100 =$ **98.135 %**

ii) kVA at $\eta_{max}\ =\ $ kVA rating $\times\sqrt{\dfrac{P_i}{(P_{cu})\,\text{F.L.}}} = 250\times\sqrt{\dfrac{1800}{2000}} =$ **237.1708 kVA**

iii) $\eta_{max}\ =\ \dfrac{\text{kVA at }\eta_{max}\times\cos\phi}{\text{kVA at }\eta_{max}\times\cos\phi + P_i + P_i}$ $P_{cu} = P_i = 1800$ W

$\therefore$ $\% \ \eta_{max}\ =\ \dfrac{237.1708\times10^3\times0.8}{237.1708\times10^3\times0.8+2\times1800}\times100 =$ **98.137%**

Example 8.16.5 *The maximum efficiency of a 100 kVA transformer is 98.40 % and operates at 90 % full load unity power factor. Calculate the efficiency of a transformer at unity power factor at full load.*   **2010-11, Marks 5**

Solution : 100 kVA, $\eta_{max} = 98.4$ %, kVA for $\eta_{max} = 90$ % of full load while $\cos\phi = 1$

$\% \ \eta_{max}\ =\ \dfrac{(\text{VA}) \text{ for } \eta_{max}\times\cos\phi}{(\text{VA}) \text{ for } \eta_{max} + 2\,P_i}\times100$ i.e. $0.984 = \dfrac{0.9\times100\times10^3\times1}{0.9\times100\times10^3\times1+2\,P_i}$

$\therefore$ $P_i\ =\ 731.7073$ W

At η_{max}, Copper losses = Iron losses

$\therefore$ $P_{cu}\ =\ 731.7073$ W at 0.9 of full load i.e. n = 0.9.

Now $P_{cu}\ \propto\ I^2 \propto (\text{VA})^2$ i.e. $\dfrac{(P_{cu})_{FL}}{P_{cu}} = \left[\dfrac{(\text{VA})_{FL}}{0.9\,(\text{VA})_{FL}}\right]^2$

$$\therefore \qquad (P_{cu})_{FL} \; = \; 731.7073 \times \left(\frac{1}{0.9} \right)^2 = 903.3423 \text{ W}$$

$$\% \, \eta_{FL} \; = \; \frac{(VA) \cos \phi}{(VA) \cos \phi + P_i + (P_{cu})_{FL}} \times 100$$

$$= \; \frac{100 \times 10^3 \times 1}{100 \times 10^3 \times 1 + 731.7073 + 903.3423} \times 100 = \textbf{98.3912 \%}$$

Example 8.16.6 *The maximum efficiency of a 100 kVA, 1100/440 volt 50 Hz transformer is 96 %. This occurs at 75 % of full load at 0.8 pf lagging. Find the efficiency of transformer at $\frac{3}{4}$ FL at 0.6 p.f. leading.* **2011-12, Marks 5**

Solution : 100 kVA, η_{max} = 96 % at 75 % of load, $\cos\phi$ = 0.8

$$\therefore \qquad \% \, \eta_{max} \; = \; \frac{nVA \cos \phi}{nVA \cos \phi + 2\,P_i} \times 100 \qquad \text{i.e.} \quad 0.96 = \frac{0.75 \times 100 \times 10^3 \times 0.8}{0.75 \times 100 \times 10^3 \times 0.8 + 2P_i}$$

$$\therefore \qquad P_i \; = \; 1250 \text{ W} = \text{Iron loss}$$

$$P_{cu} \; = \; 1250 \text{ W is copper loss at n = 0.75 i.e 75 \% of full load}$$

To find efficiency at $\frac{3}{4}^{th}$ load i.e. 75 % of full load at $\cos \phi$ = 0.6 leading

$$\therefore \qquad \% \, \eta \; = \; \frac{n \, VA \cos \phi}{nVA \cos \phi + P_i + [n^2 \times P_{cu}(FL)]} \times 100$$

But n = 0.75 hence $n^2 \, P_{cu}$(FL) = Copper loss at 75 % load = 1250 W

$$\therefore \qquad \% \, \eta \; = \; \frac{0.75 \times 100 \times 10^3 \times 0.6}{0.75 \times 100 \times 10^3 \times 0.6 + 1250 + 1250} \times 100 = \textbf{94.736 \%}$$

Review Questions

1. *Define efficiency of a transformer. How to obtain efficiency at different loads ?*
   2010-11, 2011-12, Marks 5

2. *Derive the condition for the maximum efficiency for a transformer.*

3. *A 40 kVA single phase transformer has core loss of 450 W and full load copper loss of 850 W. If the power factor of the load is 0.8 calculate :*
   i) Full load efficiency   ii) Maximum efficiency at u.p.f.
   iii) Load for maximum efficiency. **[Ans. : 29.1 kVA, 97 %, 29.1 kVA]**

4. *A single phase 25 kVA 1000/2000 V, 50 Hz transformer has maximum efficiency of 98 % at full load u.p.f. Determine its efficiency at :*
   i) 3/4 full load u.p.f. ii) 1/2 full load 0.8 p.f iii) 1.25 full load 0.9 p.f.
   [Ans. : 255.102 watts, 97.918 %, 96.909 %, 97.728 %]

5. *A 600 kVA, 1 φ transformer has an efficiency of 92 % both at full load and half full load, u.p.f. Determine its efficiency at 75 % full load, 0.9 p.f.* **[Ans. : 91.64 %]**

6. *A 25 kVA transformer has an efficiency of 94 % at full load unity p.f. and at half full load, 0.9 p.f. Determine the iron loss and full load copper loss.* **[Ans. : 1170.2126 W, 425.5319 W]**

7. *In a 50 kVA, 11 kV/400 V transformer, the iron and copper looses are 500 W and 600 W respectively under rated conditions. a) Calculate the efficiency on full load at unity p.f. b) Find the load for maximum efficiency.* **[Ans. : 97.847 %, 45.6435 kVA, 114.1088 A]**

8. *The efficiency of a 250 kVA, single phase transformer is 96 % when delivering full load at 0.8 p.f. lagging and 97.2 % when delivering half load at unity p.f. Determine the efficiency at 75 % of full load at 0.8 p.f. lagging.* **[Ans. : 2023.319 W, 6310.013 W, 96.4179 %]**

9. *Obtain the condition for maximum efficiency of a transformer and find kVA required for maximum efficiency.* **2012-13, Marks 5**

8.17 Effect of Power Factor on Efficiency   2011-12

The efficiency of a transformer is given by,

$$\eta = \frac{\text{Output}}{\text{Input}} = \frac{\text{Input} - \text{Losses}}{\text{Input}} = 1 - \frac{\text{Losses}}{\text{Input}} \qquad \dots (8.17.1)$$

Now,   Input = Output + Losses = $V_2 I_2 \cos\phi + \text{Losses}$

Using in equation (8.17.1), $\eta = 1 - \dfrac{\text{Losses}}{V_2 I_2 \cos\phi + \text{Losses}}$

$$\therefore \qquad \eta = 1 - \frac{\dfrac{\text{Losses}}{V_2 I_2}}{\cos\phi + \dfrac{\text{Losses}}{V_2 I_2}} \qquad \dots (8.17.2)$$

Let $\dfrac{\text{Losses}}{V_2 I_2} = x$ and using in equation (8.17.2),

$$\therefore \qquad \eta = 1 - \frac{x}{x + \cos\phi} = 1 - \frac{\dfrac{x}{\cos\phi}}{1 + \dfrac{x}{\cos\phi}} \qquad \dots (8.17.3)$$

Thus as the power factor of the load is more i.e. $\cos\phi$ is higher, $x / \cos\phi$ is lesser. Hence the second term in the equation (8.17.3) becomes lesser and efficiency will be more.

As power factor increases, the efficiency increases.

Thus the family of efficiency curves are obtained as power factor increases, as shown in the Fig. 8.17.1.

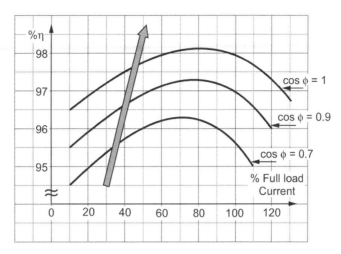

Fig. 8.17.1 Effect of p.f. on efficiency

Review Question

> 1. *How transformer efficiency is affected by change in power factor ?*   **2011-12, Marks 5**

8.18 Predetermination of Efficiency and Regulation

2001-02, 2002-03, 2004-05, 2005-06

The efficiency and regulation of a transformer on any load condition and at any power factor condition can be predetermined by indirect loading method. In this method, the actual load is not used on transformer. But the equivalent circuit parameters of a transformer are determined by conducting two tests on a transformer which are,

1   Open Circuit Test (O.C. Test)

2.   Short Circuit Test (S.C. Test)

Key Point *The parameters calculated from these test results are effective in determining the regulation and efficiency of a transformer at any load and power factor condition, without actually loading the transformer.*

The advantage of this method is that without much power loss the tests can be performed and results can be obtained. Let us discuss in detail how to perform these tests and how to use the results to calculate equivalent circuit parameters.

8.18.1 Open Circuit Test (O.C. Test)

The experimental circuit to conduct O.C. test is shown in the Fig. 8.18.1.

The transformer primary is connected to a.c. supply through ammeter, wattmeter and variac. The secondary of transformer is kept open. Usually low voltage side is used as primary and high voltage side as secondary to conduct O.C. test.

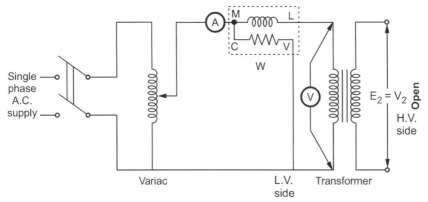

Fig. 8.18.1 Experimental circuit for O.C. test

The primary is excited by rated voltage, which is adjusted precisely with the help of a variac. The wattmeter measures input power. The ammeter measures input current. The voltmeter gives the value of rated primary voltage applied at rated frequency.

Sometimes a voltmeter may be connected across secondary to measure secondary voltage which is $V_2 = E_2$ when primary is supplied with rated voltage. As voltmeter resistance is very high, though voltmeter is connected, secondary is treated to be open circuit as voltmeter current is always negligibly small.

When the primary voltage is adjusted to its rated value with the help of variac, readings of ammeter and wattmeter are to be recorded.

The observation table is as follows

V_0 volts	I_0 amperes	W_0 watts
Rated		

V_0 = Rated voltage, W_0 = Input power, I_0 = Input current = No load current

As transformer secondary is open, it is on no load. So current drawn by the primary is no load current I_0. The two components of this no load current are,

$$I_m = I_0 \sin \phi_0, \quad I_c = I_0 \cos \phi_0$$

where $\cos \phi_0$ = No load power factor

And hence power input can be written as,

$$W_0 = V_0 I_0 \cos \phi_0$$

The phasor diagram is shown in the Fig. 8.18.2.

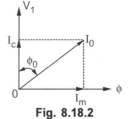

Fig. 8.18.2

As secondary is open, $I_2 = 0$. Thus its reflected current on primary is also zero. So we have primary current $I_1 = I_0$. The transformer no load current is always very small, hardly 2 to 4 % of its full load value. As $I_2 = 0$, secondary copper losses are zero. And $I_1 = I_0$ is very low hence copper losses on primary are also very very low. Thus the total copper losses in O.C. test are negligibly small. As against this the input voltage is rated at rated frequency hence flux density in the core is at its maximum value. Hence iron losses are at rated voltage. As output power is zero and copper losses are very low, the total input power is used to supply iron losses. This power is measured by the wattmeter i.e. W_0. Hence the wattmeter in O.C. test gives iron losses which remain constant for all the loads.

∴

$$W_0 = P_i = \text{Iron losses}$$

Calculations : We know that,

$$W_0 = V_0 I_0 \cos \phi$$

∴

$$\cos \phi_0 = \frac{W_0}{V_0 I_0} = \text{No load power factor}$$

Once $\cos \phi_0$ is known we can obtain,

$$I_c = I_0 \cos \phi_0 \qquad \text{and} \qquad I_m = I_0 \sin \phi_0$$

Once I_c and I_m are known we can determine exciting circuit parameters as,

$$R_0 = \frac{V_0}{I_c} \ \Omega \qquad \text{and} \qquad X_0 = \frac{V_0}{I_m} \ \Omega$$

Key Point *The no load power factor $\cos \phi_0$ is very low hence wattmeter used must be low power factor type otherwise there might be error in the results. If the meters are connected on secondary and primary is kept open then from O.C. test we get R_0' and X_0' and with which we can obtain R_0 and X_0 and knowing the transformation ratio K.*

8.18.2 Short Circuit Test (S.C. Test)

In this test, primary is connected to a.c. supply through variac, ammeter and voltmeter as shown in the Fig. 8.18.3.

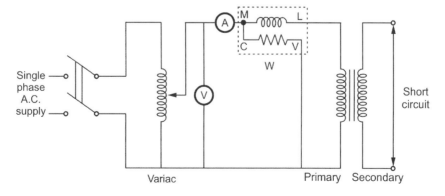

Fig. 8.18.3 Experimental circuit for S.C. test

The secondary is short circuited with the help of thick copper wire or solid link. As high voltage side is always low current side, it is convenient to connect high voltage side to supply and shorting the low voltage side.

As secondary is shorted, its resistance is very very small and on rated voltage it may draw very large current. Such large current can cause overheating and burning of the transformer. To limit this short circuit current, primary is supplied with low voltage which is just enough to cause rated current to flow through primary which can be observed on an ammeter. The low voltage can be adjusted with the help of variac. Hence this test is also called low voltage test or reduced voltage test. The wattmeter reading as well as voltmeter, ammeter readings are recorded. The observation table is as follows,

V_{sc} volts	I_{sc} amperes	W_{sc} watts
	Rated	

Now the currents flowing through the windings are rated currents hence the total copper loss is full load copper loss. Now the voltage applied is low which is a small fraction of the rated voltage. The iron losses are function of applied voltage. So the iron losses in reduced voltage test are very small. Hence the wattmeter reading is the power loss which is equal to full load copper losses as iron losses are very low.

$$W_{sc} = (P_{Cu}) \text{ F.L.} = \text{Full load copper loss}$$

Calculations : From S.C. test readings we can write,

$$W_{sc} = V_{sc} I_{sc} \cos \phi_{sc}$$

$\therefore \quad \cos \phi_{sc} = \dfrac{V_{sc} I_{sc}}{W_{sc}} = \text{Short circuit power factor}$

$$W_{sc} = I_{sc}^2 R_{1e} = \text{Copper loss}$$

$\therefore \quad \boxed{R_{1e} = \dfrac{W_{sc}}{I_{sc}^2}}$ while $\boxed{Z_{1e} = \dfrac{V_{sc}}{I_{sc}} = \sqrt{R_{1e}^2 + X_{1e}^2}}$ $\boxed{X_{1e} = \sqrt{Z_{1e}^2 - R_{1e}^2}}$

Thus we get the equivalent circuit parameters R_{1e}, X_{1e} and Z_{1e}. Knowing the transformation ratio K, the equivalent circuit parameters referred to secondary also can be obtained.

Important note : If the transformer is step up transformer, its primary is L.V. while secondary is H.V. winding. In S.C. test, supply is given to H.V. winding and L.V. is shorted. In such case we connect meters on H.V. side which is transformer secondary though for S.C. test purpose H.V. side acts as primary. In such case the parameters calculated from S.C. test readings are referred to secondary which are R_{2e}, Z_{2e} and X_{2e}. So before doing calculations it is necessary to find out whether the readings are recorded on transformer primary or secondary and accordingly the parameters are to be determined. In step down transformer, primary is high voltage itself to which supply is given in S.C. test. So in such case test results give us parameters referred to primary i.e. R_{1e}, Z_{1e} and X_{1e}.

Key Point *In short, if meters are connected to primary of transformer in S.C. test, calculations give us R_{1e} and Z_{1e}. If meters are connected to secondary of transformer in S.C. test calculations give us R_{2e} and Z_{2e}.*

8.18.3 Calculation of Efficiency from O.C. and S.C. Tests

We know that,

From O.C. test, $W_0 = P_i$

From S.C. test, $W_{sc} = (P_{Cu})$ F.L.

∴   % η on full load $= \dfrac{V_2\,(I_2)\,\text{F.L.}\cos\phi}{V_2\,(I_2)\,\text{F.L.}\,\cos\phi + W_0 + W_{sc}} \times 100$

Thus for any p.f. $\cos\phi_2$ the efficiency can be predetermined. Similarly at any load which is fraction of full load then also efficiency can be predetermined as,

$$\% \ \eta \text{ at any load} = \dfrac{n\times(\text{VA rating})\times\cos\phi}{n\times(\text{VA rating})\times\cos\phi + W_0 + n^2\,W_{sc}} \times 100$$

where   n = Fraction of full load

or $\% \ \eta = \dfrac{n\,V_2\,I_2\,\cos\phi}{n\,V_2\,I_2\,\cos\phi + W_0 + n^2\,W_{sc}} \times 100$

where $I_2 = n\,(I_2)$ F.L.

8.18.4 Calculation of Regulation

From S.C. test we get the equivalent circuit parameters referred to primary or secondary.

The rated voltages V_1, V_2 and rated currents (I_1) F.L. and (I_2) F.L. are known for the given transformer. Hence the regulation can be determined as,

$$\% \ R = \dfrac{I_2\,R_{2e}\cos\phi \pm I_2\,X_{2e}\sin\phi}{V_2}\times100 = \dfrac{I_1\,R_{1e}\cos\phi \pm I_1\,X_{1e}\sin\phi}{V_1}\times100$$

where I_1, I_2 are rated currents for full load regulation.

For any other load the currents I_1, I_2 must be changed by fraction n.

∴ I_1, I_2 at any other load = n (I_1) F.L., n (I_2) F.L.

Thus regulation at any load and any power factor can be predetermined, without actually loading the transformer.

Example 8.18.1 *Open and short-circuit tests on a 5 kVA, 220 V / 400 V, 50 Hz, single phase transformer gave the following results : O.C. test (meters on l.v. side) 2 A, 100 W S.C. test (meters on h.v. side) : 40 V, 11.4 A, 200 W. Determine the efficiency and voltage regulation of the transformer at full load 0.9 power factor lagging.*

2001-02, Marks 5

Solution : From O.C. test, P_i = Iron loss = **100 W**

From S.C. test, as meters are on h.v. side,

$$R_{2e} = \frac{W_{sc}}{I_{sc}^2} = \frac{200}{(11.4)^2} = 1.5389 \ \Omega, \quad Z_{2e} = \frac{V_{sc}}{I_{sc}} = \frac{40}{11.4} = 3.5087 \ \Omega$$

∴ $$X_{2e} = \sqrt{Z_{2e}^2 - R_{2e}^2} = 3.1532 \ \Omega, \quad (I_2)_{FL} = \frac{VA}{V_2} = \frac{5 \times 10^3}{400} = 12.5 \ A$$

Cu loss $\propto I^2$

∴ $$\frac{W_{sc}}{(P_{cu})_{FL}} = \left[\frac{I_{sc}}{(I_1)_{FL}}\right]^2 \quad \text{i.e.} \quad \frac{200}{(P_{cu})_{FL}} = \left(\frac{11.4}{12.5}\right)^2$$

∴ $(P_{cu})_{FL}$ = **240.4586 W**   ...Full load copper loss

For $\cos \phi$ = 0.9 lag, $\sin \phi$ = 0.4358

∴ $$\% \ R = \frac{(I_2)_{FL}[\ R_{2e} \cos \phi + X_{2e} \sin \phi\ ]}{V_2} \times 100 = \textbf{8.622 \%}$$

$$\% \ \eta_{FL} = \frac{VA \cos \phi}{VA \cos \phi + P_i + (P_{cu})_{FL}} \times 100 = \frac{5 \times 10^3 \times 0.9}{5 \times 10^3 \times 0.9 + 100 + 240.4586} \times 100 = \textbf{92.966 \%}$$

Example 8.18.2 *Following results were obtained on a 100 kVA, 11000 / 220 V single-phase transformer :- i) O.C. Test (L.V. side) : 220 V, 45 A, 2 kW ii) S.C. Test (H.V. side) : 500 V, 9.09 A, 3 kW. Determine equivalent circuit parameters of the transformer referred to low-voltage side.*   **2002-03, 2005-06, Marks 10**

Solution : O.C. test : As is performed on L.V. side, the **parameters are also referred to low voltage side**

$$W_0 = 2 \ kW, \quad V_0 = 220 \ V, \quad I_0 = 45 \ A$$

∴ $$\cos \phi_0 = \frac{W_0}{V_0 I_0} = \frac{2 \times 10^3}{220 \times 45} = 0.202$$

$\therefore$ $I'_c = I_0 \cos \phi_0 = 9.09$ A   and $I'_m = I_0 \sin \phi_0 = 44.0723$ A

$\therefore$ $R'_0 = \dfrac{V_2}{I_c} = \mathbf{24.2024 \ \Omega}$ and $X'_0 = \dfrac{V_2}{I_m} = \mathbf{4.9918 \ \Omega}$

S.C. test : As is performed on H.V. side, the parameters to be obtained from results are referred to high voltage side i.e. primary and must be transferred to low voltage side i.e. secondary.

$$W_{sc} = 3 \text{ kW}, \quad V_{sc} = 500 \text{ V}, \quad I_{sc} = 9.09 \text{ A}$$

$\therefore$ $R_{1e} = \dfrac{W_{sc}}{I_{sc}^2} = \dfrac{3000}{(9.09)^2} = 36.3072 \ \Omega, \ Z_{1e} = \dfrac{V_{sc}}{I_{sc}} = \dfrac{500}{9.09} = 55 \ \Omega$

$\therefore$ $X_{1e} = \sqrt{Z_{1e}^2 - R_{1e}^2} = \sqrt{55^2 - (36.3072)^2} = 41.3132 \ \Omega, \ K = \dfrac{220}{11000} = 0.02$

$\therefore$ $R_{2e} = K^2 R_{1e} = (0.02)^2 \times 36.3072 = \mathbf{0.0145 \ \Omega}$

$\therefore$ $X_{2e} = K^2 X_{1e} = (0.02)^2 \times 41.3132 = \mathbf{0.01652 \ \Omega}$

$\therefore$ $Z_{2e} = K^2 Z_{1e} = (0.02)^2 \times 55 = \mathbf{0.022 \ \Omega}$

Example 8.18.3 *An open circuit (oc) test and short circuit (sc) test are performed on a single phase transformer in standard manner with results in table. Quantities not measured are noted as 'NM'.*

	OC	OC	SC
Quantity	Side-1	Side-2	Side-1
Voltage, V	7500	220	210
Current, I	NM	3.00	2
Power, W	NM	250	200

i) What is voltage rating of transformer ?

ii) What is transformer's apparent power rating ?

iii) Draw an equivalent circuit referred to the HV side with impedance.

iv) Find the magnetising current, if excited from HV side.   **2004-05, Marks 10**

Solution : i) In open circuit test, on secondary side meters are connected while primary is kept open.

Thus

   $V_1 = 7500$ V and $V_2 = 220$ V

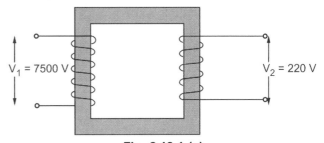

Fig. 8.18.4 (a)

$\therefore$ Voltage rating of the transformer is **7500 V / 220 V**

  ii) S.C. test is performed on side 1 i.e. H.V. side with $I_{sc} = 2$ A. It is full load current.

$\therefore$ Apparent power rating $= V_1 \, I_1 = 7500 \times 2 = $ **15 kVA**

iii) The test results are,

O.C. test (L.V. side) : $V_0 = 220$ V, $I_0 = 3$ A, $W_0 = 250$ W

S.C. test (H.V. side) : $V_{sc} = 210$ V, $I_{sc} = 2$ A, $W_{sc} = 200$ W

  As in O.C. test, meters are on L.V. side, the parameters to be obtained are referred to L.V. side.

$$\therefore \qquad \cos\phi_0 = \frac{W_0}{V_0 I_0} = \frac{250}{220 \times 3} = 0.3787$$

$$\therefore \qquad I'_c = I_0 \cos\phi_0 = 1.1363 \text{ A}, \qquad I'_m = I_0 \sin\phi_0 = 2.7765 \text{ A}$$

$$\therefore \qquad R'_0 = \frac{V_2}{I'_c} = \frac{220}{1.1363} = 193.61 \ \Omega, \quad X'_0 = \frac{V_2}{I'_m} = \frac{220}{2.7765} = 79.2364 \ \Omega$$

$$K = \frac{N_2}{N_1} = \frac{V_2}{V_1} = \frac{220}{7500} = 0.02933$$

$$\therefore \qquad R_0 = \frac{R'_0}{K^2} = \textbf{225.016 k}\Omega, \quad X_0 = \frac{X'_0}{K^2} = \textbf{92.108 k}\Omega \quad \text{...Referred to H.V. side}$$

$$\text{From S.C. test,} \quad R_{1e} = \frac{W_{sc}}{I_{sc}^2} = \frac{200}{(2)^2} = 50 \ \Omega, \ Z_{1e} = \frac{V_{sc}}{I_{sc}} = \frac{210}{2} = 105 \ \Omega$$

$$\therefore \qquad X_{1e} = \sqrt{Z_{1e}^2 - R_{1e}^2} = 92.33 \ \Omega$$

  All are referred to H.V. side. Hence equivalent circuit referred to H.V. side is shown in the Fig. 8.18.4 (b).

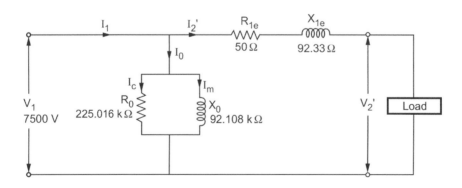

Fig. 8.18.4 (b)

iv) If excited from H.V. side, the magnetising current is,

$$I_m = \frac{V_1}{X_0} = \frac{7500}{92.108 \times 10^3} = 0.08142 \text{ A}$$

Example 8.18.4 *The following readings were obtained from O.C. and S.C. tests on 8 kVA, 400/100 V, 50 Hz transformer : O.C. Test (L.V. side) : 100 V, 4 A, 60 W S.C. Test (H.V. side) : 10 V, 20 A, 100 W Calculate i) Voltage regulation at full load and 0.8 power factor lagging. ii) Full load efficiency at same power factor* **2004-05, Marks 5**

Solution : Refer example 8.17.2 for the procedure and verify the answer as **2.3 %, 97.56 %.**

Example 8.18.5 *Obtain equivalent circuit of a 200/400 V 50 Hz 1-phase transformer from the following test data :*

O.C. test (on LV side)	200 V, 0.7 A, 70 W
S.C. test (on HV side)	15 V, 10 A, 85 W

Calculate the secondary voltage when delivering 5 kW at 0.8 pf lagging, the primary voltage being 200 V.

Solution : From O.C. test : $V_0 = 200$ V, $I_0 = 0.7$ A, $W_0 = 70$ W

$$\therefore \quad \cos \phi_0 = \frac{W_0}{V_0 I_0} = 0.5, \quad \sin \phi_0 = 0.866$$

$$\therefore \quad I_c = I_0 \cos \phi_0 = 0.35 \text{ A}, \quad I_m = I_0 \sin \phi_0 = 0.6062 \text{ A}$$

$$\therefore \quad R_0 = \frac{V_0}{I_c} = 571.428 \ \Omega, \quad X_0 = \frac{V_0}{I_m} = 329.9241 \ \Omega$$

From S.C. test : $V_{sc} = 15$ V, $I_{sc} = 10$ A, $W_{sc} = 85$ W

The meters are H.V. side i.e. secondary hence,

$$R_{2e} = \frac{W_{sc}}{I_{sc}^2} = 0.85 \ \Omega, \quad Z_{2e} = \frac{V_{sc}}{I_{sc}} = 1.5 \ \Omega, \quad X_{2e} = 1.2359 \ \Omega$$

As $K = \frac{V_2}{V_1} = \frac{400}{200} = 2$, the equivalent circuit parameters referred to primary are,

$$R_{1e} = \frac{R_{2e}}{K^2} = 0.2125 \ \Omega, \quad X_{1e} = \frac{X_{2e}}{K^2} = 0.3089 \ \Omega$$

Power delivered = 5 kW = $V_2 I_2 \cos \phi_2$

$$\therefore \quad V_2 I_2 = \frac{5 \times 10^3}{0.8} = 6250 \qquad \qquad \dots \cos \phi_2 = 0.8 \text{ lagging}$$

$$\therefore \qquad I_2 = \frac{6250}{V_2}$$

Total voltage drop = $I_2 [R_{2e} \cos \phi + X_{2e} \sin \phi]$

$$\therefore \qquad E_2 - V_2 = \frac{6250}{V_2} [0.85 \times 0.8 + 1.2359 \times 0.6] \qquad \qquad \ldots E_2 = 400 \text{ V}$$

$$\therefore \quad V_2 (400 - V_2) = 8884.625 \quad \text{i.e.} \quad V_2^2 - 400 \, V_2 + 8884.625 = 0$$

Solving, $\qquad V_2 = \textbf{376.395 V} \qquad \qquad \qquad \ldots$ Secondary voltage

Example 8.18.6 *The parameters of a 10 kVA, 500/250 V, 50 Hz, single phase transformer are as follows :*

Primary resistance = 0.2 Ω, Primary reactance = 0.4 Ω

Secondary resistance = 0.5 Ω, Secondary reactance = 0.1 Ω

Exciting circuit resistance and reactance = 1500 Ω, 750 Ω respectively. Find out the results of open circuit test and short circuit test.

Solution : The given values are,

$R_1 = 0.2 \, \Omega$, $R_2 = 0.5 \, \Omega$, $X_1 = 0.4 \, \Omega$, $X_2 = 0.1 \, \Omega$, $R_0 = 1500 \, \Omega$, $X_0 = 750 \, \Omega$

$$K = \frac{250}{500} = 0.5$$

$$\therefore \qquad R_2' = \frac{R_2}{K^2} = \frac{0.5}{(0.5)^2} = 2 \, \Omega \quad \text{i.e.} \quad R_{1e} = R_1 + R_2' = 0.2 + 2 = 2.2 \, \Omega$$

$$X_2' = \frac{X_2}{K^2} = \frac{0.1}{(0.5)^2} = 0.4 \, \Omega \quad \text{i.e.} \quad X_{1e} = X_1 + X_2' = 0.4 + 0.4 = 0.8 \, \Omega$$

$$\therefore \qquad Z_{1e} = \sqrt{R_{1e}^2 + X_{1e}^2} = 2.3409 \, \Omega$$

Now $\qquad R_0 = \dfrac{V_1}{I_c} \quad \text{i.e.} \quad 1500 = \dfrac{500}{I_c}$

$$\therefore \qquad I_c = 0.3333 = I_0 \cos \phi_0 \qquad \qquad \ldots (8.18.1)$$

$$X_0 = \frac{V_1}{I_m} \quad \text{i.e.} \quad 750 = \frac{500}{I_m}$$

$$\therefore \qquad I_m = 0.6666 = I_0 \sin \phi_0 \qquad \qquad \ldots (8.18.2)$$

Dividing equations (8.18.2) by (8.18.1),

$$\tan \phi_0 = \frac{0.6666}{0.3333} = 2 \quad \text{i.e.} \quad \phi_0 = 63.43°$$

$\therefore \qquad \cos\phi_0 = 0.4472$ lagging

$\therefore \qquad I_c = I_0 \cos\phi_0$ i.e. $I_0 = \dfrac{0.3333}{0.4472} = 0.7453$ A

$\therefore \qquad W_0 = V_0 I_0 \cos\phi_0$ where $V_0 = V_1$ = rated

$\qquad\qquad = 500 \times 0.7453 \times 0.4472 = \mathbf{166.67\ W}$

So O.C. test results are,

$$\boxed{W_0 = 166.67\ W,\ \ V_0 = 500\ V,\ I_0 = 0.7453\ A}$$

Now $\qquad Z_{1e} = \dfrac{V_{sc}}{I_{sc}}$

$\qquad\qquad I_{sc} = (I_1)\ F.L. = \dfrac{VA\ rating}{V_1} = \dfrac{10\times10^3}{500} = \mathbf{20\ A}$

$\therefore \qquad 2.3409 = \dfrac{V_{sc}}{20}$ i.e. $V_{sc} = \mathbf{46.818\ V}$

$\qquad\qquad W_{sc} = I_{sc}^2 R_{1e} = (20)^2 \times 2.2 = \mathbf{880\ W}$

So S.C. test results are,

$$\boxed{W_{sc} = 880\ W,\ V_{sc} = 46.818\ V,\ I_{sc} = 20\ A}$$

The S.C. test is conducted with L.V. winding shorted.

Review Questions

1. *Explain the short circuit test and open circuit test on transformer. Why these tests are to be performed ?*

2. *Explain transformer tests to find the following parameters of transformer :*
   i) Equivalent resistance as referred to primary   ii) Equivalent core-loss resistance
   iii) Equivalent leakage reactance as referred to primary
   iv) Magnetizing reactance.

3. *A 5 kVA, 500 / 250 V, 50 Hz, single phase transformer gave the following readings,*
   O.C. Test : 500 V, 1 A, 50 W (L.V. side open)
   S.C. Test : 25 V, 10 A, 60 W (L.V. side shorted)
   Determine : i) The efficiency on full load, 0.8 lagging p.f.
   ii) The voltage regulaion on full load, 0.8 leading p.f.
   iii) The efficiency on 60 % of full load, 0.8 leading p.f.
   iv) Draw the equivalent circuit referred to primary and insert all the values in it.
   [Ans. : 97.32 %, – 1.95 %, 97.103 %]

4. The results obtained from open circuit and short circuit tests on 10 kVA, 450/120 V, 50 Hz transformer are

O.C.test	120 V	4.2 A	80 W	Instruments placed on L.V. side
S.C.test	9.65 V	22.2 A	120 W	With L.V. winding short circuited

Compute :

i) *Equivalent circuit constants.* ii) *Efficiency and voltage regulation at full load 0.8 p.f. lag.*

iii) *Efficiency at half full load and 0.8 lagging p.f.*   **[Ans. : 97.56 %, 2.028 %, 97.323 %]**

5. *A 10 kVA, 2500/250 V, 1 - ϕ transformer gave the following test results :*

   O.C. test : 250 V, 0.8 V, 50 W

   S.C. test : 60 V, 3 A, 45 W

   i) *Calculate the efficiency at 75 % of F.L. and 125 % of F.L., at 0.8 p.f. lag.*

   ii) *Calculate the load kVA at which maximum efficiency occurs and also the value of maximum efficiency at 0.8 p.f.*

   iii) *Compute the voltage regulation and secondary terminal voltage under rated full load at*
      i) 0.8 p.f. lag and ii) 0.8 p.f. leading.

      [Ans. : 98.441 %, 98.28 %, 98.442 %, 2.5 %, − 1.219 %, 243.902 V, 253.085 V]

6. *Obtain the equivalent circuit parameters of a 200/2000 V single phase, 30 kVA step up transformer having the following test results.*

O.C. test	200 V, 6.2 A, 360 W	L.V. Side
S.C. test	75 V, 18 A, 600 W	H.V. Side

Write the equivalent circuit referred to L.V. side.

Ans. :

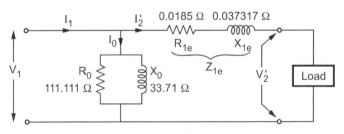

Fig. 8.18.5

7. *A 12 kVA, 220V/440 V, 50 Hz single phase transformer gave the following test data*

   No load : 220 V, 2 A, 165 W (L.V. Side)

   SC Test : 12 V,   15 A, 60 W (H.V. Side)

   Draw the equivalent circuit as referred to LV side and insert the appropriate values. Find the secondary terminal voltage on full load and as a power factor of 0.8 lag.

   [Ans. : 0.8 Ω, 0.2667 Ω, 0.067 Ω, 0.1885 Ω, 0.2 Ω, 421.8414 V]

8. *A 2500/250 V, 50 Hz, 50 kVA, single phase transformer has a resistance of 0.8 ohm and 0.012 ohm and a reactance of 4 ohm and 0.04 ohm for high and low voltage windings respectively.*

Transformer gives 96 % maximum efficiency at 75 % full-load at unity p.f. The magnetizing component of no-load current is 1.2 A on 2500 V side. Find out ammeter, voltmeter and wattmeter readings on O.C. and S.C. test, if supply is given to 2500 V side in both cases.

[Ans. : 2500 V, 1.24 A, 781.25 W, 164.924 V, 20 A, 800 W]

8.19 Autotransformer   2009-10, 2010-11, 2011-12

An autotransformer is a special type of transformer such that a part of the winding is common to both primary as well as secondary. It has only winding wound on a laminated magnetic core. With the help of autotransformer the voltage can be stepped down or can be stepped up also, to any desired value.

Fig. 8.19.1 (a) shows the step down autotransformer. AB acts as a primary winding while part of the primary winding BC acts as a secondary winding. The position of C called as % tapping point, can be selected as per the requirement of the secondary voltage.

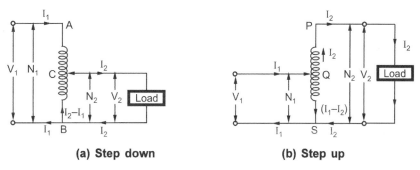

(a) Step down   (b) Step up

Fig. 8.19.1

Fig. 8.19.1 (b) shows the step up autotransformer where QS acts as a primary winding while PS acts as a secondary winding.

The operating principle of the autotransformer is same as that of two winding transformer.

The current in the portion CB i.e. secondary, in case of step down auto transformer is the vector difference of I_2 and I_1 while the current in the portion QS i.e. primary, in case of step up autotransformer is the vector difference of I_2 and I_1.

Neglecting the losses, the leakage reactance and the magnetising current we can write the transformation ratio of the autotransformer as

$$K = \frac{V_2}{V_1} = \frac{I_1}{I_2} = \frac{N_2}{N_1}$$

Due to the use of single winding, compared to normal two winding transformer, for the same capacity and voltage ratio, there is substantial saving in copper, in autotransformer.

8.19.1 Copper Saving in Autotransformer

For any winding, the cross-section of winding is proportional to the current I. While the total length of the winding is proportional to the number of turns N. Hence the weight of copper is proportional to the product of N and I.

Weight of copper $\propto$ N I

In two winding transformer,

Weight of copper of winding 1 $\propto N_1 I_1$

Weight of copper of winding 2 $\propto N_1 I_2$

$\therefore$ Total weight of copper $\propto N_1 I_1 + N_2 I_2$

In case of step down autotransformer the,

Weight of copper of section AC $\propto (N_1 - N_2) I_1$

Weight of copper of section BC $\propto N_2 (I_2 - I_1)$

$\therefore$ Total weight of copper $\propto (N_1 - N_2) I_1 + N_2 (I_2 - I_1)$

Refer Fig. 8.19.1 (a) for currents in various sections.

$$\therefore \frac{\text{Weight of copper in autotransformer}}{\text{Weight of copper in two winding transformer}} = \frac{(N_1 - N_2) I_1 + N_2 (I_2 - I_1)}{N_1 I_1 + N_2 I_2}$$

$$= \frac{N_1 I_1 - N_2 I_1 + N_2 I_2 - N_2 I_1}{N_1 I_1 + N_2 I_2}$$

$$= 1 - \frac{2 N_2 I_1}{N_1 I_1 + N_2 I_2} = 1 - \frac{2}{\left(\frac{N_1}{N_2}\right) + \left(\frac{I_2}{I_1}\right)}$$

But $\quad \dfrac{N_1}{N_2} = \dfrac{I_2}{I_1} = \dfrac{1}{K}$

Substituting in above, $= 1 - \dfrac{2}{\left(\frac{1}{K}\right) + \left(\frac{1}{K}\right)} = 1 - K$

$\therefore$ Weight of copper in autotransformer $= (1 - K) \times$ Weight of copper in two winding transformer.

$\therefore$ Saving in copper $=$ Weight of copper in two winding transformer

$\quad\quad\quad - (1 - K)$ Weight of copper in two winding transformer

$\therefore$ Saving in copper $= K \times$ Weight of copper in two winding transformer   ... Step down

In **step up** autotransformer this expression becomes,

$$\text{Saving in copper} = \frac{1}{K} \times \text{Weight of copper in two winding transformer} \qquad \text{... Step up}$$

Key Point *As transformation ratio K approaches to unity, greater is the saving in copper.*

8.19.2 Advantages of Autotransformer

1) Copper required is very less.

2) The efficiency is higher compared to two winding transformer.

3) The size and hence cost is less compared to two winding transformer.

4) The resistance and leakage reactance is less compared to two winding transformer.

5) The copper losses $I^2 R$, are less.

6) Due to less resistance and leakage reactance, the voltage regulation is superior than the two winding transformer.

8.19.3 Limitations of Autotransformer

1) Low impedance hence high short circuit currents for short circuits on secondary side.

2) If a section of winding common to primary and secondary is opened, full primary voltage appears across the secondary resulting in higher voltage on secondary and danger of accidents.

3) No electrical separation between primary and secondary which is risky in case of high voltage levels.

8.19.4 Applications of Autotransformer

1) For interconnecting systems which are operating roughly at same voltage.

2) For starting rotating machines like induction motors, synchronous motors.

3) To give a small boost to a distribution cable to correct for the voltage drop.

4) As a furnace transformer for getting required supply voltage.

5) As a variac, to vary the voltage to the load, smoothly from zero to the rated value. Such variacs are commonly used for dimming the lights in cinema halls. Hence the variacs are also called **dimmerstats.** The principle of dimmerstat is shown in the Fig. 8.19.2.

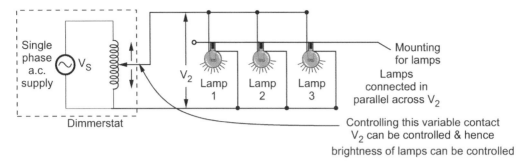

Fig. 8.19.2 Autotransformer as dimmerstat

Review Questions

1. *Explain the working of autotransformer. And state its applications.*

    2009-10, 2010-11, 2011-12, Marks 5

2. *Explain how copper saving is achieved in autotransformer.*

8.20 Short Answered and Objective Type Questions

Q.1 What is typical use of an autotransformer ?   **2012-13, Marks 2**

(Ans. : Dimmerstat)

Q.2 What happens if DC supply is given to a transformer ? **(Refer section 8.2.1)**

    2012-13, Marks 2

Q.3 Name the constant losses taking place in a transformer. **(Refer section 8.15)**

    2011-12, Marks 2

Q.4 A single phase transformer working at maximum efficiency. The copper losses are 100 W, the iron losses would be _____ .   **2008-09, Marks 2**

Ans. : $P_i = P_{cu} = 100$ W at maximum efficiency

Q.5 A 100 kVA single phase transformer operating at 0.9 power factor has 90 % maximum efficiency. The iron loss will be _____.   **2009-10, Marks 2**

Ans. : 100 kVA, $\cos\phi = 0.9$, $\eta_{max} = 90$ %

For η_{max}, $P_i = P_{cu}$.

$\therefore$ % η_{max} $= \dfrac{VA\,\cos\phi}{VA\,\cos\phi + 2P_i} \times 100$

$\therefore$ $P_i = \textbf{5000 W}$ = iron loss

Assuming that the maximum efficiency occurs at 100 kVA.

Q.6   Autotransformer can do the following : _____ .   `2009-10, Mark 1`
a) Step up voltage   b) Step down voltage

c) Both (a) and (b)   d) None of these   **(Ans. : c)**

Q.7   A transformer transforms : _____ .   `2009-10 Mark 1`
a) Voltage   b) Current   c) Voltage and current

d) Frequency   **(Ans. : c)**

Q.8   A transformer can be connected to DC : _____ .   `2009-10 Mark 1`
a) Yes   b) No   **(Ans. : b)**

Q.9   Open circuit test is usually conducted on : _____ .   `2009-10 Mark 1`
a) Slip ring motors   b) Wound rotor motor

c) Either of (a) and (b)   d) None of above   **(Ans. : a)**

Q.10   The short circuit test of transformer is done to determine :   `2010-11 Marks 2`
a) Iron loss   b) Eddy current loss

c) Copper loss at full load   d) Copper loss at desired load.   **(Ans. : c)**

Q.11   A transformer is a _____ device.

a) A.C.   b) D.C.

c) Both A.C and D.C.   d) None of these   **(Ans. : a)**

Q.12   A transformer works on the principle of _____.

a) Faraday's law   b) Mutual induction

c) Ferrari   d) Superposition   **(Ans. : b)**

Q.13   The primary and secondary windings of a transformer are _____ coupled to each other.

a) electrically   b) magnetically

c) electrically and magnetically   d) none of these   **(Ans. : b)**

Q.14   The frequency of secondary voltage is _____ that of the primary voltage.

a) greater than   b) less than   c) same as   d) none of these
                                                                               (Ans. : c)

Q.15   The vertical portion on which coils are wound in a transformer is called _____.

a) core   b) yoke   c) joint   d) limb   **(Ans. : d)**

Q.16   Generally _____ is used for laminations of a transformer core.

a) high grade silicon steel   b) copper

c) iron   d) manganin   **(Ans. : a)**

Q.17   In a core type transformer _____.

a) the core encircles the winding.   b) the winding encircles the core.

c) the limb encircles the yoke.   d) none of the above   (Ans. : b)

Q.18   The _____ on both sides of a transformer remains same .

a) voltage   b) current   c) power   d) impedance

(Ans. : c)

Q.19   _____ construction has a double magnetic circuit.

a) core type   b) shell type   c) berry type   d) three phase

(Ans. : b)

Q.20   The flux produced in the core is _____.

a) directly proportional to the supply frequency

b) directly proportional to the supply voltage

c) inverse proportional to the square of the frequency

d) none of the above   (Ans. : b)

Q.21   The average e.m.f. per turn in a transformer is _____.

a) $4 f \phi_m$ b) $4.44 f \phi_m$ c) $2 f \phi_m$ d) $f \phi_m$ (Ans. : a)

Q.22   The turns ratio is _____ to current ratio.

a) directly proportional   b) equal

c) inversely proportional   d) none of these.   (Ans. : c)

Q.23   The transformer rating is expressed on VA because _____.

a) on both sides it is constant.

b) losses are independent of load power factor.

c) the frequency is constant on the load side.

d) the flux in the core remains constant.   (Ans. : b)

Q.24   The flux in the transformer core is _____.

a) rotating   b) partly rotating   c) partly alternating   d) purely alternating

(Ans. : d)

Q.25   If transformer is connected to d.c. supply _____.

a) primary may burn out .

b) primary voltage will increase.

c) the primary impedance will increase.

d) none of these.   (Ans. : a)

Q.26 For a 250/25 V transformer having 1 kVA rating, the full load primary current is _____.

a) 40 A   B) 4 A   c) 0.4 A   d) 0.04 A   **(Ans. : b)**

Q.27 For a 10 kVA, 2000/200 V transformer, the half load secondary current is _____.

a) 50 A   b) 5 A   c) 25 A   d) 10 A   **(Ans. : c)**

Q.28 The _____ component of no load current is required to produce flux in the core.

a) wattful   b) power   c) core loss   d) magnetizing
                                                                              (Ans. : d)

Q.29 The core losses are dissipated in the form of _____.

a) heat   b) magnetic hum

c) light   d) electric energy   **(Ans. : a)**

Q.30 A transformer core is laminated to reduce the _____.

a) hysteresis loss b) eddy current loss c) leakage reactance d) all of these.
                                                                              (Ans. : b)

Q.31 Which loss is not common between rotating machines and transformer ?

a) Copper loss   b) Eddy current loss

c) Core loss   d) Friction loss   **(Ans. : d)**

Q.32 The no load current in a transformer is usually _____ of the full load current

a) 0.2 to 0.4 %   b) 1 to 5 %   c) 11 to 15 %   d) 25 to 30 %
                                                                              (Ans. : b)

Q.33 In a transformer, as load increases _____.

a) flux in the core remains constant.   b) flux in the core decreases
c) flux in the core increases   d) none of these .   **(Ans. : a)**

Q.34 For a transformer, the turns ratio is 10 : 1 then its primary resistance of 10 Ω will be _____ when referred to secondary.

a) 1 Ω b) 0 . 01 Ω c) 0.1 Ω d) 10 Ω **(Ans. : c)**

Q.35 A high voltage side is _____.

a) low current, low impedance side,
b) high current, low impedance side,
c) low current, high impedance side,
d) none of the above   **(Ans. : c)**

Q.36 The core provides _____ path to the flux produced.

a) low resistance   b) low reluctance

c) low voltage   d) none of these   **(Ans. : b)**

Q.37 _____ test is used to obtain iron losses.

a) Short circuit   b) Back to back   c) Polarity   d) Open circuit

                                                 (Ans. : d)

Q.38 _____ test is used to obtain copper losses.

a) Short circuit   b) Back to back   c) Polarity   d) Open circuit

                                                 (Ans. : a)

Q.39 For leading power factor loads, the regulation of transformer is _____.

a) positive   b) negative   c) zero   d) unity   **(Ans. : b)**

Q.40 For better performance of transformer, the regulation must be _____.

a) high   b) infinite   c) very low   d) none of these

                                                  (Ans. : c)

Q.41 The voltage regulation of a transformer is zero for _____ load.

a) lagging   b) resistive   c) inductive   d) capacitive

                                                  (Ans. : d)

Q.42 The transformer efficiency is maximum when _____.

a) $P_i > P_{cu}$ b) $P_i < P_{cu}$ c) $P_i = P_{cu}$ d) None of these

                                                  (Ans. : c)

Q.43 The main advantage of indirect loading test on transformer is _____.

a) the meters required are less   b) the results are accurate

c) the results can be predetermined with reduced power loss

d) none of the above   **(Ans. : c)**

Q.44 The wattmeter used in O.C. test must be _____.

a) low power factor   b) dynamometer type

c) of very high range   d) none of these   **(Ans. : a)**

Q.45 The short circuit test readings for a transformer are 40 V, 20 A, 400 W then its equivalent leakage reactance is _____.

a) 1.414 Ω b) $\sqrt{3}$ Ω c) 2 Ω d) 1 Ω **(Ans. : b)**

Q.46 The value of transformation ratio must be _____ for greater copper saving in autotransformer.

a) zero   b) 10   c) 5   d) unity   **(Ans. : d)**

Q.47   An autotransformer _____.

a) used in power transformer   b) converts single phase to three phase.

c) uses common winding between primary and secondary

d) none of the above.   **(Ans. : c)**

Q.48   In which of the following application, an autotransformer is used ?

a) Dimmerstat   b) Bulbs

c) Traction   d) Leath machine   **(Ans. : a)**

Q.49   The advantage of an autotransformer is _____.

a) Saving in copper   b) Reduced losses

c) Saving in core material   d) All of the above   **(Ans. : d)**

Q.50   The Hysteresis loss in a transformer varies as _____.

a) B_m b) B_m^2 c) $B_m^{1.67}$ d) $B_m^{2.4}$ **(Ans. : c)**

Q.51   The eddy current loss in a transformer varies as

a) B_m b) B_m^2 c) $B_m^{1.67}$ d) $B_m^{2.4}$ **(Ans. : b)**

Q.52   For 400 V/100 V transformer, the secondary turns are 16 then the primary turns are _____.

a) 4   b) 64   c) 16   d) 8   **(Ans. : b)**

Q.53   In a transformer, the resistance between its primary and secondary winding is _____.

a) infinite   b) zero   c) 1000 Ω d) 1 Ω **(Ans. : a)**

Q.54   A transformer has maximum efficiency at full load when iron losses are 1600 W then its half load copper losses are _____.

a) 1600 W   b) 6400 W   c) 400 W   d) none of these
                                                                                     (Ans. : c)

Q.55   The full load copper losses of transformer are 500 W then the copper losses on full load at 0.8 power factor lagging are _____.

a) 1000 W   b) 250 W   d) 125 W   d) 500 W **(Ans. : d)**

Q.56   Which loss is variable in a transformer ?

a) Eddy current   b) Copper   c) Hysteresis   d) Friction **(Ans. : b)**

Q.57   While conducting short circuit test, _____ side is short circuited.

a) L.V.   b) H.V.   c) Both   d) Primary **(Ans. : a)**

Q.58 The value of flux used in an e.m.f. equation of a transformer is _____.

     a) R.M.S.   b) average   c) maximum   d) instantaneous

                                                                                  (Ans. : c)

Q.59 If the transformer regulation is positive, _____ load is connected to the transformer.

     a) capacitive   b) inductive   c) resistive   d) none of these

                                                                                         (Ans. : b)

Q.60 For a 50 Hz transformer, the primary turns are 100 and maximum flux in the core is 0.08 Wb then the primary induced e.m.f. is _____.

     a) 1856 V   b) 1276 V   c) 176 V   d) 1776 V   **(Ans. : d)**

□□□

9 D.C. Machines

Syllabus

Concept of electro mechanical energy conversion D.C. Machines : Types, E.M.F. equation of generator and torque equation of motor, Characteristics and applications of dc motors (Simple numerical problems).

Contents

9.1 Introduction

An electrical machine, deals with the energy transfer either from mechanical to electrical form or from electrical to mechanical form. This process is called **electromechanical energy conversion**. An electrical machine which converts mechanical energy into an electrical energy is called an **electric generator**.

While an electrical machine which converts an electrical energy into the mechanical energy is called an **electrical motor**. The d.c. machines are thus classified as,

1. **D.C. Generators** : These machines convert mechanical input power into d.c. electrical power.

2. **D.C. Motors** : These machines convert d.c. electrical power into mechanical power.

The construction of both the types of d.c. machines basically remains same.

9.2 Electromechanical Energy Conversion

The generator is a well known device which converts mechanical energy into an electrical energy. Thus there involves a process of energy conversion. Similarly in many devices it is necessary to convert electrical energy into some other form of energy such as mechanical, sound, light etc.

Key Point *Thus the electromechanical energy conversion process involves the transfer of energy between electrical and mechanical systems, via the electric field or magnetic field.*

The process of electromechanical energy conversion is basically reversible in nature, apart from the losses taking place in the device. **The energy cannot be created or destroyed but it can be transformed from one form to other.** Hence practically electromechanical energy conversion devices are very important.

In practice, three types of electromechanical energy conversion devices are in use.

1. The various transducers such as microphones, loudspeakers, strain guage, thermocouples etc. These devices handle low energy signals. These devices mostly operate on vibrating motion.

2. The devices which produce the mechanical force or torque based on translatory motion such as electromagnets, relays, solenoids, actuators etc. These devices handle large energy signals than the transducers.

3. The devices used for continuous energy conversion using rotational motion such as generators, motors etc. These devices handle very large energy signals.

Key Point *Though energy conversion can take place via electric or magnetic field, the* **magnetic field** *is practically used as is most suited for practical devices and the energy storing capacity of magnetic field is much higher than that of electrical field.*

The fields involved in such electromechanical devices must be slow varying due to inertia associated with the mechanical parts. Such fields are called **quasistatic fields.**

The Fig. 9.2.1 (a) shows the representation of an electromechanical energy conversion device which converts mechanical energy to electrical. It is a **generator.** While the Fig. 9.2.1 (b) shows the representation of an electromagnetical energy conversion device which converts electrical energy into mechanical. It is a **motor.**

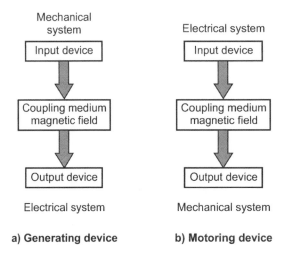

a) **Generating device**   b) **Motoring device**

Fig. 9.2.1 Representation of electromechanical energy conversion device

9.2.1 Energy Balance Equation

According to the principle of conservation of energy, the energy cannot be created or destroyed but it can be transformed from one form to another. The process of energy transformation is reversible but there are certain losses due to practical devices. Hence in energy conversion process the entire energy cannot be transformed from one form to another. The loss in the process is called **energy loss.** In addition to the loss, some part of energy gets stored in the medium like magnetic field. This is called **energy stored.** There exists a perfect energy balance in the process of electromechanical energy conversion. Thus the input energy has three parts, transformed energy, energy loss and stored energy. The energy loss gets converted to heat energy in the electromechanical devices. Thus the **energy balance equation** for generating and motoring actions can be written as,

$$\begin{bmatrix} \text{Electrical energy} \\ \text{input from} \\ \text{electrical system} \end{bmatrix} = \begin{bmatrix} \text{Mechanical} \\ \text{transformed} \\ \text{output energy} \end{bmatrix} + \begin{bmatrix} \text{Change} \\ \text{in energy} \\ \text{stored} \end{bmatrix} + \begin{bmatrix} \text{Total energy loss} \\ \text{i.e. energy dissipated} \\ \text{in the form of heat} \end{bmatrix}$$

... For motor (1)

$$\begin{bmatrix} \text{Mechanical energy} \\ \text{input from} \\ \text{mechanical system} \end{bmatrix} = \begin{bmatrix} \text{Electrical} \\ \text{transformed} \\ \text{energy output} \end{bmatrix} + \begin{bmatrix} \text{Change in} \\ \text{energy} \\ \text{stored} \end{bmatrix} + \begin{bmatrix} \text{Total energy loss} \\ \text{i.e. energy} \\ \text{dissipated} \end{bmatrix}$$

... For generator (2)

In these energy balance equations, the transformed energy terms are always positive but change in energy stored may be positive or negative. If energy stored increases, it is positive while if it decreases it is negative. The energy dissipated in the form of heat can be because of copper loss (I^2R) due to current flowing in winding, eddy current loss, hysteresis loss, mechanical friction etc.

Review Questions

1. *What is electromechanical energy conversion ? State the types of electromechanical energy conversion devices.*

2. *Write and explain the energy balance equations for generator and motor.*

9.3 Working Principle of a D.C. Machine as a Generator

All generators work on the principle of dynamically induced e.m.f. This principle is nothing but the Faraday's law of electromagnetic induction. It states that, 'whenever the number of magnetic lines of force i.e. flux linking with a conductor or a coil changes, an electromotive force is set up in that conductor or coil.'

The magnitude of induced e.m.f. in a conductor is proportional to the rate of change of flux associated with the conductor. This is mathematically given by,

$$e \text{ (magnitude)} \propto \frac{d\phi}{dt}$$

The relative motion can be achieved by rotating conductor with respect to flux or by rotating flux with respect to a conductor. So a voltage gets generated in a conductor, as long as there exists a relative motion between conductor and the flux. Such an induced e.m.f. which is due to physical movement of coil or conductor with respect to flux or movement of flux with respect to coil or conductor is called **dynamically induced e.m.f.**

So a generating action requires following basic components to exist, i) The conductor or a coil ii) The flux iii) The relative motion between conductor and flux.

To have a large voltage as the output, the number of conductors are connected together in a specific manner, to form a winding. This winding is called **armature winding** of a d.c. machine. The part on which this winding is kept is called **armature** of a d.c. machine.

To have the rotation of conductors, the conductors placed on the armature are rotated with the help of some external device. Such an external device is called a **prime mover**. The commonly used prime movers are diesel engines, steam engines, steam turbines, water turbines etc. The necessary magnetic flux is produced by current carrying winding which is called **field winding**. The direction of the induced e.m.f. can be obtained by using Fleming's right hand rule.

If angle between the plane of rotation and the plane of the flux is 'θ' as measured from the axis of the plane of flux then the induced e.m.f. is given by,

$$E = B\,l\,(v \sin \theta) \text{ volts}$$

where v sin θ is the component of velocity which is perpendicular to the plane of flux and hence responsible for the induced e.m.f.

If the plane of rotation is parallel to the plane of the flux, θ = 0° hence induced e.m.f. is zero. If the plane of rotation is perpendicular to the plane of the flux, θ = 90° hence induced e.m.f. is maximum.

From the equation of the induced e.m.f., it can be seen that the basic nature of the induced e.m.f. in a d.c. generator is purely sinusoidal i.e. alternating. To have d.c. voltage, a device is used in a d.c. generator to convert the alternating e.m.f. to unidirectional e.m.f. This device is called **commutator**.

Review Question

1. *Explain the working principle of d.c. generator.*

9.4 Constructional Details of a D.C. Machine

Whether a machine is **d.c. generator or a motor** the construction basically remains the same as shown in the Fig. 9.4.1.

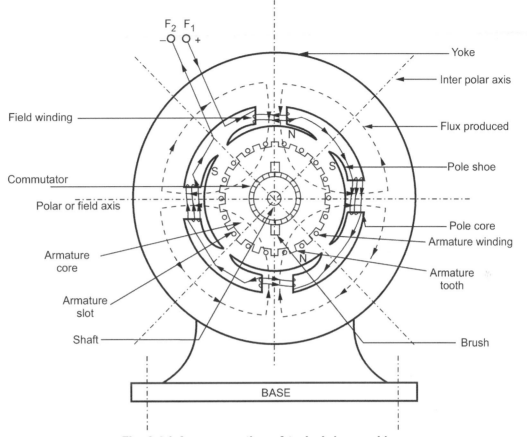

Fig. 9.4.1 A cross-section of typical d.c. machine

It consists of the following parts :

9.4.1 Yoke

a) Functions :

1. It serves the purpose of outermost cover of the d.c. machine. So that the insulating materials get protected from harmful atmospheric elements like moisture, dust and various gases like SO_2 , acidic fumes etc.

2. It provides mechanical support to the poles.

3. It forms a part of the magnetic circuit. It provides a path of low reluctance for magnetic flux. The low reluctance path is important to avoid wastage of power to provide same flux. Large current and hence the power is necessary if the path has high reluctance, to produce the same flux.

b) Choice of material : It is prepared by using cast iron because it is cheapest and provides low reluctance path. For large machines rolled steel, cast steel, silicon steel is used which provides high permeability i.e. low reluctance and gives good mechanical strength.

9.4.2 Poles

Each pole is divided into two parts namely, I) Pole core and II) Pole shoe

This is shown in the Fig. 9.4.2.

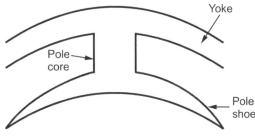

Fig. 9.4.2 Pole structure

a) Functions of pole core and pole shoe :

1. Pole core basically carries a field winding which is necessary to produce the flux.

2. It directs the flux produced through air gap to armature core, to the next pole.

3. Pole shoe enlarges the area of armature core to come across the flux, which is necessary to produce larger induced e.m.f. To achieve this, pole shoe has been given a particular shape.

b) Choice of material : It is made up of magnetic material like cast iron or cast steel.

As it requires a definite shape and size, laminated construction is used. The laminations of required size and shape are stamped together to get a pole which is then bolted to the yoke.

9.4.3 Field Winding (F1 - F2)

The field winding is wound on the pole core with a definite direction.

a) Functions : To carry current due to which pole core, on which the field winding is placed behaves as an electromagnet, producing necessary flux.

As it helps in producing the magnetic field i.e. exciting the pole as an electromagnet it is called **Field winding** or **Exciting winding**.

b) Choice of material : It has to carry current hence obviously made up of some conducting material. So aluminium or copper is the choice. But field coils are required to take any type of shape and bend about pole core and copper has good pliability i.e. it can bend easily. So copper is the proper choice.

Field winding is divided into various coils called field coils. These are connected in series with each other and wound in such a direction around pole cores, such that alternate 'N' and 'S' poles are formed. The total number of poles is denoted as P.

9.4.4 Armature

The armature is further divided into two parts namely,

I) Armature core and II) Armature winding

I) Armature core : Armature core is cylindrical in shape mounted on the shaft. It consists of slots on its periphery and the air ducts to permit the air flow through armature which serves cooling purpose.

a) Functions :

1. Armature core provides house for armature winding i.e. armature conductors.

2. To provide a path of low reluctance to the magnetic flux produced by the field winding.

b) Choice of material : As it has to provide a low reluctance path to the flux, it is made up of magnetic material like cast iron or cast steel.

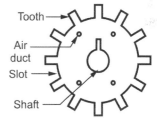

It is made up of laminated construction to keep eddy current loss as low as possible. A single circular lamination used for the construction of the armature core is shown in the Fig. 9.4.3.

Fig. 9.4.3 Single circular lamination of armature core

II) Armature winding : Armature winding is nothing but the interconnection of the armature conductors, placed in the slots provided on the armature core periphery.

When the armature is rotated, in case of generator, magnetic flux gets cut by armature conductors and e.m.f. gets induced in them.

a) Functions :

1. Generation of e.m.f. takes place in the armature winding in case of generators.

2. To carry the current supplied in case of d.c. motors.

3. To do the useful work in the external circuit.

b) Choice of material : As armature winding carries entire current which depends on external load, it has to be made up of conducting material, which is copper.

9.4.5 Commutator

The basic nature of e.m.f. induced in the armature conductors is alternating. This needs rectification in case of d.c. generator, which is possible by a device called commutator.

a) Functions :

    1. To facilitate the collection of current from the armature conductors.

    2. To convert internally developed alternating e.m.f. to unidirectional (d.c.) e.m.f.

    3. To produce unidirectional torque in case of motors.

b) Choice of material : As it collects current from armature, it is also made up of copper segments.

It is cylindrical in shape and is made up of wedge shaped segments of hard drawn, high conductivity copper. These segments are insulated from each other by thin layer of mica.

Each commutator segment is connected to the armature conductor by means of copper lug or strip. This construction is shown in the Fig. 9.4.4.

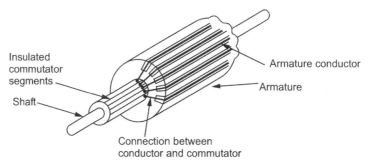

Fig. 9.4.4 Commutator

9.4.6 Brushes and Brush Gear

Brushes are stationary and resting on the surface of the commutator.

a) Function : To collect current from commutator and make it available to the stationary external circuit.

b) Choice of material : Brushes are normally made up of soft material like carbon.

To avoid wear and tear of commutator, the brushes are made up of soft material like carbon.

9.4.7 Bearings

Ball-bearings are usually used as they are more reliable. For heavy duty machines, roller bearings are preferred.

Review Questions

    1. Draw the neat sketch representing the cut section of a d.c. machine. Explain the important features of different parts involved there on.

    2. Why pole shoe has been given a particular shape ?

    3. What are the functions of field winding ? State the choice of material for the field winding.

4. *Explain the construction of commutator in brief.*

5. *Explain brushes of a d.c. machine.*

9.5 Types of Armature Winding

The number of armature conductors are connected in a specific manner to give armature winding. According to way of connecting the conductors, the armature winding has two types, a) Lap and b) Wave. In lap type, the connections overlap each other as the winding proceeds as shown in the Fig. 9.5.1.

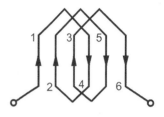

Fig. 9.5.1 Lap winding

Due to the this, number of parallel paths in which conductors are divided is P where P = Number of poles in the machine.

∴   A = P = Number of parallel paths for lap

Large number of parallel paths indicate high current capacity of machine hence lap winding is preferred for high current rating generators. In wave type, the winding travels ahead avoiding the overlapping as shown in the Fig. 9.5.2 in a progressive fashion.

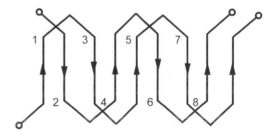

Fig. 9.5.2 Wave winding

Due to this, the armature conductors always get divided into two parallel paths, irrespective of number of poles.

∴   A = 2 = Number of parallel paths for wave

9.5.1 Comparison of Lap and Wave Type Windings

Sr. No.	Lap winding	Wave winding
1.	Number of parallel paths (A) = poles (P)	Number of parallel paths (A) = 2 (always)
2.	Number of brush sets required is equal to number of poles.	Number of brush sets required is always equal to two.
3.	Preferable for high current, low voltage capacity generators.	Preferable for high voltage, low current capacity generators.
4.	Normally used for generators of capacity more than 500 A.	Preferred for generators of capacity less than 500 A.

5.   If Z = total number of conductors then,   If Z = total number of conductors then,

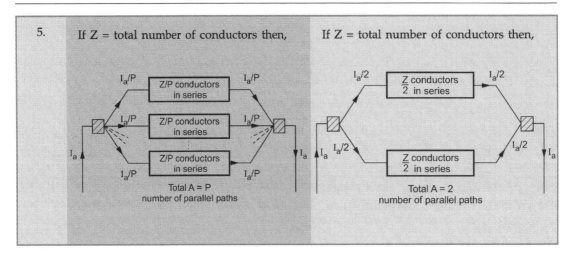

9.5.2 Winding Terminologies

a) Conductor : It is the actual armature conductor which is under the influence of the magnetic field, placed in the armature slot.

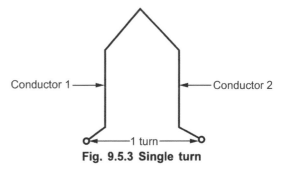

b) Turn : The two conductors placed in different slots when connected together, forms a turn. While describing armature winding the number of turns may be specified from which, the number of conductors can be decided.

Fig. 9.5.3 Single turn

$$Z = 2 \times \text{Number of turns}$$

c) Coil : For simplicity of connections, the turns are grouped together to form a coil.

If coil contains only one turn it is called single turn coil while coil with more than one turn is called multiturn coil.

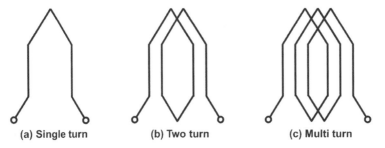

(a) Single turn   (b) Two turn   (c) Multi turn

Fig. 9.5.4 Armature coils

Hence if number of coils, alongwith number of turns per coil are specified, it is possible to determine the total number of turns and hence total number of armature conductors 'Z' required to calculate generated e.m.f.

d) Pole-pitch : The distance between the two adjacent poles is called a **pole pitch**. It is measured interms of number of slots. Thus total slots along the periphery of armature divided by the total number of poles is called a pole pitch.

Review Questions

1. *Explain the armature winding of a d.c. machine.*
2. *Compare lap and wave type armature winding.*

9.6 E.M.F. Equation of D.C. Generator   2001-02, 2005-06, 2006-07, 2010-11

Let   P = Number of poles of the generator

ϕ = Flux produced by each pole in webers (Wb)   N = Speed of armature in r.p.m.

Z = Total number of armature conductors

A = Number of parallel paths in which the 'Z' number of conductors are divided

So A = P for **lap** type of winding and A = 2   for **wave** type of winding

Induced e.m.f. gets induced in the conductor according to Faraday's law of electromagnetic induction. Hence average value of e.m.f. induced in each armature conductor is,

$$e = \text{Rate of cutting the flux} = \frac{d\phi}{dt}$$

Consider one revolution of conductor. In one revolution, conductor will cut total flux produced by all the poles i.e. $\phi \times P$. While time required to complete one revolution is $\frac{60}{N}$ seconds as speed is N r.p.m.

$\therefore$ $e = \dfrac{\phi P}{\dfrac{60}{N}} = \phi P \dfrac{N}{60}$ ... The e.m.f. induced in one conductor

Now the conductors in one parallel path are always in series. There are total Z conductors with A parallel paths, hence $\dfrac{Z}{A}$ number of conductors are always in series and e.m.f. remains same across all the parallel paths.

$\therefore$ Total e.m.f. can be expressed as, $E = \phi P \dfrac{N}{60} \times \dfrac{Z}{A}$ volts

This is nothing but the e.m.f. equation of a d.c. generator.

So,

$$E = \frac{\phi PNZ}{60\,A}$$ e.m.f. equation with A = P for Lap and A = 2 for wave

Example 9.6.1 *A 4 pole, 1500 r.p.m. d.c. generator has a lap wound armature having 24 slots with 10 conductors per slot. If the flux per pole is 0.04 Wb, calculate the e.m.f. generated in the armature. What would be the generated e.m.f. if the winding is wave connected?*

Solution :   P = 4, N = 1500 r.p.m., Lap i.e. A = P, ϕ = 0.04 Wb

$$Z = \text{Slots} \times \text{Conductors/Slot} = 24 \times 10 = 240$$

$\therefore$

$$E_g = \frac{\phi\,PNZ}{60\,A} = \frac{0.04 \times 4 \times 1500 \times 240}{60 \times 4} = \mathbf{240\ V}$$

If winding is wave connected, A = 2

$\therefore$

$$E_g = \frac{0.04 \times 4 \times 1500 \times 240}{60 \times 2} = \mathbf{480\ V}$$

Example 9.6.2 *A d.c. generator has an armature e.m.f. of 100 V when the useful flux per pole is 20 mWb, and the speed is 800 rpm. Calculate the generated e.m.f. i) With the same flux and a speed of 1000 rpm. ii) With a flux per pole of 24 mWb, and a speed of 900 rpm.*   **2001-02, Marks 5**

Solution : E_{g1} = 100 V, ϕ_1 = 20 mWb, N_1 = 800 r.p.m.

i) N_2 = 1000 r.p.m.

$$E_g \propto \phi N$$

$\therefore$ $\dfrac{E_{g1}}{E_{g2}} = \dfrac{\phi_1}{\phi_2} \times \dfrac{N_1}{N_2}$ but $\phi_1 = \phi_2$ i.e. $\dfrac{100}{E_{g2}} = \dfrac{800}{1000}$

$\therefore$ $E_{g2} = \mathbf{125\ V}$

ii) ϕ_2 = 24 mWb, N_2 = 900 r.p.m.

$\therefore$ $\dfrac{100}{E_{g2}} = \dfrac{20 \times 10^{-3}}{24 \times 10^{-3}} \times \dfrac{800}{900}$ i.e. $E_{g2} = \mathbf{135\ V}$

Example 9.6.3 *What will be change in e.m.f. induced if flux is reduced by 20 % and the speed is increased by 20 % in case of a d.c. generator.*   **2005-06, Marks 5**

Solution : For a d.c. generator,

$$E_g \propto N\phi$$

$$N_2 = N_1 + 0.2\, N_1 = 1.2\, N_1 \qquad\qquad \text{... Increased by 20 \%}$$

$$\phi_2 = \phi_1 - 0.2\, \phi_1 = 0.8\, \phi_1 \qquad\qquad \text{... Decreased by 20 \%}$$

$$\therefore \qquad \frac{E_{g1}}{E_{g2}} = \frac{N_1}{N_2} \times \frac{\phi_1}{\phi_2} = \frac{1}{1.2} \times \frac{1}{0.8} = 1.041$$

$$\therefore \qquad E_{g2} = 0.96\, E_{g1}$$

The e.m.f. will change to 96 % of the original value.

$$\% \text{ decrease in e.m.f.} = \frac{E_{g2} - E_{g1}}{E_{g1}} \times 100 = -\mathbf{4\ \%}$$

The negative sign indicates decrease in e.m.f.

Example 9.6.4 *Calculate flux/pole required for 4 pole generator with 360 conductors generating 250 V at 1000 r.p.m. when i) Armature is lap wound ii) Armature is wave wound.* **2006-07, Marks 5**

Solution : P = 4, Z = 360, N = 1000 r.p.m., E_g = 250 V

i) Lap wound, A = P = 4

$$E_g = \frac{\phi\, PNZ}{60\, A} \qquad \text{i.e.} \qquad 250 = \frac{\phi \times 4 \times 1000 \times 360}{60 \times 4}$$

$$\therefore \qquad \phi = \mathbf{0.04166\ Wb = 41.66\ mWb}$$

ii) Wave wound, A = 2

$$E_g = \frac{\phi PNZ}{60\, A} \qquad \text{i.e} \qquad 250 = \frac{\phi \times 4 \times 1000 \times 360}{60 \times 2}$$

$$\phi = \mathbf{0.02083\ Wb = 20.83\ mWb}$$

Example 9.6.5 *The armature of a four-pole DC machine has 100 turns and runs at 600 r.p.m. The e.m.f. generated in open circuit is 220 V. Find the useful flux per pole when armature is i) Lap connected ii) Wave connected.* **2010-11, Marks 10**

Solution : P = 4, N = 600 r.p.m., E_g = 220 V, Turns = 100

Two conductors constitute one turn.

$$\therefore \qquad Z = \text{Number of conductors} = 2 \times 100 = 200$$

$$E_g = \frac{\phi\, PNZ}{60\, A}$$

i) Lap connected hence A = P

$$\therefore \qquad 220 = \frac{\phi \times 4 \times 600 \times 200}{60 \times 4} \quad \text{hence} \quad \phi = \textbf{0.11 Wb}$$

ii) Wave connected hence A = 2

$$\therefore \qquad 220 = \frac{\phi \times 4 \times 600 \times 200}{60 \times 2} \quad \text{hence} \quad \phi = \textbf{0.055 Wb}$$

Review Questions

1. *With usual notations derive the e.m.f. equation of a d.c. generator.*

2. *A 4 pole generator with wave wound armature has 51 slots, each having 24 conductors. The flux per pole is 0.01 weber. At what speed must the armature rotate to give an induced emf of 220 V ? What will be the voltage developed if the winding is lap and the armature ratates at the same speed ?* **(Ans. : 539.21 r.p.m., 110 V)**

3. *A 4 pole, lap wound, d.c. generators has 42 coils with 8 turns per coils. It is driven at 1120 r.p.m. If useful flux per pole is 21 mWb, calculate the generated e.m.f. Find the speed at which it is to be driven to generate the same e.m.f. as calculated above, with wave wound armature.* **(Ans. : 263.42 V, 560 r.p.m.)**

9.7 Symbolic Representation of D.C. Generator

The armature is denoted by a circle with two brushes. Mechanically it is connected to another device called prime mover. The two ends of armature are denoted as A_1-A_2. The field winding is shown near armature and the two ends are denoted as F_1- F_2. The representation of field vary little bit, depending on the type of generator.

The symbolic representation is shown in the Fig. 9.7.1. Many times an arrow ($\uparrow$) is indicated near armature. This arrow denotes the direction of current which induced e.m.f. will set up, when connected to an external load.

Every practical generator needs a **prime mover** to rotate its armature. Hence to avoid complexity of the diagram, prime mover need not be included in the symbolic representation of generator.

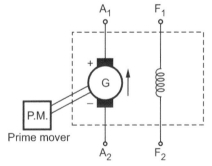

Fig. 9.7.1 Symbolic representation of D.C. generator

9.8 Types of D.C. Generators

The field winding is also called **exciting winding** and current carried by the field winding is called an **exciting current.** Thus supplying current to the field winding is called excitation and the way of supplying the exciting current is called **method of excitation.**

Depending on the method of excitation used, the d.c. generators are classified as,

1. Separately excited generator   2. Self excited generator

In **separately excited generator**, a separate external d.c. supply is used to provide exciting current through the field winding. The d.c. generator produces d.c. voltage. If this generated voltage itself is used to excite the field winding of the same d.c. generator, it is called **self excited generator**. The Fig. 9.8.1 shows the various types of d.c. generators.

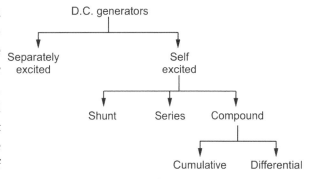

Fig. 9.8.1 Types of d.c. generators

Review Question

> 1. *State the various types of d.c. generators.*

9.9 Separately Excited Generator

When the field winding is supplied from external, separate d.c. supply i.e. excitation of field winding is separate then the generator is called separately excited generator. The schematic representation of this type is shown in the Fig. 9.9.1.

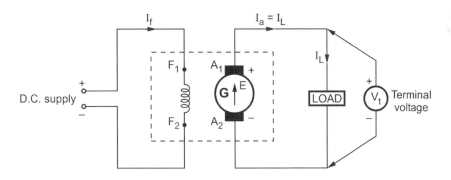

Fig. 9.9.1 Separately excited generator

The field winding of this type of generator has large number of turns of thin wire. So length of such winding is more with less cross sectional area. So resistance of this field winding is high in order to limit the field current.

In the terminology of a d.c. machine the various currents are denoted as,

I_a = Armature current I_L = Load current I_f = Field current

Voltage and Current Relations :

The field winding is excited separately, so the field current depends on supply voltage and resistance of the field winding. For armature side, we can see that it is supplying a load, demanding a load current of I_L at a voltage of V_t which is called **terminal voltage**.

Now, $$I_a = I_L$$

The internally induced e.m.f. E is supplying the voltage to the load hence terminal voltage V_t is a part of E. But E is not equal to V_t while supplying a load. This is because when armature current I_a flows through armature winding, due to armature winding resistance R_a ohms, there is a voltage drop across armature winding equal to $I_a R_a$ volts. The induced e.m.f. has to supply this drop, along with the terminal voltage V_t. To keep $I_a R_a$ drop to minimum, the resistance R_a is designed to be very very small.

In addition to this drop, there is some voltage drop at the contacts of the brush called brush contact drop. But this drop is negligible and hence generally neglected. When armature carries current, it produces its own flux which distorts the main flux. Due to this, there is small voltage drop called armature reaction drop. But as small, this drop is also practically neglected.

So in all, induced e.m.f. E has components namely,

i) Terminal voltage V_t ii) Armature resistance drop $I_a R_a$

iii) Brush contact drop V_{brush} iv) Armature reaction drop

So voltage equation for separately excited generator can be written as,

$$E = V_t + I_a R_a + V_{brush} + \text{Armature reaction drop}$$

where $$E = \frac{\phi P N Z}{60 A} = \text{Generated e.m.f.}$$

Generally V_{brush} is taken as 1 V per brush but many times it is neglected.

Example 9.9.1 *A 250 V, 10 kW, separately excited generator has an induced e.m.f. of 255 V at full load. If the brush drop is 2 V per brush, calculate the armature resistance of the generator.*

Solution : Consider separately excited generator as shown in the Fig. 9.9.2.

$$I_a = I_L$$

Note that 250 V, 10 kW generator means the full load capacity of generator is to supply 10 kW load at a terminal voltage $V_t = 250$ V.

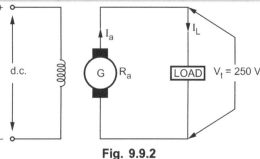

Fig. 9.9.2

$$\therefore \qquad V_t \; = \; 250 \text{ V and P} = 10 \text{ kW}$$

$$\text{and} \qquad P \; = \; V_t \times I_L$$

$$\therefore \qquad I_L \; = \; \frac{10 \times 10^3}{250} = 40 \text{ A}$$

$$\therefore \qquad I_a \; = \; I_L = 40 \text{ A} \qquad\qquad \text{... as separately excited}$$

$$\text{Now} \qquad E \; = \; V_t + I_a \, R_a + V_{brush}$$

There are two brushes and brush drop is 2 V/brush, i.e. $V_{brush} = 2 \times 2 = 4$ V

$$\therefore \qquad E \; = \; 250 + 40 \times R_a + 4 \quad \text{i.e.} \quad 255 = 250 + 40\,R_a + 4$$

$$\therefore \qquad R_a \; = \; \mathbf{0.025 \; \Omega}$$

Review Question

1. *Draw the schematic representation of a seperately excited d.c. generator. State its voltage and current equations.*

9.10 Shunt Generator
2003-04, 2006-07

When the field winding is connected in parallel with the armature and the combination across the load then the generator is called **shunt generator.** The Fig. 9.10.1 shows the symbolic representation of d.c shunt generator. The field winding has large number of turns of thin wire so it has high resistance denoted as R_{sh}.

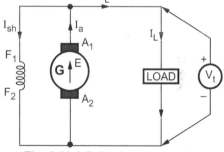

Fig. 9.10.1 D.C. shunt generator

From the Fig. 9.10.1, we can write

$$I_a = I_L + I_{sh}$$

Now voltage across load is V_t which is same across field winding as both are in parallel with each other.

$$\therefore \qquad I_{sh} = \frac{V_t}{R_{sh}}$$

While induced e.m.f. E, still requires to supply voltage drop $I_a R_a$ and brush contact drop.

$$\therefore \qquad E = V_t + I_a R_a + V_{brush}$$

Armature reaction drop is practically neglected.

Example 9.10.1 *A 200 V, 8 pole, lap connected d.c. shunt generator supplies sixty, 40 W, 200 V lamps. It has armature and field circuit resistance of 0.2 Ω and 200 Ω respectively. Calculate the generated emf, armature current and current in each armature conductor.*

2003-04, Marks 5

Solution : $V = 200$ V, $P = 8$, $R_a = 0.2$ Ω, $R_{sh} = 200$ Ω, lap i.e. $A = P$

$$V_t = 200 \text{ V}, \quad P = 40 \text{ W}$$

$$I_{Lamp} = \frac{P}{V_t} = \frac{40}{200} = 0.2 \text{ A}$$

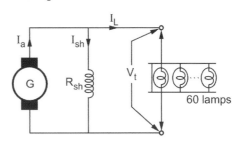

∴ $\quad I_L = 60 \times I_{lamp} = 60 \times 0.2 = 12$ A

$$I_{sh} = \frac{V_t}{R_{sh}} = \frac{200}{200} = 1A$$

Fig. 9.10.2

∴ $\quad I_a = I_L + I_{sh} = 12 + 1 = \mathbf{13}$ **A**

$$E_g = V_t + I_a R_a = 200 + 13 \times 0.2 = \mathbf{202.6 \text{ V}}$$

I_a in each conductor $= \dfrac{\text{Total } I_a}{\text{Number of parallel paths (A)}} = \dfrac{13}{8}$ ... A = P = 8

$$= \mathbf{1.625 \text{ A}}$$

Note *Conductors in each parallel path are in series hence the current in each parallel path gives current in each armature conductor.*

Example 9.10.2 *A 20 kW, 200 V shunt generator has an armature resistance of 0.05 Ω and a shunt field resistance of 200 Ω. Calculate the power developed in the armature when it delivers rated output.*   **2006-07, Marks 5**

Solution : The generator is shown in the Fig. 9.10.3.

$$P_L = V_t \times I_L$$

∴ $\quad 20 \times 10^3 = 200 \ I_L$

∴ $\quad I_L = 100$ A

$$I_{sh} = \frac{V_t}{R_{sh}} = \frac{200}{200} = 1 \text{ A}$$

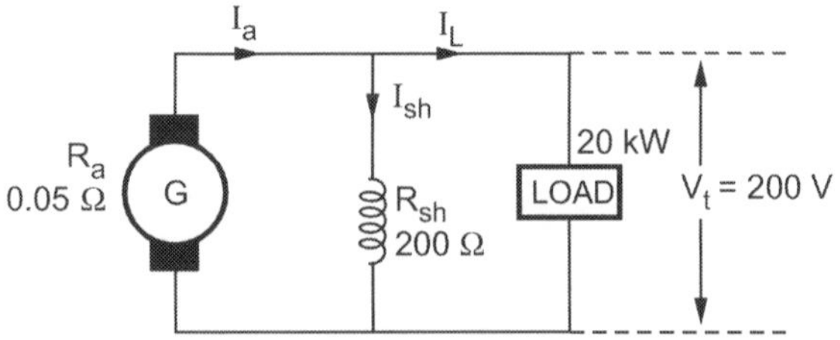

∴ $\quad I_a = I_L + I_{sh} = 100 + 1$

$$= 101 \text{ A}$$

Fig. 9.10.3

$$E_g = V_t + I_a R_a = 200 + 101 \times 0.05 = 205.05 \text{ V}$$

∴ $\quad P_a = $ Power developed by armature $= E_g \times I_a = 205.05 \times 101 = \mathbf{20.71 \text{ kW}}$

Review Questions

1. *Draw the circuit diagram of a d.c. generator. State its voltage and current equations.*

2. *A 4-pole d.c. shunt generator with lap connected armature has field and armature resistances of 80 Ω and 0.1 Ω respectively. It supplies power to 50 lamps rated for 100 volts, 60 watts each. Calculate the total armature current and the generated e.m.f. by allowing a contact drop of 1 volt per brush.*   **2003-04**

   (Ans. : 31.25 A, 105.125 V)

3. *A shunt generator supplies a load of 10 kW at 200 V, through a pair of feeders of total resistance 0.05 Ω. The armature resistance is 0.1 Ω. The shunt field resistance is 100Ω. Find the terminal voltage and the generated e.m.f.*   (Ans. : 202.5 V, 207.702 V)

9.11 Series Generator

When the field winding is connected in series with the armature winding while supplying the load then the generator is called **series generator**. It is shown in the Fig. 9.11.1. The field winding, in this case is denoted as S_1 and S_2.

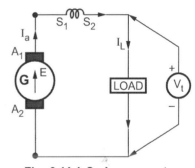

Fig. 9.11.1 Series generator

The resistance of series field winding is very small and hence naturally it has less number of turns of thick cross-section wire as shown in the Fig. 9.11.1. Let R_{se} be the resistance of the series field winding.

As all armature, field and load are in series they carry the same current.

∴ $I_a = I_{se} = I_L$ where I_{se} = Current through series field winding.

Now in addition to drop $I_a R_a$, induced e.m.f. has to supply voltage drop across series field winding too. This is $I_{se} R_{se}$ i.e. $I_a R_{se}$ as $I_a = I_{se}$. So voltage equation can be written as,

∴ $E = V_t + I_a R_a + I_a R_{se} + V_{brush}$

Example 9.11.1 *A d.c. series generator has armature resistance of 0.5 Ω and series field resistance of 0.03 Ω. It drives a load of 50 A. If it has 6 turns/coil and total 540 coils on the armature and is driven at 1500 r.p.m., calculate the terminal voltage at the load. Assume 4 poles, lap type winding, flux per pole as 2 mWb and total brush drop as 2 V.*

Solution : Consider the series generator as shown in Fig. 9.11.2.

$$R_a = 0.5 \ \Omega, \ R_{se} = 0.03 \ \Omega$$

$$V_{brush} = 2 \ V$$

$$N = 1500 \text{ r.p.m.}$$

Total coils are 540 with 6 turns/coil.

$\therefore$ Total turns $= 540 \times 6 = 3240$

$\therefore$ Total conductors $Z = 2 \times$ Turns

$$= 2 \times 3240 = 6480$$

$\therefore$ $E = \dfrac{\phi \, P \, N \, Z}{60 \, A}$

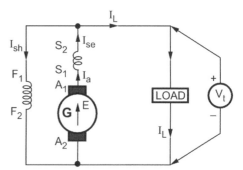

Fig. 9.11.2

For lap type, $A = P$

and $\phi = 2 \text{ mWb} = 2 \times 10^{-3} \text{ Wb}$

$\therefore$ $E = \dfrac{2 \times 10^{-3} \times 1500 \times 6480}{60} = 324 \text{ V}$

$E = V_t + I_a (R_a + R_{se}) + V_{brush}$ ... Total V_{brush} given

where $I_a = I_L = 50 \text{ A}$

$\therefore$ $324 = V_t + 50 (0.5 + 0.03) + 2$

$\therefore$ $V_t = \mathbf{295.5 \ V}$

Review Question

1. *Draw the circuit diagram of d.c. series generator. State its voltage and current equations.*

9.12 Compound Generator

In this type, the part of the field winding is connected in parallel with armature and part in series with the armature. Both series and shunt field windings are mounted on the same poles.

Depending upon the connection of shunt and series field winding, compound generator is further classified as :

i) Long shunt compound generator   and   ii) Short shunt compound generator

9.12.1 Long Shunt Compound Generator

In this type, shunt field winding is connected across the entire series combination of armature and series field winding as shown in the Fig. 9.12.1.

From the Fig. 9.12.1, $I_a = I_{se}$.

$$\boxed{I_a = I_{sh} + I_L}$$

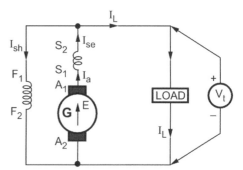

Fig. 9.12.1 Long shunt compound generator

Voltage across shunt field winding is V_t .

$$I_{sh} = \frac{V_t}{R_{sh}} \text{ where } R_{sh} = \text{Resistance of shunt field winding}$$

And voltage equation is,

$$\therefore \quad E = V_t + I_a R_a + I_a R_{se} + V_{brush} \text{ where } R_{se} = \text{Resistance of series field winding}$$

9.12.2 Short Shunt Compound Generator

In this type, shunt field winding is connected, only across the armature, excluding series field winding as shown in the Fig. 9.12.1.

For the Fig. 9.12.2, $I_a = I_{se} + I_{sh}$

and $I_{se} = I_L$

$$\therefore \quad I_a = I_L + I_{sh}$$

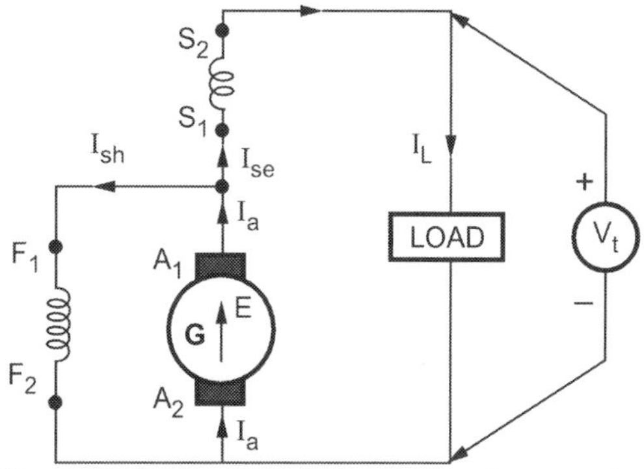

Fig. 9.12.2 Short shunt compound generator

The drop across shunt field winding is drop across the armature only and not the total V_t, in this case.

So drop across shunt field winding is $E - I_a R_a$.

$$\therefore \quad I_{sh} = \frac{E - I_a R_a}{R_{sh}}$$

Now the voltage equation is $E = V_t + I_a R_a + I_{se} R_{se} + V_{brush}$

Now, $\quad I_{se} = I_L \text{ hence } E = V_t + I_a R_a + I_L R_{se} + V_{brush}$

Neglecting V_{brush}, we can write, $\quad E = V_t + I_a R_a + I_L R_{se} \text{ i.e. } E - I_a R_a = V_t + I_L R_{se}$

$$\therefore \quad I_{sh} = \frac{V_t + I_L R_{se}}{R_{sh}}$$

Any of the two above expressions of I_{sh} can be used, depending on the quantities known while solving the problems.

9.12.3 Cumulative and Differential Compound Generator

The two windings, shunt and series field are wound on the same poles.

Depending on the direction of winding on the pole, two fluxes produced by shunt and series field may help or may oppose each other. This fact decides whether generator is cumulative or differential compound.

If the two fluxes help each other as shown in Fig. 9.12.3 (a) the generator is called **cumulative compound generator**.

If the two windings are wound in such a direction that the fluxes produced by them oppose each other then the generator is called **differential compound generator**. This is shown in the Fig. 9.12.3 (b).

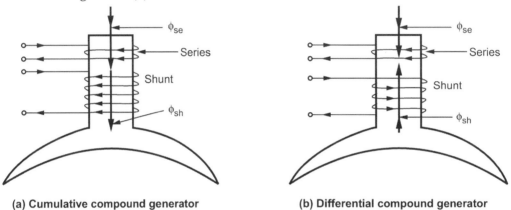

(a) Cumulative compound generator   (b) Differential compound generator

Fig. 9.12.3

Example 9.12.1 *A long shunt d.c. compound generator drives 20 lamps, all are connected in parallel. Terminal voltage is 550 V with each lamp resistance as 500 Ω. If $R_{sh} = 25\ \Omega$, $R_a = 0.06\ \Omega$ and $R_{se} = 0.04\ \Omega$, calculate the armature current and the generated e.m.f.*

Solution : Consider the arrangement as shown in the Fig. 9.12.4 (a).

As all lamps are in parallel, the voltage across all of them is same which is terminal voltage of generator $V_t = 550$ V.

Consider only one lamp as shown in the Fig. 9.12.4 (b).

So current drawn by each lamp is

$$I = \frac{V_t}{R_{\text{lamp}}} = \frac{550}{500} = 1.1 \text{ A}$$

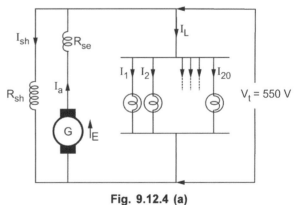

Fig. 9.12.4 (a)

Such 20 lamps are used as a load.

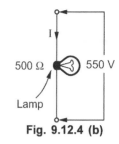

Fig. 9.12.4 (b)

$$\therefore \quad I_L = 20 \times I_{lamp} = 20 \times 1.1 = 22 \text{ A}$$

$$\text{Now} \quad I_{sh} = \frac{V_t}{R_{sh}} = \frac{550}{25} = 22 \text{ A}$$

$$\therefore \quad I_a = I_L + I_{sh} = \mathbf{44 \ A}$$

$$\therefore \quad E = V_t + I_a R_a + I_a R_{se} = 550 + 44 \times 0.06 + 44 \times 0.04$$

$$= \mathbf{554.4 \ V}$$

Example 9.12.2 *A short shunt compound d.c. generator supplies a current of 75 A at a voltage of 225 V. Calculate the generated voltage if the resistance of armature, shunt field and series field windings are 0.04 Ω, 90 Ω and 0.02 Ω respectively.*

Solution : Consider a short shunt generator as shown in the Fig. 9.12.5.

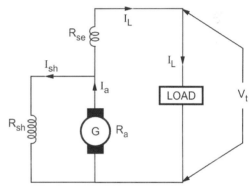

Fig. 9.12.5

$$R_a = 0.04 \ \Omega, \ R_{sh} = 90 \ \Omega, \ R_{se} = 0.02 \ \Omega$$

$$V_t = 225 \text{ V}$$

$$I_L = 75 \text{ A}$$

$$I_a = I_L + I_{sh}$$

$$\text{Now} \quad E = V_t + I_a R_a + I_L R_{se}$$

and drop across armature terminals is,

$$E - I_a R_a = V_t + I_L R_{se} = 225 + 75 \times 0.02 = 226.5 \text{ V}$$

$$\therefore \quad I_{sh} = \frac{E - I_a R_a}{R_{sh}} = \frac{V_t + I_L R_{se}}{R_{sh}} = \frac{226.5}{90} = 2.5167 \text{ A}$$

$$\therefore \quad I_a = I_L + I_{sh} = 75 + 2.5167 = 77.5167 \text{ A}$$

$$\therefore \quad E = V_t + I_a R_a + I_L R_{se} = 225 + 77.5167 \times 0.04 + 75 \times 0.02 = \mathbf{229.6 \ V}$$

Review Questions

1. What is compound generator ? State its two types.
2. Draw the circuit diagram of long shunt compund generator. Write its voltage and current equations.
3. Draw the circuit diagram of short shunt compound generator. Write its voltage and current equations.
4. What are cumulative and differential compound generators ?

9.13 Applications of Various Types of D.C. Generators

Separately excited generators :

As a separate supply is required to excite field, the use is restricted to some special applications like electro-plating, electro-refining of materials etc.

Shunt generators :

Commonly used in battery charging and ordinary lighting purposes.

Series generators :

Commonly used as boosters on d.c. feeders, as a constant current generators for welding generator and arc lamps.

Cumulatively compound generators :

These are used for domestic lighting purposes and to transmit energy over long distance.

Differential compound generator :

The use of this type of generators is very rare and it is used for special application like electric arc welding.

Review Question

> 1. *State the applications of various types of d.c. generators.*

9.14 Principle of Operation of a D.C. Machine as a Motor

The principle of operation of a d.c. motor can be stated in a single statement as 'when a current carrying conductor is placed in a magnetic field; it experiences a mechanical force'.

In a practical d.c. motor, field winding produces a required magnetic field while armature conductors play a role of a current carrying conductors and hence armature conductors experience a force.

Consider a single conductor placed in a magnetic field as shown in the Fig. 9.14.1 (a).

Now this conductor is excited by a separate supply so that it carries a current in a particular direction. Consider that it carries a current away from an observer as shown in the Fig. 9.14.1 (b).

Any current carrying conductor produces its own magnetic field around it, hence this conductor also produces its own flux, around. The direction of this flux can be determined by right hand thumb rule. For direction of current considered, the direction

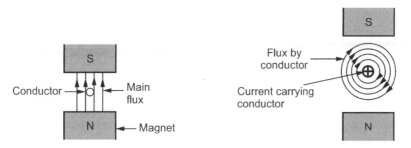

(a) Conductor in a magnetic field   **(b) Flux produced by current carrying conductor**

Fig. 9.14.1

of flux around a conductor is clockwise. For simplicity of understanding, the main flux produced by the permanent magnet is not shown in the Fig. 9.14.1 (b).

Now there are two fluxes present,

1. The flux produced by the permanent magnet called main flux.

2. The flux produced by the current carrying conductor.

These are shown in the Fig. 9.14.2 (a).

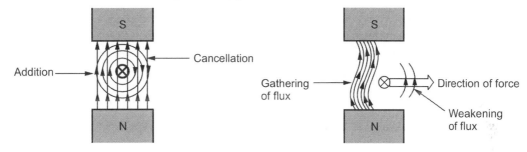

(a) Interaction of two fluxes   **(b) Force experienced by the conductor**

Fig. 9.14.2

From this, it is clear that on one side of the conductor, both the fluxes are in the same direction. In this case, on the left of the conductor there is gathering of the flux lines as two fluxes help each other.

As against this, on the right of the conductor, the two fluxes are in opposite direction and hence try to cancel each other. Due to this, the density of the flux lines in this area gets weakened. So on the left, there exists high flux density area while on the right of the conductor there exists low flux density area as shown in the Fig. 9.14.2 (b).

This flux distribution around the conductor acts like a stretched rubber band under tension. This exerts a mechanical force on the conductor which acts from high flux density area towards low flux density area, i.e. from left to right for the case considered as shown in the Fig. 9.14.2 (b).

In the practical d.c. motor, the permanent magnet is replaced by a field winding which produces the required flux called main flux and all the armature conductors, mounted on the periphery of the armature drum, get subjected to the mechanical force.

Due to this, overall armature experiences a twisting force called torque and armature of the motor starts rotating.

The magnitude of the force experienced by the conductor in a motor is given by,

$$F = B \, l \, I \quad \text{Newtons (N)}$$

B = Flux density due to the flux produced by the field winding.

l = Active length of the conductor.

I = Magnitude of the current passing through the conductor.

The direction of such force i.e. the direction of rotation of a motor can be determined by **Fleming's left hand rule.**

To reverse the direction of rotation of a d.c. motor, either direction of main field produced by the field winding is reversed or direction of the current passing through the armature is reversed.

Review Question

1. *Explain the working principle of d.c. motor. How to reverse the direction of rotation ?*

9.15 Significance of Back E.M.F.

It is seen in the generating action, that when a conductor cuts the lines of flux, e.m.f. gets induced in the conductor. In a d.c. motor, after a motoring action, armature starts rotating and armature conductors cut the main flux.

Thus, there exists a generating action. There is an induced e.m.f. in the rotating armature conductors according to Faraday's law of electromagnetic induction. This induced e.m.f. in the armature always acts in the opposite direction of the supply voltage. This is according to the **Lenz's law** which states that the direction of the induced e.m.f. is always, so as to oppose the cause producing it. In a d.c. motor, electrical input i.e. the supply voltage is the cause and hence this induced e.m.f. opposes the supply voltage. This e.m.f. tries to set up a current through the armature which is in the opposite direction to that, which supply voltage is forcing through the conductor.

So as this e.m.f. always opposes the supply voltage, it is called **back e.m.f.** and denoted as E_b. Though it is denoted as E_b, basically it gets generated by the generating action which we have seen earlier in case of generators. So its magnitude can be determined by the e.m.f. equation which is derived earlier. So,

$$E_b = \frac{\phi \, P \, N \, Z}{60 \, A} \text{ volts}$$

where all symbols carry the same meaning as seen earlier in case of generators.

This e.m.f. is shown schematically in the Fig. 9.15.1 (a). So if V is supply voltage in volts and R_a is the value of the armature resistance, the equivalent electric circuit can be shown as in the Fig. 9.15.1 (b).

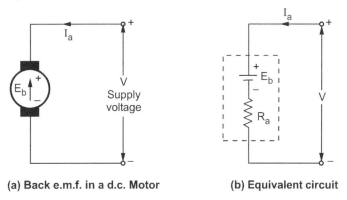

(a) Back e.m.f. in a d.c. Motor   (b) Equivalent circuit

Fig. 9.15.1

9.15.1 Voltage Equation of a D.C. Motor

In case of d.c. motor, supply voltage V has to overcome back e.m.f. E_b which is opposing V and also various drops as armature resistance drop $I_a \, R_a$, brush drop etc. Hence the voltage equation of a d.c. motor can be written as,

$$V = E_b + I_a \, R_a + \text{brush drop}$$

The back e.m.f. is always less than supply voltage ($E_b < V$). But R_a is very small hence under normal running conditions, the difference between back e.m.f. and supply voltage is very small. The net voltage across the armature is the difference between the supply voltage and back e.m.f. which decides the armature current. Hence from the voltage equation we can write,

$$I_a = \frac{V - E_b}{R_a}$$

Key Point *Voltage equation gets changed a little bit depending upon the type of the motor, which is discussed later.*

Example 9.15.1 *A 4 pole, d.c. motor has lap connected armature winding. The flux per pole is 30 mWb. The number of armature conductors is 250. When connected to 230 V d.c. supply it draws an armature current of 40 A. Calculate the back e.m.f. and the speed with which motor is running. Assume armature resistance is 0.6 Ω.*

Solution : $P = 4$, $A = P = 4$ as lap, $V = 230$ V, $Z = 250$, $\phi = 30$ mWb $= 30 \times 10^{-3}$ Wb

$$I_a = 40 \text{ A}.$$

From voltage equation, $V = E_b + I_a R_a$

∴ $230 = E_b + 40 \times 0.6$ i.e. $E_b = 206$ V

And $E_b = \dfrac{\phi\, P\, N\, Z}{60\, A}$ i.e. $206 = \dfrac{30 \times 10^{-3} \times 4 \times N \times 250}{60 \times 4}$

∴ $N = \mathbf{1648 \text{ r.p.m.}}$

9.15.2 Back E.M.F. as a Regulating Mechanism

Due to the presence of back e.mf. the d.c. motor becomes a regulating machine i.e. motor adjusts itself to draw the armature current just enough to satisfy the load demand. The basic principle of this fact is that the back e.m.f. is proportional to speed, $E_b \propto N$.

When load is suddenly put on to the motor, motor tries to slow down. So speed of the motor reduces due to which back e.m.f. also decreases. So the net voltage across the armature $(V - E_b)$ increases and motor draws more armature current. As $F = B\, l\, I$, due to increased current, force experienced by the conductors and hence the torque on the armature increases. The increase in the torque is just sufficient to satisfy increased load demand. The motor speed stops decreasing when the armature current is just enough to produce torque demanded by the new load.

When load on the motor is decreased, the speed of the motor tries to increase. Hence back e.m.f. increases. This causes $(V - E_b)$ to reduce which eventually reduces the current drawn by the armature. The motor speed stops increasing when the armature current is just enough to produce the less torque required by the new load.

Key Point *So back e.m.f. regulates the flow of armature current and it automatically alters the armature current to meet the load requirement. This is the practical significance of the back e.m.f.*

Review Questions

1. *What is back e.m.f. ? Explain its significance.*

2. *Write and explain the voltage equation of a d.c. motor.*

3. *A 220 V, d.c. motor has an armature resistance of 0.75 Ω. It is drawing an armature current of 30 A, driving a certain load. Calculate the induced e.m.f. in the motor under this condition.*

(Ans. : 197.5 V)

9.16 Power Equation of a D.C. Motor   2008-09

The voltage equation of a d.c. motor is given by,

$$V = E_b + I_a R_a$$

Multiplying both sides of the above equation by I_a we get,

$$\boxed{V I_a = E_b I_a + I_a^2 R_a}$$

This equation is called **power equation** of a d.c. motor.

$V I_a$ = Net electrical power input to the armature measured in watts.

$I_a^2 R_a$ = Power loss due to the resistance of the armature called **armature copper loss**.

So difference between $V I_a$ and $I_a^2 R_a$ i.e. input-losses gives the output of the armature.

So $E_b I_a$ is called **electrical equivalent of gross mechanical power developed** by the armature. This is denoted as P_m.

∴ Power input to the armature − Armature copper loss = Gross mechanical power developed in the armature.

Example 9.16.1 *Calculate the voltage induced in the armature winding of a 4-pole, lap wound d.c. machine having 728 active conductors and running at 1800 r.p.m. The flux per pole is 30 mWb. If the armature is designed to carry a maximum line current of 100 A, what is the maximum electromagnetic power developed by the armature ?*

2008-09, Marks 5

Solution : P = 4, lap wound so A = P, Z = 728, N = 1800 r.p.m., ϕ = 30 mWb, $I_{a\ max}$ = 100 A

∴ $$E_b = \frac{\phi\ PNZ}{60\ A} = \frac{30 \times 10^{-3} \times 4 \times 1800 \times 728}{60 \times 4} = \textbf{655.2 V}$$

The maximum electromagnetic power developed by the armature is,

$$P_{m(max)} = E_b \times I_{a\ max} = 655.2 \times 100 = \textbf{65.52 kW}$$

Review Question

1. *State the power equation of a d.c. motor.*

9.17 Torque Equation of a D.C. Motor

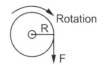

2009-10

The turning or twisting force about an axis is called torque. Consider a wheel of radius R meters acted upon by a circumferential force F newtons as shown in the Fig. 9.17.1.

The wheel is rotating at a speed of N r.p.m. then its angular speed is,

Fig. 9.17.1

$$\omega = \frac{2\pi N}{60} \text{ rad/sec}$$

So workdone in one revolution is,

$$W = F \times \text{Distance travelled in one revolution} = F \times 2\pi R \text{ Joules}$$

$$P = \text{Power developed} = \frac{\text{Workdone}}{\text{Time}} = \frac{F \times 2\pi R}{\text{Time for 1 rev}} = \frac{F \times 2\pi R}{\left(\dfrac{60}{N}\right)} = (F \times R) \times \left(\frac{2\pi N}{60}\right)$$

$$\therefore \qquad \boxed{P = T \times \omega \ \text{ watts}}$$

where   T = Torque in Nm   and ω = Angular speed in rad/sec.

Let T_a be the gross torque developed by the armature of the motor. It is also called **armature torque**. The gross mechanical power developed in the armature is $E_b I_a$, as seen from the power equation.

So if speed of the motor is N r.p.m. then,

Power in armature = Armature torque $\times \omega$ i.e. $E_b I_a = T_a \times \dfrac{2\pi N}{60}$

But E_b in a motor is given by, $E_b = \dfrac{\phi P N Z}{60 A}$

$$\therefore \quad \frac{\phi P N Z}{60 A} \times I_a = T_a \times \frac{2\pi N}{60}$$

$$\therefore \qquad \boxed{T_a = \frac{1}{2\pi} \phi I_a \times \frac{PZ}{A} = 0.159 \ \phi I_a \cdot \frac{PZ}{A} \quad \text{Nm}}$$

This is the **torque equation** of a d.c. motor.

9.17.1 Types of Torque in the Motor

The mechanical power developed in the armature is transmitted to the load through the shaft of the motor. It is impossible to transmit the entire power developed by the armature to the load. This is because while transmitting the power through the shaft, there is a power loss due to the friction, windage and the iron loss.

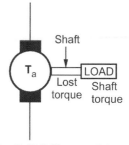

The torque required to overcome these losses is called **lost torque**, denoted as T_f. These losses are also called **stray losses**. The torque which is available at the shaft for doing the useful work is known as **load torque** or **shaft torque** denoted as T_{sh}.

Fig. 9.17.2 Types of torque

∴
$$T_a = T_f + T_{sh}$$

The shaft torque magnitude is always less than the armature torque, $(T_{sh} < T_a)$.

The speed of the motor remains same all along the shaft say N r.p.m. Then the product of shaft torque T_{sh} and the angular speed ω rad/sec is called power available at the shaft i.e. net output of the motor. The maximum power a motor can deliver to the load safely is called **output rating** of a motor. Generally it is expressed in H.P. It is called **H.P. rating** of a motor.

$$\text{Net output of motor} = P_{out} = T_{sh} \times \omega$$

9.17.2 No Load Condition of a Motor

On no load, the load requirement is absent. So $T_{sh} = 0$. This does not mean that motor is at halt. The motor can rotate at a speed say N_0 r.p.m. on no load. The motor draws an armature current of I_{a0}.

$$I_{a0} = \frac{V - E_{b0}}{R_a}$$

where E_{b0} is back e.m.f. on no load, proportional to speed N_0.

Now armature torque T_a for a motor is,

$$T_a \propto \phi I_a$$

As flux is present and armature current is present, hence T_{a0} i.e. armature torque exists on no load.

Now $T_a = T_f + T_{sh}$ but on no load, $T_{sh} = 0$

∴
$$T_{a0} = T_f$$

So on no load, motor produces a torque T_{a0} which satisfies the friction, windage and iron losses of the motor.

$\therefore$ Power developed $(E_{b0} \times I_{a0})$ = Friction, windage and, iron losses.

where E_{b0} = Back e.m.f. on no load.

and I_{a0} = Armature current drawn on no load.

This component of stray losses i.e. $E_{b0}I_{a0}$ is practically assumed to be constant though the load on the motor is changed from zero to the full capacity of the motor.

Example 9.17.1 *A 4 pole d.c. motor takes a 50 A armature current. The armature has lap connected 480 conductors. The flux per pole is 20 m Wb. Calculate the gross torque developed by the armature of the motor.*

Solution :   P = 4, A = P = 4, Z = 480

$$\phi = 20 \text{ mWb} = 20 \times 10^{-3} \text{ Wb}, I_a = 50 \text{ A}$$

Now $T_a = 0.159 \times \phi \; I_a . \dfrac{PZ}{A} = 0.159 \times 20 \times 10^{-3} \times 50 \times \dfrac{4 \times 480}{4} = \textbf{76.394 N-m}$

Example 9.17.2 *A 4 pole, lap wound d.c. motor has 540 conductors. Its speed is found to be 1000 r.p.m. when it is made to run light. The flux per pole is 25 mWb. It is connected to 230 V d.c. supply. The armature resistance is 0.8 Ω. Calculate i) Induced e.m.f. ii) Armature current iii) Stray losses iv) Lost torque*

Solution : P = 4, A = P = 4 Running light means it is on no load.

$\therefore$ $N_0 = 1000$ r.p.m., Z = 540 and $\phi = 25 \times 10^{-3}$ Wb

$\therefore$ $E_{b0} = \dfrac{\phi \; PN_0 Z}{60 \; A} = \dfrac{25 \times 10^{-3} \times 4 \times 1000 \times 540}{60 \times 4} = \textbf{225 V}$

i) Induced e.m.f., $E_{b0} = 225$ V

ii) From voltage equation, $V = E_b + I_a \; R_a$

$\therefore$ $V = E_{b0} + I_{a0} \; R_a$ i.e. $230 = 225 + I_{a0} \times 0.8$ i.e. $I_{a0} = \textbf{6.25 A}$

iii) On no load, power developed is fully the power required to overcome stray losses.

$\therefore$ Stray losses = $E_{b0} \; I_{a0} = 225 \times 6.25 = \textbf{1406.25 W}$

iv) Lost torque $T_f = \dfrac{E_{b0} \; I_{a0}}{\omega_0} = \dfrac{1406.25}{\dfrac{2\pi N_0}{60}} = \dfrac{1406.25 \times 60}{2\pi \times 1000} = \textbf{13.428 N-m.}$

Review Questions

1. *Derive the expression of arrmature torque develped in a d.c. motor.*   **2009-10, Marks 5**

2. *A 240 V, 4 pole, shunt motor running at 1000 r.p.m. gives 15 H.P. with an armature current of 50 A and a field current of 1.0 A. The armature winding is wave-connected and has 540 conductors. Its resistance is 0.1 Ω and drop at each brush is 1 V. Find a) Useful torque ; b) Total torque ; c) Useful flux per pole and d) Rotational losses.*

                 (Ans. : 105.35 Nm, 112.249 Nm, 12.95 mWb, 617.77 W)

9.18 Types of D.C. Motors   **2002-03, 2004-05**

Similar to the d.c. generators, the d.c. motors are classified depending upon the way of connecting the field winding with the armature winding.

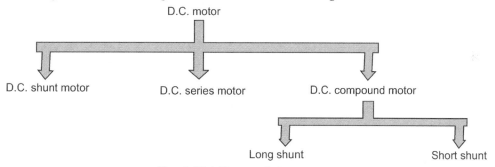

Fig. 9.18.1 Types of d.c. motors

9.18.1 D.C. Shunt Motor

In this type, the field winding is connected across the armature winding and the combination is connected across the supply, as shown in the Fig. 9.18.2.

Let R_{sh} be the resistance of shunt field winding and R_a be the resistance of armature winding.

The value of R_a is very small while R_{sh} is quite large. Hence shunt field winding has more number of turns with less cross-sectional area.

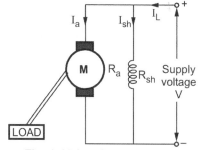

Fig. 9.18.2 D.C. shunt motor

Voltage and Current Relationship :

The voltage across armature and field winding is same **equal** to the supply voltage V.

The total current drawn from the supply is denoted as line current I_L.

$$I_L = I_a + I_{sh} \quad \text{and} \quad I_{sh} = \frac{V}{R_{sh}}$$

$$V = E_b + I_a R_a + V_{brush}$$

Now flux produced by the field winding is proportional to the current passing through it i.e. I_{sh}.

$$\phi \propto I_{sh}$$

As long as supply voltage is constant, which is generally so in practice, the flux produced is constant. Hence *d.c. shunt motor is called constant flux motor*.

9.18.2 D.C. Series Motor

In this type of motor, the series field winding is connected in series with the armature and the supply, as shown in the Fig. 9.18.3.

Let R_{se} be the resistance of the series field winding then the value of R_{se} is very small and it is made of small number of turns having large cross-section area.

Voltage and Current Relationship :

Let I_L be the total current drawn from the supply.

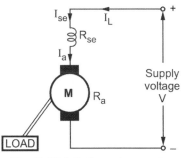

Fig. 9.18.3 D.C. series motor

So

$$I_L = I_{se} = I_a \qquad \text{and}$$

$$V = E_b + I_a R_a + I_{se} R_{se} + V_{brush}$$

$$V = E_b + I_a (R_a + R_{se}) + V_{brush}$$

Supply voltage has to overcome the drop across series field winding in addition to E_b and drop across armature winding.

In series motor, entire armature current is passing through the series field winding. So flux produced is proportional to the armature current.

$$\phi \propto I_{se} \propto I_a \qquad \text{for series motor}$$

9.18.3 D.C. Compound Motor

The compound motor consists of part of the field winding connected in series and part of the field winding connected in parallel with armature. It is further classified as short shunt compound and long shunt compound motor.

1. Long Shunt Compound Motor :

In this type, the shunt field winding is connected across the combination of armature and the series field winding as shown in the Fig. 9.18.4.

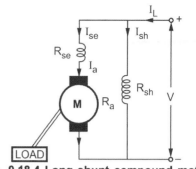

Fig. 9.18.4 Long shunt compound motor

Voltage and Current Relationship :

Let R_{se} be the resistance of series field and R_{sh} be the resistance of shunt field winding.

The total current drawn from supply is I_L.

So
$$I_L = I_{se} + I_{sh}$$

But $\quad I_{se} = I_a \text{ i.e. } I_L = I_a + I_{sh} \quad$ and $\quad I_{sh} = \dfrac{V}{R_{sh}}$

and $\quad V = E_b + I_a R_a + I_{se} R_{se} + V_{brush} \quad$ but as $\quad I_{se} = I_a,$

∴
$$V = E_b + I_a (R_a + R_{se}) + V_{brush}$$

2. Short Shunt Compound Motor :

In this type, the shunt field is connected purely in parallel with armature and the series field is connected in series with this combination shown in the Fig. 9.18.4 (a).

The entire line current is passing through the series field winding.

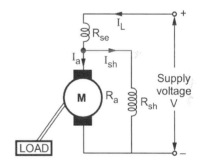

Fig. 9.18.4 (a) Short shunt compound motor

$$I_L = I_{se} \quad \text{and} \quad I_L = I_a + I_{sh}$$

Now the drop across the shunt field winding is to be calculated from the voltage equation.

So $\quad V = E_b + I_{se} R_{se} + I_a R_a + V_{brush} \quad$ but $\quad I_{se} = I_L$

∴ $\quad V = E_b + I_L R_{se} + I_a R_a + V_{brush}$

Drop across shunt field winding $= V - I_L R_{se} = E_b + I_a R_a + V_{brush}$

∴
$$I_{sh} = \frac{V - I_L R_{se}}{R_{sh}} = \frac{E_b + I_a R_a + V_{brush}}{R_{sh}}$$

A long shunt compound motor can be of cumulative or differential type. Similarly short shunt compound motor can be cumulative or differential type.

Example 9.18.1 *A 4 pole, 250 V, d.c. series motor has a wave connected armature with 200 conductors. The flux per pole is 25 mWb when motor is drawing 60 A from the supply. Armature resistance is 0.15 Ω while series field winding resistance is 0.2 Ω. Calculate the speed under this condition.*

Solution : $P = 4$, $Z = 200$, $A = 2$, $\phi = 25 \times 10^{-3}$ Wb, $I_a = I_L = 60$ A, $R_a = 0.15\ \Omega$,

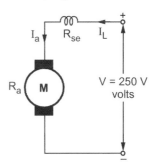

$$R_{se} = 0.2\ \Omega$$

$$V = E_b + I_a R_a + I_a R_{se}$$

$$250 = E_b + 60\,(0.15 + 0.2)$$

$$\therefore \quad E_b = 229V$$

Now $\quad E_b = \dfrac{\phi\,P\,N\,Z}{60\,A}$

$$\therefore \quad 229 = \dfrac{25 \times 10^{-3} \times 4\,N \times 200}{60 \times 2}$$

$$\therefore \quad N = \textbf{1374 r.p.m.}$$

Fig. 9.18.5

Example 9.18.2 *A 250 V, d.c. shunt motor takes a line current of 20 A. Resistance of shunt field winding is 200 Ω and resistance of the armature is 0.3 Ω. Find the armature current and the back e.m.f.*

Solution : $V = 250$ V, $I_L = 20$ A, $R_a = 0.3\ \Omega$, $R_{sh} = 200\ \Omega$

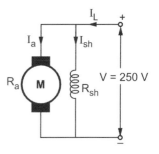

$$I_L = I_a + I_{sh} \quad \text{and} \quad I_{sh} = \dfrac{V}{R_{sh}} = \dfrac{250}{200} = 1.25 \text{ A}$$

$$\therefore \quad I_a = I_L - I_{sh} = 20 - 1.25 = \textbf{18.75 A}$$

Now $\quad V = E_b + I_a R_a$

$$\therefore \quad E_b = V - I_a R_a = 250 - 18.75 \times 0.3 = \textbf{244.375 V}$$

Fig. 9.18.6

Example 9.18.3 *A d.c. shunt machine connected to 230 volts supply has resistance of armature as 0.115 Ω and of field winding as 115 Ω. Find the ratio of the speed as a generator to the speed as a motor with the line current in each case being 100 amperes.*

2002-03, Marks 5

Solution :

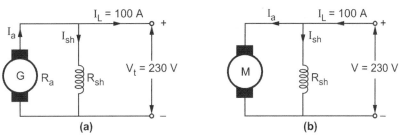

(a)   **(b)**

Fig. 9.18.7

$$I_{sh} = \frac{V}{R_{sh}} = \frac{230}{115} = 2 \text{ A}$$ ... In both cases

As I_{sh} is constant 2 A, $\phi \propto I_{sh}$ is also same for both cases.

For generator : $I_a = I_L + I_{sh} = 100 + 2 = 102$ A

$\therefore$ $E_g = V_t + I_a R_a = 230 + 102 \times 0.115 = 241.73$ V

For motor : $I_a = I_L - I_{sh} = 100 - 2 = 98$ A

$\therefore$ $E_b = V_t - I_a R_a = 230 - 98 \times 0.115 = 218.73$ V

Now $\dfrac{N_g}{N_m} = \dfrac{E_g}{E_b}$ as $N \propto \dfrac{E}{\phi}$ and ϕ is constant

$\therefore$ $\dfrac{N_g}{N_m} = \dfrac{241.73}{218.73} = \textbf{1.105}$

Example 9.18.4 *A d.c. shunt generator running at 1200 r.p.m. supplies a load of 60 kW at 250 volts. Find the speed at which it runs as a shunt motor when taking 60 kW from 250 volts supply. Take armature resistance at 0.1 ohm and field winding resistance as 50 ohm. Neglect brush drop.*   **2004-05, Marks 5**

Solution : As a generator, $P_{out} = 60$ kW, $V_t = 250$ V, $N_g = 1200$ r.p.m.

$\therefore$ $I_L = \dfrac{P_{out}}{V_t} = \dfrac{60 \times 10^3}{250} = 240$ A

        $I_{sh} = \dfrac{V_t}{R_{sh}} = \dfrac{250}{50} = 5$A

$\therefore$ $I_a = I_L + I_{sh} = 245$ A

$\therefore$ $E_g = V_t + I_a R_a = 250 + 245 \times 0.1$

           $= 274.5$ V

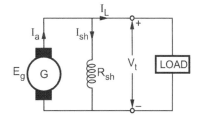

Fig. 9.18.8

As a motor, $P_{in} = 60$ kW,   V = 250 V

$$\therefore \qquad I_L = \frac{P_{in}}{V} = 240 \ A$$

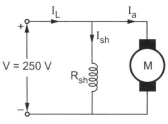

Fig. 9.18.9

$$\text{and} \qquad I_{sh} = \frac{V}{R_{sh}} = \frac{250}{50} = 5 \ A \quad \ldots \text{constant}$$

$$\therefore \qquad I_a = I_L - I_{sh} = 240 - 5 = 235 \ A$$

$$\therefore \qquad E_b = V_t - I_a R_a = 250 - 235 \times 0.1$$

$$= 226.5 \ V$$

$$\text{Now} \qquad N \propto \frac{E}{\phi} \propto E \qquad\qquad \ldots \phi \text{ is constant as } I_{sh} \text{ is constant}$$

$$\therefore \qquad \frac{N_g}{N_m} = \frac{E_g}{E_b}$$

$$\therefore \qquad N_m = \frac{226.5 \times 1200}{274.5} = \textbf{990.1639 r.p.m.} \qquad \ldots \text{Speed as motor}$$

Review Questions

1. State the various types of d.c. motors.

2. Draw the circuit diagram of d.c. shunt motor and give its voltage and current relation.

3. Draw the circuit diagram of d.c. series motor and give its voltage and current relations.

4. Draw the diagram of long shunt compound d.c. motor and give its voltage and current relations.

5. Draw the diagram of short shunt compound d.c. motor and give its voltage and current relations.

6. A 200 V, 4 pole, lap wound, d.c. shunt motor has 800 conductors on its armature. The resistance of the armature winding is 0.5 Ω and that of shunt field winding is 200 Ω. The motor takes a current of 21 A, the flux per pole is 30 mWb. Find the speed and the gross torque developed in the motor. **(Ans. : 475 r.p.m., 76.38 Nm)**

7. A 4 pole, 220 V, lap connected, D.C. shunt motor has 36 slots, each slot containing 16 conductors. It draws a current of 40 A from the supply. The field resistance and armature resistance are 110 Ω, 0.1 Ω respectively. The motor develops an output power of 6 kW. The flux per pole is 40 mWb. Calculate, a) The speed b) The torque developed by the armature and c) The shaft torque. **(Ans. : 563.02 r.p.m., 139.21 Nm, 101.73 Nm)**

8. A 4 pole, 250 V series motor has wave connected armature with 1254 conductors. The flux per pole is 22 mWb when the motor is taking 50 A. The armature and series field coil resistance are respectively 0.3 Ω and 0.2 Ω. Calculate the speed and torque of the motor and also the power developed in watts. **(Ans. : 244.67 r.p.m., 438.65 Nm, 11.25 kW)**

9. A 4 pole DC shunt motor takes 22 A from 220 V supply. The armature and field resistances are respectively 0.5 Ω and 100 Ω respectively. The armature is lap connected with 300 conductors. If the flux per pole is 20 mWb , calculate the speed and gross torque. **(Ans. : 2101 r.p.m., 18.89 Nm)**

9.19 Torque and Speed Equations

2002-03, 2007-08, 2009-10, 2011-12, 2012-13

Before analysing the various characteristics of motors, let us revise the torque and speed equations as applied to various types of motors.

$$T \propto \phi I_a \qquad \text{from torque equation.}$$

This is because, $0.159 \dfrac{PZ}{A}$ is a constant for a given motor.

Now ϕ is the flux produced by the field winding and is proportional to the current passing through the field winding.

$$\phi \propto I_{field}$$

For a d.c. shunt motor, I_{sh} is constant as long as supply voltage is constant. Hence ϕ flux is also constant.

$$\therefore \qquad T \propto I_a \quad \text{for shunt motors}$$

For a d.c. series motor, I_{se} is same as I_a. Hence flux ϕ is proportional to the armature current I_a.

$$\therefore \qquad T \propto I_a \phi \propto I_a^2 \quad \text{for series motors}$$

Similarly as $E_b = \dfrac{\phi P N Z}{60 A}$, we can write the speed equation as,

$$\therefore \qquad E_b \propto \phi N \quad \text{i.e.} \quad N \propto \frac{E_b}{\phi}$$

But $\qquad V = E_b + I_a R_a \quad$ i.e. $\quad E_b = V - I_a R_a$

$\therefore$ Speed equation becomes,

$$N \propto \frac{V - I_a R_a}{\phi}$$

So for shunt motor as flux ϕ is constant,

$$\therefore \qquad N \propto V - I_a R_a$$

While for series motor, flux ϕ is proportional to I_a

$$\therefore \qquad N \propto \frac{V - I_a R_a - I_a R_{se}}{I_a}$$

These relations play an important role in understanding the various characteristics of different types of motors.

9.19.1 Speed Regulation

The speed regulation for a d.c. motor is defined as the ratio of change in speed corresponding to no load and full load condition to speed corresponding to full load.

Mathematically it is expressed as,

$$\% \text{ speed regulation} = \frac{N_{\text{no load}} - N_{\text{full load}}}{N_{\text{full load}}} \times 100$$

Example 9.19.1 *A 4-pole D.C. shunt motor working on 220 V D.C. supply takes a line current of 3 A at no load while running at 1500 r.p.m. Determine the speed when the motor takes a line current of 50 A. Assume armature and field resistances as 0.2 ohm and 400 ohm respectively.* **2002-03, Marks 5**

Solution : P = 4, V = 220 V, I_{L0} = 3 A, N_0 = 1500 r.p.m., I_{L1} = 50 A,

R_a = 0.2 Ω, R_{sh} = 400 Ω

For d.c. shunt motor,

$$I_{sh} = \frac{V}{R_{sh}} = \frac{220}{400} = 0.55 \text{ A}$$

On no load, I_{a0} = $I_{L0} - I_{sh}$ = 3 - 0.55 = 2.45 A

$\therefore$ E_{b0} = V - $I_{a0} R_a$ = 220 - 2.45 × 0.2 = 219.51 V

On load, I_{a1} = $I_{L1} - I_{sh}$ = 50 - 0.55 = 49.45 A ... I_{sh} is constant

$\therefore$ E_{b1} = V - $I_{a1} R_a$ = 220 - 49.45 × 0.2 = 210.11 V

Now $N \propto \dfrac{E_b}{\phi} \propto E_b$ ... $\phi \propto I_{sh}$ and is constant

$\therefore$ $\dfrac{N_0}{N_1} = \dfrac{E_{b0}}{E_{b1}}$

$\therefore$ $N_1 = \dfrac{E_{b1}}{E_{b0}} \times N_0 = \dfrac{210.11}{219.51} \times 1500 = \mathbf{1435.766 \ r.p.m.}$ ... New speed

Example 9.19.2 *A D.C. shunt motor runs at 600 r.p.m. taking 60 A from a 230 V supply. Armature resistance is 0.2 ohm and field resistance is 115 ohms. Find the speed when the current through the armature is 30 A.* **2007-08, Marks 5**

Solution :

$$I_{sh} = \frac{V}{R_{sh}} = \frac{230}{115} = 2 \text{ A}$$

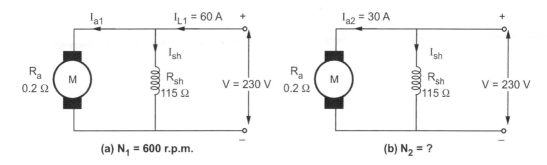

(a) $N_1 = 600$ r.p.m.   (b) $N_2 = ?$

Fig. 9.19.1

∴ $\quad I_{a1} = I_{L1} - I_{sh} = 60 - 2 = 58$ A

∴ $\quad E_{b1} = V - I_{a1} R_a = 230 - 58 \times 0.2 = 218.4$ V

$\quad E_{b2} = V - I_{a2} R_a = 230 - 30 \times 0.2 = 224$ V

$$ N \propto \frac{E_b}{\phi} \propto \frac{E_b}{I_{sh}} \propto E_b \qquad \qquad \ldots I_{sh} \text{ is constant} $$

∴ $\quad \dfrac{N_1}{N_2} = \dfrac{E_{b1}}{E_{b2}} \quad$ i.e. $\quad \dfrac{600}{N_2} = \dfrac{218.4}{224}$

∴ $\quad N_2 = \textbf{615.3846 r.p.m.} \qquad \qquad \ldots$ New speed

Example 9.19.3 *A 140 V d.c. shunt motor has an armature resistance of 0.2 ohm and a field resistance 70 ohm. The full load line current is 40 A and the full load speed is 1800 r.p.m. If the brush contact drop is 3 V, find the speed of the motor at half load.*

2009-10, Marks 5

Solution : $V = 140$ V, $R_a = 0.2\ \Omega$, $R_{sh} = 70\ \Omega$, $I_{FL} = 40$ A, $N_{FL} = 1800$ r.p.m., Brush drop = 3 V, $N_{HL} = ?$

$$ I_{sh} = \frac{V}{R_{sh}} = \frac{140}{70} = 2 \text{ A} $$

∴ $\quad I_{aFL} = I_{FL} - I_{sh} = 40 - 2 = 38$ A

$\quad T \propto \phi I_a \propto I_a \qquad \qquad \ldots \phi$ is constant

∴ $\quad \dfrac{T_1}{T_2} = \dfrac{I_{a1}}{I_{a2}} \quad$ i.e. $\quad \dfrac{T_{FL}}{T_{HL}} = \dfrac{I_{aFL}}{I_{aHL}}$

But $\quad T_{HL} = \dfrac{1}{2} T_{FL} \quad$ i.e. $\quad 2 = \dfrac{I_{aFL}}{I_{aHL}}$

∴ $\quad I_{aHL} = \dfrac{1}{2} \times 38 = 19$ A

$\therefore \qquad E_{bFL} = V - I_{aFL}R_a - \text{Brush drop} = 129.4 \text{ V}$

$\therefore \qquad E_{bHL} = V - I_{aHL}R_a - \text{Brush drop} = 133.2 \text{ V}$

$\therefore \qquad N \propto \dfrac{E_b}{\phi} \propto E_b \qquad\qquad\qquad \dots \phi \text{ is constant}$

$\dfrac{N_{FL}}{N_{HL}} = \dfrac{E_{bFL}}{E_{bHL}} \quad \text{i.e.} \quad \dfrac{1800}{N_{HL}} = \dfrac{129.4}{133.2}$

$\therefore \qquad N_{HL} = \mathbf{1852.859 \ r.p.m.} \qquad\qquad \dots \text{Half load speed}$

Example 9.19.4 *The armature resistance of a 200 V DC shunt motor is 0.12 ohm. It runs at 600 r.p.m. at constant torque load and draws a current of 21 ampere. Calculate its new speed if the field current of the motor is reduced by 10 %.* **2011-12, Marks 5**

Solution : $V = 200 \text{ V}, R_a = 0.12 \ \Omega, N_1 = 600 \text{ r.p.m.}, I_{a1} = 21 \text{ A}$

$\therefore \qquad E_{b1} = V - I_{a1}R_a = 200 - 21 \times 0.12 = 197.48 \text{ V}$

$\qquad T \propto \phi I_a \text{ and torque is constant}$

$\therefore \qquad \dfrac{\phi_1 I_{a1}}{\phi_2 I_{a2}} = 1 \quad \text{and filed current reduced by 10 \%.}$

As $\phi \propto I_f$, flux will get reduced by 10 %.

$\therefore \qquad \phi_2 = \phi_1 - 0.1\phi_1 = 0.9\,\phi_1 \quad \text{i.e.} \quad \dfrac{\phi_1}{\phi_2} = \dfrac{1}{0.9}$

$\therefore \qquad \dfrac{1}{0.9} \times \dfrac{21}{I_{a2}} = 1 \qquad \text{i.e.} \qquad I_{a2} = 23.333 \text{ A}$

$\therefore \qquad E_{b2} = V - I_{a2}R_a = 200 - 23.333 \times 0.12 = 197.2 \text{ V}$

$\qquad N \propto \dfrac{E_b}{\phi} \qquad \text{i.e.} \qquad \dfrac{N_1}{N_2} = \dfrac{E_{b1}}{E_{b2}} \times \dfrac{\phi_2}{\phi_1}$

$\therefore \qquad \dfrac{600}{N_2} = \dfrac{197.48}{197.2} \times 0.9 \qquad \text{i.e.} \qquad N_2 = \mathbf{665.72 \ r.p.m.}$

Example 9.19.5 *A DC shunt motor runs at 600 rpm taking 60 A from a 230 V supply. Armature resistance is 0.2 ohm and field resistance is 115 ohms. Find the speed when the current through the armature is 30 A.* **2012-13, Marks 10**

Solution : $N_1 = 600 \text{ r.p.m.}, I_{L1} = 60 \text{ A}, V = 230 \text{ V}, R_a = 0.2 \ \Omega, R_{sh} = 115 \ \Omega$

$\qquad I_{sh} = \dfrac{V}{R_{sh}} = \dfrac{230}{115} = 2 \text{ A} \quad \text{and} \quad I_{L1} = I_{sh} + I_{a1}$

$\therefore$ $\qquad$ $I_{a1} = 60 - 2 = 58$ A $\quad$ i.e. $\quad E_{b1} = V - I_{a1} R_a = 218.4$ V

$\qquad \qquad I_{a2} = 30$ A (Given) $\quad$ i.e. $\quad E_{b2} = V - I_{a2} R_a = 224$ V

$\qquad \qquad N \propto \dfrac{E_b}{\phi} \propto E_b$ $\qquad \qquad \qquad$ ... ϕ is constant for d.c. shunt motor

$\therefore$ $\qquad \dfrac{N_1}{N_2} = \dfrac{E_{b1}}{E_{b2}}$ $\quad$ i.e. $\quad \dfrac{600}{N_2} = \dfrac{218.4}{224}$ $\quad$ i.e. $\quad$ **N₂ = 615.384 r.p.m.**

Example 9.19.6 *A series motor runs at 600 r.p.m. when taking 110 A from a 250 V supply. The resistance of the armature circuit is 0.12 Ω, and that of series winding is 0.03 Ω. The useful flux per pole for 110 A is 0.024 Wb, and that for 50 A is 0.0155 Wb. Calculate the speed when the current has fallen to 50 A.*

Solution : $N_1 = 600$ r.p.m., $\quad I_{a1} = 110$ A, $\quad V = 250$ V, $\quad R_a = 0.12$ Ω, $\quad R_{se} = 0.03$ Ω

For $\qquad I_{a1} = 110$ A, $\qquad \phi_1 = 0.024$ Wb $\;$ and $\;$ $I_{a2} = 50$ A, $\quad \phi_2 = 0.0155$ Wb

$\qquad \qquad E_{b1} = V - I_{a1}(R_a + R_{se}) = 250 - 110\,(0.12 + 0.03) = 233.5$ V

$\qquad \qquad E_{b2} = V - I_{a2}(R_a + R_{se}) = 250 - 50\,(0.12 + 0.03) = 242.5$ V

Now, $\qquad N \propto \dfrac{E_b}{\phi}$

$\therefore$ $\qquad \dfrac{N_1}{N_2} = \dfrac{E_{b1}}{E_{b2}} \times \dfrac{\phi_2}{\phi_1}$

$\therefore$ $\qquad \dfrac{600}{N_2} = \dfrac{233.5}{242.5} \times \dfrac{0.0155}{0.024}$

$\therefore$ $\qquad N_2 = \dfrac{600 \times 242.5 \times 0.024}{233.5 \times 0.0155} =$ **964.8407 r.p.m.**

Review Questions

1. *Define speed regulation of a d.c. motor.*

2. *A 120 V d.c. shunt motor has an armature resistance of 0.2 Ω and shunt field resistance of 60 Ω. It runs at 1800 r.p.m. when it takes full load current of 40 A. Find the speed of the motor while it is operating at half the full load, with load terminal voltage remaing same.* **(Ans. : 1860.85 r.p.m.)**

3. *A 440 V d.c. shunt motor takes an armature current of 20 A and runs at 500 r.p.m. The armature resistance is 0.6 Ω. If the flux is reduced by 30 % and the torque is increased by 40 %. What are the new values of armature current and speed ?* **(Ans. : 694.26 r.p.m.)**

4. *A 6 pole, d.c. shunt motor has a lap-connected armature with 492 conductors. The resistance of the armature is 0.2 Ω and the flux per pole is 50 mWb. The motor runs at 20 revolutions per second when it is connected to a 500 V supply for a particular load. What will be the speed of the motor when the load is reduced by 50 %. Neglect contact drop and magnetic saturation.*

(Ans. : 1209.76 r.p.m.)

5. *A 440 V d.c. shunt motor takes an armature current of 20 A and runs at 500 r.p.m. The armature resistance is 0.6 ohms. If the flux is reduced by 40 %, calculate the new values of armature current and speed.* **(Ans. : 33.33 A, 817.761 r.p.m.)**

6. *A d.c. series motor is running with a speed of 1000 r.p.m., while taking a current of 22 amps from the supply. If the load is changed such that the current drawn by the motor is increased to 55 amps, calculate the speed of the motor on new load. The armature and series winding resistances are 0.3 Ω and 0.4 Ω respectively. Assume supply voltage as 250 V.*

(Ans. : 360.613 r.p.m.)

9.20 D.C. Motor Characteristics

The performance of a d.c. motor under various conditions can be judged by the following characteristics.

i) Torque-Armature current characteristics (T Vs I_a) :

The graph showing the relationship between the torque and the armature current is called a torque-armature current characteristic. These are also called electrical characteristics.

ii) Speed-Armature current characteristics (N Vs I_a) :

The graph showing the relationship between the speed and armature current characteristics.

iii) Speed-Torque characteristics (N Vs T) :

The graph showing the relationship between the speed and the torque of the motor is called speed-torque characteristics of the motor. These are also called mechanical characteristics.

The nature of these characteristics can easily be obtained by using speed and torque equations derived in section 9.19. These characteristics play a very important role in selecting a type of motor for a particular application.

9.21 Characteristics of D.C. Shunt Motor   2009-10, 2012-13

i) Torque-Armature current characteristics

For a d.c. motor $T \propto \phi I_a$

For a constant values of R_{sh} and supply voltage V, I_{sh} is also constant and hence flux is also constant.

∴
$$T_a \propto I_a$$

The equation represents a straight line, passing through the origin, as shown in the Fig. 9.21.1. Torque increases linearly with armature current. It is seen earlier that armature current is decided by the load. So as load increases, armature current increases, increasing the torque developed linearly.

Now if shaft torque is plotted against armature current, it is known that shaft torque is less than the armature torque and the difference between the two is loss torque T_f as shown. On no load T_{sh} = 0 but armature torque is present which is just

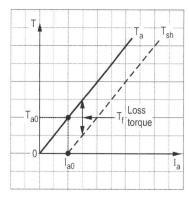

Fig. 9.21.1 T Vs I_a for shunt motor

enough to overcome stray losses shown as T_{a0}. The current required is I_{a0} on no load to produce T_{a0} and hence T_{sh} graph has an intercept of I_{a0} on the current axis.

To generate high starting torque, this type of motor requires a large value of armature current at start. This may damage the motor hence d.c. shunt motors can develop moderate starting torque and hence suitable for such applications where starting torque requirement is moderate.

ii) Speed-Armature current characteristics

From the speed equation we get,

$$N \propto \frac{V - I_a R_a}{\phi} \propto V - I_a R_a \qquad \text{as } \phi \text{ is constant.}$$

So as load increases, the armature current increases and hence drop $I_a R_a$ also increases.

Hence for constant supply voltage, V - $I_a R_a$ decreases and hence speed reduces. But as R_a is very small, for change in I_a from no load to full load, drop $I_a R_a$ is very small and hence drop in speed is also not significant from no load to full load.

So the characteristics is slightly droping as shown in the Fig. 9.21.2.

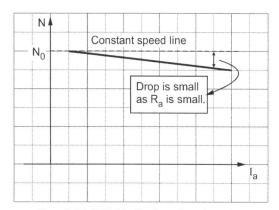

Fig. 9.21.2 N Vs I_a for shunt motor

Key Point *But for all practical purposes these type of motors are considered to be a constant speed motors.*

iii) Speed-Torque characteristics

These characteristics can be derived from the above two characteristics. This graph is similar to speed-armature current characteristics as torque is proportional to the armature current. This curve shows that the speed almost remains constant though torque changes from no load to full load conditions. This is shown in the Fig. 9.21.3.

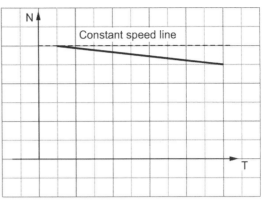

Fig. 9.21.3 N Vs T for shunt motor

Review Question

1. *Explain the characteristics of d.c. shunt motor.*	**2009-10, 2012-13, Marks 5**

9.22 Characteristics of D.C. Series Motor   **2009-10, 2012-13**

i) Torque-Armature current characteristics

In case of series motor the series field winding is carrying the entire armature current. So flux produced is proportional to the armature current.

$$\therefore \qquad \phi \ \propto \ I_a$$

Hence $\boxed{T_a \ \propto \ \phi \, I_a \ \propto \ I_a^2}$

Thus torque in case of series motor is proportional to the square of the armature current. This relation is parabolic in nature as shown in the Fig. 9.22.1.

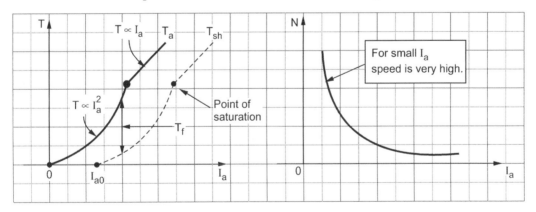

Fig. 9.22.1 T Vs I_a for series motor   **Fig. 9.22.2 N Vs I_a for series motor**

As load increases, armature current increases and torque produced increases proportional to the square of the armature current upto a certain limit.

As the entire I_a passes through the series field, there is a property of an electromagnet called **saturation**, may occur. Saturation means though the current through the winding increases, the flux produced remains constant. Hence after saturation the characteristics take the shape of straight line as flux becomes constant, as shown. The difference between T_a and T_{sh} is loss torque T_f which is also shown in the Fig. 9.22.1.

At start as $T \propto I_a^2$, these types of motors can produce high torque for small amount of armature current hence the series motors are suitable for the applications which demand high starting torque.

ii) Speed-Armature current characteristics

From the speed equation we get,

$$N \propto \frac{E_b}{\phi} \propto \frac{V - I_a R_a - I_a R_{se}}{I_a} \qquad \text{as } \phi \propto I_a \text{ in case of series motor}$$

Now the values of R_a and R_{se} are so small that the effect of change in I_a on speed overrides the effect of change in $V - I_a R_a - I_a R_{se}$ on the speed.

Hence in the speed equation, $E_b \cong V$ and can be assumed constant. So speed equation reduces to,

$$N \propto \frac{1}{I_a}$$

So speed-armature current characteristics is rectangular hyperbola type as shown in the Fig. 9.22.2.

iii) Speed-Torque characteristics

In case of series motors, $T \propto I_a^2$ and $N \propto \dfrac{1}{I_a}$

Hence we can write, $$N \propto \frac{1}{\sqrt{T}}$$

Thus as torque increases when load increases, the speed decreases. On no load, torque is very less and hence speed increases to dangerously high value. Thus the nature of the speed-torque characteristics is similar to the nature of the speed-armature current characteristics.

The speed-torque characteristics of a series motor is shown in the Fig. 9.22.3.

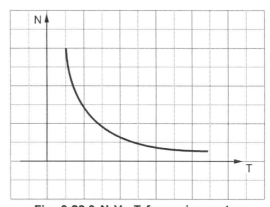

Fig. 9.22.3 N Vs T for series motor

Review Question

1. *Sketch and explain the various characteristics of d.c. series motors.* **2009-10, 2012-13, Marks 5**

9.23 Why Series Motor is Never Started on No Load ?

It is seen earlier that motor armature current is decided by the load. On light load or no load, the armature current drawn by the motor is very small.

In case of a d.c. series motor, $\phi \propto I_a$ and

on no load as I_a is small hence flux produced is also very small.

According to speed equation,

$$N \propto \frac{1}{\phi}$$ as E_b is almost constant.

So on very light load or no load as flux is very small, the motor tries to run at dangerously high speed which may damage the motor mechanically. This can be seen from the speed-armature current and the speed-torque characteristics that on low armature current and low torque condition motor shows a tendency to rotate with dangerously high speed.

This is the reason why series motor should never be started on light loads or no load conditions. For this reason it is not selected for belt drives as breaking or slipping of belt causes to throw the entire load off on the motor and made to run motor with no load which is dangerous.

Review Question

1. *A series motor should never be started on no load. Justify the above statement with proper reasoning.*

9.24 Characteristics of D.C. Compound Motor   **2006-07, 2009-10**

Compound motor characteristics basically depends on the fact whether the motor is cumulatively compound or differential compound. All the characteristics of the compound motor are the combination of the shunt and series characteristic.

Cumulative compound motor is capable of developing large amount of torque at low speeds just like series motor. However it is not having a disadvantage of series motor even at light or no load. The shunt field winding produces the definite flux and series flux helps the shunt field flux to increase the total flux level.

So cumulative compound motor can run at a reasonable speed and will not run with dangerously high speed like series motor, on light or no load condition.

In differential compound motor, as two fluxes oppose each other, the resultant flux decreases as load increases, thus the machine runs at a higher speed with increase in the load. This property is dangerous as on full load, the motor may try to run with dangerously high speed. So differential compound motor is generally not used in practice.

The various characteristics of both the types of compound motors cumulative and the differential are shown in the Fig. 9.24.1 (a), (b) and (c).

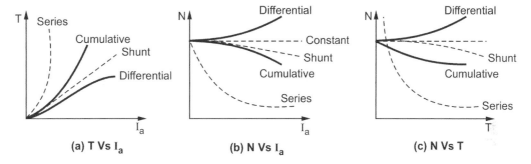

Fig. 9.24.1 Characteristics of d.c. compound motor

The exact shape of these characteristics depends on the relative contribution of series and shunt field windings. If the shunt field winding is more dominant then the characteristics take the shape of the shunt motor characteristics. While if the series field winding is more dominant then the characteristics take the shape of the series characteristics.

Review Question

> 1. *Sketch and explain the characteristics of d.c. compound motors.*   **2006-07, 2009-10, Marks 5**

9.25 Applications of D.C. Motors

Instead of just stating the applications, the behaviour of the various characteristics like speed, starting torque etc., which makes the motor more suitable for the applications, is also stated in the Table 9.25.1.

Types of motor	Characteristics	Applications
Shunt	Speed is fairly constant and medium starting torque.	1) Blowers and fans 2) Centrifugal and reciprocating pumps 3) Lathe machines 4) Machine tools 5) Milling machines 6) Drilling machines

Series	High starting torque. No load condition is dangerous. Variable speed.	1) Cranes 2) Hoists, Elevators 3) Trolleys 4) Conveyors 5) Electric locomotives and electric traction.
Cumulative compound	High starting torque. No load condition is allowed.	1) Rolling mills 2) Punches 3) Shears 4) Heavy planers 5) Elevators
Differential compound	Speed increases as load increases.	Not suitable for any practical application.

Table 9.25.1

Review Question

1. *State the applications of various types of d.c. motors.*

9.26 Factors Affecting the Speed of a D.C. Motor

According to the speed equation of a d.c. motor we can write,

$$N \propto \frac{E_b}{\phi} \propto \frac{V - I_a R_a}{\phi}$$

The factors Z, P, A are constants for a d.c. motor.

But as the value of armature resistance R_a and series field resistance R_{se} is very small, the drop $I_a R_a$ and $I_a (R_a + R_{se})$ is very small compared to applied voltage V. Hence neglecting these voltage drops the speed equation can be modified as,

$$N \propto \frac{V}{\phi} \qquad \text{as } E_b \approx V$$

Thus the factors affecting the speed of a d.c. motor are,

1. The flux ϕ

2. The voltage across the armature

3. The applied voltage V

Depending upon these factors the various methods of speed control are,

1. Changing the flux ϕ by controlling the current through the field winding called **flux control** methods.

2. Changing the armature path resistance which in turn changes the voltage applied across the armature called **rheostatic control**.

3. Changing the applied voltage called **voltage control** method.

Before studying how these methods are used for various types of d.c. motors, let us study the ratings of a d.c. motor. These ratings decide the range in which the speed of a particular d.c. motor can be varied.

9.27 Ratings of a D.C. Motor

To change the speed as per the requirements, it is not possible to increase the voltage or currents beyond certain limit. These limits are called ratings of the motor.

The maximum voltage that can be applied to the motor, safely is called **rated voltage** or **normal voltage** of the motor. While changing the applied voltage, one should not apply the voltage more than the rated voltage of the motor.

Similarly maximum current that field winding can carry, safely is called **rated field current** of the motor. Hence while changing the flux, one should not increase field current beyond its rated value. This is important rating as far as shunt motor is concerned. In a series motor, the entire armature current flows through the series field winding. The armature current is decided by the load and it cannot be changed by changing the resistance of the armature circuit. So the maximum current that armature winding can carry safely is decided by the load called **full load current** or **full load rating** of the motor. Motor should not be loaded more than its full load capacity indicated by its full load armature current.

Exceeding the rating is dangerous from the motor point of view as due to high currents, the heat produced, which is proportional to the square of the current is very large. This may damage the windings electrically.

Now $\qquad N \propto \dfrac{V}{\phi}$

So for $V = V_{rated}$ and $\phi \propto I_f$ rated i.e. when there is no external resistance in the armature and field circuit and motor is excited by normal rated voltage, the speed obtained is called **rated speed** or **normal speed**.

$\therefore \qquad \boxed{N_{rated} \propto \dfrac{V_{rated}}{I_{f\,rated}}}$

Key Point *Note that the rated or normal speed is not the maximum speed with which motor can run safely but it is the speed when the electrical parameters controlling the speed are at their rated values.*

Practically a motor speed can be increased to approximately twice its normal speed safely.

Thus while controlling the speed, the voltage applied should not be more than rated voltage of a motor, the field current should not be more than its rated value and the current carried by armature should not be more than its full load value. All the ratings are provided by the manufacturer in the form of name plate of a d.c. motor. Let us study now the various methods as applied to different types of d.c. motors.

9.28 Speed Control of D.C. Shunt Motor   2010-11

Out of the three methods, let us study flux control method.

9.28.1 Flux Control

As indicated by the speed equation, the speed is inversely proportional to the flux. The flux is dependent on the current through the shunt field winding. Thus flux can be controlled by adding a rheostat (variable resistance) in series with the shunt field winding, as shown in the Fig. 9.28.1.

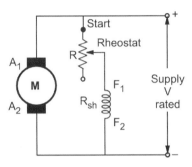

Fig. 9.28.1 Flux control of shunt motor

At the beginning the rheostat R is kept at minimum indicated as start in the Fig. 9.28.2. The supply voltage is at its rated value. So current through shunt field winding is also at its rated value. Hence the speed is also rated speed also called normal speed. Then the resistance R is increased due to which shunt field current I_{sh} decreases, decreasing the flux

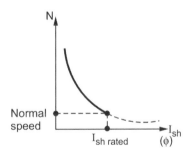

Fig. 9.28.2 N Vs I_{sh} (ϕ) for shunt motor

produced. As $N \propto (1/\phi)$, the speed of the motor increases beyond its rated value.

Thus by this method, the speed control above rated value is possible. This is shown in the Fig. 9.28.2, by speed against field current curve. The curve shows the inverse relation between N and ϕ as its nature is rectangular hyperbola.

It is mentioned that the rated values of electrical parameters should not be exceeded but the speed which is mechanical parameter can be increased upto twice its rated value.

9.28.2 Armature Voltage Control Method or Rheostatic Control

The speed is directly proportional to the voltage applied across the armature. As the supply voltage is normally constant, the voltage across the armature can be controlled by adding a variable resistance in series with the armature as shown in the Fig. 9.28.3.

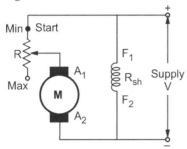 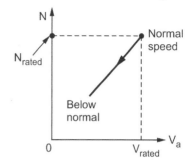

Fig. 9.28.3 Rheostatic control of shunt motor   **Fig. 9.28.4 N Vs voltage across armature**

The field winding is excited by the normal voltage hence I_{sh} is rated and constant in this method. Initially the rheostat position is minimum and rated voltage gets applied across the armature. So speed is also rated. For a given load, armature current is fixed. So when extra resistance is added in the armature circuit, I_a remains same and there is voltage drop across the resistance added (I_a R). Hence voltage across the armature decreases, decreasing the speed below normal value. By varying this extra resistance, various speeds below rated value can be obtained.

So for a **constant load torque**, the speed is directly proportional to the voltage across the armature. The relationship between speed and voltage across the armature is shown in the Fig. 9.28.4.

9.28.2.1 Potential Divider Control

The main disadvantage of the above method is, the speed up to zero is not possible as it requires a large rheostat in series with the armature which is practically impossible. If speed control from zero to the rated speed is required, by rheostatic method then voltage across the armature can be varied by connecting rheostat in a potential divider arrangement as shown in the Fig. 9.28.5.

When the variable rheostat position is at 'start' point shown, voltage across the armature is zero and hence speed is zero. As rheostat is moved towards 'maximum' point shown, the voltage across the armature increases, increasing the speed. At maximum point the voltage is maximum i.e. rated hence maximum speed possible is rated speed. The relationship is shown in the Fig. 9.28.6.

When the voltage across the armature starts increasing, as long as motor does not overcome inertial and frictional torque, the speed of the motor remains zero. The motor requires some voltage to start hence the graph of voltage and the speed does not pass through the origin as shown in the Fig. 9.28.6.

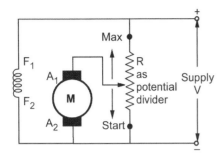

Fig. 9.28.5 Potential divider arrangement

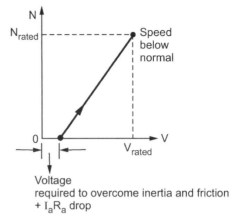

Fig. 9.28.6 N Vs V

9.28.3 Applied Voltage Control

Multiple voltage control :

In this technique the shunt field of the motor is permanently connected to a fixed voltage supply, while the armature is supplied with various voltages by means of suitable switch gear arrangements.

The Fig. 9.28.7 shows a control of motor by two different working voltages which can be applied to it with the help of switch gear.

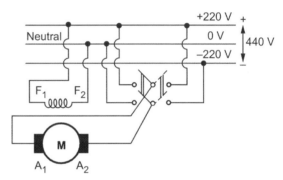

Fig. 9.28.7 Multiple voltage control

In large factories, various values of armature voltages and corresponding arrangement can be used to obtain the speed control.

> *** General steps to solve problems on speed control**
>
> 1. Identify the method of speed control i.e. in which winding of the motor, the external resistance is to be inserted.
>
> 2. Use the torque equation, $T \propto \phi I_a$ to determine the new armature current according to the condition of the torque given. Load condition indicates the condition of the torque.
>
> 3. Use the speed equation $N \propto \dfrac{E_b}{\phi}$ to find the unknown back e.m.f. or field current.
>
> 4. From the term calculated above and using voltage current relationship of the motor, the value of extra resistance to be added, can be determined. The above steps may vary little bit according to the nature of the problem but are always the base of any speed control problem.

Example 9.28.1 *A 250 V d.c. shunt motor runs at 1000 r.p.m. on no load and takes 5 A. The armature and shunt field resistances are 0.2 Ω and 250 Ω respectively. Calculate the speed when loaded and taking a current of 50 A. Due to armature reaction the field weakens by 3 %.*

Solution : $V = 250$ V, $N_0 = 1000$ r.p.m., $I_0 = 5$ A, $R_a = 0.2$ Ω, $R_{sh} = 250$ Ω

$$I_{sh} = \frac{V}{R_{sh}} = \frac{250}{250} = 1 \text{ A}$$

∴ $$I_{a0} = I_0 - I_{sh} = 5 - 1 = 4 \text{ A}$$

∴ $$E_{b0} = V - I_{a0}R_a = 250 - 4 \times 0.2 = 249.2 \text{ V}$$

$$I_L = 50 \text{ A on load}$$

$$I_{sh} = \frac{V}{R_{sh}} = 1 \text{ A}$$

∴ $$I_a = I_L - I_{sh} = 50 - 1 = 49 \text{ A}$$

Key Point *Note that I_{sh} remains same though flux weakens.*

∴ $$E_{b1} = V - I_a R_a = 250 - 49 \times 0.2 = 240.2 \text{ V} \qquad \text{... On load}$$

Now $$N \propto \frac{E_b}{\phi} \qquad \text{i.e.} \qquad \frac{N_0}{N_1} = \frac{E_{b0}}{E_{b1}} \times \frac{\phi_1}{\phi_0}$$

Now $$\phi_1 = \phi_0 - 0.03\phi_0 = 0.97\,\phi_0 \qquad \text{... Weakens by 3 \%}$$

∴ $$\frac{1000}{N_1} = \frac{249.2}{240.2} \times 0.97 \qquad \text{i.e.} \qquad N_1 = \textbf{993.695 r.p.m.}$$

Example 9.28.2 *A 100 H.P., 500 V d.c. shunt motor has 4 poles and a 2 circuit wave winding with 492 conductors. The flux/pole is 50 mWb and full load efficiency is 92 %. The armature and the commutating pole winding have a total resistance of 0.1 Ω, shunt field resistance is 250 ohms. Calculate for full load, (a) The speed and (b) The useful torque.*

Solution : $P_{out} = 100$ H.P., $V = 500$ V, $P = 4$, $A = 2$, $Z = 492$,

$$\phi = 50 \text{ mWb}, \qquad \eta = 92 \text{ \%}, \qquad R_a = 0.1 \text{ Ω}, \qquad R_{sh} = 250 \text{ Ω}.$$

Assume 1 H.P. = 735.5 W i.e. $P_{out} = 73550$ W

∴ $$P_{in} = \frac{P_{out}}{\eta} = \frac{73550}{0.92} = 79945.652 \text{ W}$$

Now $$I_L = \frac{P_{in}}{V} = \frac{79945.652}{500} = 159.8913 \text{ A}$$

$$I_{sh} = \frac{V}{R_{sh}} = \frac{500}{250} = 2 \text{ A}$$

∴ $\qquad I_a = I_L - I_{sh} = 159.8913 - 2 = 157.8913 \text{ A}$ $\qquad$ ... Shunt motor

∴ $\qquad E_b = V - I_a R_a = 500 - 157.8913 \times 0.1 = 484.01 \text{ V}$

But $\qquad E_b = \dfrac{\phi\, P\, N\, Z}{60\, A}$

∴ $\qquad 484.01 = \dfrac{50 \times 10^{-3} \times N \times 492}{60 \times 2}$

∴ $\qquad N = \textbf{590.2571 r.p.m.}$ $\qquad$ ... Speed of motor

$$T_{sh} = \text{Useful torque} = \frac{P_{out}}{\omega} = \frac{P_{out}}{\dfrac{2\pi N}{60}}$$

$$= \frac{73550}{\left(\dfrac{2\pi \times 590.2571}{60} \right)} = \textbf{1189.90 Nm}$$

Review Question

1. *Discuss the various methods of speed control of d.c. shunt motor.* **2010-11, Marks 5**

9.29 Speed Control of D.C. Series Motor

The flux produced by the winding depends on the m.m.f. i.e. magnetomotive force which is the product of current and the number of turns of the winding through which current is passing. So flux can be changed either by changing the current by adding a resistance or by changing the number of turns of the winding. Let us study the various methods based on this principle.

9.29.1 Flux Control

The various methods of flux control in a d.c. series motor are explained below :

9.29.1.1 Field Divertor Method

In this method the series field winding is shunted by a variable resistance (R_x) known as **field divertor**. The arrangement is shown in the Fig. 9.29.1 (a).

Due to the parallel path of R_x, by adjusting the value of R_x, any amount of current can be diverted through the divertor. Hence current through the field winding can be adjusted as per the requirement. Due to this, the flux gets controlled and hence the speed of the motor gets controlled.

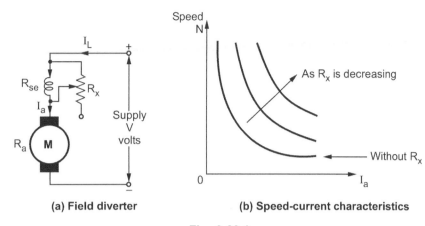

(a) Field diverter   (b) Speed-current characteristics

Fig. 9.29.1

By this method the speed of the motor can be controlled above rated value. The speed armature current characteristics with change in R_x is shown in the Fig. 9.74 (b).

9.29.1.2 Armature Divertor Method

This method is used for the motor which require constant load torque. An armature of the motor is shunted with an external variable resistance (R_x) as shown in the Fig. 9.29.2. This resistance R_x is called **armature divertor**.

Any amount of armature current can be diverted through the divertor. Due to this, armature current reduces. But as $T \propto \phi\ I_a$ and

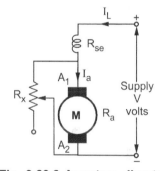

Fig. 9.29.2 Armature divertor

load torque is constant, the flux is to be increased. So motor reacts by drawing more current from the supply. So current through field winding increases, so flux increases and speed of the motor reduces. The method is used to control the speed below the normal value.

9.29.1.3 Tapped Field Method

In this method, flux change is achieved by changing the number of turns of the field winding. The field winding is provided with the taps as shown in the Fig. 9.29.3.

The selector switch 'S' is provided to select the number of turns (taps) as per the requirement. When the switch 'S' is in position 1 the entire field winding is in the circuit and motor runs with normal speed. As switch is moved from position 1

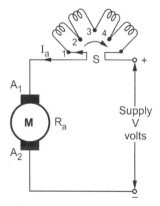

Fig. 9.29.3 Tapped field

to 2 and onwards, the number of turns of the field winding in the circuit decreases. Due to this m.m.f. required to produce the flux, decreases. Due to this flux produced decreases, increasing the speed of the motor above rated value. The method is often used in electric traction.

9.29.1.4 Series - Parallel Connection of Field

In this method, the field coil is divided into various parts. These parts can then be connected in series or parallel as per the requirement. The Fig. 9.29.4 (a) and (b) show the two parts of field coil connected in series and parallel.

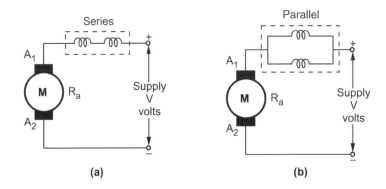

Fig. 9.29.4 Series-parallel grouping of field coils

For the same torque, if the field coil is arranged in series or parallel, m.m.f. produced by the coils changes, hence the flux produced also changes. Hence speed can be controlled. Some fixed speeds only can be obtained by this method. In parallel grouping, the m.m.f. produced decreases, hence higher speed can be obtained by parallel grouping. The method is generally used in case of fan motors.

9.29.2 Rheostatic Control

In this method, a variable resistance (R_x) is inserted in series with the motor circuit. As this resistance is inserted, the voltage drop across this resistance $(I_a R_x)$ occurs. This reduces the voltage across the armature. As speed is directly proportional to the voltage across the armature, the speed reduces. The arrangement is shown in the Fig. 9.29.5 (a). As entire current passes through R_x, there is large power loss. The speed-armature current characteristics with change in R_x are shown in the Fig. 9.29.5 (b).

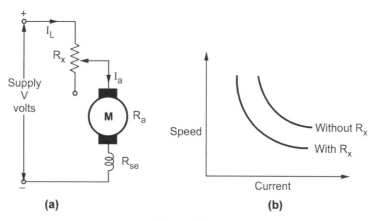

(a)   **(b)**

Fig. 9.29.5

9.29.3 Applied Voltage Control

In this method, a series motor is excited by the voltage obtained by a series generator as shown in the Fig. 9.29.6.

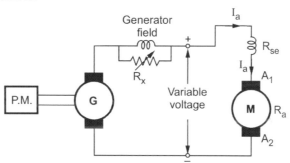

Fig. 9.29.6 Variable voltage control

The generator is driven by a suitable prime mover. The voltage obtained from the generator is controlled by a field divertor resistance connected across series field winding of the generator.

As $E_g \propto \phi$, the flux change is achieved, gives the variable voltage at the output terminals. Due to the change in the supply voltage, the various speeds of the d.c. series motor can be obtained.

Note *Note that all the advantages and disadvantages of various methods, discussed as applied to shunt motor are equally applicable to speed control of series motor.*

Example 9.29.1 *A 200 V d.c. series motor drives a load at a certain speed and takes a current of 30 A. The resistance between its terminals is 1.5 Ω. Find the extra resistance to be added in series with the motor circuit to reduced the speed to 60 % of its original value. Assume that the torque produced is proportional to the cube of the speed.*

Solution : $V = 200\ V$, $I_{a1} = 30\ A$

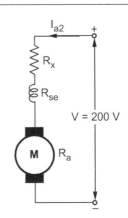

Fig. 9.29.7

Resistance across terminals $= R_a + R_{se} = 1.5\ \Omega$

$\therefore \qquad\qquad E_{b1} = V - I_{a1}\ (R_a + R_{se})$

$\qquad\qquad\qquad = 200 - 30 \times 1.5 = 155\ V$

$\qquad\qquad N_2 = 0.6\ N_1$

$\therefore \qquad\qquad \dfrac{N_1}{N_2} = \dfrac{1}{0.6}$

Use torque equation,

$\qquad T \propto \phi\ I_a \propto I_a^2 \qquad\qquad\qquad\qquad \text{... as } \phi \propto I_a$

$\therefore \qquad \dfrac{T_1}{T_2} = \left(\dfrac{I_{a1}}{I_{a2}}\right)^2 = \left(\dfrac{30}{I_{a2}}\right)^2 \qquad\qquad \text{... (9.29.1)}$

Also $T \propto N^3$ given, $\dfrac{T_1}{T_2} = \left(\dfrac{N_1}{N_2}\right)^3 = \left(\dfrac{1}{0.6}\right)^3 \qquad \text{... (9.29.2)}$

Equating (9.29.1) and (9.29.2), $\left(\dfrac{1}{0.6}\right)^3 = \left(\dfrac{30}{I_{a2}}\right)^2$

$\therefore \qquad I_{a2} = 13.9427\ A$

$\therefore \qquad E_{b2} = V - I_{a2}\ (R_a + R_{se} + R_x)$

$\qquad\qquad\quad = 200 - 13.9427\ (1.5 + R_x) \qquad\qquad \text{... (9.29.3)}$

Use speed equation, $\qquad N \propto \dfrac{E_b}{\phi} \propto \dfrac{E_b}{I_a} \qquad\qquad \text{... } \phi \propto I_a$

$\dfrac{N_1}{N_2} = \dfrac{E_{b1}}{E_{b2}} \times \dfrac{I_{a2}}{I_{a1}} \qquad \text{i.e.} \qquad \dfrac{1}{0.6} = \dfrac{155}{E_{b2}} \times \dfrac{13.9427}{30}$

$E_{b2} = 43.22\ V \qquad\qquad\qquad\qquad\qquad\qquad \text{... (9.29.4)}$

Equating (9.29.1) and (9.29.2), $\qquad 43.22 = 200 - 13.9427\ (1.5 + R_x)$

$\therefore \qquad\qquad\qquad R_x = \mathbf{9.745\ \Omega}$

Example 9.29.2 *A d.c series motor has an armature resistance of 0.5 Ω. It runs at 800 r.p.m. at 220 V with a current of 15 A. Find the speed at which it will run when connected in series with a 5 Ω resistance and taking the same current.*

Solution : $R_a = 0.5\ \Omega$, $N_1 = 800$ r.p.m., $V = 220$ V, $I_1 = 15$ A

As resistance of series field winding R_{se} is not given, neglect it. The two conditions are shown in the Fig. 9.29.8 (a) and (b).

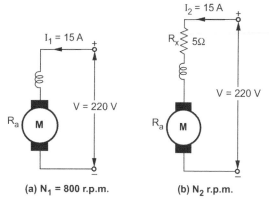

(a) $N_1 = 800$ r.p.m.   (b) N_2 r.p.m.

Fig. 9.29.8

$$E_{b1} = V - I_1 R_a = 220 - 15 \times 0.5$$

$$= 212.5\ V$$

$$E_{b2} = V - I_2 (R_a + R_x)$$

$$= 220 - 15\ (5 + 0.5) = 137.5\ V$$

$$I_{se1} = I_1 = I_{se2} = I_2 = 15\ A$$

Now $\qquad N \propto \dfrac{E_b}{\phi} \propto \dfrac{E_b}{I_{se}}$ i.e. $\dfrac{N_1}{N_2} = \dfrac{E_{b1}}{E_{b2}} \times \dfrac{I_{se2}}{I_{se1}}$

$\therefore \qquad \dfrac{800}{N_2} = \dfrac{212.5}{137.5} \times 1$ i.e. $\qquad N_2 = \mathbf{517.647\ r.p.m.}$ ... New speed of motor

Review Question

1. *Discuss the various methods of speed control of d.c. series motor.*

9.30 Losses in a D.C. Machine

The various losses in a d.c. machine whether it is a motor or a generator are classified into three groups as :

1. Copper losses   2. Iron or core losses   3. Mechanical losses

9.30.1 Copper Losses

The copper losses are the losses taking place due to the current flowing in a winding. There are basically two windings in a d.c. machine namely armature winding and field winding. The copper losses are proportional to the square of the current flowing through these windings. Thus the various copper losses can be given by,

$$\text{Armature copper loss} = I_a^2\ R_a$$

where $\qquad R_a$ = Armature winding resistance

and $\qquad I_a$ = Armature current

$$\text{Shunt field copper loss} = I_{sh}^2 \, R_{sh}$$

where $\quad R_{sh}$ = Shunt field winding resistance

and $\quad I_{sh}$ = Shunt field current

$$\text{Series field copper loss} = I_{se}^2 \, R_{se}$$

where $\quad R_{se}$ = Series field winding resistance

and $\quad I_{se}$ = Series field current

In a compound d.c. machine, both shunt and series field copper losses are present. In addition to the copper losses, there exists brush contact resistance drop. But this drop is usually included in the armature copper loss.

The power loss at the brush is obtained as the product of the voltage drop at the brush and the current passing through the brush. Hence this loss is proportional to the armature current in a d.c. machine.

$$\text{Brush contact loss} \propto I_a$$

9.30.2 Iron or Core Losses

These losses are also called magnetic losses. These losses include hysteresis loss and eddy current loss.

The hysteresis loss is proportional to the frequency and the maximum flux density B_m in the air gap.

This loss is basically due to reversal of magnetisation of the armature core.

The eddy current loss exists due to eddy currents. When armature core rotates, it cuts the magnetic flux and e.m.f. gets induced in the core. This induced e.m.f. sets up eddy currents which cause the power loss.

The hysteresis loss is minimised by selecting the core material having low hysteresis coefficient. While eddy current loss is minimised by selecting the laminated construction for the core. These losses are almost constant for the d.c. machines.

9.30.3 Mechanical Losses

These losses consist of friction and windage losses. Some power is required to overcome mechanical friction and wind resistance at the shaft. This loss is nothing but the friction and windage loss. The mechanical losses are also constant for a d.c. machine.

The magnetic and mechanical losses together are called **stray losses.**

Thus for a d.c. machine,

> Total losses = Constant losses + Variable losses

The power flow and energy transformation diagrams at various stages, which takes place in a d.c. machine are represented diagrammatically in Fig. 9.30.1 (a) and (b).

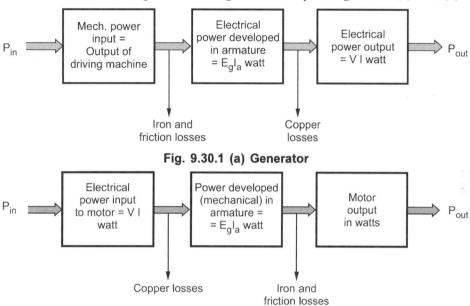

Fig. 9.30.1 (a) Generator

Fig. 9.30.1 (b) Motor

1. *Which are the various losses taking place in a d.c. machine ? Explain.*

2. *Explain the power flow diagram of generator and motor.*

9.31 Efficiencies of a D.C. Machine   2004-05

In case of a d.c. generator, following three efficiencies are defined.

i) Mechanical efficiency : It is the ratio of total power generated in armature to the total mechanical power input to the generator.

$\therefore$

$$\% \, \eta_m = \frac{E_g I_a}{P_{in} \text{ (mechanical)}} \times 100 = \frac{E_g I_a}{\text{Output of driving machine}} \times 100$$

ii) Electrical efficiency : It is the ratio of total power supplied to the load to the total power generated in armature.

$\therefore$

$$\% \, \eta_e = \frac{V_t I_L}{E_g I_a} \times 100$$

iii) Overall or commercial efficiency : This is the ratio of total power supplied to the load to the total mechanical power input to the generator. This is called efficiency of a d.c. machine which is generally obtained.

$$\therefore \quad \boxed{\% \ \eta = \frac{P_{out}}{P_{in}} \times 100 = \frac{V_t I_L}{P_{in}} \times 100}$$

It can be seen that $\% \eta = \% \eta_m \times \% \eta_e$

The overall efficiency of a generator and motor are obtained as,

$$\therefore \quad \boxed{\begin{aligned} \% \ \eta_g &= \frac{Output}{Output + Losses} \times 100 \qquad \dots \text{Generator} \\[2mm] \% \ \eta_m &= \frac{Input - Losses}{Input} \times 100 \qquad \dots \text{Motor} \end{aligned}}$$

Such three efficiencies can be defined for a d.c. motor also.

9.31.1 Condition for Maximum Efficiency

In case of a d.c. generator the output is given by,

$$P_{out} = V I$$

$$P_{Cu} = \text{Variable losses} = I_a^2 \ R_a = I^2 \ R_a$$

$$I_a = I \qquad\qquad\qquad\qquad\qquad \dots \text{neglecting shunt field current}$$

$$\therefore \quad \% \ \eta = \frac{V I}{V I + I^2 \ R_a + P_i} \times 100 = \frac{1}{1 + \left(\dfrac{I R_a}{V} + \dfrac{P_i}{V I} \right)} \times 100$$

The efficiency is maximum, when the denominator is minimum. According to maxima-minima theorem,

$$\frac{d}{d I} \left[1 + \left(\frac{I R_a}{V} + \frac{P_i}{V I} \right) \right] = 0$$

$$\therefore \quad \frac{R_a}{V} - \frac{P_i}{V I^2} = 0$$

$$\therefore \quad I^2 \ R_a - P_i = 0$$

$$\therefore \quad I^2 \ R_a = P_i = P_{Cu}$$

Thus for the maximum efficiency, the condition is,

$$\boxed{\textbf{Variable losses } = \textbf{ Constant losses}}$$

Example 9.31.1 *A 230 V d.c. shunt motor having an armature resistance of 0.5 Ω takes 3 A excluding a field current of 1 A when running on no load. Determine its efficiency taking currents as i) 30 A ii) 50 A iii) 70 A.*

Solution : No load input to motor $= V \cdot I_0 = (230)\,(3) = 690$ W

$$I_{a0} = I_0 - I_{sh} = 3 - 1 = 2 \text{ A}$$

No load armature copper loss $= I_{a0}^2 \cdot R_a = (2)^2\,(0.3) = 1.2$ W

Constant losses $=$ No load input $-$ No load armature copper loss

$$= 690 - 1.2 = 688.8 \text{ W}$$

i) $\quad I_{L1} = 30$ A, $I_{a1} = I_{L1} - I_{sh} = 30 - 1 = 29$ A

Armature copper loss $= I_{a1}^2 \cdot R_a = (29)^2\,(0.3) = 252.3$ W

Motor input $= V \cdot I_{L1} = (230)\,(30) = 6900$ W

Motor output $=$ Motor input $-$ Armature copper loss $-$ Constant losses

$$= 6900 - 252.3 - 688.8$$

$$= 5958.9 \text{ W}$$

Motor efficiency, $\eta_m = \dfrac{\text{Motor output}}{\text{Motor input}} \times 100 = \dfrac{5958.9}{6900} \times 100$

$\therefore \qquad \eta_m = \mathbf{86.36 \ \%}$

ii) $\quad I_{L2} = 50$ A; $\quad I_{a2} = I_{L2} - I_{sh} = 50 - 1 = 49$ A

Armature copper loss $= I_{a2}^2 \cdot R_a = (49)^2\,(0.3) = 720.3$ W

Motor input $= V \cdot I_{L2} = (230)\,(50) = 11500$ W

Motor output $=$ Motor input $-$ Armature copper loss $-$ Constant losses

$$= 11500 - 720.3 - 688.8$$

$$= 10090.9 \text{ W}$$

Motor efficiency, $\eta_m = \dfrac{\text{Motor output}}{\text{Motor input}} \times 100 = \dfrac{10090.9}{11500} \times 100$

$\therefore \qquad \eta_m = \mathbf{87.74 \ \%}$

iii) $\quad I_{L3} = 70$ A; $I_{a3} = I_{L3} - I_{sh} = 70 - 1 = 69$ A

Armature copper loss $= I_{a3}^2 \cdot R_a = (69)^2\,(0.3) = 1428.3$ W

Motor input $= V \cdot I_{L3} = (230)\,(70) = 16100$ W

Motor output   =   Motor input − Armature copper loss − Constant losses

$$= 16100 - 1428.3 - 688.8$$

$$= 13982.9 \text{ W}$$

Motor Efficiency, $\eta_m = \dfrac{\text{Motor Output}}{\text{Motor Input}} \times 100 = \dfrac{13982.9}{16100} \times 100$

$\therefore \qquad \eta_m = \textbf{86.85 \%}$

Example 9.31.2 *A 10 kW, 200 V, 1200 r.p.m. series d.c. generator has armature resistance of 0.1 Ω, field winding resistance of 0.3 Ω. The frictional and windage loss of the machine is 200 W and brush contact drop is 1 volt per brush. Find the efficiency of the machine and the load current at which this machine has maximum efficiency.* **2004-05, Marks 10**

Solution : $V_t = 220$ V, N = 1200 r.p.m. $R_a = 0.1$ Ω, $R_{se} = 0.3$ Ω, $V_{brush} = 1$ V/brush

$$P_{out} = 10 \text{ kW}$$

Now $\qquad P_{out} = V_t \times I_L$ i.e. $I_L = \dfrac{P_{out}}{V_t} = \dfrac{10 \times 10^3}{200} = 50$ A

$\therefore \qquad I_L = I_a = I_{se} = 50$ A $\qquad\qquad\qquad\qquad\qquad$ ... Series generator

$\therefore \qquad$ Armature copper loss $= I_a^2 \, R_a = 250$ W

$\therefore \qquad$ Field copper loss $= I_{se}^2 \, R_{se} = 750$ W

$\therefore \qquad$ Loss at brushes $= 2 \, I_a \times V_{brush} = 2 \times 50 \times 1 = 100$ W $\qquad$ ... 2 brushes

$\qquad$ Frictional losses $= 200$ W $\qquad\qquad\qquad\qquad\qquad\qquad\qquad\qquad$ ... given

$\therefore \qquad$ % $\eta = \dfrac{P_{out}}{P_{out} + \text{Total losses}} \times 100 = \dfrac{10 \times 10^3}{10 \times 10^3 + 250 + 750 + 100 + 200} \times 100$

$$= \textbf{88.49 \%}$$

Variable losses $= I_a^2 R_a + I_a^2 \, R_{se} + 2V_{brush} \, I_a$

Constant losses $= 200$ W

For η_{max}, variable and constant losses must be equal.

$\therefore \qquad 200 = I_a^2 \, [0.1 + 0.3] + 2 \, I_a$ i.e $I_a^2 + 5 \, I_a - 500 = 0$

$\therefore \qquad I_a = \textbf{20 A}$ $\qquad\qquad\qquad\qquad\qquad$ ... Neglecting negative value

This is the load current required for η_{max}.

Review Questions

1. Define : i) Electrical efficiency ii) Mechanical efficiency iii) Overall or commercial efficiency. Derive the condition for maximum efficiency.

2. A 400 V shunt motor takes 4.1 A when running light at 950 r.p.m. The armature resistance is 0.8 Ω, the total brush drop is 2 V and R_{sh} = 250 Ω. Determine full load efficiency, full load regulation and h.p. output when full load current is 50 A. Assume 5 % armature reaction.

(Ans. : 82.03 %, 5.26 %, 22.3 h.p.)

9.32 Short Answered and Objective Type Questions

Q.1 _____ motor has self load properties. 2009-10, Mark 1

(Ans. : Shunt)

Q.2 _____ motor will be preferred for elevators. 2009-10, Mark 1

(Ans. : Series)

Q.3 The back e.m.f. of DC motor is given by E_b = _____ . 2010-11, Marks 2

(Ans. : $V - I_a R_a$ (neglecting brush drop)

Q.4 The current drawn by a 120 V dc motor of armature resistance 0.4 Ω and back e.m.f. 112 V is _____ . 2008-09

Ans. : $I_a = \dfrac{V - E_b}{R_a} = \dfrac{120 - 112}{0.4} = 20 \text{ A}$

Q.5 A 4-pole lap wound d.c. generator generates 200 V at 1000 r.p.m. If this generator is now wave wound and runs at 500 r.p.m., the generated voltage will be _____. 2009-10

Ans. : P = 4, E_g = 200 V, N = 1000 r.p.m., Lap hence A = P

$\therefore$ $\quad E_g = \dfrac{\phi PNZ}{60 A}$ i.e. $200 = \dfrac{\phi \times 4 \times 1000 \times Z}{60 \times 4}$

$\therefore$ $\quad \phi Z = 12$

Now A = 2 for wave and N = 500 r.p.m.

$\therefore$ $\quad E_g = \dfrac{\phi PNZ}{60A} = \dfrac{(12)(4)(500)}{60 \times 2} = 200 \text{ V.}$

Q.6 What will happen if the back e.m.f. of d.c. motor vanishes ? 2009-10, Mark 1

Ans. : The motor will draw very high current and motor will burn.

Q.7 Explain voltage building process in self excited generator.

Ans. : The field winding has some residual magnetism. When generator rotates, small e.m.f. gets induced due to residual magnetism. This drives some current through field winding. So flux increases hence induced e.m.f. increased. The process is cumulative and finally rated voltage is available.

Q.8   Define speed regulation of d.c. motor. **(Refer section 9.19.1)**

Q.9   Why a shunt motor should not be put on with its field winding open ?

Ans. :   In shunt motor, $N \propto \dfrac{E_b}{\phi}$ If the shunt motor is started with field winding open, the flux ϕ is not zero but having very small value equal to residual flux. Due to this, the motor tries to achieve dangerously high speeds and may get damaged. To avoid high speeding action, shunt motor should not be put on with its field winding open.

Q.10   State the advantages of flux control method for controlling speed of d.c. motor.

Ans. :

1. It provides relatively smooth and easy control.

2. Speed control above rated speed is possible.

3. As the field winding resistance is high, the field current is small. Hence power loss ($I_{sh}^2 R$) in the external resistance is very small, which makes the method more economical and efficient.

4. As the field current is small, the size of the rheostat required is small.

Q.11   State the disadvantages of flux control method.

Ans. :

1. The speed control below normal rated speed is not possible as flux can be increased only upto its rated value.

2. As flux reduces, speed increases. But high speed affects the commutation making motor operation unstable. So there is limit to the maximum speed above normal, possible by this method.

Q.12   In electromechanical energy conversion _____ field is mainly used for transfer of energy.

     a) electric   b) electromechanical   c) magnetic   d) none of these

                                                                                (Ans. : c)

Q.13   The generator works on the principle of _____.

     a) statically induced e.m.f.   b) mutual induction

     c) dynamically induced e.m.f.   d) Kirchhoff's laws   **(Ans. : c)**

Q.14   The direction of induced e.m.f. in a generator is given by _____.

     a) Fleming's right hand rule   b) Right hand thumb rule

     c) Fleming's left hand rule   d) Cork screw rule.   **(Ans. : a)**

Q.15   In Fleming's right hand rule, the index finger indicates _____.

     a) E.M.F.   b) lines of flux

     c) direction of relative motion   d) current   **(Ans. : b)**

Q.16 If the angle between the plane of flux and plane of relative motion is $0°$ then the induced e.m.f. is _____.

a) zero   b) maximum   c) infinite   d) none of these

(Ans. : a)

Q.17 _____ provides mechanical support to the d.c. machine.

a) Poles   b) Armature   c) Yoke   d) Bearings **(Ans. : c)**

Q.18 Yoke is made up of _____.

a) copper   b) aluminium   c) cast steel   d) cast iron

(Ans. : d)

Q.19 Air ducts are provided in armature core to _____.

a) increase the core area   b) cool the machine
c) to accommodate the winding   d) none of these   **(Ans. : b)**

Q.20 The generation of e.m.f. takes place in _____ of a d.c. machine.

a) armature winding   b) field winding

c) pole core   d) interpoles   **(Ans. : a)**

Q.21 The brushes are made up of _____.

a) copper   b) iron   c) silver   d) carbon **(Ans. : d)**

Q.22 A. d.c. machine having _____ poles has four magnetic circuits.

a) 8   b) 2   c) 4   d) 16   **(Ans. : c)**

Q.23 The armature of a d.c. machine is laminated because _____.

a) to reduce hysteresis loss   b) to reduce eddy current loss
c) to reduce copper loss   d) to reduce mechanical loss   **(Ans. : b)**

Q.24 The basic nature of induced e.m.f. in the armature is _____.

a) pure d.c.   b) A.C.
c) rotating   d) D.C. with pulsating d.c.   **(Ans. : b)**

Q.25 The brushes are made up of soft material because _____.

a) it is easy to collect e.m.f.   b) they are rotating
c) to avoid wear and tear of commutator   d) to reduce friction losses **(Ans. : c)**

Q.26 The number of parallel paths equal to number of poles in _____ winding.

a) wave   b) distributed   c) concentrated   d) lap   **(Ans. : d)**

Q.27 In wave type winding, the number of parallel paths of armature winding is _____.

a) P   b) 2   c) 4   d) $\dfrac{P}{2}$

(Ans. : b)

Q.28 In an e.m.f. equation of a d.c. generator, Z indicates _____.

a) conductors　　　b) brushes　　　c) field turns　　d) commutator segments

(Ans. : a)

Q.29 The brush drop in d.c. machine is about _____ V/brush.

a) 2　　　　　　b) 4　　　　　　c) 1　　　　　　d) zero　　**(Ans. : c)**

Q.30 _____ number of conductors constitute one turn.

a) 2　　　　　　b) 4　　　　　　c) 1　　　　　　d) zero　　**(Ans. : a)**

Q.31 The function of commutator is _____.

a) collection of voltage　　　　　　b) production of flux

c) production of torque　　　　　　d) convert a.c. e.m.f. to d.c.　　**(Ans. : d)**

Q.32 Practically number of commutator segments is _____.

a) more than field coils　　　　　　b) less than armature coils

c) equal to armature coils　　　　　d) less than field coils　　**(Ans. : d)**

Q.33 In a separately excited d.c. generator _____ is not necessary.

a) armature　　　b) residual magnetism　　c) field flux　　　d) rotor　**(Ans. : b)**

Q.34 In a shunt generator, which of the following relations is true ?

a) $I_a = I_L + I_{sh}$　　　b) $I_L = I_a + I_{sh}$　　　c) $I_L - I_a = I_{sh}$　　　d) $I_L + I_a + I_{sh} = 0$

(Ans. : a)

Q.35 When the fluxes produced by series and shunt field windings help each other, the compound generator is called _____.

a) differential compound　　　　　　b) long shunt compound

c) cumulatively compound　　　　　　d) short shunt compound　　**(Ans. : c)**

Q.36 Which is the cause of failure to excite self excited generator ?

a) Absence of residual flux　　　　　b) Wrong field connections

c) Driven in opposite direction　　　d) All of the above　　**(Ans. : d)**

Q.37 Which graph of the following is called external characteristics of a d.c. generator ?

a) E_g Vs I_L　　　b) V_t Vs I_L　　　c) E_g Vs I_{sh}　　　d) E_g Vs V_t

(Ans. : b)

Q.38 Which graph of the following is called internal characteristics of a d.c. generator ?

a) E_g Vs I_L　　　b) V_t Vs I_L　　　c) E_g Vs I_{sh}　　　d) E_g Vs V_t

(Ans. : a)

Q.39 To control the flux in separately excited generator _____ is used.

a) three point starter　　　　　　b) four point starter

c) commutator　　　　　　　　　d) field regulator　　**(Ans. : d)**

Q.40 The internal characteristics of d.c. series generator is _____.

a) drooping nature
b) straight line parallel to x-axis
c) rising nature
d) straight line parallel to y-axis **(Ans. : c)**

Q.41 In level compounded d.c. generator, the no load voltage is _____ that of full load voltage.

a) greater than   b) same as   c) less than   d) none of these
(Ans. : b)

Q.42 _____ generator is used for boosters on d.c. feeders.

a) D.C. series
b) D.C shunt
c) Cumulatively compound
d) None of these   **(Ans. : a)**

Q.43 _____ generator is used for battery charging.

a) D.C. series
b) D.C shunt
c) Cumulatively compound
d) None of these   **(Ans. : b)**

Q.44 The bearings used to support the rotor shaft are _____.

a) bush bearings
b) roller bearings
c) magnetic bearings
d) ball bearings   **(Ans. : d)**

Q.45 If B is the flux density, l is active length of conductor and v is velocity of conductor, then induced e.m.f. is given by, _____.

a) $E = Bl^2v$ b) $E = B^2lv$ c) $E = Blv$ d) $E = Blv^2$ **(Ans. : c)**

Q.46 In generators, lap winding is preferred for _____.

a) low voltage, low current
b) low voltage, high current
c) high voltage, low current
d) high voltage, high current   **(Ans. : b)**

Q.47 In generators, wave winding is preferred for _____.

a) low voltage, low current
b) low voltage, high current
c) high voltage, low current
d) high voltage, high current   **(Ans. : c)**

Q.48 In a d.c. generator, if speed of prime mover is halved and flux per pole is doubled, the induced e.m.f. will _____.

a) remain constant
b) increase by 2 times
c) increase by 4 times
d) none of these   **(Ans. : a)**

Q.49 The direction of force in a motoring action is determined by _____.

a) Fleming's right hand rule
b) end rule
c) Fleming's left hand rule
d) right hand thumb rule   **(Ans. : c)**

Q.50 In Fleming's left hand rule, the middle finger indicates _____.

a) direction of rotation
b) direction of current
c) direction of flux
d) direction of force   **(Ans. : b)**

Q.51 The back e.m.f. in a motor is due to _____ .

     a) generating action   b) motoring action

     c) reverse action   d) none of these   **(Ans. : a)**

Q.52 In a 240 V d.c. motor, the back e.m.f. is 220 V and $R_a = 0.5 \ \Omega$ then its armature current is _____ .

     a) 20 A   b) 10 A   c) 80 A   d) 40 A   **(Ans. : d)**

Q.53 An electrical equivalent of gross mechanical power developed in a d.c. motor is _____ .

     a) VI_L b) $E_b I_L$ c) $E_b I_a$ d) $E_b I_{sh}$ **(Ans. : c)**

Q.54 The condition for maximum power developed in a d.c. motor is _____ .

     a) $E_b = V$ b) $E_b = 0.5 \ V$ c) $V = 0.5 \ E_b$ d) $E_b = \sqrt{V}$ **(Ans. : b)**

Q.55 A 4 pole d.c. motor has lap winding with 360 conductors. It takes armature current of 20 A and flux is 10 mWb. It develops gross torque of _____ .

     a) 11.44 Nm   b) 1.44 Nm   c) 8 Nm   d) 5.4 Nm **(Ans. : a)**

Q.56 As the speed of a d.c. motor increases, the armature current _____ .

     a) increases   b) decreases   c) remains same   d) none of these

                                                                       (Ans. : b)

Q.57 The armature torque is _____ that of shaft torque.

     a) less than   b) same as   c) greater than   d) none of these

                                                                       (Ans. : c)

Q.58 The no load power drawn by a d.c. motor is used to overcome _____ losses.

     a) constant   b) variable   c) copper   d) friction **(Ans. : a)**

Q.59 The speed of a d.c. motor is _____ .

     a) directly proportional to E_b b) directly proportional to I_a

     c) inversely proportional to flux   d) inversely proportional to R_a **(Ans. : c)**

Q.60 _____ motor has constant speed characteristics.

     a) D.C. series   b) D.C. compound   c) D.C. shunt   d) None of these

                                                                       (Ans. : c)

Q.61 _____ motor cannot be started on no load.

     a) D.C. series   b) D.C. compound   c) D.C. shunt   d) None of these

                                                                       (Ans. : a)

Q.62 _____ motor has best speed regulation.

     a) D.C. series   b) D.C. compound   c) D.C. shunt   d) None of these

                                                                       (Ans. : c)

Q.63 _____ motor is used for rolling mills.

     a) D.C. series   b) D.C. compound   c) D.C. shunt   d) None of these

                                                                       (Ans. : b)

Q.64 When constant speed and medium starting torque is necessary, _____ motor is used.

     a) D.C. series   b) D.C. compound   c) D.C. shunt   d) None of these

                                                                               (Ans. : c)

Q.65 As load current increases, the speed of _____ motor increases.

     a) shunt   b) cumulative compound

     c) series   d) differential compound   **(Ans. : d)**

Q.66 _____ motor is not suitable for any practical application.

     a) Shunt   b) Cumulative compound

     c) Series   d) Differential compound   **(Ans. : d)**

Q.67 When the motor carries the rated field current at the rated voltage then its speed is _____.

     a) full load   b) no load   c) rated   d) none of these

                                                                               (Ans. : c)

Q.68 _____ method is used to control the speed above rated.

     a) Rheostatic control   b) Flux control

     c) Armature diverter   d) None of these   **(Ans. : b)**

Q.69 Easy and smooth speed control below rated is possible by _____ method of speed control.

     a) rheostatic control   b) flux control

     c) armature diverter   d) none of these   **(Ans. : a)**

Q.70 Large power losses is the disadvantage of _____ method of speed control.

     a) rheostatic control   b) flux control

     c) armature diverter   d) none of these   **(Ans. : a)**

Q.71 _____ method of speed control is commonly used for electric traction.

     a) Field diverter   b) Armature diverter

     c) Tapped field   d) Series-parallel grouping   **(Ans. : c)**

Q.72 Condition for maximum efficiency for a d.c. motor is _____.

     a) constant losses greater than variable losses

     b) constant losses less than variable losses

     c) friction losses equal to iron losses

     d) constant losses equal to variable losses   **(Ans. : d)**

Q.73 Which of the following application requires very high starting torque ?

     a) Air blower   b) Locomotive   c) Lathe machine   d) Fan   **(Ans. : b)**

Q.74 The speed of d.c. motor falls from 1500 r.p.m. to 1425 r.p.m. from no load to full load then its speed regulation is _____.

     a) 2.263 %   b) 1.263 %   c) 5.263 %   d) 10.263 %**(Ans. : c)**

Q.75 Which of the following graphs represents efficiency of a motor ? **(Ans. : d)**

(a)   (b)   (c)   (d)

Q.76 If the field of a d.c. shunt motor is opened while running then _____.

a) speed will reduce   b) speed will be dangerously high

c) motor will stop   d) motor will run as it is   **(Ans. : b)**

Q.77 If the back e.m.f. of a d.c. motor gets vanished suddenly during running then _____.

a) armature will burn   b) field will burn

c) motor will stop   d) motor will make noise   **(Ans. : a)**

Q.78 Residual magnetism is necessary in a d.c. _____.

a) shunt generator   b) separately excited generator

c) shunt motor   d) series motor.   **(Ans. : a)**

Q.79 The field winding of _____ generator has thin wire of large number of turns.

a) series   b) shunt   c) compound   d) none of these
(Ans. : b)

Q.80 The field winding of _____ generator has thick wire of less number of turns.

a) series   b) shunt   c) compound   d) none of these
(Ans. : a)

Q.81 The back e.m.f. of a motor at the moment of starting is _____.

a) zero   b) maximum   c) low   d) optimum.
(Ans. : a)

Q.82 The relationship between the applied voltage and back e.m.f. in D.C. motors is _____ .

a) $V = E_b + I_a R_a$ b) $V = E_b - I_a R_a$ c) $V = E_b$ d) none of these.
(Ans. : a)

Q.83 Which D.C. motor will be preferred for constant speed line shafting ?

a) Cumulatively compound motor   b) Differentially compound motor

c) Shunt motor   d) Series motor.   **(Ans. : c)**

Q.84 The speed of a d.c. shunt motor _____ from no load to full load.

a) falls slightly   b) improves slightly

c) remains unchanged   d) falls rapidly.   **(Ans. : a)**

□□□

10 Three Phase Induction Motor

Syllabus

Types, Principle of operation, Slip-torque characteristics, Applications (Numerical problems related to slip only).

Contents

10.1 Introduction

An electric motor which operates on a.c. supply is called a.c. motor. As a.c. supply is commonly available, the a.c. motors are very popularly used in practice. The a.c. motors are classified as single and three phase induction motors, synchronous motors and some special purpose motors.

Out of all these types, three phase induction motors are widely used for various industrial applications. The important advantages of three phase induction motors over other types are self starting property, no need of starting device, higher power factor, good speed regulation and robust construction.

10.2 Rotating Magnetic Field

Three phase induction motor works on the principle of rotating magnetic field (R.M.F.). The rotating magnetic field can be defined as the field or flux having constant amplitude but whose axis is continuously rotating in a plane with a certain speed.

In three phase induction motors such a rotating magnetic field is produced by supplying currents to a set of three phase **stationary** windings, with the help of three phase a.c. supply. The current carrying windings produce the magnetic field or flux. The three phase stator winding produces three alternating fluxes which are seperated from each other by 120°.

Due to interaction of three fluxes produced due to three phase supply, resultant flux has a constant magnitude and its axis rotating in space, without physically rotating the windings.

Thus when stationary three phase winding is excited by a three phase supply then,

a) The resultant of the three alternating fluxes, separated from each other by 120°, has a constant amplitude of 1.5 ϕ_m where ϕ_m is maximum amplitude of an individual flux due to any phase.

b) The resultant always keeps on rotating with a certain speed in space.

Such a magnetic field is called **rotating magnetic field.**

There exists a fixed relation between frequency f of a.c. supply to the windings, the number of poles P for which winding is wound and speed N r.p.m. of rotating magnetic field. For a standard frequency whatever speed of R.M.F. results is called **synchronous speed**, in case of induction motors. It is denoted as N_s.

∴
$$N_s = \frac{120f}{P} = \textbf{Speed of R.M.F.}$$

where   f = Supply frequency in Hz

             P = Number of poles for which winding is wound.

The direction of rotating magnetic field depends on the phase sequence of the three phase supply.

> By interchanging any two terminals of three phase winding while connecting it to three phase a.c. supply, direction of rotation of R.M.F. gets reversed.

Thus by changing the supply phase sequence, the direction of three phase induction motor can be reversed.

The detail theory of production of rotating magnetic field is included in the appendix A.

Review Question

> 1. *What is rotating magnetic field ? What is the speed of rotating magnetic field ?*

10.3 Construction

Basically, the induction motor consists of two main parts, namely

1.   The part i.e. three phase windings, which is stationary called **stator**.

2.   The part which rotates and is connected to the mechanical load through shaft called **rotor**.

The conversion of electrical power to mechanical power takes place in a rotor. Hence rotor develops a driving torque and rotates.

10.3.1 Stator

Discuss the construction of stator of three phase induction motor. The stator has a laminated type of construction made up of stampings which are 0.4 to 0.5 mm thick.

The stampings are slotted on its periphery to carry the stator winding. The stampings are insulated from each other. Such a construction essentially keeps the iron losses to a minimum value. The number of stampings are stamped together to build the stator core. The built up core is then fitted in a casted or fabricated steel frame. The choice of material for the stampings is generally silicon steel, which minimises the hysteresis loss.

The slots on the periphery of the stator core carries a **three phase winding**, connected either in star or delta. This three phase winding is called **stator winding**. It is wound for definite number of poles. The radial ducts are provided for the cooling purpose. The Fig. 10.3.1 shows a stator lamination.

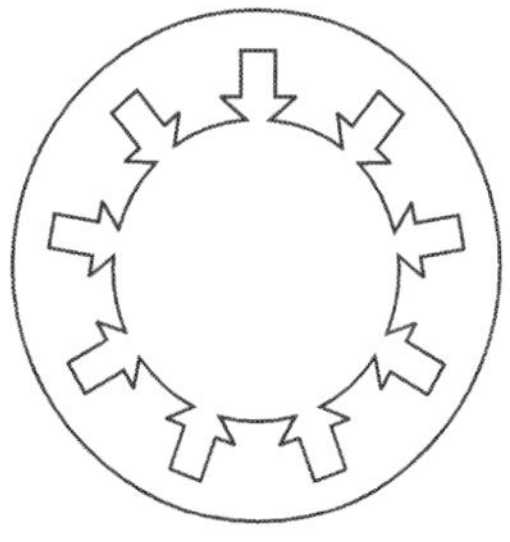

Fig. 10.3.1 Stator lamination

10.3.2 Rotor

The rotor is placed inside the stator. The air gap between stator and the rotor is 0.4 mm to 4 mm. The two types of rotor constructions which are used for induction motors are,

    1. Squirrel cage rotor   and   2. Slip ring or phase wound rotor

1. Squirrel Cage Rotor

The rotor core is cylindrical and slotted on its periphery. The rotor consists of uninsulated copper or aluminium bars called rotor conductors. The bars are placed in the slots.

These bars are permanently shorted at each end with the help of conducting copper ring called **end ring**. The bars are usually brazed to the end rings to provide good mechanical strength.

The entire structure looks like a cage, forming a closed electrical circuit. So the rotor is called squirrel cage rotor. The construction is shown in the Fig. 10.3.2. As the bars are permanently shorted to each other through end ring, the entire rotor resistance is very very small. Hence this rotor is also called **short circuited rotor**.

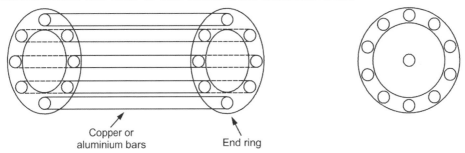

Copper or aluminium bars   End ring

(a) Cage type structure of rotor   **(b) Symbolic representation**

Fig. 10.3.2 Squirrel cage rotor

As rotor itself is short circuited, no external resistance can have any effect on the rotor resistance. Hence no external resistance can be introduced in the rotor circuit. So slip ring and brush assembly is not required for this rotor. Hence the construction of this rotor is very simple.

Fan blades are generally provided at the ends of the rotor core. This circulates the air through the machine while operation, providing the necessary cooling. In this type of rotor, the slots are not arranged parallel to the shaft axis but are skewed as shown in the Fig. 10.3.3.

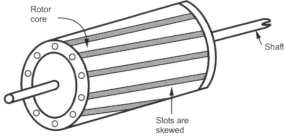

Fig. 10.3.3 Skewing in rotor construction

The **advantages of skewing** are,

1. A magnetic hum i.e. noise gets reduced due to skewing hence skewing makes the motor operation quiter.

2. It makes the motor operation smooth.

3. The stator and rotor teeth may get magnetically locked. Such a tendency of magnetic locking gets reduced due to skewing.

4. It increases the effective transformation ratio between stator and rotor.

2. Slip Ring Rotor or Phase Wound Rotor

In this type of construction, rotor winding is exactly similar to the stator. The rotor carries a three phase star or delta connected, distributed winding, wound for same number of poles as that of stator.

The rotor construction is laminated and slotted. The slots contain the rotor winding.

The three ends of three phase winding, available after connecting the winding in star or delta, are permanently connected to the slip rings.

With the help of slip rings, the external resistances can be added in series with each phase of the rotor winding. This arrangement is shown in the Fig. 10.3.4.

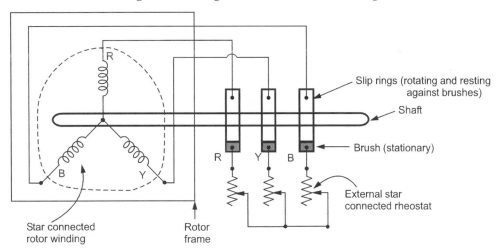

Fig. 10.3.4 Slip rings or wound rotor

> This way the value of rotor resistance per phase can be controlled. This helps us to control some of the important characteristics of the motor like starting torque, speed etc.

In the running condition, the slip rings are shorted. The possibility of addition of an external resistance in series with the rotor, with the help of slip rings is the main feature of this type of rotor.

10.3.3 Comparison of Squirrel Cage and Wound Rotor

Sr. No.	Wound or slip ring rotor	Squirrel cage rotor
1.	Rotor consists of a three phase winding similar to the stator winding.	Rotor consists of bars which are shorted at the ends with the help of end rings.
2.	Construction is complicated.	Construction is very simple.
3.	Resistance can be added externally.	As permanently shorted, external resistance cannot be added.
4.	Slip rings and brushes are present to add external resistance.	Slip rings and brushes are absent.
5.	The construction is delicate and due to brushes, frequent maintenance is necessary.	The construction is robust and maintenance free.
6.	The rotors are very costly.	Due to simple construction, the rotors are cheap.
7.	Only 5 % of induction motors in industry use slip ring rotor.	Very common and almost 95 % induction motors use this type of rotor.
8.	High starting torque can be obtained.	Moderate starting torque which cannot be controlled.
9.	Rotor resistance starter can be used.	Rotor resistance starter cannot be used.
10.	Rotor must be wound for the same number of poles as that of stator.	The rotor automatically adjusts itself for the same number of poles as that of stator.
11.	Speed control by rotor resistance is possible.	Speed control by rotor resistance is not possible.
12.	Rotor copper losses are high hence efficiency is less.	Rotor copper losses are less hence have higher efficiency.
13.	Used for lifts, hoists, cranes, elevators, compressors etc.	Used for lathes, drilling machines, fans, blowers, water pumps, grinders, printing machines etc.

Review Questions

1. *Discuss the construction of stator of three phase induction motor.*
2. *Discuss the important features of squirrel cage and phase wound rotor constructions in an induction motor.*
3. *State the advantages of skewing.*
4. *Compare squirrel cage and phase wound type of rotors.*

10.4 Working Principle   2001-02, 2003-04, 2011-12

Induction motor works on the principle of electromagnetic induction. When a three phase supply is given to the three phase stator winding, a rotating magnetic field of constant magnitude is produced. The speed of this rotating magnetic field is synchronous speed, N_s r.p.m.

$$N_s = \frac{120\ f}{P} = \text{Speed of rotating magnetic field.}$$

This rotating field produces an effect of rotating poles around a rotor. Let direction of rotation of this rotating magnetic field is **clockwise** as shown in the Fig. 10.4.1 (a).

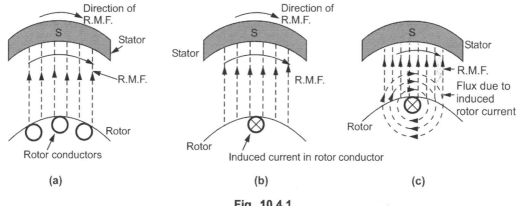

Fig. 10.4.1

Now at this instant rotor is **stationary** and stator flux R.M.F. is **rotating**. So its obvious that there exists a relative motion between the R.M.F. and rotor conductors. Whenever conductor cuts the flux, e.m.f. gets induced in it. So e.m.f. gets induced in the rotor conductors called **rotor induced e.m.f.** This is electro-magnetic induction.

As rotor forms closed circuit, induced e.m.f. circulates current through rotor called **rotor current** as shown in the Fig. 10.4.1 (b). Let direction of this current is going into the paper denoted by a cross as shown in the Fig. 10.4.1 (b). Any current carrying conductor produces its own flux. So rotor produces its flux called **rotor flux**. For assumed direction of rotor current, the direction of rotor flux is clockwise as shown in the Fig. 10.4.1 (c). Both the fluxes interact with each as shown in the Fig. 10.4.1 (d).

On left of rotor conductor, two fluxes are in same direction hence add up to get high flux area. On right side, two fluxes cancel each other to produce low flux area.

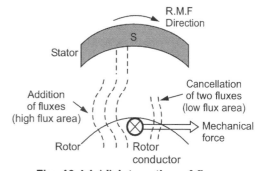

Fig. 10.4.1 (d) Interaction of fluxes

As flux lines act as stretched rubber band, high flux density area exerts a push on rotor conductor towards low flux density area. So rotor conductor experiences a force from left to right in this case, as shown in the Fig. 10.4.1 (d), due to **interaction of the two fluxes**. As all the rotor conductors experience a force, the overall rotor experiences a torque and starts rotating. So **interaction of the two fluxes is very essential for a motoring action**.

According to Lenz's law the direction of induced current in the rotor is so as to oppose the cause producing it. The cause of rotor current is the induced e.m.f. which is induced because of relative motion present between the rotating magnetic field and the rotor conductors. Hence to oppose the relative motion i.e. to reduce the relative speed, the rotor experiences a torque in the same direction as that of R.M.F. and tries to catch up the speed of rotating magnetic field.

N_s = Speed of rotating magnetic field in r.p.m.   N = Speed of rotor i.e. motor in r.p.m.

$N_s - N$ = Relative speed between the two, rotating magnetic field and the rotor

Thus rotor always rotates in same direction as that of R.M.F.

10.4.1 Can N = N$_s$?

When rotor starts rotating, it tries to catch the speed of rotating magnetic field. If it catches the speed of the rotating magnetic field, the relative motion between rotor and the rotating magnetic field will vanish ($N_s - N = 0$).

In fact the relative motion is the main cause for the induced e.m.f. in the rotor. So induced e.m.f. will vanish and hence there cannot be rotor current and the rotor flux which is essential to produce the torque on the rotor. Eventually motor will stop. But immediately there will exist a relative motion between rotor and rotating magnetic field and it will start. But due to inertia of rotor, this does not happen in practice and rotor continues to rotate with a speed slightly less than the synchronous speed of the rotating magnetic field in the steady state.

The **induction motor never rotates at synchronous speed**. The speed at which it rotates is hence called **subsynchronous speed** and motor sometimes called **asynchronous motor**.

∴ $N < N_s$

So it can be said that rotor slips behind the rotating magnetic field produced by stator. The difference between the two is called **slip speed** of the motor.

$N_s - N$ = Slip speed of the motor in r.p.m.

This speed decides the magnitude of the induced e.m.f. and the rotor current, which in turn decides the torque produced.

10.4.2 Slip of Induction Motor

The slip speed ($N_s - N$) is generally expressed as the percentage of the synchronous speed. Slip of the induction motor is defined as the difference between the synchronous speed (N_s) and actual speed of rotor i.e. motor (N) expressed as a fraction of the synchronous speed (N_s). This is also called **absolute slip or fractional slip and is denoted as 's'.**

Thus

$$s = \frac{N_s - N}{N_s}$$

... (Absolute slip)

The percentage slip is expressed as,

$$\% \; s = \frac{N_s - N}{N_s} \times 100$$

... (Percentage slip)

In terms of slip, the actual speed of motor (N) can be expressed as,

$$N = N_s \, (1 - s)$$

... (From the expression of slip)

At start, motor is at rest and hence its speed N is zero.

$\therefore$

$$s = 1 \text{ at start}$$

This is maximum value of slip s possible for induction motor which occurs at start. While s = 0 gives us $N = N_s$ which is not possible for an induction motor. So **slip of induction motor cannot be zero** under any circumstances. Practically motor operates in the slip range of 0.01 to 0.05 i.e. 1 % to 5 %. The slip corresponding to full load speed of the motor is called **full load slip.**

Example 10.4.1 *A 3 phase, 50 Hz, 6 pole induction motor has a full load percentage slip of 3 %. Find i) Synchronous speed and ii) Actual speed.*

Solution : f = 50 Hz, P = 6, s = 3 % = 0.03.

i)
$$N_s = \frac{120 \; f}{P} = \frac{120 \times 50}{6} = \textbf{1000 r.p.m.}$$
... Synchronous speed

ii)
$$\% \; s = \frac{N_s - N}{N_s} \times 100$$

i.e.
$$N = N_s \, (1 - s) = 1000 \, (1 - 0.03) = \textbf{970 r.p.m.}$$
... Actual speed

Example 10.4.2 *A 6 pole induction motor is supplied by a 10 pole alternator which is driven at 600 r.p.m. If the motor is running at 970 r.p.m., determine the percentage slip.*

Solution : For alternator, $N_s = \dfrac{120\,f}{P_A}$

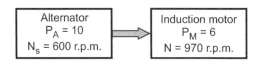

$\therefore \qquad f = \dfrac{600 \times 10}{120} = 50 \text{ Hz}$

For induction motor,

$$N_s = \dfrac{120\,f}{P} = \dfrac{120 \times 50}{6} = 1000 \text{ r.p.m.}$$

$\therefore \qquad \% \, s = \dfrac{N_s - N}{N_s} \times 100 = \dfrac{1000 - 970}{1000} \times 100 = \mathbf{3\ \%}$

Example 10.4.3 *A 12-pole, 3-phase alternator driven at a speed of 500 r.p.m. supplies power to an 8-pole, 3-phase induction motor. If the slip of the motor is 0.03 p.u., calculate its speed.* **2001-02, Marks 5**

Solution : $\quad P_A = 12, \quad N_s = 500 \text{ r.p.m.}, \quad P_M = 8, \quad s = 0.03$

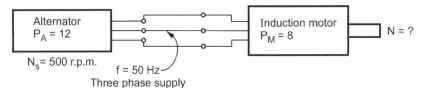

Fig. 10.4.2

For alternator, $\quad N_s = \dfrac{120\,f}{P_A} \quad$ i.e. $\quad 500 = \dfrac{120\,f}{12}$

$\therefore \qquad f = 50 \text{ Hz}$

For induction motor,

$$N_s = \dfrac{120\,f}{P_M} = \dfrac{120 \times 50}{8} = 750 \text{ r.p.m.}$$

$\therefore \qquad N = N_s(1 - s) = 750\,(1 - 0.03) = \mathbf{727.5\ r.p.m.}$

Example 10.4.4 *A 3 phase, 4 pole, 50 Hz, induction motor runs at 1460 r.p.m. Determine its percentage slip.* **2003-04, Marks 5**

Solution : $\qquad P = 4, \quad N = 1460 \text{ r.p.m.}, \quad f = 50 \text{ Hz}$

$$N_s = \dfrac{120\,f}{P} = \dfrac{120 \times 50}{4} = 1500 \text{ r.p.m.}$$

$$s = \dfrac{N_s - N}{N_s} \times 100 = \dfrac{1500 - 1460}{1500} \times 100 = \mathbf{2.667\ \%}$$

Review Questions

1. *Explain the working principle of three phase induction motor.*   **2011-12, Marks 5**

2. *What is the direction of rotation of rotor ?*

3. *Why induction motor can not run at synchronous speed ?*

4. *Explain synchronous speed, slip speed and motor speed in case of three phase induction motor. Why slip is never zero in an induction motor ?*

5. *A 4 pole, 3 phase induction motor is supplied from 50 Hz supply. Determine its synchronous speed. On full load, its speed is observed to be 1410 r.p.m. Calculate its full load slip.* **(Ans. : 6 %)**

6. *A 4 pole, 3 phase, 50 Hz, star connected induction motor has a full load slip of 4 %. Calculate full load speed of the motor.* **(Ans. : 1440 rpm)**

7. *Define slip of induction motor.*   **2011-12, Marks 2**

10.5 Effect of Slip on the Rotor Frequency   **2000-01, 2002-03, 2005-06, 2006-07, 2008-09, 2009-10**

In case of induction motor, the speed of rotating magnetic field is,

$$N_s = \frac{120\, f}{P} \qquad \qquad \ldots (10.5.1)$$

At start when N = 0, s = 1 and stationary rotor has maximum relative motion with respect to R.M.F. Hence maximum e.m.f. gets induced in the rotor at start. **The frequency of this induced e.m.f. at start is same as that of supply frequency.**

As motor actually rotates with speed N, the relative speed of rotor with respect R.M.F. decreases and becomes equal to slip speed of $N_s - N$. The induced e.m.f. in rotor depends on rate of cutting flux i.e. relative speed $N_s - N$.

Hence in running condition magnitude of induced e.m.f. decreases so as its frequency. The **rotor is wound for same number of poles as that of stator i.e. P.**

If f_r is the frequency of rotor induced e.m.f. and rotor currents, in running condition at slip speed $N_s - N$ then there exists a fixed relation between $(N_s - N)$, f_r and P similar to equation (10.5.1). So we can write for rotor in running condition,

$$(N_s - N) = \frac{120\, f_r}{P}, \text{ Rotor poles = Stator pole = P} \qquad \ldots (10.5.2)$$

Dividing equation (10.5.2) by equation (10.5.1) we get,

$$\frac{N_s - N}{N_s} = \frac{(120 f_r / P)}{(120 f / P)} \quad \text{but} \quad \frac{N_s - N}{N_s} = \text{Slip s} \quad \text{i.e.} \quad s = \frac{f_r}{f}$$

$$\therefore \qquad \boxed{f_r = s\, f}$$

Thus frequency of rotor induced e.m.f. in running condition (f_r) is slip times the supply frequency (f).

As slip of the induction motor is in the range 0.01 to 0.05, rotor frequency is very small inthe running condition.

Example 10.5.1 *A 3-phase, 4-pole induction motor is supplied from 3-phase, 50 Hz a.c. supply. Calculate : i) The synchronous speed, ii) The rotor speed when slip is 4% iii) The rotor frequency when rotor runs at 600 r.p.m.* **2005-06, Marks 5**

Solution : P = 4, f = 50 Hz, s = 4 % = 0.04

i) $N_s = \dfrac{120f}{P} = \dfrac{120 \times 50}{4} = \textbf{1500 r.p.m.}$

ii) $N = N_s (1 - s) = 1500 \times (1 - 0.04) = \textbf{1440 r.p.m.}$

iii) $f_r = sf = 50 \times 0.04 = \textbf{2 Hz}$

Example 10.5.2 *In a three-phase slip-ring, four-pole induction motor, the rotor frequency is found to be 2.0 Hz, while connected to a 400 V, 3-phase, 50 Hz supply. Determine motor-speed in r.p.m.* **2002-03, Marks 5**

Solution : P = 4, $f_r = 2$ Hz, f = 50 Hz

$$f_r = sf \qquad \text{i.e. } s = \frac{f_r}{f} = \frac{2}{50} = \textbf{0.04}$$

∴ $N = N_s (1 - s)$ where $N_s = \dfrac{120\, f}{P} = 1500$ r.p.m.

∴ $N = 1500 \times (1 - 0.04) = \textbf{1440 r.p.m.}$

Example 10.5.3 *A 3-phase, 50 Hz induction motor has 6 poles and operates with a slip of 5 % at a certain load. Determine, i) The speed of the rotor with respect to the stator. ii) The frequency of rotor current. iii) The speed of the rotor magnetic field with respect to the rotor. iv) The speed of rotor magnetic field with respect to the stator.* **2000-01, Marks 5**

Solution : f = 50 Hz, s = 0.05, P = 6

∴ $N_s = \dfrac{120\, f}{P} = \dfrac{120 \times 50}{6} = 1000$ r.p.m.

i) $N = N_s (1 - s) = 1000 \times (1 - 0.05) = \textbf{950 r.p.m.}$

ii) $f_r = sf = 0.05 \times 50 = \textbf{2.5 Hz}$

iii) Speed of rotor magnetic field with respect to rotor

$$= \text{Slip speed} = 1000 - 950 = \textbf{50 r.p.m.}$$

iv) Speed of rotor magnetic field with respect to stator

$$= N_s = \textbf{1000 r.p.m.}$$

Example 10.5.4 *A three phase slip ring, 4 pole induction motor has rotor frequency 2.0 Hz while connected to 400 V, 3 phase, 50 Hz supply. Determine slip and rotor speed.*

2006-07, Marks 5

Solution : $P = 4$, $f_r = 2$ Hz, $V_L = 400$ V, $f = 50$ Hz

For an induction motor,

$$f_r = sf \quad \text{i.e.} \quad 2 = s \times 50$$

$\therefore \qquad s = \dfrac{2}{50} = 0.04 = \textbf{4 \%} \qquad\qquad\qquad\qquad\qquad$ `... Slip

$$N_s = \dfrac{120\,f}{P} = \dfrac{120 \times 50}{4} = 1500 \text{ r.p.m.}$$

$\therefore \qquad N = N_s (1 - s) = 1500 (1 - 0.04) = \textbf{1440 r.p.m.} \qquad$ ... Rotor speed

Example 10.5.5 *A 4-pole, 3-phase induction motor is energized from a 60 Hz supply, and is running at a load condition for which the slip is 0.03. Determine : a) Rotor speed, in r.p.m. b) Rotor current frequency, in Hz c) Speed of the rotor's rotating magnetic field with respect to the stator frame, in r.p.m.* 2008-09, Marks 10

Solution : $P = 4$, $f = 60$ Hz, $s = 0.03$

$$N_s = \dfrac{120\,f}{P} = \dfrac{120 \times 60}{4} = 1800 \text{ r.p.m.}$$

a) $\quad N = N_s (1 - s) = 1800 (1 - 0.03) = \textbf{1746 r.p.m.} \qquad$ ... Rotor speed

b) $\quad f_r = sf = 0.03 \times 60 = \textbf{1.8 Hz} \qquad\qquad\qquad$ ... Rotor frequency

c) The speed of the rotor's magnetic field with respect to stator frame is 1800 r.p.m.

Example 10.5.6 *A three phase, 50 Hz induction motor has a full load speed of 960 r.p.m. Calculate i) Slip ii) Frequency of rotor induced e.m.f. iii) Number of poles iv) Speed of rotor field with respect to rotor structure v) Speed of rotor field with respect to stator field.* 2009-10, Marks 10

Solution : The induction motor runs at a speed which is just below the synchronous speed. Hence synchronous speed close to 960 r.p.m. is 1000 r.p.m. Hence $N_s = 1000$ r.p.m.

i) $\quad \% \, s = \dfrac{N_s - N}{N_s} \times 100 = \dfrac{1000 - 960}{1000} \times 100 = \textbf{4 \%}$

ii) $\quad f_r = sf = 0.04 \times 50 = \textbf{2 Hz}$

iii) $\quad N_s = \dfrac{120 f}{P} \quad \text{i.e.} \quad 1000 = \dfrac{120 \times 50}{P}$

$\therefore \qquad \textbf{P = 6}$

iv) Speed of rotor field w.r.t. rotor structure $= \dfrac{120 f_r}{P} = \dfrac{120 \times 2}{6} = $ **40 r.p.m.**

v) Both stator and rotor fields are rotating at N_s with respect to stator structure hence speed of the rotor field with respect to stator field is zero.

Review Questions

1. *Explain the effect of slip on the rotor frequency.*

2. *A 4 pole, 3 phase, 50 Hz induction motor runs at a speed of 1470 r.p.m. speed. Find the frequency of the induced e.m.f. in the rotor under this condition.* **(Ans. : 1 Hz)**

3. *A 8 pole, three phase induction motor is supplied from 50 Hz, a.c. supply. On full load, the frequency of induced e.m.f. in rotor is 2 Hz. Find the full load slip and the corresponding speed.* **(Ans. : 4 %, 720 rpm)**

10.6 Effect of Slip on other Rotor Parameters

As the rotor frequency in running condition is slip times supply frequency, it affects other rotor parameters such as induced e.m.f., rotor reactance, rotor current and rotor power factor.

10.6.1 Effect on Magnitude of Rotor Induced E.M.F.

We have seen that when rotor is standstill, s = 1, relative speed is maximum and maximum e.m.f. gets induced in the rotor. Let this e.m.f. be,

E_2 = Rotor induced e.m.f. per phase on standstill condition

As rotor gains speed, the relative speed between rotor and rotating magnetic field decreases and hence induced e.m.f. in rotor also decreases as it is proportional to the relative speed $N_s - N$. Let this e.m.f. be,

E_{2r} = Rotor induced e.m.f. per phase in running condition

Now $E_2 \propto N_s$ while $E_{2r} \propto N_s - N$

Dividing the two proportionality equations,

$$\frac{E_{2r}}{E_2} = \frac{N_s - N}{N_s} \qquad \text{But } \frac{N_s - N}{N_s} = \text{Slip s}$$

$\therefore \qquad \dfrac{E_{2r}}{E_2} = s$

$\therefore \qquad \boxed{E_{2r} = s\, E_2}$

The magnitude of the induced e.m.f. in the rotor also reduces by slip times the magnitude of induced e.m.f. at standstill condition.

10.6.2 Effect on Rotor Resistance and Reactance

The rotor winding has its own resistance and the inductance. In a case of squirrel cage rotor, the rotor resistance is very very small and generally neglected but slip ring rotor has its own resistance which can be controlled by adding external resistance through slip rings. In general let,

$$R_2 = \text{Rotor resistance per phase on standstill}$$

$$X_2 = \text{Rotor reactance per phase on standstill}$$

Now at standstill, $f_r = f$ hence if L_2 is the inductance of rotor per phase,

$$X_2 = 2\pi f_r\, L_2 = 2\pi f L_2 \ \Omega/ph$$

while $R_2 = \text{Rotor resistance in } \Omega/ph$

Now in running condition,

$$f_r = sf \quad \text{hence,}$$

$$X_{2r} = 2\pi f_r\, L_2 = 2\pi f s L_2 = s \cdot (2\pi f L_2)$$

$\therefore$ $\boxed{X_{2r} = s\, X_2}$

where $X_{2r} = \text{Rotor reactance in running condition}$

Thus resistance as independent of frequency remains same at standstill and in running condition. While the rotor reactance decreases by slip times the rotor reactance at standstill.

Hence we can write rotor impedance per phase as :

$$Z_2 = \text{Rotor impedance on standstill (N = 0) condition}$$

$$= R_2 + j X_2 \ \ \Omega/ph$$

$\therefore$ $Z_2 = \sqrt{R_2^2 + X_2^2} \ \ \Omega/ph$ ... Magnitude

while $Z_{2r} = \text{Rotor impedance in running condition}$

$$= R_2 + j X_{2r} = R_2 + j\,(s X_2) \ \ \Omega/ph$$

$\therefore$ $\boxed{Z_{2r} = \sqrt{R_2^2 + (s X_2)^2} \ \ \Omega/ph}$ ... Magnitude

10.6.3 Effect on Rotor Power Factor

From rotor impedance, we can write the expression for the power factor of rotor at standstill and also in running condition.

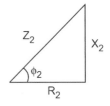

Fig. 10.6.1

The impedance triangle on standstill rotor condition is shown in the Fig. 10.6.1. From it we can write,

∴

$$\cos \phi_2 = \text{Rotor power factor on standstill} = \frac{R_2}{Z_2} = \frac{R_2}{\sqrt{R_2^2 + X_2^2}}$$

The impedance in running condition becomes Z_{2r} and the corresponding impedance triangle is shown in the Fig. 10.6.2. From Fig. 10.6.2 we can write,

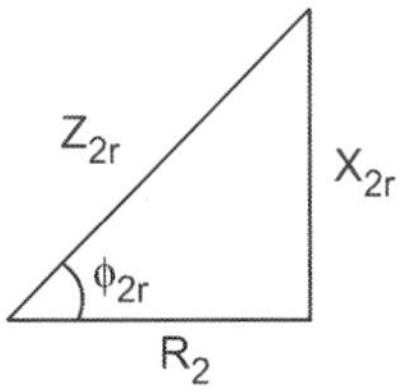

$$\cos \phi_{2r} = \text{Rotor power factor in running condition}$$

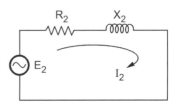

∴

$$\cos \phi_{2r} = \frac{R_2}{Z_{2r}} = \frac{R_2}{\sqrt{R_2^2 + (s X_2)^2}}$$

Fig. 10.6.2

Key Point *As rotor winding is inductive, the rotor p.f. is always lagging in nature.*

10.6.4 Effect on Rotor Current

Let I_2 = Rotor current per phase on standstill condition

The magnitude of I_2 depends on magnitude of E_2 and impedance Z_2 per phase.

$$I_2 = \frac{E_2 \text{ per phase}}{Z_2 \text{ per phase}} \text{ A}$$

Substituting expression of Z_2 we get,

$$I_2 = \frac{E_2}{\sqrt{R_2^2 + X_2^2}} \text{ A}$$

The equivalent rotor circuit on standstill is shown in the Fig. 10.6.3.

The ϕ_2 is the angle between E_2 and I_2 which determines rotor p.f. on standstill.

In the running condition, Z_2 changes to Z_{2r} while the induced e.m.f. changes to E_{2r}. Hence the

Fig. 10.6.3 Rotor equivalent circuit on standstill

magnitude of current in the running condition is also different than I_2 on standstill. The equivalent rotor circuit on running condition is shown in the Fig. 10.6.4.

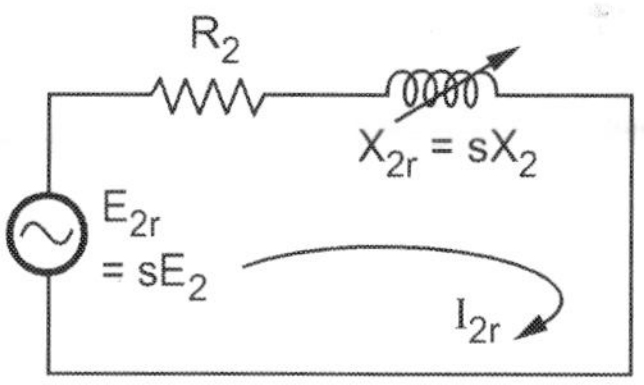

All values are phase

Fig. 10.6.4 Rotor equivalent circuit in running condition

I_{2r} = Rotor current per phase in running condition.

The value of slip depends on speed which inturn depends on load on motor hence X_{2r} is shown variable in the equivalent circuit. From the equivalent circuit we can write,

$$I_{2r} = \frac{E_{2r}}{Z_{2r}} = \frac{s\,E_2}{\sqrt{R_2^2 + (s\,X_2)^2}}$$

ϕ_{2r} is the angle between E_{2r} and I_{2r} which decides p.f. in running condition.

Key Point *Putting s = 1 in the expressions obtained in running condition, the values at standstill can be obtained.*

Review Question

1. *Explain the effect of slip on following rotor parameters :*
   i) Rotor induced e.m.f. ii) Rotor power factor iii) Rotor impedance iv) Rotor current.

10.7 Induction Motor as a Transformer   2002-03, 2004-05

In general, an induction motor can be treated as a generalized transformer.

So if E_1 = Stator e.m.f. per phase in volts

         E_2 = Rotor induced e.m.f. per phase in volts at start when motor

           is at standstill.

Then according to general transformer there exists a fixed relation between E_1 and E_2 called **transformation ratio**.

$\therefore$ At start when $\boxed{N = 0 \,,\; s = 1}$

And we get, $\boxed{\dfrac{E_2}{E_1} = K = \dfrac{\text{Rotor turns / phase}}{\text{Stator turns / phase}}}$

Key Point *So if stator supply voltage is known and ratio of stator to rotor turns per phase is known then the rotor induced e.m.f. on standstill can be obtained.*

Example 10.7.1 *For a 4 pole, 3 phase, 50 Hz induction motor ratio of stator to rotor turns is 2. On a certain load, its speed is observed to be 1455 r.p.m. when connected to 415 V supply. Calculate, i) frequency of rotor e.m.f. in running condition. ii) magnitude of induced e.m.f. in the rotor at standstill. iii) magnitude of induced e.m.f. in the rotor under running condition. Assume star connected stator.*

Solution : The given values are, K = Rotor turns/Stator turns = 1/2 = 0.5 and

P = 4, f = 50 Hz, N = 1455 r.p.m., E_{1line} = 415 V

$$N_s = \frac{120f}{P} = \frac{120 \times 50}{4} = 1500 \text{ r.p.m.}$$

For a given load, N = 1455 r.p.m.

$$\therefore \qquad s = \frac{N_s - N}{N_s} = \frac{1500 - 1455}{1500} = 0.03 \text{ i.e. } 3\%$$

i) $\qquad f_r = s f = 0.03 \times 50 = \textbf{1.5 Hz}$

ii) At standstill, induction motor acts as a transformer so,

$$\frac{E_{2ph}}{E_{1ph}} = \frac{\text{Rotor turns}}{\text{Stator turns}} = K$$

But ratio of stator to rotor turns is given as 2, i.e.

$$\frac{N_1}{N_2} = 2 \qquad \therefore \frac{N_2}{N_1} = \frac{1}{2} = K$$

and $\qquad E_{1\,line} = 415$ V

The given values are always line values unless and until specifically stated as per phase.

$$\therefore \qquad E_{1ph} = \frac{E_1}{\sqrt{3}} = \frac{415}{\sqrt{3}} = 239.6 \text{ V} \qquad \ldots \text{As star connection } E_{line} = \sqrt{3} \, E_{ph}$$

$$\therefore \qquad \frac{E_{2ph}}{E_{1ph}} = \frac{1}{2} \quad \text{i.e.} \quad E_{2ph} = \frac{1}{2} \times 239.6 = \textbf{119.8 V}$$

iii) In running condition,

$$E_{2r} = s E_2 = 0.03 \times 119.8 = \textbf{3.594 V}$$

The value of rotor induced e.m.f. in the running condition is also very very small.

Example 10.7.2 *A 3-phase, 440 V, 50 h.p., 50 Hz induction motor runs at 1450 r.p.m. w... it delivers rated output power. Determine : i) Number of poles in the machine. ii) Spe... of rotating air gap field. iii) Rotor induced voltage if stator to rotor turns ratio is 1 : 0.80. Assume the winding factors are the same. iv) Frequency of rotor current.*

2004-05, Marks 10

Solution : f = 50 Hz, N = 1450 r.p.m.

The nearest synchronous speed is 1500 r.p.m.

i) $\qquad N_s = \dfrac{120\, f}{P}$ i.e. $1500 = \dfrac{120 \times 50}{P}$

∴ $\qquad\qquad$ P = **4** $\qquad\qquad\qquad\qquad\qquad\qquad$ ... Poles in the machine

ii) Speed of rotating air gap field = N_s = **1500 r.p.m.**

iii) $\qquad \dfrac{E_{1ph}}{E_{2ph}} = \dfrac{N_1}{N_2}$

Assume that the motor is delta connected.

∴ $\qquad E_{1ph} = V_1 = 440$ V   hence $\dfrac{440}{E_{2ph}} = \dfrac{1}{0.8}$

∴ $\qquad E_{2ph} = $ **352 V** $\qquad\qquad\qquad\qquad\qquad$ ... Rotor induced voltage

iv) $\qquad f_r = sf$ where $s = \dfrac{N_s - N}{N_s} = \dfrac{1500 - 1450}{1500} = 0.03$

∴ $\qquad f_r = 0.03 \times 50 = $ **1.5 Hz**

Example 10.7.3 *A 3-phase delta connected 440 volts, 50 Hz, 4-pole induction motor has a rotor standstill e.m.f. per phase of 130 volts. If the motor is running at 1440 r.p.m., calculate for this speed - i) the slip, ii) the frequency of rotor induced e.m.f., iii) the value of the rotor induced e.m.f. per phase, and iv) stator to rotor turns ratio.*

2002-03, Marks 5

Solution : V_L = 440 V,   Delta, f = 50 Hz, P = 4, E_2 = 130 V, N = 1440 r.p.m.

i) $\qquad N_s = \dfrac{120\, f}{P} = \dfrac{120 \times 50}{4} = 1500$ r.p.m.

∴ $\qquad s = \dfrac{N_s - N}{N_s} \times 100 = \dfrac{1500 - 1440}{1500} \times 100 = $ **4 %** i.e. **0.04**

ii) $\qquad f_r = sf = 0.04 \times 50 = $ **2 Hz**

iii) $\qquad E_{2r} = s\, E_2 = 0.04 \times 130 = $ **5.2 V**

iv) $\qquad V_{ph} = V_L = $ **440 V**

$$\frac{N_1}{N_2} = \frac{V_{ph}}{E_{2ph}} = \frac{440}{130} = \textbf{3.3846}$$

Question

1. *Justify that an induction motor is generalized transformer.*

10.8 Torque Equation

The torque of a three phase induction motor is given by,

$$T = \frac{ksE_2^2 R_2}{R_2^2 + (sX_2)^2} \quad \text{N.m} \quad \text{where} \quad k = \frac{3}{2\pi n_s}$$

n_s = Synchronous speed in r.p.s., s = Slip

R_2 = Standstill resistance, X_2 = Standstill reactance

The torque produced in the induction motor depends on the following factors :

1. The part of rotating magnetic field which reacts with rotor and is responsible to produce induced e.m.f. in rotor.

2. The magnitude of rotor current in running condition.

3. The power factor of the rotor circuit in running condition.

10.8.1 Starting Torque

Starting torque is nothing but the torque produced by an induction motor at start. At start, $N = 0$ and slip $s = 1$. So putting $s = 1$ in the torque equation we can write expression for the starting torque T_{st} as,

$$T_{st} = \frac{3}{2\pi n_s} \cdot \frac{E_2^2 R_2}{(R_2^2 + X_2^2)} \qquad \qquad \dots (10.8.1)$$

Key Point *From the equation (10.8.1), it is clear that by changing R_2 the starting torque T_{st} can be controlled. The change in R_2 at start is possible in case of slip ring induction motor only.*

This is the principle used in case of slip induction motor to control the starting torque T_{st}.

Example 10.8.1 *A 3 phase, 400 V, 50 Hz, 4 pole induction motor has star connected st. winding. The rotor resistance and reactance are 0.1 Ω and 1 Ω respectively. The full lo. speed is 1440 r.p.m. Calculate the torque developed on full load by the motor. Assumi stator to rotor ratio as 2 : 1.*

Solution : The given values are,

$$P = 4, \quad f = 50 \text{ Hz}, \quad R_2 = 0.1 \ \Omega, \quad X_2 = 1 \ \Omega, \quad N = 1440 \text{ r.p.m.}$$

$$\frac{\text{Stator turns}}{\text{Rotor turns}} = \frac{2}{1}$$

$\therefore \qquad\qquad K = \dfrac{E_2}{E_1} = \dfrac{\text{Rotor turns}}{\text{Stator turns}} = \dfrac{1}{2} = 0.5$

$$N_s = \frac{120 f}{P} = \frac{120 \times 50}{4} = 1500 \text{ r.p.m.}$$

$$E_{1line} = 400 \text{ V} \qquad\qquad\qquad\qquad \dots \text{Stator line voltage given}$$

$\therefore \qquad\qquad E_{1ph} = \dfrac{E_{1 line}}{\sqrt{3}} = \dfrac{400}{\sqrt{3}} = 230.94 \text{ V}$

But $\qquad \dfrac{E_{2ph}}{E_{1ph}} = 0.5 = K$

$\therefore \qquad\qquad E_{2ph} = 0.5 \times 230.94 = 115.47 \text{ V}$

Full load slip, $s = \dfrac{N_s - N}{N_s} = \dfrac{1500 - 1440}{1500} = 0.04$

$\qquad\qquad n_s = \text{Synchronous speed in r.p.s.}$

$\qquad\qquad\quad = \dfrac{N_s}{60} = \dfrac{1500}{60} = 25 \text{ r.p.s.}$

$$T = \frac{3}{2\pi n_s} \cdot \frac{s E_2^2 R_2}{R_2^2 + (sX_2)^2}$$

$$= \frac{3}{2\pi \times 25} \times \frac{0.04 \times (115.47)^2 \times 0.1}{[(0.1)^2 + (0.04 \times 1)^2]} = \textbf{87.81 N-m}$$

10.9 Torque-Slip Characteristics   `2009-10`

As the induction motor is loaded from no load to full load, its speed decreases hence slip increases. Due to the increased load, motor has to produce more torque to satisfy load demand. The torque ultimately depends on slip as explained earlier. The behaviour of motor can be easily judged by sketching a curve obtained by plotting torque produced against slip of induction motor. The curve obtained by plotting torque against

= 1 (at start) to s = 0 (at synchronous speed) is called **torque-slip** ics of the induction motor. It is very interesting to study the nature of characteristics.

ave seen that for a constant supply voltage, E_2 is also constant. So we can write equation as,

∴
$$T \propto \frac{s R_2}{R_2^2 + (sX_2)^2}$$

Now to judge the nature of torque-slip characteristics let us divide the slip range (s = 0 to s = 1) into two parts and analyse them independently.

i) Low slip region : In low slip region, 's' is very very small. Due to this, the term $(s X_2)^2$ is so small as compared to R_2^2 that it can be neglected.

∴
$$T \propto \frac{s R_2}{R_2^2} \propto s$$ as R_2 is constant.

Hence in **low slip region torque is directly proportional to slip**. So as load increases, speed decreases, increasing the slip. This increases the torque which satisfies the load demand.

Hence the graph is straight line in nature.

At $N = N_s$, s = 0 hence T = 0. As no torque is generated at $N = N_s$, motor stops if it tries to achieve the synchronous speed. Torque increases linearly in this region, of low slip values.

ii) High slip region : In this region, slip is high i.e. slip value is approaching to 1. Here it can be assumed that the term R_2^2 is very very small as compared to $(s X_2)^2$. Hence neglecting R_2^2 from the denominator, we get

$$T \propto \frac{s R_2}{(sX_2)^2} \propto \frac{1}{s}$$ where R_2 and X_2 are constants

So in high slip region torque is inversely proportional to the slip. Hence its nature is like rectangular hyperbola.

Now when load increases, load demand increases but speed decreases. As speed decreases, slip increases. In high slip region as $T \propto 1/s$, torque decreases as slip increases. But torque must increase to satisfy the load demand. As torque decreases, due to extra loading effect, speed further decreases and slip further increases. Again torque decreases as $T \propto 1/s$ hence same load acts as an extra load due to reduction in torque produced. Hence speed further drops. Eventually motor comes to standstill condition. **The motor cannot continue to rotate at any point in this high slip region**. Hence this region is called **unstable region** of operation.

So torque - slip characteristics has two parts,

1. Straight line called **stable region of operation**.

2. Rectangular hyperbola called **unstable region of operation**.

Now the obvious question is upto which value of slip, torque-slip characteristic represents stable operation ?

In low slip region, as load increases, slip increases and torque also increases linearly. Every motor has its own limit to produce a torque. The maximum torque, the motor can produce as load increases is T_m which occurs at $s = s_m$. So linear behaviour continues till $s = s_m$.

If load is increased beyond this limit, motor slip acts dominantly pushing motor into high slip region. Due to unstable conditions, motor comes to standstill condition at such a load. Hence T_m i.e. maximum torque which motor can produce is also called **breakdown torque** or **pull out torque**. So range $s = 0$ to $s = s_m$ is called low slip region, known as stable region of operation. Motor always operates at a point in this region. And range $s = s_m$ to $s = 1$ is called high slip region which is rectangular hyperbola, called unstable region of operation. Motor cannot continue to rotate at any point in this region.

At $s = 1$, $N = 0$ i.e. at start, motor produces a torque called **starting torque** denoted as T_{st}.

The entire torque-slip characteristics is shown in the Fig. 10.9.1.

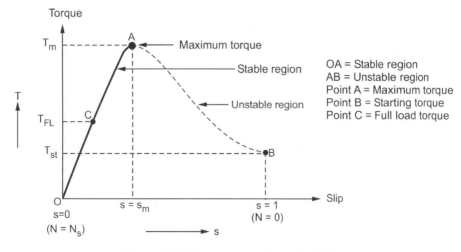

Fig. 10.9.1 Torque-slip characteristics

10.9.1 Full Load Torque

When the load on the motor increases, the torque produced increases as speed decreases and slip increases. The increased torque demand is satisfied by drawing more current from the supply.

The load which motor can drive safely while operating continuously and due to such load, the current drawn is also within safe limits is called **full load condition** of motor. When current increases, due to heat produced the temperature rises. The safe limit of current is that which when drawn for continuous operation of motor, produces a temperature rise well within the limits. Such a full load point is shown on the torque-slip characteristics as point C in the Fig. 10.9.1 and corresponding torque as $T_{F.L.}$.

The interesting thing is that the load on the motor can be increased beyond point C till maximum torque condition. But due to high current and hence high temperature rise there is possibility of damage of winding insulation, **if motor is operated for longer time** duration in this region i.e. from point C to B. But motor can be used to drive loads more than full load, producing torque upto maximum torque for short duration of time. Generally full load torque is less than the maximum torque.

So region OC upto full load condition allow motor operation continuously and safely from the temperature point of view. While region CB is possible to achieve in practice but only for short duration of time and not for continuous operation of motor. This is the difference between full load torque and the maximum or breakdown torque. The breakdown torque is also called stalling torque.

$\therefore$

$$T_{\text{Full load}} < T_m$$

Review Question

> 1. *Draw the torque-slip characteristics of a three phase induction motor and explain its various regions.*   **2009-10, Marks 5**

10.10 Applications

i) Squirrel cage type of motors having moderate starting torque and constant speed characteristics preferred for driving fans, blowers, water pumps, grinders, lathe machines, printing machines, drilling machine.

ii) Slip ring induction motors can have high starting torque as high as maximum torque. Hence they are preferred for lifts, hoists, elevators, cranes, compressors.

Review Question

> *1. State the applications of squirrel cage induction motor and slip ring induction motor.*

10.11 Necessity of Starter in Induction Motor   `2012-13`

In a three phase induction motor, magnitude of induced e.m.f. in the rotor circuit depends on the slip of the induction motor. At start the value of slip is at its maximum equal to unity. The rotor current at start is given by,

$$I_2 = \frac{E_2}{\sqrt{R_2^2 + X_2^2}} \quad \text{at start as } s = 1$$

where E_2 = Rotor induced e.m.f. per phase at start

The magnitude of induced e.m.f. at start is maximum as slip speed i.e. relative speed between rotor and the rotating magnetic field is maximum.

Hence at start, large e.m.f. gets induced in the rotor.

As rotor conductors are short circuited in most of the motors, due to squirrel cage construction, this e.m.f. circulates very high current through rotor at start.

The induction motors acts as a transformer having short circuited secondary, at start.

Hence as rotor current is high at start, consequently stator draws a very high current of the order of 5 to 8 times full load current at start.

Due to such high current at start there is possibility of damage of the motor winding. Similarly due to sudden in rush of current, other appliances connected to the same line may be subjected to voltage spikes which may affect their working.

To avoid such effects it is necessary to limit current drawn by the motor at start. Hence starter is necessary for an induction motor. In the running condition, the relative speed of rotor with respect to rotating magnetic field becomes slip speed which is very small.

Hence the magnitude of the induced e.m.f. in the rotor also reduces by slip times the magnitude of induced e.m.f. at standstill condition. Hence in the running condition, the rotor current is not very high.

Starters not only limit the starting current but also provide protection to the induction motor against over loading and low voltage conditions. The starters also provide single phasing protection too.

Review Questions

1. *Explain why an induction motor needs starter ?*   **2012-13, Marks 5**

2. *Why induction motor draws high starting current ?*

10.12 Starters used for Induction Motor   **2012-13**

The various starters used for induction motor are,

1. Stator resistance starter   2. Star-delta starter

3. Rotor resistance starter   4. Autotransformer starter

5. Direct on line starter.

10.12.1 Stator Resistance Starter

In order to apply the reduced voltage to the stator of the induction motor, three resistances are added in series with each phase of the stator winding. Initially the resistances are kept maximum in the circuit. Due to this, large voltage gets dropped across the resistances. Hence a reduced voltage gets applied to the stator which reduces the high starting current. The schematic diagram showing stator resistances is shown in the Fig. 10.12.1.

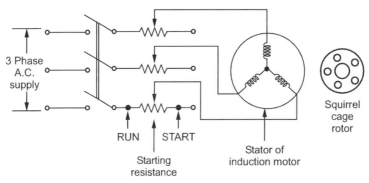

Fig. 10.12.1 Stator resistance starter

When the motor starts running, the resistances are gradually cut-off from the stator circuit. When the resistances are entirely removed from the stator circuit i.e. rheostats in RUN position then rated voltage gets applied to the stator. Motor runs with normal speed.

The starter is simple in construction and cheap. It can be used for both star and delta connected stator. But there are large power losses due to resistances. Also the starting torque of the motor reduces due to reduced voltage applied to the stator.

10.12.2 Autotransformer Starter

A three phase star connected autotransformer can be used to reduce the voltage applied to the stator. Such a starter is called an autotransformer starter. The schematic diagram of autotransformer starter is shown in the Fig. 10.12.2.

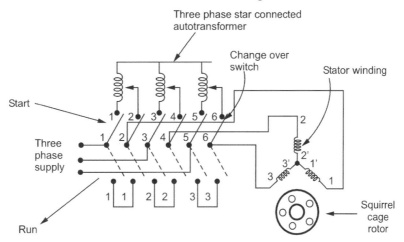

Fig. 10.12.2 Autotransformer starter

It consists of a suitable change over switch.

When the switch is in the start position, the stator winding is supplied with reduced voltage. This can be controlled by tappings provided with autotransformer.

The reduction in applied voltage by the fractional percentage tappings x, used for an autotransformer is shown in the Fig. 10.12.3.

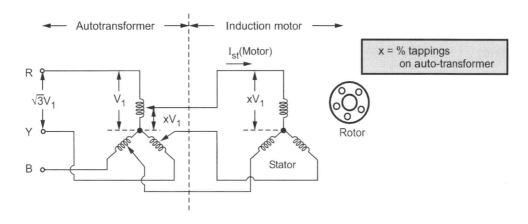

Fig. 10.12.3 Use of autotransformer to reduce voltage at start

When motor gathers 80 % of the normal speed, the change over switch is thrown into run position.

Due to this, rated voltage gets applied to stator winding. The motor starts rotating with normal speed. Changing of switch is done automatically by using relays. The power loss is much less in this type of starting. It can be used for both star and delta connected motors. But it is expensive than stator resistance starter.

10.12.3 Star - Delta Starter

This is the cheapest starter of all and hence used very commonly for the induction motors. It uses Tripple Pole Double Throw (TPDT) switch. The switch connects the stator winding in star at start. Hence per phase voltage gets reduced by the factor $1/\sqrt{3}$. Due to this reduced voltage, the starting current is limited.

When the switch is thrown on other side, the winding gets connected in delta, across the supply. So it gets normal rated voltage. The windings are connected in delta when motor gathers sufficient speed.

The arrangement of star-delta starter is shown in the Fig. 10.12.4.

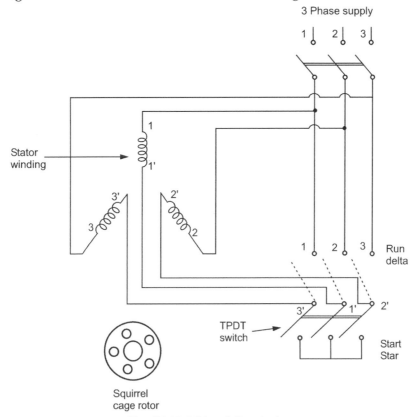

Fig. 10.12.4 Star-delta starter

The operation of the switch can be automatic by using relays which ensures that motor will not start with the switch in Run position. The cheapest of all and maintenance free operation are the two important advantages of this starter. While its limitations are, it is suitable for normal delta connected motors and the factor by which voltage changes is $1 / \sqrt{3}$ which can not be changed.

10.12.4 Rotor Resistance Starter

To limit the rotor current which consequently reduces the current drawn by the motor from the supply, the resistance can be inserted in the rotor circuit at start. This addition of the resistance in rotor is in the form of 3 phase star connected rheostat. The arrangement is shown in the Fig. 10.12.5.

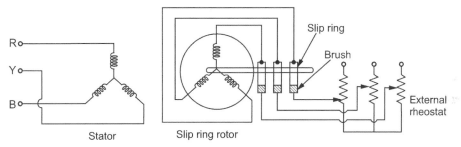

Fig. 10.12.5 Rotor resistance starter

The external resistance is inserted in each phase of the rotor winding through slip ring and brush assembly. Initially maximum resistance is in the circuit. As motor gathers speed, the resistance is gradually cutoff. The operation may be manual or automatic.

We have seen that the starting torque is proportional to the rotor resistance. Hence important advantage of this method is not only the starting current is limited but starting torque of the motor also gets improved. The only limitation of the starter is that it can be used only for slip ring induction motors as in squirrel cage motors, the rotor is parmanently short circuited.

10.12.5 Direct On Line Starter (D.O.L.)

In case of small capacity motors having rating less than 5 h.p., the starting current is not very high and such motors can withstand such starting current without any starter. Thus there is no need to reduce applied voltage, to control the starting current. Such motors use a type of starter which is used to connect stator directly to the supply lines without any reduction in voltage. Hence the starter is known as direct on line starter.

Though this starter does not reduce the applied voltage, it is used because it protects the motor from various severe abnormal conditions like over loading, low voltage, single phasing etc.

The Fig. 10.12.6 shows the arrangement of various components in direct on line starter.

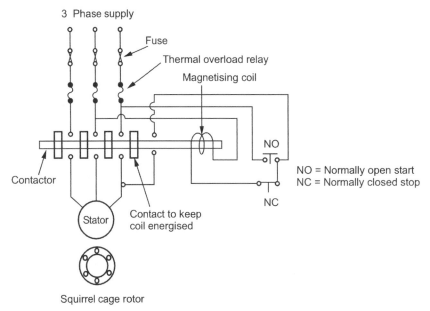

Fig. 10.12.6 D.O.L. starter

The NO contact is normally open and NC is normally closed. At start, NO is pushed for fraction of second due to which coil gets energised and attracts the contactor. So stator directly gets supply. The additional contact provided, ensures that as long as supply is ON, the coil gets supply and keeps contactor in ON position. When NC is pressed, the coil circuit gets opened due to which coil gets de-energised and motor gets switched OFF from the supply.

Under over load condition, current drawn by the motor increases due to which there is an excessive heat produced, which increases temperature beyond limit. Thermal relays get opened due to high temperature, protecting the motor from overload conditions.

Review Question

1. *Explain the various types of starters used for induction motors.*   **2012-13, Marks 5**

10.13 Short Answered and Objective Type Questions

Q.1 The rotor speed of a six pole 50 Hz induction motor is 960 r.p.m. The percentage slip is _____.   **2008-09**

a) 3 %   b) 4 %   c) 5 %   d) 2 %

Ans. :

$$N_s = \frac{120f}{P} = \frac{120 \times 50}{6} = 1000 \text{ r.p.m.}$$

$$\therefore \qquad \% \ s \ = \ \frac{N_s - N}{N_s} \times 100 \ = \ \frac{1000 - 960}{1000} \times 100 \ = \ \textbf{4 \%} \quad \textbf{i.e. (b)}$$

Q.2 A 3-phase induction motor connected from a 3-phase, 50 Hz a.c. supply runs at 720 r.p.m. and has 4 % slip. The number of poles in the motor are _____.

`2009-10`

   a) 4   b) 6   c) 8   d) 16

Ans. : f = 50 Hz,   N = 720 r.p.m. ,   s = 4 %

$$s \ = \ \frac{N_s - N}{N_s} \qquad \text{i.e.} \qquad 0.04 \ = \ \frac{N_s - 720}{N_s}$$

$$\therefore \qquad N_s \ = \ 750 \text{ r.p.m.} \ = \ \frac{120\,f}{P}$$

$$\therefore \qquad P \ = \ \frac{120 \times 50}{750} \ = \ \textbf{8}$$

Hence answer is (c).

Q.3 Slip rings are made of aluminium : _____ .   `2009-10`
   a) Yes   b) No   **(Ans. : b)**

Q.4 Three phase induction motor has a low efficiency : _____ .   `2009-10`
   a) Yes   b) No   **(Ans. : a)**

Q.5 The torque developed in an induction motor is nearly proportional to _____ .
   a) $1/V$ b) V c) V^2 d) None of these
                                                                       (Ans. : c)

Q.6 The wound rotor induction motor is mainly used due to _____.   `2010-11`
   a) high starting torque   b) speed control

   c) high rotor resistance   d) none of these.   **(Ans. : a)**

Q.7 Define the term "slip". **(Refer section 10.4)**   `2011-12`

Q.8 An induction motor works with _____ .

   a) d.c. only   b) a.c. only

   c) both a.c. and d.c.   d) none of the above.   **(Ans. : b)**

Q.9 When a 3-φ supply is given to the stator of 3-φ induction motor, a _____ magnetic field is produced.

   a) stationary   b) alternating   c) rotating   d) none of these
                                                                       (Ans. : c)

Q.10 The frame of induction motor is usually made of _____ .

   a) silicon steel   b) cast iron   c) aluminium   d) bronze   **(Ans. : b)**

Q.11 The number of poles in a 3 ϕ induction motor is determined by the _____ .

     a) supply frequency   b) motor speed

     c) supply voltage   d) both (a) and (b)   **(Ans. : d)**

Q.12 The air gap between the stator and the rotor of a 3-ϕ. I.M. ranges from _____.

     a) 2 cm to 4 cm   b) 0.4 mm to 4 mm

     c) 1 cm to 2 cm   d) 4 cm to 6 cm   **(Ans. : b)**

Q.13 Phase wound induction motors are less extensively used than squirrel cage induction motors because _____ .

     a) slip rings are required on the rotor circuit

     b) rotor windings are generally star connected

     c) they are costly and require greater maintenance

     d) none of the above   **(Ans. : c)**

Q.14 Synchronous speed of three phase induction motor is given by ____ .

     a) $N_s = 120\ f\ P$ b) $N_s = 120\ f/P$ c) $N_s = 120\ P/f$ d) $N_s = f\ P/120$

                                                                     (Ans. : b)

Q.15 The slip of an induction motor at stand still is _____ .

     a) zero   b) one

     c) infinity   d) none of the above.   **(Ans. : b)**

Q.16 An induction motor under full load has a slip of about _____ .

     a) 0.03   b) 0.1   c) 0.3   d) zero   **(Ans. : a)**

Q.17 A 4 pole, 440 V, 50 Hz induction motor is running at a slip 4 %. The speed of motor is ____ .

     a) 1260 r.p.m.   b) 1440 r.p.m.   c) 1500 r.p.m.   d) 1560 r.p.m.

                                                                      (Ans. : b)

Q.18 If N_s is the synchronous speed and 's' is the slip, then actual running speed of an induction motor will be _____ .

     a) N_s b) $s\ N_s$ c) $(1-s)\ N_s$ d) $(N_s -1)\ s$

                                                                 (Ans. : c)

Q.19 In a 3-ϕ induction motor, the slip speed is given by _____.

     a) N_s b) N   c) $N_s - N$ d) $N - N_s$ **(Ans. : c)**

Q.20 A supply of 50 Hz is given to a 3-ϕ I.M. having 4 poles. If the I.M. runs at 1440 rpm the slip is _____ .

     a) 3 %   b) 4 %   c) 5 %   d) 3.33 % **(Ans. : b)**

Q.21 A 4 pole, 50 Hz induction motor runs at a speed of 1440 r.p.m. The frequency of the rotor induced e.m.f. is _____ .

a) 3 Hz   b) 2.5 Hz   c) 2 Hz   d) 1 Hz.   **(Ans. : c)**

Q.22 The relation between rotor frequency (f') and stator frequency (f) is given by___.

a) f' = s f   b) f' = f/s   c) f' = $\sqrt{sf}$ d) f' = (1 – s) f.

(Ans. : a)

Q.23 A 3 ϕ, 440 V, 50 Hz, induction motor has 4 % slip. The frequency of rotor e.m.f. is _____ .

a) 200 Hz   b) 50 Hz   c) 2 Hz   d) 0.2 Hz   **(Ans. : c)**

Q.24 External resistance is connected to the rotor of a 3 ϕ phase wound induction motor in order to _____.

a) reduce starting current   b) collector current

c) as a star connected load   d) none of these   **(Ans. : a)**

Q.25 The stator winding of three phase induction motor produces _____ magnetic field.

a) alternating   b) rotating   c) pulsating   d) constant

(Ans. : b)

Q.26 The magnitude of rotating magnetic field is _____ times the maximum flux of any individual phase.

a) 1.5   b) $\sqrt{3}$ c) 2.5   d) $\dfrac{1}{\sqrt{3}}$

(Ans. : a)

Q.27 _____ rotor is permanently short circuited.

a) Slip ring   b) Wound   c) Squirrel cage   d) Cup type

(Ans. : c)

Q.28 For a 4 pole, 50 Hz, three phase induction motor, the synchronous speed is _____ r.p.m.

a) 1000   b) 1200   c) 1800   d) 1500   **(Ans. : d)**

Q.29 Speed of the induction motor is _____ that of N_s.

a) greater than   b) less than   c) same as   d) none of these

(Ans. : b)

Q.30 The slip speed of an induction motor is _____ r.p.m.

a) N_s b) N   c) N_s-N   d) N - N_s **(Ans. : c)**

Q.31 The value of slip is _____ at start.

a) zero   b) infinite   c) 100   d) 1   **(Ans. : d)**

Q.32 For a 6 pole, 50 Hz induction motor, the full load speed is 950 r.p.m. hence full load slip is _____.

a) 0.05   b) 0.02   c) 0.01   d) 0.08   **(Ans. : a)**

Q.33 For a 4 pole, 50 Hz induction motor, the full load slip is 0.03 hence its full load speed is _____ r.p.m.

a) 1420   b) 1455   c) 1495   d) 1500   **(Ans. : b)**

Q.34 In squirrel cage rotor, the slots are skewed _____.

a) to reduce losses   b) to give support
c) to reduce magnetic hum   d) to reduce friction   **(Ans. : c)**

Q.35 The slip rings are usually made up of _____.

a) copper   b) iron   c) carbon   d) phosphor-bronze
                                                            (Ans. : d)

Q.36 A 440 V, 50 Hz induction motor has a slip of 5 % then the frequency of rotor currents is _____.

a) 1.5 Hz   b) 2.5 Hz   c) 0.5 Hz   d) 50 Hz   **(Ans. : b)**

Q.37 The rotor standstill resistance and reactance of an induction motor are 0.5 Ω and 2.5 Ω hence the rotor impedance at 5 % slip is _____.

a) 0.5 Ω b) 0.025 Ω c) 0.5154 Ω d) 0.125 Ω **(Ans. : c)**

Q.38 The rotor power factor is _____ in nature.

a) unity   b) leading   c) zero   d) lagging **(Ans. : d)**

Q.39 In _____ motor, the speed can be controlled from rotor side.

a) a.c. series   b) slip ring   c) squirrel cage d) universal
                                                            (Ans. : b)

Q.40 An induction motor is a generalized _____.

a) generator   b) capacitor   c) transformer   d) none of these
                                                            (Ans. : c)

Q.41 The condition for maximum torque is s_m = _____.

a) $\dfrac{X_2}{R_2}$ b) $\dfrac{R_2}{X_2}$ c) $R_2 X_2$ d) none of these
                                                            (Ans. : b)

Q.42 The magnitude of maximum torque is independent of _____.

a) rotor induced e.m.f.   b) rotor standstill reactance
c) rotor resistance   d) synchronous speed   **(Ans. : c)**

Q.43 In low slip region, the torque of an induction motor is _____.

a) directly proportional to the slip

b) inversely proportional to the slip

c) directly proportional to square of the slip

d) none of the above   **(Ans. : a)**

Q.44 In high slip region, the torque of an induction motor is _____.

a) directly proportional to the slip

b) inversely proportional to the slip

c) directly proportional to square of the slip

d) none of the above   **(Ans. : b)**

Q.45 If the rotor resistance is increased, the starting torque of slip ring induction motor _____.

a) decreases   b) remains same   c) increases   d) none of these
                                                          (Ans. : c)

Q.46 The direction of rotation of an induction motor depends on _____.

a) phase sequence   b) supply frequency

c) supply voltage   d) none of these   **(Ans. : a)**

Q.47 If any two phases of an induction motor are interchanged then _____.

a) motor will burn   b) motor will stop

c) motor speed will reduce   d) direction of rotation will change
                                                          (Ans. : d)

Q.48 The rotor of an induction motor rotates in the same direction as that of rotating magnetic field, according to _____.

a) Coulombs law   b) Lenz's law   c) Faraday's law   d) Ohm's law
                                                          (Ans. : b)

Q.49 In an induction motor, the number of rotor poles is _____.

a) greater than the stator poles   b) less than the stator poles.

c) equal to the stator poles.   d) zero   **(Ans. : c)**

Q.50 For a delta connected slip ring rotor, the number of slip rings required are _____.

a) 3   b) 2   c) 1   d) 0   **(Ans. : a)**

Q.51 _____ induction motor is preferred when maintenance is the main consideration.

a) Slip ring   b) Wound rotor   c) Split phase   d) Squirrel cage
                                                          (Ans. : d)

Q.52 The rotor speed is more than the synchronous speed in a three phase induction motor when _____.

a) slip is positive   b) slip is negative   c) slip is zero   d) slip is one.

(Ans. : b)

Q.53 If the synchronous speed of the 50 Hz induction motor is 750 r.p.m., it has _____ stator poles.

a) 8   b) 4   c) 2   d) 6   **(Ans. : a)**

◻◻◻

11 Single Phase Induction Motors

Syllabus

Principle of operation and introduction to methods of starting, Applications.

Contents

11.1 Introduction

For general lighting purpose in shops, offices, houses, schools etc. single phase a.c. supply is commonly used. Hence instead of d.c. motors, the motors which work on single phase a.c. supply are very popularly in use. These a.c. motors are called **single phase induction motors**. The numerous domestic applications use single phase induction motors. The power rating of such motors is very small. Some of them are even fractional horse power motors, which are used in applications like small toys, small fans, hair dryers etc.

The single phase induction motors have two parts called stator and rotor. The stator is stationary which carries single phase winding. The rotor is rotating part. The stator winding is called main winding which is excited by single phase a.c. supply. The rotor is generally squirrel cage type.

The single phase induction motors are not self starting hence the stator has one more winding to make it self starting, called starting winding or auxiliary winding.

The stator is made up of laminations and wound for certain number of poles. The rotor automatically adjusts itself for same number of poles as that of stator.

The double revolving field theory explains why single phase induction motors are not self starting.

11.2 Double Revolving Field Theory   2012-13

According to this theory, any **alternating** quantity can be resolved into two **rotating** components which rotate in **opposite directions** and each having magnitude as half of the maximum magnitude of the alternating quantity.

In case of single phase induction motors, the stator winding produces an alternating magnetic field having maximum magnitude of ϕ_{1m}.

According to double revolving field theory, consider the two components of the stator flux, each having magnitude half of maximum magnitude of stator flux i.e. $(\phi_{1m}/2)$. Both these components are rotating in opposite directions at the **synchronous speed** N_s which is dependent on frequency and stator poles.

Let ϕ_f is forward component rotating in anticlockwise direction while ϕ_b is the backward component rotating in clockwise direction. The resultant of these two components at any instant gives the instantaneous value of the stator flux at that instant. So resultant of these two is the original stator flux.

The Fig. 11.2.1 shows the stator flux and its two components ϕ_f and ϕ_b. At start both the components are shown opposite to each other in the Fig. 11.2.1 (a). Thus the resultant $\phi_R = 0$. This is nothing but the instantaneous value of stator flux at start. After $90°$, as shown in the Fig. 11.2.1 (b), the two components are rotated in such a way that both are pointing in the same direction. Hence the resultant ϕ_R is the algebraic sum of the magnitudes of the two components. So $\phi_R = (\phi_{1m}/2) + (\phi_{1m}/2) = \phi_{1m}$. This is nothing but the instantaneous value of the stator flux at $\theta = 90°$ as shown in the Fig. 11.2.1 (c). Thus continuous rotation of the two components gives the original alternating stator flux.

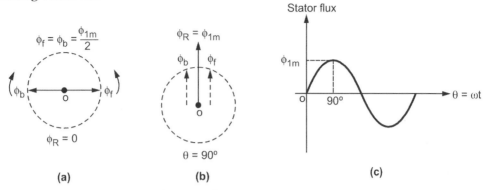

Fig. 11.2.1 Stator flux and its two components

Both the components are rotating and hence get cut by the rotor conductors. Due to cutting of flux, e.m.f. gets induced in rotor which circulates rotor current. The rotor current produces rotor flux. This flux interacts with forward component ϕ_f to produce a torque in one particular direction say anticlockwise direction. While rotor flux interacts with backward component ϕ_b to produce a torque in the clockwise direction. So if anticlockwise torque is positive then clockwise torque is negative.

At start these two torques are equal in magnitude but opposite in direction. Each torque tries to rotate the rotor in its own direction. Thus **net torque** experienced by the rotor is **zero at start**. And hence the single phase induction motors are not self starting.

11.2.1 Torque-Speed Characteristics

The two oppositely directed torques and the resultant torque can be shown effectively with the help of torque-speed characteristics. It is shown in the Fig. 11.2.2.

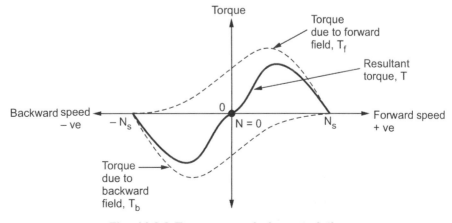

Fig. 11.2.2 Torque-speed characteristics

It can be seen that at start N = 0 and at that point resultant torque is zero. So single phase motors are not self starting.

However if the rotor is given an initial rotation in any direction, the resultant average torque increases in the direction in which rotor is initially rotated. And motor starts rotating in that direction. But in practice it is not possible to give initial torque to rotor externally hence some modifications are done in the construction of single phase induction motors to make them self starting.

Review Question

> 1. *Using double revolving field theory, explain why single phase induction motors are not self starting.*   **2012-13, Marks 5**

11.3 Phase Splitting Technique   **2011-12**

To make the single phase induction motor self starting, it is necessary to produce rotating magnetic field by the stator.

To produce rotating magnetic field, it is necessary to have minimum two alternating fluxes having a phase difference between the two. The interaction of such two fluxes produce a resultant flux which is rotating magnetic flux, rotating in space in one particular direction. So an attempt is made in all the single phase induction motors to produce an additional flux other than stator flux, which has a certain phase difference with respect to stator flux. Such two fluxes are shown in the Fig. 11.3.1 having phase difference of α between them.

More the phase difference angle α, more is the starting torque produced. Thus **production of rotating magnetic field** at start is important to make the single phase induction motors self starting. Once the motor starts, then another flux ϕ_2 may be removed and motor can continue to rotate under the influence of stator flux or main flux alone.

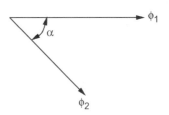

Fig. 11.3.1

Let us see how the rotating magnetic field is produced in various types of single phase induction motors.

To produce flux ϕ_2, another winding is used on the stator of single phase induction motor, called starting winding. And to have phase difference between ϕ_1 and ϕ_2, the winding is made highly resistive or highly capacitive. Thus as main winding is inductive, there will be large phase difference between main winding current and starting winding current. Due to this, there will be phase difference between ϕ_1 and ϕ_2 and the rotating magnetic field is produced. This is called phase splitting technique used to make single phase induction motors self starting. Once the motor starts, starting winding is removed using centrifugal switch.

Review Question

> 1. *What is phase splitting in single phase induction motors ?*   **2011-12, Marks 3**

11.4 Types of Single Phase Induction Motors   **2010-11, 2011-12**

Depending upon the method of making the motor self starting, the various types of single phase induction motors are,

1. Split phase induction motor

2. Capacitor start induction motor

3. Capacitor start capacitor run induction motor

4. Shaded pole induction motor

11.4.1 Split Phase Induction Motor

This type of motor has single phase stator winding called **main winding**. In addition to this, stator carries one more winding called **auxiliary winding** or **starting winding**. The auxiliary winding carries a series resistance such that its impedance is highly resistive in nature. The main winding is inductive in nature.

Let I_m = Current through main winding

and I_{st} = Current through auxiliary winding

As main winding is inductive, current I_m lags voltage V by a large angle ϕ_m while I_{st} is almost in phase in V as auxiliary winding is highly resistive. Thus there exists a phase difference of α between the two currents and hence between the two fluxes produced by the two currents. This is shown in the Fig. 11.4.1 (c). The resultant of these two fluxes is a rotating magnetic field. Due to this, the starting torque, which acts only in one direction is produced.

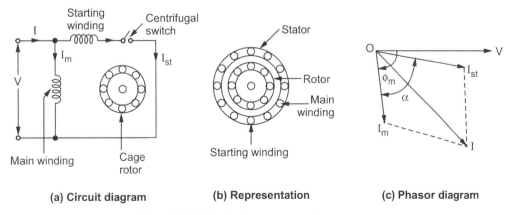

(a) Circuit diagram   (b) Representation   (c) Phasor diagram

Fig. 11.4.1 Split phase induction motor

The auxiliary winding has a centrifugal switch in series with it. When motor gathers a speed upto 75 to 80 % of the synchronous speed, centrifugal switch gets opened mechanically and in running condition auxiliary winding remains out of the circuit. So motor runs only on stator winding. So auxiliary winding is designed for short time use while

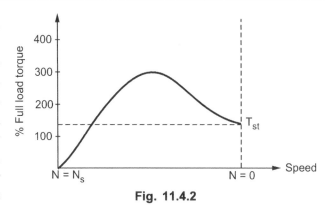

Fig. 11.4.2

the main winding is designed for continuous use. As the current I_m and I_{st} are splitted from each other by angle 'α' at start, the motor is commonly called **split phase motor**.

The torque-speed characteristics of split phase motors is shown in the Fig. 11.4.2.

The starting torque T_{st} is proportional to the split angle 'α'. But split phase motors give poor starting torque which is 125 to 150 % of the full load torque.

The direction of rotation of this motor can be reversed by reversing the terminals of either main winding or auxiliary winding. This changes the direction of rotating magnetic field which in turn changes the direction of rotation of the motor.

11.4.1.1 Applications

These motors have low starting current and moderate starting torque. These are used for easily started loads like fans, blowers, grinders, centrifugal pumps, washing machines, oil burners, office equipments etc. These are available in the range of 1/20 to 1/2 kW.

11.4.2 Capacitor Start Induction Motors

The construction of this type of motor is similar to the resistance split phase type. The difference is that in series with the auxiliary winding the capacitor is connected. The capacitive circuit draws a leading current, this feature used in this type to increase the split phase angle α between the two currents I_m and I_{st}.

Depending upon whether capacitor remains in the circuit permanently or is disconnected from the circuit using centrifugal switch, these motors are classified as,

1. Capacitor start motors and   2. Capacitor start capacitor run motors

The construction of capacitor start motor is shown in the Fig. 11.4.3 (a). The current I_m lags the voltage by angle ϕ_m while due to capacitor the current I_{st} leads the voltage by angle ϕ_{st}. Hence there exists a large phase difference between the two currents which is almost 90°, which is an ideal case. The phasor diagram is shown in the Fig. 11.4.3 (b).

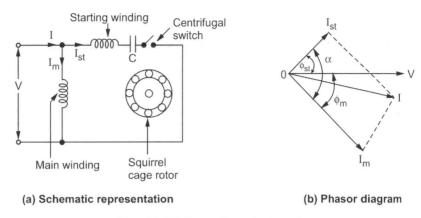

(a) Schematic representation   (b) Phasor diagram

Fig. 11.4.3 Capacitor start motor

The starting torque is proportional to 'α' and hence such motors produce very high starting torque.

When speed approaches to 75 to 80 % of the synchronous speed, the starting winding gets disconnected due to operation of the centrifugal switch. The capacitor remains in the circuit only at start hence it is called capacitor start motors.

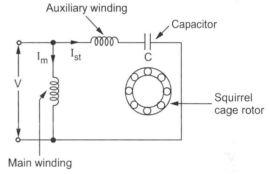

Fig. 11.4.4 Capacitor start capacitor run motor

In case of capacitor start capacitor run motor, there is no centrifugal switch and capacitor remain parmanently in the circuit. This improves the power factor. The schematic representation of such motor is shown in the Fig. 11.4.4.

The phasor diagram remains same as shown in the Fig. 11.4.3 (b). The performance not only at start but in running condition also depends on the capacitor C hence its value is to be designed so as to compromise between best starting and best running condition. Hence the starting torque available in such type of motor is about 50 to 100 % of full load torque. The torque-slip characteristics is shown in the Fig. 11.4.5.

The direction of rotation, in both the types can be changed by interchanging the connections of main winding or auxiliary winding. The capacitor permanently in the circuit improves the power factor. These motors are more costly than split phase type motors.

The capacitor value can be selected as per the requirement of starting torque, the starting torque can be as high as 350 to 400 % of full load torque. The torque-speed characteristics is as shown in the Fig. 11.4.5.

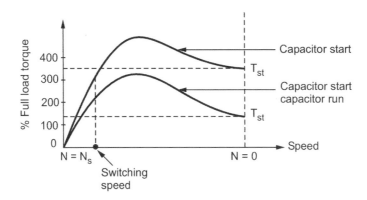

Fig. 11.4.5 Torque-speed characteristics of capacitor split phase motor

11.4.2.1 **Applications**

These motors have high starting torque and hence are used for hard starting loads. These are used for compressors, conveyors, grinders, fans, blowers, refrigerators, air conditioners etc. These are most commonly used motors. The capacitor start capacitor run motors are used in ceiling fans, blowers and air-circulators. These motors are available upto 6 kW.

11.4.3 **Shaded Pole Induction Motors**

This type of motor consists of a squirrel cage rotor and stator consisting of salient poles i.e. projected poles. The poles are shaded i.e. each pole carries a copper band on one of its unequally divided part called **shading band**. Fig. 11.4.6 (a) shows 4 pole shaded pole construction while Fig. 11.4.6 (b) shows a single pole consisting of copper shading band.

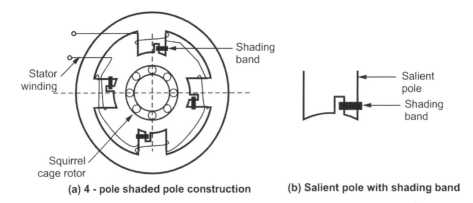

(a) 4 - pole shaded pole construction   **(b) Salient pole with shading band**

Fig. 11.4.6

When single phase a.c. supply is given to the stator winding, due to shading provided to the poles, a rotating magnetic field is generated. The production of rotating magnetic field can be explained as below :

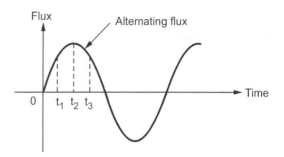

Fig. 11.4.7 (a) Waveform of stator flux

The current carried by the stator winding is alternating and produces alternating flux. The waveform of the flux is shown in the Fig. 11.4.7 (a).

The distribution of this flux in the pole area is greatly influenced by the role of copper shading band. Consider the three instants say t_1, t_2 and t_3 during first half cycle of the flux as shown, in the Fig. 11.4.7 (a).

At instant $t = t_1$, rate of rise of current and hence the flux is very high. Due to the transformer action, large e.m.f. gets induced in the copper shading band. This circulates current through shading band as it is short circuited, producing its own flux. According to Lenz's law, the direction of this current is so as to oppose the cause i.e. rise in current. Hence shading ring flux is opposing to the main flux. Hence there is crowding of flux in nonshaded part while weakening of flux in shaded part. Overall magnetic axis shifts in nonshaded part as shown in the Fig. 11.4.7 (b).

At instant $t = t_2$, rate of rise of current and hence the rate of change of flux is almost zero as flux almost reaches to its maximum value. So $\dfrac{d\phi}{dt} = 0$. Hence there is very little induced e.m.f. in the shading ring. Hence the shading ring flux is also negligible, hardly affecting the distribution of the main flux. Hence the main flux distribution is uniform and magnetic axis lies at the centre of the pole face as shown in the Fig. 11.4.7 (c).

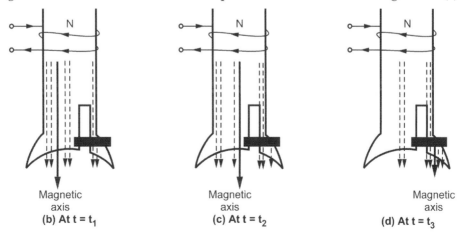

Fig. 11.4.7 (b), (c) & (d) Production of rotating magnetic field in shaded pole motor

At instant $t = t_3$, the current and the flux is decreasing. The rate of decrease is high which again induces a very large e.m.f. in the shading ring. This circulates current through the ring which produces its own flux. Now direction of the flux produced by the shaded ring current is so as to oppose the cause which is decrease in flux. So it oppose the decrease in flux means its direction is same as that of main flux, strengthening it. So there is crowding of flux in the shaded part as compared to nonshaded part. Due to this the magnetic axis shifts to the middle of the shaded part of the pole. This is shown in the Fig. 11.4.7 (d).

This sequence keeps on repeating for negative half cycle too. Consequently this produces an effect of rotating magnetic field, the direction of which is from nonshaded part of the pole to the shaded part of the pole. Due to this, motor produces the starting torque and starts rotating. The starting torque is low which is about 40 to 50 % of the full load torque for this type of motor. The torque speed characteristics is shown in the Fig. 11.4.8.

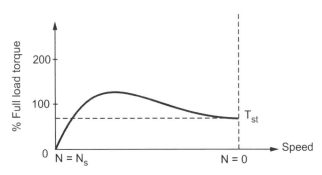

Fig. 11.4.8 Torque-speed characteristics of shaded pole motor

Due to absence of centrifugal switch the construction is simple and robust but this type of motor has a lot of limitations as :

1. The starting torque is poor.

2. The power factor is very low.

3. Due to I^2R, copper losses in the shading ring the efficiency is very low.

4. The speed reversal is very difficult. To achieve the speed reversal, the additional set of shading rings is required. By opening one set and closing other, direction can be reversed but the method is complicated and expensive.

5. The size and power rating of these motors is very small. These motors are usually available in a range of 1/300 to 1/20 kW.

11.4.3.1 Applications

These motors are cheap but have very low starting torque, low power factor and low efficiency. These motors are commonly used for the small fans, toy motors, advertising displays, film projectors, record players, gramophones, hair dryers, photocopying machines etc.

Review Questions

1. *How phase splitting is achieved in capacitor start single phase induction motor ?*

   2011-12, Marks 3

2. *Explain the starting methods of single phase induction motors.*   **2010-11, Marks 5**

3. *Explain the various types of single phase induction motors alongwith their applications.*

4. *What are the limitations of shaded pole induction motor ?*

11.5 Short Answered and Objective Type Questions

Q.1 Match the following (marks will be awarded if all matching are correct) :

2008-09

i) Series resonance	a) Electric fan
ii) Single phase induction motor	b) Condenser
iii) Overexcited synchronous motor	c) Unity power factor
iv) Eddy current loss	d) Thin laminated plates

Ans. :

i)	Series resonance	Unity power factor
ii)	Single phase induction motor	Electric fan
iii)	Overexcited synchronous motor	Condenser
iv)	Eddy current loss	Thin laminated plates

Q.2 Match the following (marks will be awarded if all matching are correct) :

2009-10

Sr. No.	Type of Motor		Application
i)	DC series motor	a)	Centrifugal pumps
ii)	Synchronous motor	b)	Cranes
iii)	3-phase squirrel cage induction motor	c)	Hair dryer
iv)	Single phase shaded pole motor	d)	Condenser

Ans. :   i)   D.C. series motor → (b)

ii)   Synchronous motor → (d)

iii)   3-phase squirrel cage induction motor → (a)

iv)   Single phase shaded pole motor → (c)

Q.3   What is the use of condenser in single-phase a.c. motor ?   `2012-13`

Ans. :   Due to condenser, there is phase difference between starting current and main winding current. Due to this, rotating magnetic field is produced and motor becomes self starting. Condenser also improves the power factor.

Q.4   What is split phasing technique ?

Ans. :   In this technique an additional starting winding is used which is highly resistive in nature. The main winding is inductive in nature. Due to this, the starting winding current and the main winding current are splitted from each other by some angle 'α' at start. The resultant of the two fluxes produced by these currents is a rotating magnetic field. Due to this, the starting torque, which acts only in one direction is produced. Thus the motor becomes self starting. This technique is called split phasing.

Q.5   State the applications of split phase induction motor.

Ans. :   The split phase induction motors have low starting current and moderate starting torque. These are used for easily started loads like fans, blowers, grinders, centrifugal pumps, washing machines, oil burners, office equipments etc.

Q.6   What is the difference between capacitor start motors and capacitor start capacitor run motors ?

Ans. :   In capacitor start motors the capacitor used at start to produce rotating magnetic field is removed once the motor gathers sufficient speed. The capacitor remains in the circuit only at start hence it is called capacitor start motors.

In case of capacitor start capacitor run motor, there is no centrifugal switch and capacitor remain permanently in the circuit for the entire operation of the motor. This improves the overall power factor.

Q.7   State the applications of capacitor start motors and capacitor start capacitor run motors.

Ans. :   The capacitor start motors are used for compressors, conveyors, grinders, fans, blowers, refrigerators, air conditioners etc. These are most commonly used motors. The capacitor start capacitor run motors are used in ceiling fans, blowers and air-circulators.

Q.8   State the limitations of shaded pole induction motor.

Ans. :
1. The starting torque is poor.
2. The power factor is very low.
3. Due to I^2R, copper losses in the shading ring, the efficiency is very low.
4. The speed reversal is very difficult.
5. The size and power rating of these motors is very small. These motors are usually available in a range of 1/300 to 1/20 kW.

Q.9   State the applications of shaded pole induction motor.

Ans. :   The shaded pole induction motors are cheap but have very low starting torque, low power factor and low efficiency. These motors are commonly used for the small fans, toy motors, advertising displays, film projectors, record players, gramophones, hair dryers, photo copying machines etc.

Q.10   Ceiling fan is : _____ .   `2009-10`
   a) three phase IM   b) single phase IM
   c) single phase synchronous motor   d) none of these   **(Ans. : b)**

Q.11   The rotor construction of single phase induction motor is _____.
   a) squirrel cage   b) slip ring   c) salient pole   d) cylindrical
                                                                           (Ans. : a)

Q.12   The rotor of single phase induction motor automatically adjusts itself for _____.
   a) same supply frequency   b) same number of stator poles
   c) same supply voltage   d) none of these   **(Ans. : b)**

Q.13   The single phase induction motors are _____.
   a) of large size   b) of large power rating
   c) unity power factor motors   d) not self starting.   **(Ans. : d)**

Q.14   The net torque experienced by rotor of a single phase induction motor at start is _____.
   a) maximum   b) moderate   c) zero   d) none of these
                                                                           (Ans. : c)

Q.15   The single phase induction motors are not self starting because _____.
   a) rotating magnetic field is absent
   b) the power rating is small
   c) the power factor is low
   d) the efficiency is low   **(Ans. : a)**

Q.16   For the same rating, size of a single phase induction motor is _____ that of three phase induction motor.
   a) $\sqrt{3}$ times   b) 1.5 times   c) same as   d) 2 times. **(Ans. : b)**

Q.17   The auxiliary winding of a split phase induction motor is _____.
   a) highly inductive b) highly capacitive c) highly resistive   d) none of these
                                                                           (Ans. : c)

Q.18   The starting torque in a split phase induction motor is proportional to the _____.
   a) stator frequency b) stator poles   c) stator voltage   d) split phase angle α
                                                                           (Ans. : d)

Q.19 At about 80 % of synchronous speed, the starting winding is disconnected in a single phase induction motor by _____.

a) knife switch   b) centrifugal switch

c) isolating switch   d) triple pole switch   **(Ans. : b)**

Q.20 For a 2 pole, 50 Hz single phase induction motor the synchronous speed is _____.

a) 1500 r.p.m.   b) 750 r.p.m.   c) 3000 r.p.m.   d) 1200 r.p.m.

                                                (Ans. : c)

Q.21 In shaded pole induction motor, the stator has _____.

a) salient poles   b) cylindrical poles

c) square poles   d) none of these   **(Ans. : a)**

Q.22 The material used for shading band in a shaded pole induction motor is _____.

a) iron   b) silver   c) manganin   d) copper **(Ans. : d)**

Q.23 The direction of rotation of shaded pole induction motor is _____.

a) clockwise   b) from nonshaded part to shaded part of pole

c) counter clockwise   d) from shaded part to nonshaded part of pole   **(Ans. : b)**

Q.24 If I_m and I_{st} are the main winding and starting winding currents, separated by angle α then the torque produced is given by _____.

a) $T \propto I_m\, I_{st} \cos \alpha$ b) $T \propto I_m\, I_{st}$

c) $T \propto I_m\, I_{st} \sin \alpha$ d) $T \propto I_m\, I_{st} \tan \alpha$ **(Ans. : c)**

Q.25 The direction of split phase induction motor can be reversed by _____.

a) reversing the connections of main or winding

b) reversing the connections of both the windings

c) changing the rotor construction

d) changing the stator frequency   **(Ans. : a)**

Q.26 The starting torque in capacitor start induction motor is _____.

a) very low   b) moderate   c) very high   d) none of these

                                                (Ans. : c)

Q.27 The starting torque in split phase induction motor is _____.

a) very low   b) moderate   c) very high   d) none of these

                                                (Ans. : b)

Q.28 The starting torque in shaded pole induction motor is _____.

a) very low   b) moderate   c) very high   d) none of these

                                                (Ans. : a)

Q.29 In shaded pole induction motor , the rotating magnetic field is produced due to
_____ .

     a) capacitance   b) inductance

     c) resistance   d) shading bands   **(Ans. : d)**

Q.30 The efficiency of shaded pole induction motor is _____ .

     a) high   b) moderate   c) very low   d) zero   **(Ans. : c)**

Q.31 Which of the following motor does not have a centrifugal switch ?

     a) split phase   b) capacitor start

     c) capacitor start capacitor run   d) none of these   **(Ans. : c)**

Q.32 The shaded pole induction motor is used in _____ .

     a) toy motors   b) record players   c) hair dryers   d) all the above
                                                               (Ans. : d)

Q.33 The rating of ceiling fan induction motor is about _____ .

     a) 200 to 500 W   b) 50 to 150 W   c) 0.5 to 10 W   d) 750 W   **(Ans. : b)**

Q.34 _____ motor gives relatively high starting torque.

     a) Capacitor start   b) Split phase   c) Shaded pole   d) Capacitor run
                                                               (Ans. : a)

Q.35 In a capacitor start motor, the phase angle between starting winding current and
main winding current is nearly _____ .

     a) 30°   b) 60°   c) 90°   d)0°   **(Ans. : c)**

□□□

Notes

12 Three Phase Synchronous Machines

Syllabus

Principle of operation of alternator and synchronous motor and their applications.

Contents

12.1 Introduction

It is known that the electric supply used, now a days for commercial as well as domestic purposes, is of alternating type.

Similar to d.c. machines, the a.c. machines associated with alternating voltages, are also classified as generators and motors.

The machines generating a.c. e.m.f. are called **alternators** or **synchronous generators**. While the machines accepting input from a.c. supply to produce mechanical output are called **synchronous motors**. Both these machines work at a specific constant speed called **synchronous speed** and hence in general called **synchronous machines**.

In d.c. machines, the armature is rotating while field is stationary. But in case of synchronous machines, the armature is kept stationary while field is kept rotating. This rotating field arrangement has certain advantages.

12.2 Advantages of Rotating Field over Rotating Armature

1) As everywhere a.c. is used, the generation level of a.c. voltage may be higher as 11 kV to 33 kV. This gets induced in the armature. For stationary armature large space can be provided to accommodate large number of conductors and the insulation.

2) It is always better to protect high voltage winding from the centrifugal forces caused due to the rotation. So high voltage armature is generally kept stationary. This avoids the interaction of mechanical and electrical stresses.

3) It is easier to collect larger currents at very high voltages from a stationary member than from the slip ring and brush assembly. The voltage required to be supplied to the field is very low (110 V to 220 V d.c.) and hence can be easily supplied with the help of slip ring and brush assembly by keeping it rotating.

4) The problem of sparking at the slip rings can be avoided by keeping field rotating which is low voltage circuit and high voltage armature as stationary.

5) Due to low voltage level on the field side, the insulation required is less and hence field system has very low inertia. It is always better to rotate low inertia system than high inertia, as efforts required to rotate low inertia system are always less.

6) Rotating field makes the overall construction very simple. With simple, robust mechanical construction and low inertia of rotor, it can be driven at high speeds. So greater output can be obtained from an alternator of given size.

7) If field is rotating, to excite it by an external d.c. supply two slip rings are enough. One each for positive and negative terminals. As against this, in three

phase rotating armature, the minimum number of slip rings required are three and can not be easily insulated due to high voltage levels.

8)   The ventilation arrangement for high voltage side can be improved if it is kept stationary.

Due to all these reasons the most of the **synchronous machines** in practice use rotating field type of arrangement.

Review Question

1. *List the advantages of rotating field used in synchronous machines.*

12.3 Construction of Alternator (Synchronous Generator)   `2011-12`

Most of the alternators have stator as armature and rotor as field.

12.3.1 Stator

The stator is a stationary armature. This consists of a core and the slots to hold the armature winding similar to the armature of a d.c. generator. The stator core uses a laminated construction. It is built up of special steel stampings insulated from each other with varnish or paper. The laminated construction is basically to keep down eddy current losses. Generally choice of material is steel to keep down hysteresis losses. The entire core is fabricated in a frame made of steel plates. The core has slots on its periphery for housing the armature conductors. Frame does not carry any flux and serves as the support to the core. Ventilation is maintained with the help of holes cast in the frame. The section of an alternator stator is shown in the Fig. 12.3.1.

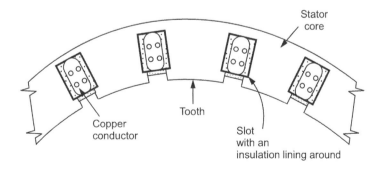

Fig. 12.3.1 Section of an alternator stator

12.3.2 Rotor

There are two types of rotors used in synchronous machines,

i) Salient pole type   and   ii) Smooth cylindrical type.

12.3.2.1 Salient Pole Type Rotor

This is also called **projected pole type as all the poles are projected out from the surface of the rotor.**

The poles are built up of thick steel laminations. The poles are bolted to the rotor as shown in the Fig. 12.3.2. The pole face has been given a specific shape as discussed earlier in case of d.c. generators. The field winding is provided on the pole shoe. These rotors have large diameters and small axial lengths. The limiting factor for the size of the rotor is the

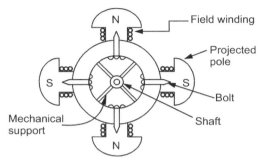

Fig. 12.3.2 Salient pole type rotor

centrifugal force acting on the rotating member of the machine. As mechanical strength of salient pole type is less, this is preferred for low speed synchronous machines ranging from 125 r.p.m. to 500 r.p.m. The prime movers used to drive such rotor are generally water turbines and I.C. engines.

12.3.2.2 Smooth Cylindrical Type Rotor

This is also called **non salient type** or **non-projected pole type of rotor.**

The rotor consists of smooth solid steel cylinder, having number of slots to accommodate the field coil. The slots are covered at the top with the help of steel or manganese wedges. The unslotted portions of the cylinder itself act as the poles. The poles are not projecting out and the surface of the rotor is smooth which maintains uniform air gap between stator and the rotor. These rotors have small diameters and large axial lengths. This is to keep peripheral speed within limits. The main advantage of this type is that these are mechanically very strong and thus preferred for high speed synchronous machines ranging between 1500 to 3000 r.p.m. Such high speed synchronous machines are called **'turboalternators'**. The prime movers used to drive such type of rotors are generally steam turbines, electric motors.

The Fig. 12.3.3 shows smooth cylindrical type of rotor.

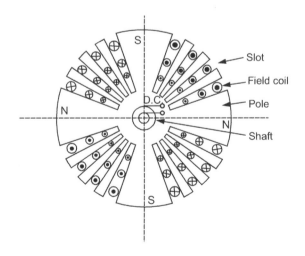

Fig. 12.3.3 Smooth cylindrical rotor

Let us list down the differences between the two types in tabular form.

12.3.2.3 **Difference between Salient and Cylindrical Type of Rotor**

Sr. No.	Salient Pole Type	Smooth Cylindrical Type
1.	Poles are projecting out from the surface.	Unslotted portion of the cylinder acts as poles hence poles are non projecting.
2.	Air gap is non uniform.	Air gap is uniform due to smooth cylindrical periphery.
3.	Diameter is high and axial length is small.	Small diameter and large axial length is the feature.
4.	Mechanically weak.	Mechanically robust.
5.	Preferred for low speed synchronous machines.	Preferred for high speed synchronous machines i.e. for turboalternators.
6.	Prime mover used are water turbines, I.C. engines.	Prime movers used are steam turbines, electric motors.
7.	For same size, the rating is smaller than cylindrical type.	For same size, rating is higher than salient pole type.
8.	Separate damper winding is provided.	Separate damper winding is not necessary.

Review Questions

1. *Explain the construction of synchronous generator.* **2011-12, Marks 5**

2. *Compare between salient and nonsalient rotors used in alternators.*

12.4 Principle of Operation of an Alternator   **2005-06, 2009-10, 2010-11**

The alternators work on the principle of **electromagnetic induction**. When there is a relative motion between the conductors and the flux, e.m.f. gets induced in the conductors. The d.c. generators also work on the same principle. The only difference in practical alternator and a d.c. generator is that in an alternator the conductors are stationary and field is rotating. But for understanding purpose we can always consider relative motion of conductors with respect to the flux produced by the field winding.

Consider a relative motion of a single conductor under the magnetic field produced by two stationary poles. The magnetic axis of the two poles produced by field is vertical, shown dotted in the Fig. 12.4.1.

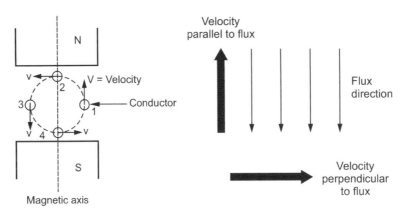

Fig. 12.4.1 Two pole alternator

Let conductor starts rotating from position 1. At this instant, the entire velocity component is **parallel** to the flux lines. Hence there is no cutting of flux lines by the conductor. So $\dfrac{d\phi}{dt}$ at this instant is zero and hence induced e.m.f. in the conductor is also zero.

As the conductor moves from position 1 towards position 2, the part of the velocity component becomes perpendicular to the flux lines and proportional to that, e.m.f. gets induced in the conductor. The magnitude of such an induced e.m.f. increases as the conductor moves from position 1 towards 2.

At position 2, the entire velocity component is **perpendicular** to the flux lines. Hence there exists maximum cutting of the flux lines. And at this instant, the induced e.m.f. in the conductor is at its maximum.

As the position of conductor changes from 2 towards 3, the velocity component perpendicular to the flux starts decreasing and hence induced e.m.f. magnitude also starts decreasing. At position 3, again the entire velocity component is parallel to the flux lines and hence at this instant induced e.m.f. in the conductor is zero.

As the conductor moves from position 3 towards 4, the velocity component perpendicular to the flux lines again starts increasing. But the direction of velocity component now is opposite to the direction of velocity component existing during the movement of the conductor from position 1 to 2. Hence an induced e.m.f. in the conductor increases but in the opposite direction.

At position 4, it achieves maxima in the opposite direction, as the entire velocity component becomes **perpendicular** to the flux lines.

Again from position 4 to 1, induced e.m.f. decreases and finally at position 1, again becomes zero. This cycle continues as conductor rotates at a certain speed.

So if we plot the magnitudes of the induced e.m.f. against the time, we get an alternating nature of the induced e.m.f. as shown in the Fig. 12.4.2.

This is the working principle of an alternator.

As the alternator completes one mechanical revolution, an induced e.m.f. completes one cycle. This is applicable for 2 pole alternator.

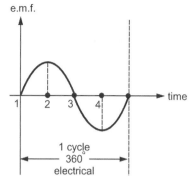

Fig. 12.4.2 Alternating nature of the induced e.m.f.

12.4.1 Mechanical and Electrical Angle

For 2 pole alternator, one mechanical revolution of alternator corresponds to one electrical cycle of an induced e.m.f.

Consider 4 pole alternator as shown in the Fig. 12.4.3. Magnetic axis exists diagonally due to 4 poles.

In this case, as conductor rotates, it experiences maximum cutting of flux at the instants 2, 4, 6 and 8 while velocity component is parallel to the flux at the instants 1, 3, 5 and 7. This is shown in the Fig. 12.4.3 (b).

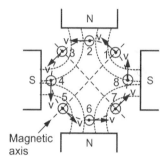

Fig. 12.4.3 (a) 4 Pole alternator

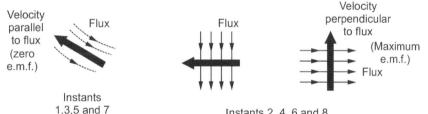

Fig. 12.4.3 (b) Velocity components at different instants

Hence for one mechanical rotation, induced e.m.f. achieves maximum twice and achieves zero twice, in either directions. This is shown in the Fig. 12.4.4.

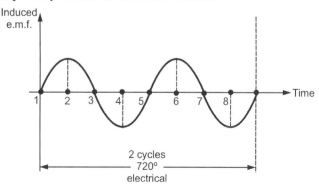

Fig. 12.4.4 Nature of the induced e.m.f.

Hence induced e.m.f. completes 2 cycles for one mechanical rotation for 4 pole synchronous generator. Thus for 4 pole machine, 360° mechanical corresponds to 720° electrical (2 cycles).

In general, $$360° \text{ mechanical} = \frac{P}{2} \times 360° \text{ electrical}$$

∴

$$1° \text{ mechanical} = \left(\frac{P}{2}\right)° \text{ electrical, P = Number of poles}$$

12.4.2 Frequency of Induced E.M.F.

Let   P = Number of poles

             N = Speed of the rotor in r.p.m.

and   f = Frequency of the induced e.m.f.

From the discussion, we can write,

One mechanical revolution of rotor = $\frac{P}{2}$ cycles of e.m.f. electrically

Thus there are P/2 cycles per revolution.

As speed is N r.p.m., in one second, rotor will complete $\left(\frac{N}{60}\right)$ revolutions.

But cycles/sec. = frequency = f

∴   Frequency f = (No. of cycles per revolution) × (No. of revolutions per second)

∴ $$f = \frac{P}{2} \times \frac{N}{60}$$

∴

$$f = \frac{PN}{120} \quad \text{Hz (cycles per sec).}$$

So there exists a fixed relationship between three quantities, the number of poles P, the speed of the rotor N in r.p.m. and f the frequency of an induced e.m.f. in Hz (Hertz).

Key Point *Such a machine bearing a fixed relationship between P, N and f is called* **synchronous machine** *and hence alternators are also called* **synchronous generators.**

12.4.3 Synchronous Speed (N_s)

From the above expression, it is clear that for fixed number of poles, alternator has to be rotated at a particular speed to keep the frequency of the generated e.m.f. constant at the required value. Such a speed is called synchronous speed of the alternator denoted as N_s.

So
$$N_s = \frac{120\,f}{P}$$

where   f = Required frequency

In our nation, the frequency of an alternating e.m.f. is standard equal to 50 Hz. To get 50 Hz frequency, for different number of poles, alternator must be driven at different speeds called synchronous speeds. Following table gives the values of the synchronous speeds for the alternators having different number of poles.

Number of poles P	2	4	8	12	24
Synchronous speed N_s in r.p.m.	3000	1500	750	500	250

Table 12.4.1

From the table, it can be seen that minimum number of poles for an alternator can be two hence maximum value of synchronous speed possible in our nation i.e. for frequency of 50 Hz is 3000 r.p.m.

Review Questions

1. *Explain the principle of operation of synchronous generator.*

     2005-06, 2009-10, 2010-11, Marks 5

2. *Derive the relation between mechanical and electrical angle.*

3. *Derive the relation between poles, speed and frequency for a synchronous generator.*

12.5 E.M.F. Equation of a Synchronous Machine

Let ϕ = Flux per pole, in Wb, P = Number of poles

          N_s = Synchronous speed in r.p.m., f = Frequency of induced e.m.f. in Hz

          Z = Total number of conductors

          Z_{ph} = Conductors per phase connected in series

∴ $Z_{ph} = \dfrac{Z}{3}$ as number of phases = 3.

Consider a single conductor placed in a slot.

The average value of e.m.f. induced in a conductor $= \dfrac{d\phi}{dt}$

For one revolution of a conductor,

$$e_{avg} \text{ per conductor} = \frac{\text{Flux cut in one revolution}}{\text{Time taken for one revolution}}$$

Total flux cut in one revolution is $\phi \times P$.

Time taken for one revolution is $\dfrac{60}{N_s}$ seconds.

$\therefore \qquad e_{avg}$ per conductor $= \dfrac{\phi P}{\left(\dfrac{60}{N_s}\right)} = \phi\,\dfrac{PN_s}{60}$ 　　　　　　　　　　...(12.5.1)

But $\qquad\qquad\qquad f = \dfrac{PN_s}{120}$

$\therefore \qquad\qquad\qquad \dfrac{PN_s}{60} = 2f$ Substituting in equation (12.5.1),

$\qquad e_{avg}$ per conductor $= 2\,f\,\phi$ volts

Assume full pitch winding for simplicity i.e. this conductor is connected to a conductor which is 180° electrical apart. So these two e.m.f.s will try to set up a current in the same direction i.e. the two e.m.f. are helping each other and hence resultant e.m.f. per turn will be twice the e.m.f. induced in a conductor.

$\therefore$ e.m.f. per turn $= 2 \times$ (e.m.f. per conductor) $= 2 \times (2f\,\phi) = 4\,f\,\phi$ volts.

Let T_{ph} be the total number of turns per phase connected in series. Assuming concentrated winding, we can say that all are placed in single slot per pole per phase. So induced e.m.f.s in all turns will be in phase as placed in single slot. Hence net e.m.f. per phase will be algebraic sum of the e.m.f.s per turn.

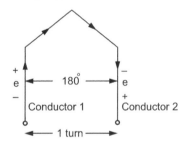

Fig. 12.5.1 Turn of full pitch coil

$\therefore$ Average $E_{ph} = T_{ph} \times$ (Average e.m.f. per turn) $= T_{ph} \times 4\,f\,\phi$

But in a.c. circuits R.M.S. value of an alternating quantity is used for the analysis. The form factor is 1.11 of sinusoidal e.m.f.

$$K_f = \dfrac{R.M.S.}{Average} = 1.11 \qquad \text{for sinusoidal}$$

$\therefore$ R.M.S. value of $E_{ph} = K_f \times$ Average value

$\therefore \qquad\qquad\qquad E_{ph} = 1.11 \times 4\,f\,\phi\,T_{ph}$

$$\boxed{E_{ph} = 4.44\,f\,\phi\,T_{ph} \qquad \text{volts}}$$

Key Point *This is the basic e.m.f. equation for an induced e.m.f. per phase for full pitch, concentrated type of winding.*

Where T_{ph} = Number of turns per phase

$$T_{ph} = \frac{Z_{ph}}{2}$$ ... as 2 conductors constitute 1 turn

The winding of a synchronous machine is distributed and short pitched. Due to this, the generated e.m.f. slightly decreases. The factors by which the generated e.m.f. slightly decreases are,

K_c = Coil span factor or pitch factor

K_d = Distribution factor.

Both K_c and K_d are less than unity. Hence the e.m.f. equation of a synchronous machine is,

$$E_{ph} = 4.44 \ K_c K_d \ \phi \ f T_{ph}$$

Depending upon the connection of the winding whether star or delta, the line value of the induced e.m.f. is $\sqrt{3} \ E_{ph}$ or E_{ph} respectively.

Review Question

> 1. *Deduce the e.m.f. equation of a synchronous machine.*

12.6 Synchronous Motor

If a.c. supply is given to stator of three phase alternator, it will start rotating at synchronous speed and will work as a motor. Such a device, which converts alternating type of electric supply into mechanical form, running at synchronous speed N_s, is called **synchronous motor**.

Key Point *The synchronous motor works **only at synchronous speed** and cannot work at a speed other than the synchronous speed.*

The rotating magnetic field, getting produced when three phase supply is given to a three phase stationary winding is the base of working principle of a synchronous motor.

12.7 Construction of Three Phase Synchronous Motor

Similar to d.c. machine where there is no constructional difference between a generator and motor, there is no difference between the construction of synchronous motor and the alternator both being the synchronous machines.

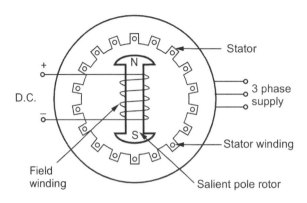

Fig. 12.7.1 Schematic representation of three phase synchronous motor

The synchronous motor construction is basically similar to rotating field type alternator. It consists of two parts :

i) Stator : Consisting of a three phase star or delta connected winding. This is excited by a three phase a.c. supply.

ii) Rotor : Rotor is a field winding, the construction of which can be salient (projected pole) or non salient (cylindrical) type. Practically most of the synchronous motors use salient i.e. projected pole type construction. The field winding is excited by a separate d.c. supply through slip rings.

Review Question

> 1. *Explain the construction of three phase synchronous motor.*

12.8 Working Principle of Synchronous Motor   2009-10, 2010-11

Synchronous motor works on the principle of the **magnetic locking**. When two unlike poles are brought near each other, if the magnets are strong, there exists a tremendous force of attraction between those two poles. In such condition the two magnets are said to be magnetically locked.

If now one of the two magnets is rotated, the other also rotates in the same direction, with the same speed due to the force of attraction i.e. due to magnetic locking condition. The principle is shown schematically in the Fig. 12.8.1.

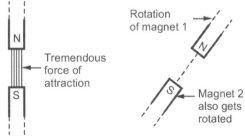

Fig. 12.8.1 Principle of magnetic locking

Consider a three phase synchronous motor, whose stator is wound for 2 poles. The two magnetic fields are produced in the synchronous motor by exciting both the windings, stator and rotor with three phase a.c. supply and d.c. supply respectively.

When three phase stator winding is excited by a three phase a.c. supply then the flux produced by the three phase winding is **rotating magnetic field** rotating in space at a speed called synchronous speed. The rotating magnetic field creates the effect similar to the physical rotation of magnet in space with a synchronous speed.

$$N_s = \frac{120\,f}{P} \text{ r.p.m.} \qquad \text{Speed of rotating magnetic field}$$

For simplicity of understanding let us assume that the stator poles are N_1 and S_1 which are rotating at a speed of N_s. The direction of rotation of rotating magnetic field is say clockwise.

When the field winding on rotor is excited by a d.c. supply, it also produces two poles, assuming rotor construction to be two pole, salient type. Let these poles be N_2 and S_2.

Now one magnet is rotating at N_s having poles N_1 and S_1 while at start rotor is stationary i.e. second magnet is stationary having poles N_2 and S_2. If somehow the unlike poles N_1 and S_2 or S_1 and N_2 are brought near each other, the magnetic locking may get established between stator and rotor poles. As stator poles are rotating, due to magnetic locking, rotor will also rotate in the same direction as that of stator poles i.e. in the direction of rotating magnetic field, with the same speed i.e. N_s. Hence synchronous motor rotates at one and only one speed i.e. synchronous speed.

This is shown in the Fig. 12.8.2.

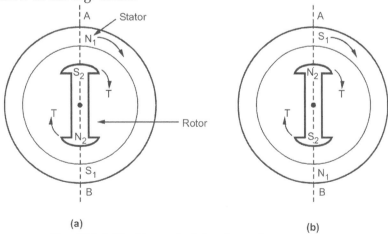

(a)   (b)

Fig. 12.8.2 Working principle of synchronous motor

Practically it is not possible for stator poles to pull the rotor poles from their stationary position into magnetic locking condition because of rotor inertia. Hence synchronous motors are not self starting.

12.8.1 Why Synchronous Motor is Not Self Starting ?

Consider the rotating magnetic field as equivalent to physical rotation of two stator poles N_1 and S_1. Consider an instant when two poles are at such a position where stator magnetic axis is vertical, along A-B as shown in the Fig. 12.8.3 (a).

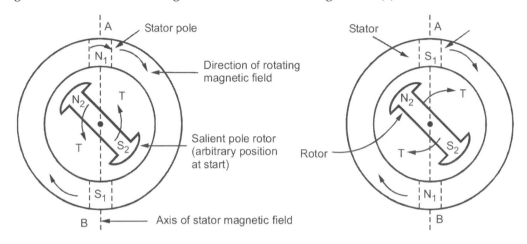

(a) Action of synchronous motor   **(b) Action of synchronous motor**

Fig. 12.8.3

At this instant, rotor poles are arbitrarily positioned as shown in the Fig. 12.8.3 (a).

At this instant, rotor is stationary and unlike poles will try to attract each other. Due to this rotor will be subjected to an instantaneous torque in anticlockwise direction as shown in the Fig. 12.8.3 (a).

Now stator poles are rotating very fast i.e. at a speed N_s r.p.m. Due to inertia, before rotor hardly rotates in the direction of anticlockwise torque, to which it is subjected, the stator poles change their positions. Consider an instant half a period latter where stator poles are exactly reversed but due to inertia rotor is unable to rotate from its initial position. This is shown in the Fig. 12.8.3 (b).

At this instant, due to the unlike poles trying to attract each other, the rotor will be subjected to a torque in clockwise direction. This will tend to rotate rotor in the direction of rotating magnetic field.

But before this happens, stator poles again change their positions reversing the direction of the torque exerted on the rotor.

As a result, the **average torque exerted on the rotor is zero. And hence the synchronous motor is not self starting.**

Review Questions

1. *Explain the principle of operation of synchronous motor.* **2009-10, 2010-11, Marks 5**
2. *Why synchronous motor is not self starting ?*

12.9 Methods of Starting Synchronous Motor

As seen earlier, synchronous motor is not self starting. It is necessary to rotate the rotor at a speed very near to synchronous speed. This is possible by various methods in practice. The various methods to start the synchronous motor are,

1. Using pony motors   2. Using damper winding

3. As a slip ring induction motor   4. Using small d.c. machine coupled to it.

12.9.1 Using Pony Motors

In this method, the rotor is brought to the synchronous speed with the help of some external device like small induction motor. Such an external device is called **'Pony Motor'**.

Once the rotor attains the synchronous speed, the d.c. excitation to the rotor is switched on. Once the synchronism is established pony motor is decoupled. The motor then continues to rotate as a synchronous motor.

12.9.2 Using Damper Winding

In a synchronous motor, in addition to the normal field winding, the additional winding consisting of copper bars is placed in the slots in the pole faces. The bars are short circuited with the help of end rings. Such an additional winding on the rotor is called **damper winding**. This winding as short circuited, acts as a squirrel cage rotor winding of an induction motor. The schematic representation of such damper winding is shown in the Fig. 12.9.1.

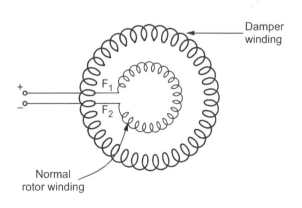

Fig. 12.9.1 Starting as a squirrel cage I.M.

Once the stator is excited by a three phase supply, the motor starts rotating as an induction motor at subsynchronous speed. Then d.c. supply is given to the field winding. At a particular instant motor gets pulled into synchronism and starts rotating at a synchronous speed. As rotor rotates at synchronous speed, the relative motion between damper winding and the rotating magnetic field is zero. Hence when motor is running as synchronous motor, there cannot be any induced e.m.f. in the damper winding. So damper winding is active only at start, to run the motor as an induction motor at start. Afterwards it is out of the circuit. As damper winding is short circuited and motor gets started as induction motor, it draws high current at start so induction motor starters like star-delta, autotransformer etc. are used to start the synchronous motor as an induction motor.

12.9.3 As a Slip Ring Induction Motor

The above method of starting synchronous motor as a squirrel cage induction motor does not provide high starting torque. So to achieve this, instead of shorting the damper winding, it is designed to form a three phase star or delta connected winding. The three ends of this winding are brought out through slip rings. An external rheostat then can be introduced in series with the rotor circuit. So when stator is excited, the motor starts as a slip ring induction motor and due to resistance added in the rotor, provides high starting torque. The resistance is then gradually cut off, as motor gathers speed. When motor attains speed near synchronous, d.c. excitation is provided to the rotor, then motor gets pulled into synchronism and starts rotating at synchronous speed. The damper winding is shorted by shorting the slip rings. The initial resistance added in the rotor not only provides high starting torque but also limits high inrush of starting current. Hence it acts as a rotor resistance starter.

The synchronous motor started by this method is called a slip ring induction motor as shown in the Fig. 12.9.2.

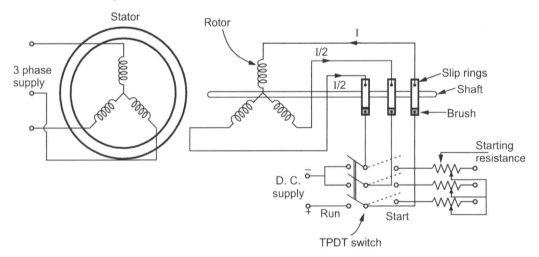

Fig. 12.9.2 Starting as a slip ring I.M.

It can be observed from the Fig. 12.9.2 that the same three phase rotor winding acts as a normal rotor winding by shorting two of the phases. From the positive terminal, current 'I' flows in one of the phases, which divides into two other phases at star point as I/2 through each, when switch is thrown on d.c. supply side.

12.9.4 Using Small D.C. Machine

Many a times, a large synchronous motors are provided with a coupled d.c. machine. This machine is used as a d.c. motor to rotate the synchronous motor at a synchronous speed. Then the excitation to the rotor is provided. Once motor starts running as a synchronous motor, the same d.c. machine acts as a d.c. generator called exciter. The field of the synchronous motor is then excited by this exciter itself.

Review Question

> 1. *Explain the various methods of starting synchronous motor.*

12.10 Behaviour of Synchronous Motor on Loading

As the load on the motor increases the speed of the synchronous motor remains same as synchronous but the rotor field axis falls back with respect to stator field axis maintaining the magnetic locking condition.

So the rotor axis falls back with respect to stator axis by angle 'δ' on loading, as shown in Fig. 12.10.1.

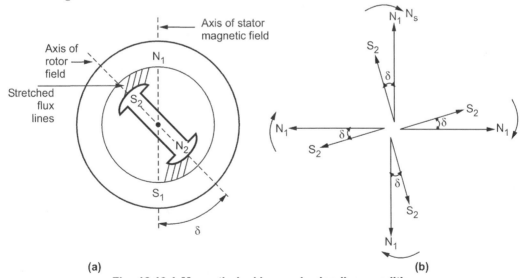

(a)   (b)

Fig. 12.10.1 Magnetic locking under loading condition

This angle decides the amount of current required to produce the torque to supply various load conditions.

Hence this angle is called **load angle, power angle, coupling angle, torque angle or angle of retardation** and denoted as δ .

12.10.1 Back e.m.f. in Synchronous Motor

In case of synchronous motor, once rotor starts rotating at synchronous speed, the stationary stator conductors cut the flux produced by rotor. The conductors are stationary and flux is rotating. Due to this there is an induced e.m.f. in the stator which according to Lenz's law opposes the supply voltage. This induced e.m.f. is called **back e.m.f.** in case of synchronous motor. It is denoted as E_{bph} i.e. back e.m.f. per phase. This gets generated as the principle of alternator and hence alternating in nature and its magnitude can be calculated by the equation,

$$E_{bph} = 4.44 \ K_c \ K_d \ \phi \ f \ T_{ph}$$

or $\qquad E_{bph} \ \propto \ \phi \ \text{(excitation)}$

As speed is always synchronous, the frequency is constant and hence magnitude of such back e.m.f. can be controlled by changing the flux ϕ produced by the rotor.

So **back e.m.f. in case of synchronous motor depends on the excitation given to the field winding and not on the speed, as speed is always constant.**

The impedance of the stator is called synchronous impedance of synchronous motor consisting of R_a as the stator winding resistance and X_s as the synchronous reactance. All the values are generally expressed on per phase basis.

$$Z_s \ = \ R_a + j \ X_s \ \Omega \ \text{per phase}$$

The voltage equation for a synchronous motor is,

$$\overline{V}_{ph} \ = \ \overline{E}_{bph} + \overline{I}_{aph} \ \overline{Z}_s = \overline{E}_{bph} + \overline{E}_{Rph} \qquad \text{... Phasor addition}$$

This equation is vector equation as each quantity is alternating and has different phases. So addition is to be performed vectorially to obtain the result.

$$\therefore \qquad \overline{I}_{aph} \ = \ \frac{\overline{V}_{ph} - \overline{E}_{bph}}{\overline{Z}_s}$$

where V_{ph} is the supply voltage per phase.

The magnitude of E_{bph} is adjusted almost equal to V_{ph}, on no load by controlling flux produced by rotor i.e. field winding.

For an ideal synchronous motor the losses are zero and on no load $E_{bph} = V_{ph}$ and E_{bph} opposes the supply voltage. Thus the difference $\overline{V}_{ph} - \overline{E}_{bph} = 0$ and the current drawn by the motor is zero. Hence the phasor diagram for an ideal synchronous motor on no load is as shown in the Fig. 12.10.2. Pratically motor draws very small current to meet the no load losses.

Fig. 12.10.2 Phasor diagram for ideal no load condition

12.10.2 Synchronous Motor on Load

As the load on the synchronous motor increases, there is no change in its speed. But what gets affected is the load angle 'δ' i.e. the angle by which rotor axis retards with respect to stator axis.

Hence as load increases, δ increases but speed remains synchronous.

As δ increases, though E_{bph} and V_{ph} magnitudes are same, displacement of E_{bph} from its ideal position increases. Hence the vector difference $\overline{V}_{ph} - \overline{E}_{bph}$ increases i.e. $\overline{E}_{Rph} = \overline{I}_{aph}\overline{Z}_s$ increases. As synchronous impedance is constant, the magnitude of I_{aph} drawn by the motor increases as load increases.

This current produces the necessary torque which satisfies the increased load demand. The magnetic locking still exists between the rotor and stator.

The phasor diagrams showing E_{Rph} increases as load increases are shown in Fig. 12.10.3 (a) and (b).

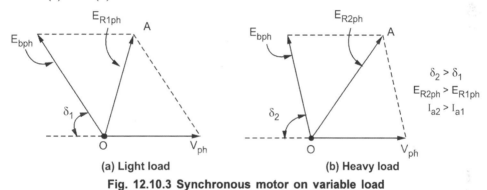

(a) Light load   (b) Heavy load

Fig. 12.10.3 Synchronous motor on variable load

Thus the torque produced in synchronous motor depends on load angle δ.

As angle δ increases, the magnetic flux lines producing the force of attraction between the two get more and more stretched. This weakens the force maintaining the magnetic locking, though torque produced by the motor increases. As δ reaches upto $90°$ electrical i.e. half a pole pitch, the stretched flux lines get broken and hence magnetic locking between the stator and rotor no longer exists. The motor comes out of synchronism. So torque produced at 'δ' equal to $90°$ electrical is the maximum torque, a synchronous motor can produce, maintaining magnetic locking i.e. synchronism. Such a torque is called **pull out torque**. The relationship between torque produced and load angle δ is shown in the Fig. 12.10.4.

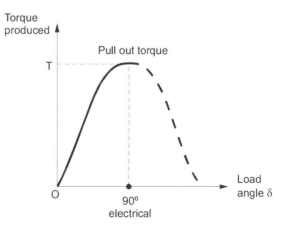

Fig. 12.10.4 Torque-angle characteristics

Let us summarize the details to show them in a single phasor diagram as shown in the Fig. 12.10.5.

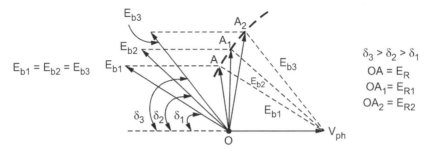

Fig. 12.10.5 Constant excitation variable load condition

As load increases, the angle δ increases while as excitation is constant, E_b remains constant in magnitude. But as δ changes from δ_1 to δ_2 and so on due to increase in the load, so the resultant E_R increases.

$$E_{R2} \; > \; E_{R1} > E_R$$

But as $E_R = I_a Z_s$ and Z_s is constant, the current drawn by the motor increases.

$$\therefore \qquad I_{a3} \; > \; I_{a2} > I_{a1}$$

So as load increases, current drawn by the motor increases.

The locus of tip of the phasor E_R as load on the motor increases, is a circle shown dotted in the Fig. 12.10.5.

As seen earlier such increase in the load permissible without loss of synchronism till δ becomes 90° electrical.

Review Questions

> 1. *Explain why synchronous motor draws more current as load increases.*
> 2. *Explain the behaviour of synchronous motor on constant excitation variable load condition.*

12.11 Operation at Constant Load Variable Excitation

In the last article we have seen that when load changes, for constant excitation, current drawn by the motor increases. But if excitation i.e. field current is changed keeping load constant, the synchronous motor reacts by changing its power factor of operation. This is most interesting feature of synchronous motor. Let us see the details of such operation.

Consider a synchronous motor operating at a certain load. The corresponding load angle is δ.

At start, consider normal behaviour of the synchronous motor, where excitation is adjusted to get $E_b = V$ i.e. induced e.m.f. is equal to applied voltage. Such an excitation is called **Normal Excitation** of the motor. Motor is drawing certain current I_a from the supply and power input to the motor is say P_{in}. The power factor of the motor is lagging in nature as shown in the Fig. 12.11.1 (a).

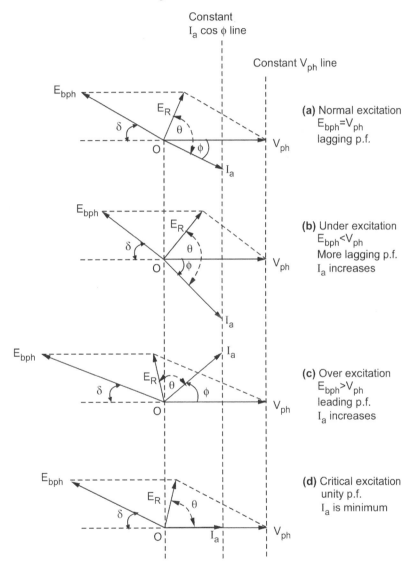

Fig. 12.11.1 Constant load variable excitation operation

Now when excitation is changed, E_b changes but there is hardly any change in the losses of the motor. So the power input also remains same for constant load demanding same power output.

Now $\qquad P_{in} = \sqrt{3}\, V_L\, I_L\, \cos\phi = 3\,(V_{ph}\, I_{aph}\, \cos\phi)$

Most of the times, the voltage applied to the motor is constant. Hence for constant power input as V_{ph} is constant, '$I_{aph}\cos\phi$' remains constant.

So for this entire operation of variable excitation it is necessary to remember that the cosine component of armature current, '$I_a \cos\phi$ ' **remains constant**.

So motor adjusts its $\cos\phi$ i.e. p.f. nature and value of I_a so that $I_a \cos\phi$ remains constant when excitation of the motor is changed, keeping load constant. This is the reason why synchronous motor reacts by changing its power factor to variable excitation conditions.

12.11.1 Under Excitation

When the excitation is adjusted in such a way that the magnitude of induced e.m.f. is less than the applied voltage ($E_b < V$) the excitation is called **Under excitation.**

Due to this, E_R increases in magnitude. This means for constant Z_s, current drawn by the motor increases. But E_R phase shifts in such a way that, phasor I_a also shifts (as $E_R \wedge I_a = \theta$) to keep $I_a \cos\phi$ component constant. This is shown in the Fig. 12.11.1 (b). So in under excited condition, current drawn by the motor increases. The p.f. $\cos\phi$ decreases and becomes more and more lagging in nature.

12.11.2 Over Excitation

The excitation to the field winding for which the induced e.m.f. becomes greater than applied voltage ($E_b > V$), is called **Over excitation.**

Due to increased magnitude of E_b, E_R also increases in magnitude. But the phase of E_R also changes. Now $E_R \wedge I_a = \theta$ is constant, hence I_a also changes its phase. So ϕ changes. The I_a increases to keep $I_a \cos\phi$ constant as shown in Fig. 12.11.1 (c). The phase of E_R changes so that I_a becomes leading with respect to V_{ph} in over excited condition. So power factor of the motor becomes leading in nature. So overexcited synchronous motor works on leading power factor. So power factor decreases as over excitation increases but it becomes more and more leading in nature.

12.11.3 Critical Excitation

When the excitation is changed, the power factor changes. The excitation for which the power factor of the motor is unity ($\cos\phi = 1$) is called **Critical excitation.** Then I_{aph} is in phase with V_{ph}. Now $I_a \cos\phi$ must be constant, $\cos\phi = 1$ is at its maximum hence motor has to draw **minimum current** from supply for unity power factor condition.

So for critical excitation, $\cos \phi = 1$ and current drawn by the motor is minimum compared to current drawn by the motor for various excitation conditions. This is shown in the Fig. 12.11.1 (d).

Under excitation	Lagging p.f.	$E_b < V$
Over excitation	Leading p.f.	$E_b > V$
Critical excitation	Unity p.f.	$E_b \cong V$
Normal excitation	Lagging	$E_b = V$

Table 12.11.1

12.11.4 V-Curves and Inverted V-Curves

From the above discussion about variable excitation operation of motor, it is clear that if excitation is varied from very low (under excitation) to very high (over excitation) value, then current I_a decreases, becomes minimum at unity p.f. and then again increases. But initial lagging current becomes unity and then becomes leading in nature. This can be shown as in the Fig. 12.11.2.

Excitation can be increased by increasing the field current passing through the field winding of synchronous motor. If graph of

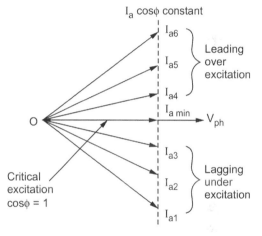

Fig. 12.11.2

armature current drawn by the motor (I_a) against field current (I_f) is plotted, then its shape looks like an english alphabet V. If such graphs are obtained at various load conditions we get family of curves, all looking like V. Such curves are called V-curves of synchronous motor. These are shown in the Fig. 12.11.3 (a).

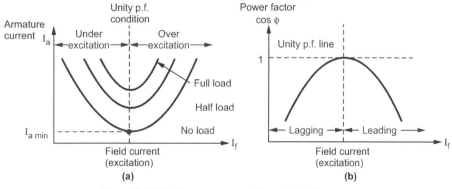

Fig. 12.11.3 V-curves and inverted V-curves

As against this, if the power factor (cos ϕ) is plotted against field current (I_f), then the shape of the graph looks like an inverted V. Such curves obtained by plotting p.f. against I_f, at various load conditions are called Inverted V-curves of synchronous motor. These curves are shown in the Fig. 12.11.3 (b).

As over excited synchronous motor works on leading power factor, it is used as a synchronous condenser to improve power factor.

Review Question

1. *Explain the operation of synchronous motor at constant load variable excitation.*

12.12 Applications of Three Phase Synchronous Motor

2009-10, 2010-11

The important characteristics of the synchronous motor is its constant speed irrespective of the load conditions, and variable power factor operation. As seen earlier its power factor can be controlled by controlling its excitation. For overexcitation its power factor is leading in nature, which is very important from the power factor correction point of view.

Due to constant speed characteristics, it is used in machine tools, motor generator sets, synchronous clocks, stroboscopic devices, timing devices, belt driven reciprocating compressors, fans and blowers, centrifugal pumps, vacuum pumps, pulp grinders, textile mills, paper mills line shafts, rolling mills, cement mills etc.

The synchronous motors are often used as a power factor correction device, phase advancers and phase modifiers for voltage regulation of the transmission lines. This is possible because the excitation of the synchronous motor can be adjusted as per the requirement.

The disadvantages of synchronous motors are their higher cost, necessity of frequent maintenance and a need of d.c. excitation source, auxiliary device or additional winding provision to make it self starting. Overall their initial cost is very high.

Review Question

1. *State the applications of synchronous motor.*   2009-10, 2010-11, Marks 2

12.13 Comparison between Synchronous and Induction Motor

Sr. No.	Synchronous motor	Induction motor
1	Construction is complicated.	Construction is simple, particularly in case of cage rotor.
2	It is not self starting.	It is self starting.
3	A separate d.c. excitation source is required to excite the rotor.	A separate d.c. excitation to the rotor is not necessary.
4	The speed is always synchronous irrespective of the load.	The speed decreases as the load increases.
5	It operates at synchronous speed and never at speed other than synchronous.	It operates below the synchronous speed and never at the synchronous speed.
6	Speed control is not possible.	Though difficult, speed control is possible.
7	By changing its excitation, can be made to operate with wide range of power factors both lagging and leading.	It always operates at lagging power factors and power factor control is not possible.
8	It can be used as synchronous condenser for power factor improvement.	It cannot be used as a synchronous condenser.
9	Motor is more sensitive to sudden load changes. Hunting starts as load changes suddenly.	Less sensitive to sudden load changes. Phenomenon of hunting is absent.
10	Motor is very much costlier and requires the maintenance.	Motor is much cheaper and almost maintenance free particularly in case of squirrel cage rotors.

Review Question

> 1. *Compare synchronous motor with induction motor.*

12.14 Short Answered and Objective Type Questions

Q.1 A device which converts an electrical energy into a mechanical energy running only at synchronous speed is called _____.   **(Ans. : synchronous motor)**

Q.2 Synchronous motor works on the principle of _____**(Ans. : magnetic locking)**

Q.3 Synchronous motor is not _____.   **(Ans. : self starting)**

Q.4 Separate _____ is required for the rotor of synchronous motor.   **(Ans. : d.c. supply)**

Q.5 As the load increases the _____ increases but _____ remains constant in synchronous motor.   **(Ans. : load angle, speed)**

Q.6 The induced e.m.f. in the stator of synchronous motor is called _____.
(Ans. : back e.m.f.)

Q.7 The back e.m.f. in case of synchronous motor depends on the _____ given to the field winding and not on the _____. **(Ans. : excitation, speed)**

Q.8 The excitation for which $E_b = V$ is called _____ excitation. **(Ans. : normal)**

Q.9 The excitation for which $E_b < V$ is called _____ excitation. **(Ans. : under)**

Q.10 The excitation for which $E_b > V$ is called _____ excitation. **(Ans. : over)**

Q.11 The excitation for which power factor is unity is called _____ excitation.
(Ans. : critical)

Q.12 For critical excitation the _____ is minimum and _____ is maximum.
(Ans. : current, power factor)

Q.13 If graph of armature current drawn by the motor (I_a) against field current (I_f) is called _____. **(Ans. : Vee curve)**

Q.14 If graph of power factor of the motor against field current (I_f) is called _____.
(Ans. : inverted Vee curve)

Q.15 The maximum torque occurs when load angle is _____ in synchronous motors.
(Ans. : 90)

Q.16 External motor used to start synchronous motor is called _____.
(Ans. : pony motor)

Q.17 Over excited synchronous motor operating on no load condition is called _____. **(Ans. : synchronous condenser)**

Q.18 The _____ is used for the power factor impovement.
(Ans. : synchronous condenser)

Q.19 In normal and under excitation the power factor is _____ in nature.
(Ans. : lagging)

Q.20 Name two motors used for constant speed operation.   2011-12
Ans. : 1. D.C. shunt motor 2. Synchronous motor

Q.21 Write the name of different types of rotor of an alternator.   2012-13
Ans. : Salient pole rotor and nonsalient or cylindrical rotor.

Q.22 Under no load running condition of synchronous machine, what will be the angle between the induced voltage and supply voltage ?   2012-13
Ans. : Under no load condition, induced e.m.f. and supply voltage are in antiphase i.e. angle between them is $180°$.

Q.23 Synchronous motor can be used as power factor improving device : _____ .

a) Yes   b) No   **(Ans. : a)**

Q.24 The range of speed for salient pole synchronous machines is _____.

a) above 500 r.p.m.   b) above 1000 r.p.m.

c) 125 to 500 r.p.m.   d) None of these   **(Ans. : c)**

Q.25 _____ rotor construction is used for turbo alternators.

a) Nonsalient   b) Salient   c) Squirrel cage   d) Slip ring

                                                                                      (Ans. : a)

Q.26 If an alternator has 8 poles then for one mechanical rotation, the number of cycles of induced e.m.f. is _____.

a) 2   b) 4   c) 8   d) 1   **(Ans. : b)**

Q.27 For an alternator, $1°$ mechanical = _____ electrical.

A) $P°$ b) $2P°$ c) $4P°$ d) $\dfrac{P°}{2}$

                                                                                            (Ans. : d)

Q.28 The maximum value of the synchronous speed for an alternator is _____.

a) 1500 r.p.m.   b) 2000 r.p.m.   c) 3000 r.p.m.   d) 4000 r.p.m.

                                                                                             (Ans. : c)

Q.29 The synchronous motor always runs at _____ speed.

a) subsynchronous   b) synchronous   c) more than synchronous

d) none of these.   **(Ans. : b)**

Q.30 The working principle of synchronous motor is _____.

a) magnetic locking   b) magnetic huming

c) magnetic induction   d) none of these   **(Ans. : a)**

Q.31 The slip of a synchronous motor in running condition is _____.

a) one   b) 5 %   c) zero   d) 10 %   **(Ans. : c)**

Q.32 For a 50 Hz, 250 r.p.m. synchronous motor, the number of poles is _____.

a) 20   b) 16   c) 8   d) 24   **(Ans. : d)**

Q.33 _____ motor is used to start the synchronous motor.

a) Pony motor   b) Universal motor

c) A.C. series motor   d) None of these   **(Ans. : a)**

Q.34 _____ winding is used to start the synchronous motor which helps to prevent hunting.

a) Compensating   b) Damper   c) Field   d) Armature

                                                                                             (Ans. : b)

Q.35 The back e.m.f in synchronous motor depends on _____.

a) speed   b) stator poles   c) excitation   d) frequency
                                                                    (Ans. : c)

Q.36 The torque at which synchronous motor comes out of synchronism is called _____.

a) shaft torque   b) armature torque   c) pull out torque   d) slip torque
                                                                    (Ans. : c)

Q.37 The pull out torque occurs when the load angle δ = _____.

a) 90°   b) 45°   c) 60°   d) 0°   **(Ans. : a)**

Q.38 If the excitation of synchronous motor is varied, its _____ varies.

a) voltage   b) power factor   c) power   d) none of these
                                                                    (Ans. : b)

Q.39 The over excited synchronous motor works at _____ power factor.

a) lagging   b) zero   c) leading   d) unity   **(Ans. : c)**

Q.40 The under excited synchronous motor works at _____ power factor.

a) lagging   b) zero   c) leading   d) unity   **(Ans. : a)**

Q.41 The excitation at which power factor is unity is called _____ excitation.

a) under   b) over   c) normal   d) critical **(Ans. : d)**

Q.42 The graph of I_a against I_f at various excitation is called _____.

a) A curve   b) V curve   c) C curve   d) None of these
                                                                    (Ans. : b)

Q.43 At critical excitation, the armature current drawn by the synchronous motor is _____.

a) maximum   b) zero   c) minimum   d) none of these
                                                                    (Ans. : c)

Q.44 The synchronous motor is used as _____.

a) transformer   b) power factor correction device
c) induction motor   d) universal motor   **(Ans. : b)**

Q.45 To change the direction of rotation of synchronous motor, _____.

a) increase the field excitation   b) interchange any two stator terminals

c) decrease the supply voltage.   d) increase the supply frequency **(Ans. : b)**

Q.46 As the load on the synchronous motor increases _____.

a) load angle increases, current drawn decreases.
b) load angle decreases, current drawn decreases.
c) load angle increases, current drawn increases.
d) none of the above.   **(Ans. : c)**

Q.47   As the load on the synchronous motor increases, its speed _____.

a) increases   b) remains constant

c) decreases   d) none of these   **(Ans. : b)**

Q.48   If the synchronous motor is switched on to the supply with field windings shorted then _____.

a) it will not start   b) its speed will be dangerously high

c) it will start and continue to run as an induction motor

d) it will start as induction motor but later will run as synchronous motor.

(Ans. : c)

Q.49   A _____ synchronous motor is used as a synchronous capacitor.

a) over excited   b) under excited   c) normal excited   d) critically excited

(Ans. : a)

Q.50   The operating speed of synchronous motor can be changed by _____.

a) changing the load   b) changing the voltage

c) changing the frequency   d) none of these   **(Ans. : c)**

Q.51   In V curve, the power factor to the left of unity p.f. line is _____.

a) leading   b) lagging   c) zero   d) depends on load

(Ans. : b)

Q.52   The slip rings in synchronous motor carry _____.

a) alternating current   b) direct current

c) pulsating current   d) none of these   **(Ans. : b)**

❑❑❑

Notes

13 Introduction to Power System

Syllabus (Only for MMTU)

General layout of electrical power system and functions of its elements, Standard transmission and distribution voltages, Concept of grid (Elementary treatment only).

Contents

13.1 Introduction

The energy is neither be created nor be destroyed but it can be converted from one form to another. The generation of an electrical energy is nothing but the conversion of various other forms of energy into an electrical energy. The various energy sources which are used to generate an electrical energy on the large scale are steam obtained by burning coal, oil, natural gas, water stored in dams, diesel oil, nuclear power and other nonconventional energy sources. The electrical power is generated in bulk at the generating stations which are also called power stations. Depending upon the source of energy used, these stations are called thermal power station, hydroelectric power station, diesel power station, nuclear power station etc.

This generated electrical energy is demanded by the consumers. Hence the generated electrical power is to be supplied to the consumers. Generally the power stations are located too far away from the town and cities where electrical energy is demanded. Hence there exists a large network of conductors between the power stations and the consumers. This network is broadly classified into two parts,

1. Transmission   2. Distribution

In this chapter, let us discuss the basic elements of a typical transmission and distribution scheme. The chapter also includes the various elements of power system.

13.2 A Typical Transmission and Distribution Scheme

The flow of electrical power from the generating station to the consumer is called an electrical power system or electrical supply system. It consists of the following important components :

1. Generating station

2. Transmission network

3. Distribution network

All these important networks are connected with the help of conductors and various step up and step down transformers. A typical transmission and distribution scheme is shown in the Fig. 13.2.1.

A scheme shows a generating station which is located too far away from cities and towns. It is generating an electrical power at 11 kV. It is required to increase this level for the transmission purpose. Hence a step up transformer is used which steps up the voltage level to 220 kV. This level may be 132 kV, 220 kV or more as per the requirement.

Then with the help of **transmission lines** and the towers, the power is transmitted at very long distances. Design of the transmission lines is based on the factors like transmission voltage levels, constants like resistance, reactance of the lines, line

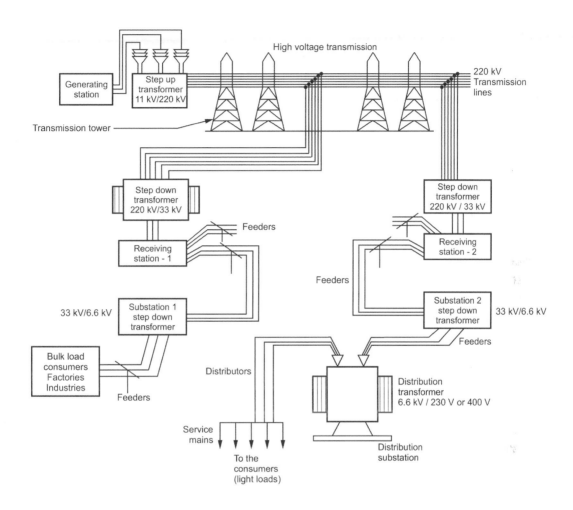

Fig. 13.2.1 Schematic representation of a typical transmission distribution scheme

performance, interference with the neighbouring circuits etc. Its mechanical features are strength of the supports, sag calculations, tension etc. Transmission of power by the overhead lines is very much cheaper. Similarly the repairs also can be carried out comparatively more easily. The transmission is generally along with additional lines in parallel. These lines are called **duplicate lines**. Thus two sets of three phase lines work in parallel. This ensures the continuity during maintenance and also can be used to satisfy future demand. The power is then transmitted to the receiving station via step down transformer. This transformer is 220/33 kV or 220/22 kV transformer.

The power is then transmitted to the substations. A substation consists of a step down transformer of rating 33 kV to 6.6 kV or 3.3 kV. The transfer of power from receiving station to the substation is with the help of conductors called **feeders**. This is called **secondary transmission**.

From the substations, power is distributed to the local distribution centres with the help of **distributors**. Sometimes for bulk loads like factories and industries, the distributors transfer power directly. For the light loads, there are distribution centres consisting of distribution transformers which step down the voltage level to 230 V or 400 V. This is called **primary distribution**. In the crowded areas like cities, overhead system of bare conductors is not practicable. In such cases insulated conductors are used in the form of underground cables, to give supply to the consumers. These cables are called **service mains**. This is called **secondary distribution**.

All the elements involved in the transmission and distribution together is called a **power grid**.

Let us study the line diagram of such a typical scheme of transmission and distribution and discuss the various components and voltage levels at the various stages in detail. The Fig. 13.2.2 shows the line diagram of a typical transmission and distribution scheme.

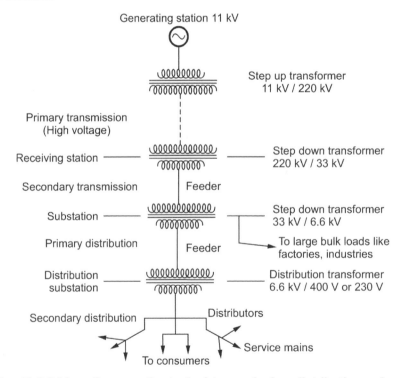

Fig. 13.2.2 Line diagram of a typical transmission distribution scheme

At the generating station, an electrical power is generated with the help of three phase alternators running in parallel. In the scheme shown, the voltage level is 11 kV but the voltage level may be 6.6 kV, 22 kV or 33 kV depending upon the capacity of the generating station. After the generating station, actual transmission and distribution starts. The overall scheme can be divided into four sections which are,

1. **Primary transmission :** It is basically with the help of overhead transmission lines. For the economic aspects, the voltage level is increased to 132 kV, 220 kV or more, with the help of step up transformer. Hence this transmission is also called **high voltage transmission**. The primary transmission uses 3 phase 3 wire system.

2. **Secondary transmission :** The primary transmission line continues via transmission towers till the receiving stations. At the receiving stations, the voltage level is reduced to 22 kV or 33 kV using the step down transformer. There can be more than one receiving stations. Then at reduced voltage level of 22 kV or 33 kV, the power is then transmitted to various substations using overhead 3 phase 3 wire system. This is secondary transmission. The conductors used for the secondary transmission are called feeders.

3. **Primary distribution :** At the substation the voltage level is reduced to 6.6 kV, 3.3 kV or 11 kV with the help of step down transformers. It uses three phase three wire underground system. And the power is further transmitted to the local distribution centres. This is primary distribution, also called high voltage distribution. For the large consumers like factories and industries, the power is directly transmitted to such loads from a substation. Such big loads have their own substations.

4. **Secondary distribution :** At the local distribution centres, there are step down distribution transformers. The voltage level of 6.6 kV, 11 kV is further reduced to 400 V using distribution transformers. Sometimes it may be reduced to 230 V. The power is then transmitted using distributors and service mains to the consumers. This is secondary distribution, also called low voltage distribution. This uses 3 phase 4 wire system. The voltage between any two lines is 400 V while the voltage between any of the three lines and a neutral is 230 V. The single phase lighting loads are supplied using a line and neutral while loads like motors are supplied using three phase lines.

Review Questions

1. *Write a note on typical transmission and distribution scheme.*
2. *Draw and explain the line diagram of a typical transmission and distribution scheme. Indicate clearly the voltage levels used at different stages.*
3. *Explain primary and secondary transmission.*
4. *Explain primary and secondary distribution.*

13.3 Components of Distribution

The distribution scheme consists of following important components

1. **Substation :** Transmission lines bring the power upto the substations at a voltage level of 22 kV or 33 kV. At the substation the level is reduced to 3.3 kV or 6.6 kV. Then using feeders, the power is given to local distribution centres.

2. **Local distribution station :** It consists of distribution transformer which steps down the voltage level from 3.3 kV, 6.6 kV to 400 V or 230 V. Then it is distributed further using distributors. This is also called **distribution substation**.

3. **Feeders :** These are the conductors which are of large current carrying capacitor. The feeders connect the substation to the area where power is to be finally distributed to the consumers. No tappings are taken from the feeders. The feeder current always remains constant. The voltage drop along the feeder is compensated by compounding the generators.

4. **Distributors :** These are the conductors used to transfer power from distribution centre to the consumers. From the distributors, the tappings are taken for the supply to the consumers. The voltage drop along the distributors is the main criterion to design the distributors.

5. **Service mains :** These are the small cables between the distributors and the actual consumer premises.

The interconnection of feeders, distributors and service mains is shown in the Fig. 13.3.1.

There is no tapping on feeders. PQ, QR, RS and PS are the distributors which are supplied by the feeders. No consumer is directly connected to the feeder. The service mains are used to supply the consumers from the distributors. Tappings are taken from the distributors.

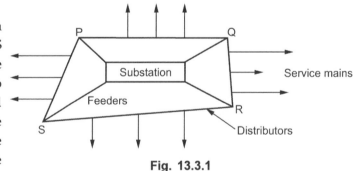

Fig. 13.3.1

Review Question

1. *Explain the following components of distribution :*
   a. Substation   b. Distribution substation
   c. Feeder   d. Distributor   e. Service mains

13.4 Elements of Power System   `2009-10`

The power system is comprised of various elements such as generator, transformer, transmission lines, bus bars, circuit breakers, isolators etc. Now we will discuss in brief about these elements.

13.4.1 Generators

The generator or alternator is the important element of power system. It is of synchronous type and is driven by turbine thus converting mechanical energy into electrical energy. The two main parts of generator are stator and rotor. The stationary part is called **stator** or **armature** consisting of conductors embedded in the slots. The conductors carry current when load is applied on the generator. The rotating part or **rotor** is mounted on the shaft and rotates inside the stator. The winding on rotor is called **field winding**. The field winding is excited by d.c. current. This current produces high m.m.f. The armature conductors react with the m.m.f. produced by the field winding and e.m.f. gets induced in the armature winding. The armature conductors carry current when the load is connected to an alternator. This current produces its own m.m.f. This m.m.f. interacts with the m.m.f. produced by the field winding to generate an electromagnetic torque between stator and rotor.

The d.c. current required for field winding is supplied through exciter which is nothing but a generator mounted on the same shaft on which alternator is mount. The separate d.c. source may also be used sometimes to excite the field windings through brushes bearing on slip rings.

The generators are driven by prime mover which is normally a steam or hydraulic turbine. The electromagnetic torque developed in the generator while delivering power opposes the torque provided by the prime mover.

With properly designed rotor and proper distribution of stator windings around the armature, it is possible to get pure sinusoidal voltage from the

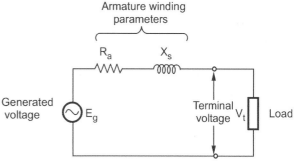

Fig. 13.4.1 Representation of alternator

generator. This voltage is called no load generated voltage or generated voltage. The representation of generator is shown in the Fig. 13.4.1.

13.4.2 Transformers

For stepping up or down the system voltage, power transformers are used in the substations. At generating end, the voltage is only stepped up for transmission of power while at all the subsequent substations the voltage is gradually stepped down to reach finally to working voltage level.

Instead of using a bank of 3 single phase transformers, a single three phase transformer is used now a days. The advantage of using this transformer is the easiness in its installation and only one three phase load tap changing mechanism can be used.

Generally naturally cooled, oil immersed, two winding, three phase transformers upto the rating of 10 MVA are installed upon lengths of rails fixed on concrete slabs having foundations 1 to 1.5 m deep. For more than 10 MVA ratings, forced oil, water cooling and air blast cooling type may be used. The tap changers are used for regulating the voltage of transformers.

13.4.3 Transmission Line

The transmission line forms the connecting link between the generating stations and the distribution systems. It carries the power generated by generating stations and makes it available for distribution through distribution network.

Any electrical transmission line has four major parameters which are important from the point view of its proper operation. These parameters are namely resistance, inductance, capacitance and conductance.

The resistance and inductance is uniformly distributed along the line. It forms series impedance. The resistance of a line is responsible for power loss. It is expected that the resistance of a line should be as low as possible so that the transmission system will be more efficient. Due to flux linkage, the conductor is associated with inductance which is distributed along the length of the line. For analysis, both resistance and inductance are assumed to be lumped.

The capacitance also exists between the conductors and is the charge on the conductors per unit of potential difference between them. The conductance between conductors or between conductors and the ground is due to leakage current at the insulators of overhead lines and through the insulation of cables. The leakage at conductors is negligible so the conductance between conductors of an overhead line is taken as zero. The conductance and capacitance between conductors of a single phase line or from conductor to neutral of a three phase line form the shunt admittance.

Depending upon the length of the transmission line it is classified as short transmission line, medium transmission line and long transmission line. For short line, its length is small so capacitance effects are small and are neglected.

13.4.4 Bus Bars

Bus bars are the common electrical component that connect electrically number of lines which are operating at the same voltage directly. These bars are of either copper or aluminium generally of rectangular cross-section. They can be of other shapes such as round tubes, round solid bars or square tubes.

The outdoor bus bars are of two types viz the rigid type or strain type.

In the rigid type of bus bars, pipes are used. The pipes are also used for making connections among different components. The pedestal insulators support the bus bars and the connections. The equipments and bus bars are spread out and it requires large space. The clearances remain constant as the bus bars are rigid.

It has following **advantages**

1) The maintenance is easy as bus bars and connections are not very high from ground.

2) As pipe diameter is large, the corona loss is less.

3) Reliability is more than strain type.

Following are its **limitations**

1) Larger area is required.

2) It requires comparatively high cost.

In strain type, bus bars are an overhead system of wires between two supporting structure and supported by strain type insulators. As per the size of the conductor, the stringing tension can be limited (500 - 900 kg).

The advantage of this type is its economy and it is recommended presently due to general shortage of aluminium pipes.

The material used in case of rigid type bus bars is aluminium pipes. The general sizes of pipes commonly used for voltages are as given below.

33 kV	40 mm
66 kV	65 mm
132 kV	80 mm
220 kV	80 mm
400 kV	100 mm

Due to rapid oxidization of aluminium, proper care must be taken while doing connections. In order to avoid strain of supporting insulators due to thermal expansion or contraction of pipe, joints should be provided.

In case of strain type arrangement, material used is ACSR (Aluminium conductors with steel reinforcement) and all aluminium conductors. For high ratings of bus bars bundled conductors are used. The commonly used sizes are as below.

66 kV	37/2.79 mm	ACSR
132 kV	37/4.27 mm	ACSR
220 kV	61/3.99 mm	ACSR
400 kV	61/4.27 mm	ACSR in duplex

13.4.5 Circuit Breaker

The circuit breakers are used to open or close a circuit under normal and faulty conditions. It can be designed in such a way that it can be manually operated or by remote control under normal conditions and automatically operated during fault. For automatic operation, relay circuit is used.

The circuit breakers are essential as isolators cannot be used to open a circuit under normal conditions as it has no provision to quench arc that is produced after opening the line. It has to perform following functions.

i)   Full load current is to be carried continuously.

ii)   Opening and closing the circuit on no load.

iii)   Making and breaking the normal operating current.

iv)   Making and breaking the fault currents of magnitude upto which it is designed for.

Upto 66 kV voltages, bulk oil circuit breakers are used. Voltages greater than 66 kV, low oil circuit breakers are used. For still high voltages, air blast, vacuum or SF_6 circuit breakers are used.

13.4.6 Isolators

In order to disconnect a part of the power system for maintenance and repair purposes, isolating switches are used. These are operated after switching off the load by means of a circuit breaker. The isolators are connected on both sides of circuit breakers. Thus to open isolators, circuit breakers are to be opened first.

An isolator is essentially a knife switch and is designed to open a circuit under no load that is lines in which they are connected should not be carrying any current.

Use of isolators in a substation is shown in the Fig. 13.4.2.

As shown in the Fig. 13.4.2, there are 5 sections. With the help of isolators, each section can be disconnected for repair and maintenance. If it is required to do maintenance in section 4, then the circuit breaker in that section is to be opened first and then open the isolators 3 and 4. Thus section 4 is open for maintenance. After maintenance, the isolators 3 and 4 are to be closed first and then circuit breaker is closed.

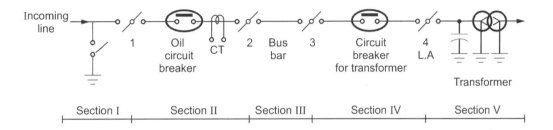

Fig. 13.4.2 Line diagram of substation with use of isolating switches

In some cases, isolators are used as circuit breaking devices. But it is limited by particular conditions such as power rating of given circuit. The isolators are of two types viz single pole and three pole isolators.

Review Question

1. *List out the main components of power supply system with brief description.*
   2009-10, Marks 10

13.5 Short Answered and Objective Type Questions

Q.1   The transfer of power from receiving station to the substation is with the help of _____.

a) transformers   b) transmission lines   c) interconnectors   d) feeders
   (Ans. : d)

Q.2   In a power system a 6.6 kV/ 400 V transformer is installed on _____.

a) primary transmission side   b) secondary transmission side
c) secondary distribution side   d) primary distribution side   **(Ans. : c)**

Q.3   Which of the following is not a standard transmission voltage in India ?

a) 66 kV   b) 109 kV   c) 220 kV   d) 33 kV   **(Ans. : b)**

Q.4   The maximum transmission voltage in India is _____.   **2008-09**

a) 220 kV   b) 765 kV   c) 400 kV   d) 1200 kV **(Ans. : c)**

Q.5 The conductors used to transfer power from distribution centre to consumers is called _____.

a) distributors   b) feeders   c) transformers   d) none of these

(Ans. : a)

Q.6 The three phase, four wire system is commonly used on _____.

a) primary transmission   b) secondary transmission
c) primary distribution   d) secondary distribution   (Ans. : d)

Q.7 _____ are used for regulating the voltage of the transformers.

a) Capacitors   b) Tap changers   c) Circuit breakers   d) None of these

(Ans. : b)

Q.8 The material used for rigid type of bus bars is _____.

a) steel   b) nickel   c) aluminium   d) iron   (Ans. : c)

Q.9 Upto 66 kV, _____ type of circuit breakers are used.

a) air blast   b) vacuum   c) SF$_6$ d) bulk oil (Ans. : d)

Q.10 The switches which are used only after switching off the load are called _____.

a) circuit breakers   b) insulators
c) isolating switches   d) double pole switches   (Ans. : c)

❑❑❑

14

Additional Measuring Instruments

Syllabus (Only for MMTU)

Induction type energy meter, Block diagram of multi-meter and megger.

Contents

14.1 Single Phase Induction Type Energy Meter

Induction type instruments are most commonly used as energy meters. Energy meter is an integrating instrument which measures quantity of electricity. Induction type of energy meters are universally used for domestic and industrial applications. These meters record the energy in kilo-watt-hours (kWh). The Fig. 14.1.1 shows the induction type single phase energy meter.

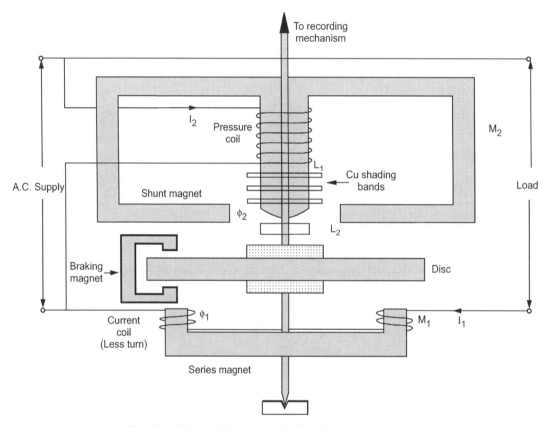

Fig. 14.1.1 Induction type single phase energy meter

It consists of two electromagnets whose core is made up of silicon steel laminations. The coil of one of the electromagnets, called **current coil,** is excited by load current which produces flux. This is called a **series magnet.** The coil has few turns of heavy guage wire. The coil of another electromagnet is connected across the supply and it carries current proportional to supply voltage. This coil is called **pressure coil.** This is called **shunt magnet.** This coil has large number of turns of fine wire.

The flux produced by shunt magnet is brought in exact quadrature with supply voltage with the help of **copper shading bands placed over the central limb,** whose position is adjustable. The **moving system** consists of a light aluminium disc mounted on a light alloy shaft. This disc is positioned in between series and shunt magnets. It is supported between jewel bearings. The moving system runs on hardened steel pivot. A pinion engages the shaft with the counting mechanism.

There are no springs and no controlling torque.

The **braking system** consists of a permanent magnet placed near the aluminium disc for braking mechanism. This magnet is used to control the speed of the disc.

The **registering mechanism** records continuously a number which is proportional to the revolutions made by the aluminium disc. By a suitable system, a train of reduction gears, the pinion on the shaft drives a series of pointers.

14.1.1 Working

The current coil produces the alternating flux ϕ_1 which is proportinal and in phase with the current through the current coil. The pressure coil carries the current and produces the flux ϕ_2 which proportional to the supply voltage V and lags behind it by 90° which is achieved by the copper shading bands.

Major portion of the flux ϕ_2 crosses the narrow gap between the central and the side limbs of the shunt magnet and only small amount passes through the disc which is the useful flux. Both the fluxes ϕ_1 and ϕ_2 induce e.m.f.s in the disc which produce the eddy currents in the disc.

The interaction between these fluxes and the eddy currents produce the necessary driving torque and the disc starts rotating.

The speed of disc is controlled by the C shaped magnet called braking magnet. When the peripheral portion of the disc rotates in the air gap, eddy currents are induced in the disc which oppose the cause producing them i.e. relative motion of disc with respect to magnet. Hence braking torque T_b is generated. This is proportional to speed N of the disc.

By adjusting position of this magnet, desired speed of disc is obtained. Spindle is connected to recording mechanism through gears which record the energy supplied.

14.1.2 Mathematical Analysis

Let, V = Supply voltage

I_2 = Current through pressure coil proportional to V and

ϕ_2 = Flux produced by I_2

I_1 = Current through current coil i.e. load and ϕ_1 = Flux produced by I_1

Now I_2 lags V by $90°$ while ϕ_2 and I_2 are in phase.

While I_1 lags V by angle ϕ where ϕ is decided by the load connected.

The flux ϕ_1 and I_1 are in phase.

The phasor diagram is shown in the Fig 14.1.2.

E_1 = Induced e.m.f. in disc due to ϕ_1

E_2 = Induced e.m.f. in disc due to ϕ_2

I_{sh} = Eddy current due to E_1

I_{se} = Eddy current due to E_2.

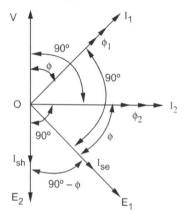

The induced e.m.f. lags the respective flux producing it by $90°$.

The eddy currents are in phase with the induced e.m.f. producing them.

Fig. 14.1.2

There is interaction between ϕ_1 and I_{sh} which produces torque T_1 and the interaction between ϕ_2 and I_{se} which produces torque T_2.

T_2 is in opposite direction to T_1. Hence net deflecting torque is,

$$T_d \; \propto \; T_2 - T_1 \propto \phi_2 I_{se} \cos\left(\phi_2 {}^\wedge I_{se}\right) - \phi_1 I_{sh} \cos\left(\phi_1 {}^\wedge I_{sh}\right)$$

Now $\qquad \phi_2 {}^\wedge I_{se} = \phi$ and $\phi_1 {}^\wedge I_{sh} = 180 - \phi$ $\qquad$ ... From Fig 14.1.2

$\therefore \qquad T_d \; \propto \; \phi_2 I_{se} \cos\phi - \phi_1 I_{sh} \cos(180 - \phi) \propto \phi_2 I_{se} \cos\phi + \phi_1 I_{sh} \cos\phi$

$$\text{as } \cos(180 - \phi) = -\cos\phi$$

But $\qquad \phi_2 \propto I_2 \propto V, \quad I_{se} \propto E_1 \propto I_1, \quad \phi_1 \propto I_1, \quad I_{sh} \propto E_2 \propto I_2 \propto V$

$\therefore \qquad T_d \; \propto \; K_1 V I_1 \cos\phi + K_2 I_1 V \cos\phi \propto (K_1 + K_2) V I_1 \cos\phi$

$\therefore \qquad T_d \; \propto \; V I_1 \cos\phi \quad$ i.e. power consumed by load.

Now braking torque is proportional to speed N with which disc rotates.

$\therefore \qquad T_d \; \propto \; N$

For constant speed, $T_b = T_d \quad$ i.e. $N \propto V I_1 \cos\phi$

Multiplying both side by t, $\qquad N t \propto V I_1 t \cos\phi \propto P t \propto$ energy

Number of revolutions in time $t \propto$ energy supplied

The power $P \times t$ is energy supplied in time t while Nt are the number of revolutions in time t.

Thus by counting number of revolutions, electrical energy consumed can be measured.

Without any current through current coil, disc has a tendency to rotate due to the supply voltage exciting its pressure coil. This is called **creeping.** This creeping may be because of overfriction compensation.

> To eliminate creeping two holes are drilled in the disc 180° opposite to each other.

When this holes comes under the shunt magnet pole, it gets acted upon by a torque opposite to its rotation. This restricts its rotation, on no load condition.

To have the flux produced by the pressure coil lagging the voltage V exactly by 90° the copper shading ring is provided on central limb. This ensures the accurate measurement at all the power factors of the load.

The permanent magnet surrounding the peripheral portion of the disc is braking magnet which is used to control the speed of rotation of the disc. The speed of the disc can be adjusted by means of changing the effective radius of the braking magnet. This ensures the accurate measurement.

Review Questions

1. *With the help of neat diagram explain the construction and principle of operation of single phase energy meter.* **2009-10, 2010-11, 2011-12, Marks 10**

2. *Prove that the number of revolutions of the disc is proportional to the energy supplied.*

3. *As applied to an energy meter give the reasons for the following :*
    i) There is a permanent magnet surrounding a portion of the rotating disc.
    ii) Diagonally opposite holes are cut on the disc.
    iii) A copper shading ring is provided on the central limb of the shunt magnet.

14.2 Calibration of an Energy Meter

Calibrating the energy meter means to find out the error in the measurement of energy by energy meter.

Every energy meter has its own characteristic constant specified by the manufacturer which relates the energy measured in joules and the number of revolutions of the disc. For example say 'x' revolutions corresponds to the measurement of 'y' joules. But practically the value of 'x' is very large and can not be measured in the laboratory. Hence using this constant, energy recorded for certain less number of revolutions say 5, is calculated in the laboratory for the calibration purpose. This energy is denoted as E_r. Thus E_r can be calculated from 'x' as,

$$E_r = \frac{5 \, x}{y} \quad \text{joules}$$

To have zero error, the actual energy consumed by the load for the time corresponding to the 5 revolutions must be same as E_r. This energy is called actual energy consumed or the true energy denoted as E_t. Experimental set up used in the laboratory to obtain the value of E_t is shown in the Fig. 14.2.1.

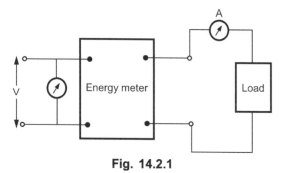

Fig. 14.2.1

For various loads, the time required to complete the 5 revolutions of disc is measured with the help of stop watch. The voltage and current readings are observed on the ammeter and voltmeter connected in the circuit. The readings can be tabulated as :

Sr. No.	Voltage (V)	Current (A)	Time for 5 revolutions	True enrgy $E_t = VI \cos \phi \, t$ J
1				
2				
3				

Now E_r is fixed for the 5 revolutions, while E_t is obtained practically. Hence error for each load condition can be obtained as,

$$\% \text{ error } = \frac{E_r - E_t}{E_t} \times 100$$

The graph of % error against the load current I can be obtained, which is called **calibration curve** for the energymeter. When there is no load, I = 0 and hence true energy E_t is also zero. While E_r is also zero. Hence the error is also zero. Thus calibration curve passes through origin. The errors can be positive or negative. Such a curve is shown in the Fig. 14.2.2.

Once the calibration curve is obtained, by observation of the curve, in which range of the load current error is severe, can be easily predicted. And if error is not within the permissible limits then by using the various adjustments discussed earlier, the error can be minimised.

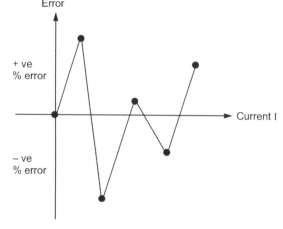

Fig. 14.2.2

Review Question

> 1. *Explain the calibration of energy meter.*

14.3 Advantages of Energy Meter

The various advantages of induction type energy meters are,

1. Its construction is simple and strong.

2. It is cheap in cost.

3. It has high torque to weight ratio, so frictional errors are less and we can get accurate reading.

4. It has more accuracy.

5. It requires less maintenance.

6. Its range can be extended with the help of instrument transformers.

14.4 Disadvantages of Energy Meter

1. The main disadvantage is that it can be used only for a.c. circuits.

2. The creeping can cause errors.

3. Lack of symmetry in magnetic circuit may cause errors.

14.5 Adjustments in Energy Meter   2000-01, 2004-05, 2005-06

The adjustments are required in the energy meters so that they read accurately with minimum possible errors.

i) **Main speed adjustment :** The measurement of energy is dependent on the speed of the rotating disc. For accurate measurement, speed of the disc must be also proportionate. The speed of the meter can be adjusted by means of changing the effective radius of the braking magnet shown in Fig. 5.21. Moving the braking magnet in the direction of the spindle, decreases the value of the effective radius, decreasing the braking torque. This increases the speed of the meter. While the movement of the braking magnet in the outward direction i.e. away from the centre of the disc, increases the radius, decreasing the speed of the disc. The fine adjustments of the speed can be achieved by providing an additional flux divertor.

ii) **Power factor adjustment :** It is absolutely necessary that meter should measure correctly for all power factor conditions of the loads. This is possible when the flux produced due to current in the pressure coil lags the applied voltage by 90°. But the iron loss and resistance of winding do not allow the flux to lag by exact 90° with respect to the voltage.

To have this adjustment, the shading ring called quadrature loop is provided on the centre limb of shunt magnet carrying pressure coil. The fine adjustments can be achieved by the movement of this loop upwards or downwards and meter can be made to read accurately at all the power factors.

iii) **Friction adjustment** : Inspite of proper design of the bearings and registering mechanism, there is bound to exist some friction. Due to this speed of the meter gets affected which cause the error in the measurement of the energy.

To compensate for this, a metallic loop or strip is provided between central limb of shunt magnet and the disc. Due to this strip an additional troque independent of load is produced which acts on the disc in the direction of rotation. This compensates for the friction and meter can be made to read accurately. This is shown as L_2 in the Fig. 14.1.1.

iv) **Creep adjustment** : It is seen that, without any current through current coil, disc rotates due to the supply voltage exciting its pressure coil. This is called creeping. This creeping may be because of overfriction compensation.

To eliminate this, two holes are drilled in the disc 180° opposite to each other. When this holes comes under the shunt magnet pole, it gets acted upon by a torque opposite to its rotation. This restricts its rotation, on no load condition.

Remember :

$$E_r = \frac{\text{Number of revolutions}}{\text{Constant in rev / kWh}} \text{ in kWh} = \text{Recorded energy}$$

$$E_t = V \, I \cos \phi \times t \text{ in Wsec} = \text{True energy}$$

where t = Time in sec.

i.e. $$E_t = \frac{V \, I \cos\phi \, t}{3600} \times 10^{-3} \text{ kWh}$$

Example 14.5.1 *A 50 A, 230 V meter on full load test makes 61 revolutions in 37 seconds. If the normal disc speed is 500 revolutions per kWh, find the percentage error.*

2005-06, **Marks 5**

Solution : I = 50 A,   V = 230 V,   t = 37 sec, 500 rev/kWh, 61 revolutions

$$E_r = \text{Recorded energy} = \frac{\text{Number of revolutions}}{\text{rev / kWh}} = \frac{61}{500} = 0.122 \text{ kWh}$$

$$E_t = \text{True energy} = VI \cos \phi \times t \qquad \qquad ...\cos \phi = 1$$

$$= 230 \times 50 \times 1 \times 37 = 425500 \text{ Wsec}$$

$$= \frac{425500}{3600} \times 10^{-3} \text{ kWh} = 0.1182 \text{ kWh}$$

$$\therefore \quad \% \text{ error} = \frac{E_r - E_t}{E_t} \times 100 = \frac{0.122 - 0.1182}{0.1182} \times 100 = \mathbf{3.2196 \% \ (Fast)}$$

The positive sign indicates meter is fast.

Example 14.5.2 *An energy meter revolves 100 revolutions of disc for one unit of energy. Find the number of revolutions made by it during an hour when connected across load which takes 20 A, at 210 V and 0.8 power factor leading. If energy meter revolves 350 revolutions, find the percentage error.* **2004-05, Marks 5**

Solution : 100 revolutions for 1 kWh, I = 20 A, V = 210 V, $\cos \phi = 0.8$, N = 350

$$E_t = \text{Energy consumed} = VI \cos \phi \times t \quad \text{where t = 1 hour}$$

$$= 210 \times 20 \times 0.8 \times 1 \text{ Wh} = 3.36 \text{ kWh}$$

As meter constant is 100 rev/kWh,

Number of revolutions = 3.36×100 = **336**

But actually it makes 350 revolutions hence,

$$E_r = \text{Energy recorded} = \frac{350}{100} \text{ kWh} = 3.5 \text{ kWh}$$

$$\therefore \quad \% \text{ error} = \frac{E_r - E_t}{E_t} \times 100 = \frac{3.5 - 3.36}{3.36} \times 100 = \mathbf{4.16 \%}$$

As error is positive, meter is **fast**.

Example 14.5.3 *A single phase energy meter has a registration constant of 100 rev/kWh. If the meter is connected to a load carrying 20 A at 230 V and 0.8 power factor for an hour; find the number of revolutions made by it. If it actually makes 360 revolutions, find the percentage error.* **2000-01, Marks 5**

Solution : I = 20 A, V = 230 V, $\cos \phi = 0.8$, t = 1 hour = 3600 sec

$$\therefore \qquad E_t = VI \cos \phi \times t = 20 \times 230 \times 0.8 \times 3600 = 13.248 \times 10^6 \text{ J}$$

$$= 3680 \text{ Wh} = 3.68 \text{ kWh}$$

Meter constant = 100 rev/kWh

∴   Number of revolutions = 3.68 × 100 = **368**

Actually it makes 360 revolutions,

∴ $E_r = \dfrac{360}{100}$ kWh = 3.6 kWh

∴   % error $= \dfrac{E_r - E_t}{E_t} \times 100 = \dfrac{3.6 - 3.68}{3.68} \times 100 = $ **– 2.173 % (slow)**

Review Question

> 1. *Explain the adjustments in energy meter.*

14.6 Megger

Resistances of the order of 0.1 MΩ and upwards are classified as high resistances. These high resistances are measured by portable, instrument known as **megger**. It is also used for testing the insulation resistance of cables.

14.6.1 Principle of Operation

It is based on the principle of electromagnetic induction. The Fig 14.6.1 shows the construction of megger.

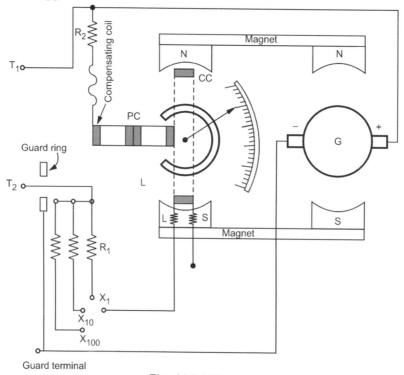

Fig. 14.6.1 Megger

When a current carrying conductor is placed in a uniform magnetic field it experiences a mechanical force whose magnitude depends upon the strength of current and magnetic field. While its direction depends on the direction of current and magnetic field.

14.6.2 Construction

It consist of a permanent magnet which provides the field for both the generator G and ohm meter. The moving element of the ohm meter consist of three coil viz. current or deflection coil, pressure or control coil and compensating coil. These coils are mounted on a central shaft which are free to rotate over a stationary C-shaped iron core.

The coils are connected to the circuit through flexible leads called ligaments which do not produce a restoring torque on the moving element, consequently the moving element takes up any position over the scale when the generator handle is stationary.

The current coil is connected in series with resistance R_1 between one generator terminal and the test terminal T_2. The series resistance R_1 protects the current coil in the event of the test terminals getting short circuited and also controls the range of the instrument. The pressure coil, in series with a compensating coil and protection resistance R_2 is connected across the generator terminals. The compensating coil is included in the circuit to ensure better scale proportions. The scale is calibrated reversely means the normal position of pointer indicates infinity while full scale deflection indicates zero resistance.

14.6.3 Working

When the current flows from the generator, through the pressure coil, the coil tends to set itself at right angles to the field of the permanent magnet.

When the test terminals are open, corresponding to infinite resistance, no current flows through deflection coil. Thus the pressure coil governs the motion of the moving element making it move to its extreme anticlockwise position. The pointer comes to rest at the infinity end of the scale.

When the test terminals are short circuited i.e. corresponding to zero resistance, the current from the generator flowing through the current coil is large enough to produce sufficient torque to overcome the counter-clockwise torque of the pressure coil. Due to this, pointer moves over a scale showing zero resistance.

When the high resistance to be tested is connected between terminals T_1 and T_2 the opposing torques of the coils balance each other so that pointer attains a stationary position at some intermediate point on scale. The scale is calibrated in megaohms so that the resistance is directly indicated by pointer.

The guard ring is provided to eliminate the error due to leakage current. The supply to the meter is usually given by a hand-driven permanent magnet d.c. generator sometimes motor-driven generator may also be used.

14.6.4 Applications

The megger can be used to determine whether there is sufficiently high resistance between the conducting part of a circuit and the ground. This resistance is called insulation resistance.

The megger can also be used to test continuity between any two points. When connected to the two points, if pointer shows full deflection then there is an electrical continuity between them.

Review Question

1. *Explain construction, working and applications of megger.*

14.7 Analog Multimeter

For the measurement of d.c. as well as a.c. voltage and current, resistance, an electronic multimeter is commonly used. It is also known as Voltage-Ohm Meter (VOM). The important salient features of VOM are as listed below.

1) The basic circuit of VOM includes balanced bridge d.c. amplifier.

2) To limit the magnitude of the input signal, RANGE switch is provided. By properly adjusting input attenuator input signal can be limited.

3) It also includes rectifier section which converts a.c. input signal to the d.c. voltage.

4) It facilitates resistance measurement with the help of internal battery and additional circuitry.

5) The various parameters measurement is possible by selecting required function using FUNCTION switch.

6) The measurement of various parameters is indicated with the help of Indicating Meter.

A multimeter measures a.c. and d.c. voltage, a.c. and d.c. currents and resistance.

The Fig. 14.7.1 shows the modern laboratory type multimeter.

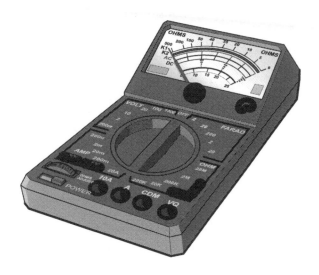

Fig. 14.7.1 Laboratory type multimeter

14.7.1 Use of Multimeter for D.C. Voltage Measurement

The Fig. 14.7.2 shows the arrangement used in multimeter to measure the d.c. voltages.

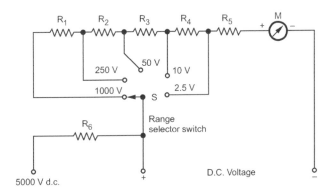

Fig. 14.7.2

For getting different ranges of voltages, different series resistances are connected in series which can be put in the circuit with the range selector switch. We can get different ranges to measure the d.c. voltages by selecting the proper resistance in series with the basic meter.

14.7.2 Use of Multimeter as an Ammeter

To get different current ranges, different shunts are connected across the meter with the help of range selector switch. The working is same as that of PMMC ammeter.

The Fig. 14.7.3 shows the arrangement used in the multimeter to use is as an ammeter.

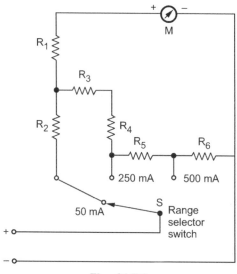

Fig. 14.7.3

14.7.3 Use of Multimeter for Measurement of A.C. Voltage

The Fig. 14.7.4 shows voltmeter section of a multimeter.

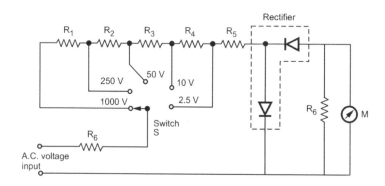

Fig. 14.7.4

The rectifier used in the circuit rectifies a.c. voltage into d.c. voltage for measurement of a.c. voltage before current passes through the meter. The other diode is used for the protection purpose.

14.7.4 Use of Multimeter for Resistance Measurement

The Fig. 14.7.5 shows ohmmeter section of multimeter for a scale multiplication of 1. Before any measurement is made, the instrument is short circuited and "zero adjust" control is varied until the meter reads zero resistance i.e. it shows full scale current. Now the circuit takes the form of a variation of the shunt type ohmmeter. Scale multiplications of 100 and 10,000 can also be used for measuring high resistances. Voltages are applied to the circuit with the help of battery.

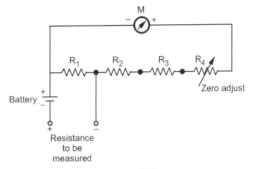

Fig. 14.7.5

Review Question

1. *Explain the use of multimeter for various measurements.*

14.8 Short Answered and Objective Type Questions

Q.1 What is accuracy and resolution of an instrument ?   2010-11

Ans. : The degree of closeness with which the instrument reading approaches the true value of the quantity to be measured is called its accuracy. The smallest measurable input change by an instrument is called its resolution.

Q.2 In energymeters _____ torque is absent.

    a) deflecting   b) controlling   c) breaking   d) damping

                                                                 (Ans. : b)

Q.3 In energymeters, the number of revolutions in time t of disc is proportional to the _____.

    a) current   b) voltage   c) power   d) energy **(Ans. : d)**

Q.4 The graph of % error against load current is called _____ for an energy meter.

    a) characteristic curve   b) transfer curve

    c) calibration curve   d) none of these   **(Ans. : c)**

Q.5 The rotation of the disc without any current through the current coil is called _____.

    a) creeping   b) cogging   c) crawling   d) none of these

                                                                   (Ans. : a)

Q.6 The average torque acting on the aluminium disc of an energy meter is proportional to the _____ consumed by the circuit.

    a) current   b) voltage

    c) power   d) none of the above   **(Ans. : c)**

Q.7   In the energy meter, constant speed of rotation of disc is provided by _____.

a) shunt magnet   b) series magnet

c) braking magnet   d) none of these   **(Ans. : c)**

Q.8   In an energy meter, the moving system attains the steady speed when, _____ .

a) braking torque is zero   b) braking torque is equal to operating torque

c) braking torque is maximum   d) operating torque is constant.   **(Ans. : b)**

Q.9   In energy meter, _____ effect is used.

a) thermal   b) induction   c) hall   d) magnetic
                                                                            (Ans. : b)

Q.10 One unit of electrical energy is equivalent to _____.

a) 1 kWH   b) 3600 W-sec   c) 100 WH   d) 10 kWH **(Ans. : a)**

Q.11 Under no load condition, the revolution of the disc due to kinetic energy of an energy meter can be blocked by _____.

a) brake magnet   b) electromagnet

c) creeping hole with brake magnet   c) copper shading band   **(Ans. : c)**

□□□

A

Production of Rotating Magnetic Field

A.1   Rotating Magnetic Field (R.M.F.)

The rotating magnetic field can be defined as the field or flux having constant amplitude but whose axis is continuously rotating in a plane with a certain speed. So if the arrangement is made to rotate a permanent magnet, then the resulting field is a rotating magnetic field. But in this method, it is necessary to rotate a magnet physically to produce rotating magnetic field.

But in three phase induction motors such a rotating magnetic field is produced by supplying currents to a set of **stationary** windings, with the help of three phase a.c. supply. The current carrying windings produce the magnetic field or flux. And due to interaction of three fluxes produced due to three phase supply, resultant flux has a constant magnitude and its axis rotating in space, without physically rotating the windings. This type of field is nothing but rotating magnetic field. Let us study how it happens.

A.1.1   Production of R.M.F.

A three phase induction motor consists of three phase winding as its stationary part called **stator**. The three phase stator winding is connected in star or delta. The three phase windings are displaced from each other by 120°. The windings are supplied by a balanced three phase a.c. supply. This is shown in the Fig. A.1.1. The three phase windings are denoted as R-R′, Y-Y′ and B-B′.

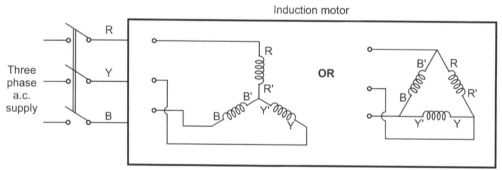

Star or delta connected 3 phase winding

Fig. A.1.1

The three phase currents flow simultaneously through the windings and are displaced from each other by 120° electrical. Each alternating phase current produces its own flux which is sinusoidal. So all three fluxes are sinusoidal and are separated from each other by 120°. If the phase sequence of the windings is R-Y-B, then mathematical equations for the instantaneous values of the three fluxes ϕ_R, ϕ_Y and ϕ_B can be written as,

$$\phi_R = \phi_m \sin (\omega t) = \phi_m \sin \theta \qquad \qquad \dots (A.1.1)$$

$$\phi_Y = \phi_m \sin(\omega t - 120°) = \phi_m \sin(\theta - 120°) \qquad \ldots (A.1.2)$$

$$\phi_B = \phi_m \sin(\omega t - 240°) = \phi_m \sin(\theta - 240°) \qquad \ldots (A.1.3)$$

As windings are identical and supply is balanced, the magnitude of each flux is ϕ_m. Due to phase sequence R-Y-B, flux ϕ_Y lags behind ϕ_R by 120° and ϕ_B lags ϕ_Y by 120°. So ϕ_B ultimately lags ϕ_R by 240°. The flux ϕ_R is taken as reference while writing the equations.

The Fig. A.1.2 (a) shows the waveforms of three fluxes in space. The Fig. A.1.2 (b) shows the phasor diagram which clearly shows the **assumed positive directions** of each flux. Assumed positive direction means whenever the flux is positive it must be represented along the direction shown and whenever the flux is negative it must be represented along the opposite direction to the assumed positive direction.

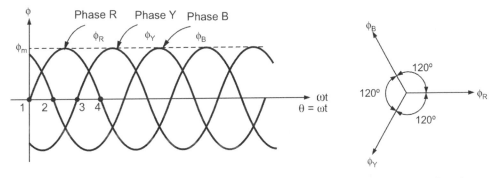

(a) Waveforms of three fluxes   (b) Assumed positive directions

Fig. A.1.2

Let ϕ_R, ϕ_Y and ϕ_B be the instantaneous values of three fluxes. The resultant flux ϕ_T is the phasor addition of ϕ_R, ϕ_Y and ϕ_B.

$$\therefore \qquad \bar{\phi}_T = \bar{\phi}_R + \bar{\phi}_Y + \bar{\phi}_B$$

Let us find ϕ_T at the instants 1, 2, 3 and 4 as shown in the Fig. A.1.2 (a) which represents the values of θ as 0°, 60°, 120° and 180° respectively. The phasor addition can be performed by obtaining the values of ϕ_R, ϕ_Y and ϕ_B by substituting values of θ in the equations (A.1.1), (A.1.2) and (A.1.3).

Case 1 : $\theta = 0°$

Substituting in the equations (A.1.1), (A.1.2) and (A.1.3) we get,

$$\phi_R = \phi_m \sin 0° = 0$$

$$\phi_Y = \phi_m \sin(-120°) = -0.866 \; \phi_m$$

$$\phi_B = \phi_m \sin(-240°) = +0.866 \; \phi_m$$

The phasor addition is shown in the Fig. A.1.3 (a). The positive values are shown in assumed positive directions while negative values are shown in opposite direction to the assumed positive directions of the respective fluxes. Refer to assumed positive directions shown in the Fig. A.1.2 (b).

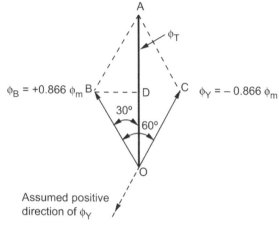

Fig. A.1.3 (a) Vector diagram for $\theta = 0°$

BD is drawn perpendicular from B on ϕ_T. It bisects ϕ_T.

$$\therefore \quad OD = DA = \frac{\phi_T}{2}$$

In triangle OBD,

$$\angle BOD = 30°$$

$$\therefore \quad \cos 30° = \frac{OD}{OB} = \frac{\phi_T/2}{0.866\phi_m}$$

$$\therefore \quad \phi_T = 2 \times 0.866\phi_m \times \cos 30°$$

$$= 1.5\,\phi_m$$

So magnitude of ϕ_T is 1.5 ϕ_m and its position is vertically upwards at $\theta = 0°$.

Case 2 : $\theta = 60°$

Equations (A.1.1), (A.1.2) and (A.1.3) give us,

$$\phi_R = \phi_m \sin 60° = +\,0.866\,\phi_m$$

$$\phi_Y = \phi_m \sin(-\,60°) = -\,0.866\,\phi_m$$

$$\phi_B = \phi_m \sin(-\,180°) = 0$$

So ϕ_R is positive and ϕ_Y is negative and hence drawing in appropriate directions we get phasor diagram as shown in the Fig. A.1.3 (b).

Doing the same construction, drawing perpendicular from B on ϕ_T at D we get the same result as,

$$\phi_T = 1.5\,\phi_m$$

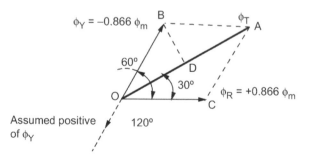

Fig. A.1.3 (b) Vector diagram for $\theta = 60°$

But it can be seen that though **its magnitude is 1.5 ϕ_m it has rotated through 60° in space, in clockwise direction, from its previous position.**

Case 3 : $\theta = 120°$

Equations (A.1.1), (A.1.2) and (A.1.3) give us,

$$\phi_R = \phi_m \sin 120 = + 0.866 \, \phi_m$$

$$\phi_Y = \phi_m \sin 0 = 0$$

$$\phi_B = \phi_m \sin (- 120) = - 0.866 \, \phi_m$$

So ϕ_R is positive and ϕ_B is negative. Showing ϕ_R and ϕ_B in the appropriate directions, we get the phasor diagram as shown in the Fig. A.1.3 (c).

After doing the construction same as before i.e. drawing perpendicular from B on ϕ_T, it can be proved again that,

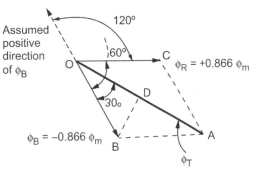

$$\phi_T = 1.5 \, \phi_m$$

Fig. A.1.3 (c) Vector diagram for $\theta = 120°$

But the position of ϕ_T is such that **it has rotated further through 60° from its previous position, in clockwise direction.** And from its position at $\theta = 0°$, it has rotated through 120° in space, in clockwise direction.

Case 4 : $\theta = 180°$

From the equations (A.1.1), (A.1.2) and (A.1.3),

$$\phi_R = \phi_m \sin (180°) = 0$$

$$\phi_Y = \phi_m \sin (60°) = + 0.866 \, \phi_m$$

$$\phi_B = \phi_m \sin (- 60°)$$

$$= - 0.866 \, \phi_m$$

So $\phi_R = 0$, ϕ_Y is positive and ϕ_B is negative. Drawing ϕ_Y and ϕ_B in the appropriate directions, we get the phasor diagram as shown in the Fig. A.1.3 (d).

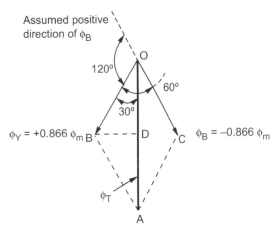

Fig. A.1.3 (d) Vector diagram for $\theta = 180°$

From phasor diagram, it can be easily proved that,

$$\phi_T = 1.5 \phi_m$$

Thus the magnitude of ϕ_T once again remains same. But it can be seen that **it has further rotated through 60° from its previous position in clockwise direction**.

So for an electrical half cycle of 180°, the resultant ϕ_T has also rotated through 180°. This is applicable for the windings wound for 2 poles.

From the above discussion we have following conclusions :

a)   The resultant of the three alternating fluxes, separated from each other by 120°, has a constant amplitude of 1.5 ϕ_m where ϕ_m is maximum amplitude of an individual flux due to any phase.

b)   The resultant always keeps on rotating with a certain speed in space.

Key Point *This shows that when a three phase stationary windings are excited by balanced three phase a.c. supply then the resulting field produced is **rotating magnetic field**. Though nothing is physically rotating, the field produced is rotating in space having constant amplitude.*

Review Question

1. *Explain the production of rotating magnetic field.*

□□□

Made in the USA
Middletown, DE
14 May 2021